NINTH EDITION

PURCHASING

Selection and Procurement for the Hospitality Industry

ANDREW H. FEINSTEIN | JEAN L. HERTZMAN | JOHN M. STEFANELLI

VP AND EDITORIAL DIRECTOR	George Hoffman
EDITORIAL DIRECTOR	Veronica Visentin
EDITORIAL MANAGER	Gladys Soto
EDITORIAL ASSISTANT	Ethan Lipson
CONTENT MANAGEMENT DIRECTOR	Lisa Wojcik
CONTENT MANAGER	Nichole Urban
SENIOR CONTENT SPECIALIST	Nicole Repasky
PRODUCTION EDITOR	Christian Arsenault
PHOTO RESEARCHER	Alicia South
COVER PHOTO CREDIT	(top left): MNStudio / Shutterstock; (top right): laurasiens / Shutterstock; (bottom left): Tavee Adam / Shutterstock; (bottom right): nanD_Phanuwat / Shuttersock

This book was set in Adobe Garamond Pro 11/15 by SPi Global and printed and bound by Quad/Graphics.

Founded in 1807, John Wiley & Sons, Inc. has been a valued source of knowledge and understanding for more than 200 years, helping people around the world meet their needs and fulfill their aspirations. Our company is built on a foundation of principles that include responsibility to the communities we serve and where we live and work. In 2008, we launched a Corporate Citizenship Initiative, a global effort to address the environmental, social, economic, and ethical challenges we face in our business. Among the issues we are addressing are carbon impact, paper specifications and procurement, ethical conduct within our business and among our vendors, and community and charitable support. For more information, please visit our website: www.wiley.com/go/citizenship.

Evaluation copies are provided to qualified academics and professionals for review purposes only, for use in their courses during the next academic year. These copies are licensed and may not be sold or transferred to a third party. Upon completion of the review period, please return the evaluation copy to Wiley. Return instructions and a free of charge return shipping label are available at: www.wiley.com/go/returnlabel. If you have chosen to adopt this textbook for use in your course, please accept this book as your complimentary desk copy. Outside of the United States, please contact your local sales representative.

ISBN: 9781119148517 (PBK/BRV)
ISBN: 9781119299554 (EVALC)

The inside back cover will contain printing identification and country of origin if omitted from this page. In addition, if the ISBN on the back cover differs from the ISBN on this page, the one on the back cover is correct.

V10010497_052319

Contents

4 Forces Affecting the Distribution Systems 51

5 An Overview of the Purchasing Function 85

6 The Organization, Administration, and Evaluation of Purchasing 105

7 The Purchase Specification: An Overall View 131

8 The Optimal Amount 155

9 Determining Optimal Purchase Prices and Payment Policies 177

10 The Optimal Supplier 213

11 Typical Ordering Procedures 243

12 Typical Receiving Procedures 257

Preface

Nicholas, the general manager of a large independent foodservice operation had recently decided to employ a variety of social media marketing tools to build a regular customer base and keep it up to date with restaurant specials and events. Dinner business had been steadily declining over the past several months. His marketing campaign included a new Facebook page, offering half off meals through Groupon and a certificate for $10 on Restaurant.com.

Business had been particularly slow on Monday nights. One Monday morning, he decided to tweet his 600 followers that the restaurant would be offering 50 percent off on all entrees that evening. He also posted this on his Facebook page. Around 5:30 P.M., Nicholas was pleasantly surprised to notice a steady increase of walk-in customers. Shortly thereafter, the restaurant filled up and the wait for a table exceeded 45 minutes. While he smiled, Rachel, the restaurant's purchasing manager, approached him and said, "It sure would have been nice if you let me know about your half-off idea. I estimate that in about one hour, we will run out of food." Nicholas learned a very valuable lesson that evening—one that stuck with him for years—the importance of the purchasing function in the hospitality industry.

This text is not written necessarily for those who wish to become managers or directors of purchasing in the hospitality industry. It is written for those who will be involved with some phase of purchasing throughout their careers, and as the preceding scenario illustrates, most individuals involved in the management of a hospitality operation will interact with the purchasing function. In essence, this book is a purchasing book for nonpurchasing agents. It provides a comprehensive and understandable view of the activity, as well as its relationship to the management of a successful operation.

Although the text is primarily written as the foundation of a hospitality purchasing course, it is structured in a way that also acts as a comprehensive reference guide to the selection and procurement functions within the hospitality industry. This structure is particularly evident in the later chapters, which provide specific details on numerous categories of items and services commonly procured in this industry. Another reference attribute is the comprehensive glossary of key terms used throughout the text and the detailed index that provides context to many hospitality purchasing terms and concepts.

The text has a storied history, spanning numerous editions. In that time, we have maintained the original objectives of the text, while keeping up to date with this evolving field. Along with our staff, we spend thousands of hours on each new edition, ensuring that you are provided with current information and insights into the purchasing field from both academics and industry professionals.

Purchasing: Selection and Procurement for the Hospitality Industry, Ninth Edition is the most comprehensive and up-to-date hospitality purchasing text on the market today.

ORGANIZATION OF THE TEXT

This ninth edition of *Purchasing: Selection and Procurement for the Hospitality Industry* continues its successful recipe of balancing purchasing activities with product and information from a management perspective. Moreover, each chapter is revised so that it includes the most current concepts available, while providing even more in-depth coverage of hospitality purchasing. In essence, great care has been taken to maintain the integrity and readability of the original text while modernizing the discussions of purchasing techniques and practices currently being employed in the hospitality industry.

The text is divided into two parts. The first 14 chapters focus on the theory and application of selection and procurement concepts. The chapters are structured in a way that allows the reader to first gain insight into the typical organizational structure of a hospitality operation and the integration of the purchasing function. A discussion of concepts then progresses to provide the reader an expanding understanding of many of the facets of this complex, intertwined, and integral part of the industry. Along the way, the reader is provided numerous examples, questions, and exercises to reinforce these concepts. Although the organizational structure of the first 14 chapters provides an effective instructional path through hospitality purchasing theory, each chapter is written with the insight that some may wish to reorganize their order and/or select only a few to read. Because of this structure, the hospitality professional can also find significant value in this text by using the detailed table of contents or index to identify a particular concept to refresh or learn.

The remaining 11 chapters focus on items and services commonly procured in the hospitality industry. They are written in a modular and self-contained manner, and their sequence can be easily restructured by the instructor. Further, the hospitality professional can use these chapters as a reference guide when procuring these items and services.

Although many of the theoretical underpinnings of the purchasing function have not changed in the years since the text was created—product distribution channels and forces that affect the price of goods remain relatively unchanged, and specifications and purchase orders are still required to order these goods—the use of technology when implementing and maintaining effective purchasing policies and procedures has changed drastically. To inform readers about these changes, technology applications in the purchasing function are discussed throughout the majority of the first 14 chapters that encompass purchasing principles. Chapter 2, "Technology Applications in Purchasing," also covers this topic in depth.

We have also significantly expanded the number of discussions and interviews with industry executives who are purchasing experts. More than 25 experts discuss topics as diverse as the role of the broker, handling waste, green purchasing opportunities and responsibilities, and energy cost considerations, to name a few. We hope that these short stories provide even more insight into this complex and rapidly evolving field.

WHAT'S NEW FOR THE EDITION

Many important changes and additions have been made to *Purchasing: Selection and Procurement for the Hospitality Industry* to make the text even more useful. Among the most significant changes are the following:

- The former Chapter 6—The Organization and Administration of Purchasing—is combined with former Chapter 7—The Buyer's Relations with Other Company Personnel. This revision builds on the importance of staffing, training, directing, and overall administration of the purchasing function.

- The former Chapter 10—The Optimal Price—is combined with Chapter 11—The Optimal Payment Policy. This new chapter, "Determining Optimal Purchasing Prices and Payment Policies," more accurately reflects the interrelationship between price and payment policies.

- Industry Insights throughout the text have been updated. More than 27 discussions and interviews with industry executives are interwoven throughout. These stories include insights that provide insider information about current and future trends related to purchasing. All are written by experts in the purchasing field, providing perspectives of the future of purchasing, novel approaches to procurement, and new techniques for calculating the amount of products to purchase.

- Chapter 1 now includes definitions of the concepts of supply chain management and logistics. Chapter 2 has been updated to include more information on purchasing technology. Technology applications in purchasing—such as online ordering and group purchasing organizations—are addressed in chapters throughout the text.

- There is much more discussion of sustainability, green practices, and corporate social responsibility throughout the text. We also added substantial new information about organic and natural products in product chapters where appropriate.

- Chapter 4 contains new information on ethical concerns and procurement laws, such as the Food Safety Modernization Act.

- The updated glossary contains hundreds of purchasing-specific terms and detailed definitions. This glossary is a vital reference for students and those already working as purchasing professionals.

- New, revised, and updated illustrations and photographs of concepts, companies, and products relating to the purchasing function have been included.

- The end-of-chapter Questions and Problems have been updated and are now organized with the problems at the end to make it easier for instructors to decide which to assign to their classes. There are now Experiential Exercises for each chapter.

FEATURES

Purchasing: Selection and Procurement for the Hospitality Industry, Ninth Edition is a learning-centered textbook that includes several pedagogical enhancements in an effort to help the reader quickly acquire and retain important information.

- Each chapter begins with a **Purpose** section, which provides several learning objectives. These objectives, written using Bloom's Taxonomy of Educational Objectives – Cognitive Domain, direct readers' attention to the major headings and important themes discussed throughout the chapter.

- **Industry** interviews and insights are interspersed throughout all chapters of this text. Some of the interviews are "day-in-the-life" features that demonstrate how a typical purchasing agent functions day-to-day, whereas others are detailed discussions of specific areas within the purchasing function and how the purchasing agent makes an impact on decisions made for the benefit of the hospitality organization.

- At end of each chapter, a list of **Key Words and Concepts** provides the reader with an additional resource to assist in the retention of important topics. Readers can review these terms to ensure that they have grasped all relevant information from the chapter. Further, all Key Words are available in the glossary at the end of the text.

- The **Questions and Problems** section can be used for classroom discussion or assigned to students as homework. The accompanying Instructor's Manual provides detailed answers to each of these questions.

- Most chapters also include a **References** section. Along with citing sources of information within the chapter, these entries provide additional articles, websites, and texts should the reader wish to explore further particular topics.

- All chapters include **Experiential Exercises**. These allow the reader to actively learn about the function of purchasing through hands-on activities and projects.

SUPPLEMENTS

A completely revised *Instructor's Manual* accompanies this book; it provides several syllabus examples, teaching suggestions, test questions, answers to the book questions, and term projects. It can be obtained by contacting your Wiley sales representative. If you don't know who your representative is, please visit www.wiley.com, click on "Resources for Instructors," and then click on "Who's My Rep?" An electronic version of the *Instructor's Manual* is available to qualified instructors on the companion website, at www.wiley.com/college/feinstein.

Revised and updated *PowerPoint slides* are also available to students and instructors on the companion website. These graphically rich presentations are classroom tested and provide a detailed outline of each chapter. They can be easily modified to suit any instructor's preferences.

The *Test Bank* for this text has been specifically formatted for Respondus, an easy-to-use software for creating and managing exams that can be printed to paper or published directly to Blackboard, Canvas, Desire2Learn, eCollege, ANGEL, and other eLearning systems. Instructors who adopt *Purchasing: Selection and Procurement for the Hospitality Industry, Ninth Edition*, can download the *Test Bank* for free. Additional Wiley resources also can be uploaded into your Learning Management System (LMS) course at no charge. To view and access these resources and the Test Bank, visit www.wiley.com/college/feinstein, select *Purchasing: Selection and Procurement for the Hospitality Industry, Ninth Edition*, click on the "visit the companion sites" link.

ACKNOWLEDGMENTS

The authors would like to thank the following individuals for their continued assistance in developing and refining this text:

Audrey Alonzo for research and writing assistance.

Tanya Ruetzler for her work on updating the *Instructor's Manual.*

Ryan Kirk-Bautista for providing student input and research assistance.

Abigail Lorden at *Hospitality Technology Magazine*

Robert Grimes at Constrata Tech

Glenn Millar at Red Rock Capital Management

Danny Campbell at Cannery Casino Resorts

Camille Godwin-Austen at IHOP

Robert Hartman at Robert Hartman Consulting

Mark Mignogna at Sysco

Jerry Burawski at Lake Tahoe's Squaw Valley USA

Rebecca Kohn at San Jose State University

John Howeth at the American Egg Board

Joe Micatrotto Jr. at MRG Marketing and Management, Inc.

George Baggott, Baggott Consulting, Ltd., formerly at Cres Cor

Lisa Hogan at Santa Monica Seafood

Seth Larson at Newport Meat Company

John Smith and Drew Levinson at Wirtz Beverage Nevada

Wayne Bach at Four Queens Hotel and Casino

Dennis Lambertz at Nevada Food Brokerage

Robert Lindsay at House of Blues, Live Nation Entertainment

Mark Kelnhofer at Return on Investments

Mark Perigen at the USDA, AMS, Livestock, Poultry, and Seed Program

Don Odiorne at the Idaho Potato Commission

Daniel Celeste at University of Nevada, Las Vegas

Mark Lawson, Bill Leaver, and Jeff Bradach at Nevada Beverage Company

Sara Janovsky at Open Table

JoAnna Turtletaub, James Metzger, and Julie Kerr at John Wiley & Sons.

CHAPTER 1

THE CONCEPTS OF SELECTION AND PROCUREMENT

The Purpose of This Chapter

After reading this chapter, you should be able to:

- Define several terms associated with selection and procurement.

- Distinguish among different types of hospitality operations, and describe purchasing functions within those operations.

INTRODUCTION AND PURCHASING, SELECTION, AND PROCUREMENT DEFINITIONS

There is not a single job in the hospitality industry that does not involve purchasing in one way or another. A flight attendant must keep careful inventories of bottled water and soft drinks to know how much to request for restocking. The manager of a hotel must be able to find the best price for sheets and pillows in a reasonable quantity for her size of operation. An accountant for a hotel chain must know enough about the company's purchasing agreements to take advantage of discounts based on timely payments. An event designer must know the current price for flowers and décor so that he can make appropriate recommendations in the guest's price range. These are just a few of hundreds of scenarios where purchasing plays a critical role in the hospitality industry. Think about it for just a moment; it is the person in charge of purchasing who spends the majority of the money made by a hospitality operation, and it is this person's skills and knowledge that significantly assist in achieving profitability in an operation. It could easily be said that purchasing is one of the most important functions in any hospitality operation.

This book has been designed for those students who expect to have careers in the hospitality industry, but we realize not everyone will specialize in hospitality purchasing.

We emphasize the managerial principles of the purchasing function and intertwine the purchasing function with the other related management duties and responsibilities that the hospitality operator faces on a day-to-day basis.

This book includes enough product information so that you can easily prepare the product specifications required to select and procure an item if necessary, but also includes information on related purchasing activities, such as bill paying, that most purchasing agents do not perform. The typical hospitality manager eventually becomes involved with many of these related activities.

We also incorporate a great deal of information on technology applications related to the purchasing function that will enable a hospitality student to learn the technological aspects of procurement. Similarly, in areas where appropriate, particularly the specific product chapters, the concepts of sustainable and green practices and organic and natural products will be addressed.

It is our goal that wherever your career takes you within the hospitality industry, you will be adequately prepared to interact with the selection and procurement functions of an operation. With this in mind, we begin our discussion of selection and procurement for the hospitality industry.

purchasing Paying for a product or service.

selection Choosing from among various alternatives.

For most people, the term **purchasing** means simply paying for an item or service. For hospitality professionals, this meaning is far too restrictive because it fails to convey the complete scope of the buying function. For our use, the terms *selection* and *procurement* better define the processes involved.

Selection can be defined as choosing from among various alternatives on a number of different levels. For example, a buyer can select from among several competing brands of chicken, various grades of chicken, particular suppliers, or fresh and processed chicken products. One person, generally referred to as a buyer or purchaser, may not perform all these activities or make all these choices at one time. But they may be involved in most of them at some level.

Procurement, as opposed to selection, can be defined as an orderly, systematic exchange between a seller and a buyer. It is the process of obtaining goods and services, including all the activities associated with determining the types of products needed, making purchases, receiving and storing shipments, and administering purchase contracts.

Procurement activities are the nuts and bolts of the buyer's job. Once buyers know what is needed, they set about locating the suppliers who can best fulfill their needs. Buyers then attempt to order the correct amounts of products or services at the appropriate times and best prices, see to it that shipments are timely, and ensure that the delivered items meet company requirements. A host of related duties surrounding these activities include: being on the lookout for new items and new ideas, learning the production needs of the departments they serve, appraising the reliability of suppliers, identifying new technologies for procurement, and so on.

Not all operations have full-time buyers. Many have managers and supervisors who do the buying in addition to their other duties. To these employees, buying means more than what the term *procurement* by itself implies. These employees must also be aware of the relationship between purchasing and the other activities in the hospitality operation.

Because there are so few full-time purchasing agents in our field, a textbook that focuses solely on hospitality buying principles and procedures or product identification, although useful to some, would unnecessarily restrict operating managers and supervisors in hospitality. For example, it is not enough to simply know how to procure chicken. The typical operating manager must also consider what form of chicken to purchase, as well as whether or not chicken should even be on the menu.

procurement An orderly, systematic exchange between a seller and a buyer. The process of obtaining goods and services, including all activities associated with determining the types of products needed, making purchases, receiving and storing shipments, and administering purchase contracts.

■ Supply Chain Management

In today's complex world, even the term *procurement* does not reflect the full range of activities that are involved in obtaining the products and services necessary to accommodate our hospitality guests. A much wider concept is that of **supply chain management**. The Council of Supply Chain Management Professionals (CSCMP) defines supply chain management in the following way: "Supply chain management encompasses the planning and management of all activities involved in **sourcing** and procurement, **conversion**, and all logistics management activities." These may sound like big words, but in essence supply chain management means that businesses are concerned with knowing and coordinating everything starting with where the product is made or grown, to how it moves through distribution channels (discussed in Chapter 3), to how it is handled within the business, and how it is utilized by the end-user, our hospitality guest. Supply chain

supply chain management Process encompassing the planning and management of all activities involved in sourcing and procurement, conversion, and all logistics management activities.

sourcing Procurement practices aimed at finding, evaluating, and engaging suppliers of goods and services.

conversion Converting supplies into finished products.

management integrates supply and demand management within and across companies. Supply chain activities focus on product development, sourcing, production, and logistics, as well as the information systems needed to coordinate these activities. The CSCMP advocates that supply chain management is successful when the goal of getting the right product to the right customer at the lowest costs is achieved.

> **logistics management**
> The part of the supply chain management that plans, implements, and controls the efficient, effective flow and storage of goods, services, and related information between point of origin and the point of consumption in order to meet customer requirements.

The concept of **logistics management**, which is part of a company's supply chain, involves the movement of products and services to the customers. The CSCMP defines logistics management as "that part of the supply chain management that plans, implements and controls the efficient, effective flow and storage of goods, services and related information between point of origin and the point of consumption in order to meet customer requirements" (p. 1). From the definition, the core idea of logistics management is to meet customers' needs through optimizing movement of products and services within the company. Some activities in logistics management include controlling the flow of goods into the operation and out to the guest, sourcing and procurement, planning and customer service at strategic, tactical, and operational levels.[1]

■ Technology

Today, operating managers must also deal with technology that has revolutionized how buyers and suppliers procure products and services. This technology enables purchasing managers to complete complex procurement functions online with a few clicks.

> **e-commerce** Refers to transactions done online.
>
> **B2B e-commerce**
> Online interaction between businesses. Typically involves the sale and purchase of merchandise or services.
>
> **B2C e-commerce**
> Online interaction between businesses and consumers. Typically involves the sale and purchase of merchandise and services.
>
> **e-procurement** Ordering products and services from various purveyors online. Alternately, ordering these things from a particular vendor who provides proprietary software to the buyer, who is then allowed to enter the vendor's electronic system.

Transactions done electronically are commonly referred to as **e-commerce**, for electronic commerce. **B2B e-commerce** is the term used for business-to-business electronic transactions, and **B2C e-commerce** refers to business-to-consumer e-commerce. Amazon.com, for example, relies on B2C e-commerce to sell its products to consumers. B2B e-commerce that focuses specifically on procurement activities is referred to as **e-procurement**, for electronic procurement. Examples of companies that make e-procurement applications available to a wide variety of industry segments include Perfect Commerce, Ariba, and Sterling Commerce (a subsidiary of IBM).

These companies have successfully revolutionized the way procurement is conducted. One major company that focuses on the development of e-procurement applications in the food industry is iTradeNetwork (ITN). Companies such as Aramark, Sodexo, CKE Enterprises, Subway, Smash Burger, and PF Chang's, rely on ITN's supply chain solutions to streamline their selection and procurement functions.[2] Avendra, one of the largest procurement services companies,[3] has primarily focused on developing e-procurement applications for hotels. The company was formed by ClubCorp USA, Inc., Fairmont Hotels & Resorts, Hyatt Hotels Corporation, Marriott International, Inc., and Six Continents Hotels.

SUSTAINABILITY AND CORPORATE SOCIAL RESPONSIBILITY

No purchasing textbook can be relevant today without including the importance of **sustainability** and **corporate social responsibility**. Whether referring to an independent restaurant that buys produce and meats from local farms or a corporation, like Marriott, whose core values and heritage statement includes "Serve our World," hospitality companies must evaluate the effect of all their practices on the environment, people, and the global economy. We will discuss these concepts in more detail in the chapters detailing the forces that affect purchasing, supplier considerations, and purchasing specific types of products.

> **sustainability** The ability to not harm the environment or deplete natural resources.
>
> **corporate social responsibility** The practice of a company self-regulating the effect of their practices on the environment, people, and the global economy.

PURCHASING FUNCTIONS IN DIFFERENT TYPES OF HOSPITALITY OPERATIONS

The hospitality industry includes three major segments (see Figure 1.1). The first segment is **commercial hospitality operations**—the profit-oriented companies (see Figure 1.2). The second is the on-site segment, which used to be commonly known as institutional—those facilities that are operated on a break-even basis. The third is the military segment—those operations that include troop feeding and housing, as well as the various military clubs and military exchanges that exist within military installations. The second and third segments are collectively referred to as **noncommercial hospitality operations**.

> **commercial hospitality operations** Profit-oriented company.
>
> **noncommercial hospitality operations** Another term for on-site or military hospitality operation.

The following types of operations are generally considered part of the commercial segment:

- Hotels
- Motels
- Casinos
- Resorts
- Lodges
- Spas
- Quick-service (limited-service, casual service, or fast-food) restaurants
- Table-service (full-service) restaurants
- Snack bars
- Food courts
- Taverns, lounges, and bars
- Cafeterias

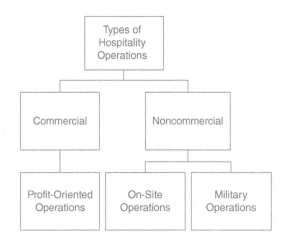

FIGURE 1.1 A major segment outline of the hospitality industry.

- Buffets
- On-premises caterers
- Off-premises caterers
- Vending-machine companies
- Ice cream parlors and stands
- In-transit foodservices (e.g., cruise ships and airlines)
- Contract foodservice companies, which typically operate in plants, office buildings, day care facilities, assisted care facilities, senior care facilities, schools, recreation centers, hospitals, and sports centers

FIGURE 1.2   An example of a commercial hospitality operation. ©atmoomoo/Shutterstock

- Convenience stores with foodservices
- Supermarkets with foodservices
- Department stores and discount stores with foodservices

The following types of operations are generally considered part of the noncommercial division of the hospitality industry:

- Employee-feeding operations
- Public and parochial elementary- and secondary-school foodservices
- College and university housing and foodservices
- Transportation foodservices, such as the Meals on Wheels program
- Hospitals
- Assisted living facilities
- Extended-care facilities
- Clubs
- Self-operated community centers, such as senior centers and day care centers
- Military installations
- Camps
- Public institutions, such as the foodservices in some government facilities
- Adult communities
- Correctional facilities
- Religious facilities
- Shelters

In Chapter 6, we offer a detailed discussion of the purchasing functions found in the various types of hospitality operations. In this introductory chapter, however, we provide you with sufficient understanding to get you started. When we discuss traditional hospitality operations, we think first of the independent operation. In addition, those in the trade usually group the independent operations according to size: the small, medium, and large independents. The other major type of hospitality operation includes the multiunits and the **franchises**.

> **franchises** A business form where the owner (franchisor) allows others (franchisees) to use his or her operating procedures, name, and so forth, for a fee.

■ The Independent Operation

The small independent, such as a local Chinese restaurant or a bed and breakfast inn, is typically run by an owner–manager, who usually does all the buying for the business. He or she also oversees the other related purchasing activities, such as receiving deliveries and paying the bills.

The medium-sized independent generally involves more than one person in the purchasing function. Usually, the general manager coordinates the various activities that other management personnel perform. For instance, he or she typically coordinates the purchases of department heads, such as the dining room manager who needs china and glassware, the bartender who requires alcoholic beverages, and the chef who needs food. The general manager also oversees other related purchasing activities.

The large independent, such as a hotel, implements the purchasing function in much the same way that the medium independent does, except that it may employ a full-time buyer. This buyer purchases for the various production departments, such as housekeeping, maintenance, engineering, and foodservice. Alternately, a designated employee from each of these departments may be doing the purchasing; for example, a hotel may employ an **executive steward** to order supplies and to supervise the sanitation crew. Often the large independent operation has a full-time food buyer, a beverage buyer, and a buyer who purchases equipment and other nonfood supplies. A purchasing vice president or an equivalent official may or may not supervise these three buyers. The buyers are, almost certainly, supervised by a management person.

> **executive steward** Oversees cleaning crews. Typically also has purchasing responsibilities for things such as soaps, chemicals, and other cleaning supplies. May also control the china, glass, flatware inventories, and single-use (paper, plastic, etc.) products.

In the past, small and medium-sized businesses may have had a tough time competing in the same markets as larger companies. This was mainly because these smaller businesses had to pay higher prices for many of the products that they procured because they were not afforded the same discounts as large companies (we talk more about these discounts in Chapter 6). However, e-procurement has leveled the playing field in many instances by enabling these smaller hospitality companies to procure products at more competitive prices and, therefore, to be more competitive pricewise with larger hospitality operations. Today, hospitality buyers can select and procure goods and services from suppliers and distributors all over the world.

An idea addressed more completely in Chapter 6 is co-op buying, a concept that enjoys popularity among some independent hospitality operations, particularly some foodservice operations.

co-op buying   The banding together of several small operators to consolidate and enhance their buying power.

referral group   A type of co-op where independent operators join together to send business to one another. For instance, Best Western is a referral group that has a central reservations system available to each member. In addition, these groups typically provide some purchasing advantages, as well as other types of support, to its members.

aggregate purchasing company   Another term for buying club.

group purchasing organization (GPO)   Another term for buying club.

real estate investment trust (REIT)   A legal business entity that buys, sells, and manages commercial and residential properties.

portal   Web access point. Presents a starting point and access to multiple sources of similar online information.

e-commerce marketplace   An online application allowing buyers to locate vendors, research products and services, solicit competitive bids, and place orders electronically.

commissary   Similar to a central distribution center. The major difference is that at a commissary, raw foods are processed into finished products, which is not the case in a central distribution center. Could be considered a restaurant company's personal convenience food processing plant.

As the phrase implies, **co-op buying** is a system whereby hospitality operations come together to achieve savings through the purchase of food and supplies in bulk. Either the operations rotate the purchasing duties among themselves, or they hire someone (or a company) to coordinate all of the purchasing for them. Another type of co-op involves **referral groups**, which are independent operators joining together to send business to one another. For instance, Best Western is a lodging referral group that has a central reservations system available to each member.

E-commerce has significantly affected co-op buying. Companies are currently aggregating purchasing processes for similar hospitality organizations throughout the country. These companies are commonly referred to as **aggregate purchasing companies** or **group purchasing organizations (GPOs)**. Examples of GPOs include Entegra, Foodbuy, and Dining Alliance.

GPOs do not buy or sell products. Instead, they negotiate contracts on behalf of restaurants, hotels, management companies, resorts, and **real estate investment trusts (REITs)**. Each company enrolling in this group might receive a purchasing guide that includes the names, e-mail addresses, websites, and telephone numbers of suppliers, along with a brief description of the programs negotiated on purchasing companies' behalf. Buyers can then access a private **e-commerce marketplace**—or **portal**—to conduct business with approved distributors or suppliers. As more buyers become members of the GPO, purchasing power increases and so do savings. Typically, either buyers pay a participation fee that provides access to the aggregate purchasing companies' pricing or the GPO takes a percentage of the savings.

■ The Multiunits and Franchises

The second major category of hospitality operations in the purchasing function includes multiunit companies, franchises, and chains. These interlocking operations organize their purchasing somewhat differently from independent organizations. One usually finds, when examining a chain of hospitality operations, for example, a centrally located vice president of purchasing. Moreover, the company may maintain one or more central distribution points, such as a **commissary** or distribution warehouse. The managers of the company-owned outlets receive supplies from the central distribution points under the authority of the vice president of purchasing. Often these managers may also do a minimal amount of purchasing from local or national suppliers that this vice president approves; in some cases the managers may order from approved suppliers without consulting the vice president of purchasing, or they may order everything from a commissary.

In company-owned outlets, the internal organization for buying, particularly for restaurants, stipulates that the unit manager order most products from the central commissary or approved suppliers. The unit managers may, however, have the authority to make a few purchases on their own, such as a cleaning service or a locally produced beer. When the unit managers do this sort of purchasing, however, they nevertheless need to follow company policies and procedures.

In company-owned, large-hotel properties, a system similar to that of the large independents generally exists while applying the broader concepts of supply chain management. That is, the vice president of purchasing at corporate headquarters may draw up some national contracts, research and buy **commodity** items such as coffee or shrimp in consideration of global supply and demand, establish purchase specifications, and set general purchasing policy. He or she may also purchase the stock for the company's central distribution warehouses and/or central commissaries. By and large, however, vice presidents of purchasing handle overall policy, while the individual hotel units, although they do not have complete freedom, exercise a great deal of purchasing discretion within established limitations.

The typical franchisee receives many supplies from a central commissary, but many of these non-company-owned units try to do some purchasing locally— to maintain good relations in the community, if nothing else. However, they quickly discover that they save considerable time, money, and energy by using the commissary and/or **central distribution center** as much as possible. If no central commissaries and distribution centers are available, the franchisees usually order their needed stock from suppliers that the vice president of purchasing has prescreened and approved. Franchisees are, however, usually free to buy from anyone as long as that supplier meets the company's requirements.

> **commodity** A basic, raw food ingredient. It is considered by buyers to be the same regardless of which vendor sells it. For instance, all-purpose flour is often considered a commodity product, for which any processor's product is acceptable.
>
> **central distribution center** A large warehouse owned by a multiunit hospitality company that orders merchandise directly from primary sources, takes delivery, stocks the merchandise, and then delivers it to company-affiliated units in the area.

A DAY IN THE LIFE
Wayne Bach, Purchasing Manager

■ THE FOUR QUEENS HOTEL AND CASINO, LAS VEGAS, NEVADA

Opened in 1966, the Four Queens Hotel and Casino is one of the classic gaming hotels on Fremont Street in downtown Las Vegas. The property has 690 rooms including 45 suites, three full-service restaurants, two fast-service restaurants, three cocktail lounges, 22,000 square feet of meeting and event space, and a gift shop to accompany its 32,000 square feet of casino space. Wayne Bach and Karen Ashe comprise the tag team that ensures that there are enough food, beverage, and supplies to provide superior products and services to their guests 24 hours a day.

Wayne holds the title of purchasing manager. He reports directly to the controller and then to the financial director. Wayne is responsible for buying all food and beverage products so he also indirectly reports to the chef and the food and beverage directors.

Wayne starts his day early; he arrives at 6:00 a.m. to his office right inside the receiving and storage warehouse. Wayne feels that being right on the floor is essential to have control over the operation and to know exactly what is happening in his department. When he arrives, the first thing he does is check e-mails for notices from the chef regarding special needs and from suppliers regarding any product shortages or the product bid sheets he receives an average of twice per week. Then he grabs his inventory sheet and walks through all the storage areas, refrigerators, and freezers. Because he manages the four receiving clerks, he checks to see that they are doing their jobs to keep the areas clean and the product rotated. He makes sure they check the weight and quality of all deliveries, especially fresh meat and seafood items. Twice a week he does a check to see that the par stocks on hand match the amounts that the computer shows should be available.

The Four Queens does not have as sophisticated a computer system as some of the ones that will be discussed later in this book, but it does use a Stratton-Warren inventory system. After the food products are received, an inventory control clerk enters the quantities of products and prices from the invoices into the system.

Wayne spends 20–25 percent of his time placing orders. He emphasizes that it takes a lot of research to ensure that he is buying the proper products and that he is helping the chef and food and beverage director learn about new products in the marketplace or that might fulfill existing needs better. He attends many trade shows such as restaurant association shows, Catersource, the Nightclub and Bar show, and distributor shows as well as reads as many trade magazines as possible. He also arranges for brokers and vendors to provide samples and perform taste tests.

Food items get bid sheets twice per week. Due to the relatively small size of the warehouse, Wayne orders produce and some dairy items daily, meat and liquor three times a week, and grocery items/dry goods twice a week.

The inventory control system is not as strict as in some of the larger properties where Wayne has worked such as the Plaza Hotel in New York. About 75 percent of the product used from inventory is issued from a requisition, but chefs and others can enter the storeroom, especially in the evening hours when the receiving clerks are not present, and still grab what they need.

One of the biggest parts of the job is deciding how much and when to order. The hotel sets pars (the minimum amount that you always need to have on hand) for all products. But these pars can be greatly affected by the amount of banquet business. At the Four Queens, the chef decides how much extra food is needed to let Wayne know how much to order. With all the special events on Fremont Street such as concerts and festivals, Wayne says that for beverages, they often need to order as much as 50 percent over the pars, especially beer to satisfy all the people thirsty from the heat in Las Vegas.

Another employee maintains par stocks for all the nonfood items for the hotel, such as plates, glassware, flatware, disposable items, linens, towels, and even the coffeemakers. Some of the biggest challenges are keeping enough glassware because the breakage is so high. Pillowcases are another high demand item as on a busy weekend the housekeepers may change out as many as 1,000 of them in an hour. The hotel buys many logo items that require special procedures. It has blanket purchase orders with the companies that supply items such as logo cocktail napkins and glasses. Because the price is cheaper to buy the items in large quantities but there is not enough storage space to hold that much product, it uses stockless purchasing where the supplier keeps the product in its warehouse until needed. When soliciting bids for these items every six months, the ability of the company to store the product is even more important than the price.

Wayne says that the hardest part of his job is accommodating and finding products for last-minute requests. But the best part is the job is lots of fun. "There is always something different to do and new things to learn. Know your products, know your vendors, know your menu/recipes, know your customer."

A DAY IN THE LIFE (continued)

Wayne is a Culinary Institute of America trained chef and worked for the Plaza Hotel in New York for 20 years prior to moving to Las Vegas. The major differences between his job at the Plaza and at the Four Queens are that the Plaza had stricter inventory controls and also had many early morning and off-hours deliveries.

Key Words and Concepts

Aggregate purchasing companies
Business-to-business (B2B) e-commerce
Business-to-consumer (B2C) e-commerce
Central distribution center
Commercial hospitality operations
Commissary
Commodity
Conversion
Co-op buying
Corporate social responsibility
E-commerce
E-commerce marketplace
E-procurement
Executive steward

Franchise
Group purchasing organization (GPO)
Logistics management
Noncommercial hospitality operations
Portal
Procurement
Purchasing
Real estate investment trust (REIT)
Referral group
Selection
Sourcing
Supply chain management
Sustainability

Questions and Problems

1. Define the term *selection*.

2. Define the term *procurement*.

3. Define the term *supply chain management*.

4. Define the term *logistics*.

5. Explain the advantages of studying the broad view of the purchasing function.

6. What is an e-procurement application?

7. Briefly describe the major segments of the hospitality industry.

8. Briefly differentiate among the ways in which the small and the large independents generally do their purchasing.

9. Briefly describe co-op buying.

10. How has e-commerce affected co-op buying?

Questions and Problems (continued)

11. Briefly describe two typical purchasing procedures found in multiunits and franchises.

12. Briefly describe how a local restaurant that is part of a large restaurant chain probably does its purchasing.

13. Name one reason why a franchise might do some local buying.

14. Describe three duties of a vice president of purchasing in a large hotel or restaurant chain.

15. Why might a small, independent hospitality operation be interested in co-op buying?

16. Under what conditions do you think a franchise operation might be interested in co-op buying?

17. Define the term *purchasing*.

18. What is a referral group?

19. Briefly describe the benefits of e-commerce.

20. How do you think e-commerce has changed the hospitality industry?

Experiential Exercises

1. Ask a manager of a local franchise operation the five following questions. Write a report detailing your findings.

   > Do you currently purchase items from a commissary?
   > If so: What items are you required to purchase from the commissary?
   > Do you have to follow specific guidelines on the other products you purchase outside of the commissary?
   > What are the benefits of purchasing from a commissary?
   > What are the drawbacks of purchasing from a commissary?

2. Interview a noncommercial hospitality operator. Ask him or her to describe the job and explain how the responsibilities differ from those of a commercial hospitality operator. Write a report detailing your discussion with the operator.

3. Shadow (follow around) a purchasing agent for a day. Prepare a diary of all duties and responsibilities performed by the agent.

References

1. Council of Supply Chain Management Professionals (CSCMP), *Logistics Management*, 2010. Retrieved from http://cscmp.org/aboutcscmp/definitions.asp. See also, R. Handfield, *What Is Supply Chain Management?* 2011. Retrieved from http://scm.ncsu .edu/scm-articles/article/what-is-supply-chain-management.

TECHNOLOGY APPLICATIONS IN PURCHASING

The Purpose of This Chapter

After reading this chapter, you should be able to:

- Describe how distributors utilize technology to assist in the management of their products and to streamline their services.

- Explain how technologies are used by hospitality operators in the selection, procurement, and inventory management process.

- Discuss what may lie ahead for the future of hospitality selection and procurement.

TECHNOLOGIES THAT DISTRIBUTORS USE

Technology applications in the selection and procurement function continue to evolve rapidly. Today, many forms of technology are available to help distributors and buyers transact business. Very few businesses can do without these tools that can considerably streamline the cycle of purchasing, distribution, receiving, storage, issuing, and product usage.

middleman or **intermediary** Other terms for vendor.

Distributors use software applications to track and analyze many business functions. A distributor is the **middleman** or **intermediary** between a source and retailer (to be discussed further in Chapter 3) and, therefore, must keep track of information such as customers, sources, costs, and specifications.[1]

■ Customer Databases

Typically, distributors use specialized software that integrates with the hospitality operation's point-of-sale (POS) system that buyers use to input their orders. The distributors also use their management information systems to build valuable customer databases. For example, these databases can help predict the hospitality business's product needs and behavior so the right products will always be available and can even forecast profitability by analyzing the buyer's food costs of items sold. Customer databases also provide information to the marketing department for the development of special promotions. This software is also used to estimate, or forecast, the number and types of hospitality operations that might, or should, open in a particular area, allowing the distributor to make informed decisions regarding hiring and expansion.

customer relationship management (CRM) Another term for customer. Sometimes also referred to as customer relationship marketing. Forming personal alliances that will lead to the sale and purchase of products and services.

These days, the development and management of customer databases is more commonly included in an operation's **customer relationship management (CRM)** strategy that places the emphasis on the customer. CRM is "all the tools, technologies and procedures to manage, improve, or facilitate sales, support and related interactions with customers, prospects, and business partners" throughout the business. This could include customer contact information, product preferences, buying habits, and satisfaction levels regarding service, just to name a few elements.[2] Using CRM in this type of business-to-business (B2B) environment assists in developing critical masses of information and can be integrated with other technology solutions to make all processes more efficient. Salesforce.com is one of the largest CRM systems according to Softwareadvice.com. Its hospitality clients include distributors and producers such as Sysco, Coca-Cola, and Pernod Ricard (a premium wine and spirits company).

■ Ordering Systems

Distributors also utilize software applications to facilitate the sales process. For instance, most distributors now have all inventories counted, priced, organized, and stored in product databases that their customers can access online. This detailed information enables distributors to manage and price their products quickly and easily. It is much more convenient for everyone than the old method, whereby buyers would receive printed product lists from distributors that noted product names, manufacturers, identification numbers, and other descriptive information. To obtain the **product status**—availability or current prices—buyers had to call either the sales representative or the distributor directly and in some cases had to receive daily fax order sheets to update prices, especially dairy, meat, fish, poultry, produce, and bread prices. The buyer then had to call in the order or place it with the sales representative. This old method is still used, although most buyers now go online to procure products or request them from their central warehouses.

> **product status**   Indicates whether a product is available from the vendor or if it is on backorder.

When buyers go online to acquire products, they utilize an **online ordering system**, commonly referred to as a **web order entry system**. Through this type of system, buyers and distributors communicate directly with one another online. This method of communication permits buyers to order products directly and receive instant feedback on pricing and availability. Such systems also minimize the ordering function and the paper trail for buyers and distributors. Distributors commonly provide these services free of charge. Companies using these types of Web order entry systems include U.S. Foodservice and Sysco. These companies are two of the largest broadline foodservice distributors in the United States. Examples of other companies that utilize Web order entry systems include the following:

> **online ordering system**   Ordering products from vendors over the Internet or directly from a purveyor using his or her proprietary software.
>
> **web order entry system**   Refers to a method of ordering products online.

Cheney Brothers, Inc.

iTradeNetwork

HFM Foodservice (Pacific region and Hawaii)

J. Kings Food Service Professionals, Inc.

Phoenix Wholesale Foodservice

Schoenmann Produce Co.

FreshPoint

Preferred Meats

GFS—Gordon Foodservice

Ecolab

Coca-Cola

■ GPS

With the rapid development of inexpensive global positioning systems (GPS), many distributors use **logistics and mapping software** to outline the routing sequences their delivery drivers must follow when delivering products.[3] This technology is commonly referred to as a "GPS vehicle tracking system." A distributor can enter into the GPS all the locations

> **logistics and mapping software**   Software used by vendors to outline the routing sequences its delivery drivers must follow when delivering shipments. Intended to increase delivery efficiency.

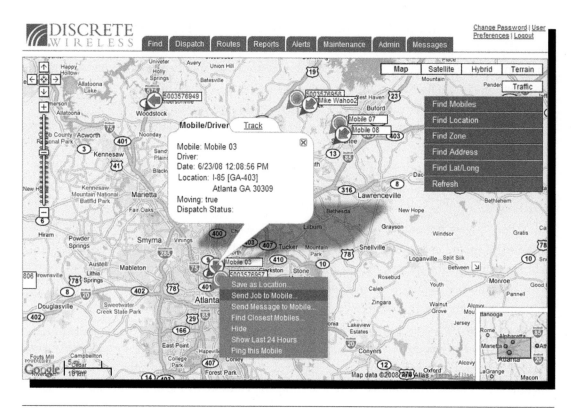

FIGURE 2.1 GPS screen as seen by a delivery driver.
Courtesy of Discrete Wireless, Inc.

drivers need to visit the following day simply by typing an address or placing a marker on a digital map (such as Google Maps or Mapquest). The sequence of deliveries and routing also impacts how the trucks and items are loaded and placed within the vehicles.

fleet management software Software that suppliers use to schedule vehicles and other equipment usage, required repair and maintenance work, and preventive maintenance activities.

roadside sensor network Vehicles that contain a variety of onboard sensors that collect real-time data on current traffic conditions that can then be used to reroute automatically the vehicles' scheduled routes. Some networks also include safety warning features.

Fleet management software can then be utilized to determine the most efficient route to take and will assist in determining the optimal number of delivery trucks to use (Figure 2.1). This software can also estimate both driver downtime and the amount of product that should be delivered per hour by taking into account street traffic flow (utilizing **roadside sensor networks** or applications such as Waze), various times of day, and the expected time spent loading and unloading shipments. Software can then compare these estimates with actual results. Companies such as Fleetgistics and USA Fleet Solutions specialize in providing these types of technologies.

Related software can be utilized to track delivery errors, discrepancies, and complaints or comments by customers, receiving agents, or salespersons. All of these software programs can be integrated to form one information technology (IT) solution. This enables the distributor to minimize order-placing and delivery costs, as well as to resolve problems quickly, ultimately increasing margins and profitability.

RFID

Although a relatively new technology in the hospitality industry, RFID is predicted to be able to dramatically change the management and distribution of products (see Figure 2.2). **RFID (radio frequency identification) tags** are miniscule microchips, some as small as a grain of sand, that can be utilized in tracking everything from cars to basic inventory, and even people. For instance, they can be attached to apples to transmit location information and monitor temperature throughout the channel of distribution. RFID can also be useful in overall supply chain management and can assist with more accurate inventory counts and order reconciliations, ensuring product is fresh and free from organisms that cause foodborne illness, and reducing out-of-stock situations.[4] More information on the basics of RFID can be found in the online RFID Journal.

FIGURE 2.2 An RFID scanner.
©ermingut/Getty Images

> **RFID tags**   Radio frequency identification tags placed on boxes, crates, pallets, and the like. They are used by distributors and retailers to monitor automatically inventory and storage areas. A wireless technology is used—the same technology that allows electronic wireless toll payment in many states or the ExxonMobil SpeedPass wireless payment system—to transmit data wirelessly to a sensor. It could be argued that RFID tags are a major improvement over the bar code technology used by most distributors and retailers today.

TECHNOLOGIES THAT HOSPITALITY OPERATORS USE

Many technological products have been developed to streamline the selection and procurement process and make life easier for buyers. Hospitality operators have generally been eager to adopt labor- and time-saving electronic equipment to enhance the purchasing function and the overall inventory control process.

Fax Machine

It is hard to believe that just 30 years ago, fax machines were one of the most innovative types of technology used in purchasing. The ability to send documents over phone lines significantly reduced the confusion and mistakes sometimes associated with verbal orders and allowed printed output to be stored for historical records, used to verify orders and prove they were sent, and establish usage patterns. Today, most fax machines are multipurpose devices that can scan, print, fax, email, and copy at incredible speeds in high resolution and color. eFax documents can also be sent from within various applications and via email. However, they have been almost fully displaced by personal computers (PCs), notebooks, tablets, smart phones, and other smart devices.

■ Personal Computers, Tablets, Smart Phones, and Other Smart Devices

The personal computer (PC) is certainly the most powerful and useful tool that a hospitality owner–manager can have. Although the majority of students reading this book cannot imagine a time without computers, PCs in 1979 (VisiCalc) revolutionized how hospitality operators could analyze huge amounts of data and manage inventories more effectively. Previously, the majority of inventory costing and counting had been done by individuals armed with calculators, paper, and pencils. PCs have also made it possible for hospitality operators to base their purchasing decisions on the most up-to-date data, such as current food costs, item availability, and menu item popularity. Today, the mobility, flexibility, and convenience of wireless devices mean supply chain managers can coordinate processes at every link in the chain, regardless of their physical location. They also can access data on all devices that can support browser applications such as Internet Explorer, Google Chrome, Apple Safari, and other proprietary applications. Although some would argue that the PC is becoming obsolete, others feel that it will still have a place for business and personal use for many more years.[5]

■ Point-of-Sale Systems

point-of-sale (POS) system Computerized device used to record sales revenue and maintain a considerable amount of management information, such as number of guests served, server productivity statistics, amount of cash collected, number of each menu item sold, and so forth.

Before the introduction of the **point-of-sale (POS) system**, it was very difficult to track sold menu items. The gear-driven cash register merely stored cash and provided some limited sales information on printed receipts while reporting based on how many times a specific key was hit on the keyboard.

Today, POS systems are networked PCs that are highly integrated in the daily functions of operations (see Figure 2.3). These systems can tabulate and organize tremendous amounts of sales data very quickly Many POS systems actually include a back-office PC or access to cloud computing, where all data are stored, reported, manipulated, and integrated with other hardware and software applications inside and outside the operation. Most POS systems use touch-screen PCs that allow authorized users to delete menu items, track employee activity, analyze worker productivity, force **order modifiers** (such as doneness of a steak), and up-sell (upgrade

FIGURE 2.3 POS system.
©*Oracle Corporation, used with permission*

your meal to a large Coke and fries?). Some POS systems allow a waiter to carry a wireless ordering system to the table. There are also POS systems on top of or embedded at the table, allowing customers to order themselves and complete other functions such as comment cards, server paging, nutritional information, wine ordering, and games. Jack in the Box was one of the first quick-service restaurants (QSRs) to install kiosks at which guests can order their food.[6] Stacked in California is a great example of a restaurant company that allows guests to build their own menu item on a tabletop computer and send the order directly to the kitchen.

POS systems are networked and communicate with a central computer, referred to as a **server**, or through the Internet. This system can track sales from the connected computers in all departments or areas within the hospitality operation and instantly provide vital information to managers. These systems integrate with inventory-tracking systems that automatically delete from inventory the standard amount of each ingredient used to make each menu item. The integration of POS and inventory systems provides the manager with a **theoretical inventory usage** figure that can later be compared with actual physical counts. Furthermore, some POS systems facilitate the ability to send purchase orders directly to the distributors, based on sales and inventory reduction information.[7] Back-office systems and applications often include additional software modules such as production forecasting, training, labor scheduling, time and attendance, and human resource information systems (HRIS) that includes all human resource and employee-related functionality.

> **order modifier** Point-of-sale (POS) software prompt that forces the server to answer questions about a guest's order. For instance, if the server enters one steak into the system, the computer will ask, "What temperature?" The server will then answer the question to complete the order before sending it to the kitchen.
>
> **server** Central computer to which other computers, such as individual PCs, are networked. It communicates with all the other computers on the network.
>
> **theoretical inventory usage** Expected amount of inventory usage based on recorded sales. For instance, if 100 steaks are recorded as sold, there should be only 100 steaks missing from inventory.

■ Bar Code Reader

Many hospitality operations are now placing bar code labels on their inventory items (or use those the distributors applied) to streamline the inventory-control process (see Figure 2.4). Bar code labels are vertical lines of varying thicknesses separated by blank spaces. These lines and spaces, or "elements," provide a bar code reader with an identification code (ID). This ID is used to look up the product on a database. **Bar code elements**, IDs, and corresponding product information are based on a standard that associates these pieces of information. The most commonly used standard is the Universal Product Code (UPC) in the United States. However, other standards include EAN, Code 128, Code 39, Interleaved 2-of-5, PDF417, MaxiCode, Data Matrix, and QR Code. Information on these standards is available on the websites of GS1 US, Scandit, and Barcode Graphics.

> **bar code element** The lines and spaces on a bar code label.

When a bar code system is used, the physical inventory count of a hospitality operation usually consists of scanning each product in the storeroom with a portable bar code reader.[8] Bar code readers of today sometimes are specialized devices, but also can be an add-on or an application to a smart phone or other tablet device. There is no need to spend large amounts of time locating a product on a lengthy printed inventory list and recording, by hand, the total number of units in inventory at the end of the month. Instead, the portable bar code reader quickly gathers and

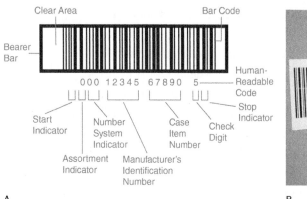

A   B

FIGURE 2.4 (A) A UPC description. (B) Using a bar code reader for inventory.
©Bacho/Shutterstock

| **bar code reader** Device used to read labels that contain bar code elements. | downloads the data to the computer for instant analysis. **Bar code readers** provide wireless communication to a computer and can instantaneously download and upload information over radio frequencies (RFs). |

The bar code reader also automates the counting of in-process inventories and in particular is used frequently in beverage operations to control inventory. This will be discussed in more detail in Chapter 22.

■ Product Identification and Specifications

Buyers have many options available to "spec out" or compare similar products for their hospitality operations. Traditional forms include buyers' guides, such as the **North American Meat Processors Association (NAMP)** publication, *The Meat Buyer's Guide (MBG)*, originally published in 1963. This printed guidebook, with specific product information, contains many full-color photographs. The newest version of this guide (March 2011) can be purchased in print or for online access, or a combination of both at the association's website.

North American Meat Processors Association (NAMP) Trade organization representing meat-processing companies and associates who share a continuing commitment to provide their customers with safe, reliable, and consistent meat, poultry, seafood, game, and other related products.

product identification Another term for product specification.

specification A description of a product's required characteristics.

Other products on the market can also streamline the **product identification** and **specification** process. These resources enable users to search products and product categories and may also provide information about the distributors who sell them. They can contain a seemingly endless amount of information. If a product is made somewhere in the world and is distributed, chances are it can be found online.

An example is the Food and Beverage Market Place, started in print form 100 years ago as the *Thomas Food Industry Register* (TFIR). This subscription-based service (also available in print) brings buyers and sellers together through a searchable database of more than 40,000 company listings and nearly 6,000 product categories. All company listings are cross-indexed, and one may search by product, location, company, or brand name. The Thomas Register produced a printed version of this product for more than 100 years. Websites can also help buyers spec out products. For example, many marketing boards in the United States provide information about a particular product. The California Avocado Commission, for instance, is responsible for promoting the sale and purchase of avocados. This board, as well as many others, such as the Australian Pork Corporation, the National Paper Trade Association, and the British Contract Furniture Association, have websites to distribute information about their products. The sites might feature product specifications, availability reports, trends, and other information. These sites also enable viewers to engage in question/answer activities with the board administrators.

■ Product Ordering

As discussed in Chapter 1, several companies have developed systems that permit buyers to order products online. These **e-procurement applications**, often made available by the distributors, streamline and minimize a buyer's ordering procedure, thereby creating a value-added service for the buyer.[9] At the same time, when a buyer uses this ordering system, he or she streamlines the order-taking process at the distributor's end. Previously, a distributor had to enter a buyer's order manually from a fax, telephone call, or written purchase order. The new system eliminates the inefficiencies of the "multiple-ordering" process. Instead, a buyer enters the order and sends it directly to the distributor. This process reduces labor costs and time on the buyer's and the distributor's ends. For the buyer, the goal is to have "perfect orders." The payoff for companies with high rates of "perfect orders"—those that are complete, in the right place, undamaged, and on time—can be substantial. An AMR Research survey cited by the American Hotel and Lodging Association (AHLA) concluded that increasing the total number of perfect orders would result in a one-percent profit increase for an organization. Companies that ranked high in the amount of perfect orders carried less inventory, had shorter times between when they purchased products and when the product was sold to the hospitality companies' guests, and were more profitable overall.[10] Another distributor benefit of the process is the likelihood that users of this easy-to-use ordering system will become loyal customers who are sometimes referred to as **house accounts** or **prime-vendor accounts**.

> **e-procurement application** Software that allows customers to select and purchase products online.

Large, multiunit hospitality operations leverage this technology by negotiating contractual pricing agreements on selected products prior to ordering. A unit operator can then go online to order products that have been approved by the main office. Upon entering the distributor's ordering site and logging in, the unit operator would see only a list of items that they are approved to buy.

Product information on e-procurement applications can typically be retrieved in several formats, unlike the typical printed catalog in which everything is listed alphabetically and/or by product categories. For instance, databases on the e-marketplace enable users to search for and evaluate all of the types of hot dogs a particular vendor sells. Buyers might view hot dogs by size, types of ingredients, and packers' brands. Users can

> **house account** Term used by a vendor to identify a very loyal customer. A customer who continually buys from a vendor and is not interested in buying from competing vendors.
>
> **prime-vendor account** A consistent and significantly large account a buyer has with a vendor that, because of its size and the loyalty of the buyer, may be eligible for discounts and/or other special privileges.

also narrow the search, for example, to 4–1 (four hot dogs per pound), pure-beef, or Oscar Mayer® brand hot dogs. From this narrow list, users can then choose the desired product or continue to refine and narrow the search. Once users find the desired product, the hospitality operators can then "tag," or choose, products they want to procure. Orders are then instantly communicated to the vendor, who might forward this information to a local distribution center for processing and delivery.

■ Inventory-Tracking and Storage Management

If product orders have been made online, ordering information can be utilized to streamline the inventory process. For instance, it can be linked to other software and used in the equations and formulas noted in Chapters 8, 9, and 13.

Today, almost all hospitality operators use technology to increase their inventory-control and cost-control efforts. For example, some small operators develop elaborate spreadsheets using generic spreadsheet software, most commonly in Microsoft Excel®. They list all their products in inventory and then develop mathematical formulas to calculate costs and usage. On the last day of each month, they physically count their storeroom and in-process inventories and enter this information on the spreadsheet. They also enter all product costs, which usually come from typing in invoice receipts for the month or from directly downloading the information from an ordering system they are using. The information currently entered is the "ending inventory," and the information entered the previous month becomes the "beginning inventory." Once the major variables have been entered (beginning inventory, ending inventory, purchases, and other end-of-month adjustments), cost of goods sold calculations are automatic.

Some hospitality operators use off-the-shelf software packages and services that manage inventory in a hospitality environment, such as Eatec®, CrunchTime!, Compeat, MenuLink by NCR, and Stratton Warren system by Agilysys. These software packages can streamline the back-of-the-house hospitality operation and be linked to an operator's POS system, whether it is on a server or in the cloud. These packages can also cost recipes, analyze a recipe's nutritional information, calculate food and beverage costs, evaluate a food item's sales history, forecast sales, develop audit trails, allow instant stock level information, and enhance menu planning efforts (see Figure 2.5). In addition, many of these software packages can track employee work schedules, attendance patterns, and work-hour accumulations.

When generic spreadsheet programs and off-the-shelf software do not meet a hospitality operator's needs, he or she might hire a software-consulting firm that specializes in the hospitality industry. A specialist can develop customized software applications to satisfy almost any need. Alternately, the developers of some off-the-shelf software products can customize some or all of their software packages, but in today's environment this is becoming less and less a requirement. Two large consulting groups specializing in hospitality procurement and software are Hospitality Purchasing Consultants and the Parker Company. This brings up the concept of "all-in-one" solutions versus "best-of-breed" solutions. The all-in-one is where all the various applications are provided by a single back-office software provider. In a best-of-breed solution, the operator chooses the best individual software applications for each specific purchasing function and then

FIGURE 2.5 A wireless free-pour liquor inventory management system.
©*Skyflo™ Automatic Bar Controls, Inc.*

provides integration between the systems to allow them to share and use the data collected by each individual application.

WHAT LIES AHEAD?

It is hard to believe that the use of computer technology in the selection and procurement function is only in its infancy. In the future, technology will bring more ideas, tools, and information to hospitality operators. And it cannot come too soon because hospitality operators will continue to experience more competitive markets, slimmer profit margins, and a shrinking labor force. As the American Hotel and Lodging Association states, purchasing technology offers substantial return on investment (ROI) by more precise ordering through managed par levels, instant access to lowest price information, the ability to hold people accountable for differences in sales versus product used, and better communication with vendors.

In a competitive environment, hospitality operators have less time to make key managerial decisions. Making the correct decisions quickly can be done, but only if operators have access to the necessary technological tools.

In the future, distributors will probably bear more of the burden of providing hospitality operators with the proper technology to suit a more technical selection and procurement process, as well as the burden of helping operators control their businesses more efficiently. Because hospitality businesses are the distributors' customers, it is in their best interests to ensure that these companies make the correct purchasing and other key management decisions. Distributors, therefore, will be more actively involved with their customers, helping them to develop and evaluate new menus, substitution possibilities, inventory management procedures, and marketing strategies, as well as assisting them with streamlining the process of electronic commerce.

In the future, the distinguishing factors between distributors most likely will be the services they provide and the technology they use and can share with hospitality operators. In addition, because of time constraints, competition, and economies of scale, many industry experts feel that more hospitality operators will practice **one-stop shopping**, thereby teaming with prime vendors to enhance their competitive positions.

BETTER PROCUREMENT
Abigail A. Lorden, editor-in-chief, Hospitality Technology

■ FIVE KEY FEATURES FOR AN EFFECTIVE INVENTORY MANAGEMENT SOLUTION

Managing food and beverage inventories is a critical element in operating a restaurant. Whether following a philosophy of long-term contract negotiation, or buying in bulk when the price is right, all well-run restaurant operations share at least one common denominator: controlling their inventories. A procurement system is a central component in any effective inventory management strategy. More and more restaurant operators are turning to Web-based procurement systems for ordering and tracking their inventory, and members of the technology vendor community are adding procurement and inventory management to their point-of-sale and back-office systems.

Before settling on any procurement or inventory management solution, restaurant operators should work to understand their operations' specific needs and choose a vendor that can offer a tailored solution. Although the features and functions of the "right" inventory management solution will vary by restaurant operation, here's a lineup of five important features that aid in effective procurement and inventory management.

User-friendly. As with most technology systems within the restaurant, it's not the IT directors, but the managers and front-line staff that regularly interface with systems. As such, any procurement solution should offer a user interface that's easy to understand. Though complex algorithms might be used to calculate food costs per unit, or determine quantities needed, the algorithms should remain on the back end of the system so that the day-to-day user can easily navigate the software. Considering the high degree of turnover in the foodservice industry, the system should also require minimal training and be intuitive to use.

Life cycle product tracking. Restaurant ingredients tend to be purchased in larger quantities or cases, are then broken down into individual units (such as cans of sauce or corn), and then applied in recipes by smaller units of measure. For this reason, a procurement solution should be able to track the product's life cycle from receipt through consumption. The software should use conversion tables and algorithms that can account for and relate different units for the same ingredient.

Integration into the POS. Most inventory cost control systems use information that is captured from the point of sale to make projections about inventory. The systems track items on hand and ongoing sales to monitor inventory and can be set up to automatically generate a purchase order when the inventory of a specific item drops below a preset minimum. Managing the procurement process also requires that

BETTER PROCUREMENT (continued)

restaurants account for the lead and lag time required in shipping an item. Integration into the POS can give an inventory management system the real-time data needed to avoid out-of-stocks.

Customized reporting. To get the most from an inventory management solution, restaurant operators should have the ability to create customized reporting that can help them address operational concerns, including the optimization of on-hand inventory based on supplier lead and lag times. Comprehensive systems often offer a dashboard view of consumption and pricing trends and can be customized to include the entire portfolio of restaurants, specific regions, or even certain suppliers or departments. Remote access and real-time data increases the usability of such dashboard reporting tools.

Nutritional information. With the social push toward health-conscious eating, and several state governments mandating that nutritional information be made available to customers, inventory and procurement solutions are starting to incorporate a nutrition module. In this case, the software would assign nutritional values to individual inventory items as well as recipes. Having this information available can be helpful to restaurants when building customized menus for special events or adding healthy food choices to their regular menus.

Key Words and Concepts

Bar code element	Online ordering system
Bar code reader	Order modifier
Customer relationship management (CRM)	Point-of-sale system (POS system)
E-procurement applications	Prime-vendor account
Fleet management software	Product identification
House account	Product specifications
Intermediary	Product status
Logistics and mapping software	RFID tags
Middleman	Roadside sensor network
North American Meat Processors Association (NAMP)	Server
	Theoretical inventory usage
One-stop shopping	Web order entry system

Questions and Problems

1. How has a Web order entry system changed the ordering process?

2. Explain what a customer relationship management (CRM) system is and how it would be used by a hospitality supplier.

Questions and Problems (continued)

3. Explain how the use of global positioning systems (GPS) has affected the distribution process.

4. How can a spreadsheet program, such as Microsoft Excel, assist managers in controlling their inventories?

5. How could a wireless ordering system improve customer service in a hospitality operation?

6. How can placing bar codes on all products in inventory streamline the order-taking process?

7. What are the advantages and disadvantages of using online versions of product guides such as *The Meat Buyers Guide* or the *Fresh Produce Manual* versus the hard copy versions?

8. What type of considerations would a hospitality operation have when deciding whether to buy off-the-shelf purchasing software and systems or whether to develop the program itself?

Experiential Exercises

1. Visit a local distributor to view its ordering, routing, delivering, and invoicing system.

2. Research a current hospitality-related purchasing and inventory system. Provide a one-page report explaining the capabilities of the system.

3. Research a current hospitality-related POS system. Provide a one-page report explaining the capabilities of the system.

4. Visit the website for a food and beverage marketing board. Just a few examples are the National Cattleman's Beef Association, the Distilled Spirits Council of the United States (DISCUS), California Avocado Commission, and the American Egg Board. Write a one-page report evaluating the site based on the following criteria:
   * Graphical design
   * Ease of use
   * How this information would be used to guide the purchasing process

References

1. Susan Avery, "Distributor Technology Tools Can Remove Costs from Supply Chain," October 18, 2007, www.purchasing.com/article/225377-Distributor_technoloSusgy_tools_can_remove_costs_from_supply_chain.php.

References (continued)

2. T. H. Davenport, J. G. Harris, and A. K. Kohli, "How Do They Know Their Customers So Well?" *MIT Sloan Management Review*, 2001, 42(2), pp. 63–73. See also, Matthew Schwartz. "From Short Stack to Competitive Advantage: IHOP's Pursuit of Data Quality," *Business Intelligence Journal,* 2006, 11(3), pp. 44–51. See also Yun E. Zeng, H. Joseph Wen, and David C. Yen, "Customer Relationship Management (CRM) in Business-to-Business (B2B) e-Commerce," *Information Management and Computer Security*, 2003, 11(1), pp. 39–44.

3. Diane M. Gayeski and Michael J. Petrillose, "No Strings Attached: How the Gaming and Hospitality Industry Uses Mobile Devices to Engineer Performance," *Performance Improvement,* 2005, 44(2), pp. 25–31. See also Brian Schiavo, "More Fleets Are Calling on Smartphones," *Food Logistics*, 2008, 108, pp. 30–31; Tom Kelley, "Well Positioned," *Beverage World,* 2009, 128(1), pp. 46–47.

4. April Terreri, "Cover Assets with Low-Cost RFID Tags," *Food Logistics,* 2009, 116, p. 34. See also Marianna Sigala, "RFID Applications for Integrating and Informationalizing the Supply Chain of Foodservice Operators: Perspectives from Greek Operators," *Journal of Foodservice Business Research,* 2007, 10(1), pp. 7–29; Yahia Mehrjerdi, "RFID-Enabled Systems; A Brief Review," *Assembly Automation,* 2008, 28(3), pp. 234–245; Antonio Rizzi, "Monitoring the Fresh Food Supply Chain. RFID-Tracking Pallets and Cases of Perishable Goods Can Enable Retailers to Reduce Costs and Improve Customer Satisfaction," *RFID Journal,* Jan. 19, 2014. See also Dean Vella, "Using Technology to Improve Supply Chain Management," *Global Purchasing,* November 12, 2012, http://globalpurchasing.com/supply-chain/using-technology-improve-supply-chain-management.

5. Jon Phillips, "When the PC Is Obsolete, How Will You Do This and This and This?" www.pcworld.com/article/2034842/when-the-pc-is-obsolete-how-will-you-do-this-and-this-and-this-.html. See also Bob Evans, "Personal Computers Becoming Obsolete Says IBM PC Architect," www.forbes.com/sites/sap/2011/08/11/personal-computers-becoming-obsolete-says-ibm-pc-architect/. See also Harry McCracken, "They Keep Killing the PC," http://techland.time.com/2011/03/11/they-keep-killing-the-pc/.

6. Cherryh A. Butler, "Kiosks Order Up Faster Fast Food," *Kiosk Marketplace,* www.kioskmarketplace.com/article/179307/Kiosks-order-up-faster-fast-food.

7. Ken Burgin, "Wide World of POS Possibilities," *Hospitality,* 208, 635, pp. 26–30. See also T. H. Strenk, "The Future of POS," *Restaurant Business,* 2008, 107(3), pp. 26–32; Ralph Johns and Kent Rain, "Embracing POS Technology," *FoodService Director,* 2006, 19(10), p. 50.

References (continued)

8. Robert Barrese, "Bar Codes Make Headway in Foodservice Channel," *Food Logistics,* 2001, 45, p. 12. See also "The Bar Code Turns 35 Years Old," *Modern Materials Handling,* 2009, 64(6), p. 11.

9. Jimmy LeFever. "E-procurement software uses cloud to its fullest abilities," 2016, searchfinancialapplications.techtarget.com/feature/E-procurement-software-uses-cloud-to-its-fullest-abilities. See also Ross Bentley, "Buying Power," *Caterer and Hotelkeeper,* 2008, 198(4533), p. 46. Tanvi Kothari, Clark Hu, and Wesley Roehl, "Adopting e-Procurement Technology in a Chain Hotel: An Exploratory Case Study," *International Journal of Hospitality Management,* 2007, 26(4), pp. 886–898.

10. John Inge. *Food and Beverage Systems: A Technology Primer.* Produced by the American Hotel and Lodging Association's E-Business and Technology Committee, 2006.

CHAPTER 3

DISTRIBUTION SYSTEMS

The Purpose of This Chapter

After reading this chapter, you should be able to:

- Differentiate between sources and intermediaries in the distribution system for food, nonalcoholic beverages, and nonfood supplies.

- Differentiate between sources and intermediaries in the distribution system for beer, wine, and distilled spirits.

- Describe the distribution systems for furniture, fixtures, and equipment and for services.

- Distinguish between the economic values added to products and services as they journey through the channel of distribution.

- Explain the buyer's place in the channel of distribution.

DISTRIBUTION SYSTEM FOR FOOD, NONALCOHOLIC BEVERAGES, AND NONFOOD SUPPLIES

distribution channel
The people, organizations, and procedures involved in producing and delivering products and services from primary sources to ultimate consumers.

primary source A supplier at the beginning of a product's channel of distribution. For instance, a farmer is a primary source for fresh produce items. This supplier typically sells items to an intermediary that resells them to hospitality operations.

intermediary Another term for vendor.

Food, beverages, nonfood supplies, furniture, fixtures, equipment, and services follow relatively specific **distribution channels**. In most instances, an item goes from its **primary source** through various **intermediaries** to the retailer, which is you, the hospitality operator, as Figure 3.1 illustrates. As shown by the broken line, however, the possibility of a retailer's bypassing the intermediaries and dealing directly with the primary source also exists.

The distribution system for food, nonalcoholic beverages, and nonfood supplies involves a tremendous number of primary sources, intermediaries, and hospitality retailers. In the United States, thousands of primary sources and intermediaries compete to serve approximately 980,000 food-service operations and 52,000 lodging facilities.[1] The typical nonchain hospitality property uses about 10 to 12 types of suppliers, but chain units generally use only about 6 to 8.[2] As the number of suppliers in the global supply chain decreases due to bankruptcies and consolidations, it is even more important for hospitality operators to understand the dynamics of distribution systems.[3]

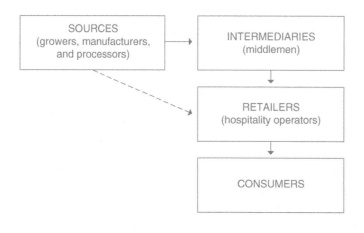

FIGURE 3.1 A general channel of distribution.

■ Sources

Three major primary sources supply products to hospitality operations:

grower Primary source providing fresh, raw foods.

farm-to-table The food on the table (served to the guest) comes directly from a specific farm.

1. **Growers:** Many farmers and ranchers, referred to as **growers**, provide fresh food and floral products to the hospitality industry (see Figure 3.2). Buying directly from the grower is an expanding trend as more hospitality operators and consumers are concerned with knowing exactly where their food comes from. Restaurants and events that feature food directly from the grower are known as **farm-to-table** operations.

FIGURE 3.2 Harvested iceberg lettuce.
© *GomezDavid/GettyImages*

2. **Manufacturers:** A manufacturer controls the production of an item from raw materials. For example, a paper products manufacturer can take wood materials and create paper napkins, bags, and placemats (see Figure 3.3).

3. **Processors:** A **processor**, sometimes referred to as a **fabricator**, takes one or more foods and assembles them into a new end product. For example, a processor could combine flour, water, yeast, tomato sauce, cheese, and seasonings to produce frozen pizzas. The new end product is usually referred to as a "convenience," "efficiency," or **value-added food**. Some processors are also manufacturers, but not all manufacturers are processors. The difference is that processors always work with food products.

> **processor** or **fabricator**
> Company that takes raw foods and assembles them into a new product.
>
> **value-added food**
> Another term for convenience food.

FIGURE 3.3 Cheese processing.
© *Monty Rakusen/GettyImages*

■ Intermediaries

middleman An antiquated term for vendor.

distributor or **merchant wholesaler** A term for a vendor that purchases directly and resells to customers.

Eight intermediaries or **middlemen** (an antiquated gender-specific term still in use today) can be found in this distribution system:

1. **Distributors: Distributors**, sometimes referred to as **merchant whole-salers**, purchase products directly from growers, manufacturers, and/or processors for resale and delivery to customers. It is more than likely that hospitality buyers purchase most of their product requirements from one or more distributors. There are three major types of distributors:

   a. **Specialty distributor:** A company that handles only one type or classification of products, for example, coffee and tea.

full-line distributor A vendor that provides food products and nonfood supplies.

broadline distributor Intermediary that provides food, nonfood supplies, and equipment.

broker Person who represents one or more primary sources. A broker does not buy or resell products, but promotes products to potential buyers. A broker usually represents manufacturers and processors that do not employ their own sales force.

   b. **Full-line distributor:** A **full-line distributor** is a company that provides food and nonfood supplies.

   c. **Broadline distributor:** A company that provides food, nonfood supplies, and equipment. **Broadline distributors** are commonly referred to as "broadliners." (See Figure 3.4 .)

2. **Brokers:** Agents who represent one or more primary sources. **Brokers** neither buy nor resell. Their job is to promote products and put sellers in contact with buyers. Brokers usually represent primary sources that do not employ their own sales force.

   A broker most often works among hospitality operation buyers, generating enthusiasm for a particular product. A successful broker convinces a distributor that a good "market" for the product exists and that the distributor can easily resell that product. In this example, the broker provides the sales effort, and the distributor provides the "end-user" services, that is, everything but the sales effort. Most brokers generally specialize in a specific department, such as frozen food, confection, or deli products. The broker earns a sales commission, and the distributor earns a profit on the resale.

Top Broadline Distributors Based on U.S. Sales
Sysco
US Foods
Performance Food Group
Gordon Food Service
Reinhart Food Service
Maines Paper & Food Service
Shamrock Foods Co.
Ben E. Keith
Cheney Brothers Inc.
Labatt Food Service

FIGURE 3.4 Ten of the largest broadline foodservice distributors in the United States.
Courtesy of Hale Group

3. **Manufacturer's representatives:** These middlemen serve a function similar to that of brokers. One major difference is that **manufacturer's representatives**, also known as outsourced field sales professionals, do more than simply get sellers and buyers together. They often provide such additional **end-user services** as actually carrying items in stock themselves, perhaps delivering items, and possibly even providing additional service to the buyers. Representatives—or "reps" for short—seem to work more frequently with the equipment and furnishings trade, whereas brokers are usually found in the food and nonfood supplies trade.

4. **Manufacturer's agents:** These intermediaries are similar to manufacturer's representatives. The major differences, though, are that primary sources employ agents to represent them in a specific geographic area, and that agents typically work exclusively for one source. Usually, the agent is a manufacturer or processor who agrees to take on another primary source's products and works to sell them. This other primary source typically is a very small company that cannot afford to market and distribute its own products to a wide market area.

   Recently, the differences in responsibilities between many manufacturer's representatives and **manufacturer's agents** have become very slight, and many people now use these two terms interchangeably. The Manufacturers' Agents National Association provides an excellent website that provides more detailed information on the responsibilities of a manufacturer's agent. There is even a specific organization, the Manufacturers' Agents Association for the Foodservice Industry, that represents more than 2,200 foodservice sales and marketing agents.

5. **Commissaries:** A **commissary** is usually owned and operated by a large foodservice company. A commissary processes food products according to exact requirements that the company has determined. It is intended to sell and ship products to company-owned restaurants or approved franchisees. Some commissaries may also serve other types of hospitality properties that are not affiliated with the parent company.

6. **Wholesale clubs: Wholesale clubs** are **cash-and-carry** operations that are patronized primarily by small businesses that do not order enough products from distributors to qualify for deliveries. Distributors usually cannot make a profit on small-order deliveries. Some distributors have storefronts in their warehouses to provide cash-and-carry services, thereby accommodating the small businessperson, as well as the large.

   Costco originally started as a wholesale club, where small businesses could go to select and procure products (see Figure 3.5). Over the last decade, Costco has reduced its requirements for becoming a member and now just about anyone willing to pay the annual membership fee can benefit from the low prices. Other wholesale clubs that provide

manufacturer's representative Similar to a broker, but not the same; main difference is that the rep will typically provide end-user services, whereas the broker will not. Also similar to a manufacturer's agent, but not the same; main difference is that the agent typically works for only one primary source, whereas the manufacturer's representative typically works for several.

end-user services Support functions provided to buyers by vendors. Includes everything except the sales effort, which is provided by a sales rep, such as a food broker.

manufacturer's agent Similar to a manufacturer's representative, but not the same. Main difference is that the agent typically works for only one primary source, whereas the manufacturer's representative typically works for several.

commissary Similar to a central distribution center. The major difference is that at a commissary, raw foods are processed into finished products, which is not the case in a central distribution center. Could be considered a restaurant company's personal convenience food processing plant.

wholesale club or **cash-and-carry** A type of buying club. It is a cash-and-carry operation patronized primarily by small hospitality operations that do not order enough from vendors to qualify for free delivery. Buyers usually have to pay a membership fee.

services to both the small hospitality operator and the public include Sam's Club, BJ's Wholesale Club, and Smart & Final.

buying club A type of co-op purchasing. Instead of co-op members organizing and administering their own co-op, they join a buying club that, for a fee, streamlines the process and makes it more efficient.

price club Another term for buying club.

contract house Another term for buying club.

7. **Buying clubs: Buying clubs** (sometimes referred to as **price clubs**) are groups of independent purchasers who join together to purchase collectively to obtain more competitive prices by placing larger orders than they would be able to do independently.[4] The most typical kind of buying club is the purchasing co-op, which usually includes several small, independent foodservices and lodging properties. Some buying clubs, such as **contract houses**, are operated by third parties that pass on some of the savings obtained through bulk purchasing to member buyers. Buying clubs typically purchase directly from primary sources to obtain the lowest possible prices. As discussed in Chapter 1, aggregate purchasing companies and group purchasing organizations (GPOs) can be considered buying clubs.

8. **Group Purchasing Organizations (GPOs):** Group purchasing organizations utilize many small, independent businesses as a group to combine their purchasing power to receive better discounts than they would as individual businesses. Although the benefits of receiving discounts are useful, there are other factors to consider. GPOs are not afforded the same discounts and promotional programs that larger individual accounts may be offered. Also, the discount one GPO receives will be nearly identical to another GPO, meaning there is a set discount for GPOs that is not based on static pricing. Finally, GPOs are often locked into long-term contracts for their products and cannot switch vendors. This causes the loss of a competitive pricing scheme, which can invalidate the discount over the term of the contract.[5]

Some examples of GPOs include Entegra Procurement Services, which can create a customized procurement program to suit a customer's needs. They include services for bakery, meats, disposables, dairy, and seafood, to name a few.[6] Another GPO is Foodbuy Innovative Procurement. Foodbuy offers a variety of services to many different types of businesses, including food, beverages, technology, small wares, and maintenance.[7]

FIGURE 3.5 Example of a wholesale club.
©Spencer Grant/GettyImages

■ DENNIS LAMBERTZ, CORPORATE EXECUTIVE CHEF

Courtesy of Dennis Lambertz

Dennis Lambertz is the corporate executive chef for Nevada Food Brokerage (NFB), the only independent, locally owned food brokerage in Las Vegas. The company's philosophy is, "We take care of the end user." His job is to consult, assist with menu development, and provide service to foodservice establishments. He works with all types of operations—everything from grocery stores and gas stations to health care facilities and contract foodservices, like Aramark, to independent restaurants to the large chain restaurants and casino hotels. When working with such a diverse group of customers Dennis must perform a lot of research regarding their menu and style of operation so he will know exactly which products to recommend.

Dennis visits an average of five customers on a normal day, more during busy times such as around the holidays or when special events and conferences are coming to town. He will bring samples of food products and demonstrate how they can be prepared and used. The best and most cost-effective products are usually the ones that operations can use to prepare multiple menu items. For example, a lobster bisque base can be used for the soup, but also as a sauce for other seafood dishes, or even in a salad dressing.

Dennis uses bacon as another example of the importance of educating his accounts' buyers about edible portion costs and value of a product for its intended use. When he does tastings of bacon, not only does he open and count several cases to see the exact number of pieces in a 14–17 count per pound case, but he also weighs the box and the parchment paper to show that a 10-pound case does actually have 10 pounds of bacon. He even opens the box at room temperature to show how much fat weight may be lost due to it sticking to the parchment paper or temperature.

NFB represents more than 45 different food companies. Because some of those companies are corporate giants, which in itself may supply hundreds of different brands and products, Dennis must have a vast knowledge of all types of foods and cooking. Fortunately, his many years as an executive chef for casino companies including MGM Grand and Harrah's prepared him well.

The broker acts as the middleman between the food manufacturing and supply companies and the distributor such as Sysco or US Foods. One of the most difficult parts of the job is managing the product lines. Because most suppliers do not sell directly to the foodservice establishments, they must find a distributor in each local market to carry the product. Sometimes, the distributor will ask the manufacturer for money to carry the item, which will cover administrative costs like shipping.

Brokers also have to make sure that there are no product conflicts between lines and in types of food sold. Dennis gives the example of NFB's representation of a vegetable line. Because NFB does not work with commodity products, it does not sell some of the company's items such as 50-pound bags of white onions. It only sells specialty cut items and further processed products such as sliced onions or breaded onion rings.

As the broker, Dennis can also take his clients' special requests for customized products, such as proteins or vegetables cut to a specific size or shape or with a new seasoning or sauce mix, to the manufacturer. Especially when one of the large casino accounts wants something new, it is worth the supplier's time to accommodate them. Dennis says that vegetable blends developed for one of his Las Vegas clients are now being sold nationwide.

NFB and its employees such as Dennis and its ten salespeople collect its revenues from the manufacturers. NFB receives payment through the manufacturers it represents and whose products they are able to sell to the end users and place through local distributors. Payments could be calculated by the pound, by the case, or by a percentage of the price of all the manufacturers' products that are shipped to town.

Dennis emphasizes that NFB works for the end user, making sure they can get products that fulfill their business needs, rather than for the distributor. Because all the company's employees have different tastes and food preferences, another philosophy it goes by is, "You don't have to like it, you just have to sell it."

DISTRIBUTION SYSTEM FOR BEER, WINE, AND DISTILLED SPIRITS

■ Sources

Three major sources supply beverage alcohol products:

> **brewer** Primary source of fermented beverages made primarily from grains.

1. **Brewers: Brewers** provide fermented beverages made primarily from grains (see Figure 3.6).

FIGURE 3.6 Example of a brewer.
Raymond Boyd/Michael Ochs Archives/Getty Images

2. **Wine makers: Winemakers** provide fermented beverages made primarily from grapes (see Figure 3.7)

3. **Distillers: Distillers** provide beverage alcohol that has undergone a distillation process. They may also supply other similar high-alcohol-content items (see Figure 3.8).

winemaker Beverage alcohol company that produces fermented alcoholic products made primarily from grapes.

distiller Primary source that produces alcoholic beverages, such as whisky, that have undergone a distillation process.

FIGURE 3.7 Winemaker at work.
©*Jaroslaw Pawlak/Shutterstock*

FIGURE 3.8 Distiller.
©*JoffreyM/Shutterstock*

■ Intermediaries

Three major intermediaries, or middlemen, are part of this distribution system:

importer–wholesaler
Intermediary in the beverage alcohol distribution channel. Responsible for importing products into the United States, as well as into each state and local municipality. Also responsible for distribution to retail establishments, such as bars, restaurants, and liquor stores.

liquor distributor
Another term for vendor. Purchases beverage alcohol from primary sources or liquor retailers.

tied-house laws
Legislation that prohibits liquor distributors from becoming liquor primary sources or liquor retailers.

exclusive territory The geographical area in which an exclusive seller is allowed to operate as the sole vendor of certain brands of merchandise.

Alcohol Beverage Commission (ABC) A liquor control authority that regulates the sale and purchase of beverage alcohol.

control state A state that sells beverage alcohol. It is the only purveyor of beverage alcohol in that state.

license state A state that grants licenses to importer–wholesalers, distributors, and retailers, who then handle the distribution and sale of beverage alcohol.

1. **Importer–wholesalers:** **Importer–wholesalers** are responsible for importing alcoholic beverages into the United States, as well as into each state and local municipality. Most of these intermediaries also act as **liquor distributors** in that they buy the liquor from primary sources for resale to retail establishments, such as restaurants, hotels, taverns, and supermarkets.

2. **Liquor distributors:** Liquor distributors are specialized wholesalers who operate under a variety of legal sanctions. These distributors purchase from primary sources and sell to retailers, and they are careful not to overstep their legal boundaries because their businesses are continually examined by regulatory authorities. In most states, so-called **tied-house laws** prohibit these distributors from becoming primary sources or retailers; the laws mandate separate ownership for primary sources, intermediaries, and retailers. A more thorough discussion of the distribution of beverages will be presented in Chapter 22.

   In many states, liquor distributors operate in **exclusive territories**; that is, they are the only suppliers to carry and offer particular brands to hospitality buyers. As a result, little competition exists in the wholesale liquor trade.[8] In fact, the alcoholic beverage distribution system is defined so precisely that an individual purchaser has very little discretion in buying these items and almost no control over how the channel of distribution operates.

3. **Alcohol Beverage Commissions:** All states have one or more liquor control authorities, often referred to as the **Alcohol Beverage Commission (ABC)**, or some similar title. The ABC rigidly controls the sale and purchase of alcoholic beverages. In some states, control is so tight that the state itself is the only purveyor of alcoholic beverages. When the state alone can sell alcoholic beverages, it is called a **control state** (as opposed to a **license state**, in which the ABC grants licenses to importer–wholesalers, distributors, and retailers, who then handle the distribution of these products). When operating in a control state, purchasers have no discretion. They must adhere exactly to the purchasing, receiving, and bill-paying procedures the governmental authority sets forth.[9]

DISTRIBUTION SYSTEMS FOR FURNITURE, FIXTURES, AND EQUIPMENT AND FOR SERVICES

The distribution systems for **furniture, fixtures, and equipment (FFE)** and for services are slightly less complex than for the items previously discussed.

■ Sources for FFE

There is one major source for FFE items: the manufacturer. The number of manufacturers of these items tends to be smaller than the number of sources in the other distribution systems.

■ Intermediaries for FFE

Seven major intermediaries can be found in this distribution system:

1. **Dealers:** An **equipment dealer** typically functions much like a food distributor. Dealers usually buy equipment items from primary sources, earning profits when they resell to hospitality buyers. There are four major types of dealers:[10]

   a. **Catalog house:** A **catalog house** is typically a very small dealer that carries no inventory, or very little inventory, in stock. Items are selected by customers from one or more catalogs, and the dealer handles the ordering, delivery, setup, and so forth. Some of these catalogs are now available online.

   b. **Storefront dealer:** **Storefront dealers** (sometimes referred to as **discount operations**) usually carry a minimum amount of inventory. They typically specialize in handling small, portable types of FFE.

   c. **Heavy equipment dealer:** **Heavy equipment dealers** specialize in handling large equipment installations. They carry inventory and are usually involved in the layout and design of new hospitality properties or major renovations.

   d. **Full-service dealer:** **Full-service dealers** typically carry a full line of inventory and are able to provide all end-user services to their customers.

2. **Brokers:** FFE brokers are similar to brokers working in the distribution system for food, nonalcoholic beverages, and nonfood supplies. However, FFE brokers are not as numerous as their counterparts in other distribution systems.

FFE
Acronym for furniture, fixtures, and equipment.

equipment dealer
Company that purchases equipment from a primary source and resells it to hospitality buyers.

catalog house A very small equipment dealer that carries no inventory, or very little inventory, in stock. Buyers select items from one or more catalogs, and the dealer handles the ordering, delivery, setup, installation, and so forth.

storefront dealer FFE company that carries a minimum amount of inventory. Usually specializes in handling small, portable types of FFE.

discount operation
Another term for storefront dealer.

heavy equipment dealer
Specializes in handling large equipment installations. Carries inventory. Usually involved in the layout and design of new hospitality properties or major renovations.

full-service dealer FFE vendor that typically carries a full line of inventory and is able to provide all end-user services.

designers In the hospitality industry, designers are persons typically hired to originate and develop a process for creating suitable work spaces and/or themes for the interiors of hospitality operations.

architect Person who designs buildings and develops plans for their construction.

construction contractor Term used in the building trade. One who takes the plans and designs produced by architects and designers and turns them into finished products.

leasing companies Firm that purchases FFE and leases them to other companies. The typical rental plan is a rent-to-own arrangement. May be a more expensive form of financing a FFE purchase than borrowing the money and buying the items outright.

3. **Designers:** **Designers** typically work as consultants for hospitality operators. They are hired to design, say, an addition to an existing kitchen. During their work, they see to it that the appropriate FFE are ordered from the primary sources. Designers also make sure that the required end-user services, such as delivery, are provided in a timely manner. Designers earn their income from the hospitality operator who employs them; they work for a fee.

4. **Architects:** **Architects** are trained and licensed to plan, design, and oversee the construction of buildings, additions, or modifications to existing structures.

5. **Construction Contractors:** **Construction contractors** are also known as general contractors. They are construction site managers employed by clients to carry out the architect's designs and plans.

6. **Distributors:** Many distributors of food, nonalcoholic beverages, and nonfood items often supply several of the most commonly purchased FFE items. They typically sell replacement items and are not normally involved with the design and construction of new hospitality operations.

7. **Leasing companies:** It is relatively common for retailers to lease FFE from **leasing companies**. (Some dealers may also offer this option.) For example, expensive kitchen equipment such as ice machines, ovens, and ranges can often be leased or purchased on a rent-to-own plan.

■ Services

Services such as advertising, consulting, and waste removal follow slightly different distribution patterns. Retailers generally purchase them directly through the source without going through an intermediary. Few large national sources exist, and most sources are local and consist of many mom-and-pop operations or small partnerships. A few of these may be local offices of a national firm or franchisees of a national firm. For instance, major accounting firms, technology, and printing companies have local offices or franchisees.

It is important to make sure that these small companies have the expertise you are seeking. Anyone can claim to be an accountant, for example, but a person qualified to provide a complete range of accounting, bookkeeping, and financial services usually is a certified public accountant (CPA).

Two ways to source information about the background and legitimacy of a company are through the local Chamber of Commerce or the Council of the Better Business Bureau (BBB; www.bbb.org). The local Chamber of Commerce offers programs that allow businesses to advertise and help members connect their services to consumers. The Council of the BBB is a consumer-focused service that allows for businesses and consumers to build relationships based on ratings and reviews. In this way, the BBB builds consumer confidence in businesses and creates trust among consumers.[11]

WHAT HAPPENS THROUGHOUT THE CHANNEL OF DISTRIBUTION?

We often hear that "the middleman makes all the money." It is, for example, suggested that the loaf of bread we buy contains only a few pennies' worth of food ingredients. What accounts for the rest of the price we pay for it? As with most items purchased, the price paid is the sum total of several costs. Some cost is tacked on during the bread's journey through the distribution channel each time someone adds value to the original food ingredients. Four kinds of **economic values** may be added to a product as it passes from the primary source to the retailer: time, form, place, and information.

> **economic value**
> Represents the increase in AP (as purchased) price that occurs as a product journeys through the distribution channel. For example, 10 pounds of preportioned steak is more valuable, and more expensive, than 10 pounds of meat that has to be processed further in a restaurant's kitchen.

■ Time Value

If you want to buy a product at the time you select, you must be willing to pay for this privilege. If, for instance, you wish to buy canned vegetables a little at a time instead of in bulk, your supplier will have to store these products and wait for you to order them. This is a major problem for the supplier because he or she must assume the risk and cost of storing the items. The supplier also will have money sitting on the shelf.

Whoever pays money for a product, regardless of where it is in the distribution channel, loses the use of that money for a while. For example, a vegetable canner may have to pay cash for raw vegetables and may also have to store the finished products, the canned vegetables, for many weeks. During this time, the canner's money is tied up. And the longer money is tied up, the more the vegetable canner has to charge for the canned vegetables. In other words, processors add an interest cost for capital tied up in processing because they probably borrow money from a bank to carry inventory.

The time economic value can also include other types of financing. For example, the typical intermediary often provides credit financing to hospitality buyers. It is a generally accepted procedure in the industry for suppliers to grant credit terms to their customers. These terms usually allow buyers about 30 to 45 days after delivery before they must pay the bill. Obviously, these purveyors must earn an interest income for capital tied up in accounts receivable.

Some restaurant operators follow the same practice when they price wines. They usually start with a certain price, and for every year they must keep the wine in their wine cellar waiting for a buyer, they add a percentage markup to the price.

Thus, members of the distribution channel consider financing an investment. If they invest money in products, they cannot invest it elsewhere. Consequently, this investment must offer them a certain return at least equal to the amount of interest they would have to pay to borrow these same funds. And in a productive, profitable business, the expected rate would exceed the cost of borrowed capital.

■ Form Value

Form is usually the most expensive value added to the products our industry purchases. Form is what turns a raw ingredient into something more user friendly. For instance, a precut steak is much easier to purchase, store, and use than a large cut of beef that must undergo quite a bit of processing in a restaurant kitchen. Unfortunately, the processed item is much more expensive than the raw, unprocessed product due to expensive testing requirements.[12]

The form value is also very expensive because highly processed items are usually packaged in costly containers. In fact, packaging becomes more expensive every day, especially for products that can be reconstituted in their own packages. In addition, buyers pay close attention to frozen-food packaging, particularly if these products are to be stored on their premises for any period of time. The demand and the need for stronger and more effective packaging have raised the price that retailers must pay.

One way to minimize the cost of packaging is to pay attention to the array of package sizes from which to choose. For example, catsup comes in several package types and sizes. One must be ready to pay more for individual servings of catsup than for catsup in large containers because of the amount of packaging involved.

In addition, package size and the cost of packaging are important in the development of a sustainability plan. Packaging that will be disposed of en masse, including small single-use items, can be purchased in a way to minimize packaging cost and its environmental impact. The use of reusable shipping and storage containers and recyclables are a few ways to accomplish this. Each hotel, restaurant, and foodservice outlet should consider the use of packaging that will reduce waste so that it can reduce the costs of the packaging itself as well as its disposal.[13]

■ Place Value

If you want an item delivered to the place of your choice, you must pay for this convenience. For instance, all other things being equal, it costs less to buy produce from a local farmer than to have it shipped from across the country. However, as the hospitality industry has become more global, our guests demand that we serve foods and beverages sourced from particular areas that might have significant transportation costs. Whoever moves a product from one place to another must recoup these costs in the selling price. This value is very expensive, especially when items such as fresh seafood and frozen products must be shipped.

■ Information Value

This is the least understood and, quite often, the most controversial economic value. An operator may be willing to pay more for a product if some information—for example, directions for use—comes with it. This operator might not mind paying a little more for a dishwashing machine if the company sends an instructor for three or four days to show workers how to use the machine. On the other hand, most hospitality operators would not care to pay anything extra for the recipes on the backs of flour bags. Also, now that so much information is available easily, 24 hours a day online, operators may not need or be willing to pay for as much information from the supplier.

supplier services
Services, such as free delivery, generous credit terms, and so forth, provided by vendors to buyers who purchase their products.

■ Supplier Services Value

In addition to the four economic values discussed earlier, intangible **supplier services** accompany the items you purchase. When you purchase something, you purchase not only whatever you desire, but also any additional services that come with it. For instance, a salesperson who puts a rush order in his or her car and runs it over to your operation in an emergency is a good friend; an accountant who prepares a special report "overnight" also is valuable to you. But how much more are you willing to pay for such additional supplier services? This is not an easy question to answer, but you can be sure that the cost of supplier services (sometimes referred to as **support functions**) work their way into an item's final price tag. GPOs provide substantial supplier services. They balance the increase in cost necessary for their services with the advantage of providing substantial quantity discounts and ability to provide products that operators may be unable to purchase on their own.

> **support functions**
> Another term for supplier services.

■ Ultimate Value

In the final analysis, a product's ultimate value consists of its quality and the values added to it. This final analysis does not always apply, especially when a perishable product must be price-discounted before it spoils. But, more often than not, the largest component of a product's final cost to the hospitality buyer can be attributed to the values added to that item as it journeys through the channel of distribution.

THE BUYER'S PLACE IN THE CHANNEL OF DISTRIBUTION

The buyers for most hospitality operations deal with several middlemen, and the typical middleman is the distributor. Buyers for large corporations normally break out of this strict pattern and purchase many of their items directly from the primary source. In effect, they bypass some intermediaries. These buyers feel that buying directly from the primary source offers considerable cost savings. For example, buyers find car prices in Detroit to be generally cheaper than those in San Francisco simply because Detroit buyers can take advantage of the place value; in effect, they are compensated for receiving the car at its place of manufacture.

Consider, too, buyers who pick up food supplies in their own vehicles instead of waiting for the deliveries. In this case, the price of the food should be lower because the buyers are providing the transportation value. (Notice, though, that the practice of picking up food yourself uses time and gasoline and has the associated risk of accident.) Assuming, however, that the primary sources and middlemen would permit this choice, can you provide the economic values more cheaply yourself? Many large multiunit corporations think so and have moved into what is called "**direct buying** with central distribution." They buy from the primary sources, take delivery of the products at **central distribution centers**, perhaps add some form value to the raw ingredients in their commissaries (e.g., clean, cut, and package raw vegetables), and then deliver the products to their restaurants or hotel properties via their own transportation.

> **direct buying** Bypassing intermediaries and purchasing directly from the primary source.
>
> **central distribution center** A large warehouse owned by a multiunit hospitality company that orders merchandise directly from primary sources, takes delivery, stocks the merchandise, and then delivers it to company-affiliated units in the area.

Some hospitality companies claim that buying directly in this manner saves a great deal of money.[14] In addition to benefiting from this cost reduction, these firms feel that they enjoy supply assurances, greater quality control, improved coordination, and an ability to overcome local suppliers' lack of technological capabilities.

Buyers in other firms, though, do not agree that eliminating the intermediaries necessarily makes their operations easier and less costly.[15] For instance, many of them fear the considerable investment that may be necessary to launch such ventures. Some companies also feel that they may lack the necessary expertise and, thus, could become very inefficient and inflexible over time. Furthermore, these firms are not always eager to cut out local suppliers who may be able to provide unique supplier services, purchase discounts, introduce them to new products, and offer other competitive advantages.

E-procurement, which enables companies to buy and sell products and services online, can provide access to hundreds of thousands of products and services. Businesses that participate can often purchase products without dealing with faxes, copies, or time out of the office. In essence, these applications can be a significant time-saver, allowing customers to order products from their desktops.

Direct procurement or e-procurement, central distribution, and the surrounding issues are controversial. The major problem seems to be that everyone has a different view of the importance of various aspects of the supply chain. Historically, few companies have been able to increase profitability by "eliminating the middleman." Disintermediation can divert operators' attention from the major part of their businesses—their core competencies—thereby causing them to lose sight of their customers.

THE OPTIMAL ECONOMIC VALUES AND SUPPLIER SERVICES

When the hospitality business is doing well, hospitality company officials are not usually eager to provide too many economic values and supplier services themselves. They would rather spend their time, for example, convincing retail customers to purchase hamburgers than concern themselves with the care and feeding of steers. But when business takes a nosedive, hospitality company officials begin to examine, for instance, the

> **as-purchased**
> **(AP) price** Price charged
> by the vendor.

as-purchased (AP) price of preportioned steak per pound versus the AP price of a side of beef per pound. In other words, in recessionary periods, management may try to provide some of its own economic values and supplier services with the hope of restoring prerecessionary profits.

This type of thinking has cost many companies quite a bit of money. Middlemen are experts, and in the long run, they can usually provide these values and services less expensively than the individual hospitality operation.

■ Selecting Economic Values

Full-time buyers do not normally have complete control over which economic values their company provides for itself. As with the determination of quality of a particular item, the owner–manager must make these decisions. In large hospitality companies, many of the decisions are made by corporate purchasing teams that negotiate purchase prices and deal directly with the suppliers. Full-time buyers may, of course, make suggestions and help inform the decision-making process.

Part-time buyers, especially those who have other management responsibilities, often are expected merely to maintain the economic values top management has decided upon. Like full-time buyers, however, part-time buyers may also make relevant suggestions and recommendations.

When managements do consider the feasibility of providing their own economic values, they tend to slant the analyses in the direction they desire. This skewing is easily done because everyone has a particular idea of what it costs, for example, to cut his or her own steaks. Some managers include an extra labor expense; others assume no extra labor expense, thinking existing employees can absorb this extra task

There is no doubt that it is very costly to provide your own economic values, particularly the form economic value. There are sound reasons that a precut, preportioned New York sirloin steak sells for about 60 percent more per pound than the wholesale cut of beef (the short loin) that contains this type of steak, along with extra fat and trim. To obtain the convenience of prefabrication, a buyer must compensate a primary source and/or a middleman for the cost of payroll, payroll-related administrative expenses, the waste associated with meat processing, and the cost of energy needed to process and store the finished products.

But factors other than the "hard-cost" figures can enter the picture and haunt the manager later. The following are four of them:

1. Does the manager really want to get into the meat packing business? Does he or she really want to buy a truck? Does the manager have the long-term desire, the expertise, and the time to engage in these activities?

2. Will antitrust problems arise? Large companies must consider this possibility. For instance, some supermarket chains have expressed an interest in going way back in the channel of distribution for meat and becoming their own primary source, but no one is quite sure what the U.S. Justice Department would say about this plan—and it does not seem that too many want to find out.

3. What will other company employees, especially hourly employees and supervisors, say about taking on additional burdens? What will the labor unions say about this?

4. How do guest perceptions of the quality of the meats and menu marketing and merchandising factors affect the decision?

■ Selecting Supplier Services

Buyers usually do have something to say about which supplier services their company should be willing to pay for. These supplier services are correlated with AP prices. Because buyers are not normally restricted to exact AP price limitations, they have a bit more discretion in deciding how much they are willing to pay for supplier services.

Generally, the arguments for and against supplier services are the same as those that center on the economic-values issue. On one hand, some owner–managers and buyers are convinced that they can do it all. On the other hand, others regard the supplier as a kind of "employee," and if the "employee" performs additional "services," he or she should be compensated for it. Thus, if the supplier performs additional services, these owner–managers are willing to pay for it—and choose to do so if the supplier's cost for the service is less than the in-house cost.

Many analysts have searched futilely for a middle ground between these extremes. Perhaps there is no middle ground, but it is undoubtedly worthwhile to accept, and pay for, many supplier services. An executive in the hospitality industry once put it this way:

Let's try to relate purchasing dollars to sales dollars to help us judge how much service is worth. Look at some hypothetical figures.

Purchases Per Month	
Distributor's cost	$5,000.00
Average distributor markup of 15%	+$750.00
	$5,750.00
Hospitality property monthly sales	$90,000.00
12 hours per day, 30 days per month	12 × 30 = 360 hours
$90,000 / 360 = $250.00 sales per hour	

Let's say we find a really great distributor who provides all those extras that we like, but who asks for a 17 percent markup on the same $5,000 monthly purchases. That's $850, or $100 more per month, or 28 cents per operating hour. Where should we devote our time and attention? To satisfying our customers and earning $250 worth of sales per operating hour? Or riding hard on our distributor to save 28 cents per operating hour? If you are picky about your products, have rigid receiving hours, and generally have a one-way relationship with your distributor, you'll probably wind up paying more for less and spend more time at it.

We believe that if we are to make a profit, we must give something of value to our customers. We know what we give our customers and [what we] must do to satisfy them. We hope that our distributors do also.[16]

In this example, it is assumed that the manager can increase sales if he or she spends more time with the restaurant's customers. Of course, many factors contribute to sales revenue; however, the point is well taken, and this example's approach is an honest attempt to quantify the difficult decision-making factors that surround the supplier–services issue.

 ## Key Words and Concepts

Alcohol Beverage Commission (ABC)	Construction contractor	Fabricator
Architect	Contract house	Farm-to-table
As-purchased (AP) price	Control state	Full-line distributor
Brewer	Designers	Full-service dealer
Broadline distributor	Direct buying	Furniture, fixtures, and equipment (FFE)
Broker	Discount operation	Grower
Buying club	Distiller	Heavy equipment dealer
Cash-and-carry	Distribution channel	Importer–wholesaler
Catalog house	Distributor	Intermediary
Central distribution center	Economic value	Leasing companies
Commissary	End-user services	License state
	Equipment dealer	Liquor distributor
	Exclusive territory	

Key Words and Concepts (continued)

Manufacturer's agent	Price club	Support functions
Manufacturer's	Primary source	Tied-house laws
representative	Processor	Value-added food
Merchant wholesaler	Storefront dealer	Wholesale club
Middleman	Supplier services	Winemaker

 Questions and Problems

1. Define the major primary sources in the hospitality channels of distribution, and explain how they differ from one another.

2. Describe the various intermediaries (the middlemen) with whom hospitality operators deal. How do these middlemen differ from one another?

3. How does the channel of distribution for services differ from the distribution channel for food?

4. Define the four economic values. Give an example of each. Why might buyers be reluctant to pay for the information value?

5. Would it be profitable for a small restaurant owner to buy directly from a primary source? What specific items do you feel lend themselves particularly to this sort of buying?

6. Discuss how the need for financing adds to the end cost of a product.

7. Assume that you are the buyer for a large corporation. Of the four specific values discussed in this chapter, which do you think you can provide more cheaply than the middleman? Why? Which do you think a middleman can provide more cheaply? Why?

8. What is the buyer's normal role in determining which economic values the company should provide for itself?

9. What is the buyer's normal role in determining which supplier services should be "purchased"?

10. What is the difference between a price club and a wholesale club?

11. What is a group purchasing organization? What are some of the advantages and disadvantages of purchasing through one?

12. Assume that you have been purchasing your produce from one supplier for several years. You have been satisfied during this time. A new produce supplier seeks your business and offers you a 3½ percent discount from what you currently are paying. What would you do?

13. Define the term *end-user services*.

14. Give an example of a supplier service.

15. Briefly describe the typical distribution system for fresh meat.

16. What is the difference between a broker and a food distributor?

Questions and Problems (continued)

17. The food distributor normally earns a larger percentage of profit than the broker. What are some of the reasons you feel might account for this?

18. List three typical intermediaries you will find in the distribution system for FFE.

19. What is the primary function of a commissary?

20. Assume that you are a small restaurateur. You have the opportunity to purchase your precut steaks less expensively from a competing restaurant chain's central commissary. Should you do this? Why?

21. What is the difference between a control state and a license state?

22. What does the term *farm-to-table* mean?

Experiential Exercises

1. Interview a purchasing manager at a hospitality operation. Determine how this company is using e-procurement to purchase products.

2. Select a website for a group purchasing organization. Write a one-page report detailing what services it provides, what type of products it carries, and what hospitality companies it works with.

3. Interview a food broker. Find out what products he/she represents. What does he/she feel is the most important part of the job? Does he/she consider it more difficult to work with the food suppliers or the hospitality buyers? Write a one-page paper detailing your findings.

4. Interview two sales representatives of different local liquor distributors. Ask each sales representative for a list of distilled spirit brands that they sell. Determine if there is any crossover of distilled spirit brands between the distributors; there should be none. Ask one sales representative if they can provide you with a particular brand that another distributor sells. If he or she says no—which most certainly will be the case—ask that representative for suggestions of an alternative brand. Write a one-page report detailing how you would purchase distilled spirits for a bar in your local area.

References

1. National Restaurant Association (NRA [www.restaurant.org] estimate as of July 2013) and American Hotel and Lodging Association (AH&LA [www.ahla.com] estimate as of year end 2012).

2. Patt Patterson, "Single Source of Supply: Does It Really Work?" *Nation's Restaurant News*, July 19, 1993, p. 109. See also Catherine H. Strohbehn and Mary B. Gregoire, "Case Studies of Local Food Purchasing by Central Iowa Restaurants and Institutions," *Foodservice*

References (continued)

Research International, June 2003, 14(1), p. 53, 12 p. 4 charts. Consider updating with Amit Sharma, Joonho Moon, and Catherine Strohbehn, "Restaurant's Decision to Purchase Local Foods: Influence of Value Chain Activities," *International Journal of Hospitality Management*, 39, no. 0 (5, 2014): 130–143. doi:10.1016/j.ijhm.2014.01.009.

3. CFO Research Services, "Supply Chain Consolidation: Gaining Efficiencies, Minimizing Risks," March 2009, https://www.fmglobal.com/assets/pdf/P09180 .pdf. See also David Butcher, "How Many Suppliers Are in the Global Supply Chain?" August 25, 2010, http://news.thomasnet.com/IMT/2010/08/25/how-many -suppliers-are-there-throughout-global-supply-chain-cvm-solutions-report/. This article reports on the top foodservice distributors in the United States as of January 2014, "Top Foodservice Distributors," *Restaurant, Food & Beverage Market Research Handbook* 15 (March 2014): 260–261. Hospitality & Tourism Complete, EBSCOhost.

4. See www.ica.coop.

5. Janine Roberts, "The Pros and Cons of Group Purchasing Organizations," *Hotel Business Review*, 2014, http://hotelexecutive.com/business_review/2330/the-pros-and -cons-of-group-purchasing-organizations.

6. Entegra Procurement Services, *Programs Offered*, November 2008, https://www .entegraps.com/public/programs-offered/food-supplies.aspx.

7. Foodbuy Innovative Procurement, *Our Programs*, 2011, http://www.foodbuy.com/ Pages/Our-Programs.aspx.

8. Jerry Hirsch, "Wine: Limit on Interstate Sales Sobers Retailers," *Los Angeles Times*, January 7, 2008, p. C1. See also Jerry Hirsch, "Is Wholesale Change in Alcohol Pricing on Tap?" *Los Angeles Times*, April 10, 2005, p. C1; Sara Schorske and Alex Heckathorn, "Three Tier or Free Trade?" *Vineyard and Winery Management*, 2005, www.csa-compliance. com/html/Articles/ThreeTierFreeTrade.html; Sharon Gerrie, "Liquor Market: Liquid Gold. Two Companies Dominate Nevada's Lucrative Wholesale Liquor Market," *Sunday*, June 17, 2001, www.reviewjournal.com/lvrj_home/2001/Jun-17-Sun-2001/ business/16219020.html; Sarah Theodore, "New Strategies for Distribution," *Beverage Industry*, January 2006, 97(1), p. 4.

9. See, for example, the California Department of Alcoholic Beverage Control, www .abc.ca.gov, or the Pennsylvania Liquor Control Board, www.lcb.state.pa.us. See also State of Tennessee, "Rules of the Alcohol Beverage Commission," www.state.tn.us/ sos/rules. See also Dennis Reynolds and Carlye Knowles, "Do U.S. State Laws Affect per Capita Wine Purchases?" *Journal of Foodservice Business Research*, 17, no. 1 (2014): 19–27.

10. Alan Benjamin, "Rely on Professionals to Navigate FF&E Purchasing Process," *Hotel & Motel Management*, November 21, 2005, 220(20), pp. 8, 23. Patt Patterson, "Dealer Evolution Gives Rise to Many New Options," *Nation's Restaurant News*,

References (continued)

September 21, 1992, p. 128. See also John Tracy, "Food House Redistribution: Boon or Bane? BOON," *Foodservice Equipment & Supplies*, January 2004, 57(1), pp. 44–46; Fred Singer, "Food House Redistribution: Boon or Bane? BANE," *Foodservice Equipment and Supplies*, January 2004, 57(1), pp. 45–46. See also Joseph M. Carbonara, "Understanding Total Cost of Ownership." *Foodservice Equipment & Supplies* 63, no. 1 (2010): 12, http://search.proquest.com.libaccess.sjlibrary.org/docview/235171594?accountid=10361.

11. See Better Business Bureau, "Consumer Education," www.bbb.org/council/consumer-education/. See also Las Vegas Metro Chamber of Commerce, "The Chamber," 2012, www.lvchamber.com/chamber/about.

12. B. Hurst, "The Future of Processed Foods—Management Briefing: Why Do We Rely on Processed Food?" *Just-food*, April 2005, pp. 4–6. See also Megan Pellegrini, "Revolutionizing Formed Products," *National Provisioner*, 228, no. 7 (July 2014): 64–66.

13. P. Sloan, W. Legrand, and J. Chen, *Sustainability in the Hospitality Industry: Principles of Sustainable Operations*, 2nd ed. (New York: Elsevier, 2013).

14. See, for example, Bob Luder, "Restaurants, Foodservice Picking up on Locally Grown," June 5, 2009, www.thepacker.com/Restaurants—foodservice-picking-up-on-locally-grown/Article.aspx?oid=367113&aid=342&fid=PACKER-FOODSERVICE; Foster Frable Jr., "More for Your Buck: Manufacturers Need to Show Potential Buyers Better Value," *Nation's Restaurant News*, August 7, 2000, p. 26. See also Ron Ruggless, "Furr's/Bishop's Tackles Food Manufacturing," *Nation's Restaurant News*, January 11, 1993, p. 7; Jack Hayes, "CHPD Cuts Costs, Maintains Quality," *Nation's Restaurant News*, March 29, 1993, p. 74.

15. Jim Yardley, "A Revolution in the Fish Industry That Hasn't Quite Taken Hold," *New York Times*, June 7, 2000, p. H19. The company cited in this article, GoFish.com, is out of business. However, several food broker alliances exist, such as http://www.ibafoodservice.com/about.php or producer broker co-ops such as the one described in this article: Lihlani Skipper and Alfonso Morales, "The Right Blend," *Rural Cooperatives*, 81, no. 3 (2014): 13–45.

16. George Topor, "What Price Service?" *Restaurant Business*, February 1977, p. 101.

CHAPTER 4

FORCES AFFECTING THE DISTRIBUTION SYSTEMS

The Purpose of This Chapter

After reading this chapter, you should be able to:

- Identify and differentiate the economic forces and the intangible forces that affect the channel of distribution.

- Describe the role of political forces and ethics in the channel of distribution.

- Explain legal restrictions related to food distribution and labeling.

- Explain the legal forces that regulate competition and how companies conduct business.

- List examples of technological advances that impact product distribution.

ECONOMIC AND INTANGIBLE FORCES

In Chapter 3, we discussed the overall pattern of distribution in the hospitality business, as well as the values added throughout the distribution channel. That discussion did not take into consideration the forces that might interfere with the flow of products and services or with the final purchase price retailers must pay. In other words, several forces in the environment can have some effect on the price and availability of the products needed by a hospitality operation. Figure 4.1 shows the major forces that affect the distribution channel, and the next sections discuss these forces.

■ Economic Force

economic force The effects of supply and demand, and other forms of competitive pressure, on businesses.

supply and demand Refers to a competitive environment that exists for producers of commodity items. If supply exceeds demand, purchase prices will decrease. If demand exceeds supply, purchase prices will increase.

The first of these forces is **economic force**. Supply-and-demand considerations have a powerful effect on purchase prices, particularly the prices of perishable items. At the beginning of the channel of distribution, at the primary source level, **supply and demand** can be extremely important. Generally, at this level, the products are in their initial stages of production and are not readily distinguishable, regardless of the producer. Little value has been added to these products; as a result, the prices at this stage are often set through a bidding procedure.

For example, many of the food products that eventually reach the retailer start out as basic commodities such as wheat, corn, cattle, and poultry. Within the same product quality class, little or no differences may exist between Farmer Jones's wheat and Farmer Smith's. Consequently, if the amount of wheat available exceeds the demand, the price drops until all the wheat is sold. Conversely, if the demand exceeds the supply, prices rise until people stop bidding for the wheat. Supply-and-demand forces exert a major impact on commodity prices.

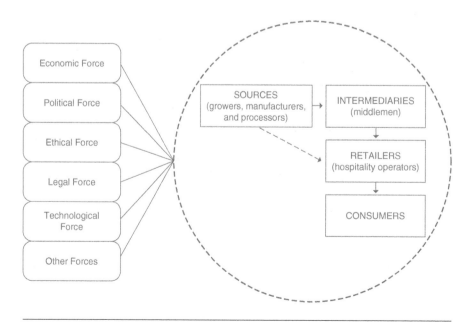

FIGURE 4.1 Major forces affecting the distribution channels.

In many respects, the wheat farmers in this example occupy a precarious position unless they can do something to differentiate their products. This differentiation usually occurs when each primary source, or a middleman, attempts to apply his or her own version of the economic values. For instance, manipulating the form in which the product comes to market can earn a seller a stronger competitive position. Consequently, once a **basic commodity** gets into the channel of distribution, the pressure is on to do something to make the product unique in the buyer's eyes.

> **basic commodity**
> A product for which there is demand, but which is sold by many suppliers without qualitative differentiation. It is a product that is the same no matter who produces it.

If all products were sold strictly on a supply-and-demand basis, sellers would be forced to accept the price that supply-and-demand conditions set. Thus, sellers would worry constantly about producing an excessive supply. Generally speaking, wheat is wheat. Consequently, the wheat farmer must accept the established market price. For farmers, raising natural or organic products versus genetically modified foods or mass-production of produce or farm animals can give them a niche, and they can command higher prices due to the smaller supplies of those products available. However, there are trade-offs, as there may be current and potentially higher costs to grow or produce the items.

As products move along in the channel, they acquire different values. In fact, by the time products reach middlemen, once-similar products may have pronounced differences. This variety means that a seller begins to exercise a bit of control over the price and does not always need to accept the price determined by supply and demand.[1]

But sellers cannot forget supply-and-demand conditions entirely. When overstocked, for example, they may have to lower the price to generate a demand—a situation often associated with perishable goods. Sellers try to avoid this problem, but they remain aware of the old axiom, "Sell it or smell it." And most of them would rather sell.

Buyers can expect to see varying prices for apparently similar products, even products that are in the same quality class. This situation is not so surprising once you realize that each seller can do something to differentiate the product.

The amount of sellers can affect prices also. If there are few distributors of a product in an area, they can charge higher prices. Of primary concern is the prospect of consolidation and mergers among the broadline distributors. For example, in December 2013, Sysco offered to buy US Foods at a value of $8.2 billion. However, the Federal Trade Commission (discussed later in this chapter) called for an injunction against the merger because the combined company would have been 75 percent of the foodservice marketplace. In June 2015, a district court judge granted the injunction due to the possible extreme negative effect on the competitive marketplace, and the merger was cancelled.[2]

Sellers usually strive to emphasize the product's overall value. Value is directly related to the quality of a product, as well as to the supplier services. Hence, a buyer supposedly would be willing to pay more for a product if the price included additional supplier services that the buyer felt provided increased value.

We use the term *value* intentionally, but to be even more accurate, we should use the term *perceived value*, because value means different things to different people. Perceived value is equal to the "perceived quality" of a product or service plus the "perceived supplier services" divided by the "perceived edible-portion (EP) cost" (see Figure 4.2 for a diagram of this equation).

edible-portion (EP)
cost   Equal to the
AP price per portion
divided by its edible
yield percentage. (See
Chapter 10.)

as-purchased (AP)
price   Price charged by
the vendor.

The perceived **edible-portion (EP) cost** is the final cost to you of providing, for example, a finished steak dinner. Usually, it is not equal to the **as-purchased (AP) price** because some products must normally have some waste: fat may have to be trimmed from the steak, resulting in an EP cost per pound that is higher than the AP price per pound, or, depending on the style in which you purchase steak—for example, precut and preportioned versus a whole beef carcass—you incur different labor costs, as well as different energy costs utilized in the preparation of a steak dinner.

Traditionally, the EP cost of food included only the food-ingredient cost, and the cost of nonfood supplies included only the cost of the usable product. Although the EP cost is difficult to assess, we think that it is more appropriate to expand the tradition and think of the EP cost in a different way. For instance, the labor cost associated with some food items may be higher than that for other similar items. Or perhaps the amount and cost of energy utilized in preparation can differ among similar

as-served cost   Another
term for edible-portion
(EP) cost.

as-used cost   Another
term for edible-portion
(EP) cost.

perceived value
equation   Perceived value
of a product is equal to:
(perceived quality + the
perceived supplier services)
divided by its perceived
edible (i.e., usable or servable) cost.

monopolistic competi-
tion   Refers to a competitive environment where
each competitor is affected
by supply-and-demand
conditions because their
businesses are very similar.
However, each competitor
is able to differentiate its
products and/or services
enough to establish a competitive advantage. Typical
economic conditions faced
by vendors and hospitality
businesses.

food products. Even the labor and energy required to clean can vary according to the type of cleaning solution used. Various costing procedures such as prime costing and activity-based costing take more of these factors into account. However, they require more information and time to calculate than the average independent operation has. They tend to be used by larger, corporate operations that have more accounting and cost control employees.

Throughout this book, we refer to the EP cost, not necessarily as the edible-portion cost of food or beverage, but in the context of an **as-served cost** of a food or beverage or an **as-used cost** per gallon of liquid cleaner. Our intent is not to provide mathematical formulas to compute these costs, but we want you to adopt a more panoramic view of the AP price—we wish to use the term "EP cost" to mean that the final cost of anything you buy includes several aspects, the least of which might be the initial AP price.

$$\text{Perceived value} = \frac{\text{Perceived quality} + \text{Perceived supplier services}}{\text{Perceived EP cost}}$$

FIGURE 4.2 Value as related to quality, supplier services, and EP cost.

The relationship shown in Figure 4.2 is not a mathematical formula. We present it as an equation to emphasize the point that value is directly related to quality and supplier services, but inversely related to the EP cost. For example, if quality and the supplier services remain the same while the EP cost drops, the value of the product increases. Conversely, if quality decreases and the supplier services and EP cost remain constant, the value of the product decreases.

The possibilities for sellers' attempts to manipulate how buyers perceive the elements of the **value equation**, and the many supply-and-demand conditions that exist, create a market situation that economists refer to as **monopolistic competition**. Monopolistic competition refers to the idea that each seller enjoys some sort of monopoly to the extent that he or she can manipulate products and services and make them seem to be unique. But the specter of supply and demand remains, and, ultimately, so does the need to be sensitive to price competition: suppliers cannot raise their prices that much higher than their competitors. Thus, most competitors have some sort of monopoly, but just enough to give them some control over prices and some flexibility in attracting customers.

Monopolistic competition is the most common type of marketing environment found throughout the hospitality industry. From the primary source to the retail level, all members of the distribution system strive to highlight value over price. Suppliers do this in an attempt to convince retailers that no substitute suppliers are capable of satisfying their needs. Restaurant managers similarly manipulate product quality, customer services, and menu prices and offerings to create repeat patronage. Hotel operators are quick to emphasize their unique sets of room quality, customer services, and room rates. In today's world, technology, sophisticated revenue management systems, and social media have a major impact on operators' abilities to customize and market their products to an increasingly diverse and segmented customer base while adding value to their hospitality offerings.

Buyers must realize that they might need to pay a bit more for a certain unique set of quality, supplier services, and EP cost. But this can easily be the most cost-effective alternative. There is no reason that buyers cannot enjoy considerable financial success by throwing in their lot with only those suppliers who provide the best perceived value. In the long run, a slightly higher AP price can very well generate the most profitable results.

■ Intangible Forces

Intangible forces include such factors as a supplier's advertising and promotion effectiveness, pricing policy, credit terms, and the conviviality of salespersons, and they can certainly affect the channel of distribution. Buyers must continually guard against reacting disproportionately to these intangible forces because both primary sources and middlemen use them to differentiate the products and services they sell. The buyer must be a "rational buyer."

> **intangible force** Factors that impact the distribution channels in ways that cannot be easily determined, nor can they be easily categorized.

Buyers and their superiors must accept all forces as part of the game they have elected to play. In the final analysis, though, the dynamic market forces that most directly affect the availability of products and their cost must be recognized and used to shape the overall purchasing strategy.

ECONOMIC FORCE—GLOBAL FOOD SUPPLY AND PRICES

The first edition of *Farmer's Almanac* was printed in 1818 by David Young and publisher Jacob Mann. Almost 200 years later, both the hard copy and online versions (www.farmersalmanac .com) still provide amazingly accurate weather predictions, guides to when to plant and harvest produce items and when to fish, and descriptions of other factors affecting our food supply. Today's savvy purchasing agent would be wise to use the latest copy as a guide to understanding climate, weather patterns, diseases, and environmental factors in North America. But they also need to know about

ECONOMIC FORCE—GLOBAL FOOD SUPPLY AND PRICES (continued)

global conditions too. With the large amount of our food supply imported from other countries, conditions all around the world affect the supply and prices of the meat, produce, and seafood items needed by the foodservice industry. Here are just a few examples of commodities that have recently been of great concern.

Beef: As of spring 2014, more than 37 percent of the 48 contiguous states in the United States were in drought conditions. The governor of California, Jerry Brown, declared a state of emergency on January 17, 2014. Many farmers could no longer afford to feed and water their animals and were reducing the size of their herds. Cattle and calves in the United States as of January 1, 2014, totaled 87.7 million head, the lowest January 1 inventory of all cattle and calves since 1951, according to data from the U.S. Department of Agriculture. This has caused prices to jump dramatically. Live cattle futures hit a closing high in January of $1.439 per pound, the highest level since 1984.[1] The Texas Beef Council reported that in April, the average retail price of beef was $5.28 per pound.[2] Barbecue restaurant owners there are worried that the price increases will kill their businesses.[3]

Limes: Who would think that the lime juice in your margarita would cost more than the tequila? But lime prices have increased dramatically over the past years. Since 2001, when much of the Florida citrus crop was depleted by a citrus canker disease, almost 90 percent of limes sold in the United States have been imported from Mexico. But now the deadly "Huanglongbing" (HLB, also known as greening) bacterial disease has devastated crops in Mexico. HLB has mostly affected the smaller key limes used in Mexico but also affected overall supplies. Then severe rains in November and December 2013 knocked lime blossoms off the trees, reducing exports to the United States by two-thirds.[4] The price for a case of limes, which used to be as low as $25, can now be as high as $147. Restaurants all around the country are being affected. One small restaurateur in Los Angeles said he paid more than $2,000 extra for limes in January alone. Many establishments are raising their drink prices and starting to substitute other citrus juices.[5] If you no longer get that wedge of lime with your fish taco, you will know the reason why.

Shrimp: Much of the world's shrimp supply is farmed in China and Southeast Asia. First seen in China in 2009, a disease called Shrimp Early Mortality Syndrome (EMS) moved to Vietnam and now is killing off farm-raised shrimp in the world's largest shrimp exporter, Thailand. The disease, caused by a bacterial infection that lives in brackish water, causes shrimp to die before they reach maturity and reproduce.[6] Fortunately, it is not directly harmful to humans.[7] Unfortunately, the huge decrease in shrimp supply has caused equivalent increases in the price of shrimp. According to the U.S. Bureau of Labor Statistics, in March 2014, the price of shrimp jumped 61 percent from a year earlier. How have restaurant companies reacted to this increase? Some are taking a hit to their profits. Red Lobster, owned by Darden Restaurants, Inc. estimated that the higher prices would add $30 million to its food costs in fiscal year 2014. Bubba Gump Shrimp Co., owned by Landry's Inc., and Cheesecake Factory also expect to take the hit to profits, rather than raise prices. But a younger chain, Noodles & Co. said it raised its price to add shellfish to a meal of pasta or pad thai from $2.59 to $3.34 rather than absorb the costs.[8]

ECONOMIC FORCE—GLOBAL FOOD SUPPLY AND PRICES (continued)

■ REFERENCES

1. Myra Saefong, "Western Drought Spells Killer Grocery Bills," *Wall Street Journal Market Watch,* February 7, 2014, www.marketwatch.com/story/us-drought-hurts-cattle -crops-prices-heat-up-2014-02-07/print?guid=12EFCFAE-8F5B-11E3-A354- 00212803FAD6.

2. Rabea Tahir, "Ongoing Drought Pushes Beef Prices to Record Levels," *Texas Tribune,* April 30, 2014, www.texastribune.org/2014/04/30/record-drought-takes-toll-dinner-tables/.

3. Brad Tuttle, "Beef: It's What's No Longer Affordable for Dinner," *Time.com,* March 8, 2014, http://web.b.ebscohost.com.ezproxy.library.unlv.edu/ehost/detail?vid=4&sid=73eadb2e-8be4 -4451-912f-1f9d7ae4291e%40sessionmgr110&hid=128&bdata=JnNpdGU9ZWhvc3QtbGl2ZQ %3d%3d#db=aph&AN=94894803.

4. Andrew Reilly, "As Lime Prices Soar, Restaurants Wonder What to Do about Cinco de Mayo," *Fox News Latino* May 1, 2014, http://latino.foxnews.com/latino/lifestyle/2014/05/01/as-lime -prices-soar-restaurants-ponder-what-to-do-about-cinco-de-mayo/.

5. David Karp, "Is the Lime an Endangered Species?" *The New York Times Sunday Review* March 30, 2014, www.nytimes.com/2014/03/30/opinion/sunday/is-the-lime-an-endangered -species.html?_r=0.

6. Nopparat Chaichalearmmongkol and Julie Jargon, "Disease Kills Shrimp, Pushes U.S. Prices Higher," *Wall Street Journal—Asian Business News,* July 12, 2013, http://online.wsj.com/news/ articles/SB10001424127887323998604578565201120674008.

7. Food and Agriculture Organization of the United Nations, "Culprit behind Massive Shrimp Die- Offs in Asia Unmasked," May 3, 2013, www.fao.org/news/story/en/item/175416/icode/.

8. Leslie Patton, "Shrimp Is Big. Now It's Sick. And Really Expensive," *Bloomberg News,* April 15, 2014, from www.bloomberg.com/news/print/2014-04-15/shrimp-price-surge-making noodles-s-pad-thai-more-costly.html.

POLITICAL AND ETHICAL FORCES

■ Political Force

Large suppliers and hospitality enterprises exercise considerable political influence in state legislatures and even in the U.S. Congress. These firms frequently lobby for legislation that favors their business and against legislation that is unfavorable to their business. Generally, the primary sources in the channel of distribution have the most political influence. There are fewer sources than middlemen and hospitality operations, thereby making it easier to reach an agreement and prepare a well-organized, concentrated effort to ensure that their interests are served.

The majority of members in the channels of distribution usually restrict their lobbying efforts to joining a local hospitality association and/or chamber of commerce. Good examples of hospitality associations include the National Restaurant Association, the American Hotel and Lodging Association, the American Gaming Association, and the Wine and Spirits Wholesalers of America. Because politics play a large part in how hospitality operators conduct their businesses, it should not be surprising to find many people trying to create easier business climates for themselves. One unfortunate aspect of this political reality is that as one channel member is accommodated, others may be hurt.

political force Refers to factors that impact the distribution channels in ways that are directly related to the amount of influence channel members have on one another.

Political force need not be restricted to local, state, and federal legislative bodies. Many political realities, or "unwritten laws," can affect a channel member's behavior. For instance, it may be politically unwise for a hospitality operator to provide some of his or her own specific values, thereby reducing some middleman's income, particularly if that operator may need to do business with the middleman later. Alternately, it may be unwise for a hospitality operator to delay paying bills.

There is nothing inherently wrong with trying to influence legislation; this behavior is natural and often beneficial. Also, operators must always remember that politics are not restricted to government. Channel members must coexist, and the political force, as invisible as it may be at times, is there to influence product availability, prices, and channel member behavior.

■ Ethical Force

ethical force The effects on businesses of fair and honest business practices and other relevant forms of competitive pressure.

What is **ethical force**? Better yet, what is "ethical"? Is it ethical for a large meat packer to restrict supply for a few days, hoping that the price for meat will rise? Is it ethical for a chef to return spoiled products if the items spoiled because the chef purchased too much and could not use them quickly enough? Is it ethical for a salesperson to keep quiet about a product's limitations if the buyer does not ask about them? Is it ethical to buy products that were produced by farmers or laborers who are paid poorly or work in unhealthy or unsafe environments? No doubt, most of us would agree that these practices would be unethical behavior, but we must recognize that not everyone would view such practices as dishonest.

Although the legality of accepting gifts from business partners and suppliers is debatable, company policy must always take precedence. Many corporations and multinational chains have strict policies regarding this behavior that can result in termination. In a recent study, event planners were asked if accepting room upgrades and gifts would cause a conflict of interest in reviewing hotels. Of the respondents, 60 percent believed that accepting gifts from suppliers was ethical, whereas the remaining 40 percent believed it unethical. When asked if allowing the gifts to influence their choice of supplier was ethical, 25 percent believed it was and 75 percent found it unethical. Of the respondents, only 2 percent thought that it was ethical to accept gifts of more than $2,000.[3]

Another study also indicated that there is no clear-cut definition of ethical behavior. Respondents were asked to indicate their perceptions of ethical issues in business practices. Interestingly enough, on average, they felt that accepting gifts from suppliers was not considered very unethical.[4] Some have suggested that questionable ethics are necessary speed bumps in the channel of distribution. The pressure on salespersons and buyers to consummate attractive deals practically compels members to behave unethically at times. The fact is that through the years, a system of **illegal rebates** and **kickbacks** has grown up among some traditional operators, and these may be thought of as an unethical force bearing on the channels. In large business firms, control systems quickly detect the inflation of cost, and the wise and ethical manager avoids these practices. An honest manager can advance more surely playing by the rules than can the dishonest ones who must constantly devote energy to covering their tracks—and who continually risk destroyed careers.[5]

> **illegal rebate** Another term for kickback.
>
> **kickback** An illegal gift given by a vendor or sales rep to someone if he or she will agree to help defraud the hospitality operation.

Several professional purchasing associations, among them the Institute for Supply Management—formerly the National Association of Purchasing Managers (NAPM)—and the International Society of Hospitality Purchasers (ISHP), have developed codes of ethics/conduct to guide their members.[6] An example of a code of ethics/conduct can be seen in the Chartered Institute & Supply (CIPS) Code of Conduct.

Legislators continue to devote considerable attention to selling and buying practices, particularly the various rebate systems and other forms of economic favoritism. Channel members' adherence to sound ethics can ease this growing pressure, but regardless of the future role of ethics in the hospitality channel of distribution, ethical and unethical forces continue to influence product availability and prices in the present.

CIPS CODE OF CONDUCT

Your commitment to the profession

INTRODUCTION

The purpose of this code of conduct is to define behaviours and actions which CIPS members must commit to maintain as long as they are members of CIPS.

USE OF THE CODE

Members of CIPS worldwide are required to uphold this code and to seek commitment to it by all the parties they engage with in their professional practice.

CIPS CODE OF CONDUCT (continued)

Members should encourage their organisation to adopt an ethical procurement and supply policy based on the principles of this code and raise any matter of concern relating to business ethics at an appropriate level within their organisation.

Members' conduct will be judged against the code and any breach may lead to action under the disciplinary rules set out in the Institute's Royal Charter. Members are expected to assist any investigation by CIPS in the event of a complaint being made against them.

AS A MEMBER OF THE CHARTERED INSTITUTE OF PURCHASING & SUPPLY, I WILL:

Enhance and protect the standing of the profession, by:

- never engaging in conduct, either professional or personal, which would bring the profession or the Chartered Institute of Purchasing & Supply into disrepute

- not accepting inducements or gifts (other than any declared gifts of nominal value which have been sanctioned by my employer)

- not allowing offers of hospitality or those with vested interests to influence, or be perceived to influence, my business decisions

- being aware that my behaviour outside my professional life may have an effect on how I am perceived as a professional

Maintain the highest standard of integrity in all business relationships, by:

- rejecting any business practice which might reasonably be deemed improper

- never using my authority or position for my own financial gain

- declaring to my line manager any personal interest that might affect, or be seen by others to affect, my impartiality in decision making

- ensuring that the information I give in the course of my work is accurate and not misleading

- never breaching the confidentiality of information I receive in a professional capacity

- striving for genuine, fair and transparent competition

- being truthful about my skills, experience and qualifications

Promote the eradication of unethical business practices, by:

- fostering awareness of human rights, fraud and corruption issues in all my business relationships

- responsibly managing any business relationships where unethical practices may come to light, and taking appropriate action to report and remedy them

- undertaking due diligence on appropriate supplier relationships in relation to forced labour (modern slavery) and other human rights abuses, fraud and corruption

- continually developing my knowledge of forced labour (modern slavery), human rights, fraud and corruption issues, and applying this in my professional life

Enhance the proficiency and stature of the profession, by:

- continually developing and applying knowledge to increase my personal skills and those of the organisation I work for

- fostering the highest standards of professional competence amongst those for whom I am responsible

- optimising the responsible use of resources which I have influence over for the benefit of my organisation

Ensure full compliance with laws and regulations, by:

- adhering to the laws of countries in which I practise, and in countries where there is no relevant law in place I will apply the standards inherent in this Code

- fulfilling agreed contractual obligations

- following CIPS guidance on professional practice

This code was approved by the CIPS Global Board of Trustees on 10 September 2013

LEGAL FORCE RELATED TO FOOD DISTRIBUTION AND LABELING

Many buyers have discovered that a lawyer is a buyer's best friend. Channel members must accept a multitude of rules and regulations if they want to engage in buying and selling. We have already seen how the political force works to influence legislation. The next section discusses the major pieces of legislation that provide **legal force** that focuses on food distribution and labeling and their relevance to the hospitality channel of distribution.

■ Meat Safety Legislation

In 1906, Upton Sinclair shocked the world with his book *The Jungle*. In it, he depicted the unspeakably unsanitary conditions then prevalent in the meat packing industry. His description of these horrendous conditions immediately led to a severe decline in meat consumption in the United States, particularly meat from the Chicago stockyards. The book also forced the federal government to pass the **Pure Food Act** (1906) and the Federal

legal force Legislative influence on the distribution channels establishing certain rules of conduct. Enforced by local, state, and/or federal governments.

Pure Food Act Along with other legislation, grants the U.S. Department of Agriculture (USDA) inspection powers throughout the food distribution channels.

Meat Inspection Act
Along with other legislation, grants the U.S. Department of Agriculture (USDA) inspection powers throughout the food distribution channels.

U.S. Department of Agriculture (USDA)
Among other responsibilities, it has inspection powers throughout the food distribution channel. Typically concentrates its inspection efforts on red meat, poultry, and egg production.

Poultry Products Inspection Act
Legislation mandating federal government inspection of poultry products sold interstate.

Wholesome Meat Act
Enhances the USDA's authority to regulate safety in the meat industry. Requires state inspection of meat production to be at least equal to the federal inspection program.

Wholesome Poultry Products Act Enhances the USDA's authority to regulate safety in the poultry industry. Requires state inspection of poultry production to be at least equal to the federal inspection program.

Hazard Analysis Critical Control Point (HACCP) Process used by food processors and others in the foodservice industry to ensure food safety. It identifies the areas at which foods are most susceptible to contamination and recommends procedures that can be used to prevent it from occurring.

Meat Inspection Act (1906). These acts gave the **U.S. Department of Agriculture (USDA)**, established by Congress in 1862, inspection powers throughout the channels of distribution. Although the USDA technically has the authority to inspect any channel member (except seafood production), it usually confines its activities to the inspection of meat, poultry, and eggs. In recent times, it has expanded its role as the USDA also has authority over organic food production.

The meat-inspection legislation requires continuous antemortem and postmortem inspection of all meat intended for interstate and international commerce. State agriculture departments normally inspect meat plants that service customers located only within the particular states.

One of the major weaknesses in the original meat inspection laws was the lack of application to poultry products. Although voluntary poultry inspection was begun in 1926, the required inspection of all poultry sold in interstate commerce did not take effect until the passage of the **Poultry Products Inspection Act** (1957) more than 30 years later.

No further federal legislation affected red meat until 1967, when consumer advocate Ralph Nader and his "Nader's Raiders" focused attention on continuing abuses in the meat industry. Nader's efforts led to the passage of the **Wholesome Meat Act** (1967).

Current USDA food-safety authority rests on a series of legislation based primarily on the Wholesome Meat Act (1967), the Poultry Products Inspection Act (1957), and the **Wholesome Poultry Products Act** (1968).[7] The USDA enforces chemical residue standards and the standards dealing with wholesomeness, general sanitation, packaging, and labeling.

Today's meat inspection system still relies on inspectors' observations of meat products. However, in 1996 the Wholesome Meat Act and the Wholesome Poultry Products Act added a Pathogen Reduction/**Hazard Analysis Critical Control Point (HACCP)** Rule. The HACCP system (similar to one promulgated by local health districts for restaurant operators) requires food processors to identify places within their production cycle where the items can become contaminated (i.e., "critical points") and institute procedures to ensure food safety. It is thought that stronger regulations could reduce the number of foodborne illness outbreaks caused by meat and poultry products.[8] The USDA also requires that **safe-handling procedures** be placed on all packages of raw meat and poultry (see Figure 4.3).

Further, the **Food Safety Inspection Service (FSIS)** division of the USDA has developed a Technical Service Center for *E. coli* testing and *Listeria monocytogenes* regulation. FSIS now requires training as a condition of employment for inspectors as proof USDA has made inspections more scientific.

FIGURE 4.3 Required safe-handling instructions sticker.
Courtesy of the United States Department of Agriculture

According to the American Meat Institute, there are approximately 6,278 federally inspected meat and poultry slaughtering and **processing** plants in the United States. In addition, more than 7,600 federal inspectors are employed to supervise the processing of approximately 8.7 billion poultry, 34.1 million cattle, and 110.9 million hogs per year.[9]

Federal inspection is under the direction of a supervising veterinarian from the FSIS. The FSIS has an annual budget of approximately $1 billion. Funding covers the costs of federal inspection of meat, poultry, and egg products; support of state inspection programs; and research and development.[10] The FSIS inspector also oversees all voluntary federal inspection for animals not covered under mandatory inspection, such as buffalo, rabbit, reindeer, elk, deer, antelope, and ratites, which are flightless birds, such as the ostrich or emu. Voluntary inspection is covered by the Agricultural Marketing Act (1946), which defined grading and inspection services. Suppliers that request this inspection pay an hourly fee.

■ The Federal Food, Drug, and Cosmetic Act (1906)

Although the USDA primarily administers meat inspection, the **Federal Food, Drug, and Cosmetic Act (FFDCA)** provides the majority of food and drug regulation in the United States. Congress created the **Food and Drug Administration (FDA)** to administer this law.

The FDA is responsible for random inspections of approximately 136,000 food-processing plants in the United States. It employs more than 7,600 inspectors worldwide but fewer than 2,000 inspectors domestically. And, like the USDA, it has adopted the HACCP system to increase quality assurance.

safe-handling procedures Instructions typically printed on a product's package label detailing the way in which the product should be handled and prepared to prevent foodborne illness.

Food Safety Inspection Service (FSIS) Division of the United States Department of Agriculture (USDA). Oversees meat inspection.

processing Producing a finished product from raw materials. Typically involves the production of convenience foods by a food processor.

Federal Food, Drug, and Cosmetic Act (FFDCA) Provides the majority of food and drug regulation in the United States.

Food and Drug Administration (FDA) Administers the Federal Food, Drug, and Cosmetic Act (FFDCA).

The FDA has the power to inspect products, records, and premises of food and drug establishments to ensure compliance with the law. Among other powers, the FDA is granted the authority to establish maximum amounts permitted for various classes of contaminants whose presence in food cannot be avoided.

The FDA's power has been increased several times over the years. The major changes occurred in 1938, 1958, 1960, 1962, 1967, 1990, and 1997, perhaps the most significant one being the

Cosmetics-Devices Act (1938). This law gave the FDA injunctive power and the authority to set food standards. Essentially, the FDA has the power to remove from the marketplace any product that does not meet agency standards. Indeed, no other governmental agency can force a company to recall its products as quickly as the FDA.

The FFDCA was amended by the **Food Quality Protection Act (FQPA)** in 1996. This new act provided a single safety standard for pesticide residuals in foods and changed the way the **Environmental Protection Agency (EPA)** regulates pesticides used in the United States.

Cosmetics-Devices Act Law granting the FDA injunctive powers and the authority to set food standards.

Food Quality Protection Act (FQPA) Provides a single safety standard for pesticide residuals in foods. It also changed the way the Environmental Protection Agency (EPA) regulates pesticides use in the United States.

Environmental Protection Agency (EPA) A U.S. agency responsible for protecting human health and the environment by writing and enforcing regulations based on laws passed by Congress.

■ FDA Food Safety Modernization Act (2011)

Even with these food safety laws in place, about 48 million Americans get sick from foodborne illnesses each year. In addition, there has been a dramatic expansion of the scale and complexity of both the U.S. and global food system. To better protect public health and strengthen the food safety system, the FDA Food Safety Modernization Act (FSMA) was signed into law in January 2011.

The FSMA changes the focus of the FDA to preventing rather than reacting to food safety problems and gives it much greater authority to regulate, inspect, and control the food safety system. The new authorities and mandates fall into five key categories: Prevention, Inspection and Compliance, Response, Imports, and Enhanced Partnerships. Due to the broad scope of the legislation and the need for extensive rule-making, public comment, and review, the new policies and procedures could not take place immediately and were being phased in over a multiyear period. By summer 2016, operational strategies had been set for implementing all categories of the law but not all were in effect.

Under prevention, the FDA will be able to require comprehensive, science-based controls for food facilities (including Hazard Analysis Critical Control Point [HACCP] plans), produce safety standards, and protect against intentional contamination of food. To ensure compliance, the FSMA establishes more frequent inspection of high-risk domestic and foreign facilities, gives access to food safety plans and records, and increases food testing by accredited laboratories.

The greatest change in response capabilities is that the FDA can now issue a mandatory recall of unsafe food products if a company does not do so voluntarily. It can also suspend registration of a food facility if it poses serious health hazards. For imports, the FSMA establishes greater accountability and the ability to require third-party certification of foreign food facilities and high-risk foods. If the FDA is denied access to a facility, it can refuse entry of food from that facility into the United States.

The FSMA explicitly recognizes that all food safety agencies need to work together to ensure public health. In the enhanced partnership category, the FDA will promote strategies to work more effectively and expand the capabilities of other federal, state, local, and foreign governmental agencies and nongovernmental agencies.

■ Seafood Safety Legislation

Seafood is not subject to the rigorous, mandatory continuous inspection required for meat and poultry products. People have lobbied for a mandatory seafood-inspection system,[11] but as of this writing, there is only a voluntary program.

However, in 1997, the FDA established HACCP requirements for all processors engaged in interstate commerce and/or the importing of seafood. In essence, these operations now have to perform at least a hazard analysis based on HACCP guidelines.

On the voluntary side, a major continuous inspection program is housed in the **U.S. Department of Commerce (USDC)**. For a fee, a fish processor can obtain continuous inspection of its processing plant from the **National Oceanic and Atmospheric Administration (NOAA**; see Figure 4.4). In return, the processor can label its packages as **Packed Under Federal Inspection (PUFI)**. For an additional fee, the Department of Commerce will provide a quality grading service.

Seafood is subject to the provisions of the FFDCA. This law permits the FDA to periodically inspect fish production to ensure that the foods are wholesome, sanitary, labeled correctly, and stored properly. According to the FDA, there are approximately 13,400 seafood-processing establishments in the United States.[12] With so many processing facilities, a mandatory continuous inspection program is not feasible. However, as stated previously, the FDA now requires seafood processors to use the HACCP system when establishing and operating their production plants.

U.S. Department of Commerce (USDC) Agency that, among other things, will, for a fee, provide to seafood processors continuous government inspection and federal grading of their fish products.

National Oceanic and Atmospheric Administration (NOAA) Agency of the U.S. Department of Commerce (USDC) that, for a fee, will provide continuous inspection of a fish processor's plant.

Packed Under Federal Inspection (PUFI) Seal placed on the product labels of fish items that have been produced and packed under continuous government inspection by the U.S. Department of Commerce (USDC).

Interstate Shellfish Sanitation Conference Voluntary program, involving federal and state agencies, that supervises the beds of water used to grow and harvest shellfish.

The FDA has the authority to examine seafood in interstate commerce and, if the product is defective, to seize it and prohibit its sale. In addition, the FDA is allowed to inspect imported seafood products before they are permitted to enter the United States.

There also is a cooperative program, involving federal and state agencies, that supervises the beds of water that are used to grow and harvest shellfish. This venture, referred to as the **Interstate Shellfish Sanitation Conference**,

FIGURE 4.4 NOAA logo.
Courtesy of the NOAA

Marine Mammal Protection Act   Law stating that tuna harvested in a way that endangers dolphins cannot be sold in the United States.

Perishable Agricultural Commodities Act (PACA)   Legislation prohibiting unfair and fraudulent practices in the sale of fresh and frozen produce.

Agricultural Adjustment Act   Legislation developed as part of the New Deal's farm relief bill. It stated that whenever the administration desired currency expansion, the president must first authorize the open market committee of the Federal Reserve to purchase up to $4 billion of federal obligations. Its primary purpose was to create an "honest dollar" that would be fair to debtors and creditors in the farming industry. Also referred to as the Thomas Amendment, named after its sponsor, Oklahoma Senator Elmer Thomas.

Agricultural Marketing Agreement Act   Law that allows primary sources and intermediaries in the produce trade to work together without violating antitrust regulations.

seller co-op   Refers to sellers, usually primary sources, who are legally allowed to join together to market their products. Typically found in the fresh produce trade.

identifies areas that are suitable for the production of clams, oysters, and mussels, and designates that they are in compliance with the Department of Commerce's voluntary inspection program. Created in 1982, this organization helps to promote cooperation and trust among the shellfish control agencies.

Some seafood products are subject to legislation that, although not necessarily focused on seafood safety, nevertheless contributes to a safe, wholesome environment. For instance, the 1972 **Marine Mammal Protection Act** (a federal law) stipulates that only tuna harvested without endangering dolphins can be sold, distributed, or bought in the United States. In 2011, new guidelines were released to make it simpler to farm fish in federal waters. It is believed that by allowing fish farms to use federal waters there would be more jobs created and less restriction on fishing wild stocks. As the United States Department of Agriculture (USDA) has suggested that Americans consume more fish, the demand has increased and so has foreign imports. The new farm fishing guidelines are the direct result of a lack of domestic supply.[13]

In addition to creating legislation, the National Oceanic and Atmospheric Administration (NOAA) also takes part in Fisheries Management through their NOAA Fisheries Office of Sustainable Fisheries. This is a process that sets annual catch limits and places regulations to avoid overfishing. This department also studies the environmental, social, and economic impact of fishing on their points of origin.[14]

■ Perishable Agricultural Commodities Act (1930)

The intent of the **Perishable Agricultural Commodities Act (PACA)** is to control interstate commerce, specifically by prohibiting unfair and fraudulent practices in the sale of fresh and frozen produce. Wholesalers are required to be licensed by the government. If an individual hospitality operation does a bit of wholesale business on the side and the products sold in this manner cross state lines, the operation also may need such a license.

■ Agricultural Adjustment Act (1933) and Agricultural Marketing Agreement Act (1937)

The **Agricultural Adjustment Act** and the **Agricultural Marketing Agreement Act** permit primary sources and intermediaries to work together in certain ways to solve their marketing problems and to ensure a steady flow of perishable products. The acts exempt these sellers from some antitrust laws. For example, in certain cases, sellers of these products may join together to form **seller co-ops**, which market the products of each individual primary source.

■ The Fair Packaging and Labeling Act (Hart Act; 1966)

The **Fair Packaging and Labeling Act** (FPLA) altered the way products are packaged.[15] It requires that a label state the identity of the product, the net quantity of the contents (in metric

Nutrition Facts

Serving Size 2/3 cup (55g)
Servings Per Container About 8

Amount Per Serving	
Calories 230	Calories from Fat 72

	% Daily Value*
Total Fat 8g	**12%**
Saturated Fat 1g	**5%**
Trans Fat 0g	
Cholesterol 0mg	**0%**
Sodium 160mg	**7%**
Total Carbohydrate 37g	**12%**
Dietary Fiber 4g	**16%**
Sugars 1g	
Protein 3g	

Vitamin A	10%
Vitamin C	8%
Calcium	20%
Iron	45%

*Percent Daily Values are based on a 2,000 calorie diet. Your daily value may be higher or lower depending on your calorie needs.

	Calories:	2,000	2,500
Total Fat	Less than	65g	80g
Sat Fat	Less than	20g	25g
Cholesterol	Less than	300mg	300mg
Sodium	Less than	2,400mg	2,400mg
Total Carbohydrate		300g	375g
Dietary Fiber		25g	30g

FIGURE 4.5 Nutrition label.

and inch/pound units), and the name and place of business of the manufacturer or distributor (see Figure 4.5). The act, which the FDA enforces, also sought to eliminate misleading descriptions and illustrations and to force companies to adopt standard packaging sizes, which it failed to accomplish.

Fair Packaging and Labeling Act (FPLA) Requires consumer products' package labels to provide an accurate description of the amount of contents in the package. It is also designed to allow consumers to make value comparisons among competing brands. Sometimes referred to as the Hart Act.

■ Package Label Regulations

The federal government requires the labels of packaged, processed foods to contain this information:[16]

a. The common or legal name of the product.

b. The name and address of the food processor, or the distributor, of the items.

c. The net contents in the package, listed according to count, weight, or other appropriate measure.

d. A listing of ingredients, in descending order, from greatest proportion to least proportion. (This requirement may be unnecessary if a **standard of identity** has been established for the product. A standard of identity essentially establishes what a food product is—for example, what a food product must be to be labeled "strawberry preserves." The federal government has developed standards of identity for more than 300 products, and the FSIS has developed around 100 for meat and poultry, specifically.)[17]

standard of identity A U.S. government regulation that establishes what a food product must be to carry a certain name. For example, what a food product must be to be labeled "strawberry preserves."

e. A notation of any artificial flavoring or chemical preservative added to the product.

f. Serving size (in typical measures, such as "cups") and number of servings per container. (The federal government has developed standard serving sizes for many food categories.)[18]

g. Number of calories per serving.

h. Number of calories derived from fat.

i. Amounts of fat, saturated fat, cholesterol, sodium, sugars, dietary fiber, protein, total carbohydrates, and complex carbohydrates.

j. Amounts of important vitamins and minerals.

k. If the product is a beverage, the amount of juice (fruit or vegetable) it contains.

standard of fill   A U.S. government regulation that indicates to the processor how full a container must be to avoid deception. It prevents the selling of excessive amounts of air or water in place of food.

standard of quality   A U.S. government regulation that states the minimum quality a product must meet to earn the federal government's lowest possible quality grade. Products below the minimum standard of quality must indicate on the package label what the problem is. For instance, if canned green beans are excessively broken, the label could read, "Below Standard of Quality, Excessively Broken."

Nutrition Labeling and Education Act   Legislation that mandates nutritional and other related information to be listed on product package labels.

l. A notation that the product falls below the standard of fill, if relevant. (A **standard of fill** indicates to the processor how full a container must be to avoid deception. This standard prevents the selling of air or water in place of food; prescribed amounts of air and water, though, are permissible.)

m. Also, if relevant, a statement that the product falls below the standard of quality. (A **standard of quality** is the minimum standard a product must meet to earn the federal government's lowest possible quality grade. For instance, if canned green beans are excessively broken, the label could read "Below Standard of Quality, Excessively Broken.")

n. All label information must be noted in English unless an imported product with a foreign-language label will not deceive consumers, or if such a product will be distributed in an area where the foreign language is the predominant language.

o. If the food processor makes any nutritional or dietary claims, the package label must carry government-approved terminology. Several terms can be used as long as the processor meets these strict definitions (see Figure 4.6).

p. A standardized list of nutrition facts, as articulated by the **Nutrition Labeling and Education Act** (1990), must be included on the package label (see Figure 4.5). (Technically, the package labels of processed foods sold only to food services that will process them further and resell them to guests do not have to include nutrition facts. Today, however, it is unusual to see a package label that does not include this standardized information.)

q. If the product is raw or partially cooked meat or poultry, it must contain safe-handling instructions on the package label, that is, instructions that indicate how the product should be handled to avoid contamination.

The federal government continues to add and modify food labeling regulations. In 2004, the Food Allergen Labeling and Consumer Protection Act, mandated that food labels provide the

NUTRITION/HEALTH CLAIM STANDARD DEFINITIONS	
Calorie free	Fewer than 5 calories
Cholesterol free	Fewer than 2 milligrams cholesterol and 2 grams (or less) saturated fat
Fat free	Less than 1/2 gram fat
Heart healthy	Contains 13 grams of oat bran or 20 grams of oatmeal and is low fat and low sodium
Light (lite)	One-third fewer calories (or 50 percent less fat)
Low calorie	40 calories (or less)
Low cholesterol	20 milligrams (or less) cholesterol and 2 grams (or less) saturated fat
Low fat	3 grams (or less) fat
Low sodium	140 milligrams (or less) sodium
Sodium free	Fewer than 5 milligrams sodium

FIGURE 4.6 Standard definitions of some nutrition/health claims.

common or usual name and food source for any ingredients containing eight categories of food allergens: milk, egg, fish, crustacean shellfish, tree nuts, wheat, peanuts, and soybeans. Effective in 2006, the FDA amended the regulations on food labeling to include the amount of trans fatty acids that are contained within a serving size. The gluten-free labeling final rule took effect in August 2014. It specifies that foods voluntarily labeled as gluten free must contain less than 20 parts per million gluten. A more detailed discussion of food labeling can be found on the FDA website. In addition to federal-government labeling requirements, many states and local municipalities issue their own label regulations. For instance, Proposition 65 (1986) in California, states that a food processor must place a health warning on any food that contains an ingredient(s) suspected of causing cancer or birth defects.

More recently, companies are implementing the certification of USDA Organic, Organic, "Made With" Organic, or listing certain ingredients as organic. This provides the consumer with certain assurances regarding the product. USDA Organic means that all ingredients contained within the package must be certified organic and any packaging aids used must also be organic. The next listing is organic. Something labeled as organic must have all agricultural ingredients as certified organic. Items labeled as organic must also contain a minimum of 95 percent organic ingredients, and those ingredients must be identified on the label. To use the label "Made With" Organic, the product must be at least 70 percent certified organic. When using the "Made With" label the packaging cannot use the USDA organic seal (Figure 4.7). The final labeling is for items with specific organic ingredients. In this case, only the items

FIGURE 4.7 Organic labeling.
Courtesy of the United States Department of Agriculture

that are certified organic can be labeled as such and the USDA organic seal cannot be used on the packaging.[19]

OTHER LEGAL FORCES

Many other laws have been put into place since the late 1800s that serve to maintain a competitive business environment and regulate how companies can conduct business. The next section outlines many of these pieces of legislation and defines terms such as contracts, warranties, patents, and rebates.

■ The Sherman Antitrust Act (1890)

The **Sherman Antitrust Act** (named for Senator John Sherman) was the United States' first piece of antitrust legislation. Basically, it forbids any action that tends to eliminate or severely reduce competition. Interestingly, the language of this law is so general that just about anything relating to unfair competition could be covered under the Sherman Antitrust Act.

> **Sherman Antitrust Act**
> The first piece of antitrust legislation enacted in the United States. Prohibits any action that tends to eliminate or severely reduce competition.

Federal Trade Commission (1914), Amended by the Wheeler-Lea Act (1938)

Federal Trade Commission (FTC) Oversees and regulates advertising, deceptive promotions, monopolies, and unprofessional conduct in the marketplace.

Clayton Act Enhances and amplifies the antitrust duties performed by the FTC. It also outlaws tying agreements and exclusive dealing.

tying agreement Illegal contract that forces a buyer to purchase from a vendor certain items he or she may not want to gain the privilege of purchasing other items the buyer does want.

exclusive dealing Occurs when a salesperson allows a buyer to purchase the brands he or she carries, only if the buyer agrees to purchase no competing brands from other vendors. An illegal practice.

exclusive selling Another term for exclusive distribution.

promotional discount Price discount awarded to the buyer if he or she allows the vendor to promote the product in the hospitality operation. Or if the hospitality operation agrees to personally help promote the sale of the product to its customers.

Robinson-Patman Act Legislation that enhanced federal antitrust powers that help protect small businesses.

The **Federal Trade Commission (FTC)** deals with: advertising, deceptive promotions, monopolies, and unprofessional conduct in the marketplace. It was established primarily to clarify the Sherman Act and to enhance its power.

The Clayton Act (1914)

The **Clayton Act** was yet another attempt by Congress to increase the federal government's control over antitrust violations. The act (named for Senator Henry De Lamar Clayton Jr.) essentially enumerates and amplifies the antitrust duties of the FTC.

Two illegal activities covered in this act are of particular importance to channel members: (1) **tying agreements**, whereby sellers once forced retailers to purchase certain items (e.g., pickles) to gain the privilege of purchasing others (e.g., mustard), and (2) **exclusive dealing**, whereby a salesperson forced a retailer to buy only his or her product (e.g., beer) and no other brands of that product. Exclusive dealing should not be confused with **exclusive selling**, which is a perfectly legal type of franchise arrangement. For example, in most cases, a beer company can legally sell its beer to only a few select retailers, which then become the retailers that customers must contact if they want that particular brand of beer.

More information on the Sherman and Clayton Acts can be found in Chapter 2 of the Antitrust Division Manual on the U.S. Department of Justice website.

The Robinson-Patman Act (1936)

This act, known as the "small-business protection act," was designed to enhance further the power of the federal government to control antitrust violations. The primary thrust of the act was the limitation placed on companies that used various types of price discounts when marketing their goods and services.

Among other things, this act addressed three specific loopholes: (1) Up until 1936, sellers could give **promotional discounts** to buyers of their choice. After 1936, this became a form of illegal price discrimination when the discounts were not offered to all qualified buyers. (2) It is legal for sellers to offer a buyer a discount if the buyer purchases in large amounts, but it has been illegal since 1936 to set this amount so high that only one or two buyers can hope to reach it. In other words, the **Robinson-Patman Act** incorporated a **quantity limits provision** so that the quantity a buyer must purchase to qualify for a discount must be reasonable. (3) A supplier cannot practice **predatory pricing**. That is to say, the supplier cannot price goods or services so low that it would drive all other competitors out of the marketplace, thereby affording this lone supplier a monopoly and the opportunity to raise prices significantly in the future.

The Clayton Act and the Robinson-Patman Act do not prohibit all types of price discrimination. Generally, two buyers can pay different prices for the same product if, for example, one buyer provides some value. For instance, purchasing large quantities of products is a way for buyers to provide their own financing as well as storage. As a reward for bulk purchasing, a supplier can legally charge a lower price. In general, sellers can manipulate the price if the goods are of unlike quality or quantity. Sellers also can reduce their prices at a moment's notice to meet a competitor's recently reduced price.

Franchise Law

A franchisor can legally require franchisees to adhere to standards of quality set forth by the franchisor. For example, franchisors normally prepare strict product specifications that franchisees must use when purchasing all food, beverage, and nonfood supplies. **Franchise laws** ensure quality and cost control as well as a consistent appearance.

Usually a franchisor will not force a franchisee to purchase from the franchisor's commissary and/or central distribution center, nor would a franchisee necessarily be required to buy from a supplier designated by the franchisor. However, it would appear that, under some circumstances, a franchisor can impose these types of restrictions on franchisees.[20] At one time, the courts found these restrictions to be illegal, citing them as violations of antitrust legislation. More recently, though, court rulings have eased these limitations on franchisors as long as they do not derive an economic benefit from requiring franchisees to carry certain specified products.

The Internal Revenue Service and the Bureau of Alcohol, Tobacco, Firearms, and Explosives

Two federal-government agencies, the **Internal Revenue Service (IRS)** and the **Bureau of Alcohol, Tobacco, Firearms, and Explosives (ATF)**, are responsible for the orderly and legal sale, distribution, and purchase of alcoholic beverages. These agencies ensure that: (1) no adulterated product enters the marketplace; (2) products are produced, sold, distributed, and purchased by duly licensed entities only; and (3) all appropriate taxes and fees are collected.

State and Local Legislation

All the laws discussed so far are federal. Some states and municipalities have adopted somewhat stricter versions of them, as well as additional legislation not found in the federal statutes. For example, although the federal government does not mandate fish plant inspection, some states do. In addition, many channel members must contend with several state and county liquor codes.

---

quantity limits provision   Part of the Robinson-Patman Act. Stipulates that the amount of product that needs to be purchased to qualify for a quantity discount must be reasonable, and not so high that only one or two favored buyers have the chance to reach it.

predatory pricing   Company pricing its products unreasonably low in an attempt to drive all other competitors out of business. An illegal practice.

franchise law   Refers to the ability of a franchisor to require franchisees to adhere to certain standards of quality set by the franchisor.

Internal Revenue Service (IRS)   Federal agency responsible for enforcing the U.S. tax code and for collecting taxes.

Bureau of Alcohol, Tobacco, Firearms, and Explosives (ATF)   Federal agency responsible for overseeing the sale and purchase of these products and ensuring that all pertinent laws and regulations are followed.

■ Contract

> **contract** Voluntary and legal agreement, by competent parties, to do or not do something. In almost every case it must be a written agreement to be legally enforceable.
>
> **Uniform Commercial Code (UCC)** Legislation outlining rules and regulations pertaining to various business transactions, such as leases, contracts, bills of lading, and so forth. Ensures consistency throughout the United States.

A **contract** is "a voluntary and lawful agreement, by competent parties, for a good consideration, to do or not do a specified thing."[21] A completed purchase order, once accepted by a supplier, becomes a legally enforceable contract. If buyers renege on their promises, they may be sued by their suppliers and forced to perform according to the terms established in their contracts.

In some instances, a buyer purchases only a small amount of merchandise at one time and may not prepare a formal purchase order document. Instead a buyer may simply call in an order to a local supplier instead of e-mailing or faxing a written order. In some cases, a verbal commitment of this type can carry the force of a written contract. Article 2–201 of the **Uniform Commercial Code (UCC)** states that a purchase order of $500 or more is not enforceable in a court of law unless the agreement is reduced to writing. Consequently, a small verbal order of, say, $100, could be considered legally binding for both parties.

After an order is made with the supplier, a buyer might request a written acknowledgment from the supplier. Technically, no contract exists if a supplier does not acknowledge his or her intent to enter into a legally binding agreement.

Presumably, once the goods are delivered, the buyer will deem them acceptable and will pay for the merchandise. However, legal problems might arise if the goods delivered do not meet the agreed-upon standards of quality, quantity, and price. A buyer is able to return these goods upon: (1) inspecting a representative sample of the goods; (2) indicating why the goods are not acceptable; and (3) informing the supplier that the goods are being rejected. If a buyer fails to inspect and reject the goods and to indicate why this action is being taken, he or she will have accepted the merchandise and will be responsible for payment.[22]

A great deal of trust must exist between buyers and suppliers. In some situations, we cannot take time to create written documentation; we must rely on our suppliers to treat us honestly and with good faith. As long as all parties have one another's best interests at heart, all of them can coexist and achieve their long-term goals.

This brief discussion highlights the major issues that a purchasing agent needs to consider when preparing purchase orders, but a buyer must consider other laws—federal, state, and local laws—as well. In fact, an operator should immediately seek legal advice whenever a question arises. For instance, there may be unique deposit and refund laws in your area that must be considered before you enter into a long-term purchase agreement.

■ Agency Law

Salespersons need to know the precise authority operators delegate to their buyers. In general, buyers have the authority, as their company's agents, to legally bind their companies to purchase

> **agency law** Law that allows employees, when acting in their official capacity, to sign contracts for their companies.

order contracts, or **agency law**. Hospitality companies usually limit a buyer's authority by setting a dollar limit on the purchases he or she can contract for. If such a limitation exists, however, salespersons and their companies must be notified; otherwise, they can rightfully assume that the buyer has unlimited authority.

■ Title to Goods

It is important for buyers to know the precise moment when the title to any product passes to their firm because, at the point of title transfer, the buyer's firm assumes responsibility for the item. **Title to goods** can pass at any one of many points in the market channel. Usually, when purchasing from intermediaries, the hospitality operation takes title when a receiving agent receives, inspects, and signs for the delivered merchandise. Under a direct-buying arrangement (i.e., purchasing directly from the primary source), the hospitality operation takes title when the merchandise leaves the primary source's premises; typically, the primary source places the merchandise on a common carrier **free on board (FOB)**, which states that, once the property is on board, the buyer now owns it and takes responsibility for its safe transit.

If the buyer takes title before actually receiving the item, even though he or she may not have actually paid for the product, it, as well as the risk, belongs to that company. (Parenthetically, when taking a risk like this earlier than necessary, the buyer may earn a slightly lower AP price.)

■ Consignment Sales

Although **consignment sales** are not common in the hospitality industry, and are not allowed for alcoholic beverages, they do appear now and then, especially in seasonal resort areas where buyers must stock up well before the doors are opened to cash-paying guests. Off-premise caterers also tend to rely on consignment sales from time to time, especially for big parties that are allowed to pay most of their catering bills after the functions are over.

A typical consignment sale stipulates that the buyer of a product need not pay until the acquiring company sells the product. This is a good way for a retailer to work with a supplier's money, but a desire to buy "on consignment" tends to imply that the buyer is in a precarious financial position.

■ Warranties and Guarantees

Warranties and guarantees may be either "expressed" or "implied." The express warranty or guarantee is written out in, ideally, straightforward language. The implied versions are, as their name suggests, either inferred by the buyer or implied by the seller. Courts of law have been known to let salespersons voice a degree of prideful exaggeration and to include a certain amount of subjectivity, or permissible puffery, in a sales pitch. Consequently, a buyer may face problems if seeking retribution when the product is not, after all, "the best in the land."

■ Patents

Retailers must be careful to avoid illegally adopting someone else's **patented** procedures. Nor can copyrights and trademarks be violated. For instance, you cannot substitute Pepsi for Coke.

---

title to goods   Represents ownership of property which is free of claims against it, and therefore can be sold, transferred, or put up as security.

free on board (FOB)   When buyers purchase merchandise, but have to arrange for their own delivery. The vendor will place the merchandise on the buyer's vehicle or a common carrier at no additional charge (i.e., "free on board"), but the buyer is then responsible for the merchandise and the cost of transportation from that point on.

consignment sale   Allows the buyer to pay a vendor for a purchase after the buyer's company has sold the merchandise to its customers.

warranty and guarantee   May be expressed or implied. Assurance that a product or service will be provided. Alternately, assurance that a product or service will meet certain specifications. Alternately, assurance that a product or service will be acceptable for a specified period of time or amount of use. Alternately, assurance that parts and/or repairs needed during a specified time period will be paid for by the vendor.

patent   A set of exclusive rights granted by a government to an inventor for a limited time period in exchange for a public disclosure of the invention.

A copyright is a form of intellectual property law that provides protection based on the U.S. Constitution. Copyright law protects original works of authorship.[23]

A trademark protects words, symbols, phrases, or designs which can aid in identifying the source of goods and services or distinguish one's goods or services from a competitor's.

Internet and social media rights with respect to intellectual property are still in their infancy. However, trademarks and copyrights still protect a company's online property. In addition to these protections, any company that advertises through the use of social media is required to disclose payment for endorsements. This is enforced through the Federal Trade Commission (FTC). The FTC is also responsible for enforcing laws that require companies to protect its consumers' privacy rights and maintain security for sensitive consumer information.[24]

■ Rebates

rebate Another term for cash rebate.

Rebates, which are gifts of cash or product, are legal as long as suppliers offer all buyers the same rebate possibility. An exception exists in the liquor trade, in which all rebates are illegal on the wholesale level. Oddly enough, a buyer could be unknowingly implicated in a legal action if he or she takes a rebate, assuming that all other buyers have had the same opportunity, when in fact he or she is the only buyer receiving the rebate.

Rebates are also against the law when a buyer and seller conspire to inflate the price of a product and the buyer takes a personal rebate after the purchase.

TECHNOLOGICAL FORCE

As discussed in Chapter 2, many technological advances in the hospitality channel of distribution have taken place. In addition to the changes in the way products are ordered, received, stored, and accounted for, there have been many other current developments.

■ Genetically Engineered Foods

genetically modified food Food modified by bioengineering techniques. Typically done to enhance flavor, appearance, and/or uniformity of size and to increase shelf life.

Food processing has advanced to the point where several foods can be **genetically modified** (i.e., bioengineered) to improve their shelf life and/or to increase their flavor and availability in the marketplace. For example, some tomatoes have been genetically engineered to remain on the vine much longer than those produced the traditional way.[25] Other types of common genetically modified foods include potatoes that are resistant to disease, wheat that can be raised in drought conditions, rice that can be grown in salt water, and corn with higher production yields.[26] Genetically engineered foods are accepted by most Americans, and there are few laws regulating their standards or labeling. They are much more controversial in other countries; for instance, they are prohibited in many parts of Europe and Latin America.[27]

■ Product Preservation

Today, foods reach us in many forms. One of the main reasons for this is our sophisticated level

of **product preservation** technology. Although some individuals are wary of preservation processes, no one can deny that we would not enjoy many of the foods we take for granted if these products deteriorated noticeably through the channel of distribution.[28]

Closely related to the genetic engineering of foods are techniques that food processors can use to increase product shelf life. For instance, government-approved **irradiation** techniques (FSIS approved in 2000) can reduce product spoilage.[29] However, the FDA requires that irradiated foods must include a label stating products have been "treated with [by] radiation," along with the now-utilized international symbol for irradiation, the Radura (Figure 4.8).

FIGURE 4.8 Radura, the international symbol for irradiation.
Courtesy of Heinz

> **product preservation**
> Refers to production, storage, and/or delivery procedures a vendor uses to ensure consistent and reliable product quality. Alternately, process used to increase an item's shelf life.
>
> **irradiation** Controversial product preservation procedure that can reduce or eliminate harmful bacteria. Used to extend a product's shelf life.

This labeling requirement does not currently apply to restaurant foods, but only foods sold in grocery stores. More information on food irradiation can be found at the FDA website and at the U.S. Environmental Protection Agency website.

High-pressure processing is a new alternative to irradiation. A scientist at Ohio State University has developed a method to compress food with a machine originally used to make industrial diamonds. It kills bacteria, but does not chemically or physically change the food. Although smaller food processors may not be able to afford the $3 million machine, it has been adopted by Hormel and Oscar Meyer and is used to produce some of their higher-priced deli meats.[30]

■ Productivity

In 1994, the FDA approved the use of a synthetic hormone in cows. The commercial name of

the hormone is **Posilac**; other names include bovine somatotropin, rbST, and rbGH. It has been found that the use of this hormone can increase milk production by roughly 10 percent. Once again, though, some people are very leery of these practices and feel they result in foods that are unsafe for human consumption. As a result, some large dairy companies are starting to eliminate use of the hormones. Most recently, Yoplait and Dannon have stopped buying rbGH milk for their yogurt, and Kroger grocery stores and Starbucks are two of the larger retailers that are committed to sourcing milk from non-rbGH cows.[31]

> **Posilac** A supplement of the naturally occurring cow hormone BST, that when administered to cows allows them to produce more milk.
>
> **convenience food**
> A food that has been processed to change its form and/or taste. It usually requires very little handling in the restaurant kitchen. It may be ready-to-use or ready-to-serve.

■ Value-Added Foods

Product processing, from primary source to retailer level, has reached higher and higher levels of sophistication. A very large number of **convenience foods**

value-added food
Another term for
convenience food.

**first-generation
convenience food**   Value-
added product that
was one of the first
convenience foods on the
market. It has been available for many years. May
be less expensive than
its fresh counterpart. An
example is frozen orange
juice.

are on the market today. It is the rare hospitality operation that does not purchase some of these products. Hospitality operators usually buy these items to save money in the long run. Although it is generally true that a **value-added food** is much more expensive than its raw counterpart, the potential savings in labor preparation time, energy usage, and storing and handling chores may reduce the EP cost to the point at which overall profit margins will be attractive.

In some cases, the AP price of a convenience food may actually be less than the AP price of the raw ingredients needed to fabricate the item. This is especially true with **first-generation convenience foods** such as those developed by frozen food pioneer Clarence Birdseye (1886–1956).[32] For instance, frozen fish fillets are a first-generation convenience food and, like many of the older convenience foods, are usually less expensive than their fresh equivalent.

Today, almost every food item purchased has some degree of form value added to it. "Convenience," then, is all a matter of degree. The hospitality buyer can look forward to having an ever-growing variety of convenience foods to choose from.

▪ Transportation

transportation   The
movement of people and
goods from one location to
another.

In many respects, faster **transportation** constitutes a form of product preservation. But it is much more. Today, buyers can expect faster, larger, and more predictable deliveries, which often reduce the number of purchase orders buyers must make. Also, the increased dependability of transportation allows the buyer companies, in turn, to fulfill more readily the promises they make to their customers. Improved transportation also has made more products available more quickly, as hospitality companies can now get specialty products shipped by FedEx and UPS from anywhere in the world. We might even get food delivered by drones in the near future. Although not approved by the Federal Aviation Administration (FAA) in the United States yet, YoSushi restaurant in London is bringing food to the table using drones.[33]

▪ Packaging

packaging   Process of
enclosing or protecting
products for distribution,
storage, sale, and use.
Alternately, the process
of design, evaluation, and
production of packages.

According to the USDA, **packaging** accounts for, on average, about 8 percent of the purchase price of food products. The USDA also estimates that in about one-fourth of all food and beverages sold, packaging costs exceed the cost of the edible ingredients. In general, the more processed or complicated a food product is, the higher the packaging costs.

Packaging is extremely important to the hospitality operator because it directly affects the quality, shelf life, and convenience of the food or beverage products. Unfortunately, the higher-quality packaging that our convenience-oriented society demands has caused a consumer backlash in the United States. Our quest for more and more processed "instant" foods has led food fabricators to create packaging materials that may pose risks of long-term harm to our environment by exponentially increasing the volume of solid waste disposal.

Today, some packaging not only can make a food product more convenient, but it can also contribute to better taste. For example, many products are packed in **controlled atmosphere packaging (CAP)**, which involves placing an item in waxboard, cardboard, aluminum, and/or plastic; removing all existing gases by creating a vacuum; and then introducing a specially formulated mixture of gases that will extend the shelf life of the particular product in the package.[34]

Some common forms of CAP—also referred to as modified atmosphere packaging (MAP)—are the **aseptic packs** that are used to package juices, wines, and unrefrigerated milk; shelf-stable, unrefrigerated convenience meals; and processed produce and other grocery products (see Figure 4.9). These items are convenient to use. They do not require expensive refrigerated storage. They tend to taste better than canned food because the aseptic sterilization process requires less heating time than the canning process. Another plus is that these types of containers usually can be stacked more readily and take up less storage space than regular cans or bottles. Some packaging can also increase the safety of the foods we purchase. For instance, some products have **time- and temperature-sensitive food labels** attached, which will change color if the products have been stored too long and/or have been subjected to unsafe storage temperatures.

As discussed in Chapter 2, other welcome packaging advances include the application of the **Universal Product Codes (UPC)** and radio frequency identification (RFID) tags to the hospitality industry. The familiar bar codes that are present on most grocery store product offerings are now being utilized in the hospitality industry, thanks to the efforts of the **International Foodservice Manufacturers Association (IFMA)** and other like-minded business organizations. RFID tags are also slowly finding their way onto products as well. Eventually, the use of these technologies will lead to more efficient order processing, improved receiving operations, more accurate inventory valuation and control, and increased opportunities to do business electronically, thereby saving a bit of labor cost.[35]

FIGURE 4.9 Aseptic packaging. *Courtesy of Hormel Foods, LLC. The VALLEY FRESH trademark and logo are registered trademarks of Hormel Foods, LLC and used with permission.*

controlled atmosphere packaging (CAP) Process that involves placing a food or beverage item in a package, removing existing gases by creating a vacuum, and introducing a specially formulated mixture of gases intended to enhance the product's shelf life.

aseptic pack A form of controlled atmosphere packaging (CAP). Sterile foods placed in an airtight, sterilized package. The package contains a hygienic environment that prolongs shelf life and makes the foods shelf-stable.

time- and temperature-sensitive food labels Labels that typically change color when the product is too old and/or when the product has been too long in the danger zone (i.e., in an unsafe storage temperature).

Universal Product Codes (UPC) Another term for bar code.

International Foodservice Manufacturers Association (IFMA) Organization whose primary membership is employed in the foodservice equipment trade. Provides relevant information and professional development opportunities to its members. Also helps ensure that their interests are represented in the marketplace.

Key Words and Concepts

Agency law

Agricultural Adjustment Act

Agricultural Marketing Agreement Act

Aseptic pack

As-purchased (AP) price

As-served cost

As-used cost

Basic commodity

Bureau of Alcohol, Tobacco, Firearms, and Explosives (ATF)

Clayton Act

Consignment sale

Contract

Controlled atmosphere packaging (CAP)

Convenience food

Cosmetics-Devices Act

Economic force

Edible-portion (EP) cost

Environmental Protection Agency (EPA)

Ethical force

Exclusive dealing

Exclusive selling

Fair Packaging and Labeling Act (FPLA)

Federal Food, Drug, and Cosmetic Act (FFDCA)

Federal Trade Commission (FTC)

First-generation convenience food

Food and Drug Administration (FDA)

Food Quality Protection Act (FQPA)

Food Safety Inspection Service (FSIS)

Franchise law

Free on board (FOB)

Genetically modified food

Hazard Analysis Critical Control Point system (HACCP system)

Illegal rebate

Intangible force

Internal Revenue Service (IRS)

International Foodservice Manufacturers Association (IFMA)

Interstate Shellfish Sanitation Conference

Irradiation

Kickback

Legal force

Marine Mammal Protection Act

Meat Inspection Act

Monopolistic competition

National Oceanic and Atmospheric Administration (NOAA)

Nutrition Labeling and Education Act

Packaging

Packed Under Federal Inspection (PUFI)

Patent

Perceived value equation

Perishable Agricultural Commodities Act (PACA)

Political force

Posilac

Poultry Products Inspection Act

Predatory pricing

Processing

Product preservation

Promotional discount

Pure Food Act

Quantity limits provision

Rebate

Robinson-Patman Act

Safe-handling procedures

Seller co-op

Sherman Antitrust Act

Standard of fill

Standard of identity

Standard of quality

Supply and demand

Time- and temperature-sensitive food labels

Title to goods

Transportation

Tying agreement

U.S. Department of Agriculture (USDA)

U.S. Department of Commerce (USDC)

Uniform Commercial Code (UCC)

Universal Product Code (UPC)

Value-added food

Warranty and guarantee

Wholesome Meat Act

Wholesome Poultry Products Act

Questions and Problems

1. Define *monopolistic competition*.

2. Give an example of how the political force affects the hospitality channel of distribution.

3. Is it ethical for a buyer to cancel an order with one supplier because he or she just found out that he or she can purchase the item at a lower price from someone else? Why or why not?

4. Define the following:

   a. Sherman Act
   b. USDA
   c. FDA
   d. FTC
   e. Tying agreement
   f. Exclusive dealing
   g. Quantity limits provision
   h. Agency law
   i. Consignment sale
   j. Rebate
   k. Value-added foods
   l. Federal Meat Inspection Act
   m. Perishable Agricultural Commodities Act
   n. Poultry Products Inspection Act
   o. Robinson-Patman Act
   p. IRS
   q. ATF

5. Do rebates foster unethical behavior among channel members? Why or why not?

6. Explain how advertising and promotion might influence buyers and sellers.

7. How do supply-and-demand conditions affect prices? Is it ethical to hold products off the market in an attempt to increase their prices? Why or why not?

8. What does the Robinson-Patman Act forbid?

9. Give an example of legal price discrimination and one of illegal price discrimination.

10. What is the major difference between the AP price and the EP cost?

11. Briefly describe the perceived value equation. How might a broker utilize this equation when selling foods?

12. How might a restaurant operator utilize the perceived value equation to increase patronage?

13. What is one difference between a basic commodity and a product that has additional form value added to it?

14. What are some advantages and disadvantages of using genetically engineered foods in a restaurant operation?

15. What are three of the guidelines that apply to labeling a food product as "organic"?

16. What is the primary duty of the FSIS division of the USDA?

17. Which federal law grants injunctive power to the FDA?

18. What is the difference between "exclusive dealing" and "exclusive selling"?

Questions and Problems (continued)

19. Which federal law is known as the "small-business protection act"?

20. What is "predatory pricing"? Why do you think the federal government outlaws it?

21. When would a verbal contract carry the same legal force as a written one?

22. What is high-pressure processing? Why might some people prefer this type of food preservation method to irradiation?

Experiential Exercises

1. Find a reference that discusses truth-in-menu regulations such as the National Restaurant Association (NRA) booklet *Accuracy in Menus* (1977); Paul J. McVety, Bradley J. Ware, and Claudette Lévesque Ware, *Fundamentals of Menu Planning*, 3rd ed. (New York: Wiley, 2008); or David T. Denney, Esq. "What You Say Is What They Get: A Truth-in-Menu and Menu Labeling Laws Primer," *Restaurant Start-up and Growth*, October 2009, www.foodbevlaw.com/images/uploads/DD_Article_1.pdf. Evaluate a restaurant menu to see if its menu item descriptions have the potential to violate any of the regulations. Are there particular words or phrases that could be problems? Write a one-page paper on your findings.

2. Select one of the other acts or laws that are discussed in this chapter. Go online and gather some information on this topic. Write a one-page report discussing the current debates that surround your selected topic.

3. Go online and research genetically altered foods. Write a one-page report discussing the current debate on this topic. Be sure to include both the benefits and negatives of using these controversial products in your hospitality operation.

References

1. Wei-yu Kevin Chiang, Dilip Chhajed, and James D. Hess, "Direct Marketing, Indirect Profits: A Strategic Analysis of Dual-Channel Supply-Chain Design," *Management Science*, January 2003, 49(1), pp. 1–20. Vivek Sehgal, *Enterprise Supply Chain Management: Integrating Best in Class Processes* (Hoboken, NJ: John Wiley & Sons, 2009).

2. Forbes, "Sysco $8.2 Billion US Foods Takeover in Big Antitrust Win for FTC," June 29, 2015, www.forbes.com/sites/antoinegara/2015/06/29/sysco-cancels-8-2-billion-us-foods -takeover-in-big-antitrust-win-for-ftc/#52dbbd631298.

3. B. Chapman, "Kickback Controversy," *Successful Meetings* [serial online], April 2003; 52(4):17, available from: Hospitality & Tourism Complete, Ipswich, MA.

References (continued)

4. Betsy Stevens, "Hospitality Ethics: Responses from Human Resource Directors and Students to Seven Ethical Scenarios," *Journal of Business Ethics*, April 2001, 30(3), pp. 233–242. See also Rachel Long, "Morals Matter," *Hospitality Design*, May/June 2006, 28(4), p. 26; Marnburg, Einar, "'I hope it won't happen to me!' Hospitality and Tourism Students' Fear of Difficult Moral Situations as Managers," *Tourism Management*, August 2006, 27(4), pp. 561–575.

5. Robert Carey, "Doing the Right Thing," *Successful Meetings*, October 2004, 53(11), pp. 34–39. See, for example, Thomas L. Trace, John F. Lynch, Joseph W. Fisher, and Jake Kanter, "20% of Buyers Have Been Offered Bribes by Suppliers," *Supply Management*, April 24, 2008, 13(9), p. 11.

6. For examples of Codes of Professional Conduct, see ISHP Code of Professional Conduct, www.ishp.org/conduct.html. McDonald's Corporation Our Story, www.mcdonalds.com/us/en/our_story.html.

7. Food Safety and Inspection Service, USDA, "Federal Inspection Programs," www.fsis.usda.gov/regulations_&_policies/federal_inspection_programs/index.asp; "A Century of Inspection," Meat & Poultry, June 1, 2006, www.meatpoultry.com/feature_stories.asp?ArticleID=79796.

8. Ezra Klein, "When Food Goes Wrong," *The Washington Post*, September 30, 2009, p. E4; See also Jared Favole, "FDA Requires Faster Food-Safety Alerts," *The Wall Street Journal*, September 9, 2009, p. A3.

9. USDA, "Agriculture Fact Book," www.usda.gov/factbook/9.

10. USDA, "FY 2010 Budget Summary and Annual Performance Plan," www.obpa.usda.gov/budsum/FY10budsum.pdf. See also American Meat Institute, "United States Meat Industry at a Glance," 2008, www.meatami.com/ht/d/sp/i/47465/pid/47465; U.S. Food and Drug Administration, "The Laws, Rules, & Guidance," www.fda.gov/Food/GuidanceRegulation/FSMA/ucm359436.htm. See also, A. Kheradia and K. Warriner, "Understanding the Food Safety Modernization Act and the Role of Quality Practitioners in the Management of Food Safety and Quality Systems," *TQM Journal*, 2013, 25(4), pp. 347–370. doi: 10.1108/17542731311314854.

11. SeafoodSource Staff, "Food Associations Say Inspection Plan Unnecessary," April 25, 2008, www.seafoodsource.com/newsarticledetail.aspx?id=1130; see also Leila Abboud, "Bad Fish Slip through FDA's Safety Net—Most Seafood Companies Ignore Standards, U.S. Says; Oy! Throw Out the Lox," *The Wall Street Journal*, October 9, 2002, p. D1.

12. Andrew C. von Eschenbach, "Enhanced Aquaculture and Seafood Inspection—Report to Congress," Food and Drug Administration, November 20, 2008, www.fda.gov/Food/FoodSafety/Product-SpecificInformation/Seafood/SeafoodRegulatoryProgram/ucm150954.htm.

References (continued)

13. J. Eilperin, "Administration Issues New Rules for Fish Farms," *Washington Post*, June 10, 2011.

14. National Oceanic and Atmospheric Administration, *NOAA Fisheries Office of Sustainable Fisheries*, 2013, www.nmfs.noaa.gov/sfa/.

15. Eric Wall, "A Comprehensive Look at the Fair Packaging and Labeling Act of 1966 and the FDA Regulation of Deceptive Labeling and Packaging Practices: 1906 to Today," May 2002, Harvard Law School, http://leda.law.harvard.edu/leda/data/444/Wall.pdf. See also FTC, "The Fair Packaging and Labeling Act," www.ftc.gov/os/statutes/fplajump.shtm.

16. Rose Gutfeld, "Food-Label 'Babel' to Fall as Uniform System Is Cleared," *The Wall Street Journal*, December 3, 1992, p. B1. See also Patricia A. Curtis, *Guide to Food Laws and Regulations* (Ames, IA: Blackwell, 2005); FDA, "General Food Labeling Requirements," www.fda.gov/Food/GuidanceComplianceRegulatoryInformation/GuidanceDocuments/FoodLabelingNutrition/FoodLabelingGuide/.

17. U.S. Food and Drug Administration, "FDA's Standards for High Quality Foods," www.fda.gov/ForConsumers/ConsumerUpdates/ucm094559.htm; Cindy Skrzycki, "New USDA Rule Changes Barbecue Standard," *Washington Post*, September 7, 2004, www.washingtonpost.com/wp-dyn/articles/A1442–2004Sep6.html; Department of Agriculture FSIS and Department of Health and Human Services FDA, "Food Standards; General Principles and Food Standards Modernization," May 17, 2005, www.fda.gov/OHRMS/DOCKETS/98fr/95n-0294-npr0001.pdf. See also Bruce Ingersoll, "Label Rules to Foster Healthful Foods," *The Wall Street Journal*, December 26, 1991, p. 9.

18. USDA, "What's in a Serving Size?" www.fns.usda.gov/tn/Healthy/Portions_Kit/serving_size.pdf. See also, for example, Elizabeth Scherer, "What Counts as a Serving?" health.discovery.com/centers/articles/articles.html?chrome=c14&article=LC_135&center=p04. U.S. Food and Drug Administration, "Food Allergen and Labeling Consumer Protection Act 2004," www.fda.gov/Food/GuidanceRegulation/GuidanceDocumentsRegulatoryInformation/Allergens/ucm106187.htm. U.S. Food and Drug Administration, "Foods Labeled Gluten-free Must Now Meet FDA's Definition," www.fda.gov/Food/NewsEvents/ConstituentUpdates/ucm407867.htm.

19. U.S. Department of Agriculture, *Labeling Organic Products*, October 2012, www.ams.usda.gov/AMSv1.0/getfile?dDocName=STELDEV3004446.

20. Ronald J. Baker, *Pricing on Purpose: Creating and Capturing Value*, (Hoboken, NJ: John Wiley & Sons, 2006).

21. James O. Eiler, "Hotel Contracts and Words," *Hotel and Casino Law Letter*, September 1990, p. 87.

References (continued)

22. John R. Goodwin and Jolie R. Gaston, "Creating Sales Contracts in the Hospitality Industry," *Hospitality & Tourism Educator*, Spring 1994, p. 23.

23. United States Copyright Office. (2006, July 12). *Copyright in General.* Copyright: www.copyright.gov/help/faq/faq-general.html#what.

24. Federal Trade Commission, *Enforcing Privacy Promises*, 2013, www.ftc.gov/news-events/ media-resources/protecting-consumer-privacy/enforcing-privacy-promises.

25. Paul Berryman, "Only the Brave Market GM," *Food Manufacturer,* August 2009, 84(8), p. 17. See also Scott Kilman, "Monsanto Resurrects Efforts to Engineer Wheat," *The Wall Street Journal,* July 15, 2009, p. B4; Jill Adams, "Biotech Animals; Scoping out a New Breed of Rules; Are Genetically Engineered Fish and Meat Coming Soon? We Examine the Food and Drug Administration's Regulations," *Los Angeles Times,* January 26, 2009, p. F1. See also Elizabeth Weise, "Four-Fifths of U.S. Soybean Crop Is Now Bioengineered," *USA Today*, April 1, 2003, p. D09.

26. MIT Technology Review, "Why We Need Genetically Modified Foods," www.technology review.com/featuredstory/522596/why-we-will-need-genetically-modified-foods/.

27. United States Food and Drug Administration, *Food: Food Labeling Guide*, January 2013, www.fda.gov/Food/GuidanceRegulation/GuidanceDocumentsRegulatoryInformation/ LabelingNutrition/ucm2006828.htm; see also D. Lynch and D. Vogel, "The Regulations of GMOs in Europe and the United States: A Case-Study of Contemporary European Regulatory Policy," *Council on Foreign Relations Press*, April 5, 2001.

28. Kevin Higgins, "Fresh Today, Safe Next Week," *Food Engineering,* February 2001, 73(2), pp. 44–48.

29. Andrew Martin, "Spinach and Peanuts, with a Dash of Radiation," *New York Times,* February 2, 2009, p. A10. See also J. Farkas, "Irradiation for Better Foods," *Trends in Food Science & Technology,* 2006, 17(4), pp 148–152; P. B. Roberts, "Irradiation of Foods: Basic Principles," *Encyclopedia of Food Sciences and Nutrition*, 2003, pp. 3381–3386.

30. David H. Freedman, "The Bright Hi-Tech Future of Food Preservation," *Discover: Science for the Curious,* September 2011, http://discovermagazine.com/2011/sep/ 17-impatient-futurist-hi-tech-future-food-preservation.

31. Bruce Horovitz, "Synthetic Hormone Cut from Dairy; Consumers Don't Want rbST in Their Products," *USA Today,* March 26, 2009, p. B4. See also the Organic Consumers Association Website, www.organicconsumers.org/rbghlink.cfm.

32. Birds Eye, "Our History: A Birds Eye Timeline," www.birdseyefoods.com/ourcompany/ history.aspx.

References (continued)

33. Sean Fitzgerald, "Sushi Restaurant Tests Drone-Driven Food Delivery," *The Guardian,* June 12, 2013, http://mashable.com/2013/06/12/sushi-drone-delivery/. See also "Burrito Bomber—The world's First Airborne Mexican Food Delivery System," www.darwin aerospace.com/burritobomber.

34. Greg Levy, "A New MAP for Natural Products Packaging," *Natural Products Insider,* March 2009, www.naturalproductsinsider.com/articles/2009/03/a-new-map-for-natural -products-packaging.aspx?tw=20091002133225. See also Anonymous, "Modified Atmosphere Meat Packaging Raises Questions; FDA Says Meat Is Safe," *Food and Drink Weekly,* February 27, 2006, http://findarticles.com/p/articles/mi_m0EUY/is_9_12/ai_ n26781633/?tag=content;col1; Amand Hesser, "Salad in Sealed Bags Isn't So Simple, It Seems," *New York Times,* January 14, 2003, p. A1. For more information about modified atmosphere packaging, see www.modifiedatmospherepackaging.net.

35. Jon Rasmussen, "Standards, Technology Continue to Evolve," *Food Logistics,* October 2007, 99, pp. 51–52. See also "Implementing Technology," *Nation's Restaurant News,* October 28, 2002, pp. T20–T22; Alan J. Liddle, "New Arena Embraces 'Nothing but Net' Outsourced Technology," *Nation's Restaurant News,* September 23, 2002, p. 34; Olin Thompson, "Supply Chain Payoffs with RFID," *Food Engineering,* April 2004, 76(4), pp. 119–120.

AN OVERVIEW OF THE PURCHASING FUNCTION

The Purpose of This Chapter

After reading this chapter, you should be able to:

- Describe the purchasing activities in a hospitality operation.

- Explain research projects and activities that can assist with improving future operations.

- Outline the objectives of the purchasing function.

- Differentiate potential problems that buyers may encounter when pursuing purchasing objectives.

PURCHASING ACTIVITIES

As we mentioned in Chapter 1, it is critical that each hospitality organization establish effective purchasing procedures. Moreover, each operation, large or small, performs many purchasing activities common to all. Finally, all operations, regardless of size, strive for similar purchasing objectives. These are the unifying facts that this chapter addresses.

The hospitality industry is made up of a surprisingly large number of small operations. For instance, the vast majority of foodservice operations have fewer than 50 employees.[1] These small establishments do not have the resources to perform each operating activity in "textbook fashion." The small operator normally has to conduct some business procedures informally, and purchasing may be one of them. Medium-size companies may employ purchasing specialists, but the normal pattern is for owner–managers to squeeze the purchasing activities into their schedules. Large corporate operations have teams of specialists at both the corporate and operational level.

As we have said, every operation performs pretty much the same activities. The difference is in the degree of attention the activities receive and the thoroughness with which they are accomplished. Large companies tend toward completeness; smaller firms must trim somewhere. This chapter discusses these purchasing activities and purchasing objectives. Not every organization adheres to our outline, but all hospitality managers or owners must at least consider a definite procedure.

purchasing activities
Tasks buyers must perform in order to obtain the right products and services, at the right price and time, from the right vendors.

Regardless of the size of a hospitality operation, someone must perform a certain number of **purchasing activities** (see Figure 5.1).

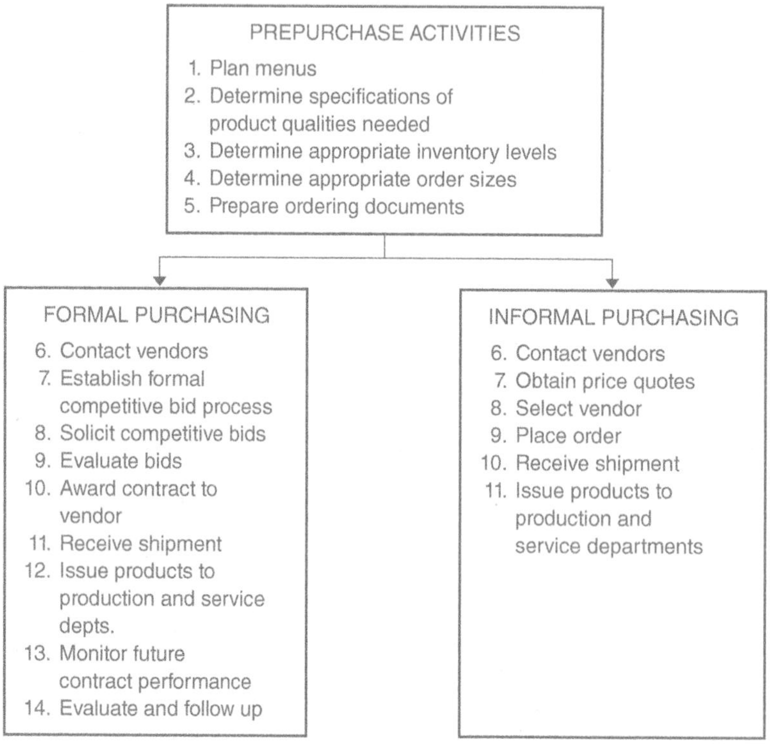

PREPURCHASE ACTIVITIES

1. Plan menus
2. Determine specifications of product qualities needed
3. Determine appropriate inventory levels
4. Determine appropriate order sizes
5. Prepare ordering documents

FORMAL PURCHASING

6. Contact vendors
7. Establish formal competitive bid process
8. Solicit competitive bids
9. Evaluate bids
10. Award contract to vendor
11. Receive shipment
12. Issue products to production and service depts.
13. Monitor future contract performance
14. Evaluate and follow up

INFORMAL PURCHASING

6. Contact vendors
7. Obtain price quotes
8. Select vendor
9. Place order
10. Receive shipment
11. Issue products to production and service departments

FIGURE 5.1 As this chart indicates, several activities must be accomplished to fulfill the purchasing function's responsibilities. Of course, the owner–manager can dictate the desired degree of formality.

One survey of hotel purchasing agents uncovered these key purchasing responsibilities: (1) determine when to order, (2) control inventory levels, (3) establish quality standards, (4) determine specifications, (5) obtain competitive bids, (6) investigate vendors, (7) arrange financial terms, (8) oversee delivery, (9) negotiate refunds, (10) handle adjustments, and (11) arrange for storage.[2]

Purchasing activities center on: (1) recipe development, (2) menu development, (3) specification writing, (4) approval of buying source, (5) designation of approved brands, (6) supplier evaluation, (7) negotiation with suppliers, (8) change of suppliers, (9) change of brands, (10) substitution of approved items, (11) approval of new products, (12) invoice approval, (13) invoice payment, and (14) order placement with supplier.[3]

To do an efficient buying job, hospitality organizations must usually perform a wide variety of activities.

■ Selection and Procurement Plan

Typically, the person charged with purchasing responsibilities needs to work with management to determine relevant policies and procedures to guide the purchasing function. The plan should contain a description of how the organization intends to select and procure the products and services needed to conduct normal business activity. The plan should also explain the methods used, why they were selected, and its major goals and objectives. Ideally, the plan should include a discussion of supplier availability, purchasing trends that will have to be considered, and a procedure that allows the plan to be revised when necessary.

■ Determine Requirements

In most cases, the buyer helps to determine the varieties and amounts of products, services, equipment, and furnishings that the hospitality enterprise requires. It is unusual, though, for a buyer to make these decisions in a vacuum. Normally, they are made collectively: the buyers consult with other management officials and with those individuals who will eventually use the purchased items to decide what the operation needs. For example, if a casino manager needs to lease staging, lighting, and sound equipment for a special three-day music festival, the buyer will be called in to help negotiate the contract. However, the person doesn't need to be a lighting specialist. There are many ways the specifications can be developed: maybe the manager will have ideas about specific equipment needs, perhaps a consultant will be called in to help "spec" out the job, or maybe there are certain equipment requirements in the musicians' contracts that must be fulfilled. Once the specifications have been confirmed, the buyer will get two or more bids and order the equipment with delivery and setup dates to coincide with the event. More information on the development of specifications will be discussed in Chapter 7.

■ Supplier Selection

Selecting dependable suppliers who will provide consistent product and service value is a very difficult task. Hospitality companies must determine their **supplier selection criteria** before beginning to locate and evaluate potential suppliers. Generally speaking, large hospitality firms wield considerable

supplier selection criteria
Characteristics a buyer considers when determining if potential vendors should be added to the approved-supplier list.

purchasing power and, therefore, receive the attention and value commensurate with this power. Unfortunately, smaller firms sometimes find it difficult to enlist this type of consistency; although no supplier would intentionally ignore a customer, a buyer who is not high on the supplier's priority list may someday be disappointed.

■ Sourcing

For most products and services, a number of suppliers are capable of meeting a buyer's needs. For some items, though, especially unique products that must be purchased in large quantities, it may be necessary for a buyer's company to help establish a supplier.[4]

sourcing The process used by a hospitality company to help establish a supplier. Typically done by large hospitality companies to help establish minority-owned primary sources and/or intermediaries. Alternately, the process a buyer undertakes to locate a vendor for a product or service that is very hard to find.

When a buyer establishes a supplier, the process is usually referred to as a type of **sourcing**. (Another type of sourcing occurs when a buyer must search high and low for the one supplier capable of handling his or her needs.) It is typically a win–win situation, in that the buyer establishes a reliable source, and the supplier enjoys a predictable amount of business.[5] It is also a good way for buyers to help establish and support minority- and women-owned suppliers.[6] With the need for and availability of products from all around the world, many companies do sourcing on a global basis. The benefits of obtaining a particular product must often be weighed against the additional shipping and environmental costs of transporting the item over long distances.

■ Maintain a Convenient and Sufficient Inventory

optimal inventory management Procedures used to maintain efficiently the quality and security of merchandise.

An operation must practice **optimal inventory management**, which is nothing more or less than ensuring that an appropriate inventory of all items is always on hand. Too small an inventory may cause run-out of some items, which often produces guest dissatisfaction. Conversely, too large an inventory ties up dollars in these items and requires extra storage space.

An operation should strive to maintain an optimal overall level of inventory items, but this is more easily said than done. As much as possible, though, a buyer must try to maintain this optimal level by determining the correct order size for each item and ordering this correct amount at the correct time.

■ Conduct Negotiations

as-purchased (AP) price Price charged by the vendor.

Someone has to negotiate specific **as-purchased (AP) prices**, delivery schedules, and other supplier services. Firm but fair bargaining builds mutual respect. We should point out that your negotiating power is determined largely by the amount of money you expect to spend. Keep in mind, though, that all things, at least theoretically, are negotiable. In many cases, suppliers will provide something extra simply because a buyer asks about it. Although negotiating may require a certain degree of time and effort, the benefits can be considerable with the results showing up in the company's bottom line. For example, you might find out that a supplier is overstocked on a specific item that you are looking for. You could negotiate for a lower price to take a significant amount of that product off their hands.

■ Maintain Supplier Diplomacy

A buyer works continually with suppliers and salespersons; meanwhile, several other suppliers may wish for the buyer's business. Keeping every potential supplier content is impossible; a buyer should not even try it. Nevertheless, diplomatic, cordial relations, known as **supplier diplomacy**, help a buyer get along with suppliers and earn the best value from each.[7]

Some operations concentrate heavily on maintaining amicable relations with all reputable suppliers, and many of these companies insist on instituting a **trade relations** function within the organization.[8] The objective of trade relations is to spread the purchase dollar among as many suppliers as possible. The goodwill generated throughout the channel of distribution from trade relations might sometimes prove valuable in the long run—and in short-run emergencies. (Several operations purchase from only one or two purveyors for other reasons. In Chapter 12, we discuss the potential advantages of "one-stop" shopping.)

> **supplier diplomacy** The art and practice of conducting negotiations between buyers and suppliers. Alternately, the employment of tact to gain a strategic advantage or to find mutually acceptable solutions to a common problem.
>
> **trade relations** The practice of spreading your purchase dollars among several vendors. Intended to create positive publicity for your hospitality operation.

■ Educate Suppliers

Buyers must attempt to keep all potential suppliers informed about anything that can help improve their performance. Suppliers who stay abreast of your changing needs can provide the service to match those needs. Moreover, a buyer can continually test a supplier's flexibility and capability.

Another dimension of this issue is the advisability of buyers maintaining close contact with suppliers and salespersons to "pick their brains." This is a time-consuming activity, but many people in the industry think that it is absolutely necessary if a buyer hopes to maintain his or her knowledge of the rapidly changing hospitality market.

■ Purchase, Receive, Store, and Issue Products

Someone must be responsible for a product until it is ready to be used. No chef, for example, will take responsibility for expensive meat cuts before they actually come within his or her domain. In some cases, a buyer assumes the duties of selecting the supplier, purchasing and receiving the products, and, often, storing and eventually issuing them to the various departments.

Some firms do not like to link these activities, especially the buying and receiving activities. These companies tend to relieve a buyer of the receiving activity and place this function under the direct supervision of the accounting department. This approach establishes a measure of control. The physical separation of these two activities substantially reduces the possibility of theft whereby a buyer would purchase items and upon delivery take them for personal use rather than placing them in the company's inventory.

■ Disposal of Excess and Unsalable Items

At times, because of menu changes, overbuying, and obsolescence, a hospitality organization finds itself overstocked with certain products. Sometimes, too, when it purchases a new piece of equipment, it must dispose of the old piece. Buyers are usually expected to shoulder these responsibilities and trade the items, sell them, or give them away. Because buyers involve themselves directly in the marketplace, it is logical to expect them to fulfill these duties.

FIGURE 5.2 Recycling logo.

■ Recycling

In addition to disposing of excess and unsalable items, buyers may be responsible for ensuring that recyclable materials are gathered efficiently and delivered to an approved **recycling** center (Figure 5.2). Buyers who can sell these items may also have the additional responsibility of accounting for the receipts.

> **recycling** Refers to taking a used product and/or its parts and reusing them after they have undergone a reconditioning process. Alternately, taking a used product and/or its parts and creating something new and different that can be used for another purpose.

■ Develop Record-Keeping Controls

The activities of purchasing, receiving, storing, and issuing normally require some sort of control. Large firms and, to a much lesser extent, small ones strive to maintain a system of overlapping receipts connecting these activities. For example, as a product moves from one activity to the next, a variety of hard copy and/or electronic forms (bills, receipts, inventory records, issue slips, etc.) may trace its movement. The objective of using these forms is to enable management to locate and monitor the product as it moves through the operation. (Chapters 11, 12, and 13 provide thorough discussions of these internal controls.)

A buyer may help design these forms. Alternately, the accounting department may take charge of this duty as part of its overall responsibility for controlling all of the company assets. It is customary, though, for a buyer to contribute to the development of these forms.

■ Organize and Administer the Purchasing Function

Where applicable, the person in charge of purchasing must plan, organize, staff, direct, and control the purchasing function, especially in large companies that maintain a separate purchasing department. In addition, purchasing must be coordinated with other company activities, including accounting, marketing, production, and service. The purchasing agent, then, must not only see to it that products and services are efficiently and effectively purchased, received, stored, and, where appropriate, issued, but he or she must also have the managerial competence to organize and administer these activities expeditiously.

■ Self-Improvement

All buyers should continually strive to improve their buying performance. Association meetings, seminars, plant visits, **trade show visits**, and continuing education courses are among some of the more traditional self-improvement methods available. Full-time buyers should seriously consider obtaining the Certified Professional in Supply Management® (CPSM®) credential from the **Institute for Supply Management™ (ISM)**. The CPSM (Figure 5.3) reflects the expanded education, skills, and experience needed to be a successful supply management professional. It also has a new program. The Certified Professional in Supplier Diversity® (CPSD™) is the certification for supply chain professionals whose responsibilities include supplier diversity.

The **American Purchasing Society** offers several levels of certification to its members: Certified Purchasing Professional (CPP), a Certified Professional Purchasing Manager (CPPM), a Certified Green Purchasing Professional (CGPP), and/or a Certified Professional Purchasing Consultant (CPPC). In addition to having minimum levels of purchasing experience for each certification, applicants must meet certain ethical standards, perform coursework, and pass an exam.

The **Certified Foodservice Professional (CFSP)** program certification, offered through the **North American Association of Food Equipment Manufacturers (NAFEM)**, is available to qualified purchasing professionals specializing in the equipment side of the business.

For each of these organizations, the coursework is performed online or through independent study of certification handbooks and then the exam is taken at a local test proctoring site. They will also offer courses at the business's own location for an established minimum number of employees. NAFEM also offers workshops several times per year at its corporate headquarters in Chicago.

Many hospitality operations reimburse their employees for this kind of self-improvement by paying for tuition charges, the cost of books, seminar fees, and travel expenses. In addition, some operators provide in-house training. In the long run, employees who increase their competence usually return management's investment many times by improving their productivity and increasing their readiness to assume more responsible positions within the firm.

FIGURE 5.3 Certified Professional in Supply Management (CPSM) *CPSM® and Certified Professional in Supply Management® are registered trademarks of the Institute for Supply Management™.*

trade show visit Attendance at exhibitions organized so that companies in a specific industry can showcase and demonstrate their latest products and services, study activities of rivals, and examine recent trends and opportunities.

Institute for Supply Management (ISM) Organization that offers relevant information, education, and training to supply management professionals.

American Purchasing Society Professional association of buyers and purchasing managers, which was the first organization to establish certification for buyers and purchasing professionals.

Certified Foodservice Professional (CFSP) Indication that the person who holds this designation has achieved a certain level of foodservice operations knowledge and experience.

North American Association of Food Equipment Manufacturers (NAFEM) Trade organization representing companies in Canada, the United States, and Mexico that manufacture commercial foodservice equipment and supplies.

■ Help Competitors

Helping the competition does not always seem to be a logical part of a purchasing agent's duties. An operation is unlikely to go out of its way to aid competitors; nevertheless, competing buyers are in a position to help each other in mutually beneficial ways.

The type of help we refer to consists, for one thing, of lending products to competitors when a crucial need arises. If we run out of a product we desperately need, we try to borrow it from a neighbor. Moreover, in the role of a lender, we have little to gain by refusing such a service: it is unlikely that a competitor's customers will flock to our door simply because the competitor temporarily cannot serve them a particular item.

When we do lend, we set up a reciprocal arrangement by which we feel justified in borrowing. Of course, management needs to make the ultimate decision about these types of loan arrangements. Lending and borrowing are reasonable activities that often come under a buyer's purview.

A buyer might also help a less-knowledgeable colleague gain the advantage of the more seasoned buyer's experience. Such cordial, professional relations will tend to make everyone's life a bit easier and will significantly increase the industry's ability to serve its customers more effectively and efficiently.

■ Other Activities

As hospitality companies continue to downsize their managerial ranks, those managers remaining often need to shoulder nontraditional duties. In today's business environment, managers should be prepared to adapt to any situation. For instance, a purchasing manager working at company headquarters may have to take on responsibility for the mailroom operation. Similarly, a buyer working at a large hotel may have to oversee a retail gift shop.

MANAGING WASTE TO REDUCE COSTS: REDUCE, REUSE, AND RECYCLE
Robert Hartman, Principal, Robert Hartman Food and Beverage Management & Consulting

Large properties can generate as much as 8 tons of waste per day, and up to 60 percent of this material may be recyclable.[1]

The disposal of waste products, such as opened beverage containers, used paper products, food scraps, and so on, can add up to hefty collection fees at the shipping dock or landfill. Furnishings, equipment, and other items that require replacement must also be disposed of from time to time. Procuring the services of waste-collection companies is part of the purchasing function, as is reducing the costs of disposal.

Understanding the options available for minimizing these costs can help a purchaser save money while enhancing an organization's reputation for environmental awareness. The slogan "Reduce, reuse, and recycle" is one that resonates with the public, but how can a purchaser implement it effectively?

MANAGING WASTE TO REDUCE COSTS: (continued)

Any system for reducing disposal costs depends on identifying items in the waste stream that need not go there and diverting them into less-costly channels. Once these items have been identified, the options for diverting them include the following:

A. Reducing the purchases of such items in the first place.

For example, if a restaurant serves bottled water with a disposable cup, it might find that serving filtered water in reusable ware can reduce food and disposal costs while benefiting the environment. Any added costs in labor (for busing and ware washing) could well be overshadowed by the combination of savings and customer goodwill.

If such items cannot be eliminated entirely, purchasing recyclable versions can also save on disposal costs. For example, disposable eating utensils made from compostable materials can now be purchased in place of nonrecyclable plastic.[2]

Another example is the use of microfiber cleaning cloths and mops that are more durable and effective than traditional cleaning implements, to cut down on purchases and waste.[3]

B. Find ways to reuse them.

Many hotels give guests the option to forgo a change of linens during their stays. Lodging operators can often find willing takers among charitable organizations for used furnishings that must be disposed of during renovations. Another way to reuse items is to purchase products made with recycled content. For example, carpeting and other decorative textiles made from recycled plastic shopping bags can be purchased or leased. If leased, the provider also maintains the carpeting by replacing portions as they wear. Thus, a recycled carpet can maintain a fresh appearance for far longer than a new one.

C. Capturing items for recycling or composting before they go to the landfill (or down the drain).

Glass containers and many other plastic and metal items can be recycled. Waste cooking oil can be sold for conversion to biodiesel fuel, or used directly as fuel for electric generators.[4] "Gray water" from kitchen sinks and guest showers can be diverted for use in cooling towers[5] or for flushing toilets.[6] Reclaimed water from municipal sources can be used to irrigate landscapes. Other strategies for conserving water include the catchment and storage of rainwater for later irrigation and the installation of water-conserving landscapes, or "xeriscapes."[7]

Waste cardboard and paper can be recycled, or combined with food waste for composting. In some cases, recyclers and compost producers pay hospitality operators for these items. In July 2008, in response to interest from employees to adopt less-wasteful ways, Microsoft switched to compostable kitchenware and started composting food waste. These moves have slashed the company's waste stream from its cafes and break rooms nearly in half.[8]

Composting is nature's way of recycling the building blocks of life. Food scraps rich in nitrogen, when combined with waste paper and other carbon-based ingredients provide an ideal food source for the microbes that break them down. When the process is complete, finished compost contains an abundance of basic nutrients that plants can use to grow. Unlike at-home compost bins, commercial compost producers accept meat scraps and other animal products as part of the mix.[9]

MANAGING WASTE TO REDUCE COSTS: (continued)

A simple recycling plan can earn a company extra points with its employees, guests, and others. Mandalay Bay Convention Center's new recycling program diverted 6,000 cubic feet of tradeshow exhibitor waste from the local landfill in its first four months of operation. During that time, with a commitment from the clients themselves, three tradeshows produced zero landfill waste, sending 100 percent of the leftover materials to recycling centers or community organizations.[10]

■ **REFERENCES**

1. D. E. Meeroff and P. D. Scarlatos, "Green Lodging Project Phase 1: Solid Waste Management, Waste Reduction, and Water Conservation," Florida Atlantic University, Department of Civil Engineering, September, 2006, pp. 4–22, passim, www.dep.state.fl.us/greenlodging/files/fau_final_report.pdf.

2. Microsoft Corporation, "Microsoft's Environmental Chief Sees Opportunity for IT to Help the Planet," *Microsoft PressPass*, http://news.microsoft.com/2009/04/21/microsofts-environmental -chief-sees-opportunity-for-it-to-help-the-planet/.

3. University of California, Davis, "Pioneers Use of Microfiber Mops in Hospitals," June 23, 2006, www.ucdmc.ucdavis.edu/publish/news/newsroom/2379.

4. April Joyner, "Owl Power Turns Restaurants into Mini Power Plants," *Inc.*, 2009, 31(5), pp. 106–107, Business Source Complete, EBSCOhost.

5. Los Alamos National Laboratory, "Lighting, HVAC, and Plumbing," 2009, pp. 110–112, passim, http://apps1.eere.energy.gov/buildings/publications/pdfs/commercial_initiative/sustainable_guide_ch5.pdf.

6. Ibid., p. 155.

7. Eric Carbonnier and Allison Okihiro, "Landscape & Grounds Case Study: Scope 3 Greenhouse Gas Reduction Strategies," unpublished paper for Regenerative Studies 599, March 2009, California Polytechnic University, Pomona, pp. 17–18, passim.

8. Op. cit., Microsoft Corporation.

9. Glenn Hasek, "S. F. Marriott's Composting Program Approaches 1 Million Pounds Annually," *Green Lodging News*, July 12, 2006, www.greenlodgingnews.com/SF-Marriotts-Composting -Program-Approaches-1-Million-Pounds-Annually.

10. William Ng, "Responsible Gaming," *Incentive*, 2010, 184(5), pp. 22–24. Business Source Complete, EBSCOhost.

RESEARCH ACTIVITIES AND PROJECTS

Buyers often find it necessary to conduct research projects. Purchasing is a very dynamic activity, and although the general principles and procedures remain the same, their applications may have to be altered to meet perceived trends. Similarly, product availability, prices, supplier services, and customer tastes may change quickly. The wise buyer will undertake research projects to improve future operations.

■ Value Analysis

One of the more common research activities, and one that is typically done on a regular basis, is **value analysis**. This involves examining a product to identify unnecessary costs that can be eliminated without sacrificing overall quality or performance. For example, a buyer who habitually purchases whole milk for cooking purposes may want to research the possibility of using less-expensive, low-fat milk instead. If the recipes can be prepared with the less-expensive milk without a discernible loss of quality, the buyer will recommend using the more economical low-fat product.

> **value analysis** Involves examining a product to identify unnecessary costs that can be eliminated without sacrificing overall quality or performance.

Value analysis usually centers on the perceived value equation noted in Chapter 4. Although the typical value analysis procedure may not be quite this formal, the ultimate purpose of this research activity is to increase value by manipulating quality, supplier services, and **edible-portion (EP) cost**.

> **edible-portion (EP) cost** Equal to the AP price per portion divided by its edible yield percentage.

A buyer performing value analysis on a product or service should make no changes without consulting the person who uses that product or service. There may be good reasons, for example, why the EP cost is a little higher than it could be—reasons known only to the user. Value analysis usually works best when it becomes a cooperative venture.

■ Forecasting

Forecasting can involve many things, but usually the buyer is most interested in predicting the kinds of products and services that will be available in the future and what their prices will be. Buyers often center their forecasting efforts on picking the brains of friendly suppliers and salespersons. Informal chats can yield accurate and useful information quickly and easily.

> **forecasting** An attempt to predict the future. Current and historical information are used to estimate what might happen over the near or long term. Referred to as sales forecasting when attempting to predict future sales.
>
> **National Restaurant Association (NRA)** Trade organization that represents, educates, and promotes the U.S. foodservice industry and the people working in it.

Today, supply availability and future pricing can be tracked with one or more online services. For instance, the **National Restaurant Association (NRA)** provides *Restaurant TrendMapper*. This subscription-based online information service provides current analysis of the U.S. restaurant industry, including current commodities pricing. *Food For Thought* provides current consumer demand information on hundreds of food products. *Foodservice .com* provides weekly market reports on commonly purchased hospitality products. Technomic is a consulting firm that focuses on the restaurant and food supplier industry. They provide several publications focusing on foodservice industry trends. Mintel also offers detailed analysis of the food and beverage industry and consumer demographics. Many colleges and universities subscribe to their database and reports services.

■ What-If Analysis

what-if analysis
Method of analyzing the potential outcome of a particular procedure without actually executing it. Normally involves the use of mathematical models.

Many buyers use computer spreadsheet software to develop mathematical models that can test various **what-if analysis** proposals. For instance, a simple model buyers can use predicts the overall effect that an increase in the purchase price of one food item will have on the overall food cost. Suppose that the price of prime rib will increase 10 percent and that prime rib represents 50 percent of a restaurant's overall food cost. We want to know what will happen to the overall food cost as a result of this increase. The model equation to use in this case is

$$
\begin{aligned}
\text{Increase in overall food cost} &= \text{Percentage price increase for the ingredient} \\
&\quad \times \text{The ingredient's percentage of overall food cost} \\
&= 10\% \times 50\% \\
&= 0.10 \times 0.50 \\
&= 0.05 \text{ or } 5\%
\end{aligned}
$$

Other, more complicated formulas can be developed to show, for instance, the effect of a purchase price increase on overall profits.

Any model is an attempt to predict the future. Some models may be based on shaky estimates, but this has not curtailed their use. Most, if not all, operations rely on models, and some of these models become highly sophisticated mathematical devices.

■ Make-or-Buy Analysis

make-or-buy analysis
A cost/benefit analysis whereby the buyer tries to determine if, for example, it is more economical to purchase raw foods and make a finished product in-house, or whether it may be less expensive to purchase a convenience, value-added food. The buyer usually considers the cost of food, labor, overhead, labor skill available, and so forth when making the decision.

At times, management may consider making a product in-house instead of buying it already prepared, even though several types of value-added products on the market can serve an operator's needs.

Make-or-buy analysis is one of the most critical types of research projects in which a buyer can become involved. There is a lot to lose when the wrong decision is made. Usually, each situation has several advantages and disadvantages.

For instance, value-added products usually offer these advantages: (1) consistent quality; (2) consistent portion control; (3) an opportunity to serve diversified menu items, regardless of the employee skill level, and, thereby, to attract patrons who enjoy diversity; (4) operating efficiencies, such as less energy needed to reconstitute, rather than prepare from scratch, a menu item; (5) less food-handler supervision, which gives the supervisor more time for merchandising, promoting, and otherwise increasing sales volume; (6) reduced employee skill requirements; (7) reduction in leftovers; (8) reduction of raw-materials inventory, which implies smaller storage costs; (9) reduction in ordering costs because you are not ordering and receiving several raw ingredients; (10) an increase in edible yields because usually there is no waste with convenience items; and (11) with convenience-foods usage, a possible reduction of the size of the storage and the kitchen facility, which leads to more room for dining patrons.

The major disadvantage of **convenience foods** is, of course, their high price.[9] Because most or all of the economic form value is included, the buyer expects to pay more for a value-added food than for the individual ingredients needed to produce the item in-house. However, there is no average rule of thumb to indicate whether the difference between these two prices favors the buyer or the food processor. Suppose, for example, that we cannot quite decide which alternative is better: cutting our own steaks from a side of beef or buying precut, portion-controlled steaks. The AP price of the uncut sides is cheaper, but considering the waste involved, additional labor costs, and investment in equipment, the precut steaks might represent the better EP cost.

> **convenience food**
> A food that has been processed to change its form and/or taste. It usually requires very little handling in the restaurant kitchen. It may be ready-to-use or ready-to-serve.

The same decision-making process can be used in housekeeping when choosing chemical cleaners. Would it be better to purchase large amounts of concentrated chemicals for your staff to mix; or would it be better to purchase ready-to-use versions of the same products? Although the concentrated forms of chemicals would be less expensive in the long run, your staff would then need to be trained in the proper handling and storage of chemicals, which could involve additional training. This additional labor cost would need to be factored into the make-or-buy analysis to get an accurate picture of the true cost.

There is no simple way to tell whether you should "make" or "buy." You need to consider so many qualitative and quantitative factors that the decision necessarily involves a great deal of research and analysis.

■ Plant Visits

Purchasing agents and buyers usually take the time to visit suppliers' facilities. Most industry members recommend using **plant visits** or audits, particularly when there is some question about a supplier's ability to fulfill a need or safety is of concern.[10] In addition, a supplier who runs a sloppy store, experiences labor–management difficulties, or keeps erratic hours may be undependable and, therefore, undesirable.

> **plant visit**   Refers to a buyer making a personal visit to a vendor's facilities to evaluate its product line and its production and distribution systems.

PURCHASING OBJECTIVES

Industry experts suggest several goals for the purchasing function. Continuing research into this issue shows that five major objectives must be achieved.

■ Maintain an Adequate Supply

No hospitality operator enjoys running out of products. **Stockouts** (running out of an item) are intolerable—they hinder an operator's customer service goals. Thus, an adequate stock level, one that prevents running out of items between deliveries, is crucial to good management. A more thorough discussion of inventory management will be presented in Chapter 9.

> **stockout**   Running out of a product; not having it available for guests who want it.

■ Minimize Investment

This objective seems to conflict with the first. How can buyers maintain an uninterrupted supply while minimizing the number of dollars tied up in inventory? This question suggests that buyers must find some kind of trade-off between the investment level and the risk of running out. Most operators expect a buyer to compromise by optimizing the investment level and, at the same time, ensuring a continual flow of products.

■ Maintain Quality

Maintaining quality is not quite the same as establishing the firm's desired level of quality. Some buyers have comparatively little to say about the quality of products they must purchase. They do, however, have a major responsibility to make sure that, once set, the quality standards vary only within acceptable limits. For some products, such as liquor and soap, brand names ensure uniform quality. Unfortunately, the quality of fresh foods can change drastically from day to day and from one supplier to the next. This situation can make it particularly difficult to maintain quality standards. In addition, occasional overbuying or a sudden breakdown in storage facilities, particularly refrigeration facilities, can wreak havoc on quality standards. Regardless of the associated difficulties, however, operators insist that their buyers maintain quality control.

■ Obtain the Lowest Possible EP Cost

As we mentioned earlier, the AP price is only the beginning. Unfortunately, some buyers are entranced by a low AP price and tend to overlook the fact that the EP cost is the relevant price consideration. Many operators think in terms of steak price per pound or liquid detergent price per gallon. What should be paramount in their thinking is the steak cost per servable pound or the liquid detergent cost per square foot of dirty tile. In other words, the EP cost is most critical, and management understandably expects its buyers to recognize this fact and endeavor to achieve the lowest possible EP cost and, ultimately, the best possible value.

■ Maintain the Company's Competitive Position

As far as we have been able to determine, management's main concern here is to get the same, or a better, deal from a supplier than any other comparable hospitality enterprise. Unfortunately, this goal is difficult to achieve. Although EP cost and quality may be more or less uniform, suppliers often apply their supplier services unevenly among buyers. You may recall that these supplier services add to the overall value of a product or service, provided that the quality and EP cost remain constant. If we receive fewer supplier services, theoretically, we receive less value for our money. This value loss places us at a competitive disadvantage.

■ The Value of the Purchasing Functions and Objectives

The purchasing function involves a great variety of activities and objectives. As noted earlier, all buyers, full-time or part-time, perform most of these activities, one way or another. Buyers also attain, or fail to attain, what we have outlined as the major purchasing objectives.

How much should we be willing to spend to discharge the purchasing activities conscientiously enough to achieve these major objectives? This is an especially difficult question because, on one hand, buyers' salaries and receiving and inventory management costs are highly visible to management, but on the other hand, the benefits associated with these costs are not so visible. A look at the income statement reveals immediately most of the costs of maintaining a top-flight purchasing function; unhappily, the benefits do not leap out quite so dramatically.

In our opinion, the benefits outweigh the costs for all but perhaps the smallest hospitality operations. The purpose of this book, however, is to present what we perceive to be the relevant aspects of selection and procurement. We leave it to you to decide, gradually, the value of the purchasing function and the relative justification for its cost.

PROBLEMS OF THE BUYER

Buyers encounter several problems while working to attain their objectives. Some of the major **problems of the buyer** are as follows:

> **problems of the buyer** Challenges buyers must overcome to perform their jobs effectively and efficiently.
>
> **backdoor selling** This happens when a sales rep bypasses the regular buyer and goes to some other employee, such as the lead line cook, to make a sales pitch. The cook then exerts pressure on the buyer to make the purchase.

1. **Backdoor selling**, whereby a salesperson bypasses the appointed buyer and goes to some other employee, such as the bartender, to make a sales pitch. The bartender then puts pressure on the buyer to consummate a sale.

2. Excessive time may be spent with salespersons. Most operators set aside certain periods during the week to receive sales presentations. On the one hand, these may be wastes of time, but occasionally you need to spend time with others to pick up a good bit of advice or information.

3. A variety of ethical traps await the buyer, such as those discussed in Chapter 4 including whether to accept samples or whether to purchase products made from producers who lack fair labor or proper environmental standards.

4. Sometimes the buyer has full responsibility for purchasing, yet may lack the commensurate authority needed to act accordingly. For example, they may have to get approval from higher-level managers or owners to purchase specialty items or place orders over a certain dollar amount.

5. The buyer might have full responsibility but does not have enough time to do the job right. This is particularly true for part-time buyers.

6. Sometimes the buyer finds it difficult to work with other department heads and to coordinate their needs.

7. Sometimes department heads, or other users of products and services, make unreasonable demands on the person in charge of buying.

8. Late deliveries and subsequent problems with receiving and storage can ruin the most efficient purchase.

9. Other company personnel do not always consider purchasing a profit-making activity. Actually, a penny saved in purchasing goes directly to the bottom line of the income statement, whereas the typical hospitality operation must sell about 50 cents worth of product or service to realize a 1-cent net profit because considerable expense must be incurred in the generation of this 50-cent sale.

10. Suppliers do not always have what the buyer orders, sending a substitute that may or may not be acceptable.

11. Some suppliers may not be interested in the buyer's business if it is a "small stop" (i.e., does a small amount of business). No salespersons will intentionally avoid the buyer, but realistically, they must service the large customers first. This means that the small buyer may not be on the top of their list of priorities.

12. Receiving and storage inadequacies make it difficult to protect the merchandise after it is purchased. Regardless of the energy expended to procure the best possible value, the effort could be wasted if these inadequacies result in excessive spoilage, waste, and/or theft.

back order When your shipment is incomplete because the vendor did not have the item in stock, the invoice will state that the item is back ordered. You will receive the item later.

returns and allowances Amount of money representing price reductions given to customers because of goods returned and defective merchandise not suited to the customers' needs.

13. When suppliers do not have something that a buyer has ordered, they may note on the delivery slip that the item is **back ordered**. This means that the buyer will usually receive the item when the next regularly scheduled delivery occurs and be charged for it at that time. The major problem here is that the buyer does not have the item ready for today's customers.

14. **Returns and allowances** occur because some delivered merchandise will be unsuitable for one reason or another. The hospitality operator must then ensure that fair credit is received for the rejected items and that this credit is ultimately reflected on the suppliers' bills. This takes time and effort, two attributes that most individuals have in short supply. Furthermore, as with back orders, there are the stockout problems that must be solved to avoid customer dissatisfaction.

15. Buyers need to understand and be able to use all the technology available today as described in Chapter 2. Although technology generally makes the procurement process more efficient and effective, what happens if the computer crashes, the Internet is not available, or the power goes out?

 ## Key Words and Concepts

American Purchasing Society
As-purchased (AP) price
Backdoor selling
Back order
Certified Foodservice Professional (CFSP)
Convenience food
Edible-portion (EP) cost
Forecasting
Institute of Supply Management (ISM)
Make-or-buy analysis
National Restaurant Association (NRA)
North American Association of Food Equipment Manufacturers (NAFEM)
Optimal inventory management

Plant visit
Problems of the buyer
Purchasing activities
Recycling
Returns and allowances
Sourcing
Stockout
Supplier diplomacy
Supplier selection criteria
Trade relations
Trade show visit
Value analysis
What-if analysis

Questions and Problems

1. Assume that two suppliers sell the same quality of meat for the same price. What type of supplier services would you seek from them? Why? Which supplier service would you value enough so that if one supplier provided it and the other did not, you would purchase your meat from the former? Why?

2. Name some potential benefits of trade relations. Name potential difficulties. Would you engage in trade relations? Why or why not?

3. Do you think it is a good idea to allow competitors to "borrow a cup of sugar" once in a while? Why?

4. Explain what is meant by the purchasing function's goal of "maintaining the company's competitive position."

5. Name the five major objectives of the purchasing function.

6. Name three types of research activities that a buyer might perform.

7. What are two resources that a buyer may use when trying to identify trends in the hospitality industry?

8. Define or explain:

   a. Value analysis
   b. Sourcing
   c. CPM
   d. Plant visits
   e. CFPM
   f. Stockouts
   g. Backdoor selling
   h. Back orders

9. What problems will a foodservice operation incur if it experiences several back orders?

10. What is a major disadvantage associated with having excess inventory on hand?

11. When should the buyer visit a supplier's facilities?

12. List three advantages and three disadvantages of using convenience foods.

13. Assume that steak represents 30 percent of your overall food cost. If the purchase price of steak increases 10 percent, by what percentage will the overall food cost increase?

14. Assume that you have decided to serve roast beef on your menu. The AP price of roast beef is $3.98 per pound. The edible yield per pound is approximately 9 ounces. You plan to serve a 4 1/2-ounce portion size.

   a. Approximately how much raw roast beef must you purchase to serve 125 portions?

Questions and Problems (continued)

b. KWG Enterprises, a statewide food-merchant wholesaler, offers a precooked, pre-sliced roast beef product for $6 per pound. The edible yield is 100 percent.

1. Under what conditions would you purchase this convenience item?

2. Under what conditions would it be advisable to purchase the raw roast beef product instead of this convenience item?

3. Approximately how much of this convenience roast beef must you purchase to serve 125 portions?

15. A purveyor has offered to sell you fudge cakes for $6 each. You try to determine whether you can make the cakes more cheaply. Assuming that you will need to pay an additional employee $9.25 per hour, plus about $1.50-per-hour fringe benefits, and further assuming that this employee can make 24 cakes per hour, what alternative should you select? Should you "make" or should you "buy"? Why?

THE RECIPE FOR ONE CAKE IS

12	ounces shortening
1	pound, 12 ounces cake flour
2	pounds sugar
¼	ounce salt
½	ounce vanilla
1	ounce baking soda
1½	pints buttermilk
5	ounces cocoa

THE AP PRICES FOR THESE INGREDIENTS ARE

Shortening: $0.32 per pound
Cake flour: $11.09 per 50 pounds
Sugar: $18.22 per 50 pounds
Salt: $0.11 per pound
Vanilla: $6.85 per pint
Baking soda: $0.24 per pound
Eggs: $1.29 per dozen
Buttermilk: $2.45 per gallon
Cocoa: $2.12 per pound

Experiential Exercises

1. Present this purchasing activity list to a purchasing manager. Ask the manager if he or she performs all of these tasks. Ask if the manager would add or remove any of these tasks from the list. Provide a report detailing your conversation.
   a. Determine when to order.
   b. Control inventory levels.
   c. Establish quality standards.
   d. Determine specifications.
   e. Obtain competitive bids.
   f. Investigate vendors.
   g. Arrange financial terms.
   h. Oversee delivery.
   i. Negotiate refunds.
   j. Handle adjustments.
   k. Arrange for storage.

2. Determine the requirements for an individual to receive these certifications:
   Certified Professional in Supply Management (CPSM)
   Certified Professional in Supplier Diversity® (CPSD™)
   Certified Purchasing Professional (CPP)
   Certified Professional Purchasing Manager (CPPM)
   Certified Green Purchasing Professional (CGPP)
   Certified Professional Purchasing Consultant (CPPC)

3. Speak with a broker, a merchant–wholesaler, and a hotel or restaurant buyer. Ask them if they think it is a good idea to allow a salesperson to assist owner–managers in carrying out the necessary purchasing activities. Why or why not? Write a one-page paper comparing their answers.

References

1. National Restaurant Association, *2009 Restaurant Industry Fact Sheet,* National Restaurant Association (NRA), www.restaurant.org/research.

2. John Lawn, "Common Mistakes that Purchasing Managers Make," *Food Management,* February 2003, 38(2), p. 6; John Lawn, "Seven More Mistakes Purchasing Managers Make," *Food Management,* March 2003, 38(3), p. 8. See also C. Lee Evans, "The Hotel Purchasing Function," in *Hotel Management and Operations,* 4th ed., ed. Denney G. Rutherford (Hoboken, NJ: John Wiley & Sons, 2006).

3. J. Biljanoska and S. Martinoska, "Supplier Selection Criteria as a Critic Point in the Menu Quality," *Tourism & Hospitality Management,* 2010, pp. 266–272.

References (continued)

4. Tamar Benzaken, "Starbucks' Responsible Sourcing Social Guidelines from the Farm to the Coffeeshop," Cal Safety Compliance Corporation, United Nations Global Compact, 2007, www.unglobalcompact.org. See also JinLin Zhao, Jacqueline De Chabert-Rios, and William Quain, "Buyer-Supplier Relationships from the Buyer Perspective," *Journal of Applied Hospitality Management,* Spring 2005, 7(1), pp. 110–120.

5. Dave Ostrander, "Purchasing Power," *Pizza Today,* June 2006, 24(6), pp. 50–52.

6. "Avendra Adds 14 Minority and Women-Owned Suppliers to Its Procurement Programs," *Hotel News Resource,* 2004, www.hotelnewsresource.com/article13641 -Avendra_Adds_Minority_And_Women_Owned_Suppliers_To_Its_Procurement_ Program. Gregg Cebrzynski, "Burger King's Ads Target Women and Minorities in Bid to Recruit New Suppliers and Franchisees," *Nation's Restaurant News,* January 7, 2008, 42(1), p. 12. "Q&A with Wright-Lacy on Diversity," *The Triangle Tribune,* July 20, 2014, http://search.proquest.com.libaccess.sjlibrary.org/docview/1550173664?account id=10361.

7. Steve Hamm, "How Do You Maintain Good Supplier Relations?" *Caterer and Hotelkeeper,* November 2007, 197(4502), p. 20.

8. M. Subramani, "How Do Suppliers Benefit from Information Technology Use in Supply Chain Relationships?" *MIS Quarterly,* 2004, 28(1), 45–73.

9. "Hasty and Tasty—Smart Use of Pre-Prepared Products," *Hospitality,* November 2008, 44(11), pp. 37–40. See also Karen Weisberg, "Speed Prep Smarts," *Foodservice Director,* September 15, 2007, 20(9), pp. 48–50. Economic Research Service, "Food Dollar Series," *United States Department of Agriculture,* May 28, 2014, http://www.ers.usda.gov/ data-products/food-dollar-series/documentation.aspx.

10. Philip Parker, "As Supply Chains Get Global, Supplier Qualification Is More Important Than Ever," *Nutraceuticals Now,* Spring 2012, pp. 10–11.

CHAPTER 6

THE ORGANIZATION, ADMINISTRATION, AND EVALUATION OF PURCHASING

The Purpose of This Chapter

After reading this chapter, you should be able to:

- Describe the methods used to plan the purchasing activities of a hospitality operator.

- Design the purchasing organizational patterns of small independent, medium independent, and multiunit hospitality operations.

- Summarize the skills and qualities typically sought after in a hospitality buyer as shown in a job specification and job description.

- Describe the buyer's relationship with other managers and employees.

- Explain the importance of budgeting and controlling inventories.

- Recognize the different types of purchasing policies and procedures and how they are used to evaluate a buyer's performance.

PLANNING

All buyers, both full-time and part-time, must plan, organize, and administer their purchasing activities. This principle is crucial in large operations, especially chain organizations, in which more than one person may be involved in purchasing. In large hotels, for example, it is common to find a full-time purchasing agent as well as several department heads who purchase specialized merchandise for their needs. Similarly, large, multiunit chain restaurants usually employ a corporate purchasing agent with a buyer or a buyer–manager at each individual unit.

In small operations, the buyer and the owner–manager are often one and the same person or one of the department heads performs the buyer duties as part of his/her overall responsibilities. In all cases, purchasing should not be done casually. All buyers need a definite plan of action. All are also members of management and usually have specific supervisory and reporting relationships with their supervisors, other managers, staff members, and hourly employees.

In the initial stages of developing a selection and procurement plan that will be consistent with the hospitality operation's overall mission and values, buyers must understand the goals and objectives of the purchasing function. For instance, the five purchasing objectives we discussed in Chapter 5—maintain adequate supply, minimize investment, maintain quality, obtain lowest possible edible-portion (EP) cost, and maintain competitive position—can serve as the initial goals to be achieved in the long run. However, individual buyers may devise different ways of working toward these goals. Thus, evaluating possible methods of achieving the goals and eventually selecting one become the major accomplishment in the **planning** stage.

planning Process of developing business goals and objectives, along with actions and systems needed to achieve them.

Consider this example. A small operator may decide that the main objective of the purchasing function is to maintain adequate supplies at all times and that all other objectives are secondary to this one. The overall buying plan, then, must be tailored to ensure the attainment of this objective: the operator may decide to select only those suppliers with the most favorable delivery schedules and, if necessary, to pay a little extra for this supplier service.

Decisions made at the initial planning stage set the tone for future activities. Planning for purchasing is not carried out in a vacuum. It is part of the overall plan of the hospitality organization and cannot exist apart from the overall goals and objectives of the operation. Furthermore, a buyer rarely determines the buying plan without receiving input from other company personnel.

One way to start such a planning process might be to have middle and upper managers think about and rate the importance of the five purchasing objectives. Ask them to make notes about how these activities will affect their area of the operation and how they see the buyer's function in the overall management scheme. Schedule a meeting in the distant enough future to give everyone time to think about the questions at hand and then come together with the goal of reaching some form of consensus and obtaining direction for the purchasing plan.

ORGANIZING

Having formulated a general plan, a buyer must **organize** the human and material resources needed to follow it. At this second stage, however, the buyer's voice may still be only one of many. In some cases, there is little to say; superiors may decide how to do the operation's purchasing.

> **organizing** Process of arranging a company's workforce to achieve its overall business objectives.

The buying activities of a hospitality firm can be organized several ways. Generally, however, we find only two major organizational patterns: one for the independent operator and one for the multiunit chain operations. Most other organizational patterns are variations of these two.

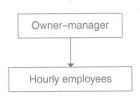

FIGURE 6.1 A typical purchasing organizational pattern for a very small independent operation.

■ Organizing for the Independent Operation

The many very small hospitality operations are often referred to as "mom-and-pop" places. Most do not have a payroll; that is, they are operated completely by the owners with, perhaps, some assistance from family members. Usually, the selection and procurement responsibilities fall directly on the owner–manager's shoulders. If these organizations have hourly employees, they normally are involved in these activities only sparingly (see Figure 6.1). For instance, an hourly employee may have receiving and storing responsibility whenever the owner–manager is absent.

Medium-size operations rarely employ full-time buyers (see Figure 6.2). Instead, these firms tend to designate one or more **user–buyers**. Ordinarily, the head bartender, the chef, the dining room supervisor, and other supervisors all do some buying as part of their responsibilities. The owner–manager acts as a coordinator of these user–buyers to control their activity and, especially, to supervise the receipt of their orders. The owner–manager also oversees receiving and storing, as well as bill paying.

In some independent properties, including large hotels and country clubs, an owner–manager may not coordinate the orders of each department head. Instead, a **steward** or assistant manager may be employed specifically to do this work. The owner–manager then controls and supervises this person's activities.

> **user–buyer** Refers to a person who is not a full-time buyer, but has some buying responsibilities. For instance, a chef who also orders the food products he or she uses in production would be considered a user–buyer.
>
> **steward** Manager who has food-buying responsibilities. May also be responsible for the food storage areas.

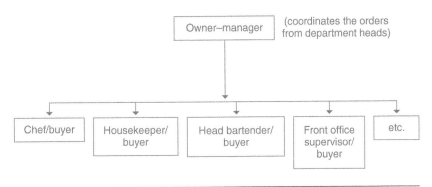

FIGURE 6.2 A typical purchasing organizational pattern for a medium-size independent hospitality operation.

Another variation of this pattern occurs when a separate steward or food buyer works in the kitchen specifically to coordinate the chef's needs. A kitchen steward may also supervise the warewashing (washing of dinnerware, silverware, etc.) and the kitchen cleaning employees. Large independents and, in some cases, large chain operations, may follow this pattern.

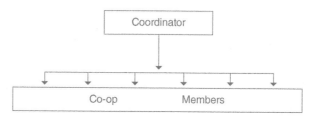

FIGURE 6.3 A typical purchasing organizational pattern for a co-op.

Organizational variations abound for independent operations; they are limited only by the imagination. As noted, however, a characteristic they share is the need for owner–managers to be directly involved in purchasing. They cannot avoid this activity, and in many cases, the purchaser is actually the owner–manager–chef, who not only buys for the kitchen but may also buy for, or at least coordinate the purchasing for, all the other departments.

Some small and medium-size hospitality operations join a communal-buying network. As this term suggests, these independents join together and agree to pool their purchases. The idea is to place one larger order, thereby qualifying for a lower as-purchased (AP) price than the pool members would be entitled to individually. This scheme works not only with food and operating supplies but also with insurance, advertising, and other service purchasing. The organizational pattern for **communal buying**, also referred to as **co-op purchasing**, or **shared buying**, is relatively simple (see Figure 6.3). Owners and managers from among the group of independents share the task of coordinating all the orders. Alternately, the independents may hire someone to perform this coordination, to place large orders, and to arrange proper delivery schedules. As discussed in Chapter 3, the groups that form for the purposes of communal buying are commonly referred to as **co-ops**, **aggregate buying groups**, buying clubs, or **group purchasing organizations (GPOs)**.

> **communal buying, co-op purchasing, or shared buying** Other terms for co-op buying.
>
> **co-op** A business organization owned and operated by a group of individuals for their mutual benefit. Another term for co-op purchasing, shared buying, and communal buying.
>
> **aggregate buying group** A group that forms for the purposes of co-op buying.
>
> **group purchasing organization (GPO)** Another term for buying club.

The concept of communal or cooperative (co-op) buying has its pros and cons.[1] We discuss the major advantages and disadvantages of co-op purchasing in Chapter 10. In the meantime, an excellent resource to learn more about co-op purchasing can be found on the *National Cooperative Business Association (NCBA)* website.

The large independent is similar to the small one, the major difference being the physical presence of one or more persons assigned full-time to the purchasing, receiving, storing, and issuing of products and services. The most typical setup is to have a purchasing director, with specialists in food buying, beverage buying, and equipment and supplies buying working in the purchasing department. In addition, a receiving clerk might be working for the accounting department and a storeroom manager for the purchasing director (see Figure 6.4).

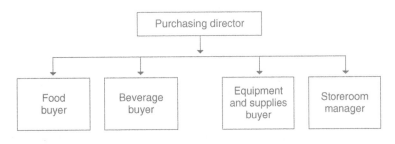

FIGURE 6.4 A typical purchasing organizational pattern for a large independent hospitality operation.

■ Organizing for Chain Operations

A major difference between independents and chains is the additional level of management found in the chain operation. The purchasing function in a hotel or restaurant that belongs to a chain operation often resembles the purchasing the independents do. What is different is the presence of a vice president of purchasing, or a corporate purchasing director, and a staff of buyers at headquarters overseeing the selection and procurement activities and, if applicable, monitoring the company-owned commissary and/or central distribution activities (see Figure 6.5).

At the local unit level, in some cases, the unit manager performs all buying activities. In other cases, he or she may serve as coordinator for the users and buyers. Chain operations with large units may have a purchasing system in each unit that is similar to the system of a large independent.

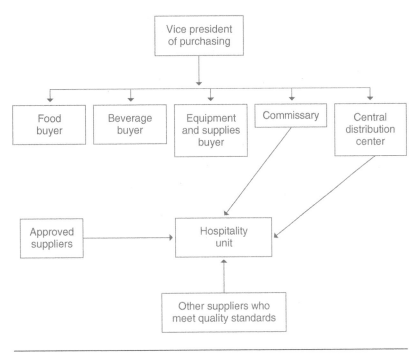

FIGURE 6.5 A typical purchasing organizational pattern for a multi-unit hospitality operation.

approved supplier A vendor that the buyer is allowed to buy from.

corporate vice president of purchasing Person responsible for all purchasing activities for the corporation. Major responsibilities include such things as: setting purchasing guidelines; negotiating long-term, national contracts for price and product availability; and researching new vendors and products. In some cases, this person is also responsible for overseeing the central commissary and/or central distribution warehouses.

The unit manager in Figure 6.5 can be a franchisee or the manager of a company-owned store. If the former, he or she usually: (1) buys from **approved suppliers** permitted by the **corporate vice president of purchasing**; (2) buys from other suppliers as long as they meet the company's quality standards; (3) buys from the franchisor's company-owned commissary and/or central distribution center; or (4) uses a combination of the three approaches. As mentioned earlier, a franchisee typically buys from the commissary and/or central distribution center whenever possible, if only for convenience.

Managers of company-owned stores have the same options as franchisees, but they usually have less flexibility. Once the company's top management determines the buying procedure, there is little chance for variation.

The vice president of purchasing serves as a central coordinator for purchases made by all of the units. His or her major responsibilities usually include (1) setting purchasing guidelines for unit managers, and (2) negotiating national, long-term contracts for items used by all of the units. The vice president normally negotiates large-quantity buys with set prices—six months of supplies or longer. (Unit managers, by contrast, order and receive just what they need when they need it and then pay the AP price that the vice president negotiated.) The corporate vice president also: (3) sets purchase specifications (to which we devote Chapter 7) for items that must be purchased at the unit level, (4) performs research activities, (5) serves as a resource person for all unit managers and unit buying personnel, and (6) if applicable, supervises the central distribution function and the commissary.

Some advantages and disadvantages accompany this kind of centralized purchasing. The major advantages are the reduction in the AP prices achieved by quantity buys, the presence of a strong negotiator, and cost and **quality control**. The main disadvantage seems to be the system's potential for alienating local suppliers, especially when the chain deals with one major supplier and bypasses all the locals.[2] Plus, because organizations are seen as "citizens," especially in small towns, the hospitality operation that doesn't purchase locally may be seen as not supporting the community. However, the corporate vice president of purchasing cannot purchase everything, nor can he or she negotiate contracts for all items. At least some buying must remain decentralized and in the hands of the local unit. This slight but inevitable degree of decentralization can soothe ruffled local suppliers and show the organization to be a good corporate citizen, as well as provide the unit personnel with some purchasing experience.

quality control Systems and procedures used by managers to ensure that the actual quality of finished items is consistent with the expected quality.

Another major difference between independents and chains is the propensity of the chains to develop a central distribution and commissary network. This network really represents an effort by the chains to provide many of their own economic values and supplier services—that is, to bypass the middlemen. The chains feel it makes sense, dollars and "sense," to centralize their buying, to have products delivered to one location, to process these products (for example, to cut portion-controlled steaks), and to deliver these processed items to each unit.

As we noted in Chapter 3, the commissary and central distribution network is not always a cost-effective system. There certainly are several quality control benefits, as well as the potential benefit of an uninterrupted supply. However, in light of the arguments for and against central

A DAY IN THE LIFE
Camille Godwin-Austen, Director, Procurement International House of Pancakes LLC (IHOP)

Courtesy of Camille Godwin-Austen

Not everyone gets to drink Lemonade Splashers and eat Blueberry Cannoli Pancakes in the middle of the day. As part of the cross-functional team for special promotions at International House of Pancakes' (IHOP's) corporate office, Camille Godwin-Austen gets to enjoy many tasty treats. However, as Director of Procurement, once a sweet-tasting themed special is approved, it is Godwin-Austen's job to ensure enough pancakes and toppings and syrups are available for the millions of hungry IHOP® guests to enjoy their favorite breakfast.

As of March 31, 2014, there were 1,627 IHOP restaurants in the United States and abroad, with continued focus on expansion internationally. The chain stretches from coast to coast in the United States and is growing overseas with locations in Canada, Mexico, Central America, the Middle East, and Asia Pacific. Only a handful of the restaurants are corporate owned—the majority of these are owned by franchisees that make most of their purchases through a jointly owned cooperative.

"One of the corporation's commitments to its franchisees is to develop, research and roll out the themed, limited time only promotions we offer each year," said Godwin-Austen. "Part of my job is to forecast all of the proposed promotions and make sure they're financially feasible and that product will be available to support the needs of the stores."

These major promotions require many feasibility tests. Godwin-Austen is part of a team that includes people from research and development, finance, marketing, training, operations, and the franchise co-op.

Proposed promotions are kitchen tested and market tested on more than one consumer group, before receiving final approval. The challenge for Godwin-Austen is forecasting the precise amount to order of each ingredient to cover each seven- to eight-week promotional period.

It's always important to calculate carefully one's needs before placing an order," she said. "But when a promotion, with specific ingredients, has a definitive timeframe, it becomes even more critical. We don't want to have anything left over because it costs the corporation money. However at the same time, we can't put franchisees in the position of having to tell their guests that they are sold out of the advertised special," she adds.

You may be thinking, "Just order more." The problem is that the promotions are unique. A recent special focused on Brioche French toast—definitely a custom order.

Plus, the numbers are staggering. Each of the restaurants can sell as many as 300 plates of each special per week. That comes to more than 4 million sweet topped pancakes or 2 million pieces of French toast during the course of a promotion.

"Just envision six or seven items that are unique to the system moving in and out of the restaurants every eight weeks," Godwin-Austen said.

Another recent project involved the transitioning of the entire purchasing system from a database on a mainframe to a web-based system. This involved writing scripts, coding data, and training people to use the new system.

"My job has evolved and continues to evolve as we've gone through many transitions here, as part of the shared services Finance group for our parent company, DineEquity, Inc., and our sister brand Applebee's Grill and Bar®," Godwin-Austen said.

Godwin-Austen's offices are on the West Coast in California, so she starts her day checking East Coast emails to ensure there are no messages regarding product outages. She then reviews the orders to be processed and may attend a cross-functional or internal orders meeting. Her afternoon may be consumed with forecasting for a promotion slated for six months in advance, or confirming that a new vendor can handle the company's high-volume demand.

Although she works hard, Godwin-Austen has time for her family, writes and plays music, and practices herbal therapy, dance, and yoga.

distribution and commissary operation, managers who face this difficult decision must undertake a good deal of careful analysis.

STAFFING AND TRAINING

staffing Process of recruiting, hiring, and training personnel to perform specific tasks in an organization.

training Procedure designed to facilitate the learning and development of new skills, and the improvement of existing skills.

Neither small nor medium-sized operations generally **staff** full-time purchasing employees. Large operations, especially chains, may hire several buyers, each an expert in one or two product areas. Such operations are also more apt to employ full-time secretarial and clerical personnel in the purchasing department. Also, they may employ receiving clerks and storeroom managers. Again, the small operation would typically settle for a chef–buyer–storeroom manager and a well-trained, generously paid kitchen worker who doubles as a receiving clerk.

A supervisor needing a full-time buyer may look among the current employees for someone with an aptitude for purchasing who can be **trained** to take on this role. Alternately, a professional buyer may be sought by advertising in the newspaper and trade journal classified-ads sections or on the Internet, by asking informally among trade association members, or by inquiring among friends and other professional colleagues. The supervisor must adhere to company policy and to federal, state, and local legislation throughout this recruiting process. The skills and qualities looked for in a candidate will vary depending on whether it is a full-time or part-time position, and if so, what percentage of their time is spent on purchasing.

job specification List of qualities, such as education, technical skill, and work experience, a person should possess to qualify for a particular job.

■ Job Specifications

The **job specification** (see Figure 6.6), which lists the skills and qualities sought in a job candidate, follows a typical pattern. It is divided into the four broad areas of technical skills, interpersonal (or human) skills, conceptual skills,

VICE PRESIDENT OF PURCHASING

Nicholas Restaurant Group, one of the world's leading restaurant firms, is seeking a Vice President of Purchasing to manage and direct all purchasing activities for its 200 restaurants worldwide. Nicholas Restaurant Group's concepts include Cheezeyburgers, Gabriella's Italian Café, and Tacos Tacos Tacos.

Responsibilities of the Vice President of Purchasing include supervising and coordinating numerous purchasing programs; communicating with manufacturers, suppliers, and distributors to establish and develop our supply chain; working with our corporate offices on major product and service negotiations and purchases; resolving a varierty of purchasing problems; assisting food and beverage departments in establishing and insuring product and service consistency; and on-going product research and development.

Candidates must have at least 5 years of purchasing experience with a restaurant or other hospitality operation, a bachelor's degree in hotel or restaurant management, proven management ability, and strong written and verbal communication skills. We are offering a competitive salary ($95,000-$115,000), excellent benefits, and a working environment that rewards hard work and creativity.

If you are interested, please send your résumé in strictest confidence to:

Andrew Hale Feinstein
1000 Dead End Road
Pomona, CA 91768

We are an Equal Opportunity Employer.

FIGURE 6.6 Example of a job specification for a purchasing position.
Courtesy of the St. Anthony Hotel

and other qualities. For some positions relating to the buying activity, technical skill and extensive experience are very important. For other positions, a desire to learn may be the only requirement. The complicating factor is that purchasing personnel often have responsibilities other than purchasing, receiving, storing, and issuing; thus, these other responsibilities may take precedence when a manager undertakes to develop overall job specifications. There are three types of skills necessary for most buyer positions.

■ Technical Skill

Buyers must be extremely familiar with the items they will purchase. At the very least, they should have the aptitude to learn the intricate aspects of all these products and services. In addition, a person cannot really aspire to a buyer's job unless familiar with the ways in which and the conditions under which chefs, bartenders, housekeepers, and so on will use the purchased items.

■ Interpersonal (or Human) Skill

The buyer must get along with other department heads and employees. After all, buyers work with employees throughout the organization who may be totally dependent on them for the supplies or food items they need to do their jobs. A buyer who is difficult to get along with, doesn't listen to the needs of others, or is dictatorial in any way may alienate fellow employees and help create an unpleasant work atmosphere. A buyer also must be firm but fair with all types of sales representatives.

■ Conceptual Skill

A buyer should be able to conceptualize the entire hospitality operation and not see things exclusively from the point of view of purchasing. Sometimes it is difficult to see how, for example, a low as-purchased (AP) price can turn into an exorbitant edible-portion (EP) cost. But it is just this type of general perspective and **systems mentality**—the ability to view the whole operation and the multitude of relationships it contains—that supervisors tend to look for in a buyer. See Figure 6.7 for examples of these skills.

> **systems mentality** Ability to view and understand the entire organization and the multitude of relationships it contains.
>
> **job description** A list of duties the job entails that the employee must perform. May also include additional information, such as the job's direct supervisor, the objective(s) of the job, and guidelines that must be followed when performing the job functions.

■ Other Qualities

The three skills we just mentioned are fairly routine. Some other characteristics looked for are not so easily discussed, but they are important. These include (1) the quality and types of an applicant's experience, (2) honesty and integrity, (3) the desire to advance and grow with the operation, (4) the ability to administer a purchasing department, if applicable, and (5) the desire to work conscientiously for the operation.[3]

■ Job Descriptions

A **job description** constitutes a list of duties an employee must perform. It is usually prepared before, or in conjunction with, the job specification. In some cases, the supervisor develops the description personally. In others, the purchasing manager may participate in this effort. Even in this situation, however, the supervisor should set the tone of the job by stating its objectives and the broad guidelines a buyer must follow. The buyer, then, is left to iron out the specific details necessary to organize and administer the purchasing function (see Figure 6.8).[4] For examples of

> **TECHNICAL SKILLS**
> Creating a recipe
> Costing a recipe
> Preparing a recipe
> Preparing a work schedule
> Developing a job description
>
> **INTERPERSONAL SKILLS**
> Conducting a performance appraisal
> Interviewing a sales representative
> Training an employee
> Handling a customer complaint
> Working with delivery agents
>
> **CONCEPTUAL SKILLS**
> Forecasting food trends
> Marketing a restaurant
> Organizing a special event
> Budgeting payroll expenses
> Researching a new food item

FIGURE 6.7 Examples of technical, interpersonal, and conceptual skills.

Establish selection and procurement policies
Forecast trends
Develop purchase specifications
Maintain supplier files, price lists, etc.
Negotiate contracts
Monitor deliveries
Select suppliers
Coordinate other departments' purchasing needs
Identify and research new products
Investigate suppliers' facilities
Establish inventory stock levels
Monitor storeroom inventories
Select and train purchasing staff
Monitor operating budget
Establish and monitor inventory and cost controls

FIGURE 6.8 An example of job description duties for a purchasing manager.
Courtesy of the Hay-Adams Hotel

purchasing job descriptions, search career websites such as hospitalitycareers.com and Monster.com.

The job description should describe how the buyer will meet the general objectives discussed in Chapter 5, and how they attain them by: (1) purchasing the appropriate quality, (2) purchasing at the right price, (3) purchasing in the right amount, (4) purchasing at the right time, and (5) purchasing from the right supplier, who provides the needed supplier services. Additional objectives may be more specific. For example, someone in the

> **quality standard** The type of quality you consistently use and that the hospitality operation is known for. Buyers typically communicate this standard to vendors by specifying brand names and government grades.

operation may decide to set rigid **quality standards** for fresh produce and looser quality standards for the remaining food products. A specific job duty and goal would then be the maintenance of these various quality standards.

■ Compensation

Full-time and part-time buyers usually receive a straight salary, but in some situations they also receive a bonus. Corporate purchasing agents can expect to receive a good salary and to occupy a top management position within the company. Buyers, too, receive good salaries. Part-time buyers, though, tend to earn salaries based on several duties, not just their buying. For example, a chef may receive a high salary primarily because of his or her staff supervision and culinary expertise.

Where purchasing has been concerned, the major aspect of the **compensation** issue has always been the bonus. A bonus can be tricky to assign because buyers may be tempted to work toward the bonus alone, while sacrificing other important aspects of the job. For example, buyers receiving bonuses based on the AP prices paid for food may be motivated to purchase foods with the lowest AP price, even if they are also the ones with the highest EP cost.

> **compensation** Financial remuneration, such as wages, salaries, bonuses, and fringe benefits, paid to people for their work.
>
> **on-the-job training (OJT)** Typical method used to teach job skills to new and continuing employees. Involves learning the skills while performing the duties in real time, usually under the direction and supervision of a trainer.

■ Training

Regardless of whether the job is full-time or part-time and how experienced a buyer is, some type of training is always necessary. New employees must be introduced to the philosophy and goals of the company, to all of its operational aspects, and to the purchasing policies. These introductions actually represent an orientation rather than training. Full-time buyers and buyer trainees undergo additional training, as needed, in the procedural elements of buying. **On-the-job training (OJT)** is probably most often used in the purchasing function.

In addition, management training seminars and courses sometimes supplement in-house training. The National Restaurant Association (NRA), The National Restaurant Association Educational Foundation (NRAEF), the Institute of Supply Management (ISM), and the North American Association of Food Equipment Manufacturers (NAFEM) normally sponsor several seminars and courses every year.

DIRECTING AND WORKING WITH OTHERS

> **directing**   Supervising and managing persons who work for you.
>
> **supervisory style**   The way in which a person watches over and guides the work or tasks of another who may lack full knowledge of the tasks that must be carried out.

In addition to fulfilling their other responsibilities, full-time and part-time buyers must **direct** the purchasing personnel assigned to them. **Supervisory style** is, of course, a personal matter; no two successful supervisors ever seem to follow identical supervisory styles. Generally speaking, though, top management, or an owner–manager, dictates some sort of supervisory policy.[5]

Buyers are often in a unique position of working with colleagues from all other areas of the hospitality business to ensure the proper items are available for each department. All colleagues should strive to help one another. At the very least, a full-time buyer who purchases items for the kitchen, bar, housekeeping department, and so on can ensure a continuous flow of supplies for all departments of the hotel or restaurant. We have stressed the fact that few operations employ a full-time buyer. Most depend on such buyer–users as the buyer–head bartender, the buyer–housekeeper, and the buyer–chef. However, the buying aspect of their jobs can create an additional bond between these colleagues.

For instance, these user–buyers may want to combine some activities. They may agree that the buyer–chef will purchase writing supplies for everyone or that the buyer–housekeeper will purchase soaps and other cleaning supplies for all departments. Sometimes the owner–general manager makes these decisions. However this process is handled, a greater need for cooperation and coordination among colleagues enters the picture.

Buyers must also work closely with colleagues who have no buying authority. For example, the buyer–chef may work with the accountant to develop various formats to be used for ordering, receiving, storing, and the like. The buyer–chef may work with the sales manager or the owner–manager whenever new menus are contemplated because he or she can advise on food prices, the availability of various items, and the operation's capability of producing the new menu items given its kitchen facilities and employee skills.

Major conflicts can occur between buyers and production supervisors who use the products and services. For example, a full-time buyer may spend a lot of time tracking down good buys, only to see excessive waste and spoilage in food preparation. Although the control of purchased items eventually passes from the buyer to the user, the chef may blame the buyer for purchasing inferior merchandise if food costs are too high because of waste. Conversely, the buyer may blame the waste on the chef's lack of control over the kitchen employees. Either way, the owner–manager has a problem deciding whom or what to believe.

This kind of conflict has encouraged some operations to create several buyer–user positions, thereby keeping control and responsibility together. For example, some restaurants employ a buyer–chef, buyer–head bartender, buyer–wine steward, and buyer–maitre d'. The drawback is that the buyer–user has no one checking up on his or her buying activities, no one to uncover buying mistakes. An alert owner–manager, though, can usually minimize this difficulty.

The buyer also has a responsibility to hourly employees to provide the resources they need to carry out their duties properly. Buyers must ensure a continuity of supply. If employees do not have the raw materials, they cannot produce. In addition, idle production workers lead to customer dissatisfaction somewhere down the line. When employees should be producing but cannot because materials are late or unavailable, at some later point, when output is expected, guests will find that their guest rooms are not ready or their food is missing.

The buyer's secondary responsibility to hourly employees involves steward sales. If the hospitality operation permits hourly employees to make personal purchases, the buyer generally incurs the responsibility for supervising and monitoring these purchases.

The major potential conflict with hourly employees can occur when a buyer tries to exert control and authority over employees someone else supervises. Generally, this conflict parallels a major conflict that occurs between a full-time buyer and colleagues. Full-time buyers may unknowingly assume more authority than they are entitled to. For instance, a buyer who also manages the storeroom might alienate the chef's employees by forcing them to follow myriad rules and regulations to obtain the food and supplies they need in their work. These rules can indirectly affect the employees' work patterns; hence, they tend to give the buyer some control over these employees. In the long run, these conflicts must be ironed out between the buyer and his or her colleagues.

BUDGETING AND CONTROLLING INVENTORIES

In operations that employ a full-time buyer, it may be necessary to fund the buying function, which means that annual operating expenses, such as buyers' salaries and clerical costs, must be **budgeted**. The operations that employ user–buyers rarely construct a separate purchasing budget. Nevertheless, because a budget is always a measure of performance, a buyer's overall contribution can be measured by comparing actual operating expenses with budgeted operating expenses.

Buyers usually take responsibility for **control** over the products they buy until a user takes them from the storeroom and places them in the production flow. It is not always clear at exactly what point this responsibility shifts to the user. Nevertheless, everyone in a hospitality operation should be concerned with controlling waste, spoilage, and theft.

Small operations use a **direct control system** in which the owner–manager keeps a close eye on everything. Larger operations use an **indirect control system**, often one in which a system of overlapping electronic or nonelectronic forms enables someone, usually the controller, to keep tabs on all the products. The manager can determine, from glancing at the controller's summary of issues and receipts, where these products are in the hospitality operation and how much of each is at its respective location. (Chapters 12, 13, and 14 contain thorough discussions of these controls.)

Controlling the purchasing process of a large organization is always a daunting task, but it is vital to the success of your operation. Today, purchasing technology enables companies with multiregional properties to track, monitor, and control the purchasing activities of its employees.

budgeting Developing a realistic statement of management's goals and objectives, expressed in financial terms. This statement is usually referred to as a budget.

control Systems and procedures used by managers to ensure that the actual costs of doing business are consistent with the expected (or budgeted or theoretical) costs.

direct control system System that does not rely on number crunching and paperwork. It relies on the supervisor's presence and personal supervision and direction.

indirect control system Process of using overlapping computerized and/or noncomputerized receipts and other records to maintain tight control over all inventory items.

Large corporations often enjoy deep discounts when they procure products from preferred or contracted vendors. However, ensuring that purchasers at different properties are using these vendors rather than purchasing from noncontracted companies is crucial to cutting costs and increasing a property's profitability. Modern technology permits companies to create systems that track purchases company-wide.

For example, a purchasing agent in Houston seeks to order 1,000 pounds of crab from a local vendor. Meanwhile, your company has entered a contract for a certain quantity of crab at a set discount from a national vendor that provides your company with seafood and other products. A corporate manager would then be notified if a purchase order is submitted to a company that has not been approved. In addition, purchasing managers could be notified if the dollar amount is excessive, thereby controlling maverick spending while maximizing company profits.

Control is further complicated in the hospitality industry by waste and spoilage factors. Furthermore, security becomes more difficult because many of the products we buy are useful, convenient, and attractive to just about everyone. The buyer must do whatever is possible to minimize losses—normally, by adhering to the control system approved by company policy.

The systems of control will be set by the buyer, upper-level management, and/or corporation. The next section will outline many of the policies and procedures that the buyer must establish and follow to ensure this control and the proper operation of the purchasing department.

ESTABLISHING AND FOLLOWING SELECTION AND PROCUREMENT POLICIES

■ Policies

selection and procurement policies   These are usually broad, flexible rules a supervisor expects a buyer to follow when selecting and procuring products and services.

These policies are usually broad, flexible rules a buyer must follow when selecting and procuring products and services. In general, **selection and procurement policies** guide a buyer in terms of how to act and what to do in several types of situations. Precise policies are in the buyers' best interest to assist them with typical situations they may face.

Accepting Gifts from a Supplier

gifts from suppliers Controversial subject in the purchasing profession. Occurs when the buyer receives an item of personal gain from suppliers in appreciation for buying their products. Buyers are usually forbidden from accepting any significant personal gift. A valuable gift could be interpreted as a kickback.

Gifts from suppliers includes accepting gifts, pooling them, and distributing them later to all company employees. Strict rules against this practice are the norm. Drawing the line can, however, be difficult. For example, accepting bottles of liquor may be taboo, but what should a buyer do about a free lunch now and then? Similarly, what should a buyer do about a supplier who always has complimentary tickets to major sports events? Whatever the policy, a buyer must realize that accepting gifts, especially those that cannot be returned (such as complimentary meals and tickets) could create a psychological obligation to purchase goods or services from these generous suppliers.[6]

Favoring Suppliers

How many potential suppliers should a buyer contact? Should a buyer stick with one or two, or should he or she consider any reputable, capable purveyor? In some cases, other department heads or employees may try to steer a buyer toward a certain supplier, usually a friend. **Favoring suppliers** puts the buyer in a difficult position. However, a strict policy can protect a buyer from undue pressure from, for example, the bartender who wants all the bar supplies to be purchased from his cousin's supply house. In most instances, the supervisor insists that an **approved supplier list** be developed along the guidelines of supplier selection criteria to be discussed further in Chapter 10, which then serves to restrict all personnel who have purchasing responsibilities.

Establishing Reciprocity

Basically, **reciprocity** means "you buy from me, I'll buy from you." It is also interpreted to mean "I'll buy from you if you do something special for me." This is a troublesome policy. Not only may the arrangement be illegal, but also the best a buyer can do, obviously, is to break even. In fact, the buyer usually winds up purchasing more items from a supplier than the supplier could ever reciprocate; for example, suppliers can refer much less food business to you than you can buy from them. If there is a reciprocal arrangement, the supervisor normally establishes it, with the buyer then expected to purchase accordingly.

Accepting Free Samples

Some buyers collect all sorts of **free samples**; others accept them only when they have a sincere interest in buying the product; still others purchase the samples they want to avoid obligating themselves to a particular supplier. Perhaps the best policy is to accept a free sample only when there is a serious interest in the product. Free **equipment testing** falls under the same guidelines: typically, you test it only if you have more than a casual interest.

The major difficulty with free samples and free equipment testing is the distinct possibility that suppliers will send their most expensive items and then pressure the user(s) of the items to pressure the buyer to purchase them. Consulting with a user of the equipment (the chef, for example) instead of the buyer is an example of **backdoor selling**. This selling strategy can be effective, but it also can undermine efficiency and friendship. In any case, hospitality companies should adhere to a strict policy on free samples and test equipment.

favoring suppliers
Giving special treatment or unfair advantages to a supplier and/or its representatives.

approved supplier list A list of all vendors who buyers are allowed to purchase from. An excellent security precaution.

reciprocity In the world of purchasing, it means, "You buy from me, and I'll buy from you."

free sample Part of the marketing strategy used by vendors to sell products. Buyers are allowed to test a product in their own facility without having to pay for it.

equipment testing Evaluating equipment to determine if the item performs as expected.

backdoor selling This happens when a sales rep bypasses the regular buyer and goes to some other employee, such as the lead line cook, to make a sales pitch. The cook then exerts pressure on the buyer to make the purchase.

Accepting Discounts

A buyer can obtain at least four separate types of discounts from a supplier:

quantity discount A price reduction for buying a large amount of one specific type of merchandise.

volume discount Similar to a quantity discount. The buyer agrees to purchase a huge volume of goods; however, unlike a quantity discount, he or she buys more than one type of merchandise.

blanket order discount Another term for volume discount.

cash discount An award for prompt payment, for paying in advance of the delivery, or using a cash-on-delivery (COD) bill-paying procedure.

cash-on-delivery (COD) Paying for a shipment when it is delivered. Payment may be in cash, check, credit card, debit card, or other acceptable means.

bill-paying procedure Method used to discharge debts in such a way that payments are made on time. Payments should not be late, as that could create penalties, yet they should not be too early unless there are incentives for early payments.

promotional discount Price discount awarded to the buyer if he or she allows the vendor to promote the product in the hospitality operation. Or if the hospitality operation agrees to personally help promote the sale of the product to its customers.

1. **Quantity discount:** A **quantity discount** is granted by the supplier if a buyer agrees to purchase a large amount of one specific type of merchandise.

2. **Volume discount:** This is similar to the quantity discount. The buyer must agree to purchase a large volume of goods; however, he or she can buy more than one type of merchandise. A **volume discount** is sometimes referred to as a **blanket order discount**, in that the purchase order contains a long list of several items, none of which is ordered in huge amounts. But, when all of these small amounts are totaled, a supplier might reward the resulting large dollar volume with a discount.

3. **Cash discount:** A **cash discount** is an award for prompt payment, for paying in advance of the delivery, or for using a **cash-on-delivery (COD) bill-paying procedure**.

4. **Promotional discount:** A supplier might grant a **promotional discount** if a buyer's company agrees to accept the discount and use it to promote the product in the operation. For example, this promotion might involve letting restaurant customers sample the product at a reduced menu price.

Quantity discounts and volume discounts are relatively common in the hospitality industry, but they often require purchasing amounts that cannot be stored easily. Buyers may or may not be permitted to bargain for cash discounts because the accounting department or the financial officer usually sets up some sort of bill-paying schedule. (We discuss this issue in Chapter 9.)

Some hospitality companies aggressively seek out suppliers who offer generous promotional discount opportunities.[7] For example, some quick-service restaurants will allow a supplier to advertise brand name merchandise in the property if the supplier agrees to give them, free of charge, beverage-dispensing equipment, menu sign boards, and/or countertop display shelving. Some table-service operations like promotional discounts because they can use them to reward servers who sell their quota of a particular item to guests. Also, caterers enjoy having suppliers construct attractive displays of their products in the caterers' sales offices that can be used to entice potential banquet customers into purchasing expensive parties.

Promotional discounts, though, represent a loaded decision. Although a buyer may want to save the money, the company may not want the obligation to promote the product or even to be identified too closely with it.

Supporting Local Suppliers

Some owner–managers like to **support local suppliers** and ensure that a certain amount of business stays in the community. Although this policy of **trade relations** can limit a buyer's alternatives, in the long run, purchasing some goods locally may be a beneficial strategy. It may also be linked to specific social responsibility concerns and marketing and promotion of the establishment.

supporting local suppliers Done to maintain good relationships with business-persons who live and work in the local community.

trade relations The practice of spreading your purchase dollars among several vendors. Intended to create positive publicity for your hospitality operation.

Adhering to Quality Standards

Usually, the owner–manager or the corporation will set the quality standards, and the person who has ordering responsibilities will abide by them and see to it that, as much as possible, he or she purchases and receives such quality. It is unusual for buyers to have the final say regarding the quality standards to be used in the hospitality operation, but quite often, the person who has the major responsibility for ordering has some leeway and flexibility.

Following Shopping Procedures

The owner–manager or the corporation will specify the **shopping procedures**, especially the procedures to be used when selecting the appropriate supplier. These will vary depending on the size of the operation, the amount and type of technology used, and the values of the operation. Considerations include how many potential suppliers to contact and how much and what types of products to be purchased from each.

shopping procedures Methods buyers use to find the correct products and services at the right prices from the right suppliers. Usually involves taking bids from several potential suppliers before deciding who to purchase from.

Limiting Quantity

The typical buyer is restricted in the amount of purchases at any one time. For a larger-than-normal amount, generally, permission must be obtained. This common policy is strictly enforced to help an operation avoid massive overstocks that tie up large sums of money and extra storage space.

Limiting Prices

A supervisor may suggest some flexible **price limits** for certain products, especially those products that represent the bulk of the purchasing dollar. And, for instance, if an item's price rises above that limit, it may be time to reevaluate the item's place in the operation.

price limits Guideline that sets the maximum AP prices a buyer is allowed to pay for products or services unless given permission to do so by a supervisor.

personal purchase Another term for steward sale.

Making Personal Purchases

Personal purchases, also referred to as **steward sales**, occur whenever the hospitality company allows its employees to take advantage of the company's purchasing power to purchase goods for their personal, private use. Buyers,

steward sale A sale of your inventory to employees. You charge them the price you paid. In effect, you allow them to take advantage of your purchasing power for their personal benefit.

for example, might be tempted to buy hams, steaks, or roasts for a personal dinner party they are planning, and other employees might like to take advantage of the wholesale price. Usually, however, a supervisor discourages this.

In some companies, employees may be permitted to take advantage of this price on such special occasions as holidays. Also, if employees must buy their own uniforms, they may be able to make these purchases through the buyer or purchasing agent, but abusing this practice can lead to confusion and dishonesty.

Following the Written Ethics Code

ethics code   A code of conduct designed to influence the behavior of employees. It typically sets out the procedures to be used in specific ethical situations, such as conflicts of interest or the acceptance of gifts.

Most hospitality companies have established written ethical guidelines for their buyers. In many cases, these guidelines are adapted from those suggested by one or more professional purchasing associations. The typical **ethics code**, though, is usually very explicit and pertains to all potential ethical dilemmas. It is normally a major part of a buyer's job description.

■ Performance Evaluation

Buyers have very complex jobs and relationships with external suppliers and internal colleagues and employees. As in any job, their supervisor will need to evaluate their performance on a regular basis. Buyers undergo two types of performance evaluations: (1) how well they operate the purchasing department, if there is one, and (2) how well they have carried out the procurement function.

operational performance Refers to a manager's (such as a buyer's) ability to run his or her department effectively and efficiently, while maintaining company standards. Important factor considered when preparing a manager's annual job evaluation.

procurement performance Refers to the buyer's ability to accomplish the purchasing objectives set by management. Important factor considered when preparing a buyer's annual job evaluation.

Operational performance refers to how well the buyer has adhered to the budget allocated to the purchasing department; that is, how efficient the buyer has been in discharging the purchasing duties. This evaluation consists of comparing actual employee salaries, postage expenses, telephone costs, and so on, with their budgeted counterparts. Small operations tend to skip this type of evaluation even though it can help a manager to isolate the operational costs of the buying function. Unfortunately, it is usually too difficult and costly to separate, for example, telephone calls to suppliers from the rest of the telephone calls. It is not impossible, but in small places it may not be economical.

Procurement performance refers to how effectively a buyer has procured products and services. Procuring items is the heart of the buyer's job; thus, procurement performance is extremely important. Unfortunately, we can find little agreement about what to look at when evaluating procurement performance. We discuss several of these performance quality indicators next. Many will just briefly be defined here as more detailed examples will be given in the appropriate chapters.

The Materials Budget

Some large companies forecast their sales and, concomitantly, the cost of goods sold. For example, the cost of food might be forecast at 35 percent of the food-sales dollar. The food buyer might be expected to spend no more than, say, 30 percent of the sales dollar for food, with the remaining

5 percent to be used to pay for the difference between the AP price and the EP cost—things such as trimming loss and other unavoidable waste.

A company could construct a **materials budget** for such items as advertising costs, detergent costs, and lobster costs. In fact, this procedure is relatively common, even in small operations, but it is uncommon to find a materials budget for all products and services. It would be convenient, however, to have these budgets; they make it easy to compare actual costs, thereby facilitating a fair procurement performance evaluation.

> **materials budget**
> Involves setting a dollar limit of how much a buyer is able to purchase over a particular time period. A method used to control and evaluate a buyer's performance.

These budgets appear more commonly in hospitality organizations that serve a "captive audience": employee feeding, college feeding, hospital and prison food services, and so on. Indeed, whenever a foodservice catering corporation bids on a foodservice contract of this type, it usually must include the projected expenses as a part of its bid. Consequently, the buyer receives what amounts to a materials budget to work with for the duration of the contract. If, for example, the costs of some foods increase, he or she may be forced to try cheaper substitutes.

Inventory Turnover

This refers to the annual cost of goods sold divided by the average dollar value of inventory kept in stock during the course of that year. (The average inventory value is equal to the inventory value at the beginning of the year, plus the inventory value at the end of the year, divided by two.) For example, if a restaurant's annual cost of goods sold equals $250,000, the **beginning inventory** is $12,000, and the **ending inventory** is $8,000, the **inventory turnover** calculation for that particular restaurant is:

> **beginning inventory**
> Amount of products available for sale at the beginning of an accounting period.

> **ending inventory**
> Amount of product on hand at the end of an accounting period.

$$\text{Average inventory} = (\$12,000 + \$8,000) / 2 = \$10,000$$
$$\text{Inventory turnover} = \$250,000 / \$10,000 = 25$$

Operators must decide on the appropriate turnover rate to ensure that the establishment does not run out of product but that there is not too much in storage. The normal food turnover is between 20 and 25 times a year on the average. This means that it takes about two weeks for all foods to move from the receiving dock to a customer's stomach; for liquor, the turnover is between 7 and 10 times a year. Because there is no generally accepted rule-of-thumb inventory turnover figure in the hospitality industry,

> **inventory turnover**
> Equal to: (actual cost of products used, or sold, divided by the average inventory value kept at the hospitality operation).

however, an operation must decide what represents a good turnover figure for its business. A full discussion of how to calculate optimal stock levels can be found in Chapter 8.

Percentage of Sales Volume

Various rules of thumb exist regarding the appropriate amount of inventory that should be on hand at any one particular point in time to accommodate the hospitality operation's expected level of business. For instance, a full-service restaurant should have an inventory of food, beverage, and nonfood supplies that is equal in dollar value to no more than 1 percent of its annual sales volume. An annual sales volume of $1 million, therefore, needs about $10,000 worth of inventory at all times to support it.

A related rule of thumb suggests that the food inventory should be no more than about one-third of the average monthly food costs. The food inventory should not exceed this level unless other financial incentives to purchase unusually large quantities exist. As with all rules of thumb, though, generalizations can be dangerous. However, they provide a quick method that can be used to evaluate the buyer's procurement performance.

Stockouts

A stockout occurs when you cannot serve a customer a particular item because you do not have it on hand. The number of stockouts an operation encounters indicates the amount of inventory held. Several stockouts suggest an unreasonably low stock level. Few or no stockouts indicate a high stock level. Again, an operation wants to reach an optimal stock level, which means it probably must accept some stockouts. How many to accept is, of course, a matter for managerial policy.

Number of Late Deliveries

late deliveries Shipments received after the time they were expected.

A buyer may or may not be able to control a supplier's delivery schedule. But he or she certainly can complain when deliveries are late. If too many **late deliveries** occur, a supervisor may rightfully ask, "Why do you continue to buy from this purveyor?"

Number of Items That Must Be Returned to Suppliers

A buyer cannot always control defective deliveries, but he or she can complain about them. Also, a supervisor can pose the question: "Why continue to buy from a supplier who delivers defective goods?" Returned and late deliveries are to be avoided in the hospitality industry. If a buyer runs out of steak because the meat was not up to standard or late, he or she can hardly tell a customer to come back for it tomorrow.

Number of Back Orders

back order When your shipment is incomplete because the vendor did not have the item in stock, the invoice will state that the item is back ordered. You will receive the item later.

This issue is similar to the previous two. Usually, a buyer does not like **back orders** and normally will not tolerate many of them.

Checking AP Prices

Some companies periodically check the AP prices of other suppliers against the AP prices they are paying their current suppliers. These prices may not always be equal because of differences in overall value between suppliers. If wide disparities appear, however, the buyer is either negligent or dishonest. It is, of course, time consuming and tedious for supervisors to make these comparisons. It is not at all easy to compare values and EP costs. Also, if supervisors do not deal in the marketplace every day, it will be hard for them to keep track of current market prices.

Other Performance Indicators

There are many other performance indicators, but they are merely variations of the ones we have discussed. For instance, some large companies go to a lot of trouble to calculate such standard ratios as average inventory as a percentage of sales, average inventory as a percentage of total assets, and average inventory as a percentage of annual purchases. These standards, all variations on the materials budget, are subsequently compared with actual percentages.

When evaluating purchasing performance, wise supervisors will establish clearly defined and easily measured goals. In view of the variety of performance evaluations used throughout the industry, the safest conclusion is that supervisors should continually evaluate a buyer's procurement performance by monitoring: (1) the number of stockouts, (2) the inventory stock levels, (3) the percentage of **returns**, (4) losses from overbuying, (5) losses from the user's refusal of an item, and (6) inventory turnover.

Another major problem in performance evaluation is how to **evaluate the part-time buyer**. The measurements we have already discussed do apply, but the thorny question of how much emphasis to place on this part-time activity remains. For instance, a buyer–chef may be primarily involved in food production. Hence, his or her purchasing performance may be less important to the operation. If buying is a part-time activity, the chef may be unable to devote sufficient attention to it. Is this the chef's fault? Should he or she be reprimanded if the stock turnover is too low? Clearly, another dimension enters the picture whenever the part-time buyer's performance is measured.

returns Items returned by the buyer to the supplier because they are unusable. Typically, something is returned because it is the wrong item, or the item is damaged in some way.

evaluating the part-time buyer Process of establishing performance objectives and appraising how well employees achieve them. In the case of part-time buyers, it is critical to establish guidelines that represent fairly the impact buying performance will have on the overall performance evaluation.

Key Words and Concepts

Aggregate buying group	Corporate vice president of purchasing
Approved supplier list	Direct control system
Approved supplier	Directing
Back order	Ending inventory
Backdoor selling	Equipment testing
Beginning inventory	Ethics code
Bill-paying procedure	Evaluating the part-time buyer
Blanket order discount	Favoring suppliers
Budgeting	Free sample
Cash discount	Gifts from suppliers
Cash on delivery (COD)	Group purchasing organization (GPO)
Compensation	Indirect control system
Communal buying	Inventory turnover
Controlling	Job description
Co-op purchasing	Job specification
Co-op	Late deliveries

Key Words and Concepts (continued)

Materials budget

On-the-job training (OJT)

Operational performance

Organizing

Personal purchase

Planning

Price limits

Procurement performance

Promotional discount

Quality control

Quality standard

Quantity discount

Reciprocity

Returns

Selection and procurement policies

Shared buying

Shopping procedures

Staffing

Steward

Steward sale

Supervisory style

Supporting local suppliers

Systems mentality

Trade relations

Training

User–buyer

Volume discount

Questions and Problems

1. Describe the typical organizational patterns for the independent operation and for the multiunit chain operation.

2. Explain how a co-op purchasing organization works.

3. Assume that you are the owner of a small restaurant and you have the opportunity to join a purchasing co-op. Should you do it? Why or why not?

4. What are the major responsibilities of a vice president of purchasing?

5. Why do you think central distribution can be unprofitable? Are there any benefits, other than monetary, associated with central distribution? If so, what are they?

6. Develop a job specification for a full-time buyer. Which three broad areas should be included in this specification?

7. What is the main difference between a direct and an indirect control system?

8. List three critical issues that should be addressed in a company's selection and procurement plan

9. A franchisee may purchase from a company commissary. List some advantages and disadvantages to this purchasing decision.

10. Briefly describe a national contract. What is the primary advantage of such a contract?

Questions and Problems (continued)

11. Define or briefly explain these terms:

    a. Job specification

    b. Job description

    c. Purchasing policies

    d. Quantity limits

    e. Price limits

    f. Reciprocal buying

    g. Performance evaluation

    h. Materials budget

    i. Inventory turnover

    j. Stockout

    k. Approved supplier list

12. Briefly describe the buyer's major working relationship with the accountant and with the sales manager.

13. What are some specific conflicts that can occur between the full-time buyer and the chef, and between the full-time buyer and the housekeeper?

14. Explain why a hospitality organization might create several buyer–user positions.

15. What is the buyer's typical responsibility regarding the personal purchases employees make?

16. Name three advantages and three disadvantages of taking the time to shop around for the best value.

17. What are some disadvantages of accepting promotional discounts from suppliers?

18. If you had your preference, which method would you use to evaluate a buyer's procurement performance? Which method would you ignore?

19. What are some advantages that a hospitality company gains when it insists that all of the company buyers use an approved supplier list?

20. What would be the approximate food, beverage, and nonfood-supplies inventory value of a full-service restaurant with an annual sales volume of $600,000?

21. Given these data, compute the inventory turnover.

    Beginning inventory: $15,000

    Cost of goods sold: $325,000

    Ending inventory: $12,000

Experiential Exercises

1. What do you think are the major advantages and disadvantages of centralizing the purchasing responsibilities in a hospitality operation?
    a. What do you think the major advantage is?
    b. What do you think the major disadvantage is?
    c. Ask an independent owner–operator of a full-service restaurant to comment on your answer.
    d. Ask the manager of a company-owned, fast-food operation that is part of a chain to comment on your answer.
    e. Prepare a report that includes your answer and the owner–operator's and manager's comments.

2. Search online, in trade magazines, and in local newspapers for two examples of job specifications and job descriptions for a food buyer or purchasing director (examples are provided in Figure 6.6).
    a. Prepare an advertisement for a food buyer to be used on an online job-posting site.
    b. Prepare an ad for a purchasing manager to be used in a local newspaper.

3. Assume that you are a hotel manager.
    a. Devise formal policies for:
        * Accepting supplier gifts
        * Establishing quantity limits
        * Accepting free samples
    b. Show your formal policies to a hotel manager and ask for comments.
    c. Prepare a report that includes your policies and the manager's comments, and the reasoning that led to your policy statements.

4. Develop a two-week buyer's training program for a bartender who soon will be promoted to liquor buyer–bartender.

5. Assume you are a hotel manager. Develop a list of performance evaluation criteria you would use to evaluate the buyer–housekeeper's procurement activity. Briefly discuss the reasoning that led to your list.

6. Assume that you are a restaurant manager. The food buyer and chef are blaming each other for the low quality of steak dinners. The chef claims that the buyer is purchasing inferior meat. The buyer contends that the chef's employees are abusing the product. How would you solve this conflict?
    a. Prepare a one-page report explaining how you would solve this conflict.
    b. Contact a local restaurant manager and ask him or her to review your answer.
    c. Submit your report and the manager's comments.

Experiential Exercises (continued)

7. Assume that you have been instructed to purchase your fresh produce from one specific supplier, who happens to be a close friend of your employer. This supplier has back-ordered you on several occasions. What would you do to improve this situation?

    a. Prepare a one-page report explaining how you would improve this situation.

    b. Contact a local restaurant manager and ask him or her to review your answer.

    c. Submit your report and the manager's comments.

 References

1. Fern Glazer, "Outsourcing Pays: Delicious Dividends," *Nation's Restaurant News,* 44, no. 14 (July 12, 2010):1. http://search.proquest.com.libaccess.sjlibrary.org/docview/73 4349724?accountid=10361. See also Catherine R. Cobb, "Midsize Operators Team up for Purchasing Power," *Nation's Restaurant News*, August 18, 2008, 42(32), pp. 1, 53; Anonymous, "Denny's Franchise Association to Form Purchasing Co-op, Marketing Advisory Council," *Marketing Weekly News*, April 18, 2009, p. 36. Lindsey Ramsey, "Strength in Numbers," *Foodservice Director,* 23, no. 12 (December 15, 2010):42–44. *Hospitality & Tourism Complete, EBSCOhost.*

2. For an in-depth discussion of the advantages and disadvantages of centralized purchasing, see M. C. Warfel and Marion L. Cremer, *Purchasing for Food Service Managers*, 5th ed. (Berkeley, CA: McCutchan, 2005). See also: David Hannon, "Purchasing Drives Deeper into Logistics," *Purchasing*, July 26, 2009; Chris Crowell, "Purchasing Partnerships," March 6, 2009, www.hotelworldnetwork.com/day5; P. F. Johnson and Michiel R. Leenders, "Building a Corporate Supply Function," *Journal of Supply Chain Management*, 44, no. 3 (07, 2008):39–52, http://search.proquest.com .libaccess.sjlibrary.org/docview/235204318?accountid=10361.

3. Patt Patterson, "What Qualities Make a Top-Notch Restaurant Food Buyer?" *Nation's Restaurant News*, January 19, 1987, p. 51. See also John Lawn, "Common Mistakes Purchasing Managers Make," *Food Management*, July 2007, 42, p. 2; Rick Obinger, "A Day in the Life Of . . . ," *Nation's Restaurant News,* June 20, 2005, 39(25), pp. 54–55.

4. Scott Williams, "The Hiring Process, from Beginning to End," *Executive Housekeeping Today*, 33, no. 10 (2011):20–22. See also "Getting Job Descriptions Down on Paper," *Hospitality Upgrade*, Fall 2005, pp. 170–171; Hank Darlington, "Why Strong Job Descriptions Are a Must for Success," *Kitchen & Bath Design News,* 31, no. 7 (2013): 26–27.

References (continued)

5. Two volumes that supervisors should consult are: John R. Walker and Jack E. Miller, *Supervision in the Hospitality Industry: Applied Human Resources*, 7th ed. (New York: John Wiley & Sons, 2012); Miki Lane, Marilynne Malkin, Wendy Shanken, and Dennis Cavendish, *Stepping Up: A Road Map for New Supervisors, Participant Workbook* (New York: John Wiley & Sons, 2007).

6. Robert Carey, "Doing the Right Thing," *Successful Meetings,* October 2004, 53(11), pp. 34–39. See also Anthony Marshall, "Nip Vendor Bribes in the Bud Before They Bloom," *Hotel and Motel Management,* October 1, 2007, 222(17), p. 8; Jake Kanter, "20% of Buyers Have Been Offered Bribes by Suppliers," *Supply Management,* April 24, 2008, 13(9), p. 11; *Buylines,* See also Laura L. Flippin, "Honing a Compliant Gifts Policy: The Trends We Are Seeing Today," *Venulex Legal Summaries* (2013):1–3; Laura Spence and Michael Bourlakis, "The Evolution from Corporate Social Responsibility to Supply Chain Responsibility: The Case of Waitrose," *Supply Chain Management*, 14, no. 4 (2009):291–302. doi:http://dx.doi.org/10.1108/13598540910970126. Stuary Pfeifer "Tomato Firm Owner Gets 6-Year Prison Sentence for Price-Fixing," *Los Angeles Times*, February 13, 2013. http://search.proquest.com/docview/1286874968?account id=10361.

7. Patt Patterson, "Distributor: Communication Key to Relationships," *Nation's Restaurant News*, February 25, 1991, p. 46.

THE PURCHASE SPECIFICATION: AN OVERALL VIEW

The Purpose of This Chapter

After reading this chapter, you should be able to:

- Recall why hospitality organizations use purchase specifications.

- Provide examples of information that should be included on purchase specifications.

- Identify factors that influence the information included on purchase specifications and who writes them.

- Analyze the potential problems related to purchase specifications.

- Evaluate how optimum quality is related to specifications.

- Compare and contrast methods for measuring quality, including the use of government grades and packers' brands.

WHY HOSPITALITY OPERATIONS USE SPECIFICATIONS

product specification
Same as a purchase specification but does not contain any information about supplier services the buyer wants.

product identification
Another term for product specification.

purchase specification A concise description of the quality, size, weight, count, and other quality factors desired for a particular item. Usually also includes some description of the desired supplier services a buyer wants.

A **product specification**, sometimes referred to as a **product identification**, is a description of all the characteristics in a product required to fill a certain production and/or service need. It typically includes product information that can be verified on delivery and that can be communicated easily from buyers to suppliers.

Unlike the product specification, which includes only information about the product, the **purchase specification** implies a much broader concept. The purchase specification includes all product information, but in addition, it includes information regarding the pertinent supplier services required by the buyer.

Large hospitality companies normally prepare purchase specifications. They usually seek long-term relationships with several primary sources and intermediaries and, before entering into these relationships, want to iron out every detail concerning product characteristics and desired supplier services. Smaller hospitality firms, on the other hand, tend to shop around for products on a day-to-day basis. These companies concentrate their efforts on preparing and using product specifications. If, for example, a particular company's supplier services are found lacking, these buyers will seek an alternative supplier who provides at least some of the desired supplier services.

Preparing detailed purchase specifications is not an easy task. It can be time consuming, and a shortage of time can be a major obstacle. If you plan to invest the time, money, and effort needed to develop adequate purchase specifications, you must be prepared to study the product's characteristics. Among the best sources here are the references distributed by the U.S. Department of Agriculture (USDA). Many libraries carry these materials, or you can acquire them from USDA offices or state agriculture offices. (These materials are particularly attractive because you can reproduce them without violating a copyright.) Further, most of these materials are now available online at the USDA's website.

Produce Marketing Association (PMA)
Trade association representing members who market fresh fruits, vegetables, and related products worldwide. Its members are involved in the production, distribution, retail, and foodservice sectors of the industry.

North American Meat Institute (NAMI) Trade association representing meat producers, packers, and processors.

Other references are available as well. A quick search online will find numerous examples of purchasing guidelines used in the hospitality industry. Further, various product sources, such as apple and potato growers, also publish literature depicting characteristics of their products. Industry associations, such as the **Produce Marketing Association (PMA)** and the **North American Meat Institute (NAMI)**, similarly publish and distribute a significant amount of information that you can use to prepare specifications for fresh produce and meats. Plus, you can always find a supplier waiting to help you, especially if you buy from that supplier.

However, you must decide for yourself the product quality and supplier services you are seeking. You cannot always expect to find a neat formula to guide you. This book offers several considerations that you should examine, but eventually you must make your own decisions concerning these other variables. You must also keep in mind that a purchase specification should contain more than just a brief description of a product.

"Specs," or specifications, have several basic purposes and advantages, the primary ones being that: (1) they serve as quality control standards and as cost control standards (in these respects, specifications are important aspects of a hospitality operation's overall control system); (2) they help to avoid misunderstandings between suppliers, buyers, users, and other company officials; (3) in a buyer's absence, they allow someone else to fill in temporarily; (4) they serve as useful training devices for assistant buyers and manager trainees; and (5) they are essential when a company wants to set down all relevant aspects of something it wants to purchase, to submit a list of these aspects to two or more suppliers, and to ask these suppliers to indicate (bid) the price they will charge for the specific product or service.

In short, specifications are sounding boards for your ideas through which you detail every relevant consideration. By contrast, purchase orders are much less involved. After you know what you want and from whom you want it, completing a purchase order is a formality. It is a legal formality, however: a contract between you and a supplier that he or she will deliver goods at a specific time, for a specific price, to a specific place. The specification lays out the parameters of what you must have. The purchase order is a written or sometimes verbal—for example, over the telephone—contract that arranges an actual transaction.

WHAT INFORMATION DOES A SPEC INCLUDE?

A spec can be very short; it might include only a product's brand name—nothing else. Alternately, it might include several pages of detailed information, which is often the case with equipment specifications.

Be aware that specifications are sometimes categorized as either **formal** or **informal specifications**. A formal specification is apt to be extremely lengthy, perhaps several pages of information. Government agencies typically prepare formal specifications. The average hospitality enterprise owner–manager may prepare informal specifications, perhaps just a bit of information regarding product **yield**, quality, and packaging. You should not assume that the person preparing an informal specification is not cognizant of all the other information normally found on a formal one. It is just that the typical operator does not spend so much time writing.

1. **The Performance Requirement, or the Intended Use, of the Product or Service.** The **intended use** is usually considered the most important piece of information. You must have a clear idea of what purpose the product serves and how it will be handled.

2. **The Exact Name of the Product or Service.** You must note the exact name, as well as the exact type of product you want. For example, you cannot simply note that you want olives; you must note that you want black olives, green olives, or anchovy-stuffed olives. In some

formal specification
Another term for purchase specification.

informal specification
Less-precise product specification. Usually includes only information the vendor uses to describe the product.

yield   The net weight or volume of a food item after it has been processed and made ready for sale to the guest.

intended use   Refers to the performance requirement of a product or service, which is noted on the specification. Considered to be the most important piece of information on a specification.

instances, you must be extremely careful to indicate the correct name and/or type of merchandise desired, or you are apt to be disappointed at delivery time.

packer's brand name
Very specific indication of product quality. More precise than a brand name. A packer's personal grading system. Usually intended to take the place of federal government grades.

brand name Indication of product quality. A typical selection factor for purchased items, especially when purchasing beverage alcohols.

equal to or better Tells the vendor that the buyer will accept a substitute item if it is the same, or better, quality.

U.S. quality grades
Rating system used by the federal government to indicate the quality of food products. Not all foods have established federal government quality grading standards.

USDA Agricultural Marketing Service (AMS)
Agency that establishes federal grading standards for several food products, under authority of the Agricultural Marketing Act.

3. **The Packer's Brand Name, if Appropriate. Packers' brand names** are an indication of quality. Some items, such as fresh produce, do not normally carry instantly recognizable **brand name** identification. Many other items do, however, and a buyer may be interested primarily in only one or two brands and not any others. If you do indicate a brand name on the spec, you may want to add the words "or equivalent" next to it. This ensures that more than one supplier can compete for your business. By noting merely the brand name, you may reduce the opportunity to shop around because usually only one supplier in your area will carry that product.

In lieu of the words "or equivalent," some buyers prefer to add the words **equal to or better** to their brand name preferences noted on the specs. This phrase is used in conjunction with a brand name to indicate that the product quality characteristics desired must be similar or "superior" to the brand identified. The drawbacks with these words are that there may be several superior brands and that it may be very difficult for buyers to make a sound purchase decision if they are unfamiliar with some of them.

At times, it is very important to insist on a certain brand name and avoid all other comparable brands. For instance, if a recipe has been developed that calls for a certain brand of mayonnaise, the buyer should not purchase another brand unless it is compatible with that recipe. In this case, the finished product may be unacceptable if a different brand is used.

4. **U.S. Quality Grade, if Appropriate.** The federal government has developed **U.S. quality grades** to allow the buyer the option of using an independent opinion of product quality when preparing specifications. A good place to view U.S. quality grades online is at the **USDA Agricultural Marketing Service (AMS).** This site provides information on how to specify numerous food products.

Unfortunately, because grading generally is a voluntary procedure, many items in the channel of distribution may not be graded. However, you can at least indicate a desired grade, along with the notation "or equivalent." This will enable suppliers who do not have graded merchandise to bid for your business. Also, these suppliers then have a quality standard to guide them. Some states also have grading systems. For example, Wisconsin was the first state to establish its own stringent grading procedures to use for some dairy items.

5. **Size Information.** In most instances, buyers must indicate the size desired for a particular item. For some products, such as portion-cut steaks, buyers can indicate an exact weight. For other items, though, such as large, wholesale cuts of beef or whole chickens, usually

buyers can only indicate the desired **weight range**. In some instances, the size of an item, such as lemons or lobster tails, is indicated by its **count**, that is, the number of items per case, per pound, or per 10 pounds.

6. **Acceptable Trim, or Acceptable Waste.** For some products, including many fresh foods, you may need to indicate the maximum amount of **waste** or **trim** you will tolerate. Another way to say this is to note the minimum edible yield of a product you will accept. For instance, fresh lettuce may have varying degrees of waste, depending on how the food distributor processes it. Some lettuce is cleaned and chopped, ready-to-serve, whereas a typical head of lettuce has an edible yield of much less than 100 percent. Of course, you expect to pay much more for the product that has little or no waste.

7. **Package Size.** In most situations, you will need to indicate the size of the container you desire. For instance, an appropriate standard can size number (such as a No. 10 can) must be noted when purchasing canned vegetables.

8. **Type of Package.** In some cases, the type of packaging materials used is highly standardized. For example, dairy products packaging must meet minimum standards. This is not the case for other items. Frozen products, for instance, should come in packaging sufficient to withstand the extreme cold without breaking. Some suppliers scrimp on this, and although the quality of the product may meet your specification, the poor packaging will result in a rapid deterioration of this once-acceptable item.

As discussed in Chapter 4, packaging can add considerable cost to the items you purchase and is a consideration when evaluating form value. In some cases, the value of the packaging may exceed the value of the food or beverage ingredient. The cost of the packaging of single-serve packets of salt, for instance, can easily be higher than the cost of the salt.

When specifying the desired type of packaging, some buyers may require suppliers to use recyclable packaging materials. Alternatively, buyers may request reusable packaging, such as the plastic tubs some suppliers use to deliver fresh fish.

9. **Packaging Procedure.** Some products are wrapped individually and conveniently layered in the case. Others are **slab-packed**, that is, tossed into the container. The more care taken in the **packaging procedure**, the higher the as-purchased (AP) price is apt to be. However, carefully packaged products will have a longer shelf life. In addition, they will tend to maintain their appearance and culinary-quality characteristics much longer than those products that are packaged indiscriminately.

Another packaging consideration concerns the number of individual containers that normally come packaged in a case lot. For instance,

weight range Indication of the approximate size of a product the buyer wishes to purchase. Used when it is impossible or impractical to specify an exact weight.

count The number of pieces in a container. Alternately, the number of smaller containers in a larger container.

waste Unusable part of a product that occurs when it is processed. Most waste is unavoidable, but sometimes avoidable waste occurs due to mistakes and carelessness.

trim Another term for waste.

slab-packed Refers to items tossed into a container in no particular order or style. An inexpensive packing procedure, though it can cause breakage and other quality deterioration for some products.

packaging procedure Way in which items are packed in a larger container capable of protecting the items while they are in-transit and storage.

broken case   Refers to the purchase of less than one case because the vendor is willing to break open a case and sell you only part of it. Few vendors will do this for you.

preservation and/or **processing method** Preservation methods are used to extend the shelf life of a food or beverage product. Processing methods are used to enhance the product's taste and other culinary characteristics.

it is traditional for No. 10 cans of foods to come packed six to a case. However, some buyers cannot afford to purchase six cans, or they cannot use six cans. Will the supplier sell fewer than six cans; that is, will he or she "break" the case? Buyers who request **broken cases** run the risk of having few suppliers willing to compete for their business.

10. **Preservation and/or Processing Method.** For some products, you will be able to identify two or more **preservation** or **processing methods**. For instance, you could order refrigerated meats or frozen meats, canned green beans or frozen green beans, and refrigerated beer or nonrefrigerated beer.

   You also could specify unique types of preservation methods, such as smoked fish instead of salted fish, irradiated poultry instead of nonirradiated poultry, oil-cured olives instead of brine-cured olives, and genetically altered tomatoes instead of natural tomatoes.

The type of preservation and/or processing method selected often influences the taste and other culinary characteristics of the finished food product. Consequently, it is important for you to be familiar with recipe requirements before altering this part of the spec.

11. **Point of Origin.** You may want to indicate the exact part of the world that a specific item must come from. This is a rather important consideration for fresh fish. For instance, you may need to specify that your lobster must come from Maine and not from Australia.

   Buyers may want to note the **point of origin** on some specs for several reasons. One is that the flavor, texture, and so forth of an item can differ dramatically among growing regions. Another reason is that you may to want to support local primary sources (see Figure 7.1). Restaurants that feature local and sustainable products are very particular regarding where their products come from. The menu may state that an item comes from a particular producing region in the world; if so, it would be a violation of **truth-in-menu** regulations to serve an alternative product. Freshness can be another important consideration because buyers may specify nearby points of origin to ensure product quality. And, finally, buyers may indicate where a product cannot come from, instead of where it must come from, to adhere to various company policies and/or legal restrictions. For instance, for political reasons, some companies may refuse to purchase products that come from certain parts of the world.

point of origin   Refers to the part of the world where a product originates. Important selection factor for some food items, as the point of origin can have a significant impact on their culinary quality.

truth-in-menu Guidelines menu planners use to avoid unintentionally misleading the customer by ensuring accurate descriptions and prices of all menu offerings. Alternately, refers to legislation prohibiting misrepresentations on the menu.

ripeness   A term used to indicate that a food or beverage product is fully developed, mature, and ready to be used in production, or ready to eat or drink.

12. **Degree of Ripeness.** This is important for fresh produce. The **ripeness** concept also applies to beef items; for example, you may desire a specific amount of "age" on the item. Wines have a similar system that reflects, among other pieces of information, the year of production.

13. **Form.** This is an important consideration for many processed items. For example, do you want your cheese in a brick, or would you rather have it sliced? Do you want your roast beef raw, or do you want it precooked?

FIGURE 7.1 California Milk Advisory Board point of origin ad.
Courtesy of the California Milk Advisory Board

BREAKFAST**BEAT**

Vol. 32 • March 2016 / An Official Newsletter of the American Egg Board

incredible!

A.M. Eats: Minneapolis

American Egg Board

A classic Minnesota joke pokes fun at local traditional German-Scandinavian cuisine by having regional alter egos, Ole and Lena, stating they find ketchup too tangy. As

today's Minneapolis restaurant breakfasts include shakshuka, housemade chorizo and harissa, someone is going to have to write a new punch line. Here's a sampling:

- **Ecuadorian Baked Eggs:** with mole-spiced black beans, queso fresco, white cheddar, avocado crème, salsa verde, llapangacho (potato cake) and choice of tortillas (The Mill Northeast)
- **Toad In a Hole:** sandwich with egg, bacon and cheddar; sides of corn cakes and piquillo pepper sauce (Sun Street Breads)
- **Walleye Benedict:** walleye & shrimp

cakes, poached eggs, house-made hollandaise and dill (Longfellow Grill)
- **Savory Waffle:** kale/quinoa/feta waffle, pineapple-pear chutney, lemon rosemary butter, bacon lardons, sunny-side egg, sunflower seeds and maple syrup (Birchwood Café)
- **Eiffel Tower:** two sausage patties stacked between three buttermilk pancakes, topped with an over-easy egg (Bon Vie)
- **Lucia's Breakfast Panini:** peppers, onions, ham, cheese, eggs and red pepper spread (Lucia's)

Raising Veggies

Both Andrew Freeman and Baum+Whiteman predict vegetables will be front and center this year. The **NRA's 2016 "What's Hot" survey** of American Culinary Federation chefs agrees, finding locally sourced veggies to be the No. 3 hottest trend.

Vegetables are seasonal items, leading to menu changes and excitement. They're attractive to health conscious diners, locavores and flexitarians. And vegetable-forward operations serving complex veggie

entrées are the culinary darlings of those concerned with sustainability.

The perfect complement for veggies?
Eggs. Eggs add protein to vegetable dishes, create well-balanced meals for vegetarians and add indulgence to grain dishes. At BEC in NYC, guests order ciabatta rolls with two eggs, roasted sweet potato, grilled zucchini, eggplant, red onion, Swiss chard and a goat cheese spread. In L.A., at Sqirl, soft eggs crown salads of market greens, chicories,

shaved root vegetables and avocado. And in Minneapolis, the Birchwood Cafe serves a scramble containing beets, pickled radish, roasted fennel, thyme and garlic chevre mousse. **Nothing wrong with steak & eggs, but veggies & eggs has a nice ring too.**

FIGURE 7.2 Trade associations provide information useful to buyers.
Courtesy of the American Egg Board

---

trade association standard Minimum performance standards for items the association members produce.

National Sanitation Foundation (NSF) International Provides sanitation certification for FFE items that meet its standards.

14. **Color.** Some items are available in more than one color. For example, buyers can order fresh red, green, or yellow peppers.

15. **Trade Association Standards.** Some trade associations establish minimum performance standards for items. These **trade association standards** can be commonly found in their trade publications (see Figure 7.2). For instance, the **National Sanitation Foundation (NSF) International** certification seal on a piece of food-production equipment testifies to the equipment's sanitary acceptability.

16. **Approved Substitutes.** Some buyers make it a habit to include on some specs a list of acceptable substitutes that the suppliers can deliver if they are out of the normal item. This can save a great deal of time and effort because suppliers would not have to call buyers every time a product shortage occurs. Buyers also may like this convenience. Unfortunately, before

determining **approved substitutes**, buyers must ensure that they are compatible with production and service needs. So, although this notation on each spec saves time and trouble eventually, it can be more difficult in the short run to spend the time needed to test all potential substitute items.

17. **Expiration Date.** Many buyers will not accept products if they are concerned about possible quality deterioration. To avoid this problem, they may indicate on some specs that suppliers must prove that the products delivered are not too old. For instance, some product labels list "sell-by" dates; these are sometimes referred to as **pull dates**, **best-if-used-by dates**, or **freshness dates**. For such items, buyers may want to add to their specs some reference to these **expiration dates**.

18. **Chemical Standards and Organic and Natural Standards.** Buyers might specify a particular level of acceptable chemical use or **chemical standard** for some of the items they purchase. Or they may prefer that products meet the optional USDA standards verifying that a product is organic. As described in Chapter 4, in order for an item to be labeled organic, it must meet certain criteria regarding how it is raised or grown and processed without chemicals and preservatives. If the grower or manufacturer does not meet all the USDA standards or does not want to pay for the extra inspection, they may still classify the item as natural or use terms such as free-range or hormone-free. If purchasing and selling organic items is part of the values and concept of an operation, products it uses must adhere to those **organic and natural standards**.

19. **The Test or Inspection Procedure.** This is the procedure you intend to use when checking the items delivered to you or the services performed for you. Generally, this is the logical outcome of specifying the intended use. After you note the intended use, you should be prepared to indicate the tests or inspection procedures you will use to see whether your purchases will perform adequately.

20. **Cost and Quantity Limitations.** Buyers might indicate how much of the item or service is to be purchased at any one time. In addition, they might require an item to be removed from production and a substitute item to be sought when the cost limits are approached.

21. **General Instructions.** In addition to specific details, buyers might include such general details as: (a) delivery procedures, if possible; (b) credit terms; (c) the allowable number of returns and **stockouts**; (d) whether the product purchased must be available to all units in the hospitality company, regardless of a unit's location; and (e) other supplier services desired, like sales help in devising new uses for a product.

22. **Specific Instructions to Bidders, if Applicable.** Suppliers who bid for your business may want to know: (a) your bidding procedures, (b) your criteria for supplier selection, and (c) the qualifications and capabilities you expect from them. This is provided in the **instructions to bidders**, which spells out the required processes vendors must follow.

approved substitute A product that a buyer can purchase in lieu of the typical one that is usually purchased.

pull date Date beyond which a product (usually food) should not be used, or should not be sold.

best-if-used-by date, freshness date, expiration date Another term for pull date.

chemical standards The amount and/or type of additives a buyer is willing to accept in purchased products.

organic and natural standards Organic products must meet specific standards established by the USDA, whereas the term natural is generally used for items that may not meet all standards or have not been voluntarily inspected by the USDA.

stockout Running out of a product; not having it available for guests who want it.

instructions to bidders Required process vendors must follow when submitting a competitive bid. Typically also includes a description of how the winning bid will be determined and the qualifications vendors need to be allowed to bid.

WHAT INFLUENCES THE TYPES OF INFORMATION INCLUDED ON THE SPEC AND WHO WRITES THEM?

Four potential decision-making entities are involved with deciding what to include in a specification: (1) the owner–manager or another top management or corporate official, (2) the buyer, (3) the user, or (4) some combination of these three. It is unlikely that the buyer would write the specs without the advice of the supervisor and of the users of the items to be purchased. All companies seem to approach this issue differently, but the buyers and users do most of the legwork, all the while staying within overall company guidelines. That is, a top company official normally sets the tone for the specs, and the buyers or users complete the details. The biggest problem with this participatory approach is agreeing on what is a main guideline and what is a minute detail.

Several factors must be assessed before determining what information to include on a specification. Eight of these are the following:

1. **Company Goals and Policies.** These are probably most important. Overall managerial guidelines must be consulted before buyers write specs. For instance, McDonald's focuses heavily on corporate responsibility. Their global "Antibiotics & Animal Cloning" policy "prohibits antibiotics belonging to classes of compounds approved for use in human medicine when used solely for growth promotion purposes." And they "do not currently support the use of animal products sourced from cloned animals in [their] supply chain."[1] It would, therefore, behoove the McDonald's buyer to include this information on their beef and poultry specs.

2. **The Time and Money Available.** Industry members continually argue the costs and benefits of written specifications. Obviously, we consider the time and money required for preparing specifications to be well spent.

3. **The Production Systems the Hospitality Operation Uses.** If, for example, a restaurant broils its hamburgers instead of grilling them, the fat content in its ground beef should be a bit higher than usual to compensate for the additional loss of juices that can occur if meat is broiled to the well-done state.

4. **Storage Facilities.** If, for example, freezer space is limited, a buyer may have to purchase larger amounts of fresh vegetables; a specification might carry this reminder.

5. **Employee Skill Levels.** Generally, the lower the skill level, the more buyers must rely on portion-controlled foods, one-step cleaners, and other convenience items. The trade-off is between a higher AP price and a lower wage scale. The balance in these issues is not always clear-cut; this is a good example of the trade-off concept that usually arises in value analysis (which we discussed in Chapter 5).

6. **Menu Requirements.** For example, live lobster on the menu forces a buyer to include the words "live lobster" on the specification.

7. **Sales Prices or Budgetary Limitations.** If, for example, a restaurant is located in a very competitive market, its menu prices may be fixed by its competition. This fact may force a buyer to include cost limits for some or all food specifications.

8. **Service Style.** A fine dining restaurant may want to use only fresh products that can be prepared to order. On the other hand, a university dining facility or a buffet restaurant

needs some food items that have a relatively long hot-holding life because the food may remain on a steam table for a while. This type of information might be included on the specs, especially the specs for prepared food entrées.

Another concern is who actually writes the specifications. Generally, five options are available to the hospitality operation, including

1. Company personnel can write the specs. This option assumes that the necessary talent to write them exists in the company somewhere.

2. Many specs can be found in **industry and government publications**. They are most commonly available online but some are still produced in print form and/or on CDs. Although they may not fit your needs exactly, they are at least a good starting point (see Figures 7.3 and 7.4).

> **industry and government publications** Materials printed and distributed by government agencies covering a variety of subjects useful to businesses and consumers. For example, some of these publications detail quality measures that can be used by buyers to help them prepare their specifications.

Agricultural Marketing Service	Juice Product Association
American Angus Association	Kashrut.com
American Association of Meat Processors	Muslim Consumer Group
American Bakers Association	National Association of Beverage Importers
American Berkshire Association	National Coffee Association of U.S.A., Inc.
American Beverage Association	National Cattlemen's Beef Association
American Beverage Institute	National Confectioners Association
American Cheese Society	National Fisheries Institute
American Egg Board	National Frozen and Refrigerated Foods Association
American Frozen Food Institute	National Marine Fisheries Institute
American Institute of Baking	National Pasta Association
American Meat Institute	National Pork Producers Council
American Meat Science Association	National Poultry and Food Distributors Association
American Poultry Association	National Turkey Federation
American Spice Trade Association	North American Association of Food Equipment Manufacturers
Beer Institute	North American Meat Processors Association
California Milk Advisory Board	Organic Trade Association
Canned Food Alliance	Produce Marketing Association
Chilled Food Association	Refrigerated Foods Association
Dairy Market News Branch	Retail Bakers of America
Florida Fruit and Vegetable Association	The Vegetarian Resource Group
Food and Drug Administration	U.S. Department of Agriculture
Foodservice Equipment Distributors Association	U.S. Department of Commerce
Grocery Manufacturers Association	U.S. Poultry and Egg Association
International Beverage Dispensing Equipment Association	United Egg Producers
International Dairy Food Association	United Produce Association
International Deli, Dairy, Bakery Association	Wine and Spirits Wholesalers of America
International Foodservice Manufacturers Association	Wisconsin Cheese Makers Association

FIGURE 7.3 Some government and private agencies that provide product information useful to buyers.

Diversified Business Communications. 2009. *Seafood Handbook*. Hoboken, NJ: John Wiley & Sons.

Dore, Ian. 1994. *The Smoked and Cured Seafood Guide*. Toms River, NJ: Urner Barry.

Dore, Ian. 2013. *New Fresh Seafood Buyer's Guide: A Manual for Distributors, Restaurants, and Retailers*. New York: Springer.

Farrell, Kenneth T. 2012. *Spices, Condiments, and Seasonings*. New York: Aspen Publishers.

Flick, George J. 2012. *Seafood Industry: Species, Products, Processing, and Safety*. Chichester: Wiley-Blackwell.

Green, Aliza. 2005. *Field Guide to Meat: How to Identify, Select, and Prepare Virtually Every Meat, Poultry, and Game Cut*. Philadelphia: Quirk Books.

Green, Aliza. 2007. *Field Guide to Seafood: How to Identify, Select, and Prepare Virtually Every Fish and Shellfish at the Market*. Philadelphia: Quirk Books.

Hui, Y. H. 2004. *Handbook of Frozen Foods*. Boca Raton, FL: CRC.

McVicar, Jekka. 2006. *New Book of Herbs*. Upper Saddle River, NJ: Prentice Hall.

McVicar, Jekka. 2008. *The Complete Herb Book*. Richmond Hill, Ont.: Firefly Books.

McVicar, Jekka. 2011. *Jekka's Herb Cookbook*. Richmond Hill, Ont.: Firefly Books.

Morin, Thomas H. 1985. *Nifda Canned Goods Specifications Manual*. West Lafayette, IN: Restaurant Hotel & Management. The USDA provides updated specs for canned goods at http://www.ams.usda.gov/selling-food/product-specs.

North American Meat Institute. 2014. *The Meat Buyer's Guide*. Washington, DC: North American Meat Association.

Pearson, A. M. and Tedford A. Gillett. 1996. *Processed Meats,* 3rd ed. New York: Chapman and Hall.

Peterson, James. 1996. *Fish & Shellfish: The Definitive Cook's Companion*. New York: William Morrow.

Peterson, John. 2006. *Farmer John's Cookbook: The Real Dirt on Vegetables,* 1st ed. Layton, UT: Gibbs Smith, Publisher.

Reed, Lewis. 2005 (Ebook edition, 2006). *SPECS: The Foodservice and Purchasing Specifications Manual,* Student Edition. Hoboken, NJ: John Wiley & Sons.

Romans, John R. 2000. *The Meat We Eat,* 14th ed. Upper Saddle River, NJ: Prentice Hall.

Schneider, Elizabeth. 2001. *Vegetables from Amaranth to Zucchini: The Essential Reference*. New York: William Morrow.

Tainter, Donna R. and Anthony T. Grenis. 2001. *Spices and Seasonings: A Food Technology Handbook,* 2nd ed. Hoboken, NJ: John Wiley & Sons.

Urner Barry Publications. 2011. *The Commercial Guide to Fish and Shellfish.* 2nd edition. Toms River NJ: Urner Barry.

Thomas, Cathy. 2006. *Melissa's Great Book of Produce: Everything You Need to Know About Fresh Fruits and Vegetables*. Hoboken, NJ: John Wiley & Sons.

Thomas, Cathy. 2010. *Melissa's Everyday Cooking with Organic Produce*. Hoboken, N.J.: John Wiley & Sons.

Thompson, Fred. 2006. *Big Book of Fish and Shellfish*. San Francisco: Chronicle Books.

FIGURE 7.4 Some comprehensive reference materials buyers can use to prepare product specifications.

3. You can hire an expert to help you write your specs. This is a reasonable alternative, as you can control the amount of money you spend for this service. Similarly, if you are part of a group purchasing organization, the organization will most likely have developed standard specifications for many products.

4. The USDA operates an "Acceptance Service" that permits hospitality operators to hire USDA inspectors to help prepare specs. The inspectors check the products you buy at the supplier's plant to make sure they comply with your specs (see Figure 7.5). They then stamp each item or sealed package to certify product compliance. This is often done for meat products. The acceptance service is provided for a fee, which the supplier usually pays.

FIGURE 7.5 An inspector from the USDA acceptance service will inspect the buyer's order on the supplier's premises. If the order meets the buyer's specifications, the government inspector will apply a stamp, such as the one shown here, to the package. *Courtesy of the United States Department of Agriculture*

Although this expense may be included in your AP price, the service could save you money by ensuring you that you receive exactly what you want.

5. The buyer and supplier can work together to prepare the specifications. The problem with this arrangement is that the buyer usually neglects to send the specs out to other suppliers for their bids. Also, the cooperating supplier may help slant the specs so that only he or she can provide the exact item wanted. Nevertheless, this is the option most independents find realistic, given their limited time resources and prospective order sizes.

The question of who writes the specs is important to hospitality operators because few part-time buyers have enough time to learn this task thoroughly. If operators want to prepare their own specs, they often consult outside expertise.

The reasonable compromise seems to be to hire someone on a consulting basis to help write the specs or, if this is too expensive, to work with the specs found in various trade and governmental sources. The usual approach, to huddle with a supplier, may actually be least advantageous, but it does allow operators to spend more time on other business activities.

POTENTIAL PROBLEMS WITH SPECS

As in most business activities, you should consider several costs in addition to benefits in specification writing. There are, for example, a number of clearly identifiable costs, and there are some cleverly hidden problems. Some potential problems with specs include the following:

- Delivery requirements, quality tolerance limits, cost limits, or quantity limits may appear in the specs. If these are unreasonable requirements, they usually add to the AP price, but it may be questionable whether they add to the overall value.

- Some inadvertent discrimination may be written into the specs. For example, the spec may read, "Suppliers must be within 15 miles to ensure dependable deliveries." Dealing with a supplier 16 miles away could cause legal trouble because of this.

- Worse, if a spec effectively cuts out all but one supplier, you will have wasted your time, money, and effort if your intention was to use the spec to obtain bids from several sources. You do, of course, still have the benefit of having specified very precisely what you want. This gives you a receiving standard and a basis for returning unacceptable product.

- The specifications may request a quality difficult for suppliers to obtain. This situation adds to cost but not always to value. In some situations, the quality you want cannot be tested or inspected adequately without destroying the item. In these cases, however, a sampling approach may ensure the requisite quality. Before you embark on such an expensive process, careful consideration is called for.

- Some specs rely heavily on government grades. Unfortunately, some may not be specific enough for a foodservice operator's needs. For example, there can be quite a bit of variation in what qualifies as USDA Choice beef. Also, grades do not usually take into account packaging styles, delivery schedules, and so forth. Thus, U.S. grades alone are not adequate for most operations.

- Food specifications are not static; they usually need periodic revision. For instance, a spec for oranges might include the term "Florida oranges," a perfectly reasonable requirement at certain times of the year, but during some seasons, Arizona oranges might be preferable. It costs time, money, and effort to revise specifications. Moreover, if you cannot determine exactly when to revise, you might receive something you do not want, plus, your customer might also be dissatisfied if you are forced to serve the food because you have no acceptable substitute.

bid buying When buyers shop around seeking current AP prices from vendors. The vendors are asked to quote, or bid, the prices they will charge. Intended to give the buyer competitive pricing information that will allow him or her to get the best possible value.

- The best specs in the world will be of no use to you if the other personnel in the hospitality operation are not trained to understand them and to use them appropriately. For example, a buyer may be adept in the use of specs, but if the receiving agent does not have similar expertise, he or she may accept the delivery of merchandise that is not in accord with the properly prepared specifications.

- The potential problems and costs multiply quickly if the spec is used in **bid buying**. Some of these additional problems are discussed here.

■ Getting Hit with the "Lowball"

lowball A competitive bid that is artificially low. Vendors may lowball a buyer hoping to get their foot in the door; later on they will try to hike the AP price substantially.

The term **lowball** refers to a bid that is low for some artificial or possibly deliberately dishonest reason. For instance, bidders may meet a buyer's spec head-on; that is, they may hit the minimum requirements and might even reduce their normal profit levels to win the bid. Once they are in, they may try to raise prices or lower quality.

Lowballing is a fairly standard way of doing business for suppliers trying to woo buyers away from their regular suppliers. These suppliers are willing to sacrifice a bit of revenue in the short run for the opportunity to establish a long-term and potentially more profitable arrangement. Suppliers know that once they get their foot in the door, buyers may get comfortable and stick with them through force of habit.

To avoid falling for lowball prices, buyers need to shop around frequently, which means they need to keep their specs current. This tends to keep suppliers competitive and more responsive.

■ Inequality among Bidders

If your specs are too loose, that is, if too many suppliers can meet the specs, you run the risk of finding several suppliers of differing reliability bidding for your business. Choosing one of the less-reliable suppliers can result in serious operational problems.

Sometimes, good suppliers may unintentionally differ significantly from others bidding for your business because of unanticipated changing business conditions. For instance, some suppliers who bid for your business may do so only when their regular business is slow. Consequently, you may be forced to continually change suppliers, which could cost you time, trouble, and money in the long run. In addition, although you may indeed change to receive an AP price break, when their regular business picks up, these suppliers may decide to stop bidding for yours.

■ Specifications That Are Too Tight

Tight specifications tend to eliminate variables and allow a buyer to concentrate on AP prices. Unfortunately, if only one supplier meets the buyer's specifications, that buyer will spend a lot of time, money, and effort writing specifications and receiving bids only to find there are only two choices available: take it or leave it.

Large hospitality companies sometimes run into a similar problem when they demand items that only one or two suppliers are able to deliver. For instance, a typical large hospitality firm wants to purchase products that are available nationally; this ensures that all units in the company use the same products, and this, in turn, ensures an acceptable level of quality control and cost control. However, the number of suppliers who can accommodate national distribution is limited. In addition, if you want specific supplier services, chances are you will severely restrict the number of purveyors who can provide what you want.

■ Advertising Your Own Mistakes

If your specifications are in error, you can look forward to being reminded of your mistake whenever a delivery comes in.

■ Redundant Favoritism

The buyer who writes several specs, sends them out for bid, and then rejects all of the bids except the one from the supplier he or she usually buys from anyway is a genuine annoyance. This practice is followed by some operations that must use bid buying. For example, the buyer solicits a bid for corn chips. Three companies bid, but the buyer decides to buy from supplier A because this supplier's product is always preferred. If this is the case, why seek bids?

■ Too Many Ordering and Delivering Schedules

Another potential problem with bid buying is the possibility that you will have to adjust to several suppliers' ordering and delivering schedules. A large hospitality organization can handle this extra burden. However, if a small firm is accustomed to receiving produce at 10:00 A.M., it can be a difficult readjustment for that operator to receive produce at 2:00 P.M. one week and at 9:00 A.M. the next. (We have seen this need to readjust operating procedures cause a great deal of trouble, especially when a delivery must sit on the loading dock for a while because no one is free to store it. When the receiving routine is broken, problems multiply.)

■ And Always Remember . . .

The object of bid buying is to obtain the lowest possible AP price. But if the lowest possible AP price does not, somehow, translate into an acceptable edible-portion (EP) cost, you have gained little or nothing.

The costs and benefits of specification writing are never clear, and the subject becomes more confusing when you complicate it with a bid-buying strategy. We believe writing specs is generally necessary because they help you to clarify your ideas on exactly what you want in an item. We are not so confident about the bid procedures, though. For some items, such as equipment, bids may be economically beneficial to the hospitality operator. Also, if you like the bid-buying activity, you must be prepared to put up with a variety of supplier capabilities. On the whole, however, the buyer who uses this buying plan had better know as much or more about the items as the supplier. Only large operations consistently enforce this requirement.

THE OPTIMAL QUALITY TO INCLUDE ON THE SPEC

You frequently hear references to "quality" products. To most people, a "quality" product represents something very valuable. However, when businesspersons talk about quality, they are referring to some "standard" of excellence. This standard could be high quality, medium quality, or low quality. In other words, suppliers offer products and services that vary in quality. In most cases, they can sell you a "high quality," "highest quality," "substandard quality," or almost any other quality you prefer.

It is important to keep in mind that quality is a standard: something to be decided on by company officials and then maintained throughout the operation.

We do not intend to second-guess the types of quality standards that hospitality operators develop or decide upon. Rather, our objective is to examine the typical process by which the optimal quality is determined.

WHO DETERMINES QUALITY?

Someone, or some group, must decide on a quality standard for every product or service the hospitality operation uses. If somebody decides to use a low thread-count type of sheet for the hotel beds, this decision should take into account several factors, such as the type of guests the operation caters to, the hotel type and location, and the frequency of buying replacement linen.

Most analysts agree that a hospitality operator can hardly decide on quality standards without measuring the types of quality standards his or her customers expect. As the AP prices are translated into menu prices and room rates, customers are affected. The quality of the product purchased affects customers' perceptions of the operation, too. On the other hand, for the most part, supplier services are apparent principally to management. It is clear that value has many facets.

Most hospitality operations conduct some sort of market research to determine the types of value their customers, or potential customers, seek. The owner–manager's greatest responsibility is to interpret the results of the market research and translate them into quality standards. In other words, he or she must examine: (1) the overall value retail customers expect; (2) "supplier" services, that is, the property's surroundings, service style, decor, and so on; and (3) the typical menu or room price ranges attributable to his or her type of operation. Then, the owner–manager must formulate a definition of quality standards. So, in the final analysis, the consumer really has the major say in determining the quality standards an operation establishes for most of its items.

The buyer's major role here is to maintain the quality standards that someone else has determined. Generally, the standards have some flexibility, but whatever the standards are, and whatever the degree of flexibility, a buyer must ensure that all the items purchased measure up to company expectations.

Company officials may have a bit more latitude in determining the quality standards for those operating supplies and services retail customers do not directly encounter—items such as washing machine chemicals and pest control service. In these instances, it is interesting to note the number of people who may become involved in these determinations. A large group of company personnel may help work out these quality standards. The owner–manager, the department heads, and the buyer often influence the decision. Hourly employees may also be consulted because they constantly work with many of the products and services and are, hence, most familiar with them.

Quality standards for supplies, services, and equipment normally come from the top of the company. Buyers exercise a great deal of influence in these areas, though, because they get involved in such technical questions as "Is the quality standard available?" "What will it cost?" and "Can it be tested easily?" The ultimate decision, though, usually rests with the owner–manager or, in the case of chain organizations, an executive officer.

IS THE QUALITY AVAILABLE?

Another aspect of quality a buyer must know is whether the quality desired is available at all. This is quite a practical question. It is useless to determine quality standards if the quality you want is unavailable. Oddly enough, some types of quality are too often unavailable to the hospitality operation. A chef who wants low-quality apples to make homemade applesauce may find that suppliers do not carry such low quality. (Food canners usually purchase them all.)

In addition, a buyer must pay particular attention to the possibility that the quality desired is available from only one supplier. This may or may not be advantageous. In some cases, an owner–manager may take this opportunity to build a long-term relationship with one supplier. However, some company officials are not especially eager to lose flexibility in their supplier selection.

It is easier than you think to restrict yourself unknowingly to one supplier. If this does not happen because of the quality standards you set, it may happen because of the AP price you are willing to accept.

MEASURES OF QUALITY

measures of quality
Various rating systems that can be used to determine the appropriate product quality needed to fulfill an intended use. For instance, federal government grades and brand names can be used to denote the quality desired on a specification.

A buyer is expected to be familiar with the available **measures of quality**, as well as their corresponding AP prices and ultimate values. Several objective measures of quality exist. Here are some of them.

■ Federal Government Grades

Under authority of the Agricultural Marketing Act of 1946 and related statutes, the Agricultural Marketing Service (AMS) of the USDA has issued quality grade standards for hundreds of food products including beef, poultry, and fruits and vegetables. These grade standards for food, along with standards for other agricultural products, such as cotton and tobacco, have been developed to identify the degrees of quality in the various products, thereby helping establish their usability or value.

Federal government grades are measurements that normally cannot be used as the sole indication of quality. This is true because federal government grading is not required by federal law, except for foods a government agency purchases for an approved feeding program, or for commodities that are stored under the agricultural price support and loan programs; as a result, a buyer must use other measures of quality for ungraded items. Where possible, though, U.S. grades are the primary measures of quality that buyers use most frequently, at least at some point in the overall purchasing procedure.

The federal government, by legal statute, inspects most members of the channel of food distribution. Generally, the federal government's role is to check the sanitation of production facilities and the wholesomeness of the food products throughout the distribution channel. In some instances, states have set up additional inspector-powered agencies that either complement the federal agencies or supplant them.

Ordinarily, to be graded, an item must be produced under continuous federal-government inspection. Meat and poultry items and items that require egg breaking during their production process are always made under continuous inspection, but other types of items may not be.

The federal government will provide grading services for food processors, usually those at the beginning of the channel of distribution, who elect to purchase this service. Some of these producers buy this service, and some do not. Some opt for U.S. government grading because their customers include these grade stipulations in their specifications. Alternately, in some cases, the state requires federal grading. For example, several states require fresh eggs to carry a federal quality grade shield.

limiting rule Federal regulation that stipulates if a product to be graded scores very low on one grading factor, it cannot receive a high grade regardless of its total score for all grading factors.

The grading procedure usually takes a scorecard approach with the products, beginning with a maximum of 100 points distributed among two or more grading factors. To receive the highest grade designation, a product must usually score 85 to 90 points or more. As the product loses points, it falls into a lower grade category. In addition, graders work under **limiting rules**, which stipulate that if a product scores very low on one particular factor, it cannot be granted a high grade designation regardless of its total score. The grader usually takes a sample of product and bases his or her decision on that sample.

Some buyers in the hospitality industry have been conditioned to purchase many food products primarily on the basis of U.S. government grades. The effect of government grading has ultimately been to create demand among retail consumers for specific quality levels; for example, consumers are conditioned to buy USDA Choice beef or USDA Select beef in the supermarket.

A major problem with grading is the emphasis graders place on appearance. Although appearance is an overriding criterion used in U.S. government grading, this sole criterion is dangerous for the foodservice industry because our customers are not making a purchase based solely on visual inspection but, rather, are purchasing and almost immediately evaluating the product based on taste and other culinary factors.

A number of other problems are associated with U.S. government grades. These additional difficulties include (1) the wide tolerance between grades—so much so that buyers quickly learn that when they indicate U.S. No. 1, they must also note whether they want a high 1 or a low 1 (this tolerance gap is especially wide for meat items); (2) grader discretion—graders operate under one or more **partial limiting rules**, which allow them to invoke a limiting rule or not; (3) the deceiving appearance of products—for example, some products can be dyed (like oranges), some can be waxed (like cucumbers), and some can be ripened artificially and inadequately

> **partial limiting rule**
> Grants the federal grader discretion to invoke a limiting rule or to ignore it.

(like tomatoes); (4) the possible irrelevance of grades to EP cost—for instance, a vine-ripened tomato may have a high grade and a good taste, but it may be difficult and wasteful to slice; (5) the fact that graders could slight such considerations as packaging and delivery schedules, which are important in preserving the grade—for example, a lemon may look good in the field, but if it is not packaged and transported correctly, it could be dry and shriveled when it arrives; (6) a raw food item is not a factory-manufactured product, and therefore, its quality, as well as its U.S. quality grade, can fluctuate and may not be consistent throughout the year; (7) the lack of uniformity among terms used to indicate the varying grade levels—for instance, some items are labeled with a letter, some with a number, and some with other terminology; and (8) the lack of a specific regional designation. There is, for instance, a big difference between Florida and California oranges, particularly during certain times of the year.

■ AP Prices

To some degree, quality and AP prices go hand in hand. The relationship, however, is not usually direct. One notch up in AP price does not always imply that the item's quality has also gone up one notch. AP prices, though, are considered good indicators of quality by many hospitality managers, especially novices.

■ Packers' Brands

Food and nonfood product manufacturers and processors produce products under brands they have created (manufacturers' brands) as well as private labels that may carry the name of an intermediary (such as a broadline distributor or hospitality operation). Depending on customers' awareness of the manufacturer's brand, it may be easily recognizable (brand awareness), and they may be distributed nationally (national brand) or limited to a particular region (regional brand). Many private-label branded products sold to distributors are often simply the manufacturer's product packaged under a distributor's name or brand, without any change to the product specifications.

FIGURE 7.6 Packer's brand packaging.
Courtesy of Sysco

Because the manufacturer may produce the same item like canned peaches for many distributors, there may not be much difference between items labeled under different names. Products branded with the name of a hospitality operation are primarily products that are co-developed by the manufacturer and the operation. They may be created to meet a need specific to the operation's concept and with proprietary specifications. In the hospitality industry, distributors may refer to a manufacturer's branded product as a packer's brand name (also referred to as a packer's brand or packer's label, Figure 7.6) if it is not a national brand or a brand with little marketplace equity. A brand with little marketplace equity may have low overall sales, brand awareness, brand reputation, and perceived value.

A packer's brand label may also include U.S. grade terminology. For example, a packer's brand box of fresh produce might have a designation of "No. 1." This would indicate that the item was not produced under continuous U.S. government inspection, and that, in the opinion of the source, who is not a government grader, the product meets all U.S. requirements for U.S. No. 1 graded products.

In addition, a packer-branded food product, unless it is a meat or poultry item or includes egg breaking in its production, may not be under continuous government inspection. However, even if a food product manufacturer or processor does not purchase the U.S. government grading service, they must still undergo an inspection procedure. This inspection is concerned only with safety and wholesomeness, however; it makes no quality statement.

■ Samples

It may be necessary to rely on **samples**, and one or more relevant tests of these samples, when assessing the quality of new items in the marketplace. Samples and testing are commonly used to measure the quality of capital equipment.

■ Endorsements

Several associations and organizations **endorse** items that we purchase. For instance, NSF International attests to the sanitary excellence of kitchen equipment. The **American Culinary Federation (ACF)** has a Seal of Approval program for products that meet superior quality standards for application, performance, physical properties, and packaging, In the services area, the **Foodservice Consultants Society International (FCSI)** is an association of foodservice consultants whose members must meet rigorous standards to be part of the group.

■ Trade Associations

Various organizations, such as the **National Cattlemen's Beef Association (NCBA)**, and other trade groups, help set quality standards that the buyer can use.

■ Your Own Specifications

A buyer may use some combination of all the measures we have been discussing and work them into an extended measure of quality. This lengthy exercise usually finds its way into the specification. In many cases, particularly when a hospitality operation needs a special cut of meat, a unique type of paper napkin, or special cleaning agents, this extended measure is the only appropriate one.

   As we imply throughout this discussion, few buyers consider only one of these quality measures. In our opinion, however, too many operators become overreliant on only one measure when it would be more appropriate to consider two or more.

> **sample**   Testing a small portion of a product or a shipment to determine its overall quality and acceptability. Alternately, see free sample.
>
> **endorsement**   Testimonial by an independent agency or person, expressing approval and satisfaction with a company's product or service.
>
> **American Culinary Federation (ACF)**   Professional organization of chefs and cooks.
>
> **Foodservice Consultants Society International (FCSI)**   Professional association consisting primarily of kitchen designers and other related professions.
>
> **National Cattlemen's Beef Association (NCBA)**   Trade organization representing the beef industry. Its primary purpose is to promote the sale and purchase of beef. It also is an information resource for members of the beef channel of distribution.

Key Words and Concepts

American Culinary Federation (ACF)	Endorsement
Approved substitute	Equal to or better
Best-if-used-by date	Expiration date
Bid buying	Foodservice Consultants Society
Brand name	International (FCSI)
Broken case	Formal spec
Chemical standards	Freshness date
Count	Informal spec

Key Words and Concepts (continued)

Industry and government publications

Intended use

Instructions to bidders

Limiting rule

Lowball

Measures of quality

National Cattlemen's Beef Association (NCBA)

National Sanitation Foundation (NSF) International

North American Meat Institute (NAMI)

Organic and natural standards

Packaging procedure

Packer's brand name

Partial limiting rule

Point of origin

Preservation and/or processing method

Produce Marketing Association (PMA)

Product identification

Product specification

Pull date

Purchase specification

Ripeness

Sample

Slab-packed

Stockout

Trade association standard

Trim

Truth-in-menu

USDA Agricultural Marketing Service (AMS)

U.S. quality grades

Waste

Weight range

Yield

Questions and Problems

1. What is a purchase specification? How does it differ from a product specification?

2. What are some of the reasons hospitality operations develop purchase specifications?

3. What information is included on a typical purchase specification?

4. Assume you are the owner of a small table-service restaurant.

   a. How much time, money, and effort would you spend to develop specifications? Why?

   b. Assume that you do not want to write specifications; you want to rely strictly on packer's brands and government grades to guide your purchasing. What are the advantages and disadvantages of this strategy?

5. Explain how these factors influence the types of information included on the specification:

   a. Company policies

   b. Storage facilities

   c. Menu requirements

   d. Budgetary limitations

   e. Employee skills

Questions and Problems (continued)

6. What are the costs and benefits of hiring an outside consultant to help you write specifications?

7. What are the costs and benefits of writing specifications and using them in a bid-buying strategy?

8. Explain the roles of various company personnel such as the owner, general manager, and buyer in determining quality standards. What is the buyer's major role once these quality standards are set?

9. Describe five measures of quality. Name some advantages and disadvantages of each.

10. Are AP prices good measures of quality? Why or why not?

11. Some industry practitioners feel that hospitality operators can set quality standards for some nonfood supplies without considering their customers' views. Do you think this is true? Why or why not?

12. A product specification for fresh meat could include these types of information:
    a.
    b.
    c.
    d.
    e.
    f.

13. Why are expiration dates important to include on fresh-food specs?

14. A food-processing plant normally must undergo continuous federal-government inspection for wholesomeness if:
    a.
    b.

15. List some problems that the buyer will encounter if he or she is overreliant on U.S. grades.

16. What is the primary difference between a brand name and a packer's brand name?

17. Should a small hospitality operation prepare detailed purchase specifications, or should it prepare product specifications? Why?

18. What is the most important piece of information that can be included on a spec?

19. When should a buyer use packer's brands as an indication of desired quality in lieu of U.S. quality grades?

20. When should a buyer include on the specification "point of origin"?

Experiential Exercises

1. What are some potential advantages of limiting yourself to one supplier, the only one who can meet your quality standards?
   a. Write a one-page answer.
   b. Provide your answer to a hotel manager, and ask for comments.
   c. Prepare a report that includes your answer and the manager's comments.

2. Why would package quality be important to a foodservice buyer? Would you be willing to pay a bit more to ensure high-quality packaging? Why or why not?
   a. Write a one-page answer.
   b. Provide your answer to a foodservice manager, and ask for comments.
   c. Prepare a report that includes your answer and the manager's comments.

3. Develop a purchase specification.
   a. Write a purchase specification using information provided from one of the agencies in Figure 7.3.
   b. Provide your answer to an executive chef, and ask for comments.
   c. Prepare a report that includes your specification and the chef's comments.

4. Identify an agency that provides product information on a website and that is not included in Figure 7.3 . Write a one-page paper explaining how the website can be used to help purchasing managers to write specifications.

Reference

1. McDonald's Corporation, "Product Safety," www.aboutmcdonalds.com/mcd/csr.html.

CHAPTER 8

THE OPTIMAL AMOUNT

The Purpose of This Chapter

After reading this chapter, you should be able to:

- Explain the importance of determining and maintaining the optimal inventory level.
- Calculate the correct order size and order times using the par stock approach.
- Calculate the correct order size and order times using the Levinson approach.
- Calculate the correct order size using the practical approach.
- Calculate the correct order size and order times using theoretical methods.
- Evaluate the benefits and problems of using only the theoretical method for determining inventory levels.

THE IMPORTANCE OF THE OPTIMAL INVENTORY LEVEL

correct order size The order size that minimizes the ordering costs, inventory storage costs, and stockout costs.

correct order time The order time that minimizes the ordering costs, inventory storage costs, and stockout costs.

optimal inventory level The amount of inventory that will adequately serve a hospitality operation's needs without having to incur the costs associated with excess inventory.

ordering procedure Standardized process used by the buyer to ensure that the correct amounts of needed products are ordered at the appropriate time.

The **correct order size** and its counterpart, the **correct order time**, are probably the most important keys to inventory management. Without a reasonable idea of the optimal order size and time, you cannot maintain an ideal inventory level of food, beverages, and nonfood supplies.

Years ago, few hospitality operators concerned themselves with inventory management concepts. When the industry was smaller, was less complex and competitive, and inventory costs were minor, the occasional overbuy or stockout was a forgivable offense. Today, such a casual attitude is rare. Ordering is no longer haphazard. The emphasis now is on holding the **optimal inventory level**; that is, management seeks to determine the amount of inventory that will adequately serve the operation without having to suffer the costs of excess inventory.

A principal objective of inventory management is to maintain only the necessary amount of food, beverages, and nonfood supplies to serve guests without running out of anything, but not to have so much inventory that occasional spoilage and other storage costs result.[1] We also need to develop a cost-effective **ordering procedure**; for example, a buyer does not want to spend an excessive amount of time, money, and effort to order merchandise because this will increase the hospitality operation's cost of doing business. The new technologies discussed in Chapter 2 greatly assist buyers in carrying out these tasks effectively.

These objectives are more easily recited than achieved. Quite commonly, an individual manager may not know the exact value of inventory that should be on hand.

Over the years, hospitality operators have tried to devise ways of computing as accurately as possible the ideal amount of inventory that should be maintained to conduct business effectively and efficiently. Nonetheless, a major portion of the inventory management efforts that are carried out in our industry still rely heavily on rules of thumb. For instance, as mentioned in Chapter 6, many practitioners rely on a percentage of sales to guide their inventory management decisions. Recall that this percentage-of-sales concept suggests, for instance, that a full-service restaurant operation requires an inventory of food, beverage, and nonfood supplies to be equal to about one percent of annual sales volume.

A buyer can use other rules of thumb to determine the amount of inventory needed to service guests adequately. As mentioned in Chapter 6, the typical foodservice operation could devise an

inventory turnover Equal to: (actual cost of products used, or sold, divided by the average inventory value kept at the hospitality operation).

inventory management strategy to ensure that the food inventory that is kept on hand at all times does not exceed about one-third of a normal month's total food costs. Also, in a fast-food restaurant, the general feeling is that the food inventory should turn over about three times per week, or about 156 times per year. Consequently, the buyer's inventory management strategy should include an ordering procedure that maintains this approximate **inventory turnover** target.

Most industry practitioners view inventory as an investment. Like any other investment, this one must offer a return. Unfortunately, an inventory investment does not lend itself to a precise calculation of return, as does, say, a certificate of deposit, whereby an investor can depend on an exact percentage of return each year.

CORRECT ORDER SIZE AND ORDER TIME: PAR STOCK APPROACH

M ost part-time and full-time buyers use a relatively simple approach to calculate the best order size and order time. This approach is sometimes referred to as the **par stock approach**. The buyer usually accepts the supplier's **delivery schedule**—for example, twice a week. The buyer then determines a **par stock**, that is, a level of inventory items that he or she feels must be on hand to maintain a continuing supply of each item from one delivery date to the next.

The buyer accepts the supplier's delivery schedule because he or she probably cannot change it without incurring an exorbitant delivery charge. If, however, the buyer's company represents a very large order size, the supplier might make concessions. In addition, the buyer normally accepts the ordering schedule the supplier dictates; he or she places the order at a certain time prior to the actual delivery. For example, a call or online order no later than Monday morning may be required to ensure a delivery on Tuesday morning.

> **par stock approach**
> Method used to determine the appropriate amount to order. Involves setting par stocks for all items and subtracting the amount of each item on hand to calculate the order sizes.
>
> **delivery schedule**
> Purveyor's planned shipping times and dates.
>
> **par stock**   The maximum amount of a product you want to have on hand. When reordering the product you want to buy just enough to bring you up to par.

Assume, for example, that the buyer feels that he or she needs six cases of tomato paste on hand to last between orders. On Monday morning, just before placing the order, the buyer counts the number of cases of tomato paste on hand and there are one and one-half cases left. If it is expected that half a case will be used that day, one case will be left on Tuesday morning. The par stock is six. The buyer then subtracts what he or she feels will be on hand Tuesday morning from the par stock (six minus one) and orders five cases.

Another way to calculate the order size is for the buyer to subtract what is on hand—in this situation, one and one-half cases—from the par stock of six cases and enter an order for four and one-half cases. Either way, the emphasis is on setting an acceptable par stock level and then ordering enough product to bring the stock up to that level. (This concept is a bedrock of our industry. For example, most bars set up a certain par stock level that must be on hand before opening for the afternoon or evening. The bartender on duty is responsible for counting what is on hand, subtracting this from what should be on hand, and then replenishing the overall inventory of beverages, foodstuffs, and nonfood supplies accordingly.)

Par stocks sometimes change. In a restaurant that does a lot of banquet business, the par stock for tomato paste might fluctuate monthly or even weekly. This fluctuation can complicate matters, but buyers usually can solve the problem just by adding to the par stock the extra amount of tomato paste needed specifically for any emergency or extra business volume, such as a banquet next week. So, for instance, buyers might order enough to reach their par stock level, plus additional product to be their "safety" stock or to use for the banquet.

The buyer, then, normally uses the following procedures when employing the par stock approach:

1. Accept the suppliers' stipulated ordering procedures and delivery schedules. In remote locations, the inability to get deliveries as often as desired may increase par stock levels significantly.

2. Decide when it would be desirable to order enough product to bring the stock level of any particular item up to par. This decision is normally influenced by the amount of storage facilities the buyer has, how expensive the inventory item is, and the shelf life of the products the buyer orders. For example, if a preferred supplier delivers meat twice a week, and if the meats are expensive, perishable items, a buyer would most likely set a par stock to last about three or four days. For some inexpensive, nonperishable operating supplies, such as paper towels, the buyer might want to order once every three months. Consequently, he or she sets the par stock large enough to last for three months under normal operating conditions.

3. Set par stocks for all food, beverages, and nonfood items—enough to last between regularly scheduled deliveries.

4. When ordering, subtract what is on hand from the par stock. Then include any additional amount necessary to cover extra banquets, increased room service, seasonal patronage, a safety stock perhaps, and so forth.

5. Shop around, if necessary, and enter this order size at the time the supplier designates or at some agreed-upon time.

6. Periodically reevaluate the stock levels, and adjust them as needed. For instance, if you change suppliers and the new purveyor's delivery schedule is different, you must adjust accordingly.

No magic formula is associated with the par stock concept. It is a trial-and-error process. If six cases are too many, the number can be adjusted downward. If it is too low, it can be increased. The trial-and-error procedure requires small amounts of management attention on a continuing basis; in time, however, these can add up to a significant amount. Nevertheless, the work involved is quite simple and lends itself to volume swings in overall sales, as well as in sales of individual products. The par stock concept works quite effectively in the hospitality industry.

The concept works well for several reasons. Most important, there is only a slight difference in annual storage and ordering costs between a theoretical order size and a more practical order size. (An extended discussion of a theoretical calculation of optimal order size and order time is included later in this chapter.) Another reason is the relative predictability of deliveries. The third reason is that most hospitality operations undergo major modifications in their customer offerings only occasionally. For the most part, menus, sleeping accommodations, and bar offerings remain unchanged, thereby giving a buyer sufficient time to determine acceptable par stock levels for each inventory item. Finally, if a considerable sum has already been invested in a hospitality operation, an inventory level that is a few hundred dollars more than a theoretical optimal amount will tend to generate little concern.

The major drawback to the par stock method is its emphasis on setting only the par stock level, to the possible detriment of the broader view of inventory management. Generally, the optimal amount of inventory on hand is related to annual storage costs, ordering costs, and stockout costs. If acceptable par stocks are achieved, these costs will probably be minimized. However, these concepts may not be examined directly, and, as a result, a buyer may be unaware of the complete picture.

This innocence, or ignorance, can cause problems. For instance, buyers often have an opportunity to purchase large amounts of a product at reasonable savings. The problem arises when buyers have little understanding of the increase in storage costs that will accompany this huge order. Regardless of its potential drawbacks, the par stock approach is common and works fairly well. It does not, however, represent the only approach to determining correct order size and order time.

DETERMINING THE IDEAL LEVELS OF PRODUCTION AND ORDERING
Mark Kelnhofer, President and CEO

■ RETURN ON INGREDIENTS®, WESTERVILLE, OHIO

Courtesy of Return on Ingredients, LLC.

Restaurant operators are probably familiar with the term just-in-time (JIT) practices. However, they more than likely do not implement them. What just-in-time (JIT) means to the restaurant operator is, "We are producing and ordering products at an optimal quantity." As an example, in most cases we are preparing products in the morning. Ideally, the amounts we prepare and produce should only be enough to get us through the shift or day. However, JIT practices for ordering and production can increase the efficiency and profitability of the restaurant. Too many times, restaurant operators attempt to run their production or ordering according to a sales mix report or their past experience. In some cases, production and ordering requirements are being made with no data at all. Naturally, the operator does not want to run out of food, but this fear also causes instances where they produce or order way beyond what they actually need. Increased production and ordering levels are two great opportunities where cost improvements can be made. When you overproduce or order, you may have created excess waste; furthermore, the clock is now ticking on the menu item's shelf life. The goal with JIT is to minimize waste and reduce expenses.

Early in the morning the production team is preparing products. However, in many cases, they are producing product in advance of their needs. This is an attempt to make product based on shelf lives and not necessarily if they need it or not. They will justify this by stating it has a 72-hour shelf life and more than likely the product will be used. In some cases, production occurs just by having inventory on the shelves. As an example, on a Monday morning I observed a prep cook making five loaves of bruschetta bread. That was way too high for the day considering that Monday was one of the slower days of the week. When asked about why he was making so much, the response was, "I saw the loaves

DETERMINING THE IDEAL LEVELS OF PRODUCTION AND ORDERING (continued)

sitting in the dry goods area, so I prepared them." That is a very dangerous method to determine what to produce. Once the product is produced, the potential for waste has been created. Excess inventory can also lead to excess production.

The JIT practice for production and ordering are very much related to each other. With JIT practices, the goal is to produce only what you need for *one* day based on a day-specific mix and forecast. What a huge shift of thought and discipline. Focus on daily needs and not necessarily on future needs. As an example, if there is a forecasted production need of a dozen lasagnas, the goal would be to produce only those dozen and nothing more.

In terms of ordering inventory items from several vendors, it becomes a little more complicated. However, the end result is the same: minimize the opportunity for waste. To obtain a JIT amount, there needs to be an established order schedule. Each order will have to last until the next one is scheduled to arrive. With some locations, an additional buffer or safety stock should be set depending on some other factors such as night drops, distance from the delivering warehouse, dependability of the vendor (time and fill accuracy), and so on. For example, if the location is in St. Louis and it is receiving shipments from a warehouse 500 miles away, it would be a gamble to assume the delivery truck is going to be on time, all the time; for example, a truck could be late or it could break down. To prepare any order, a physical inventory of product on the shelf needs to be completed. Without taking on-hand counts, you will automatically be bringing in product unnecessarily. The goal is to order only enough to last until the next order. With reduced product on the shelves, a restaurant will experience less waste.

When applying just-in-time practices in the restaurant industry, the biggest hurdle may be the discipline to change and adopt the practices. Most restaurant locations may not have systems to provide them calculated suggested orders and may be working with manually set pars. A manual par is a quantity that is generated by the user to determine ordering and production amounts. In many cases, manual pars are very burdensome to maintain and in many cases the same amounts are utilized day to day. You cannot just look at order history to determine a future order. What happens if the order has always been historically high? As a result, future orders and amounts would be inflated as well.

In order to reach just-in-time goals, you need to have dynamically calculated pars that consider the past menu mix (history) and the recipes of the mix. To establish dynamic pars, you will need to have in place several practices or tools. The first is the ability to forecast either traffic (guest counts or sales dollars). The second is the ability to gather historic sales mixes from the point-of-sale (POS) systems. Many back office systems have interfaces directly with many of the POS systems or in some cases the POS system makes it easy to export these data. Recipes would then need to be in place that represent every menu item in the POS system so that the appropriate production requirement can be determined. With these pieces the calculation for dynamic pars can be accomplished.

Having dynamic pars for both production and ordering can have a major impact on increasing efficiency and the bottom line. The goal is to reduce the opportunity for waste and create a change of mind-set to only produce and order what is needed. Combined with a forecast and an order schedule, you now have a powerful tool to reduce the inventory levels and waste. Just-in-time systems do require establishing a whole new level of discipline for the operations. Discipline of this nature can only improve the bottom line.

Mark Kelnhofer is the President and CEO of Return On Ingredients® and has more than 20 years of management accounting experience including more than 10 years in the restaurant industry. Return On Ingredients® is a cloud-based software solution for restaurants and other foodservice operations. Mark is an international speaker on recipe costing and menu engineering and has published two books as well: *Return On Ingredients* and *The Culinary Pocket Resource of Yields, Weights, Densities and Measures.* He can be reached at Mark@ReturnOnIngredients.com.

CORRECT ORDER SIZE AND ORDER TIME: THE LEVINSON APPROACH

Another approach used in the hospitality industry is just a bit more complicated than the par stock approach. We call this approach the **Levinson approach** because Charles Levinson was one of the very first persons to address these ideas formally in his book, *Food and Beverage Operation: Cost Control and Systems Management,* 2nd ed. (Englewood Cliffs, NJ: Prentice-Hall, 1989). Much of the material in this section of our text is adapted from Levinson's volume. This book is now out of print. However, you might be able to find a used copy online.

> **Levinson approach**
> Method of determining the appropriate order sizes. Takes into account forecasted sales, portion sizes, and yield percentages when calculating the amount of products to order.

Buyers using the Levinson approach will employ the following procedures:

1. Accept the suppliers' stipulated ordering procedures and delivery schedules.

2. Determine the best time to place orders with the suppliers. For instance, fresh dairy products may be ordered daily, fresh meats and produce may be ordered perhaps every third day, and other less perishable items may be ordered less frequently. Consequently, the buyers' work follows a reasonably predictable routine, in that they have enough work to keep busy each week, even though they are not ordering exactly the same items each day or each week.

> **forecasting** An attempt to predict the future. Current and historical information is used to estimate what might happen over the near or long term. Referred to as sales forecasting when attempting to predict future sales.

3. Before ordering, forecast the amount of merchandise that will be needed during the period of time between regularly scheduled deliveries. The **forecasting** procedure includes the following steps:

   a. Forecast the expected total number of customers, based usually on past history.

   b. Forecast the expected number of customers who will order each specific menu offering, also based on past history. One way to do this is to compute a **popularity index** for each menu item. To determine

> **popularity index**
> A percentage calculated by dividing the number sold of that particular menu item by the total number of all menu items sold.

a menu item's popularity index, divide the number sold of that particular menu item by the total number of all menu items sold; this will give you a percentage, which is the menu item's popularity index.

For example, if you project that you will serve 2,500 customers next week and you know that, based on past history, 25 percent of all customers eat T-bone steaks, then you can estimate that 0.25 × 2500, or 625 customers, will eat a T-bone steak.

portion factor (PF)
Equal to (16 ounces divided by the number of ounces needed for one serving). Alternately, equal to (1,000 milliliters divided by the number of milliliters needed for one serving). Alternately, equal to (1,000 grams divided by the number of grams needed for one serving).

portion divider (PD)
Equal to an item's (portion factor (PF) multiplied by its edible yield percentage).

edible yield percentage
Another term for yield percentage.

c. Determine the number of raw pounds of each ingredient needed to satisfy your projected sales. To do this, first you must figure out the **portion factor (PF)** and the **portion divider (PD)** for each ingredient that you need to satisfy your sales forecast. The PF is computed as follows:

$$PF = 16\,oz. \,/\, \text{Amount of ingredient needed for one serving}\,(\text{in ounces})$$

The PD is computed as follows:

$$PD = PF \times \left(\text{The ingredient's edible}\,(\text{i.e., servable})\,\text{yield percentage}\right)$$

The **edible yield percentage** is computed in one of three ways: (1) you accept the supplier's estimate of edible yield, (2) you use resources developed by other chefs such as *The Book of Yields: Accuracy in Food Costing and Purchasing* by Francis Lynch and *Chef's Book of Formulas, Yields, and Sizes* by Arno Schmidt,[2] or (3) you conduct your own yield tests for each and every ingredient; that is, you use the ingredients for a while and compute an average of unavoidable waste. This will give you a good idea of the edible yield percentage you can expect to derive from each ingredient.

d. Compute the order sizes for all items. An order size is equal to the number of customers you feel will consume an ingredient divided by the PD for that ingredient—this will give you the order size in raw pounds. (Essentially, the PD is the expected number of servings per pound.). Please note that the Levinson approach can be adapted for use with any food or beverage item and any purchase unit. The general formula for the PF needs to be altered to accommodate the specific purchase unit. The unit of purchase is divided by the portion size as depicted in that unit of purchase. The computation of the PD remains the same.

4. Adjust this order size, if necessary, to account for stock on hand, extra banquets, increased room service, seasonal patronage, perhaps a safety stock, and so forth.

5. Shop around, if necessary, and enter the order size at the time the supplier designates or at some agreed-upon time.

6. Periodically revise the order time if necessary, as well as the PD of each ingredient if, for instance, you decide to change suppliers and the new supplier's ingredients have a different yield percentage than those you are currently purchasing. (In Chapter 9, we discuss the procedures used to determine whether another supplier's ingredient provides more value to you, even though it might appear that it has more waste. We also revisit the concept of the EP cost.)

EXAMPLE I

Given the following data, compute the number of raw (AP) pounds needed of each ingredient for a banquet for 500 people.

Ingredient	Serving Size (oz.)	Edible Yield (%)
Steak	12	80
Beans	4	90
Potatoes	4	75

SOLUTION:

Compute each ingredient's PF:

$$PF_{(steak)} = 16 / 12 = 1.33$$
$$PF_{(beans)} = 16 / 4 = 4.00$$
$$PF_{(potatoes)} = 16 / 4 = 4.00$$

Compute each ingredient's PD:

$$PD_{(steak)} = 1.33 \times 0.80 = 1.06$$
$$PD_{(beans)} = 4.00 \times 0.90 = 3.60$$
$$PD_{(potatoes)} = 4.00 \times 0.75 = 3.00$$

Compute the order size, in raw (AP) pounds, for each ingredient:

$$\text{Order size}_{(steak)} = 500 / 1.06 = 472 \text{ lb.}$$
$$\text{Order size}_{(beans)} = 500 / 3.60 = 139 \text{ lb.}$$
$$\text{Order size}_{(potatoes)} = 500 / 3.00 = 167 \text{ lb.}$$

EXAMPLE II

Given the following data, compute the number of liters (l) needed to serve 250 customers.

    Ingredient: Gin

    Serving size: 55 milliliters

    Servable yield: 95 percent

SOLUTION:

$$PF = 1000 / 55 = 18.18$$
$$PD = 18.18 \leftrightarrow 0.95 = 17.27$$
$$\text{Number of liters needed} = 250 / 17.27 = 14.48 \left(\text{approximately } 15 \text{ liters}\right)$$

EXAMPLE III

Given the following data, compute the number of cases needed to serve 500 customers.

Ingredient: Lobster tail

Serving size: 2 tails

Servable yield: 100 percent

Number of tails per case: 50

SOLUTION:

$$PF = 50 / 2 = 25$$
$$PD = 25 \times 1.00 = 25$$
$$\text{Number of cases needed} = 500 / 25 = 20 \text{ cases}$$

A PRACTICAL APPROACH TO DETERMINING CORRECT ORDER SIZE

The PF and PD calculations may not be intuitive to most people, especially the chefs who, although they spend more and more of their time performing cost control and human resources functions, would rather cook and develop new menu items than spend a lot of time crunching numbers. Therefore, they want to use as simple a formula as possible to determine the quantity of food to purchase.

Many chefs rely on the formula of AP (As Purchased) = EP (Edible Portion) ÷ Edible Yield Percentage to determine the amount of product to order. They basically skip one step of the Levinson approach. But before we use the formula, let's make sure that you know exactly what the Edible Yield Percentage means.

Let's use the example of asparagus. If you buy whole asparagus, but use only the tips for service, you trim off a lot of stems in the process. The amount cut off would be the trim loss, and the amount left would be the edible portion. If you started with one pound (16 ounces) of asparagus and had 10 ounces of asparagus tips after cutting, your yield percentage would be 10 ounces divided by 16 ounces per pound or approximately 63 percent. If you were determining the yield percentage of other products, for example roasted meat, you might also have to take into account trimming off the fat, shrinkage during cooking, having unusable portions after cutting, and other factors.

Now let's use the yield percentage in the AP formula. Suppose a banquet chef wants to serve 4 ounces of asparagus tips as a side vegetable to 800 people. Therefore, she needs 4 ounces × 800 or 3,200 ounces (200 lbs) EP of asparagus. But she knows that the yield percentage of asparagus is only 63 percent. Therefore, she really needs 3,200 ounces divided by 0.63 or 5,080 ounces as purchased. Translate that to pounds, and she would order 318 pounds of asparagus. If she only ordered 200 pounds, she would have to skimp on the portion sizes or lots of guests would not be getting their vegetable that evening.

Chefs use this method because the most important thing for them to know is how much food to purchase, regardless of whether they are calling the order in to a supplier themselves or submitting a requisition to a central purchasing agent. It also gives the chef the ability to accurately calculate the cost of preparing a recipe and the individual cost per portion. Once you have the current AP amount for each ingredient you can multiply that amount by that ingredient's purchase price to determine the total ingredient cost. Add up the cost of all the ingredients in the recipe and divide it by the number of portions the recipe makes, and voila! you have the cost per portion. In addition, knowing how to calculate the EP costs of the food items can help the chef decide whether to buy the raw product or whether to buy a convenience product with some of the trimming and/or cooking already done. This is an example of the "make-or-buy" analysis discussed in Chapters 5 and 9.

It is reasonable to expect the typical buyer to use a combination of the procedures just discussed to determine the proper order sizes and order times. For instance, a buyer could use the par stock approach to maintain sufficient stock for the normal, predictable business needs of the hospitality operation. However, when a buyer needs stock for special events, such as banquets and other similar functions, he or she could adopt the practical approach, the Levinson approach, or some variation thereof, when determining the correct order amount and order time.

CORRECT ORDER SIZE AND ORDER TIME: A THEORETICAL APPROACH

■ Correct Order Size

In centralized, multiunit purchasing operations, economies of scale make very large purchases realistic. When inventory value reaches the multimillion-dollar level, more formalized modes of analysis are useful in determining order size. This section suggests tools available for use in such cases.

The correct order size is influenced by two costs: the **storage cost**, which is sometimes referred to as the **carrying cost**, and the **ordering cost**. The storage cost is the sum of several little costs associated with holding inventory. The cost of maintaining storage facilities, inventory insurance, and risk of spoilage or obsolescence are three aspects of the storage cost. However, the most important part of the storage cost—the largest aspect of the storage cost—is the money tied up in inventory, that is, the **capital cost**. Economists refer to this as an **opportunity cost**, which is a nice way of saying that if your money is tied up in canned goods on a shelf, you lose the opportunity to invest this money elsewhere, such as in a bank, in shares of stock, or in gold. You also may lose the opportunity to expand or make improvements to your facility.

Attempts have been made to calculate the storage cost precisely. Unfortunately, no hard figures exist. Annual estimates run from 10 to 25 percent of the value of inventory. This means that for every dollar you tie up on the shelf, you can expect a storage cost of somewhere between 10 and 25 cents per year.

storage cost   Another term for carrying cost.

carrying cost   Expenses, such as insurance, security, and spoilage, associated with holding inventory in storage.

ordering cost   The amount of money spent to make an order, receive it, and store it. Includes things such as labor needed to perform the work and administrative costs such as faxing, photocopying, and cell phone charges.

capital cost   The rate of return (e.g., interest income) that capital could be expected to earn in an alternative investment of equivalent risk.

opportunity cost   By choosing to do something, you give up the option of doing something else. For instance, if you pay a bill too early you lose the option of investing the money and earning some interest income. The loss of income in this case is considered to be the opportunity cost.

The ordering cost includes primarily the cost of paperwork, telephone, computer, fax, employee wages and salaries, receiving, and invoice processing.

Differences of opinion exist concerning the dollar value of the ordering cost. Although it is important to determine this cost, a buyer should also examine the ordering cost in relation to the dollar amount of product purchased. Some purchases will cost more than others. For example, if the ordering cost is $10, then for a $100 purchase the cost represents 10 percent of the dollar amount purchased. For a $75 order, the cost would represent 13.3 percent, making the smaller order less cost effective.[3] What is important is that you recognize that placing orders is not a cost-free exercise and that the potential savings of reducing the number of orders can and should be determined.

It is important to consider how using the latest technology as described in Chapter 2 can affect order costs. According to a technology survey conducted in Ireland in 2013, the cost of implementing new ordering technologies was found to be the main barrier for implementation. This included maintaining and upgrading software as necessary. Although hardware systems can be pricey, this survey identified cloud-based solutions to be simpler and more cost effective solutions that would likely reduce ordering costs in the next few years.[4]

A large order size would ensure a large inventory amount and, hence, a huge annual storage cost. Because you would not order a large amount as often as a small amount, however, the annual ordering cost would decrease. On the other hand, a small order size would result in a smaller inventory and a correspondingly smaller annual storage cost; however, unfortunately, your annual ordering cost would increase (see Figure 8.1).

The important point is that there is an optimal order size, one that leads to the lowest possible total cost per year (annual storage and ordering costs). Note that a small order size (any one to the left of the crosshatched area in Figure 8.1) carries a relatively high total cost per year, as does any order size to the right of the crosshatched area. The optimal range of order sizes is represented by the crosshatched area. Theoretically, there is one optimal order size in that crosshatched area at the point where the storage cost curve intersects the ordering cost curve.

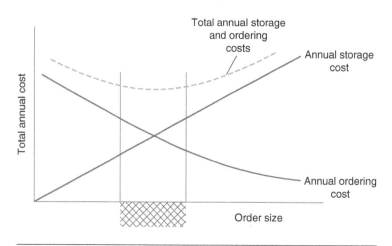

FIGURE 8.1 Annual storage and ordering costs related to order size.

When determining the optimal order size, management must take into account the influence of these two costs. Basically, the intersection of the storage cost curve and the ordering cost curve represents the best balance between the cost of carrying inventory and the benefits derived from having the inventory available for sale to the customer. When calculating this intersection, management has two options. First, a manager could attempt to graph the operation's cost curves and then try to "eyeball" the optimal order size. Second, he or she might use a formula to determine the optimal order sizes.

The most common option is summarized in the **economic order quantity (EOQ) formula**. Although relatively few hospitality operations use this formula directly, it can be used as a reference to identify the relevant costs and put them in their proper perspective. Hence, a look at this formula will immediately drive home the concept of optimal order sizes.

> **economic order quantity (EOQ) formula**   The EOQ in dollars is equal to: the square root of [(2 times the ordering cost in dollars times the amount of the item used in one year in dollars) divided by the annual storage cost expressed as a percentage of average inventory value]. The EOQ in units is equal to: the square root of [(2 times the ordering cost in dollars times the amount of the item used in one year in units) divided by the annual storage cost per unit in dollars].

You can calculate the EOQ two basic ways, as noted in Figure 8.2. Assume that an operation currently uses 600 cases of tomato paste per year, the ordering cost per order is $3, the annual storage cost is 15 percent of the value of the tomato paste, and the cost of the tomato paste is $8 per case. The question is: How many cases should the buyer purchase at one time? In other words, what is the EOQ?

Applying the formulas noted in Figure 8.2, you determine that the EOQ is about 55 cases, or approximately $440. The calculations follow:

The total cost per year (annual storage and ordering costs) associated with this EOQ of 55 cases is calculated by using the formula depicted in Figure 8.3.

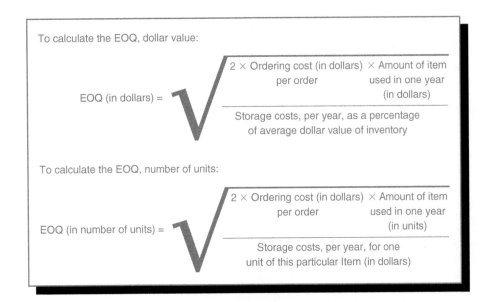

FIGURE 8.2 Ways of calculating the EOQ.

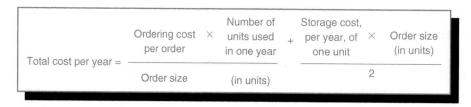

FIGURE 8.3 The calculation of the annual total cost associated with a particular order size. (This formula is used in calculating the EOQ formula.)

You have calculated the order size, 55 cases, that yields the least total cost per year. An order size of 50 cases results in a lower annual storage cost, but your annual ordering cost increases because you have to order more often during the year. Conversely, a larger order size yields a smaller annual ordering cost, but the increase in annual storage cost negates this slight savings.

As a practical matter, it may be inconvenient or impossible to order 55 cases at a time. Although it may be impractical to order 55 cases at a time, knowing what the optimal order size is can help you make decisions about other more practical order sizes. For instance, if you can order only in blocks of 50 cases, you will have an idea of the annual ordering and storage costs associated with this order size and be able to plan your expenses accordingly.

This theoretical approach is neither simple nor easy to use. However, the concept of EOQ can be used in many productive ways to ensure an optimal overall level of inventory, which is the result of the optimal order size and the topic we turn to next, the optimal order time.

■ Correct Order Time

Continuing with the tomato paste example, you should determine when to order your 55 cases, assuming 55 is a practical order size. If you could depend on instant delivery of inventory items, you might be able to wait until you are completely out of tomato paste before you order the next batch of 55 cases. Unfortunately, a lag invariably exists between the time you place an order and when it arrives. In some instances, this time lag is predictable; in others, it is not. As a result, you will want to order at some level greater than zero if you want to ensure a continuing, uninterrupted supply.

This level is sometimes referred to as the **safety stock**. It is also called the **reorder point (ROP)**. You cannot wait until you are out of stock before ordering another batch; you must maintain a safety stock. But what this safety stock should be is open to hunches, theories, and educated guesses.

The trick to calculating the ROP is first to gain some idea of the **usage pattern** of the particular product in question. In the tomato paste example, you might experience the usage pattern outlined in Figure 8.4.

safety stock Extra stock kept on hand to avoid running out and disappointing guests.

reorder point (ROP) The lowest amount of stock on hand that you feel comfortable with, the point that you will not go below before ordering more stock.

usage pattern When referring to food and beverages, it is the rate at which the products are produced and served to customers. When referring to nonfood and nonbeverage supplies, it is the rate at which the products have been exhausted and are no longer available.

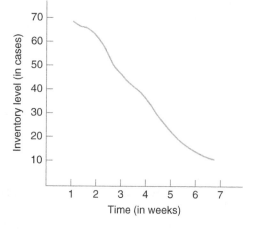

FIGURE 8.4 A hypothetical usage pattern for tomato paste.

Normally, this type of pattern is not as predictable as Figure 8.4 implies. If you keep track of your usage patterns for six months or so, however, you can determine how many cases you use, on average, every day. For discussion purposes, assume that you have determined that 40 percent of the time, you use one case of tomato paste or less per day; that 90 percent of the time, you use two cases or less; that 96 percent of the time, you use three cases or less; and that 100 percent of the time, you use four cases or less (see Figure 8.5).

Another way of looking at Figure 8.5 is to consider the possibility of using, on any given day, between one and two cases of tomato paste. Note that, in the past, you have used between one and two cases of tomato paste per day 50 percent of the time; hence, there is a 50 percent probability of selling more than one case but less than two cases per day. Similarly, you have sold less than one case per day 40 percent of the time, between two and three cases of tomato

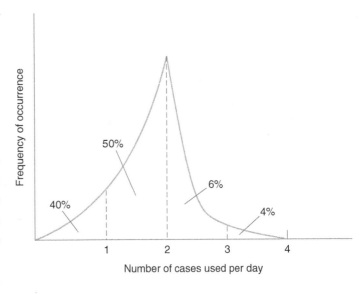

FIGURE 8.5 The percentage of times one, two, three, or four cases are used per day.

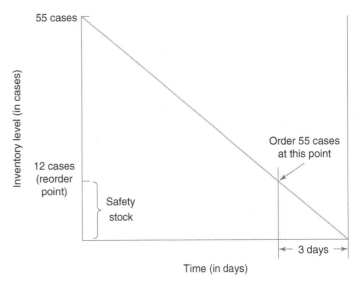

FIGURE 8.6 The graphical determination of the reorder point (ROP).

paste per day 6 percent of the time, and between three and four cases of tomato paste per day 4 percent of the time.

A conservative safety stock in this situation would be four cases for every day that lapses between the time you place your order of 55 cases and the time you receive this order. The interval of days is sometimes referred to as the **lead time**. If you can safely assume that your lead time is three days and you do not want to take a chance of running out of tomato paste, you would then place your order of 55 cases when your supply of tomato paste reaches 12 cases (see Figure 8.6).

If you use all 12 cases during the three-day lead time, you will be out of stock when your order of 55 cases arrives. If you use only 10 cases, you

lead time Period of time between when you place an order with a vendor and when you receive it.

will have 2 cases in inventory when the 55 cases are delivered. Your total inventory amount at this point would then be 57 cases.

After your order is delivered, you want to be as close as possible to a total inventory amount of 55 cases. Ideally, you will be at 55 cases exactly, that is, the moment you run out of inventory, the delivery van will be pulling up at the unloading area with the 55-case order.

just-in-time (JIT) inventory management
System that attempts to ensure that the moment the inventory level of a particular product reaches zero, a shipment of that item arrives at your back door. The main objective is to reduce carrying charges to their lowest possible level.
stockout cost The cost incurred when you do not have a product guests want. Although the cost cannot always be calculated, in the long run there will usually be a negative impact on your bottom line. For example, the guest leaves without buying anything. Or the guest stays and orders something else, but never comes back.

Hospitality operations that strive for this ideal arrangement practice use what is generally referred to in the industry as **just-in-time (JIT) inventory management**. Although these firms are trying to keep the total ordering and storage costs as low as possible, they are especially interested in minimizing the storage cost. For instance, if, using the figures in the preceding example, they have two cases of inventory in stock when the delivery van arrives, they will then have a current inventory level of 57 cases when the van pulls up. If they have 57 cases, they will incur an additional storage cost—which they are very eager to avoid. However, this additional storage cost must be weighed against the possibility of running out of tomato paste and incurring various **stockout costs**.

Stockout costs are expenses associated with being unable to serve a product because you do not have it. These costs are particularly irksome in the hospitality business: you cannot tell customers to come back for a steak tomorrow because you do not have any for them today. If you cannot provide a product, a customer usually selects another, the result being no apparent loss in profit. But a customer might be irritated when you cannot supply the product wanted. In essence, you have diminished the customer's favorable opinion of your operation. The cost of goodwill is difficult to determine, and some operators harbor a greater disdain for stockouts than do others. Another problem associated with this safety stock concept is the exactness of the lead time. In most cases, deliveries are reasonably predictable, but the supplier may not have 55 cases of tomato paste. He or she may have only 30 or 40 cases, or perhaps none at all.

The theoretical approach to the optimal order time rests on the assumptions you make about usage patterns, lead times, safety stocks, supplier capabilities, and dependability. By keeping historical records, you can determine the ROP with which you feel most comfortable. If the numbers are correct, the ROP will be optimal. If they are not, at least you will be closer to the optimal ROP than you ever could be by relying on mere hunches.

Although the formality of the approach we have been discussing would not be appropriate for a single operation of modest size, clearly, the logic of the approach has general application. This is a good way to think about ROPs, even if formulas and detailed records do not come into the picture for each hospitality operator.

CONSIDERATIONS WHEN USING THE THEORETICAL APPROACH

■ Problems

The basic overriding problem, which we alluded to earlier, is the need for certain assumptions and estimates. Any way you look at it, we deal with highly variable phenomena here. Some additional variables that tend to detract from the usefulness of these approaches are listed here:

- Usage rates vary from day to day and do not normally follow a steady pattern, unless the operation caters to a fairly predictable group of repeat customers. Although usage patterns can be approximated, they probably can never be calculated exactly.

- Storage and ordering costs can vary; in addition, several opinions exist as to the precise makeup of these costs.

- Stockout costs are extremely difficult to assess. Management philosophy is the best guide in this case; consequently, the concept of correct order time can change according to management's tolerance of risk of stockouts.

- Lead times are somewhat predictable, but you may qualify for only once-a-week delivery, which hurts any attempt to implement the EOQ and ROP concepts. In fact, the inability to control delivery times, either because of tradition or by law (e.g., some states have strict ordering and delivering schedules for alcoholic beverages), has done more to discourage the use of these concepts in the hospitality industry than any of the other difficulties. With the theoretical approach, the order size stays the same, but the order time varies. The opposite is true with the par stock and Levinson approaches. As a result, because the typical buyer has no control over order times and delivery schedules, he or she cannot implement the theoretical approach.

- What items should you consider for EOQ and ROP? All of them? This decision is not very easy when you realize that the average hospitality operation stocks a minimum of 600 to 800 items. Some people suggest considering only those few items that together represent about 80 percent of the value of the total inventory. Others feel that it is possible to construct a few item categories and develop EOQs and ROPs for them. In any case, monitoring all items is impossible without the help of sophisticated computer technology. As these types of computer applications become increasingly feasible and economical, however, it is possible that you will be able to overcome this difficulty.

- Keep in mind that your supplier normally buys from someone else. Your EOQ may not be consistent with your supplier's EOQ. As a result, you could encounter the problem of receiving an incomplete order. Alternately, you might have to settle for certain substitutions, a situation that may or may not be compatible with your EOQ calculations.

- At times, a supplier may be forced to discontinue an item that you find especially profitable in your hospitality establishment. This problem is often associated with wines, particularly those of a certain vintage. Because only so much of a certain type of wine is produced in a certain year, the stock must run out sometime. Before reaching this point, you may decide to order as much as you can in order to maintain your supply as long as possible. Needless to say, this buying decision flies in the face of the EOQ and ROP concepts.

- The EOQ assumes that you have adequate storage facilities. You may calculate an EOQ of 55 cases and then discover that you have space for only 30 cases.

- Moreover, the EOQ assumes that the products you order will be used before they spoil or become obsolete. Fewer problems concerning obsolescence exist in the hospitality industry than in other industries, but spoilage can be an enormous problem. Although you can expect 55 cases of tomato paste to maintain their quality for two or three months, you cannot assume this storage life for all products.

■ Benefits

Theories can have shortcomings, of course, but they can also have numerous benefits. The EOQ and ROP concepts are cases in point. Some potential benefits associated with these approaches are listed here:

- A theoretical approach substitutes fact for fiction. Even if some of your estimates are off, at least you have been forced to consider these variables. This discipline in itself can easily lead to a more favorable profit performance.

- A range of order sizes seems to exist in which the total cost per year (annual ordering and storage costs) does not vary dramatically. In the tomato paste example, the total cost per year for 50 cases was $66; for 55 cases, $65.73; and for 60 cases, $66. Notice that you could go down to 50 or up to 60 cases and incur an additional cost of only $0.27 per year. As a result, you gain insight by using the theory, and you will not have to be overly concerned if your estimates are a little off. And, as mentioned earlier in this chapter, this range is the major reason that the par stock approach to ordering is acceptable for many operations.

- As technology becomes more ubiquitous, it is now feasible to monitor EOQs and ROPs. This, in turn, enables you to extract maximum benefit from these theoretical approaches, while minimizing the time and paperwork involved with analyzing usage patterns, lead times, safety stock, and so on.

- Although the use of the EOQ and ROP concepts may not be feasible for a single-unit hospitality operation, the multiunit chain organizations, especially those with company-owned commissaries and/or central distribution centers, would be able to adopt these theories and use them to significantly improve their purchasing performance.

Theoretical approaches may or may not be completely useful in a specific hospitality operation. We believe, however, that all operations can derive more benefit than cost by considering these concepts. A thoughtful consideration of these concepts forces an operator to evaluate all the pertinent variables that influence an overall inventory level. By evaluating these variables, that operator comes as close as possible to an optimal overall inventory level, which is the ultimate objective of the EOQ and ROP concepts.

Key Words and Concepts

Capital cost	Optimal inventory level
Carrying cost	Ordering cost
Correct order size	Ordering procedures
Correct order time	Par stock
Delivery schedule	Par stock approach to ordering
Economic order quantity (EOQ) formula	Popularity index
Edible yield percentage	Portion divider (PD)
Forecasting	Portion factor (PF)
Inventory turnover	Reorder point (ROP)
Just-in-time (JIT) inventory management	Safety stock
Lead time	Stockout cost
Levinson approach to ordering	Storage cost
Opportunity cost	Usage pattern

Questions and Problems

1. Briefly explain how the par stock approach to ordering works. Why does it work so well? What are some of the method's drawbacks?

2. Fill in the blanks: Ordering the correct _____ at the correct _____ leads to _____.

3. Why would a general manager want to determine an optimal inventory amount?

4. Briefly describe EOQ and ROP. What benefits are there for managements that adopt these procedures? What drawbacks are there?

5. What are the elements of the ordering cost? Of the storage cost? How can either, or both, of these costs be reduced without harming the overall hospitality operation's profit performance?

6. The typical owner–operator will accept suppliers' delivery and ordering procedures. What is the primary reason he or she would not try to change them?

Questions and Problems (continued)

7. What is the most important part of the storage cost?

8. What is a safety stock? Why might an operator wish to maintain a safety stock?

9. Briefly describe the concept of an "opportunity cost."

10. Identify one reason the EOQ concept is not particularly useful to the typical hospitality operation.

11. What is the objective of using the JIT inventory management procedure?

12. You are currently using 750 cases of green beans per year. The cost of one purchase order is $75. Annual storage costs are approximately 25 percent of inventory value. The beans' wholesale price is $24 per case. Each case contains six No. 10 cans. How many cases should you purchase at one time?

13. Given the following data, determine the storage cost of the EOQ amount:
     EOQ: 500 pounds (1-month supply)
     Storage cost: 24 percent per year
     Price of the product: $6 per pound

For the next questions, you can use either the Levinson approach or the practical approach. Check with your instructor to determine which you should use. Or use both methods and see if you come up with the same answer.

14. Given the following data, compute the number of raw pounds needed to serve 250 customers:
     ingredient: PORK CHOPS
     serving size: 14 OUNCES
     edible yield: 75 PERCENT

15. Given the following data, compute the number of liters needed to serve 500 customers:
     ingredient: SCOTCH
     serving size: 60 MILLILITERS
     servable yield: 95 PERCENT

16. Given the following data, compute the number of kilograms needed to serve 750 customers:
     ingredient: BELGIAN ENDIVE
     serving size: 75 GRAMS (EP)
     edible yield: 65 PERCENT

17. Given the following data, compute the number of cases needed to serve 1,000 customers:
     ingredient: HASH BROWN POTATOES
     serving size: 4 OUNCES (EP)
     edible yield: 100 PERCENT
     weight per case: 50 POUNDS

Questions and Problems (continued)

18. Given the following data, compute the number of cases needed to serve 1,250 customers:
    ingredient: DINNER ROLLS
    serving size: 4 OUNCES (TWO ROLLS)
    servable yield: 100 PERCENT
    number of rolls per case: 250 (500 OUNCES)

19. Given the following data, compute the number of gallons needed to serve 1,500 customers:
    ingredient: ICE CREAM
    serving size: 4 OUNCES
    edible yield: 90 PERCENT
    weight per gallon: 4 1/2 POUNDS

 ## Experiential Exercises

1. What are some advantages and disadvantages of utilizing rules of thumb to direct your inventory management procedures?
    a. Interview at least two restaurant managers, and ask them what rules of thumb they use to direct their inventory management procedures (i.e., amount of inventory to have on hand). Prepare a list of all rules of thumb that you identify.
    b. Ask each manager to comment on what they think are the advantages and disadvantages of utilizing rules of thumb.
    c. Submit a list of rules of thumb used to direct inventory management procedures. Include a report detailing the advantages and disadvantages of utilizing these rules of thumb.

2. Can the economic order quantity (EOQ) model assist foodservice managers?
    a. Go online and research the EOQ model in detail. Prepare a two-page report that you will use to persuade a manager of a large or multiunit foodservice operation to incorporate the EOQ model into his or her inventory forecasting procedures.
    b. Submit the report to a foodservice manager of a large or multiunit foodservice operation.
    c. Ask the manager for comments regarding the EOQ model.
    d. Submit a report that includes your two-page persuasion and the manager's comments.

References

1. Aaron Prather, "Inventory Management—The Principles of Effective Implementation," retrieved September 2009 from ezinearticles.com/?id=640265. See also David Scott Peters, "How to Manage Your Inventory Properly," *Restaurant Hospitality,* February 2008, 92(2), p. 28; Donald Waters, *Inventory Control and Management* (Hoboken, NJ: John Wiley & Sons, 2003); Stuart Emmett, *Excellence in Warehouse Management: How to Minimise Costs and Maximise Value* (Chichester, West Sussex, England: Hoboken, NJ: John Wiley & Sons 2005).

2. See, for example, C. Barry, "Reducing Your Cost Per Order," *Catalog Age*, 17, no. 4(2000): 85–88, http://ezproxy.library.unlv.edu/login?url=http://search.proquest.com/docview/200613659?accountid=3611.

3. Francis Lynch, *The Book of Yields: Accuracy in Food Costing and Purchasing*, 8th ed. (Hoboken, NJ: John Wiley & Sons, Inc., 2010) and Arno Schmidt, *Chef's Book of Formulas, Yields, and Sizes*, 3rd ed. (Hoboken, NJ: John Wiley & Sons, Inc., 2003).

4. Technology Survey 2013. *Hospitality Ireland* [serial online], 85 (October 2013):19. Available from: Hospitality & Tourism Complete, Ipswich, MA.

CHAPTER 9

DETERMINING OPTIMAL PURCHASE PRICES AND PAYMENT POLICIES

The Purpose of This Chapter

After reading this chapter, you should be able to:

- Explain the difference between optimal price and AP price.

- Describe how suppliers determine their purchase prices.

- Differentiate between the type of discounts available and how they influence AP prices.

- Identify purchasing and receiving methods that reduce purchase prices.

- Use additional methods to reduce AP price including calculating edible portion cost, servable portion cost, and standard cost.

- Evaluate qualitative aspects of a potential opportunity buy.

- Determine the elements of the optimal payment policy, including the costs of paying sooner than necessary and of paying too late.

- Compare and contrast the bill-paying procedures that can be employed by hospitality operators.

OPTIMAL PRICE AND THE INFLUENCE OF AP PRICES

The optimal price is the price that, when combined with the optimal quality and **supplier services**, produces the optimal value. The optimal price represents the lowest possible edible-portion (EP) cost consistent with the optimal value of a product, service, furnishing, or piece of equipment. Remember, the best EP cost may or may not be the lowest as-purchased (AP) price. When a buyer assesses the optimal price, he or she should translate a quoted AP price into the hospitality organization's relevant EP cost. The buyer can quickly make this conversion by using this formula:

$$EP \ cost = AP \ price/edible - (or \ servable \ -, or \ usable \ -) \ yield \ percentage$$

For example, if a roast beef has an AP price of $2.45 per pound and an edible-yield percentage of 75 percent, the EP cost per pound is $3.27 ($2.45/0.75 = $3.27).

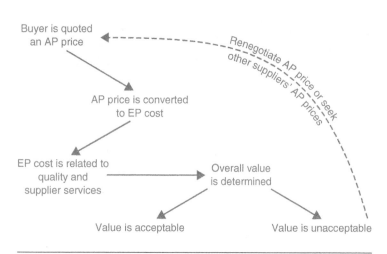

FIGURE 9.1 The conceptual process a buyer can use to relate AP price to value.

After computing the EP cost, the buyer must then relate it to product quality and supplier services and conclude with the optimal value (see Figure 9.1). The buyer must examine all these components simultaneously and must seek the optimal value. We now show how the optimal price or, more appropriately, the optimal EP cost, relates to this overall value.

The AP price can influence buyers in many ways. At one extreme are the buyers who shop entirely on the basis of AP price. This practice succeeds only when the buyers know exactly what they want in terms of quality and supplier services and can get two or more relatively similar suppliers to quote AP prices that permit adequate comparisons. At the other extreme are buyers concerned almost exclusively with quality and supplier services. These buyers do not hesitate to pay a premium AP price. The majority of buyers fall somewhere between these extremes—or, more realistically, some buyers may be close to one extreme for some products and close to the other extreme for other products.

The supplier, in turn, must obtain some measure of a buyer's reaction to AP prices. In Chapter 10, we elaborate on **buyer profiles**, which are sometimes referred to as **buyer fact sheets**. These are diaries in which suppliers and salespersons record information on buyers' purchasing habits, as well as, invariably, reactions to AP prices.

Eventually, suppliers and salespersons can accurately gauge the influence AP prices have on various buyers. However, suppliers and salespersons use certain predictable reactions to AP prices to their advantage when selling the products and services to buyers for the first time. Some of the ways that buyers' and sellers' attitudes affect the purchasing process are discussed here.

- For the most part, novice buyers, and particularly novice managers, overrate AP prices. The AP price is, after all, a number, something that can be compared and measured. Inexperienced shoppers are more apt to grasp a number until they gain sufficient practice in relating AP prices to EP costs, quality, and supplier services. Top management is usually aware of the tendency to focus on numbers, which probably explains why buyers are expected to have previous experience in other areas of the hospitality firm. This previous experience generally helps buyers relate AP prices to overall value.

- Price usually follows quality; a higher quality is normally accompanied by a higher price. To some extent, most buyers accept this reasoning. Unfortunately, at a certain point, the AP price keeps rising, but the quality fails to keep pace. Exactly when this difference between rising price and declining value occurs is not always clear, and inexperienced buyers and managers are liable to guess wrong. Even experienced purchasing personnel can be confused, especially if the products or services in question have just been introduced into the marketplace. Thus, suppliers and salespersons pushing a new item expect the AP price to receive more attention because no matter how much experience buyers have, they will have had little familiarity with new items.

- Price also may not necessarily correlate with quality if, for example, it is due primarily to the exemplary supplier services a particular supplier offers. Nor will there be a significant relationship between price and quality if a supplier encounters considerable difficulty attaining an item and, therefore, must extract a higher price to compensate for this problem.

- Generally, suppliers work under the assumption that what they sell to a hospitality firm is heavily influenced by a **derived demand**. A buyer's demand for any particular item is derived from the ultimate customer's demand on the buyer's hospitality operation. As a result, an analysis by suppliers of their customers' customers can be enlightening. For example, price-conscious hospitality customers are a signal to the supplier that the buyer might be price conscious. Suppliers, then, would expect a budget-motel buyer to be price conscious and would tailor their sales presentations and offerings accordingly.

> **derived demand** Refers to the notion that a buyer's demand for certain products and/or services is contingent on the needs and desires of the customers the buyer's company serves.

- Sometimes, price is secondary. Suppliers sense this whenever an analysis of the buyer's customers shows that the ultimate consumers are not price conscious. Salespersons react by emphasizing other factors. Prices may also be relatively unimportant to buyers when the suppliers are the exclusive distributors for one or more items. Furthermore, if suppliers feel that a buyer is in dire need of something, they may expect a corresponding decrease in concern about the AP price.

- If the products a buyer purchases represent a huge expense to the hospitality operation, chances are, the buyer will be price conscious. Similarly, the AP prices of certain items are usually scrutinized more closely than others. Meat, for example, may receive disproportionate attention from a buyer.

- Some buyers operate on a tight materials budget. If so, they are liable to become more price conscious than usual as the budget period approaches the end of its cycle. Also, some hospitality firms operate on a tight overall budget, and hard times cause them to examine AP prices more thoroughly. During difficult periods, in fact, some operators begin to assess the profit potential of providing their own economic values, such as purchasing raw food ingredients instead of a prepared menu entrée, thereby providing their own form of value in lieu of paying suppliers for it.

HOW AP PRICES ARE DETERMINED

Price determination seems to be one of the last managerial "arts." It is not entirely amenable to mathematical formulas; hunches and experience come into play. Suppliers, however, normally want to maintain some perceived differences among one another's items. As long as they can do this, you will continue to see varying AP prices for the same type of product, unless these prices are controlled, either directly or indirectly, by state or product association bylaws or by legislation. Theoretically, though, the resultant values should be acceptable to all concerned because of variations in supplier services.

In Chapter 4, we considered economic forces and their probable effects on the channels of distribution. We suggested two main effects: availability of products and services and their relevant AP prices. Availability and AP prices usually go hand in hand as one factor, particularly for perishable food products and basic commodities, but additional price-setting procedures exist. Basically, suppliers use at least four general methods for determining AP prices. These approaches are discussed in the following sections.

> **supplier's costs** Business expenses suppliers incur in order to operate their businesses effectively.

■ AP Prices as a Function of the Supplier's Cost

Suppliers add all their operating and nonoperating costs and attempt to allocate a certain portion of these costs to each product and service they sell. Then they add predetermined profit markups to these figures. The result is AP prices based on the **supplier's costs** of doing business.

Hospitality operators, too, typically start setting their retail prices this way. For example, menu prices usually begin with the cost of food. To this cost, management may add labor and other variable costs. A markup to cover profit and overhead is the final touch to reach an initial retail price for the menu item.

In practice, of course, each item is not always approached as a separate case. Instead, the average cost of doing business is known in relationship to sales volume, and a standard profit markup percentage may be derived.

> **conventional profit markup** The most typical percentage (or dollar amount) added to the cost a company pays for an item it sells, to compute the company's sales price.

Some products in the channel of distribution include **conventional profit markups,** which are sometimes referred to as "rules." A rule is a numerical factor that suppliers use to set their AP prices. For example, in the fresh-tomato market, one might find a "rule of three," which tells the supplier to take his or her cost of tomatoes, multiply this amount by three, and use the resulting figure for the AP price.

A cost-based AP price is a useful starting point. The supplier begins by applying a certain profit markup to the cost of his or her products. Then the supplier looks at his or her customers to see if they can pay, or will pay, this AP price. If they cannot, or will not, the supplier may lower the AP price, add more supplier services to justify the price, or, most typically, refuse to carry the item. The restaurant operator works much the same way: he or she will be reluctant to offer a low-profit menu item unless, of course, it is traditional and customers expect it.

It is important to keep in mind that although profit margins vary depending on the type of product, the average supplier in our industry earns an overall after-tax profit of only about 3.4 to 6 percent.[1] In many cases, a supplier earns only a few pennies per unit sold.[2]

■ AP Prices as a Function of Supply and Demand

Supply and demand have a great effect on perishable food prices and on commodity prices. Generally, the supply-and-demand force has its biggest impact at the beginning of the channel of distribution. Bread prices, for example, do not vary as much as flour prices. Similarly, flour prices do not vary as much as wheat prices. For these types of **commodity** items, buyers do not perceive differences among competing suppliers.

To a certain extent, suppliers lower some AP prices to sell a slow-moving item. Hospitality operators do this when they offer certain menu specials or special rates during the off-season.

Most sellers want to reduce the supply-and-demand effect; they consider it much too risky to carry several items other suppliers can duplicate exactly. The most common way to minimize the effect is to differentiate the products somehow. How can suppliers do this? Recall that quality is just one part of value. EP costs and supplier services are important, too. Suppliers know this, and as a result, most of them try to maintain profitable AP prices by manipulating supplier services. In other words, they make one or more attempts to differentiate the overall value, not just the AP price. This differentiation comes into play whenever suppliers use this method of determining AP prices.

■ AP Prices as a Function of Competitive Pressure

Suppliers operate in a reasonably competitive market, but they have different ways to turn various sorts of **competitive pressures** to their advantage. By differentiating a product's overall value, or by convincing buyers that a product's overall value is unique, suppliers can minimize competition.

In Chapter 4, we suggested that hospitality-related organizations operate in a market characterized by **monopolistic competition**. That is, price competition is a big factor simply because many of the products such organizations sell are so similar, but each firm has some type of monopoly. A steak served in a truck stop diner might be as good as or better than the same type of steak served in a gourmet restaurant. The menu prices will be different, however, because the supplier services—in this case, certainly, service style and physical surroundings—are

supply and demand
Refers to a competitive environment that exists for producers of commodity items. If supply exceeds demand, AP prices will decrease. If demand exceeds supply, AP prices will increase.

commodity A basic, raw food ingredient. It is considered by buyers to be the same regardless of which vendor sells it. For instance, all-purpose flour is often considered a commodity product, whereby any processor's product is acceptable.

competitive pressure
Force produced and exerted by companies on one another, to lower prices and/or to provide better products and services.

monopolistic competition
Refers to a competitive environment where each competitor is affected by supply and demand conditions because their businesses are very similar. However, each competitor is able to differentiate their products and/or services enough to establish a competitive advantage. Typical economic conditions faced by vendors and businesses.

different, so different in fact that the overall value of each product might be quite acceptable to consumers. For the most part, many people are willing to pay more for the same item served in a gourmet restaurant than in a diner because the perceived value of the different supplier services justify the higher price.

Suppliers seem more willing to operate under this method of setting AP prices. It gives them an edge because they can claim that there is no substitute for the value they provide. Moreover, it allows them numerous combinations of quality, supplier services, and AP prices sure to confuse even the most tightfisted, objective buyer. The crucial factor, then, would seem to be supplier services. Delivery schedules, sales courtesy, general reliability—all these factors, and more, work their way into a product's overall value.

■ Buyer Pricing

buyer pricing Occurs whenever a buyer does not have a clear-cut specification; the vendor then helps the buyer determine what he or she needs. Will also occur whenever you engage in panic buying. This method will significantly increase your cost of goods sold.

panic buying Occurs when a buyer is in a pinch and will pay any price to get the product immediately.

Without a doubt, suppliers prefer this type of price determination. Unfortunately, the buyer who practices this procedure is almost certain to overpay.

Buyer pricing comes about in one of two ways. It will occur if a buyer does not have a detailed purchase or product specification; in this situation, the supplier "assists" the buyer in developing the spec, which, of course, will tend to place the buyer in a precarious financial position. Buyer pricing also occurs if a buyer consistently engages in **panic buying**, that is, if he or she does not follow the principles discussed in Chapter 8 and continually runs out of products and relies on suppliers to make emergency deliveries. These emergencies will most assuredly result in significantly higher AP prices. There may also be penalties charged for unscheduled deliveries.

WAYS TO REDUCE AP PRICE AND INCREASE VALUE: DISCOUNTS

A quick way to increase a product's value is to pay less for that product yet keep the same quality and supplier services. This is not only a quick method but also leads to dramatic results: the buyer's superiors can easily see and appreciate a lower AP price, whereas a bit more quality and supplier services do not make as deep an impression, at least not immediately. Buyers in large organizations are quick to note that their superiors notice a lowered AP price. Chances are they will be asked to explain how they obtained the lower AP price, which gives them an opportunity to publicize their excellent performance. Consequently, buyers continually seek a lower AP price to increase an item's overall value.

Nevertheless, buyers should be cautious when seeking a lower AP price. The most important consideration is how well the purchased item fulfills its intended use. If a buyer pays a slightly higher AP price, all that will be lost is money. If an item performs poorly, however, a buyer will waste money and time and may create some long-run employee or customer relations problems.

When seeking a lower AP price, the buyer should emphasize increasing or maintaining overall value. At no time should a buyer accept a lower AP price if the overall value of a product or service is reduced disproportionately, unless this is done with management's approval. The buyer should also fix a value on the time it takes to find or negotiate a lower AP price.

A buyer can use several methods in an attempt to decrease an AP price. A thorough value analysis of all products and services purchased will reveal the most feasible ones. Theoretically, a buyer can use some or all of the methods discussed in the following sections of the chapter.

■ Cash Discounts

A supplier may be willing to accept a lower AP price, provided he or she receives cash in advance, at the time of delivery, or shortly thereafter. This is particularly true if the supplier is cash-starved. This practice is referred to as a **cash discount**.

The cash discount is a viable alternative only when the buyer has the authority to promise a quick payment and only when enough cash is available. In large firms, the accounting department or financial officer decides the payment schedule (in small operations, it is the owner–manager's decision) unless, of course, suppliers have strict payment demands or buyers have the authority to negotiate payment schedules that do not require a quick cash outlay. The accounting department usually does this as a part of its own **cash management** program and because it may be more efficient to pay bills on a periodic basis. In addition, companies rarely have large amounts of cash available on a moment's notice. Nevertheless, paying cash up front can be extremely economical. The immediate cash payment, sometimes coupled with the proviso that you are buying an item "as-is," can be such an attractive money-saving opportunity that sometimes it might even pay to borrow the funds to complete such a transaction.

A concept related to the cash discount is the **cash rebate**, which is sometimes also referred to as a "rebate" or a **coupon refund**. Essentially, the supplier will charge you the full AP price, but later on, after you send him or her some proof of purchase, you will receive a bit of money back—a cash rebate. It does not appear to us that this activity saves as much money as it might seem to initially. Generally, you have to pay postage, absorb the costs of reproducing bills or other proof-of-purchase records, and endure the long wait for your money. Most large hospitality organizations do not like this procedure because of the extra work involved; they prefer bargaining for lower AP prices up front. Nevertheless, these types of rebates are quite common for many items, and, if economical, they should be pursued as much as possible.

cash discount   An award for prompt payment, for paying in advance of the delivery, or using a cash-on-delivery (COD) bill-paying procedure.

cash management Procedures used to ensure that a company's cash will be tightly controlled and handled effectively and efficiently.

cash rebate   Occurs when a vendor charges the full AP price for an item, but later on, after you provide proof-of-purchase documentation, he or she will send you a check for a small amount of money, or will credit this amount to your next bill.

coupon refund   Another term for cash rebate.

■ Promotional Discounts

A **promotional discount** is a rebate from the supplier that the buyer's company must use to promote the retail sale of the product. For example, a cheesecake manufacturer might grant a 2 percent rebate if you agree to promote his or her product in your foodservice operation.

Today, the traditional promotional discount is not so common. More often, suppliers provide free promotional materials now and then. Some companies do, however, provide coupons and offers to entice the purchase of

promotional discount Price discount awarded to the buyer if he or she allows the vendor to promote the product in the hospitality operation. Or if the hospitality operation agrees to personally help promote the sale of the product to its customers.

their products. Many suppliers also like to do joint promotions with hospitality operations.[3] For example, a liquor distributor may split the cost of a special event with a local nightclub operator. In this case, although the nightclub operator does not receive a lower AP price, he or she does enjoy an increased promotional budget.

If the option to gain a promotional discount arises, management should not jump too quickly. The extra money is, of course, tempting, but you need to do some serious thinking about how such a promotion will affect your operation's reputation. This decision can have several ramifications, and some of them may prove troublesome in the long run.

■ Introductory Offers

New products continually come on the market. Some suppliers move these items by selling them for an inexpensive AP price, at least for the first one or two orders. Alternately, you might buy one and get one free. The obvious problem, of course, is that these offers are temporary. You can

> **introductory offer** AP price discount offered by suppliers to buyers who purchase an item that is newly available in the marketplace. The discount may be in the form of a cash rebate or it might include a free item for every one the buyer purchases at the regular AP price.
>
> **quantity discount** A price reduction for buying a large amount of one specific type of merchandise.

hardly make a career of moving from one **introductory offer** to the other. This strategy is inconvenient, and suppliers do not like it. However, you could take advantage of an offer and stock up on the merchandise in anticipation that you can use it later, for example, for special parties.

■ Considerations When Evaluating Discounts

Large hospitality operations tend to have more opportunity for discounts, especially promotional, volume, and **quantity discounts**—and, to a certain extent, cash discounts as well. Many chain operations can earn considerable income just by keeping track of the cash discount period, which is usually 10 days, and paying at the last possible moment before the end of this period. Discounts raise some problems, however:

1. Hospitality operations may become too intent on the discounts and may lose track of the real cost of purchases. Fortunately, keeping the books according to the *Uniform System of Accounts for Restaurants*[4] can separate the real cost from any discount.

2. Cash discounts may interfere with the firm's normal accounts payable schedule. Unless the operation has several cash discounts, which is no longer likely, it may be too much trouble to pay bills on different days.

3. The operation might stay with a "discounting" supplier longer than it should. For instance, if the supplier delivers slightly inferior foods from time to time, the firm may begin to overlook this problem to retain the discount.

4. Even if it is profitable for the hospitality operation to take advantage of a discount, it may be necessary to undergo a costly borrowing procedure to get the cash. The firms must add the interest cost of such borrowing to the cost of the purchase for decision-making purposes.

5. If the hospitality operation is lucky enough to receive a cash discount, it needs to know whether the payment due date will be extended if it has to return the delivered merchandise and wait for two or three days for an acceptable replacement. Does the cash discount period start when the replacement arrives, or does it start when the first, unacceptable delivery was made? This has caused many a strained relationship between buyers and sellers.

WAYS TO REDUCE AP PRICE AND INCREASE VALUE: PURCHASING AND RECEIVING PROCEDURES

■ Provide Your Own Supplier Services and/or Economic Values

Several possible cost-cutting opportunities exist. As is true with **make-or-buy analysis**, buyers benefit from considering the many alternatives available. For example, buyers can save money by purchasing products from a no-frills **wholesale club**, where customers are expected to pay with cash, credit card, or debit card and provide their own delivery.

Buyers may also be able to select and pay for only those supplier services or **economic values** they desire. For example, some suppliers may offer high-priority, regular, and low-priority delivery options, with payment according to the speed of delivery. Some suppliers may offer price concessions for online orders, which are more cost-effective than orders placed during personal sales visits or over the phone. These options relate to the payment policies discussed later in this chapter. Earlier, we discussed the potential costs and benefits of buyers providing many of their own supplier services and economic values. The conclusion seems to be that many firms attempting to do this have achieved mixed results and, in many cases, do not save nearly as much as they anticipated or have actually lost money.

■ Shop around More Frequently

Buyers who shop around frequently usually practice a technique that is sometimes referred to as **line-item purchasing**. This purchasing strategy is used to obtain competitive bids for several products from two or more suppliers. Buyers then select each individual product from the supplier who has given the lowest bid for it. For example, each supplier may bid on a total list of 10 products. However, the only products an individual supplier will be able to sell will be the ones he or she has priced lower than those the competing bidders have priced.

Suppliers do not like buyers to **cherry pick** their bids in this manner. They prefer buyers who use a purchasing technique that is sometimes referred to as **bottom-line, firm-price purchasing**. Using this buying procedure, buyers agree to purchase a group of products from the supplier who bids the lowest total price for the group. In this case, the successful bidder comes away with the complete order, while the unsuccessful ones leave empty-handed.

Although it takes considerable time, money, and effort to shop around, the potential rewards may make this strategy very profitable. If buyers have the time to develop specs and seek bids and do not mind dealing with

---

make-or-buy analysis A cost/benefit analysis whereby the buyer tries to determine if, for example, it is more economical to purchase raw foods and make a finished product in-house, or whether it may be less expensive to purchase a convenience, value-added food. The buyer usually considers the cost of food, labor, overhead, labor skill available, and so forth when making the decision.

wholesale club A type of buying club. It is a cash-and-carry operation patronized primarily by small hospitality operations that do not order enough from vendors to qualify for free delivery. Buyers usually have to pay a membership fee.

economic value Represents the increase in AP price that occurs as a product journeys through the distribution channel. For example, 10 pounds of preportioned steak is more valuable, and more expensive, than 10 pounds of meat that has to be processed further in a restaurant's kitchen.

line-item purchasing A practice of buying from vendors only the individual items on a competitive bid sheet that are priced lower than those submitted by competing vendors. For instance, if a purveyor bids on 10 items, but is the lowest bidder on only 1 of them, the buyer will buy only the 1 item. Sometimes referred to as *cherry picking*. The opposite of bottom-line, firm-price purchasing.

cherry picking See line-item purchasing.

several potential suppliers, generally they will obtain lower AP prices. As always, though, it is not quite clear whether the lower AP prices translate into increased values.

■ Blanket Orders

A **blanket order** is a form of **volume discount**. It usually includes quite a few miscellaneous items, no one of which is particularly expensive. However, the sum of the large number of low-cost items included in the blanket order makes it worth the supplier's time and effort, and some AP price concessions may be granted.

The basic question with blanket orders seems to be whether you should try to order on an optimal-size basis or to order these items only a few times a year. In most cases, for products such as amenities with the company logo, it would probably benefit you to place a large order once in a while because any optimal order size you might calculate would almost certainly be impractical. In fact, most buyers opt for a reasonably large par stock for these miscellaneous items and order up to par only once every three or four months.

When you place a blanket order for miscellaneous items, their AP prices may or may not decrease. Even without a reduction in AP prices, you can expect some savings if you use blanket orders because you significantly reduce your annual **ordering costs** while producing only a slight increase in annual **storage costs**.

■ Improved Negotiations

It is possible to lower the AP price by adopting a strict negotiating posture. For many products, AP prices are pretty well set and are not normally subject to **negotiation**. But supplier services and economic values can be manipulated, which might result in a higher overall value. Also, it is sometimes possible to negotiate more favorable **credit terms** or payment schedules. Although this does not lower the AP price, it does increase overall value because you can delay paying your bills and can use that money elsewhere, if only for a little while.

AP prices are generally a little more flexible for **long-term contracts** and certain types of services. The AP price of a product purchased on a six-month contract basis is usually lower than the AP price for the same item purchased on a day-to-day basis. Also, strict AP prices do not always accompany such services as contract cleaning and consulting.

■ Substitutions

When AP prices increase substantially, management can raise prices, lower the quality, drop the item from its offerings, or stop offering the item but carry a substitute.

Offering a substitute is often used in the restaurant business and, to some extent, in the lodging industry. This strategy does not necessarily lower the AP price of any item, but it can lower the total cost of operating the business. Buyers and suppliers should be encouraged to offer substitute possibilities to management because they are the first to notice price trends, availability trends, and increased costs of preparation or service. They also are the first to evaluate new items on the market. Although these substitutes can save money, guest perceptions of the item must be carefully considered.

■ Hedging

The idea behind **hedging** is to maintain a specific AP price, not to reduce it. For example, assume that you wish to maintain the AP price of chicken for the next month. To do this, you would determine how much product you need for one month and enter into an agreement, usually a **futures contract**, to purchase this amount one month from now at a specific price. During the month, you would purchase product as needed on the open market at the current AP price. If the AP price is higher than it was at the beginning of the month, you would be paying more for the product. However, your agreement, or futures contract, theoretically would be worth more. That is, the value of your agreement, which can be sold on the futures market, would increase. This increase would offset the higher, open-market AP price for the commodities. Consequently, you offset your high purchase price by selling your futures contract at a profit that you would then use to subsidize your "loss" on the open market. Where hedging is successful, the tendency is to maintain a stable AP price for the month.

> **hedging** Attempting to reduce or avoid the risk of fluctuating AP prices by taking a position in the commodity futures market.
>
> **futures contract** Agreement to purchase or sell a commodity for delivery in the future.

But buyers should consider several problems associated with hedging: (1) a lot of cash may be necessary to buy futures contracts because the minimum amount of product involved in each agreement is relatively large; (2) hedging can be done for only a few items, though these items may account for the bulk of your purchasing dollar; (3) transactions costs are involved—you must pay people to trade the contracts for you, as you cannot do this yourself unless you own a seat on a **commodity exchange**; (4) few small hospitality operations can muster the time necessary to engage in this activity; (5) the transactions costs might easily overpower the benefits you could derive from this type of protection against AP price fluctuations; and (6) it is possible, though unlikely, that no one would want to purchase your contract when you need to sell it to break even. Glenn Millar further explains the mechanics and benefits of hedging in the accompanying sidebar. Because hedging is a complicated procedure, it is more commonly practiced by larger hospitality corporations than independent operations.[5]

> **commodity exchange** An organized market for the purchase and sale of enforceable contracts to deliver a commodity, such as wheat, or a financial instrument, such as eurodollars, at some future date.

HEDGING YOUR BUDGET—A MINI-ECONOMICS LESSON
Glenn Millar, President Red Rock Capital Management, San Francisco, California

Courtesy of Glenn Millar, President, Red Rock Capital Management, San Francisco, California

It comes around every year like clockwork—budgeting time. This is when every purchasing director wishes for a crystal ball to use to see the future. What will be the price of prime rib in six months? Will the cost of paper products go up because of a new clean air act that affects paper mills? Will there be a drought that will raise the price of feed and therefore the cost of poultry?

The goal is to develop as accurate a budget as possible, neither too high nor too low. Hedging is one way to balance a budget's estimates. According

HEDGING YOUR BUDGET—A MINI-ECONOMICS LESSON   (continued)

to Glenn Millar, dairy commodity trader and risk consultant for Red Rock Capital Management LLC, "People don't hedge enough. Hedging is an appropriate way to mitigate risk when making financial plans for the future."

What is hedging, and how does it work? Using butter as an example, we'll explore the hedging process. Let's say that in the next year you know your hotel restaurant operations will use 40,000 pounds of butter. You look at the *Daily Dairy Report* (www.dailydairyreport.com), which provides a good summary of future dairy prices. You discover that the average price for butter futures in the coming year is $1.35 per pound, with prices as high as $1.40 per pound for some months and as low as $1.30 per pound for others. Your estimate for budgeting purposes will be that you will buy 40,000 pounds of butter at $1.35 per pound in the coming year for a budget line item of $54,000. You could stop right there. This is a good estimate, based on reliable information and it will probably satisfy your chief financial officer.

What if the price of butter goes up dramatically, costing more than was budgeted? You might find yourself having to cut back on the purchase of less critical items to stay within your overall budget.

There is a way to make sure that even if the price of butter rises, your budget won't be affected. Hedging involves a separate transaction where one purchases futures contracts on the exchange market. A "futures contract" is an agreement to purchase or sell a commodity (in our case butter) at a certain agreed-upon price, in a specific timeframe.

As an astute purchasing director, you buy two futures contracts for butter at $1.35 per pound, each to expire during the coming year. Butter futures are sold in 20,000-pound lots so this will cover your 40,000-pound requirement. Futures brokers generally charge a $25 fee per transaction or $50 for the two purchases. In addition, when you purchase a future, there is a margin amount or good faith deposit that is required to be in an account with your broker. For butter, that amount is $1,000, and because you are buying two futures, you will be required to have $2,000 in your account.

It is important to remember that with futures contracts you never actually take possession of the butter, you are simply buying the "right" to that amount of butter at a given price. An individual could buy two futures contracts for butter as a short-term investment just as easily. He or she will never take possession of the butter; the investor will simply sell the right to that butter at some point in the future.

Now let's say that in three months you sell the first contract at the current market price of $1.50 per pound. Your gain on the sale of the future is $0.15 per pound, but the butter you are actually buying from your supplier is also costing you $1.50 per pound. The net gain on the future offsets the "loss" you would show on your budget. The sale of the contract will net $3,000, which can be moved from your brokerage account to general funds to purchase butter at the higher rate.

Six months later you sell the other contract at $1.20 per pound, which results in a loss of $0.15 per pound. However, the price you pay to your supplier is also $0.15 lower than your budgeted amount. Your net cost—$1.35—equals your magical budget number. At this time you will need to put $3,000 back in your brokerage account to offset the loss on the sale, but at the same time you are paying $3,000 less for butter than you had budgeted.

HEDGING YOUR BUDGET—A MINI-ECONOMICS LESSON   (continued)

"Remember, when you are hedging, you are not hoping to make money by speculating in the market, you are trying to mitigate the impact of market fluctuations on your budget," said Millar. "It is important to keep in mind the reasons you are purchasing the futures contracts and focus on the budgeted amount as the goal," he added.

Once you have convinced your chief executive officer of the value of hedging, you can buy futures for a number of other big-ticket items such as beef, poultry, pork, and other dairy products besides butter. You can also buy futures for energy including gas, electricity, and gasoline for fleet vehicles.

"Hedging is a powerful tool for purchasing agents who want to make accurate budget decisions in our world of uncertainty and risk," concluded Millar.

Glenn Millar is a former partner at Kellers Creamery LLC, a $500 million butter dairy company located on the East Coast. He is currently the president of Red Rock Capital Management, market maker for the Chicago Mercantile Exchange's numerous dairy contracts.

Resources

www.dailydairyreport.com

www.investordictionary.com

■ Odd-Hour Deliveries

If suppliers deliver at night or very early in the morning, they should be able to handle more delivery stops because of the decrease in road traffic and other distractions. It is not clear just what type of AP price reduction you could expect with these **odd-hour deliveries**. Theoretically, you should gain some monetary benefit by increasing delivery efficiency. However, if these off-hours deliveries require extra personnel or existing employees to work more hours, there may not be savings.

A more practical option might be the possibility of receiving monetary considerations from a supplier if you agree to receive deliveries during the **sacred hours**. The sacred hours are those surrounding the lunch period, typically from 11:30 A.M. to 1:30 P.M. In some cases, the foodservice buyer who agrees to receive deliveries during this time period may earn some price concessions.

> **odd-hour delivery** Shipment delivered at times of the day or week when a receiving agent is not usually scheduled to work. Buyers who agree to these types of deliveries may receive a discount.
>
> **sacred hours** Time of the day when you would not want to accept deliveries. Usually these hours are from 11:30 A.M. to 1:30 P.M.

■ Co-Op Purchasing

Recall that a purchasing co-op is a group of buyers, each representing a different hospitality operation, who pool their individual small orders. The resulting single large order more than likely qualifies the group for a lower AP price.

Several advantages and disadvantages are associated with co-op purchasing, and some of these are addressed in Chapter 10. It does seem clear that AP prices decrease whenever you purchase a large amount of a product or service. However, what is not clear is the effect on EP costs.

cost-plus purchasing procedure   Under this purchasing procedure, a product's AP price is equal to the supplier's cost of the product plus an agreed-upon profit markup.

landed cost   The cost used by the vendor in a cost-plus buying arrangement.

Cost-Plus Purchasing

Under the **cost-plus purchasing procedure**, the AP price is equal to the supplier's cost of the product, which is sometimes referred to as the **landed cost**, plus an agreed-upon profit markup. The markup can be a set dollar amount or a percentage of the supplier's cost. Either way, if the supplier's cost decreases, the buyer will enjoy a price reduction. However, if the supplier's cost increases, so will the AP price.

Buyers must be willing to incur a bit of risk if they participate in this type of buying process. A sudden price increase is the most obvious risk. However, buyers must also be careful to monitor suppliers so that they do not subcontract products to their friends several times, thereby creating an artificial "daisy-chain" type of distribution channel, whereby the suppliers' costs are illegally inflated. In addition, if the profit markup is a percentage, suppliers have no incentive to control their costs. (Note that government buyers usually are not allowed to enter into a cost-plus purchase agreement if the profit markup is a percentage of cost; however, they can usually agree to a set dollar amount.) Wise buyers normally have, and exercise, the right to audit the supplier's records to determine whether the correct AP price has, in fact, been charged.

Large hospitality operations generally prefer a long-term arrangement in which both the availability of a product and its AP price are predictable. Although suppliers usually do not mind

fixed-price contract   Contract that does not allow price fluctuations.

agreeing to provide a certain amount of product to a hospitality company, they do not like to enter into a long-term, **fixed-price contract**. So, the use of a cost-plus arrangement seems to be the logical compromise. Negotiations center on the agreed-upon profit markup, not on the actual AP price itself. It appears that a hospitality corporation must follow this strategy if it wants to develop long-term contractual arrangements with its suppliers.

Exchange Bartering

Exchange bartering is simply the practice of trading your products or services for something you need. This is a relatively common practice in the hospitality industry (see Figure 9.2).[6] For

exchange bartering   Another term for barter.

barter group   A group of businesses that wish to barter for products and services and use trade dollars instead of cash money to get what they need. The group is organized and administered by a third party, and a fee is usually assessed each participant whenever they make a deal. The opposite of direct bartering, whereby two or more persons get together on their own to make a deal.

instance, it is not unusual for a hotel company to exchange room nights, restaurant meals, and beverages for radio and print advertising. Industry experts think that as long as bartering represents no more than approximately 10 to 15 percent of a hospitality operation's total sales revenue, it can be a very profitable arrangement.

Although the Internet has made bartering much easier, bartering still has its costs. For instance, you may need to join a **barter group**, an organization that connects companies that have services or products to trade. Some of these barter groups do not charge a membership fee, but others may charge hundreds of dollars just to join. Other costs may include transaction fees, which are a percentage of the value of the exchange; annual dues or charges related to account payments; late fees, and so forth.[7] A good discussion of barter clubs can be found at www.barternews.com/barterclubs.

FIGURE 9.2 An announcement by an organization that matches individual businesses that want to trade.
Courtesy of ITEX.

You may be able to avoid these costs if you engage in what is sometimes referred to as **direct bartering** whereby you personally make a deal with another business to swap goods and/or services.[8]

Bartering presents other potential difficulties. The Internal Revenue Service (IRS) may be more apt to audit your income and expense records if you engage in a significant amount of bartering because the agency suspects bartering might become the prelude to unreported income. In 1982, the IRS recognized bartering as a legitimate

> **direct bartering** When two persons trade between themselves rather than through a barter group.

purchase strategy so long as "trade" dollars are reported correctly for tax purposes. With the advent of bartering exchanges, the Internet has added some extra level of difficulty when filing with the IRS. If a bartering exchange website is used, then additional paperwork is required (Form 1099-B).[9]

The savings associated with bartering can be significant. For example, when you pay a bill of $100 with $100 worth of menu items, you have been able to discharge the obligation for much less out-of-pocket cost to you. Furthermore, if you restrict your trading partners' ability to exchange their meal credits—say, allowing them to eat during only the slow periods—you may gain even more financial benefit.

WAYS TO REDUCE AP PRICE AND INCREASE VALUE: ADDITIONAL METHODS

■ Make-or-Buy Analysis

Buyers should periodically perform make-or-buy analyses, at least for more expensive purchases. For example, a hospitality operation might find that it can save a great deal of money by cutting its own steaks instead of purchasing them precut. When performing these analyses, though, buyers must be absolutely certain to consider all relevant cost data because it is very easy to overestimate these types of cost savings.

■ Lower the Quality Standard

Although it is possible to lower the quality one notch while lowering the AP price two notches, it is unlikely that this tactic will be successful. We have suggested elsewhere that buyers seldom have the authority to reduce the **quality standard** unilaterally. Management input is normally required. In recessionary times, operators are often tempted to buy lower-quality items rather than to raise prices. However, they must be careful to consider the possible effects of lower perceived value and guest satisfaction. Whenever you do this, though, you risk incurring negative guest reaction; you especially take the chance that loyal customers will not return. Switching the quality of a product or multiple products can hold both negative and positive reactions with customers.[10] A hospitality operation's image and reputation are very fragile and could easily be tarnished irreparably if quality standards are altered.

> **quality standard** The type of quality you consistently use and that the hospitality operation is known for. Buyers typically communicate this standard to vendors by specifying brand names and government grades.

■ Economical Packaging

> **economical packaging** Packing methods and packaging materials used that will reduce overall product costs.

Buyers may look for **economical packaging** and packaging that reduces waste. As well as being environmentally friendly, large-volume packs are normally cheaper per unit of weight than their smaller counterparts. For instance, a 1-gallon container of diced tomatoes usually costs less than four 1-quart containers. Another advantage of large containers is that they tend to lessen the possibility of petty pilferage. Other types of containers such as cube-shaped boxes rather than cylindrical cans can save shelf space and storage costs. In addition, a lot of packaging contains such cosmetic touches as pictures and suggested recipes, which tend to increase the overall cost. Because you buy products for production and not, like supermarkets, for immediate resale, you gain no benefit from attractive but inefficient packaging. Theoretically, more standardized packaging should reduce the AP price.

■ Reevaluate EP Costs

As we have discussed, it is important to base purchasing decisions on EP rather than AP costs. Because products can change or intended uses may affect what EP is desired, you should reevaluate and recalculate these costs on a regular basis as well as when suppliers offer you a new product or one in a modified form.

You can never ignore an ingredient's overall value, of which the EP cost is only one factor. However, assuming that the quality and the supplier services are the same across the board, and also assuming that your other expenses will not increase if you purchase different types of ingredients, you owe it to yourself to examine the potential of purchasing another product that can be cheaper for you in the long run.[11]

You need to have a storehouse of data to perform this type of analysis. Each ingredient that you currently purchase, as well as each ingredient that you could conceivably purchase, must be listed, along with its PF and PD. As such, as we discussed in Chapter 8, hospitality operations with significant resources and using up-to-date technology are more likely to do this type of analysis.

If you have these data, you can proceed to evaluate the EP costs of each ingredient. All you really need is each ingredient's: (1) AP price per unit and (2) its edible (or servable, or usable) yield percentage. For instance, if you know that raw corned beef brisket carries an AP price of $1.38 per pound and that its edible yield percentage is 50 percent, you can determine very quickly the EP cost per pound for this item by using the formula in the practical method discussed in Chapter 8 and noted at the beginning of this chapter, which is repeated here:

$$\text{EP cost} = \text{AP price} \,/\, \text{edible- (or servable-, or usable-) yield percentage}$$
$$\text{EP cost per pound of raw corned beef brisket} = \$1.38 \,/\, 0.50 = \$2.76$$

I EXAMPLE

Given this data, determine the EP cost for one serving of each ingredient.

Ingredient	Edible Yield (%)	Serving Size (OZ.)	AP Price Per Pound
(a) -Raw corned beef brisket	50	4	$1.38
(b) -Raw corned beef round	75	4	$1.45
(c) -Cooked corned beef brisket	90	4	$2.98
(d) -Cooked corned beef round	95	4	$2.45

SOLUTION:

Compute each ingredient's PF:

   a. PF = 16 / 4 = 4

   b. PF = 16 / 4 = 4

   c. PF = 16 / 4 = 4

   d. PF = 16 / 4 = 4

Compute each ingredient's PD:

   a. PD = 4 × 0.50 = 2.00

   b. PD = 4 × 0.75 = 3.00

   c. PD = 4 × 0.90 = 3.60

   d. PD = 4 × 0.95 = 3.80

Compute each ingredient's EP cost:

   a. EP cost = $1.38 / 2.00 = $0.69

   b. EP cost = $1.45 / 3.00 = $0.48

   c. EP cost = $2.98 / 3.60 = $0.83

   d. EP cost = $2.45 / 3.80 = $0.64

II EXAMPLE

Given this data, compute the EP cost for one serving of each ingredient.

Ingredient	Edible Yield (%)	Serving Size (G)	AP Price Per Kilogram
(a) Fresh raw spinach	60	90	$1.75
(b) Frozen leaf spinach	100	90	$2.95
(c) Frozen chopped spinach	100	90	$3.25

SOLUTION:

Compute each ingredient's PF:

   a. PF = 1000 / 90 = 11.11

   b. PF = 1000 / 90 = 11.11

   c. PF = 1000 / 90 = 11.11

Compute each ingredient's PD:

   a. PD = 11.11 × 0.60 = 6.67

   b. PD = 11.11 × 1.00 = 11.11

   c. PD = 11.11 × 1.00 = 11.11

Compute each ingredient's EP cost:

   a. EP cost = $1.75 / 6.67 = $0.26

   b. EP cost = $2.95 / 11.11 = $0.27

   c. EP cost = $3.25 / 11.11 = $0.29

‖ EXAMPLE

Given this data, determine the servable portion cost for one serving of each ingredient.

Ingredient	Edible Yield (%)	Serving Size (MI)	AP Price Per Liter
(a) Scotch (750 mL bottle)	95	50	$8.25
(b) Scotch (1 liter bottle)	95	50	$7.95
(c) Scotch (1.75 liter bottle)	100	50	$7.25

SOLUTION:

Compute each ingredient's PF:

    a. PF = 1000 / 50 = 20

    b. PF = 1000 / 50 = 20

    c. PF = 1000 / 50 = 20

Compute each ingredient's PD:

    a. PD = 20 × 0.95 = 19

    b. PD = 20 × 0.95 = 19

    c. PD = 20 × 1.00 = 20

Compute each ingredient's servable portion cost:

    a. Servable portion cost = $8.25 / 19 = $0.43

    b. Servable portion cost = $7.95 / 19 = $0.42

    c. Servable portion cost = $7.25 / 20 = $0.36

This type of cost information is very useful to buyers because it provides a solid base on which they can make sound purchasing decisions. Buyers are not the only ones who will find this information useful, however; so will other managers and supervisors, who rely on product cost data to perform their jobs. Production managers, for instance, also use these data when performing their menu-planning duties. Specifically, product cost data are needed whenever a supervisor or manager has to "precost" the menu and calculate suggested menu prices.

Precosting a menu involves costing out each menu offering. This is done by first calculating the EP cost of each ingredient included in a menu offering and then obtaining a total EP cost per serving. The result of this work is the calculation of each menu item's **standard cost**, that is, the expected (or theoretical) cost of the menu item.

To see how a standard cost is calculated, consider the following example.

precosting Calculating the costs of all ingredients used in a standard recipe to determine the cost for one serving.

standard cost The expected cost. Sometimes referred to as the "potential" cost, the "planned" cost, the "budgeted" cost, or the "theoretical" cost. Typically used to help set menu prices, sleeping room prices, and so forth. Also used to compare to the actual cost incurred to determine if management is achieving its budgetary goals.

PRECOSTING EXAMPLE

Menu item: Steak Dinner

Ingredient	Servable Yield (OZ.)	Edible Yield (%)	AP Price Per Pound
Steak	12	80	$4.75
Beans	4	90	$0.65
Potatoes	4	75	$0.90

SOLUTION:

Compute each ingredient's PF:

$$PF_{(steak)} = 16/12 = 1.33$$
$$PF_{(beans)} = 16/4 = 4.00$$
$$PF_{(potatoes)} = 16/4 = 4.00$$

Compute each ingredient's PD:

$$PD_{(steak)} = 1.33 \times 0.80 = 1.06$$
$$PD_{(beans)} = 4.00 \times 0.90 = 3.60$$
$$PD_{(potatoes)} = 4.00 \times 0.75 = 3.00$$

Compute each ingredient's EP cost:

$$EP\ cost_{(steak)} = \$4.75/1.06 = \$4.48$$
$$EP\ cost_{(beans)} = \$0.65/3.60 = \$0.18$$
$$EP\ cost_{(potatoes)} = \$0.90/3.00 = \$0.30$$

Compute the standard cost:

$$
\begin{array}{r}
\$4.48 \\
0.18 \\
\underline{+0.30} \\
\underline{\$4.96}
\end{array}
$$

menu price calculation
The food cost of a menu item divided by its food cost percentage. Alternately, the beverage cost of a menu item divided by its beverage cost percentage.

product cost percentage
Equal to: [(cost of a product divided by its selling price) multiplied by 100]. A typical example would be the food cost percentage.

Once a standard cost is computed, a manager can calculate a suggested **menu price calculation** by dividing the standard cost by the target (i.e., desired) **product cost percentage**. For example, if the manager wanted the food cost of the steak dinner menu item to be 30 percent of its menu price, the suggested menu price would be $16.53 ($4.96/0.30 = $16.53).

Note that if $4.96 = 0.30 × menu price, then

$$\text{Menu price} = \$4.96/0.30 = \$16.53$$

The $16.53 figure is only a suggested menu price. The wise hospitality operator will usually begin with this price, but he or she typically will adjust it somewhat so that it is consistent with local market conditions. Furthermore, the manager would not normally adopt a menu price of $16.53; more than likely, he or she would use a price of $16.50 or $16.95, figures that are more recognizable to the typical customer.

The standard cost can also be used in a hospitality operation's overall cost control system. For instance, if you find that at the end of the month you sold 500 steak dinners, the total standard food cost for the ingredients needed to prepare and serve these meals would be $2,480 (500 × $4.96 = $2,480). This total standard cost can then be compared with the total **actual cost of food sold**, which may be calculated in this way:

> Inventory value (in dollars) at beginning
> of month for the items in the dinner
> + Purchases for the month (in dollars)
> = Inventory available for the month (in dollars)
> − Inventory value (in dollars) at the end of month
> − Other credit (e.g., food used for employee meals)
> = Actual cost (in dollars)

The actual cost should be close to the total standard cost. If a significant **variance** exists between them, the hospitality operator will need to diagnose the situation, uncover the problem(s), and take corrective action.

OPPORTUNITY BUYS

One general category of purchases that can reduce AP prices dramatically deserves a separate discussion. Some single event may occur that causes a supplier to offer a bargain. A number of examples of the kind of opportunity we refer to appear in the discussion that follows.

Suppliers offer **opportunity buys** for several reasons: (1) Sometimes they give a normal quantity discount for large purchases of one item. When you buy larger and larger amounts at one time of a particular item, the per-unit AP price decreases. For example, when you buy 50 cases at one time, the AP price per case might be $8. But if you increase your order size to 100 cases, the AP price per case might be $7.95. (The figures 50 and 100 cases are sometimes referred to as **break points**.) (2) Many suppliers offer volume discounts for large purchases that include several items. (In our experience, quantity discounts and volume discounts are the most common types of opportunity buys.) (3) Suppliers may have a **blowout sale, buyout sale,** or **closeout sale**. These "sales" generally refer to merchandise that may be unsalable for one reason or another, or merchandise that must be sold at a loss. In most instances, the buyer of these "sales" is in a position to take advantage of someone else's misfortune. (4) Some suppliers have **move lists**, or "**muzz-go**" **lists**, which include items that are on the verge of spoiling or, for one reason or another, are of poorer quality.

These items, though, are wholesome and some hospitality operations can use them. (5) Suppliers might have received an excellent buy and want to pass some of the savings on to their good customers. (6) Suppliers may be cash-starved and willing to offer cash discounts on large purchases. (7) New suppliers

actual cost of food sold Equal to: (beginning inventory + purchases − ending inventory) +/ − any adjustments, such as employee meals, complimentary items given to guests, and so forth.

variance Difference between what is expected and what actually happened. Typically used to refer to the difference between the standard cost and the actual cost.

opportunity buy A purchase intended to save a great deal of money. The products are price discounted. A quantity discount is an example of an opportunity buy.

break point The point at which a vendor will accept a lower price. For instance, if you buy from 1 to 50 cases, the AP price may be $5 per case, but if you purchase more than 50 cases, the AP price may be $4.75 per case. In this example, the break point is 50.

blowout sale Refers to the sale of old, defective, or discontinued merchandise that is usually sold at a huge discount.

buyout sale or **closeout sale** Another term for blowout sale.

move list A list of products that need to be sold ASAP. For instance, they may be on the verge of spoilage, or they might be discontinued items. If vendors have items on a move list they may call you to see if you're interested in any of them. Usually the AP prices of these items are deeply discounted.

muzz-go list Another term for move list.

may be trying to break into the market and will sell items at a loss to introduce their company. (8) Established suppliers may be introducing a new product line and, while so doing, may reduce their AP price. (This is referred to as an introductory offer when the amount you can purchase is relatively small.) To take advantage of an opportunity buy, a buyer usually must agree to purchase in very large amounts. The buyer may have to purchase the item when he or she already has a complete stock. In addition, the buyer usually has to produce the cash in advance or on delivery.

Buyers must, of course, evaluate both the quantitative and the qualitative factors when exploring the attractiveness of an opportunity buy. On the quantitative side, buyers first must consider the numbers: they must determine the potential savings. If the savings are insufficient, buyers do not need to evaluate any qualitative factors.

For example, assume that you normally purchase 600 cases of canned peaches once a month. The AP price is $5 per case, for a total of $3,000. You have an opportunity to purchase a two-month supply, or 1,200 cases, for $4.95 per case, for a total of $5,940. Your ordering cost for each order is $25. Storage costs are 24 percent per year, or 2 percent per month. What should you do?

Figure 9.3 depicts a quantitative analysis of this opportunity buy. In the usual situation, you would spend $6,050. In the proposed situation, you would spend only $6,023.80. You would save $0.05 per case and $25 with one less order. By deciding to take the option of buying 1,200 cases, you make two savings, but you also incur an additional cost. You must buy next month's supply right now and store these 600 cases for an extra month, incurring a 2 percent storage charge on $2,940, which comes to $58.80. You would not have to do this if you continued your monthly ordering schedule—that is, your normal storage costs would prevail. The upshot of this quantitative analysis, assuming that your ordering and storage cost estimates are reasonably correct, is a savings of $26.20. So, based on the numbers, which reveal a very small savings, management could either take this opportunity or leave it.

There is a simpler way to evaluate the quantitative aspects of this opportunity. In the first place, many buyers do not consider the ordering cost, mostly because of confusion about the makeup and magnitude of this cost. Basically, these buyers look at the opportunity buy as an investment. In the peach example, you must buy an additional 600 cases for $2,940 and store these cases for one month. In short, you have been asked to invest $2,940 in inventory for one month. If you do, you save $60. The return on this investment, then, is 2.04 percent ($60/$2,940) per month, or 24.48 percent per year. This percentage is normally compared with some cutoff percentage rate, usually a rate that represents the storage cost.

Regardless of which quantitative method the buyer uses, the emphasis should not be on a formula but on the estimates used in the calculations. Management must spend its time determining the relevant storage cost. (Recall

---

NORMAL SITUATION

1 month supply $3000.00 + $25.00 (order cost)
1 month supply $3000.00 + $25.00 (order cost)
Total = $6050.00

PROPOSED SITUATION

2 months supply $5940.00 + $25.00 (order cost)
$58.80 (extra storage cost for 1 month, 2% of $2940.00*)
Total = $6023.80
Savings = $6050.00 – $6023.80 = $26.20
*$2940 = $5940 – $3000

FIGURE 9.3 A quantitative analysis of an opportunity buy.

that varying opinions exist surrounding the makeup of this cost.) Management must also determine what percentage rate of return it requires to take advantage of an opportunity buy. (In our experience, a buyer may be willing to purchase an additional one-month's supply of a product if the supplier discounts the AP price by at least 2 to 3 percent.)

Normally, management takes a conservative approach when setting this percentage rate and sets a relatively high rate. That way, if the savings of an opportunity buy exceed this high rate, the buy is, indeed, an excellent opportunity. If management sets an unreasonably high rate, however, it may needlessly reject opportunity buys that, in reality, it should accept.

A buyer satisfied with the numbers can evaluate several qualitative aspects of the opportunity buy before making a purchasing decision, including

1. Is the quality the same? Does it compare favorably with the normal purchase?

2. What is the probability of a large decrease in the item's AP price after the opportunity buy?

3. Are cash reserves available? How will the purchase affect the overall cash position of the company?

4. Are storage facilities available? Will this buy pose an excessive burden on these storage facilities?

5. What is the storage life of the product?

6. Will insurance premiums, security risks, and the like increase dramatically, or will the current annual storage cost (in the peach example, 2 percent per month) remain pretty much the same?

7. Will personal property taxes increase now that the overall inventory level is higher?

8. Will the usage rate of the item remain the same over the next few weeks or months? Is it possible that management will discontinue the item? Technically, you do not save money when you buy the product; you save money only when you use it.

9. Does the opportunity buy require a change of suppliers? If so, your current supplier may become disgruntled. Also, what happens if the new supplier cannot maintain the overall value?

10. Are the supplier services the same? If not, how do they differ? Are these differences being considered when the numbers are being evaluated?

11. Is the opportunity a legitimate one? Are you buying legitimate merchandise from licensed suppliers? You should never purchase anything if you doubt the legal status of the item.

12. Furthermore, a buyer should not engage in any illegal activity when trying to save money. For example, you may save **sales taxes** on a piece of equipment if you buy it in another state and arrange to have it

> **sales taxes** Taxes a company must pay to state and local governments for things purchased, such as cleaning chemicals, that will not be resold to customers.

use tax Tax charged by the state where the buyer's hospitality operation is located (i.e., home state), on products purchased from out of state. Similar to the sales tax charged by the home state. Charged by the home state to prevent companies from going elsewhere to avoid paying sales tax to their home states.

salvage opportunity Purchase of a product that is damaged, hence sold for pennies on the dollar. Buyers must be willing to gamble that the product is usable because the item is generally sold as-is, with no guarantee.

freight-damaged item A product that has been damaged somewhat during the shipping process.

used merchandise FFE that are not new; they have been used by others but may still have some useful life left. These items are typically sold as-is, with no guarantee.

"as-is, where-is" condition Buying a product, such as a used piece of equipment, in its current condition. There usually are no guarantees. In addition, the buyer is usually responsible for the cost of packing up the product and having it delivered.

demonstration model FFE used by the purveyor or manufacturer for display purposes. Usually can be purchased at a discount.

delivered to you. Alternately, you may accomplish the same objective by purchasing equipment through an out-of-state Internet supplier. However, even though you do not pay sales taxes to the supplier's state, you are required to pay them in your state (usually in the form of **use taxes**).

13. Another problem is purchasing from unlicensed independent food distributors. You never know where they get their merchandise or whether they are under government inspection. Local producers often are not required to undergo federal inspection. Most states have laws preventing the purchase of home-canned and other home-prepared products, but local egg farmers and fishermen, who sell only in their local area market, usually require no inspection. Furthermore, they are not likely to obtain the necessary business license. Hence, you incur a risk by purchasing these products.

14. Sometimes a hospitality operation that is going out of business attempts to sell its inventories and equipment. Perhaps the operation is selling items that actually belong to its creditors.

15. Another example is the **salvage opportunity**. For instance, a refrigerated semitrailer truck overturns. Someone tries to sell the frozen-food merchandise for 20 cents on the dollar. Should you take such a deal? No, because buying food salvage or food from unlicensed purveyors is a violation of local health codes. The violation is referred to as "purchasing food from an unapproved source." It is permissible, however, to purchase nonfood and nonbeverage salvage items. For example, you could purchase a freight-damaged table if the damage will not interfere with the hospitality operation's production and service or tarnish the company's image. A buyer must realize, though, that he or she could be purchasing an item that suffers more than cosmetic bruises. Indeed, a **freight-damaged item** might be unusable and might not be a bargain at any price. Because products of this type generally are sold with no guarantee, the buyer must be willing to gamble that such a purchase will enhance the company's profits.

16. You may be able to save a great deal of money if you purchase **used merchandise**. Unfortunately, these items normally are sold or auctioned off in an **"as-is, where-is" condition** (i.e., there is no guarantee, and you would need to provide your own transportation). The high probability of a much shorter useful life for these types of items makes their purchase a risky endeavor. However, you may come out ahead if you are the lucky one who can spot a good opportunity. This is especially true if you can purchase a little-used **demonstration model** or a new one displayed only at a trade show exhibit.

Opportunity buys are clearly challenging. The quantitative aspects are relatively simple when the ordering and storage costs used are reasonably accurate, but the qualitative aspects are much more difficult to assess. This probably explains why most managers usually take a cautious approach when evaluating opportunity buys.

DETERMINING THE OPTIMAL PAYMENT POLICY

Some of the ways to evaluate and reduce AP and EP prices discussed earlier depend on the availability of cash to pay suppliers or whether the price was influenced by other payment terms. The next section of the chapter explores how hospitality organizations actually pay for the products they purchase.

Buyers usually have little influence on their company's payment procedures unless they are, themselves, the owners who pay the bills. Usually, the controller or some other financial officer is responsible for these decisions. But buyers cannot be divorced entirely from this issue for at least four reasons: (1) **Payment terms**, cash discounts, opportunity buys, and so on, represent **supplier services**, and buyers must consider them in value analyses. (2) At times, these supplier services are negotiable, implying that buyers need at least some limited authority to bargain effectively. (3) Opportunity buys normally require quick payment. (4) Buyers must continue to work with suppliers who are sometimes "stalled" at bill-paying time. Such stalling tends to place buyers in a relatively poor negotiating position in future dealings; hence, buyers need to be able to influence any such "stalling" decision (see Figure 9.4).

> **payment terms** Another name for credit terms.
>
> **supplier services** Services, such as free delivery, generous credit terms, and others, provided by vendors to buyers who purchase their products.

THE OBJECTIVE OF PAYMENT POLICY

The tenets of cash management are: (1) keep your money as long as possible; (2) pay your bills at the correct time, neither too early nor too late; and (3) collect monies due as fast as you can.

Although it is usually a good idea for a hospitality organization to hang onto its money as long as possible, sometimes it clings to its money too long, such as when financial incentives exist for paying earlier than it normally does. In some cases, it could be costly to keep your money for 30 days when, by paying on the first day, you could receive a discount of 2 percent of your bill.

The specific aim, therefore, is to determine the optimal payment policy. Such a policy dictates that you should pay your bills at that moment when you will receive the most benefit. To accomplish this, the buyer or accountant must balance the **cost of paying money too early** with the potential ill will created among suppliers who must wait too long for payment.

> **cost of paying too early** The loss of interest income that could have been collected if the cash were invested between the time the bill was paid early and the time it had to be paid.

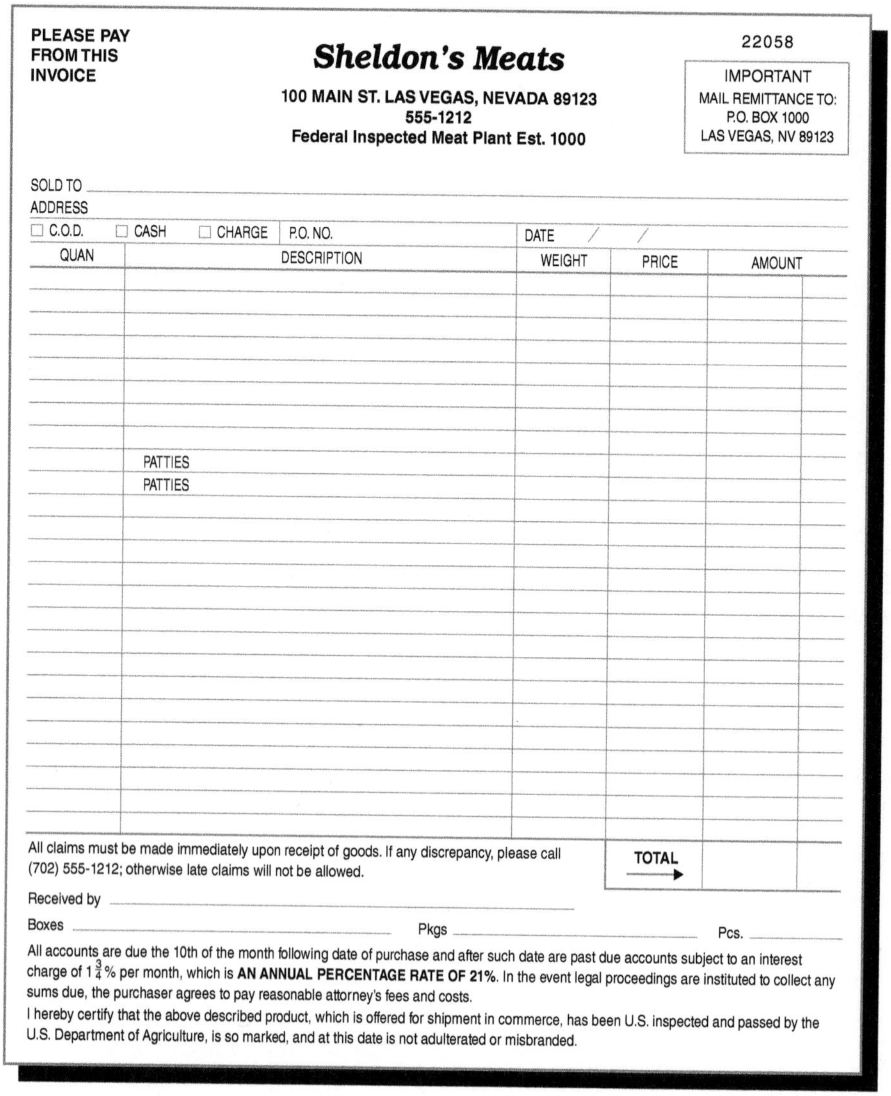

PLEASE PAY FROM THIS INVOICE

Sheldon's Meats

100 MAIN ST. LAS VEGAS, NEVADA 89123
555-1212
Federal Inspected Meat Plant Est. 1000

22058

IMPORTANT
MAIL REMITTANCE TO:
P.O. BOX 1000
LAS VEGAS, NV 89123

SOLD TO
ADDRESS

☐ C.O.D. ☐ CASH ☐ CHARGE P.O. NO. DATE / /

QUAN	DESCRIPTION	WEIGHT	PRICE	AMOUNT
	PATTIES			
	PATTIES			

All claims must be made immediately upon receipt of goods. If any discrepancy, please call (702) 555-1212; otherwise late claims will not be allowed.

TOTAL →

Received by

Boxes Pkgs Pcs.

All accounts are due the 10th of the month following date of purchase and after such date are past due accounts subject to an interest charge of $1\frac{3}{4}$% per month, which is **AN ANNUAL PERCENTAGE RATE OF 21%.** In the event legal proceedings are instituted to collect any sums due, the purchaser agrees to pay reasonable attorney's fees and costs.

I hereby certify that the above described product, which is offered for shipment in commerce, has been U.S. inspected and passed by the U.S. Department of Agriculture, is so marked, and at this date is not adulterated or misbranded.

FIGURE 9.4 Some suppliers are reluctant to allow the hospitality operator to work with their money. Notice that this supplier exacts an interest penalty if the buyer's company fails to pay in the allotted period of time.

COST OF PAYING SOONER THAN NECESSARY

Theoretically, it is easy to calculate the cost of paying too early. For example, if you pay \$40,000 today instead of one week from today, and the bank in which you keep your money pays 1.5 percent simple interest per year on deposits, you would lose approximately \$11.54:

$$\$40{,}000 \times 0.015 = \$600 \text{ interest income per year}$$
$$\$600 / 52 \text{ weeks per year} = \$11.54 \text{ interest income per week}$$

You also could invest your money in some type of alternative investment for one week and, perhaps, earn a bit more interest income than the typical rates paid on bank deposits. From this interest income, you must subtract whatever it costs to engage in this type of investment-disinvestment routine. Whatever profit you have left over is an opportunity cost incurred by paying the bill today instead of one week from today.

Investing money in this fashion, though, is not typical of the vast majority of hospitality firms, especially because few of them have cash balances large enough to justify the time and effort needed to keep cash invested productively. For the most part, if you avoid paying your bills for one week, you immediately find another use for these funds in the business. For instance, you might decide to replace an oven and hope that this week's sales receipts will be sufficient to pay the current bills seven days from now. Alternatively, you might want to use the money to prepay an insurance policy. In other words, some sort of priority within the organization always awaits an application of cold, hard cash. Shuffling the priority list—borrowing from Peter to pay Paul—is often necessary in the hospitality industry.

Another potential cost of paying sooner than necessary is that such action can leave you cash-starved and vulnerable to excessive financial risks. For example, if you needlessly drain your bank account too soon, you might be unable to take advantage of a once-in-a-lifetime opportunity buy. Another possibility is that you might find yourself in a precarious position if you suddenly need to pay cash to a service technician to make an emergency call to fix, for example, a refrigerator.

COST OF PAYING TOO LATE

Some hospitality operators attempt to preserve capital by **stretching their accounts payable**. Unfortunately, there is also a **cost of paying too late**. If a buyer abuses the suppliers' normal **credit period**, he or she will incur several potential costs. For instance, a buyer's company could: (1) gain a reputation as a slow payer, (2) jeopardize future credit potential, (3) damage **credit ratings**, (4) be put on a **cash-on-delivery (COD)** basis by all suppliers, (5) incur interest charges and/or penalty charges, (6) lose cash discounts or other favorable as-purchased (AP) price reductions, (7) incur legal difficulties, (8) find that many suppliers will not do business with a poor **credit risk**, and/or (9) be able to purchase only from those suppliers who provide shoddy merchandise and poor supplier services.

> **stretching the accounts payable** Paying bills after the credit period has expired. This might be done by a buyer's company if it is temporarily short of cash. However, suppliers may charge interest if bills are paid after the credit term expires.
>
> **cost of paying too late** Includes things such as damage to a company's credit rating, late fee charges, and being required to pay COD for future purchases.
>
> **credit period** The amount of time a borrower has before a bill must be paid.
>
> **credit rating** Another term for credit score.
>
> **cash-on-delivery (COD)** Paying for a shipment when it is delivered. Payment may be in cash, check, credit card, debit card, or other acceptable means.
>
> **credit risk** The probability that a borrower will not pay.

WHAT IS THE BEST POLICY?

The best policy is probably the one that allows you to keep your money as long as possible, unless you have an incentive, such as a cash discount, to pay early. Always keep in mind that the longer you can delay paying your bills, the more you operate with someone else's money.

Unfortunately, the average hospitality operation finds it impossible to negotiate specific payment terms. Most suppliers expect you to pay COD unless you have established credit, in which case you will normally be put on a monthly credit term period.

The typical hospitality operation also tends to incur interest charges on any balances that are not paid off at the end of the 30-day period. For instance, it is not unusual for you to be able to pay a minimum monthly payment and let the remaining balance "ride" until the end of the next month. This "ride," though, is usually accompanied by a monthly percentage charge of about 1 1⁄2 to 1 3⁄4 percent. In this situation, a buyer's company has some latitude in planning its payment schedule because suppliers allow more time. However, at these high interest rates, it probably benefits the buyer to pay his or her bills at the end of every month to avoid such charges.

Usually, large hospitality organizations are able to negotiate a more favorable set of credit terms than smaller organizations. Because large firms represent huge amounts of business, suppliers generally are willing to treat them more leniently and with more respect. In our experience, the typical large hospitality company generally seeks a 45-day credit term period; that is, it expects to pay its bills every 45 days.

Small hospitality operators should try to set up a periodic payment schedule, perhaps setting aside one day a week to pay bills. Although this may not allow them to keep their money as long as they would like, it will at least systemize their payments. This systemized procedure is often more efficient in the long run than the juggling of bills and payment periods throughout the year. The only exception should be when suppliers offer some type of discount in exchange for quick payment. In this situation, small firms should perform the appropriate opportunity buy analysis.

---

paid-outs   A method that is fairly popular with small hospitality operators. That is, assuming that everything is acceptable when the delivery is received, the receiver reaches into the cash register and pulls out the appropriate amount of cash to pay the delivery driver. Instead of pulling out cash, the receiver could pull out a preprepared check and give it to the delivery driver. Either way, the emphasis is on paying COD.

itemized bill   Invoice that indicates each item's AP price and extended price, as well as all other costs, such as delivery charges, associated with the purchase.

bank charges   Fees charged by financial institutions for various types of services provided.

THE MECHANICS OF BILL PAYING

Hospitality operators can employ four bill-paying procedures.[12] These are discussed in the sections that follow.

■ Paid-Outs

Paid-outs refer to taking money out of the cash drawer and using it to pay a bill. For example, if you run low on ice, you could take money out of the cash drawer, give it to an employee, and ask him or her to run down to the supermarket to buy some bagged ice. When the employee returns, the **itemized bill** for the bagged ice is placed in the cash drawer so that the missing cash can be accounted for at the end of the shift.

This procedure does not allow you to work with the supplier's money, but it is very convenient. You eliminate having to plan for and execute periodic payments, to spend money on postage or electronic funds transfers, and to pay for the printing cost of a check and other **bank charges**.

Some suppliers will not allow their delivery drivers to accept paid-outs for security reasons. It also is possible that paying COD is illegal for some purchases; for example, in some parts of the United States, it is illegal to pay COD for liquor purchases. However, most suppliers will agree to the paid-out procedure as long as the amount of money involved is not too large.

■ Invoices on Account

When a delivery is made, an invoice or itemized bill usually accompanies it. That is, you ordinarily receive a written description of the delivery, noting such things as items delivered, prices, and so forth (see Figure 9.4).

During this process, the receiver is normally asked to sign the delivery driver's copy of the invoice, attesting to the fact that everything is acceptable. If a problem with the delivery exists—say, some merchandise is damaged and must be sent back—the delivery driver may give the receiving agent a **credit slip**, or the hospitality operation may need to seek the appropriate credit directly from the supplier's main office. Once the driver and receiver are satisfied, the driver leaves, and the receiver arranges for storage of the shipment. No money changes hands at this point.

At the end of the credit period (e.g., at the end of the month, or at the end of a 45-day period), the hospitality operation receives a statement listing all the **invoices on account** delivered during the period; the previous balance, if any, that was left unpaid from the previous period; credits applied to the account, if any; and, if applicable, interest charges on last period's unpaid balance. The organization then needs to reconcile this statement with its copies of invoices and credit slips accumulated during the period and to report any discrepancies to the supplier.

The operation's copies of the invoices and credit slips may also be reconciled with its copies of purchase orders, or some similar order records, to ensure that it did, in fact, order all of the merchandise received. After the reconciliation, the hospitality operation then sends the supplier a check for the agreed-upon minimum payment or, perhaps, pays the entire balance.

■ Credit Card Payments

Some hospitality operations, especially small ones, prefer using a credit card to charge purchases and pay for them at the end of the credit period.[13] **Credit card payments** are very similar to the invoices-on-account system described in the preceding section, but with this procedure, the credit card company handles the billing instead of the suppliers.

When you use a credit card, suppliers must pay a fee, called a **merchant fee** or discount rate, to the credit card company. The fee is usually a percentage of the amount of money charged. The percentage amount ordinarily depends on which type of credit card you use. For instance, Visa or MasterCard, typically charge 1.5 to 3 percent and are normally less expensive than a card such as American Express, which may charge between 2 percent and 5 percent. The discount rate range is based on the supplier's volume of business, as well as how they process their charges.

Although these fees increase the suppliers' costs of doing business, many suppliers may save money in the long run if they receive their payments quickly. For example, if buyers pay with a Visa credit card, suppliers should receive payment in about 2 or 3 days instead of waiting 30 to 45 days for their money. This gives suppliers the option of investing this money and earning a

credit slip When a shipment, or partial shipment, is unsatisfactory, the driver will give a credit slip to the receiving clerk, signifying the amount of credit that will be applied to the restaurant's account. It eliminates the need for the restaurant to prepare a credit memo.

invoices on account Involves reconciling all invoices and credit slips received during the billing period with the end-of-period statement sent by the vendor. If everything is correct, the company pays the total amount listed on the end-of-period statement, or makes the minimum payment and lets the balance ride until the next period.

credit card payment Paying bills with a credit card instead of cash or check.

merchant fee Fee suppliers pay for accepting credit card payments instead of cash or check. The fee is usually some percentage of the amount charged by the buyer.

escrow account   Buyer funds held by an independent third party who releases them to the vendor once the transaction is completed satisfactorily. Commonly done when purchasing construction services.

bill-paying service   An outside company entitled to use a company's money to pay for products or services purchased by the buyer. Bills are typically paid automatically by accessing the buyer's company's bank account(s). The service is typically used to reduce administrative expenses and to increase efficiency.

bit of interest income. Furthermore, because the credit card companies handle a good deal of the paperwork, suppliers will experience some administrative savings as well.

■ Bill-Paying Service

At times, a hospitality operation might prefer depositing money into an **escrow account** and authorizing a **bill-paying service** to use this money to pay its accounts payable. For instance, if you hire a contractor to build an addition on your hotel, it is common practice for a bill-paying service to inspect the contractor's progress and pay off the project in stages—say, one-third of the price when the contractor begins work, one-third when the framing is up, and the final one-third when the addition is completed satisfactorily.

A bill-paying service will charge a fee, but in exchange it will provide an extra margin of security. In addition to handling the paperwork and other assorted details, the service ensures that purchases meet buyers' specifications.

Key Words and Concepts

"As-is where-is" condition	Commodity exchange
Actual cost of food sold	Competitive pressure
Bank charges	Conventional profit markup
Barter group	Cost of paying too early
Blanket order	Cost of paying too late
Bill-paying service	Cost-plus purchasing procedure
Blowout sale	Coupon refund
Bottom-line	Credit card payment
Firm-price purchasing	Credit period
Break point	Credit rating
Buyer fact sheets	Credit risk
Buyer pricing	Credit terms
Buyer profiles	Credit slip
Buyout sale	Demonstration model
Cash discount	Derived demand
Cash rebate	Direct bartering
Cash management	Economic value
Cash on delivery (COD)	Economical packaging
Cherry picking	Escrow account
Closeout sale	Exchange bartering
Commodity	Fixed-price contract

Key Words and Concepts (continued)

Freight-damaged item	Payment terms
Futures contract	Precosting
Hedging	Product cost percentage
Introductory offer	Promotional discount
Invoices on account	Quality standard
Itemized bill	Quantity discount
Landed cost	Sacred hours
Line-item purchasing	Sales taxes
Long-term contract	Salvage opportunity
Make-or-buy analysis	Standard cost
Menu price calculation	Storage cost
Merchant fee	Stretching the accounts payable
Monopolistic competition	Supplier services
Move list	Supplier's costs
Muzz-go list	Supply and demand
Negotiations	Use tax
Odd-hours delivery	Used merchandise
Opportunity buy	Variance
Ordering cost	Volume discount
Paid-out	Wholesale club
Panic buying	

Questions and Problems

1. Explain how a buyer relates AP price to EP cost.

2. What are the four methods that suppliers use to determine their AP prices? As a buyer, which method would you prefer? Why? Which method would the supplier prefer? Why?

3. Review the various ways of reducing AP prices. Which method do you think is best? Why? Which is worst? Why?

4. What is the major objective of hedging?

5. Briefly describe the concept of derived demand.

6. What are some major disadvantages of lowering your quality standard to reduce your costs?

7. List some advantages and disadvantages of exchange bartering.

8. What are some advantages and disadvantages of purchasing used merchandise?

Questions and Problems (continued)

9. Define or briefly explain these terms:

   a. Blanket order
   b. Cash discount
   c. Introductory offer
   d. Quantity discount
   e. Break point
   f. Move list
   g. Promotional discount
   h. Coupon refund
   i. Sacred hours
   j. Salvage buying
   k. Buyer profile
   l. Buyer pricing
   m. PD
   n. PF
   o. Make-or-buy analysis
   p. Direct bartering

10. Under what conditions would salvage buying be illegal?

11. What are the advantages and disadvantages of purchasing merchandise from a no-frills wholesale club?

12. Under what conditions would management consider a product substitution strategy in order to reduce costs?

13. What is the name of the difference between the standard cost and the actual cost? How can the actual cost be computed?

14. What is the main purpose of cash management?

15. How is cash management similar to inventory management? How do they differ?

16. What are the costs and benefits of "stalling" a supplier?

17. What should a manager do if he or she forecasts a temporary shortage of cash and will not be able to pay the bills on time next month?

18. What are some of the potential problems managers who accept discounts might experience?

19. What are the major disadvantages of paying your bills too late?

20. What are some advantages and disadvantages of using paid-outs?

21. Define or briefly explain these terms:

   a. COD
   b. Credit terms
   c. Optimal payment policy
   d. Interest charge on the unpaid balance
   e. Invoices on account
   f. Credit rating

22. When should a hospitality operator request a credit slip from the supplier?

23. What are some advantages and disadvantages of using a bill-paying service?

24. Assume that your economic order quantity (EOQ) is 500 cans. If you purchase 500 cans, you pay $343.50. If you buy 1,000 cans, you pay $650; 500 cans represent a three-month

Questions and Problems (continued)

supply, and 1,000 cans represent a six-month supply. Storage charges are 12 percent of inventory value per year. The cost of preparing one purchase order is $25.

    a. Should you purchase 500 or 1,000 cans? Why?

    b. Even if it is cheaper to purchase 1,000 cans, why might you reject such a huge order?

25. Consider this problem data:

    EOQ = 500 pounds (one-month supply)

    Normal price = $1 per pound

    Storage cost = 24% per year, or 2% per month

The product is ordered monthly. The cost of one purchase order = $20. You have an opportunity to purchase 1,000 pounds of this product this month at $0.95 per pound. How much will you save if you purchase 1,000 pounds?

26. Assume that you normally purchase 60 cases of Canadian whiskey once every three months. The cost of the whiskey is $3,600. The distributor wants to sell you a six-month supply, 120 cases, for $6,768. What do you suggest?

27. Assume that you normally purchase 100 cases of Scotch per month at an AP price of $32.50 per case. You could purchase a two-month supply at an AP price of $30 per case. Your ordering cost is $25 per order, and your storage cost is 24 percent per year. How much would you save if you purchased a two-month supply?

28. Given this data, compute the EP cost for a 6-ounce portion:

    Item: Prime rib

    AP price: $2.85 per pound

    Edible yield: 12 ounces per pound

    (One pound = 16 ounces)

29. Given this data, which lettuce would have the best EP cost?

Ingredient	Edible Yield (%)	Serving Size (OZ)	AP Price Per Pound
Lettuce A	70	3	$0.22
Lettuce B	80	3	$0.29
Lettuce C	90	3	$0.32

30. Given this data, compute the standard cost for one seafood dinner. What would the suggested menu price for the seafood dinner be assuming that the target food cost percent is 40 percent?

Ingredient	Serving Size (OZ)	Edible Yield (%)	AP Price Per Pound
Fish	12	75	$8.98
Rice	4	100	$0.22
Beans	4	90	$0.65

31. If you pay a $10,000 bill today instead of two weeks from today when it is due, approximately how much money will you lose if you have to take the $10,000 out of a bank account that pays 2.75 percent simple interest per year?

Experiential Exercises

1. How can you reduce the overall AP price and increase overall value?

   a. Interview a restaurant or hotel manager involved in purchasing for his or her operation. Ask the manager to identify which of these specific methods he or she employs to reduce the overall AP prices of products:

   Make-or-buy analysis

   Provide your own supplier services and/or economic values

   Shop around

   Lower the quality standard

   Blanket orders

   Improved negotiations

   Substitutions

   Cash discounts

   Hedging

   Economical packaging

   Odd-hours deliveries

   Co-op purchasing

   Cost-plus purchasing

   Promotional discounts

   Exchange bartering

   Introductory offers

   Reevaluate EP costs

   Opportunity buys

   b. Identify any reduction methods that the operation is not employing, and ask if they have been considered. If a particular method has been considered but not implemented, ask for an explanation. If it has not been considered, ask if the operation might benefit from this type of reduction method. Provide a report to include

      i. The identification of AP price reduction methods used by your selected hospitality operation.

      ii. A discussion of why particular reduction methods are not currently being used.

      iii. A discussion of the possible benefits of implementing new reduction methods.

2. Interview an owner–operator of a small restaurant.

   a. Ask this owner–operator to discuss how he or she does business with suppliers regarding credit.

   b. Have the owner–operator describe how he or she initially received credit from the first supplier.

   c. Prepare a one-page report detailing your interview.

Experiential Exercises (continued)

3. Interview a hotel purchasing director or hotel buyer.
   a. Ask this person to discuss how the hotel does business with its suppliers regarding credit.
   b. Have the director or buyer describe how he or she negotiates credit terms with a new supplier.
   c. Prepare a one-page report detailing your interview.

 References

1. CNN Money, "Fortune 500, Top Industries: Most profitable," *CNN Money*, May, 2009, http://money.cnn.com/magazines/fortune/fortune500/2009/industries/197/index.html.

2. Veronica Barclay, "Understanding Distributor Profit," *Wine Business Monthly*, March 2003, www.winebusiness.com/wbm/?go=getArticle&dataId=22809.

3. Katie Fairbank, "TV Advertisers Seek to Cash in on Movie Characters' Cachet," *Dallas Morning News*, June 11, 2003, p. 1A.

4. Haley Brown, "Food Processors Advised to Hedge Their Commodity Bets," *Food Manufacture*, 83, no. 9 (September 2008), p. 6. See also Andy Allen, "Trim Your Costs," *Supply Management*, 13, no. 9 (September 18, 2008):22–27; "Hedging Hurts as Market Turmoil Increases," *Business Travel World*, November 2008, p. 5.

5. Betsy Cummings, "Take Out in Trade," *Restaurant Business*, 105, no. 7 (July 2006):11–12; Karen Kelly, "Trade Fair," *Restaurant Hospitality*, 90, no. 2 (February 2006):64–65; Vijay Dandapani, "Bartering to Tide Over the Recession," www.vijaydandapani.com/2009/04/index.html. Leon Stafford, "Tourism Officials Barter to Stretch Tight Advertising Budgets," *Atlanta Journal-Constitution*, May 15, 2003, p. D1. See also Robert Selwitz, "Increased Exposure, Cash Savings Are Benefits of Bartering," *Hotel & Motel Management*, 220, no. 14 (2005):101–125.

6. Anonymous, "The 5 Rules of Bartering," *Restaurant Business*, 105, no. 7 (2006):1. See also Christopher Ostrowski, "JF Capital Finding Success with Barter/Trade Concept," *Hotel Business*, 18 no. 4 (2009):3, 39; Bob Andelman, "Barter It!" *Corporate Meetings and Incentives*, 28, no. 1 (2009):31–33; Jilian Mincer, "Web Barter's Tricks of the Trade," *Wall Street Journal*, July 3, 2008, p. B11; Justin Martin, "Fair Trade," *Fortune Small Business*, 19, no. 5 (2009):76. Ira Apfel, "Trading Places," *Restaurants USA*, May 2001, www.restaurant.org/rusa.

References (continued)

7. Enrique De Argaez, "Barter and Save Cash," www.internetworldstats.com/articles/art073.htm.

8. Internal Revenue Service, "Tax Topics: Topic 420—Bartering Income," February 27, 2014, www.irs.gov/taxtopics/tc420.html.

9. E. Manoj and S. Sahadev, "Role of Switching Costs in the Service Quality, Perceived Value, Customer Satisfaction and Customer Retention Linkage," *Asia Pacific Journal of Marketing and Logistics*, 23, no. 3 (2011):327–345. doi:http://dx.doi.org/10.1108/13555851111143240.

10. Brett Thorn, "Price Controls Pay Dividends," *Nation's Restaurant News*, 43, no. 17 (2009):43–46; see also Brett Thorn, "Get Creative with Food Costs," *Nation's Restaurant News*, 43, no. 3 (2009):48. Jacquelyn Lynn, "Profiting from Smart Purchasing," *Restaurants USA*, April 1996, www.restaurant.org/rusa. See also Marilyn Tseng, "Food Purchasing Patterns in Purchase-driven Societies," *Public Health Nutrition*, 9, no. 3 (2006):277–278.

11. A fifth method may be evolving. See William J. Lynott, "Is Desktop Banking for You?" *Restaurant Hospitality*, 90, no. 5 (2006):90–94. See also Sue Hirst, "Accentuate the Positive: Smart Use of Accounts Payable," *Hospitality*, 44, no. 2 (2008):10–11.

12. T. E. Holmes, "Used Wisely, Small-Business Cards Can Keep Business Afloat," *Creditcards.com*, February 13, 2013, www.creditcards.com/credit-card-news/small-business-credit-cards-1269.php.

CHAPTER 10

THE OPTIMAL SUPPLIER

The Purpose of This Chapter

After reading this chapter, you should be able to:

- Develop an approved supplier list.

- Assess a buying plan.

- Evaluate supplier selection criteria regarding:
  - type and size of supplier;
  - ordering and delivery policies and procedures;
  - price and payment policies and procedures; and
  - other factors.

- Describe the relationship between suppliers and buyers.

- Describe the relationship between salespersons and buyers.

- Design procedures for evaluating suppliers and salespersons.

DEVELOPING AN APPROVED SUPPLIER LIST

> **Approved supplier** A vendor that the buyer is allowed to buy from.
>
> **Approved-supplier list** A list of all vendors who buyers are allowed to purchase from. An excellent security precaution.

Buyers have a good deal more to do with selecting suppliers than fixing quality standards and economic values. The major exception to this rule occurs when another company official insists that a buyer purchase from a certain supplier. This insistence usually means that some sort of reciprocal buying arrangement has been reached or that the owner–manager has already decided on an **approved supplier** or prepared an **approved-supplier list** without consulting the buyer.

■ The Initial Survey

The first step in determining the optimal supplier is to compile a list of all the possible suppliers, or at least a reasonable number of potential suppliers. Local suppliers' names can be gathered from the Internet, local trade directories or local trade magazines, other similar publications, and other hospitality operators.

National suppliers' names can be obtained from similar sources. They also can be gathered from national buying guides, directories, and from national buying guides and directories such as:

- Grey House Publishing's Food and Beverage Market Place (see Figure 10.1)
- Foodservice Equipment & Supplies
- The National Restaurant Association's Online Buyer's Guide
- Nation's Restaurant News Marketplace
- Hotel Resource: Hospitality Industry Resources

Suppliers can also be found and evaluated at live trade shows and conventions, including

- American Culinary Federation National Convention
- National Restaurant Association Show
- Fresh Summit: Produce Marketing Association Show
- Multi-Unit Food Service Operators (MUFSO) Conference
- North American Association of Food Equipment Manufacturers (NAFEM) Show
- Hospitality Information Technology Conference (HITEC)
- International Foodservice Technology Expo (FS/TEC)
- HX: The Hotel Experience
- Multi-Unit Restaurant Technology Conference

Large corporations take the time to compile lengthy lists of suppliers. The procedure most small operators follow is to seek out a more limited number of suppliers that carry most of the required items. In some cases operators may contact only one supplier for a particular product line. This is true especially for such items as liquor and dairy products because the middlemen dealing in these product lines usually have few competitors.

Whatever initial survey is undertaken, it can present three major problems. First, it may be difficult to determine which suppliers to include on the initial list. Many potential suppliers carry several product lines; consequently, the list can become larger than you would wish.

FIGURE 10.1 The Food and Beverage Marketplace
Courtesy of Grey House Publishing, www.greyhouse.com

A second problem stems from the first. In the buyers' haste to shorten the potential supplier list, they may stop adding suppliers when they reach a certain number. The longer the list, the more time is required for interviewing, checking references, touring plants, and completing the other analytical work involved in culling the list. Indiscriminate culling can eliminate a good potential supplier. Furthermore, it tends to limit the pool of potential suppliers in the future when buyers stick with the original list. It can be costly to a hospitality firm to lock out a good supplier in this way.

The third problem is less common. It occurs when buyers need to purchase a unique item. In such situations, the search for a supplier can be extremely time consuming.

TRIMMING THE INITIAL LIST

Buyers begin to narrow their initial list into an approved-supplier list by looking closely at each supplier's product quality, as-purchased (AP) price, and supplier services. (We assume that, at this stage, a buyer knows what types of products are wanted.) These factors help to separate acceptable suppliers from the initial list.

It is relatively easy to ascertain the quality standards and AP prices of suppliers. The major obstacle occurs when buyers examine supplier services. What is the best way to evaluate these supplier services? Basically, this process becomes a matter of taste, but the important considerations come under the rubric of "performance." When evaluating performance, buyers should be interested in prompt deliveries, the number of rejected deliveries, how adjustments on rejected deliveries are handled, how well suppliers take care of one or two trial orders, the capacity of their plants, and their technological know-how.

It might be easier to narrow a supplier list by trial and error, but a supplier's poor performance can leave buyers without a product, as well as with disgruntled customers demanding that particular product. It might be best, then, to accept the list-narrowing procedure as an essential aspect of purchasing.

BUYING PLANS

buying plan Overall selection and procurement strategy. Includes reasons why it was selected and relevant policies and procedures needed to carry it out successfully.

bid buying When buyers shop around seeking current AP prices from vendors. The vendors are asked to quote, or bid, the prices they will charge. Intended to give the buyer competitive pricing information that will allow him or her to get the best possible value.

one-stop shopping Buying everything you need from one vendor. Alternately, buying everything you need from the fewest possible purveyors.

fixed bid buying Shopping around and soliciting competitive bids for long-term contracts.

daily bid buying Another term for call sheet buying.

request for bid Another term for request for quote (RFQ).

request for quote (RFQ) Used by buyers who shop around for the best possible deals. It is a list of items needed and their specifications, given to potential vendors who are then asked to quote, or bid, the AP prices they would charge for them.

The actual selection of the optimal supplier is the next logical step. Buyers cannot do this, however, without considering the type of procurement policies best for them. For instance, buyers might want to work with one particular supplier and negotiate long-term contracts for some items. If this is the case, they must keep these requirements in mind when going over the approved-supplier list. Some suppliers may wish to be accommodating; others may not.

Large corporations have a bit more latitude in formulating their preferred buying policies and then convincing suppliers to cooperate. Small operators have less discretion; that is, they may have to accept the buying procedures their suppliers prefer. However, at least a few procurement policies are available to any size operator. And, just as important, most suppliers are willing to adjust to more than one policy.

Generally speaking, the hospitality industry has two basic **buying plans**: (1) the buyer selects a supplier first, and they work together to meet the buyer's needs; or (2) the buyer prepares lengthy specifications for the items needed and then uses **bid buying** procedures.

The first plan, which involves selecting one or more suppliers to work with, is not common. Usually, a buyer chooses this plan only when: (1) a reciprocal buying policy is in effect; (2) only one supplier provides the type of item needed; (3) the buyer or owner–manager, for some reason, trusts the supplier's ability, integrity, or judgment; or (4) the buyer, for some reason, wants to establish a long-term relationship with a supplier. This plan is, however, used somewhat more often in small operations in which management, already spread thin with other operational problems, decides to limit the number of suppliers, even in some cases to a single supplier, for as many products as possible. This practice is called **one-stop shopping**.

Bid buying is more common, particularly for items that several suppliers sell.[1] It works fairly well as long as buyers realize that all suppliers are not created equal. Also, buyers must keep in mind that obtaining the lowest bid may not ensure the lowest edible-portion (EP) cost.

Deciding which plan to use is a matter of judgment for buyers. For some items, the first plan may be appropriate. For example, because the quality of fresh produce tends to vary significantly, buyers may opt to select only one or a few suppliers whom they can trust. However, those same buyers might purchase canned goods strictly on a bid-buying basis.

Buyers who use bid buying generally take two approaches: (1) **fixed bid buying**, and (2) **daily bid buying**. Typically, buyers use the fixed bid for large quantities of products purchased over a reasonably long period of time. This is usually a very formal process.

The fixed-bid buying plan usually begins with a buyer sending a **request for bid** or **request for quote (RFQ)** to prospective suppliers, asking them to submit bid prices on specific products or services. The request includes detailed specifications and outlines the process bidders need to follow, as well as the process the buyer will use to award the contract.

Buyers send bid requests only to eligible, **responsible bidders**. An **ineligible bidder** is a company that, because of financial instability, unsatisfactory reputation, poor history of performance, or other similar reasons, cannot meet the qualifications needed to be placed on the approved-supplier list.

Responsible bidders usually need to follow the **sealed-bid procedure** when participating in the fixed-bid process. A sealed bid is almost always required on major purchases to ensure fair competition among bidders. The buyer opens the sealed bids and awards the business to the responsible bidder with the lowest bid. The buyer awards the contract to this bidder because the unit price is lower, or the value per dollar bid is higher than what the other bidders quoted. Furthermore, the bid winner's reputation, past performance, and business and financial capabilities are judged best for satisfying the needs of the contract.

The daily bid is often used for fresh items, such as fresh produce. (The daily-bid method is sometimes referred to as **daily-quotation buying, call sheet buying, open-market buying,** or **market quote buying**.) Buyers also use this type of bid when purchasing a small amount—just enough to last for a few days or a week. The daily bid usually follows a simple, informal procedure: (1) the suppliers that form a list of those with whom the buyer wants to do business—the approved-supplier list—are given copies of the buyer's specifications; (2) when it is time to order some items, the buyer contacts these suppliers and asks for their bids; (3) the buyer records the bids or analyzes them electronically; and (4) the buyer usually decides on the supplier selection by choosing the supplier with the lowest AP price quote.

Some sort of **value analysis** could be used here to determine the optimal plan to use, given the types of items being purchased. The optimal procedure, though, is not an easy formula to develop because several good reasons exist for buyers to choose either plan. Convenience, degree of buyer skill, and product availability, for example, come into play

---

responsible bidder Opposite of ineligible bidder. Company that is considered large enough, has sufficient financial strength, has a good reputation and history of satisfactory performance, and so forth, and because of this, is placed on a buyer's approved-supplier list.

ineligible bidder Company that would like to bid for a buyer's business, but would not be allowed to bid because it does not meet certain qualifications set by the buyer. For instance, the company may not be large enough, it may not have sufficient financial strength, and so forth.

sealed-bid procedure Vendors' AP price quotations are secret until they are all opened by the buyer at the same time. Typically done with fixed-bid buying.

daily-quotation buying Another term for call sheet buying.

call sheet buying Used when shopping around on a day-to-day basis. The buyer contacts several purveyors seeking their AP price quotes. He or she then purchases from the one offering the lowest AP price.

open-market buying or **market quote buying** Other terms for call sheet buying.

value analysis Involves examining a product to identify unnecessary costs that can be eliminated without sacrificing overall quality or performance.

when buyers determine the optimal plan. In the final analysis, the plan used will result from examining several factors.

Regardless of the plan or combination of plans a buyer chooses, he or she must ascertain the suppliers' willingness to participate in the plan. Most suppliers will jump at the chance to be a part of the first plan. Buyers, though, normally start with some type of bid-buying procedure, if only to determine which supplier they want to use all the time. Alternately, at the very least, buyers use bid buying to select the suppliers they plan to use for the next three, four, or six months.

Not all suppliers like to become involved with bid buying. It requires their cooperation, time, and willingness to be open with their prices. These nonparticipating suppliers frequently balk at bid buying because their AP prices look high, because of the amount of supplier services they include. Generally, high AP prices do not win bids. Furthermore, the competing bidders who may or may not offer the same quality of services may inflate their AP prices to fall just under those legitimately high AP prices. High-priced, reputable suppliers do not like to be involved in this type of practice.

Many suppliers try to circumvent a buyer's desire to bid buy by offering various discounts, other opportunity buys, introductory offers, and so forth. In addition, suppliers may try to become exclusive distributors for some items: if a buyer wants to purchase them, he or she will have no choice in supplier selection.

After determining a supplier's response to the two basic buying plans, a buyer must assess the supplier's willingness to participate in additional aspects that are related to these two basic plans. Furthermore, buyers must evaluate several other related variables when developing a list of acceptable suppliers. Some of the more common **supplier selection criteria** are discussed next. They are organized by factors related to the type and size of supplier; the ordering, delivery, and pricing procedures and policies; and other factors.

> **supplier selection criteria**
> Characteristics a buyer considers when determining if potential vendors should be added to the approved-supplier list.

SUPPLIER SELECTION CRITERIA: TYPE AND SIZE OF SUPPLIER

■ Local Merchant–Wholesaler or National Source?

A small operator normally deals with local suppliers. However, larger operators sometimes bypass these middlemen and go directly to the primary source; this is especially common with equipment purchases. Large hospitality operations normally require **national distribution**, so that all of the units in the chain organization can use the same type of products. As a result, they usually seek out the large suppliers who can provide this alternative. National sources may also be more capable of offering long-term contracts for purchasing certain items, which may be an important consideration for some buyers.

> **national distribution**
> Clause in a national contract stipulating that all restaurants in the chain will be able to rely on getting the same types of products delivered to their back doors.

Operations must address the question of providing their own economic values, especially transportation and risk, before they make a decision. And, as we have already pointed out, several advantages and disadvantages must be weighed here. Sometimes, as in the case of alcohol, most states prohibit buying directly from the source.

On a dollars-and-cents basis, small operations find it economical to purchase from local suppliers. Chains and other larger operations might save money buying directly from the primary source. However, they might alienate local suppliers who in turn may not want to supply products not available nationally or needed on an emergency basis.

A compromise is possible. For instance, a vice president of purchasing might go directly to the source and negotiate a long-term contract, for, perhaps, six months. This might be followed by "hiring" local suppliers to take delivery from the sources and distribute the items to the local unit operations. Parceling out these **end-user services** is usually an acceptable and profitable compromise for all parties involved in the transaction.

> **end-user services**
> Support functions provided to buyers by vendors. Includes everything except the sales effort, which is provided by a sales rep, such as a food broker.

■ Size of Firm

Buyers with a large amount of business must be assured that suppliers are large enough to accommodate them. On the other hand, large suppliers may be more impersonal. Perhaps the buyer would prefer dealing with small firms to talk to the owners regularly. If nothing else, dealing directly with owners generally makes a buyer feel that company concerns will be met consistently.

A related issue is the amount of time suppliers have been in business. Some buyers will consider suppliers only after they have established acceptable performance track records that indicate they can handle buyers' needs and will most likely be around for a while.

■ Bonded Suppliers

A buyer is concerned about the capability of suppliers to cover the cost of any damage they might inflict on the buyer's property. Usually, before the appropriate government authority will issue a business license to a supplier, that supplier must display adequate insurance coverage; that is, it must be a **bonded supplier**. However, what is adequate for the licensing bureau may not be adequate for the buyer.

> **bonded supplier** A supplier that has adequate insurance coverage demanded by the local government that issues business licenses.

A related issue is the fact that buyers may inadvertently be dealing with an unlicensed supplier. This situation should be avoided because, if, say, a customer gets ill from products this supplier provided, the buyer's organization could become entangled in all sorts of litigation.

■ Socially Responsible Suppliers

Some buyers prefer to work with suppliers who promote socially responsible agendas. For instance, some buyers will not purchase from suppliers that sell products manufactured by employees in foreign countries who do not receive a basic level of wages and/or benefits.[2] Alternately, some buyers will not purchase from suppliers carrying products whose processing damages the earth's environment. The Green Restaurant Association provides information about suppliers that provide green products. Also, some buyers prefer to purchase from suppliers who employ minorities and deal with minority-owned subcontractors.[3]

Corporate social responsibility (CSR) is a term used to relate a corporation to practices for which they are held socially and ethically responsible by stakeholders, employees, governments, the public, the supply chain, media, and regulators. Some examples of CSR include fair trade practices, sustainability practices, animal welfare, poor wage conditions, poor working conditions, the use of biotechnology such as GMOs, and the use of fertilizers and chemicals in the growing process.[4]

CSR practices are in place in many foodservice providers; three example companies are US Foods, Perdue, and Sysco. Sysco has a listing of guiding principles that outline their corporate philosophy on CSR. It focuses on food, operations, and community. Regarding food, Sysco provides classes for its farmers, which help them incorporate Good Agricultural Practices (GAP) into their growing programs. Sysco also audits its suppliers in an effort to monitor food safety and quality programs. For sourcing food, Sysco looks at using local farmers, sustainable farming practices, animal welfare, and social compliance. Sysco also ensures the health and safety of its products by employing a full-time staff of quality assurance specialists who create best practices and inspect and monitor facilities that it utilizes. Sysco also utilizes Hazard Analysis and Critical Control Points (HACCP) in all of its facilities as well as providing controls for sanitation, foreign materials, allergen, and recall procedures. In addition to all this, Sysco even has an eye on operations where it has reduced energy usage by 35 percent and continues to increase efficiency and reduce energy use.[5]

US Foods uses donations and employee volunteerism as part of its CSR effort. The US Foods We Feed America program is the nation's leading hunger relief charity.[6] In addition to this program, US Foods is also certified by the Environmental Protection Agency (EPA) as a SmartWay Partner. This partnership was granted due to US Foods' efforts to maximize fuel economy and reduce emissions.[7]

Perdue established its corporate responsibility platform in 2011. This includes producing safe, high-quality foods for customers, utilizing forward-thinking solutions to improve products, protecting natural resources, and being a responsible employer that invests in employees' safety, growth, and well-being.[8]

socially responsible supplier Vendor who uses environmentally safe products and/or procedures. Alternately, vendor who promotes social causes, supports charities, and so forth.

Buyers can use the Web to search for **socially responsible suppliers**. For example, buyers can utilize the Thomas Publishing Company website, to obtain a list of suppliers that are owned by minorities and/or women. Suppliers are typically listed by product category, and with little more effort than picking up the phone or visiting the website, buyers can quickly secure the information they need.[9]

SUPPLIER SELECTION CRITERIA: ORDERING AND DELIVERY POLICIES AND PROCEDURES

sole-source procurement, prime-vendor procurement, or single-source procurement Other terms for one-stop shopping.

■ One-Stop Shopping and Variety of Merchandise

One-stop shopping, which is sometimes referred to as **sole-source procurement, prime-vendor procurement,** or **single-source procurement,** appeals to many buyers because of its simplicity. A one-stop shopper tries to purchase as many items as possible from one supplier. The main advantage of this procedure is the reduction of the **ordering cost**. There is considerably less effort involved with fewer orders: less paperwork, less receiving activity, fewer deliveries, and less opportunity for error. Another advantage is the possibility of qualifying for a **volume discount** when you purchase a large dollar amount of merchandise; the one-stop buyer usually enters relatively large purchase orders and, hence, is more apt to qualify for a volume discount.[10]

Unfortunately, one-stop shopping carries its share of disadvantages. One obvious disadvantage is the reduction in supplier selection flexibility. Another potential disadvantage is the possibility that the total dollars spent for purchases over the long run may be higher than if the buyer shopped around a bit.

The reason for this second disadvantage is simple. Many suppliers carry reasonably large product lines, perhaps as many as 4,000 products, under one roof. Some of these products are strong sellers, which are good-quality items that are competitively priced. Other products are not so good, nor are they as inexpensive as comparable items a competing supplier carries. As a result, although the one-stop supplier makes a minimum profit on some items, he or she typically makes up for it somewhere else, much the same as the foodservice menu that carries several items, all with varying profit potentials. The idea of shopping around is to get the minimum-profit items from each supplier, and to do this without spending more money, time, and effort than might be saved in AP prices.

No supplier can really provide complete one-stop service, just as no one supplier can carry every item an operation needs. If, for example, a buyer wants to use bid buying for most products and solicits bids from suppliers with the stipulation that the bidders must be prepared to provide all the items the buyer includes on the bid, it is likely that only one supplier will be able to meet this requirement.

One-stop shopping may be more valuable for small operators. Although some AP prices may run a bit higher, chances are that the eventual costs of items used in production will be optimal. The AP price at the back door may be higher, but if the planned EP cost holds up with the additional time the buyer can now spend in supervision and guest service, the eventual costs of products sold may be quite acceptable.

In other cases, a supplier may or may not have the one-stop shopping capability, but can, at least, offer a reasonable range of options. The supplier may offer a variety of quality grades, brand names, and/or packers' brand names for the merchandise he or she carries.

For example, a supplier who can offer buyers a variety of fresh produce qualities may conceivably be more valuable than a one-stop supplier who carries only one quality level of fresh produce along with several other product lines.

■ Stockless Purchasing

When a buyer purchases a large amount of product—for example, a three-month supply—and takes delivery of the entire shipment, the procedure is usually referred to as **forward buying**.[11]

When the buyer purchases a large amount of product, but arranges for the supplier to store it and deliver a little at a time, as needed, the procedure is

---

ordering cost The amount of money spent to make an order, receive it, and store it. Includes things such as labor needed to perform the work and administrative costs such as faxing, photocopying, and cell phone charges.

volume discount Similar to a quantity discount. The buyer agrees to purchase a huge volume of goods; however, unlike a quantity discount, he or she buys more than one type of merchandise.

forward buying When a buyer purchases a large amount of product (for example, a three-month supply) and takes delivery of the entire shipment.

stockless purchasing
When a buyer purchases a large amount of product, for example, a three-month supply, and arranges for the vendor to store it and deliver a little at a time.

called **stockless purchasing**. For instance, a buyer might foresee an impending shortage of a 2005 vintage Bordeaux wine and, in order to offer this wine to customers as long as possible, might buy all the distributor has. Because the storage area might be limited, the buyer asks that the wine distributor store the wine and deliver a bit at a time.

A buyer may also use stockless purchasing when suspecting that the AP prices for some items are about to increase drastically.

Buyers often use this procedure when purchasing such products as dinnerware, flower vases, and room amenities like soap and shampoo, especially when the hospitality operation wants a particular logo on these items. A large purchase of personalized items usually results in a lower AP price per unit. The buyer may not be able to take advantage of this tradition if there is no place to store the items, unless the supplier will provide storage.

cash-and-carry   Another term for will-call buying.

will-call   Merchandise not delivered to the restaurant; the buyer picks it up at the vendor's location. The buyer may also have to pay for it when picking it up, unless the company has established credit with the vendor.

wholesale club   A type of buying club. It is a cash-and-carry operation patronized primarily by small hospitality operations that do not order enough from vendors to qualify for free delivery. Buyers usually have to pay a membership fee.

warehouse club   Another term for wholesale club.

standing order   Under this procedure, a driver (usually referred to as a route salesperson) shows up, takes inventory of what you have, then takes off the truck enough product to bring you up to some predetermined par stock, enough to last until he or she visits you the next time. The driver writes up a delivery ticket after it's determined what you need, and the products are placed in your storage facility.

route salesperson   The driver who delivers standing orders to the restaurant.

■ Cash and Carry

The **cash-and-carry** procedure, which is sometimes referred to as **will-call** purchasing, appears to be a marginal practice in the hospitality industry because most buyers rely heavily on supplier services (especially delivery services) and are unwilling, or unable, to sacrifice them, even though it may result in price concessions.[12] Some buyers, however, like this idea if it means a considerably lower AP price in exchange for providing their own delivery.

Some hospitality buyers are very dependent on the cash-and-carry option. For instance, off-premises caterers or bed-and-breakfast owners cannot always plan their purchases as carefully as local restaurateurs who enjoy more predictable business cycles. Small independent operators may not have the purchasing power needed to negotiate purchasing and delivery discounts.[13] Cash and carry, then, is very important to these buyers.

Some suppliers resist cash and carry mainly because they have already invested heavily in the delivery function. Some do not want to deal with small buyers because of the inherent inefficiencies. Some suppliers, though, have set up one or more cash-and-carry locations, which are sometimes referred to as **wholesale clubs** or **warehouse clubs**, to service small accounts. In fact, a few suppliers have aggressively pursued this type of business, seeking small accounts as well as the large corporate and institutional buyers.[14]

■ Standing Orders

A **standing order** is an order placed with a supplier who regularly delivers just enough to bring the buyer's stock level up to par. A driver with a fully stocked truck shows up, takes inventory of what the buyer has, drops off enough merchandise to bring the buyer up to par, writes up an invoice, and leaves it with the bookkeeper. (The delivery drivers in this type of situation are usually referred to as **route salespersons**.)

Buyers like to use standing orders for items that have a standard usage pattern, such as milk, bread, and keg beer. Also, buyers sometimes like the convenience that standing orders provide. Buyers appreciate this method of purchasing even though some purchasing professionals suggest avoiding it because the procedure contradicts the basic principles of security and cost control.

With some products, such as ice cream, standing orders are traditional. However, when such orders are not traditional, buyers will probably be unable to obtain this concession from suppliers because most of them want some sort of minimum order before they schedule a delivery.

■ Use of Technology

Ordering that takes place when the buyer's computer communicates with the supplier's computer has been used for more than two decades. Some suppliers still offer complimentary software to their large customers that can be used to electronically transmit orders to the suppliers' distribution centers. This technology usually includes additional software packages that buyers can use to manage inventories, price menus, and calculate food costs.[15]

However, as discussed in Chapters 1 and 2, this system of selection and procurement is rapidly changing. Many suppliers are now moving toward the use of proprietary e-marketplaces to sell their products rather than requiring buyers to install proprietary software on their computers. A side benefit of e-marketplaces is that they do not require user-installed software. Rather, these e-marketplaces act as **application service providers (ASPs)** and permit users to download any needed software directly into their browser.

Other forms of computerization are on the increase. For example, many suppliers have armed their salespersons with tablets and smart devices with which to communicate a buyer's order directly to the supply house. This hastens the order procedure by shortening the **lead time**, verifying product availability, eliminating inaccuracies, and providing an additional supplier service to the buyer.

> **application service provider (ASP)** A company that distributes software online from a central location to customers in other locations.
>
> **lead time** Period of time between when you place an order with a vendor and when you receive it.

■ Co-Op Purchasing

Recall that co-op purchasing is the banding together of several small operators to consolidate their buying power. A lower AP price is the major advantage. Many suppliers participate in this procedure as long as no glaring inefficiencies or inconveniences result, preferring one delivery to one location and one bill payment.

The major disadvantage of co-op purchasing is the cost of developing and operating the co-op. Someone must coordinate all the members' needs and take on the challenge of supplier selection, negotiations, and so forth. A buyer also should realize that co-op purchasing may limit an individual member's influence in supplier selection. Each member surrenders a bit of flexibility as he or she goes along with the rest.

Co-op purchasing has recently enjoyed renewed popularity, primarily because it is seen as an effective way to reduce product costs.[16] In the past, when the co-op members had to do all the work, fewer buyers were interested in this type of buying plan. Lately, however, several **buying services**—which are sometimes referred to as "buying clubs," **contract houses**, or aggregate purchasing companies—have emerged to streamline the process and make it more efficient.[17]

> **buying service** Another term for buying club.
>
> **contract house** Another term for buying club.

Recall from Chapter 1 that many of these buying services have migrated to the Web. It is no longer necessary to join a local co-op and be confined to procuring food from a limited list. Instead, these international online services enable the buyer to select and procure products from a variety of suppliers, products that, many times, are delivered directly from the supplier. In essence, these buying services merely contractually negotiate prices for their members.

A buying service is a private company that buyers can join. For a fee, buyers can take advantage of the service's purchasing power, as well as other subtle benefits, such as the service's willingness to share many profitable ideas with its members. In effect, the buying service is an easy way for small, independent operators to "hire" a highly skilled, professional purchasing executive.[18]

Each buyer or owner–manager has to make his or her own decision concerning the potential costs and benefits of co-op buying. The practice is, however, worth careful investigation. In some instances, it can be a very profitable option.

■ Ordering Procedure and Lead Time

> **ordering procedures**
> Standardized process used by the buyer to ensure that the correct amounts of needed products are ordered at the appropriate time.

Buyers will be partial to those suppliers who most closely meet their needs. Suppliers who offer very convenient **ordering procedures** will most likely have a valuable competitive edge in the marketplace. The shorter the lead time, the more convenient it is, for a buyer can wait until the last possible moment before entering an order for delivery at a predetermined time. All other things being equal, buyers would probably want to deal with a purveyor who offers them the ability to call or submit electronically at night for an order to be delivered the next morning, rather than a supplier who requires two or three days' notice.

■ Delivery Schedule

All hospitality operations have preferences regarding the time(s) of day and the day(s) of the week when they accept delivery from their suppliers. For instance, if buyers had their druthers, most of them would demand morning delivery.

Realistically, hospitality operations often must make do with what is available to them. However, this does not mean that they cannot swing their purchase dollars toward the supplier(s) who most closely matches their desired **delivery schedule**. This is a valued supplier service, and

> **delivery schedule**
> Purveyor's planned shipping times and dates.

although buyers often must expect to pay a little more for a preferred delivery routine, the overall effect may prove profitable for both the hospitality operation and the supplier.

■ Minimum Order Requirement and Delivery Charges

> **minimum order requirement** The least amount of an item a buyer needs to purchase before a vendor will agree to sell it. Alternately, the least amount a buyer needs to purchase before he or she can qualify for free delivery.

Before a supplier will agree to provide buyers with "free delivery," they usually must order a certain minimum amount of merchandise, that is, a **minimum order requirement**. If the requirement is not met or buyers need delivery on a day outside the normal schedule, they may be charged a delivery fee. In times of rising product prices, and in particular, fuel prices, suppliers frequently increase delivery fees or order minimums rather than raise AP prices.

Most buyers have little trouble in meeting minimum order requirements, so it is unlikely that such a criterion would be a concern. A small operator might be very concerned with these stipulations; in this case, this aspect becomes an important supplier selection standard.

■ Outside (Independent) Delivery Service

Shopping online may yield several suppliers who do not provide delivery service personally, but who outsource it to an independent service, such as UPS, DHL, or FedEx. Buyers should be leery about suppliers who use no-name delivery services that have no verifiable track record. Delivery inconsistencies will wipe out any good deals that buyers obtain by shopping around. Furthermore, independent drivers, even from major delivery services, are unable to rectify delivery mistakes on the spot.

SUPPLIER SELECTION CRITERIA: PRICE AND PAYMENT POLICIES AND PROCEDURES

■ Cost-Plus Purchasing

A buyer might want to be charged whatever the suppliers paid, plus an agreed-upon **profit markup**. Recall from Chapter 9 the possibility of arranging this type of purchasing procedure. In this situation, the buyer may be able to negotiate with suppliers for the agreed-upon profit markup percentage or set dollar amount to be added to the suppliers' cost of obtaining the products. Large hospitality firms are usually able to negotiate, whereas smaller operators may have to settle for the suppliers' normal profit markup.

Suppliers are not always fond of **cost-plus buying** because it usually requires considerable work to alter AP prices. It also is necessary for the suppliers to share cost data with buyers, a practice on which competitive businesspersons tend to frown. Large hospitality firms, though, tend to prefer cost-plus purchasing because experience suggests that it can reduce AP prices, lessen the buyer's administrative effort, raise the level of supplier services, and improve product quality. In short, cost-plus purchasing can increase value.

> **profit markup**   The difference between the vendor's cost of a product and its sales price. Alternately, the difference between the EP cost of a menu item and its menu price.
>
> **cost-plus buying**   The AP price the buyer pays is equal to the vendor's cost of the product plus an agreed-upon profit markup.

■ Case Price

When buyers purchase a case of merchandise, such as a six-can case of tomatoes, they will pay a certain price for it, say, $12. If buyers wish to purchase one can of tomatoes and can purchase it for $2, they are receiving what is normally referred to as the **case price per unit** for that can.

Few, if any, suppliers will give a buyer a case price when purchasing less than a case. Occasionally suppliers will "bust" a case for a buyer, but they will usually charge a premium to do this. Typically, either the buyer purchases the whole case or does business elsewhere.

When a buyer purchases some items in small batches, it is important to deal with suppliers who understand meager needs. In some situations, a buyer

> **case price per unit**   Equal to the AP price for one case divided by the number of units per case. For instance, if you pay $12 for a six-can case of canned tomatoes, the case price is $2 per can. If a vendor is willing to sell you less than one case, but charges you only $2 per can, he or she is charging the case price and not a premium price for a broken (busted) case.

cannot afford to purchase a whole case of, for example, soup bases if the contents will have to sit around for a period of time losing flavor and otherwise deteriorating. This buyer will need to look for those suppliers who can and will accommodate small requests, such as warehouse-club suppliers.

■ Credit Terms

Buyers are interested in the **credit terms** available from the various suppliers with whom they might consider conducting business. It is important to note such factors as the availability of **cash discounts**, quantity discounts, volume discounts, **cash rebates**, and **promotional discounts**; when payments are due (i.e., the **credit period**); the billing procedures; the amount of interest charges buyers may have to pay on the outstanding balance; and the overall installment payment procedure available, if any.

Many hospitality operators will do what is necessary, within reason, to deal with suppliers who offer generous credit terms. This criterion conceivably could be the major consideration in supplier selection.

■ Deposits Required

For some products, buyers may need to put up a **deposit**. For example, if they purchase soft drink syrup in reusable containers, they may need to put up a cash deposit for them. Usually, deposit requirements are not burdensome, but if they are, buyers probably will want to eliminate such a demanding supplier from their approved-supplier lists.

■ Returns Policy

This is a very sensitive issue, and buyers should evaluate it well before it ever becomes necessary to return merchandise and/or refuse to pay for goods or services. Needless to say, the more liberal the **returns policy**, the more buyers expect to pay in the long run.

A related issue is the return of prepayment for merchandise that buyers ordered but for some reason must refuse its delivery. For instance, it often is necessary for buyers to put up a significant deposit for equipment purchases. If they then decide that they do not want or need the item, what happens to their deposit? It would be prudent for buyers to iron out any potential problems early.

■ Reciprocal Buying

Particularly in the area of hospitality services, such as hotel advertising, buyers may want to initiate a **reciprocal buying** arrangement, that is, an arrangement whereby "you buy from me, and I'll buy from you." If so, they should inquire as early as possible about the suppliers' willingness to do this.

A related concept is the notion of doing business only with those who do business with you, or who send other business your way. In our experience, if you allow yourself to get entangled in a web such as this, replete with so many interlocking obligations, one little slip can cause the whole situation to fall apart.

■ Willingness to Barter

As trading becomes more popular, buyers might decide to adopt it as part of their overall buying plan. If so, they must test the suppliers' willingness to accommodate this request. Internet companies such as the Hotel Buying Network and the Global Barter Corporation exist to connect companies willing to **barter**.

> **barter** The practice of trading your products or services for something you need. Intended to reduce your out-of-pocket expense.

SUPPLIER SELECTION CRITERIA: OTHER FACTORS

■ Number of Back Orders

It seems to us that a supplier who has a history of excessive **back orders** will not be part of a buyer's approved-supplier list. A buyer can probably forgive a back order once in a while. However, if this is a recurring problem, it is best not to do business with such a purveyor. The buyer will want to do business with suppliers who have very high **fill rates**. A fill rate is a ratio calculated by dividing the number of items delivered by the number ordered. Ideally, it would always equal 100 percent.

> **back order** When your shipment is incomplete because the vendor did not have the item in stock, the invoice will state that the item is back ordered. You will receive the item later.
>
> **fill rate** Equal to the amount of items delivered divided by the amount of items ordered. For instance, if you ordered 10 items and the vendor delivered 9, the fill rate is 90 percent (9 divided by 10). A fill rate less than 100 percent indicates that the vendor is out of some items and has to back order you.

■ Substitution Capability

On occasions when back orders cannot be avoided, it is nice if the supplier can provide a comparable substitute. Generally, though, only suppliers who offer a one-stop shopping opportunity are capable of doing this.

A related possibility is the supplier who runs out of an item but who is concerned enough about buyers personally to secure the products necessary to complete their order from another supplier or from one of his or her competitors. This type of purveyor is rare, but one or two of them may be in your area.

■ Buyout Policy

We can recall years ago when suppliers who wanted a buyer's business would agree to purchase his or her existing stock of competitors' merchandise. For instance, a soap salesperson soliciting a buyer's business might agree to buy out the existing stock so that the buyer could begin immediately to use the new merchandise. This type of **buyout policy** is unusual today, but it may exist somewhere. If it does exist in your area, it represents one more criterion on which to judge a potential supplier.

A related issue is the willingness of a supplier to buy back outdated or obsolete merchandise. For example, when buyers purchase replacement equipment, a major supplier selection factor would be the **trade-in allowance** that competing suppliers offer. All other things being equal, the supplier who has the most favorable policy is apt to have an edge over his or her competitors.

> **buyout policy** Vendors' willingness to purchase from a customer, a competitor's products, so that the customer can immediately begin purchasing similar products from them.
>
> **trade-in allowance** Amount of money a vendor credits your account when you buy a new piece of FFE (especially equipment) when turning in an older model.

■ Suppliers' Facilities

Buyers should be particularly concerned with a potential supplier's storage and handling facilities, the delivery facilities, and the facilities' sanitation. For instance, if the supplier uses old, dirty, and uncooled vans to deliver fresh produce, you may want to avoid that purveyor regardless of the AP price and other supplier services provided. Inadequate facilities harm product quality, and this is intolerable.

■ Consulting Service Provided

To a great extent, salespersons, and suppliers in general, are the primary sources of product and related information for the typical hospitality operator. Buyers are interested in data concerning product specifications, preparation and handling procedures, nutrition, merchandising techniques, and other similar types of advice.[19]

Small hospitality operators are especially loyal to suppliers and salespersons who willingly share their expertise. For example, a small caterer who is bidding for an unusually large banquet contract will appreciate the salesperson who takes the time to help prepare the proposal.

consulting service
Company that specializes in helping others by giving advice and/or accomplishing specific tasks that clients do not wish to do on their own.

Formal consulting, though, is not something that every purveyor is able or willing to provide. For instance, when purchasing equipment, buyers may find that some dealers stock it, sell it, and deliver it—period. Other dealers provide some additional advice, such as providing blueprints or seeking the appropriate building permits. Buyers pay more for this type of **consulting service**, but they may be willing to do so. When this is the case, buyers must seek suppliers who can provide for their needs.

■ Willingness to Sell Storage

Some suppliers will sell storage, which can be a tremendous service if, for example, a buyer needs space to house a large amount of merchandise that he or she purchased through a favorable opportunity buy. A supplier's storage space is usually better than one rented from a generic warehouse or storage locker location because it is apt to be appropriately cooled and/or heated for items the typical hospitality buyer purchases.

A supplier who will sell storage probably is a rare find, but if buyers are fortunate enough to have one in their area, they must be certain to inquire not only about the fees for this service but also about any other sort of requirements. For instance, to qualify to purchase storage, buyers may need to purchase $1,000 worth of merchandise per week. This may or may not be attractive to them, however, and they should be alert to these kinds of restrictions, which could place them in an unprofitable position.

■ Free Samples

free sample Part of the marketing strategy used by vendors to sell products. Buyers are allowed to test a product in their own facility without having to pay for it.

Suppliers will often give buyers one or two **free samples** for their evaluation, particularly if the buyers represent a potentially large amount of business. However, some suppliers may not want to do this. Also, some buyers may not feel comfortable accepting free samples because it could compromise them. Large hospitality operations may have very strict policies on whether samples can even be accepted at all.

■ References

Usually, a large part of a buyer's supplier selection work is devoted to obtaining personal references. This is normally an informal process, whereby the buyer talks with friends in the industry who may be able to provide meaningful input about certain suppliers. The buyer might also consider contacting credit-rating firms to uncover a potential supplier's financial strength. Generally, though, if a friend whose opinion the buyer trusts has had a good experience with a particular supplier, the buyer would want to do business with that firm.

It would appear that the buyer is most anxious about a potential supplier's integrity and overall dependability. These are the characteristics the buyer tries to uncover when conversing with friends. These factors can mean many things to many persons, but if a friend is impressed with a supplier's dependability and integrity, the buyer will probably want that supplier on his or her approved-supplier list.

MOST IMPORTANT SUPPLIER SELECTION CRITERIA

No one can dictate the criteria that buyers should consider when selecting their suppliers. This is something that only buyers can judge for themselves. It is interesting, though, to note those criteria that are most important to members of the hospitality industry.

Generally, most buyers are interested primarily in product quality. Suppliers must be able to consistently provide the quality needed, or else buyers cannot deal with them.

Supplier service is, usually, a close second to product quality. Dependability is critical. Suppliers must ensure that buyers receive what they need when they need it.

The AP price seems to trail quality and supplier services in most buyer surveys. Although this does not necessarily imply that buyers are unconcerned with product costs, it does emphasize the point that AP prices do not unduly influence purchase decisions in the hospitality industry.

Typical hospitality buyers seem to follow the supplier selection process that Walt Disney World food services adopted. When selecting its suppliers, Disney is concerned with product quality, supplier service, whether the purveyor is large enough to handle the account, and AP price.[20]

Regardless of the number and type of supplier selection criteria the hospitality operation employs, the common thread running through them is one of consistency, dependability, loyalty, and trust.[21] If suppliers can render consistent value, chances are they will be on the approved-supplier list of several hospitality operations. Furthermore, suppliers who consistently provide acceptable value will continue to grow and prosper.

SUPPLIER–BUYER RELATIONS

As buyers gradually complete their basic buying plan, they simultaneously reduce the potential supplier pool. Eventually, common sense and company policy guide them toward the optimal suppliers. Buyers do not want too many restrictions placed on their basic buying plan. On the other hand, they do not necessarily want to ignore all of the suppliers' needs. Buyers must strike a balance, within reason, so that both they and the seller feel confident that profit will result from the relationship. The best relationship is one in which both the buyer and the seller are satisfied.

The buyer's principal contact with suppliers is through salespersons. In the initial stages of supplier selection, the buyer may meet an officer of a supply house, but after this meeting, the top management of the supply house officer may be out of sight, but not out of the picture. Those officials work hard to improve **supplier–buyer relations**; some of their major activities include those discussed next.

■ Supply House Officers Set the Tone of Their Business

Usually, supply house officers set this tone by establishing the quality standards of the items they carry, by determining the types of economic values and supplier services they provide, and by planning their advertising and promotion campaigns. While considering these aspects of the business, moreover, suppliers seek a balance between what they want to do and what their customers, the hospitality operations' buyers, need.

■ Supply House Officers Set the Overall Sales Strategies

Two basic sales strategies exist: (1) the "push strategy," in which suppliers urge their salespersons to do whatever is necessary to entice the buyer to purchase the product—the normal push is AP price discounts of one type or another, and (2) the "pull strategy," in which suppliers cater to the preferences of those who use the items the buyer purchases. For example, suppliers may advertise heavily on television, exhorting ultimate customers to demand the suppliers' product in their favorite restaurant. If they do, the restaurant buyer has little choice but to purchase the product. In other words, the ultimate customer "pulls" the product through the channel. Alternately, if backdoor selling can be implemented successfully, a user in the company "pulls" the product through by influencing the buyer's purchasing decisions.

You have undoubtedly seen many types of pull strategies. If, for example, a restaurant customer orders a Coke®, which is a brand name, what choice does the buyer have? This also applies to something as minor as catsup on the tables. Restaurant patrons typically prefer Heinz® brand.

Of course, various shades and combinations of these two basic strategies exist, but, generally speaking, suppliers lean toward one, or, at least, they lean toward one for some items and toward the other for their remaining items.

The pull strategy can be risky and extremely costly for suppliers to implement and maintain, but if it works, the rewards are fruitful indeed. The pull strategy also is a major weapon suppliers use to steal business from one another.

■ Supply House Officers Sponsor a Great Deal of Product and Market Research

Suppliers also spend considerable time and effort evaluating the bids they make for buyers' business. Furthermore, they continually prepare and revise files that contain information about current and potential customers. These information files are sometimes referred to as **buyer fact sheets** or **buyer profiles**. They constitute a selling tool and contain as much or as little information as thought necessary to facilitate the sales effort.

These pieces of information are usually found in these files:

1. Does the buyer have a favorable impression of the supplier's reputation? Generally speaking, a favorable impression makes it easier for a salesperson to get a foot in the door on the first sales visit.

2. What are the major characteristics of the ultimate customers of the buyer's company? If, for example, the ultimate consumers are price conscious, the buyer will probably adopt a similar posture.

3. Is the buyer concerned with AP prices?

4. Is the buyer concerned with fast and dependable deliveries?

5. Will the buyer take a chance on new products? On what authority can buyers suggest new products to the respective hospitality departments?

6. Does the buyer have a great deal of confidence in the skills of purchasing, or will second-guessing prevail?

7. Does the buyer have other duties, for example, both buyer and user? Will these other duties minimize the time spent with salespersons?

8. Does the buyer insist on rigid quality control or accept certain exceptions or substitutions from time to time?

9. What is the possibility of setting up a reciprocal buying arrangement?

10. What is the payment history of the buyer's company?

11. How does the buyer treat suppliers and salespersons?

12. Do any little things irritate the buyer, such as getting annoyed if a salesperson is a few minutes late for an appointment?

■ Suppliers Train Their Sales Staffs

Suppliers expend tremendous efforts in sales training, for both new salespersons and, continually, for salespersons currently on staff. Quite often, the training materials are based on **market research**, new products, and buyer profiles.

■ Suppliers Keep Their Salespersons' Promises

Suppliers must, for example, make sure that orders are handled properly and delivered on time.

> **market research**
> Organized effort to gather information about customers. Typically used by businesses to discover what people want, need, or believe.

SALESPERSON–BUYER RELATIONS

Salespersons, who are sometimes referred to as **distributor sales representatives** (DSRs), are buyers' main contact with supplier firms. Buyers must usually meet several DSRs every week. Many of them are familiar faces; others are new. Establishing firm and fair business relations with DSRs, and particularly setting the ground rules regarding sales visits, is essential to efficient procurement.

> **distributor sales representative (DSR)** Person employed by a vendor to sell products and provide support functions to restaurant operators.

Buyers need to be aware of the sales tactics salespersons use. Generally, on the first sales call, salespersons might: (1) make some attempt, however slight, at backdoor selling (i.e., they might try to interest users in the supplier's wares), (2) attempt to use free samples and literature in an effort to interest and possibly to obligate a buyer, (3) try to establish a justification for their presence, (4) try to talk buyers away from the current supplier, or (5) try to be invited to return, thereby starting a nominal business relationship.

relationship marketing
Procedure that does not view marketing as selling products one at a time, that is, it does not view marketing as a series of individual transactions. Instead, it refers to the need for vendors and customers to form personal alliances that will lead to the sale and purchase of products and services that mutually benefit one another.

house account   Term used by a vendor to identify a very loyal customer. A customer who continually buys from a vendor and is not interested in buying from competing vendors.

Sales professionals are usually adept at practicing what is usually referred to as **relationship marketing**.[22] Salespersons after a buyer's business will bend over backward to start some type, any type, of business relationship. They will usually take any order, no matter how small, so that future sales visits are justified. Even if the buyer purchases only one item once, the salesperson still feels, as "one of your suppliers," free to drop in periodically. It may seem ludicrous that salespersons would hang around once a buyer makes it clear that future purchases are unlikely. Also, you would think that supply house officers would prohibit salespersons from taking small orders, but buyers may not always respond the same way. The next buyer, or manager, may be more receptive. Today, it may be a small order; tomorrow, who knows? Hence, salespersons continue their efforts.

Small operators enamored of one-stop shopping like to avoid excessive contacts with salespersons and to minimize their ordering procedures. These preferences turn them into **house accounts**. House accounts are regular, steady customers for whom suppliers are not always motivated to provide generous supplier services. However, they may continue to provide exceptional supplier services to keep these customers happy.

This is a touchy issue. Dealing with many salespersons is time consuming. However, never seeing them at all is poor local public relations, shuts off good sources of information, and prevents them from helping buyers check inventories, production techniques, and any equipment they may have loaned for use with their products. Good trade relations might dictate that buyers spread their orders out a bit more. This, too, can be costly, however. Each operation must, therefore, balance the potential ill will with this loss of time and make its decision in the light of such factors as order size and management availability, as well as public relations.

A full-time buyer for a large operation, though, is expected to spend a good deal of time with salespersons. The company pays the buyer to minimize the AP prices. In these large organizations, other people are responsible for the steps the product follows from purchase to use. Someone watches for pilferage, shrinkage, and spoilage in storage. Another individual is responsible for using cooking or other production techniques that prevent waste and shrinkage. Someone else is responsible for minimizing overportioning of finished product. How these responsibilities are distributed is not relevant to the present point. Our point is that, in a large operation, the achievement of a good EP cost results not only from a good AP price but also from the proper working of a complex, skilled organization.

Several volumes have been written on sales tactics, strategies, and procedures. Buyers would be wise to read some of these materials, paying particular attention to such topics as: (1) personal characteristics of good salespersons, (2) types of salespersons, (3) what to avoid when dealing with salespersons, (4) what to do when dealing with salespersons, (5) types of sales tactics, and (6) techniques for evaluating salespersons.

We do not want to suggest that an adversarial relationship necessarily exists between buyers and salespersons, but buyers must expect salespersons to go to whatever ethical lengths they can to make sales. Salespersons come to sell, not to entertain. They want to meet your expectations, but for a price.

Good salespersons will never sell a buyer something not needed. Keep in mind, however, that the main objective is to convert the buyer into a regular customer, not by pressuring the buyer but by providing satisfaction. Within reason, then, salespersons do what is necessary to turn a buyer into a house account.

An alert buyer should be able to compete in the game of sales strategy and tactics. Objectivity helps a buyer, as does an understanding supervisor. In most cases, the buyer and salesperson work together for each other's benefit. Remember, though, business being business, a buyer should never become too friendly with a sales representative.

EVALUATING SUPPLIERS AND SALESPERSONS

Suppliers and salespersons sometimes become such integral parts of a business that a buyer starts treating them as he or she would an employee. For this reason, a buyer should periodically evaluate the suppliers' and salespersons' performances and consider remedial action or rewarding them as necessary. The ultimate remedy is to switch to another source of supply. The ultimate reward is to grant the supplier a house account. (This may be no reward for salespersons, though. Some supply houses pay no sales commissions on house account sales; the theory is that little effort has gone into making the sales. These salespersons may, however, receive a bonus when they obtain a house account for their firm.) Obviously, there is a considerable range between these extremes and several discipline–reward combinations.

Most analysts agree that an operator should rate suppliers and their salespersons as part of the remedy–reward cycle. However, few analysts agree on the criteria to use in these evaluations. For instance, some buyers are appreciative of the salespersons who take the time to listen to what they have to say. Other buyers seek only those salespersons who can answer their questions completely and correctly. Still other buyers are more enamored with effective and impressive sales presentations.

In any case, once again the common thread running throughout is consistency: consistent quality, consistent supplier services, and so forth. If suppliers and salespersons consistently fulfill their part of the bargain, whether it was made yesterday or last year, buyers should have no complaint. Our suggestion, then, is for buyers to enumerate those factors on which they and the suppliers and salespersons agree and, from time to time, to use a consistency yardstick to measure performance. Although buyers look for consistency, they must remember that a high AP price often accompanies high levels of consistency, especially consistent supplier services.

If buyers expect suppliers and salespersons to be consistent, they themselves must be consistent. That is, they should never change their evaluation criteria unilaterally. Professional buyers generally try to be consistent, but users who also buy, in contrast to professional buyers, tend to be more subjective about the items they purchase, as well as more abusive toward suppliers and salespersons. User–buyers, therefore, should be especially leery of finding these traits in themselves.

In the final analysis, evaluation is probably a combination of art and science. Having evaluated consistency, buyers could examine other subjective factors, but buyers should resist being too hasty in this process. It is true that, unless buyers have a long-term contract, they can drop their supplier quite abruptly. This may do more harm than good, however. If a supplier is deficient, buyers should give him or her a chance to improve, just as they would give a poorly performing employee a chance to improve. Buyers should never drop the supplier or turn away the salesperson without allowing a second chance. If buyers acquire a reputation for rash decisions, other suppliers or salespersons may shy away, especially those who consider themselves fair and reputable performers. Buyers do not want to be left with only the poorest supply choices.

A step short of cutting a supplier off completely, a step that is often used, is suspending business for a week or so, just to make certain that this supplier realizes that possible business loss is at stake. This supposedly helps keep suppliers in line. Buyers want to be certain, though, that the supplier really did something to deserve this treatment and that the problem is not in their operation rather than the supplier's.

Supplier selection is not something to be done once and then forgotten. However, small operators often seem to think it is, even when competing suppliers and salespersons bombard them with sales pitches.

Salespersons will fight to prevent a buyer from settling in with one or two suppliers unless they are one of those selected. They do not want the buyer to enter into the "comfort stage" of the supplier selection procedure. Their sales efforts will, in fact, become increasingly insistent. On the other hand, a buyer's current suppliers and salespersons will try to increase buyer satisfaction to discourage the advances of competitors. Of course, the buyer's current sources may get comfortable themselves and need to be brought up short now and then.

Many buyers and user–buyers become comfortable with a salesperson, but at least they remain aware of the need to examine alternate suppliers and to make a switch if necessary. However, flitting continually from one supplier to another involves a certain amount of emotional strain, broken loyalties, and disrupted business patterns. The switching becomes particularly difficult when a buyer's favorite salesperson goes to work for another supplier and the buyer wants to continue doing business with that person. In effect, the buyer allows this salesperson to carry the buyer's business to a new employer.

Generally, a supplier who takes good care of buyers' needs deserves some type of reward. Suppliers and salespersons are not employees but might be accorded some of the same courtesies. Good employees are rewarded with continuous employment and a salary raise or a bonus. Suppliers and salespersons should be treated with equal consideration. We are not sure whether it is always a good idea to become a house account, but we do believe that, at the very least, good current suppliers and salespersons deserve first crack at a buyer's business, now and in the future.

■ MANDALAY BAY HOTEL AND CASINO, LAS VEGAS, NEVADA

Robert Lindsay is the purchasing and receiving manager for the House of Blues (HOB) and Foundation Room at the Mandalay Bay Hotel and Casino in Las Vegas. It has the highest sales of the 13 HOB venues due to its size and the number of special events it hosts. HOB Entertainment has been part of the Live Nation Entertainment® (LNE) Company since 2006. LNE is the world's leading entertainment company. It owns or operates over 300 concert venues and sports stadiums in North America and Europe and owns Ticketmaster Entertainment®. LNE also has a stake in about 250 artists' music, including ticket sales, promotions, and merchandise.

Robert reports to the director of venue operations and the general manager. He is responsible for buying and accounting for several categories of assets including consumables, capital items, administrative items, paper goods, other disposables, and cleaning supplies. The cost of these items are all charged directly to the operating overhead of the business.

Robert has many years of food and beverage experience that have prepared him for this position. He was a server, captain, and manager for restaurants such as Mario Batali's Carnevino and Emeril Lagasse's Delmonico Steakhouse. His first purchasing job was as a buyer for the Venetian and Palazzo resorts. Before starting with HOB, he spent a year working for a broadline distributor, which gave him a much greater understanding of the supply side of the business. Robert also has a bachelor of science degree in hotel administration from the University of Nevada, Las Vegas.

In this age of technology, Robert still does most of his ordering through e-mails. He prefers this to phoning in orders as he can see a delivery receipt and require suppliers to confirm that they received the e-mails. Although many suppliers can receive online orders sent directly from HOB's purchasing system, currently, Sysco® is the only company that is fully integrated to submit bids and create invoices within the system. Prices and weights of products on invoices from other suppliers must be updated manually from the physical invoice received with the delivery. Robert believes that the suppliers may not be in a rush to develop the systems because many of their smaller independent restaurant and hotel customer would be reluctant to use it. He predicts that online ordering will not become the norm for another five to seven years until people that grew up with technology are in buyer-management positions.

One of Robert's special projects is developing his own order template that will allow him to make his process consistent. Another item that he would love to have is an iPad that ties his inventory system into the suppliers' price lists, including how much he has to buy to get a price break on the case price. Because his purchasing ability is limited by the amount of storage space available and current amount of capital held in inventory, this type of information would help him determine the optimum time to make a purchase.

The HOB corporate purchasing department sources all branded items for the retail stores and logo glassware for the bars and restaurants. The corporation mandates which brands of beer, wine, and liquor that the venues are required to buy. However, they cannot specify which supplier to purchase them from due to the alcohol sales and control regulations discussed in Chapter 22. The individual operations can purchase additional alcoholic beverages based on regional and local customer requests. In particular, they can develop their own craft beer programs. For example, in Las Vegas, they carry local favorites such as Big Dog's, Great Basin, and Joseph James beers.

Robert says that a problem with liquor purchasing is that you have to consider logistics in addition to AP prices and EP costs. For example, buying liquor in 1.5 liter instead of the typical 750 milliliter bottle is less expensive, but the bottles do not fit in a bar's liquor wells and would be uncomfortable for the bartenders to pour. Similarly, the company switched to buying juice in cans instead of from a particular type of juice bottle because the AP price was lower. However, pouring from the can was not practical or attractive so they had an additional capital cost, which had to be expensed out over time because they had to buy new juice pourers.

Although the chef is responsible for ordering all the food for the restaurants, Robert says that the corporate purchasing is increasingly involved in finding the best buys for the company nationally. Although this will allow the operation to get the best pricing, Robert worries that it will decrease their flexibility.

A key philosophy for HOB purchasing is "no surprises." Robert has to get approval for purchases of more than $15,000–$20,000 from his director. All purchases more than $200,000 have to be approved by the corporate office. They use a purchase order system for hard items with at least three copies to ensure that all the different department managers who are responsible for different budgets and accounts have the information they need. The chain for the purchase order is: a person gives the order to Robert; it then goes to the accounting department to make sure there is money to pay for it; next stop is internal accounting; then to the department head who must sign off on it; and finally to the Director of Venue Operations.

Robert supervises three receiving clerks who work on the dock when products arrive; the products may be delivered by local distributors and suppliers or from third-party shippers such as UPS and FedEx. The receivers store the products; rotate them; check quality, temperatures, and dates on a regular basis; and deliver them to two different kitchens. They also fill other internal requests for anything kept in the storage warehouse. A big part of Robert's job is following items through the "Chain of Custody." He looks for problems within the accounting system and how the system is used.

The goal is to know where all products are all the time. More than 25 percent of his time is spent on inventory and related paperwork. He is responsible for coordinating all transfers between departments, such as fruit for cocktail garnishes sent from the kitchen to the bars. He also compares the departments' sales revenue to their cost of goods sold (COGS); the percentage cost of goods sold must fall within acceptable company guidelines. Of course, for this type of establishment, control of the liquor inventory is extremely important. The point-of-sale (POS) system tracks liquor sales and assumes that all products are used directly from the purchased inventory. Managers are the only people with keys to the liquor storage. The company restricts keys to other storage areas and the cash room as well. Managers have to check them out from a central area.

HOB uses proprietary software, CrunchTime™, which is a Web-based enterprise back office platform for multiunit foodservice operations. All managers at the venue have access to it, which allows them to cross-train in different job responsibilities and to have others be able to keep up with purchasing and accounting during people's time off. The system interfaces with the Micros point-of-sale (POS) and inventory system to do performance tracking, anticipate needs, and evaluate the numbers. Robert says that a key feature important to his job is that it allows the system to have negative balances, which take into account that there are often delays in manually entering information from the invoices into the system.

Robert stresses the importance of supplier services and getting information from the suppliers. For example, one of HOB's meat suppliers was able to save them a substantial amount of money by allowing them to buy steaks at the same price that one of the large casino companies with substantial buying power had negotiated. Robert's definition of a good supplier is one who:

- Keeps the lines of communication open.

- Answers his or her phone, text, and e-mail messages quickly.

- Sends bids on time.

- Keeps him knowledgeable about changes in the market, such as shortages, vintage changes for wines, and AP prices.

- Has subscriptions to services such as the Urner Barry Reports and passes that information on to his or her buyers.

- Can assist with finding enough products for the high-volume business in the operations where he has worked. Robert gives an example that when the Venetian needed 13,000 chicken breasts over three days for a special event, it just about wiped out the supply available in the area.

 ## Key Words and Concepts

Application service provider (ASP)	Cash-and-carry
Approved supplier	Cash discount
Approved-supplier list	Cash rebate
Back order	Consulting service
Barter	Contract house
Bid buying	Cost-plus buying
Bonded supplier	Credit period
Buyer fact sheet	Credit terms
Buyer profile	Daily bid buying
Buying plans	Daily-quotation buying
Buying services	Delivery schedule
Buyout policy	Deposits
Call sheet buying	Distributor sales representative (DSR)
Case price per unit	End-user services

Key Words and Concepts (continued)

Fill rate	Request for bid
Fixed bid buying	Request for quote (RFQ)
Forward buying	Responsible bidder
Free sample	Returns policy
House account	Route salesperson
Ineligible bidder	Sealed-bid procedure
Lead time	Single-source procurement
Market quote buying	Socially responsible supplier
Market research	Sole-source procurement
Minimum order requirement	Standing order
National distribution	Stockless purchasing
One-stop shopping	Supplier selection criteria
Open-market buying	Supplier–buyer relations
Ordering cost	Trade-in allowance
Ordering procedures	Value analysis
Prime-vendor procurement	Volume discount
Profit markup	Warehouse club
Promotional discount	Wholesale club
Reciprocal buying	Will-call
Relationship marketing	

Questions and Problems

1. What major problems are associated with the initial-survey stage of supplier selection? What would you suggest to alleviate these difficulties?

2. Why would an owner–manager take the initiative in selecting equipment suppliers over the buyer?

3. Identify the two basic buying plans. Suggest items that would be purchased under each plan.

4. Why do you think bid buying is so popular in our industry? What are the costs and benefits of this plan, as opposed to those of the other basic buying plan?

5. What are the advantages and disadvantages of one-stop shopping? Suggest the types of hospitality operations you feel would most likely benefit from one-stop shopping.

6. A buyer often takes a daily bid before placing a meat order. What does this procedure involve?

7. What are the major advantages and disadvantages of co-op purchasing?

8. What are some of the advantages and disadvantages of searching online for potential suppliers?

Questions and Problems (continued)

9. What is the difference between a formal bid procedure and an informal bid procedure?

10. What are the major advantages and disadvantages of will-call purchasing?

11. What are some advantages and disadvantages of purchasing only from socially responsible suppliers?

12. What is the difference between the push sales strategy and the pull sales strategy? Which strategy do you think a supplier prefers?

13. When is it appropriate for a buyer to use a fixed-bid buying procedure?

14. Why might a supplier be reluctant to participate in a cost-plus purchasing procedure?

15. How could a buyer save money by using the stockless purchasing procedure?

16. What are some advantages and disadvantages of the standing-order purchasing procedure?

17. Why is it important to purchase merchandise from licensed and bonded suppliers only?

18. Define or briefly explain each term:

    a. Call sheet buying
    b. Approved-supplier list
    c. Forward buying
    d. Cash rebate
    e. Credit period
    f. Buying club
    g. Direct purchase
    h. Credit terms
    i. Minimum order requirement
    j. Lead time
    k. Returns policy
    l. Buyout policy
    m. Case price
    n. Buyer fact sheet
    o. House account
    p. National distribution
    q. Trade-in allowance
    r. Corporate social responsibility

 ## Experiential Exercises

1. Assume that you are very happy with your current supplier, who has been supplying most of your needs for more than a year. A new supplier comes along with what appears to be a better deal: a promise of lower AP prices along with the same quality and supplier services.
    a. Write a one-page report regarding what you would do.
    b. Ask a hotel or restaurant manager to comment on your answer.
    c. Edit your report to include your answer and the manager's comments.

2. Select a type of hospitality operation you would like to own. Create a list of national hospitality suppliers that you might use for that type of operation. Prepare a report that explains how you identified specific national suppliers and why these would be the best for your type of operation.

Experiential Exercises (continued)

3. Select a type of hospitality operation you would like to own. Create a list of local hospitality suppliers that you might use for that type of operation. Prepare a report that explains how you identified specific local suppliers and why these would be the best for your type of operation. Explain why buying from local suppliers is a better strategy for your type of hospitality organization than using national suppliers.

4. Develop a checklist that you would use to evaluate your suppliers. Assign degrees of importance to each item on the list. If possible, ask a hotel manager and/or a food buyer to comment on your list.

References

1. Damian Beil, *Supplier Selection*, Stephan M. Ross School of Business, July 2009, http://www-personal.umich.edu/~dbeil/Supplier_Selection_Beil-EORMS.pdf.

2. The Walt Disney Company's code of conduct for manufacturers: corporate.disney.go .com/responsibility/codeofconduct.html, retrieved September 2010; Carolyn Walkup, "Burger King Hatches Its Own Humane-Sourcing Plan," *Nation's Restaurant News*, 41, no. 15 (April 7, 2007):1–2; Robin Allen, "As Environmental Concerns Go Mainstream, Clever Operators Are Joining the Crusade," *Nation's Restaurant News*, 41, no. 40 October 8, 2007):23.

3. James Morgan, "How Well Are Supplier Diversity Programs Doing?" *Purchasing*, 131, no. 13 (August 15, 2002):29–35. See also: "Avendra Adds 14 Minority and Women-Owned Suppliers to Its Procurement Programs," *Hotel News Resource*, 2004, www.hotelnewsresource .com/article13641-Avendra_Adds_Minority_And_Women_Owned_Suppliers_To_Its_ Procurement_Programs.html, retrieved September 2010; Gregg Cebrzynski, "Burger King's Ads Target Women and Minorities in Bid to Recruit New Suppliers and Franchisees," *Nation's Restaurant News*, 42, no. 1 (January 7, 2008):12.

4. M. J. Maloni and M. E. Brown "Corporate Social Responsibility in the Supply Chain: An Application in the Food Industry," *Journal of Business Ethics*, 68, no. 1 (2006):35–52.

5. Sysco, "Good Things Are Our Greatest Responsibility," Sysco Corporation 2013 Sustainability Summary Report, http://sustainability.sysco.com/pdf/syscoSR_2013.pdf.

6. US Foods, Inc., "Corporate Citizenship: Fighting Hunger," US Foods, Inc. 2013, www.usfoods.com/about-us/corporate-citizenship/strengthening-the-community .html.

7. US Foods, Inc., "Corporate Citizenship: Reducing emissions," US Foods, Inc. 2013, www.usfoods.com/about-us/corporate-citizenship/safeguarding-the-environment .html.

References (continued)

8. Perdue Farms, "Corporate Responsibility: Our Corporate Responsibility Platform," 2013, www.perduefarms.com/Corporate_Responsibility/Corporate_Responsibility_Platform.

9. Thomas Publishing Company, "Diversity and Quality," March 21, 2014, http://certifications.thomasnet.com/certifications/.

10. Lisa Bannon, "CTF Hotel's Suit Queries Purpose Behind Avendra," *The Wall Street Journal*, May 23, 2002, p. D8; "Selective Services," *Nation's Restaurant News*, 1, no. 15 (November, 2002):14.

11. Terence A. Brown and David M. Bukovinsky, "ECR and Grocery Retailing: An Exploratory Financial Statement Analysis," *Journal of Business Logistics*, 22, no. 2 (2001):77–90; Craig A. Hill, "Information Technology and Supply Chain Management: A Study of the Food Industry," *Hospital Material Management Quarterly*, 22, no. 1 (August 2000):53–58.

12. Colm O'Gorman, "The Sustainability of Growth in Small- and Medium-Sized Enterprises," *International Journal of Entrepreneurial Behaviour & Research*, 7, no. 2 (2001):60.

13. Janet Attard, *Wholesale Clubs Help Small Businesses Cut Costs* (Centereach, NY: Attard Communications, Inc., 2009), www.businessknowhow.com/money/wholesaleclubs .htm.

14. Anonymous, "Sam's Club: Back to Business—History: Twenty Years Young and Building for the Future," *DSN Retailing Today*, 42, no. 7A, (April 2003):16–20. See also Anonymous, "Focus on the Core Customer," *Chain Store Age*, 79, no. 5 (May 2003):52–56; Anonymous, "1982 to 1992: Clubs and Category Killers Arrive on the Scene," *DSN Retailing Today*, 41, no. 15 (August 2002):21–25; Doug McMillon, "Helping Small Business Is Our Higher Calling," *DSN Retailing Today*, Third Quarter (2005):6; Mike Dubb, "BJ's Launches Restaurant Supply Concept," *DSN Retailing Today*, 43, no. 18 (September 20, 2004):6–7.

15. Julie Ritzer Ross, "Challenges Abound, but Lack of Standards Slows e-Business Progress," *Nation's Restaurant News*, 35, no. 21 (May 21, 2001):28. For examples, see www.esysco.net and www.usfood.com. See also R. Burns, "Food and Beverage: Linking the Electronic Supply Chain," *Lodging*, November 2000, pp. 8–10; Tevfik Demirciftci, "An Analysis of e-Procurement Applications and Trends in Hotels: A Pilot Study," *Hosteur*, 15, no. 2 (Fall 2006):25–32; William Atkinson, "Choice Hotels Leverages In-House E-Procurement Tool," *Purchasing Magazine Online*, www.purchasing.com/article/218464-Choice_Hotels_leverages_in_house_e_procurement_ tool.php.

16. Margaret Sheridan, "Class Clout," *Restaurants & Institutions*, 113, no. 8 (April 1, 2003): 84–90. See also Anonymous, "Denny's Franchise Association to Form Purchasing Co-op, Marketing Advisory Council," *Marketing Weekly News*, April 18, 2009, p. 36.

References (continued)

17. G. Tyler, "On-line Purchasing," *Hotel and Restaurant*, November/December 2001, pp. 43–46; Paul Buisson, "Strength in Numbers: Buying Groups Can Help Independent Operators Boost Bottom Line," *Nation's Restaurant News*, 38, no. 38 (September 20, 2004):36; Catherine R. Cobb, "Midsize Operators Team up for Purchasing Power," *Nation's Restaurant News*, 42, no. 32 (August 18, 2008):1, 53.

18. "ecFood buys Master Dairies," *Dairy Foods*, 102, no. 11 (November 2001):10. See also "Beverage Media Group Launches Online Buying Service," *Empire State Foodservice News*, January 2002 (available at griffcomm.net/esfsn.htm).

19. Peter Matthews, "What Constitutes Excellence in In-Store Supplier Service?" *Retail World*, 55, no. 23 (November 25–December 6, 2002):38–45. See also Tim Dodd, Mark Gultek, and Raymond Guydosh, "Restaurateurs' Perceptions of Wine Supplier Attributes," *Journal of Foodservice Business Research*, 7, no. 3 (2004):73–92; Virginia Gerst, "Working with Suppliers," *Restaurants & Institutions*, 116, no. 2 (2006):21.

20. Stephen M. Fjellman, *Vinyl Leaves: Walt Disney World and America* (San Francisco: Westview Press, 1992), p. 390; Roger L. Ball, "Strategic Sourcing—A Recipe for Strategic Excellence," *Government Procurement*, 13, no. 1 (February, 2005):6–12.

21. Rob Johnson, "A Deal of Time and Effort," *Supply Management*, 8, no. 8 (April 10, 2003):30–31; Vijay R. Kannan and Keah Choon Tan, "Supplier Selection and Assessment: Their Impact on Business Performance," *Journal of Supply Chain Management*, 38, no. 4 (Fall 2002):11–21; Michael Tracey and Chong Leng Tan, "Empirical Analysis of Supplier Selection and Involvement, Customer Satisfaction, and Firm Performance," *Supply Chain Management*, 6, no. 3/4 (2001):174–188.

22. Susanne Frey, Roland Schegg, and Jamie Murphy, "E-Mail Customer Service in the Swiss Hotel Industry," *Tourism and Hospitality Research*, 4, no. 3 (March 2003): 197–212.

TYPICAL ORDERING PROCEDURES

The Purpose of This Chapter

After reading this chapter, you should be able to:

- Create and explain the use of a purchase requisition.

- Sequence typical ordering procedures.

- Generate a purchase order, and describe its use.

- Describe methods commonly used to expedite and streamline the ordering process.

PURCHASE REQUISITIONS

purchase requisition
Lists the products or services needed by someone in the hospitality operation. It is given to the buyer, who then goes into the marketplace to find the best deals. This requisition is typically used for things that the buyer doesn't purchase on a regular basis.

stock requisition   A formal request made by an employee for items needed to carry out necessary tasks. It is given to the person managing the storage facilities. A typical control document used by large hotels.

issuing procedure   There are two types: formal and informal. The formal procedure requires a product user, such as a chef, to requisition products from a central warehouse or storage facility. The chef signs for the items and is responsible for them. An informal procedure allows the product user to request from the manager what is needed, with the manager getting the products and handling the paperwork later on. Another informal process allows any product user to enter the warehouse or storage facility and take what's needed for production and/or service.

At times, before the buyer places any orders or the unit manager coordinates any, the department heads of the hospitality operation—for example, the chef, the executive housekeeper, the maître d'—prepare **purchase requisitions**. These forms list items or services that the particular department heads need (see Figure 11.1 for a typical purchase requisition and Figure 11.2 for a requisition sheet). Generally speaking, these requisitions grant the buyer the authority to go out into the marketplace and procure the items the department heads have listed.

Typically, a purchase requisition is used in the hospitality industry whenever a manager or supervisor needs an item that the buyer does not order regularly. For instance, if a chef wants to try a convenience item, such as par-baked bread, and if this type of item is not regularly ordered, the chef must petition the buyer, and possibly other management personnel, for permission to use this item in production.

If the hospitality operation's buyer orders an item regularly, a purchase requisition is unnecessary. If the item is kept in a separate storage facility, the employee needs to complete a **stock requisition** and give it to the storeroom manager in exchange for the item. (See Chapter 13 for a discussion of stock requisitions and **issuing procedures**.) If no separate storage facility exists, such as in a typical small restaurant unit, no formal stock requisition system may be in place. However, an employee usually must obtain permission from a supervisor before he or she is allowed to take products, especially expensive products, from the shelves for use in production and service.

PURCHASE REQUISITION		PAGE _____
DATE _____		OF _____
DEPARTMENT(S) _____		
COMPLETED BY _____		
ITEM	QUANTITY NEEDED	OTHER INFORMATION?

FIGURE 11.1 A purchase requisition.

		Estimated				Actual	
Quan.	Unit	Unit Cost	Total Cost	Item Description	Quan.	Unit	Unit Cost	Total Cost

Group: _____ Date: _____ REQUISITION SHEET

Job Code: _____ Date Needed: _____

Circle One: DAIRY   DRY GOODS   PRODUCE   MEATS/SEAFOODS

Received by: _____ Date: _____

Issued by: _____ Date: _____

FIGURE 11.2 A requisition sheet.

Potential problems are associated with the purchase requisition system. For example, it tends to dilute the selection and procurement function, in that too many people may be involved in deciding the types and qualities of products and services that the hospitality operation should purchase and use. Another problem is that the procedure tends to invite **backdoor selling**. Still another disadvantage is the time and effort required to implement and operate a purchase requisition system.

> **backdoor selling** This happens when a sales rep bypasses the regular buyer and goes to some other employee, such as the lead line cook, to make a sales pitch. The cook then exerts pressure on the buyer to make the purchase.

Certain benefits are associated with the purchase requisition system. First, it can be a useful training device for those department heads who aspire to become full-time buyers. Second, it can relieve a buyer of responsibility for ordering mistakes, simply pointing out that so-and-so improperly completed the purchase requisition. Third, this system can relieve the buyer of a good deal of paperwork. Fourth, it is a way of controlling the use of the products and services in the various departments.

This control can be easily accomplished by requiring additional information from the department head via the "other information" section (see Figure 11.1). For example, the buyer may want to know how much product the department has on hand, how much was sold yesterday, how much waste was incurred during the past week, which supplier to contact, and so on. Requiring all this information does little to endear a buyer to the department heads, but this control mechanism is, nevertheless, one of the strongest aspects of the purchase requisition systems.

ORDERING PROCEDURES

formal issues system
Process whereby all products a business uses are kept in a warehouse or storeroom overseen by a clerk or manager. Products can be obtained only by authorized persons who are required to present a properly completed stock requisition.

open storeroom An unlocked storage facility that can be accessed by employees as needed. Usually contains the less-expensive foods, beverages, and nonfood supplies.

par stock approach to ordering Method used to determine the appropriate amount to order. Involves setting par stocks for all items and subtracting the amount of each item on hand to calculate the order sizes.

in-process inventory
Products located at employee work stations; most or all will be used during the shift.

purchase order (PO) A request that the vendor deliver what you want, ideally at the time you want it, at an agreed-upon AP price and credit terms. May include other conditions, such as minimum order amount, cost of delivery (if any), and so forth.

Levinson approach to ordering Method of determining the appropriate order sizes. Takes into account forecasted sales, portion sizes, and yield percentages when calculating the amount of products to order.

When actually engaged in buying products and services, a buyer is most concerned with obtaining the right amount and the right quality at the right time with the right supplier services for the right edible-portion (EP) cost. In addition, the buying procedure is not complete until all products and services are properly received, stored, and issued to employees. In short, the buying responsibilities end only when the buyer turns these products and services over to those who will use them.

It is, of course, true that when the department head is a user–buyer, he or she may simply call in the order to an approved supplier. Actually, many hospitality operations do not use a **formal issues system**. It is important to note that even when a hospitality operation has an **open storeroom**, someone still keeps a close eye on what employees have removed from the storeroom. In very large operations, and in many smaller clubs and hotels, however, the practice of requiring written issues, approved by the department head, to draw food or supplies from a storeroom is more common. The discussion that follows describes the system found in places using a formal issues system.

Before placing an order, the buyer must determine the appropriate order size. The most common way to do this is to use the **par stock approach to ordering**, for which the buyer or user–buyer must note what is on hand in the main storeroom areas and in the department areas (stock that departments hold is normally referred to as the **in-process inventory**), subtract what is on hand from the par stock, and add products needed for banquets or other special functions. The buyer must then prepare the appropriate **purchase orders (POs)** and send them to the suppliers or call them in, keeping one or more copies as records. The buyer may interact with department heads and buyers, but the full-time buyer usually relieves the department head of the major responsibilities associated with ordering.

In operations that have sophisticated record-keeping and control systems, there is a greater tendency to use a version of the **Levinson approach to ordering** (or some variation of it), as discussed in Chapter 8.

These **ordering procedures** are commonly used in both small and large operations. The major differences between small and large properties are the degree of formality and the presence or absence of a full-time buyer. In small properties, the user–buyer is more common.

Large operations usually have at least one full-time buyer who is deeply involved in the purchasing function. In chain restaurants, for example, recall that, usually, a vice president of purchasing works in a home office and sets policies and procedures, whereas the unit manager handles only the paper-work for his or her particular store. Thus, the unit manager prepares the POs based on the format and procedure that the corporate headquarters office has designed. The unit manager then places the orders with designated suppliers, commissaries, or central distribution centers and sees to it that the products and services are properly received, stored, and issued to the respective departments.

> **ordering procedures**
> Standardized process used by the buyer to ensure that the correct amounts of needed products are ordered at the appropriate time.

The paperwork used in placing orders varies from one establishment to the next. However, among hospitality operations that use various types of forms, the information in them is reasonably standard throughout the industry.

Once the various order sizes are determined, a buyer can place the order in one of several ways. The old-fashioned method is to physically give a hard copy of the order to the supplier's salesperson or distributor sales representative (DSR). Alternatively, the buyer can telephone in the order and leave it with a person who answers or on voice mail. A more common practice is for the buyer to send the order online directly to the supplier and can obtain verification on the spot; that is, the buyer knows immediately whether the products he or she desires are available.

> **source**   Supplier at the beginning of the channel of distribution. For instance, a grower (farmer) would be at the beginning of the fresh produce channel of distribution. Also referred to as a primary source.

Unless an approved supplier has a specific requirement, management usually decides which ordering procedure to use. Small hospitality operations commonly follow one-stop shopping procedures and seek to minimize the ordering effort. Some large organizations, though, particularly the multiunit chain operations, normally contract to purchase large supplies of merchandise from several primary **sources** and/or intermediaries. Unit managers, therefore, may need to spend a bit more time when placing their orders if they must deal with several distributors.

THE PURCHASE ORDER

A purchase order (PO) can take many forms. At one extreme, an operation may not use one at all. At the other extreme, one may find a mind-boggling jumble of paper. Whatever shape it takes, a purchase order represents a request that a supplier deliver what the buyer wants, ideally at the time he or she wants it (see Figure 11.3 for a typical purchase order).

A purchase order usually resembles a purchase requisition. The date of the order enables buyers to keep track of product usage patterns and to know when to pay the bills. Some buyers may note the transportation requirement and packaging instructions. It is usual to indicate the desired **receiving** date, but as a practical matter, buyers probably have only two choices: either take the supplier's predetermined delivery schedule—or leave it. The quantity desired, the item type, the unit size (the size of the can, the weight per unit, etc.), the unit price, and the extended

> **receiving**   Process of examining shipments to determine if they should be accepted or refused.

price (the number of units times the unit price)—all these entries are clear instructions to the supplier about what buyers want, as well as their understanding of the pertinent as-purchased (AP) price, either the current AP price, or the AP price contracted for.

Recording prices also makes it easier for buyers to keep track of the value of stock on hand and serves to remind them that several thousands of dollars pass through their hands every year. The information the receiving clerk uses to compare the order with the delivery may or may not be included on the purchase order. However, if buyers send a copy of the order to the receiving clerk to be used when checking the delivery, it may be appropriate to include this information for the receiver. On the other hand, the receiving clerk may have a separate form for this purpose.

| Date _____ | Name of operation _____ | Order No. _____ |
| Account No. _____ | | Page ____ of ____ |

TO: _____

Please send the following items

Via _____

By _____

SIZE OF UNIT	QUANTITY	ITEM	UNIT PRICE	EXTENDED PRICE
			PAGE TOTAL	
			GRAND TOTAL	

TERMS OF PAYMENT _____

| For use by receiving clerk: | Rec. by _____ | Condition of goods _____ |
| | Date rec. _____ | Other remarks _____ |

FIGURE 11.3 A purchase order.

Different operators have different opinions about the number of copies of the purchase order to prepare. It is possible that one might need to prepare and use up to eight copies in extreme scenarios. If online ordering systems are being used, these copies may not always be hard-copy versions, but the appropriate people listed here would have access to view or download them. Of the eight possible copies, three may go to your supplier. The first would act as your official purchase order. The second copy might be utilized by the supplier as the bill that accompanies the delivery of the agreed-upon products or service. A third copy might need to be initialed by the supplier and sent back to the buyer; this would indicate acknowledgment of the order and the entering into of a binding contract. As for the fourth, the buyer normally keeps a copy to monitor usage patterns for future reference, as well as to keep track of which suppliers receive orders. The final four copies would go to the receiving clerk, to know what deliveries to expect and to check against the deliveries; the requisitioner, for the department's files; the accountant or bookkeeper, to keep track of bills coming due and to compare that copy with the copy of the bill that accompanies the particular delivery; and the accounting office, for its use and records.

Much more commonly, only three copies are made: one for the supplier, one for the receiving clerk, and one for the buyer's records (see Figure 11.4). A little less frequently, a fourth copy,

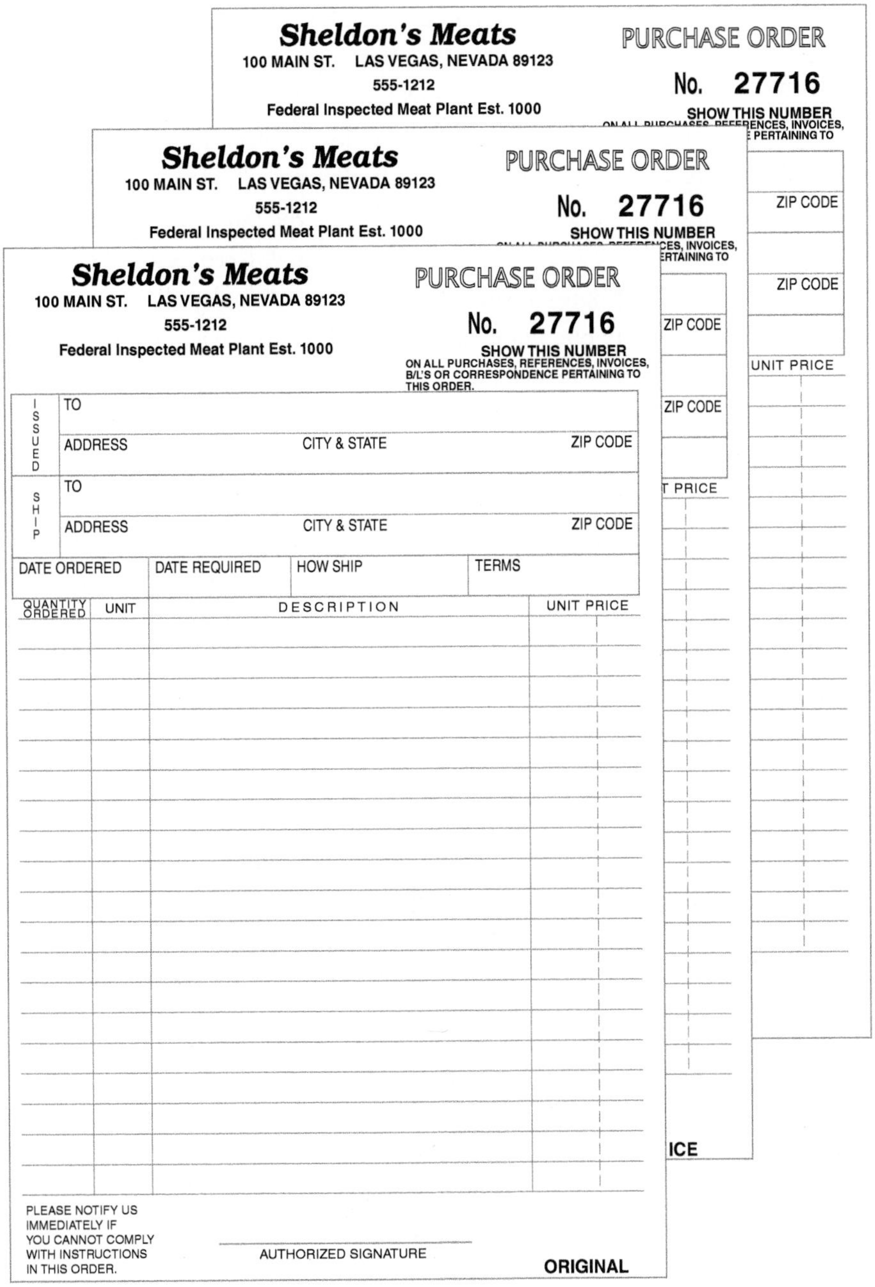

Sheldon's Meats
100 MAIN ST. LAS VEGAS, NEVADA 89123
555-1212
Federal Inspected Meat Plant Est. 1000

PURCHASE ORDER
No. 27716
SHOW THIS NUMBER
ON ALL PURCHASES, REFERENCES, INVOICES, B/L'S OR CORRESPONDENCE PERTAINING TO THIS ORDER.

ISSUED TO
ADDRESS | CITY & STATE | ZIP CODE
SHIP TO
ADDRESS | CITY & STATE | ZIP CODE

DATE ORDERED	DATE REQUIRED	HOW SHIP	TERMS

QUANTITY ORDERED	UNIT	DESCRIPTION	UNIT PRICE

PLEASE NOTIFY US IMMEDIATELY IF YOU CANNOT COMPLY WITH INSTRUCTIONS IN THIS ORDER.
AUTHORIZED SIGNATURE
ORIGINAL

FIGURE 11.4 A three-part purchase order.

which the supplier uses as the bill and sends back with the delivery, is prepared. The acknowledgment, requisitioner, accountant, and main-office copies do not appear so frequently.

The buyer's decision about how many copies to use is, however, important, as the buyer must exercise control from the moment he or she purchases an item, until the time that item is used in a productive capacity and the hospitality operation's customer pays for it. The objective is to control the cost and quality of all merchandise as it travels throughout the hospitality operation from one operating activity to another.

Another method for controlling the cost and quality of all merchandise is to use a limited purchase order (LPO). This form restricts the overall amount that a buyer can purchase on a particular purchase order form (see Figure 11.5 for an example).

Purchased products normally follow a **chain of operating activities** (see Figure 11.6). The control chain begins with buying; that is, it begins when the products and services legally become the buyer's. To control these items, a great deal of record keeping may be essential. Keep in mind that management may want to know: where the item is within the chain, how much of the item is at any one point within the chain, and whether the product is being used according to plan. The more management wants to know, the greater the potential record-keeping burden; hence, the greater the need for purchase order copies, as well as for the various other types of paperwork used. The sole reason for all this paper, or all these digitized records, is to control products and services. The greater the degree of control the buyer wants, the more complex a system is needed. Consequently, at the very least, a purchase order record should exist so that deliveries can be compared to it. This is probably the minimum control a buyer should have.

> **chain of operating activities** The sequence of day-to-day operating activities that hospitality businesses perform. Generally, they involve the following activities, in order: buying, receiving, storing, issuing, preparation, service, customer consumption, and customer payment.

It is not our purpose to present a full discussion of control concepts; many excellent discussions of this subject already exist.[1] The best buying strategy in the world will be worthless, however, if by the time the product is supposed to have reached the user department, some of it is spoiled, misplaced, stolen, or otherwise wasted. Large firms can afford the paperwork burden or

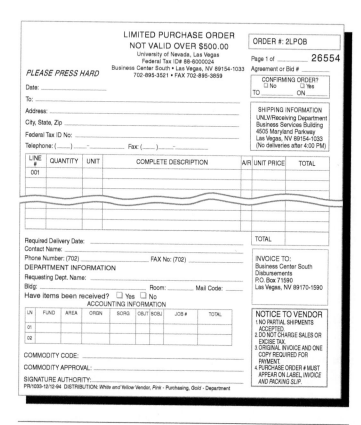

FIGURE 11.5 A limited purchase order.

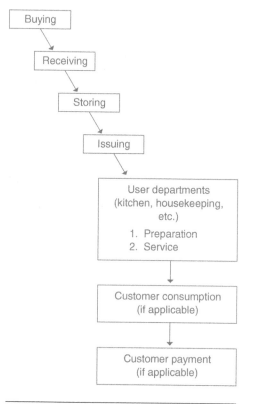

FIGURE 11.6 Typical operating activities in hospitality operation.

the digitized record-keeping procedures available in the hospitality industry. Fortunately, smaller operators can minimize the paperwork and/or computerization because, generally speaking, they can substitute eyes and ears for these more formal controls.

CHANGE ORDER

At times, a buyer may need to alter an original purchase order. Faced with this situation, a buyer normally contacts the supplier and effects changes with little difficulty. But the original purchase order, once acknowledged by the supplier, is a legal contract, and the supplier could, therefore, sue the buyer's company if any unwarranted attempt is made to alter the contract. To be on the safe side, a buyer should be sure to get it right the first time and not burden a busy supplier with **change order** requests.

> **change order** Used if a buyer wishes to alter a purchase order that was recently placed with a vendor. May be a written document, or it could be accomplished with a phone call or e-mail.

EXPEDITING AND STREAMLINING THE ORDERING PROCEDURE

Expediting is a buyer's effort to monitor suppliers from day to day to ensure that products and services arrive at the right time and in acceptable condition. Expediting is not a common practice among most buyers unless there is a chance that a large order, required at a precise time, might arrive late. For instance, a banquet for 1,000 people on a particular night might depend on a delivery of 1,000 steaks that afternoon. In this situation, an extra telephone call to the supplier is recommended.

> **expediting** To move shipments through the distribution channel at an accelerated rate. Alternately, the process used in a kitchen (or bar) to coordinate the orders from food servers (or cocktail servers) to cooks (or bartenders) to ensure efficiency and timeliness.

Expediting is most often used, at least in the hospitality industry, when purchasing furniture, fixtures, and equipment (FFE). These items have a habit of showing up late, especially, for example, long after the planned grand opening of a new restaurant. In addition, purchased services may not always be performed at the exact time desired. Expediting may be performed by the buyer, but in larger companies and those using sophisticated supply chain management processes, a separate employee or manager may be a designated expediter.[2]

Ordering is a time-consuming affair, and the paperwork and/or computerization can be costly. This process can, however, be streamlined. Unfortunately, some of the methods involved force an operation to surrender a bit of control. We do not advocate dropping all paperwork and record keeping. We suppose that small hospitality operations could omit most paperwork, but this drastic step would almost certainly encourage theft, waste, and overall employee carelessness. However, the point is well taken: if buyers can be in the hospitality operation at all times, they can use their eyes as a direct control system, instead of paperwork, an indirect control system.

Of course, larger organizations require some sort of an indirect control system, but even in these cases, some potential cost-cutting approaches exist.

▪ Blanket Order

One method of streamlining ordering procedures that we have already discussed deserves review here. Several items hospitality organizations use have a low dollar value, and the time and effort involved in ordering them can sometimes be costly, especially if they are ordered frequently. Recall that a **blanket order** is one that includes a large amount of miscellaneous items—enough products to preclude, for example, weekly ordering. In other words, if a large par stock of miscellaneous items is set, the resultant order size usually saves ordering costs, but it is not so valuable as to drastically increase the cost of storing them.

> **blanket order**   Purchase order that contains several different products.

▪ Purchase Order Draft System

A purchase order with an attached check to cover the cost of the ordered items is referred to as a **purchase order draft** and amounts to a prepaid order. Alternately, a supplier can charge a buyer's credit card or debit card number that is noted on the purchase order. This can, in some cases, save the buyer some money. For example, the supplier might be so glad to get the cash ahead of time that he or she grants a discount. Also, this system eliminates the need for a great deal of clerical work. This type of system, however, requires firm trust between the supplier and the buyer, especially in the sensitive area of returned merchandise and other adjustments that must be made. These always seem to be more difficult after the buyer paid the bill.

> **purchase order draft**   A purchase order that includes an attached check to cover the price of the goods and/or services. A form of prepaid order.
>
> **supplier's forms**
> Paperwork documents or an electronic application the supplier provides to buyers, usually at no charge. They are typically intended for use by buyers who purchase products from the company providing them for free.

▪ Supplier's Forms

Some suppliers provide preprinted paper or online order forms. These may not be exactly what buyers would like, but the **supplier's forms** may be less expensive than their own. If a hospitality operation uses several expensive multipart forms, buyers can save a considerable amount of money by using a supplier's order blanks. Of course, the cost of all "free" items and services is recaptured somehow. However, the supplier should be able to get these forms in huge quantities, thereby saving a little money, which, perhaps, is passed on to buyers.

> **Standing order**   Under this procedure, a driver (usually referred to as a route salesperson) shows up, takes inventory of what you have, then takes off the truck enough product to bring you up to some predetermined par stock, enough to last until he or she visits you the next time. The driver writes up a delivery ticket after it's determined what you need, and the products are placed in your storage facility.

▪ Standing Order

Recall that a **standing order** generally is a procedure whereby you set par stocks, and the supplier's route salesperson, who might come to your place twice a week, leaves just enough product to bring you up to par. This procedure minimizes ordering costs and eliminates the need to prepare purchase orders.

▪ Technology

E-procurement applications represent tremendous streamlining opportunities for both the supplier and the buyer. The costs associated with paper use can be drastically reduced. Purchase requisitions and purchase orders, and the purchases themselves, can all be done electronically (see Figure 11.7). There is no need for multiple paper copies of these forms; instead, an unlimited number of

Buyer POs: New PO# 123456789123

PO:	Save	Submit	Line Items:	Remove	Insert	Convert	Add Catalog Products

PO # 11522328307   Supplier   Zamar Unlimited

Order Date 06/19/2017   Subject

Line Items   Sorted By: Line Number   Ascending   Sort

Append 0   Line Items   Go

#	Qty	Description					Total
	Unit	Item #	Mfg #	Comm Code	GL Code	Price	
1 ○	4	Buffet Cart					$1,436.00
	Each	G-10034D	245726	n/a	500-49	$359	
2 ○	1	Steamer Table					$440.00
		H-30078L	838095	n/a	n/a	$44	

Subtotal		$1,876.00
Discount	% 0	$0.00
Taxes	% 0	$0.00
Shipping	0	$0.00
Grand Total		**$1,876.00**

Payment Information

Supplier Account#   Payment Terms

Internal Account#   Payment Method

Location#

Conditions - Please note that this will be printed on each purchase order.

Shipping Information

FOB   Destination   Ship To Address   EastRidge

Ship By   Streat 1   25 Main St.

Shipment Arrival Date   Streat 2   Bldg. 3

Bill to Shipping Address ?   City State Zip   Las Vegas, NV 89130

Contact   Joe Smith

Important Note Please Read Carefully

Notes

Purchase Order Message

FIGURE 11.7 Online purchase order.

electronic copies of these documents can be sent anywhere at an insignificant cost. Not only do these applications significantly reduce costs, but they also reduce the amount of time needed to complete an order, thus allowing employees and management to focus on other aspects of their jobs. Additional benefits include increased order accuracy and lead-time reduction that can result in minimizing stockouts and investment in inventories (thereby reducing opportunity costs).

■ Alternative Ways to Cut Costs

Other potential cost-cutting procedures exist, but all of these are some variation of the five just noted. Essentially, management must decide which course to follow. For many hospitality organizations, control and a certain amount of costly paperwork go hand in hand. The most economical compromise between control and record keeping seems to be an online application that can be used and viewed by whoever receives the deliveries, the buyer or user–buyer, the person who pays the bills, and the supplier. This is sufficient control at the initial stage of the cost-control chain of operating activities. The receiver knows what to expect. The buyer and bill payer can compare the PO with the bill, or invoice, that accompanies the delivery. The supplier also has a copy for his or her records.

It now remains for us to explore how control is maintained throughout the receiving, storing, and issuing functions.

Key Words and Concepts

Backdoor selling	Ordering procedures
Blanket order	Par stock approach to ordering
Chain of operating activities	Purchase order (PO)
Change order	Purchase order draft system
Expediting	Purchase requisition
Formal issues system	Receiving
In-process inventory	Source
Issuing procedure	Standing order
Levinson approach to ordering	Stock requisition
Open storeroom	Supplier's forms

Questions and Problems

1. What is the difference between a purchase requisition and a purchase order?

2. List the information that should be included on a purchase order. Why is each item important?

3. What is the purpose of expediting?

4. Describe the chain of operating activities for the typical hospitality operation.

5. What are some advantages and disadvantages of using a purchase requisitioning system?

6. What is the difference between a purchase requisition and a stock requisition?

7. Assume that a restaurant with an annual sales volume of $7.5 million can computerize its ordering procedures via an initial investment in computers, tablets, and software of $14,500. What should you know about the current ordering procedures so that you can decide whether this initial cash outlay is economically feasible?

Questions and Problems (continued)

8. Briefly describe the purchase order draft system. Do you feel that this is an advantage or a disadvantage to the hospitality operator? Why?

9. What is a change order document used for?

10. Specifically, how does a hospitality operator save money by using the standing order method of purchasing?

11. How might a buyer save money by using the blanket order procedure?

12. What are the advantages and disadvantages of the open storeroom form of issuing?

Experiential Exercises

1. Call one or more suppliers in your area. Ask the following questions:
   a. Are customers provided with order forms and, if so, how much, if anything, is charged for this supplier service?
   b. Does the supplier prefer customers to order over the telephone or through e-mail?
   c. Is an online ordering system available?

2. Contact a buyer for a hospitality establishment, and ask for an interview to discuss buying procedures. Prepare a report that provides the interviewee's answers to the following questions:
   a. How are order sizes determined?
   b. Explain the purchase order form in use.
   c. List the information the purchase order calls for, and explain why that information is needed.
   d. How many copies of a purchase order are prepared? Why?
   e. What is the estimated cost of the ordering procedure?
   f. How might that cost be reduced?
   g. Is a purchase order draft system used? Why or why not?

3. Contact a buyer for a hospitality establishment, and ask for copies of the following forms, so you can bring the documents into class and discuss them:
   a. Purchase requisition
   b. Purchase order
   c. Limited purchase order (LPO)

   Note: It might be difficult to acquire these documents, as the purchase order and the LPO can be used as legal tender if they are not voided. A suggestion would be to ask the manager of the hospitality establishment to void out the order form by writing "Void" across all copies. Another idea would be to create your own forms based on examples in this chapter.

References

1. See, for example, Lea R. Dopson, *Food and Beverage Cost Control*, 5th ed. (Hoboken, NJ: John Wiley & Sons, 2011); Paul R. Dittmer and J. Desmond Keefe, *Principles of Food, Beverage, and Labor Cost Controls*, 9th ed. (Hoboken, NJ: John Wiley & Sons, 2008); Francis T. Lynch, *The Book of Yields: Accuracy in Food Costing and Purchasing*, 8th ed. (Hoboken, NJ: John Wiley & Sons, 2010). Other texts on cost control can be found at www.amazon.com.

2. See Supply Chain Mechanic.com, "Managing Your Procurements Expediting Process," http://supplychain-mechanic.com/?p=209; Mark S. Miller and Thomas Graddy, *Purchasing and Expediting—The True Facts*, www.ism.ws/pubs/Proceedings/confproceedingsdetail.cfm?ItemNumber=11828.

TYPICAL RECEIVING PROCEDURES

The Purpose of This Chapter

After reading this chapter, you should be able to:

- Identify the objectives of receiving.

- Describe the essentials of effective receiving.

- Synthesize typical invoice receiving procedures.

- Provide examples of other receiving duties.

- Compare alternative receiving methods.

- Summarize good receiving practices, including methods that reduce receiving costs.

THE OBJECTIVES OF RECEIVING

Someone once said, "Receiving is the proof of purchasing." It's at receiving that you determine what it is you actually got—not what you ordered but what you received. And there could be a lot of difference between the order you placed and the delivery you received. That's why receiving is so important to the proper control of purchasing.[1]

accepting a delivery
Occurs when a receiving agent is satisfied that the delivered merchandise meets the company's standards. Once the shipment is accepted, the receiving agent normally signs a copy of the invoice accompanying the delivery.

route salesperson The driver who delivers standing orders to the restaurant.

Receiving is the act of inspecting and either rejecting or **accepting a delivery**. It is an activity with many facets. In any particular hospitality operation, receiving can range anywhere from a buyer letting drivers place an order in a storage facility, to having various receiving clerks waiting at the delivery entrance to check every single item to see that it meets the specifications set forth in the purchase order (PO).

Although many varieties of practice exist, the variety of correct procedures, though subject to debate, is considerably less. For instance, many operations permit the linen **route salesperson** to come into the dining room storage areas, remove tablecloths left over from the previous delivery, restock the operation, and leave the bill with someone. Purists could argue that this is poor practice on two counts: (1) the driver could cheat on both returns and delivery; and (2) the driver could steal other items while he or she was there.

Operators following this practice, however, would probably argue that the cost of a unit of product—a tablecloth, for instance—is so small that the cost of a receiving clerk or management time to physically check returns and delivery is unwarranted. Moreover, the driver in this case saves time. As for the theft issue, the driver is no more likely to steal than employees because he or she is subject to the same controls that they are. No hard-and-fast rules exist for a case like this. Each operator or company must weigh the advantages and disadvantages to arrive at a policy.

receiving objectives
Ensuring that the delivered items meet the qualities, AP prices, support functions, and quantities ordered by the buyer, and that they are delivered at the correct time.

cycle of control The day-to-day operating activities in a hospitality organization. Typically the cycle begins when products are delivered to and received by the hospitality organization and ends when they are used. Controls are established to ensure that what was received is used appropriately, with little or no loss along the way.

In contrast, consider a situation in which a supplier provides a very large portion of an operation's goods and offers, as a supplier service, to check the storeroom for all the items this supplier provides and to determine what needs to be replenished. This might be done "to save the operator some time." Most people would argue, here, that both the receiving and the purchasing functions have been turned over to a supplier, and allowing a supplier to do this is inappropriate.

These **receiving objectives** resemble the objectives of the purchasing function itself. Recall the main objectives: obtaining the correct amount and correct quality at the correct time with the correct supplier services for the correct edible-portion (EP) cost. The main objective of receiving is to check that the delivered order meets these criteria.

Another important objective of receiving is controlling these received products and services. Once the receiver accepts the items, whatever they are, they become the property of the hospitality organization. Thus, a **cycle of control** begins at this point.[2] For the most part, an owner–manager requires a certain amount of documentation during this receiving function to ascertain what was delivered and where the delivered items were sent within the organization. Keep in mind that this control activity can be simple or elaborate, depending on management's policy. The best buying plan in the world is useless if someone or something goes awry during the cycle of control and causes a reduction in quality or an increase in costs.

In some large firms, additional control is exerted in the receiving function by placing receiving personnel under the direction of the accounting department. Thus, management minimizes the possibility of any fraudulent relationship between the buyer and the receiver. Small firms cannot afford this luxury.

On the other hand, some small firms often use their very smallness—their lack of personnel—as an excuse to avoid receiving control. Although the small operator may not be able to afford the elaborate receiving department of a large hotel, he or she certainly can adapt the techniques it uses to some degree. For instance, many small- to medium-sized operations can designate a specific employee, perhaps a line cook, to act as receiver and the only person authorized to sign for received products. This person might warrant a modest salary increase for the added responsibility assumed. To make the task easier, he or she should be responsible for verifying counts and weights; quality evaluations can be left to some members of management.

ESSENTIALS FOR RECEIVING

To ensure that the receiving function is performed properly, several factors must be in place:

1. **Competent personnel.** Such personnel should be placed in charge of all receiving activity. By "competent," we mean people, full-time or part-time, who are reasonably intelligent, honest, interested in the job, and knowledgeable about the items to be received. Once such a person is designated, it is necessary to train him or her to recognize acceptable and inferior products and services. However, where the line cook–receiver combination is used, management may need to make quality checks and to supervise the receiving activity more closely.

2. **Appropriate training.** It is very important to provide the receiving agent with appropriate training. This can be a time-consuming, costly procedure, but it is absolutely essential. The receiver must be able to recognize the various quality levels of merchandise that will be delivered to the hospitality operation. He or she also must be able to adequately handle the necessary paperwork and/or computerized record keeping. Furthermore, the receiver must know what to do when something out of the ordinary arises. Although the training costs may be considerable, they will be recovered many times over if the receiver is able to prevent merely one or two receiving mistakes per month.

3. **Proper scales.** This is a must. Because many deliveries must be weighed, accurate scales are, perhaps, the most important pieces of equipment in the receiving area (see Figures 12.1 and 12.2). It is worth the money in the long run to purchase a good-quality scale and to maintain it properly. This will ensure the operation receives the proper weights.

FIGURE 12.1 Tabletop scale.
©vseb/Shutterstock

FIGURE 12.2 Floor scale.
Courtesy of Edlund Company, Inc.

4. **Other receiving equipment.** Temperature probes let receivers check the temperatures of refrigerated and frozen products. Rule measures are useful in checking trim of, for example, fat on portion-cut steaks. Calculators or wireless tablets are needed to verify costs. Cutting instruments, such as a produce knife, are handy when product sampling is part of the receiving process. Conveyor belts, hand trucks, and motorized forklift trucks can help transport the received items to the storage areas or, in some cases, directly to a production area. Also, where applicable, receiving agents must have the technology to read existing **bar codes** or radio frequency ID (RFID) tags on product packaging to process shipments correctly. In short, receivers should be provided with the proper equipment to do the most efficient, thorough job possible.

> **bar code** A computerized label attached to most food packages. The information on the bars can be read by the computer and used to track inventory amounts and values.

5. **Proper receiving facilities.** If an operation wants a receiver to perform adequately, he or she must have the facilities that will make that possible. By "facilities," we are referring to the entire receiving area. By "proper," we mean, for example, that the area should be well lit, large enough to work in comfortably, reasonably secure, and convenient for both drivers and receivers (see Figure 12.3). In some buildings, management may not be able to provide exactly what we have described, but the closer management can move to this ideal, the better the receiver can do his or her job.

6. **Appropriate receiving hours.** Deliveries should be scheduled carefully. If possible, deliveries should be staggered so that a receiver is not rushed. Also, all delivery times should be relatively predictable so that a competent receiver will be on hand and receiving will not be left to whoever happens to be handy. Remember, we mentioned that one of the biggest benefits of one-stop shopping is to minimize any difficulties and expense arising from too many deliveries. Perhaps now you can appreciate why many managers are swayed by this potential benefit. It not only reduces the number of hours a receiver must work, but it also

FIGURE 12.3 Hospitality loading dock.
©Rene Johnston/Toronto Star via Getty Images

allows for a more secure backdoor routine and, because of fewer transactions, minimized theft opportunities.

7. **Copies of all specifications.** The receiver will need these as references. This can help whenever there is a question about the product and, in particular, about substitutions. When a supplier is out of a particular brand of soap, for example, he or she might deliver what is believed to be a comparable substitute. When this occurs, it becomes necessary for the deliverer and receiver to have a reference handy, unless the buyer insists on handling any substitutions personally, in which case the receiver will ask him or her to inspect the substitute. Conveniently available specifications ensure precious time is not wasted locating them when needed.

8. **Copies of purchase orders.** Most hospitality operators feel that a receiver should know what is due to be delivered in order to be prepared. These purchase order copies are necessary to ensure that this happens.

THE TALE OF THE SCALES
Danny Campbell, Director of Corporate Purchasing Cannery Casino Resorts, Las Vegas, Nevada

One day I was visiting a supplier in his office. We were talking, but I was distracted by the large blackboard behind his desk where two distinct lists of customer names were written. Finally I just had to ask him what the lists were for. The distributor shuffled around a bit, looked embarrassed and made me promise not to tell anyone.

Then he said in effect, "The list on the left includes the customers who have scales. The list on the right is of the customers who don't have scales. Now don't get me wrong, I never short anyone on

THE TALE OF THE SCALES (continued)

weight, but if customers want 30 pounds of chicken breasts in 1/4-pound pieces, that's 120 pieces of chicken, each individually wrapped and cleaned. If that customer is on the right-hand list, I might send chicken breasts that were slightly over a 1/4-pound, maybe even up to a 1/3-pound and cut my labor and packaging costs by 25 percent. Hey, they're getting the same amount of food."

He was right, the customers in his example were getting the total weight of chicken breasts they had ordered, but their edible portion cost was higher than they had anticipated. They were serving a 1/3-pound chicken breast when they thought they were serving a 1/4-pound chicken breast. The 25 percent savings on labor and packaging that went into the supplier's pocket came straight out of the pockets of the restaurants that didn't have scales on their loading docks or in their kitchens.

I feel comfortable telling this story because the supplier has been out of business for a long time, and the lesson is a good one. An incident like this isn't restricted to chicken breasts. It could apply to cuts of beef, pears, artichokes—anything where the weight or size of an individual piece can be specified.

Let's think a minute about the opposite scenario. What if a menu reads "16-ounce T-Bone Steaks," and the supplier sends 14-ounce steaks because they were easier to find and the per-pound cost for smaller steaks was a bit less? If the receiving manager or chef doesn't have a scale and catch the "error," that restaurant will not be serving the size of steak listed on the menu. Not only could this put the restaurant in jeopardy in regard to the truth in menu guidelines, but also imagine the customer dissatisfaction if he or she realizes that the just-ordered steak isn't as big as promised.

In the story told earlier, simply having the scale would have been enough to prevent this supplier from sending the wrong weight of individual product pieces. However, it is best to have a reliable system for receiving all items and actually using the scale to ensure accurate deliveries.

INVOICE RECEIVING

invoice receiving
Common type of receiving procedure. Involves comparing the invoice with the order record, and then proceeding to check quality, quantity, and AP prices of the items delivered.

invoice A bill from a vendor for goods or services, often presented as the goods are delivered or after the services are performed.

The most popular receiving technique is sometimes referred to as **invoice receiving**. In the scheme of things, an **invoice**, or bill, accompanies the delivery (see Figure 12.4). An invoice is an itemized statement of quantity, price, and other information that usually resembles the purchase order depicted in Chapter 11. An invoice may, in fact, be nothing more than a photocopy of the original purchase order. The receiver uses the invoice to check against the quantity, quality, and prices of the items delivered and may also compare the invoice with a copy of the original purchase order as a further check. The order is either accepted or rejected. If accepted, it is stored or delivered to a production department. If rejected, appropriate credit must be obtained. Sometimes, an invoice does not accompany the delivery. In these situations, the receiver normally fills out some type of form right there on the spot and treats this completed form as the invoice. The following sections discuss the typical invoice receiving sequence in more detail.

```
                            Extra Customer Copy              Invoice:  D80568-00

                        Phoenix Wholesale Food Service       Page:     1 of 3
                               P.O. Box 707                  Route:    147-5
                            Forest Park, GA 30298
                                                            Driver:   47--JW M

   S  545035                       B  545035                Acct Mgr: 291 Avendra
   H  RITZ CARLTON/BUCKHEAD        I  RITZ CARLTON/BUCKHEAD Cust PO:  CHEF KRISTO
   I  3434 PEACHTREE RD NE         L  3434 PEACHTREE RD NE
   P                               L                        Ship Via: TRUCK/ALL ST
   T  ATLANTA GA 30326-0000        T  ATLANTA GA 30326-0000
   O  (404)240-7028                O

      Terms:   NET 14 DAYS
      Instr:   ***** ADD ON *****
               ***** STRAWBERRIES (DRISCOLL) ONLY *****

   Item#   Qty U/M Brand   Description            Pack   Weight  Price  Amount SRM Retail Ext Retai
   112110   1  CS          ORANGES 88 CT CALIF FCY *    88CT
   113130   2  CS          LEMONS 165CT FANCY *        165CT
   114070   3  CS          LIMES  54CT / 63CT           54CT
   115030   1  CS          GRAPES RED SEEDLESS          18LB
   115150   1  CS          NECTARINES                  25LB
   115160   1  CS          PEACHES                     15LB
   116030   2  CS          BANANAS PREMIUM   (STAGE 4)  CS
   116093   9  CS          PINEAPPLE *GOLD*             CS
   117120   4  CS          HONEYDEW 8CT *               8CT
   117155   4  EA          WATERMELON SEEDLESS EA.      1EA
   119055   1  CS          LETTUCE HYDROPONIC BIBB     12CT
   119083   1  CS          ROMAINE HEARTS              48CT
   119195   2  CS          SPINACH TRIPLE WASHED       4/2.5LB
   119200   2  PK          CILANTRO                     3CT
   120070   1  CS          ASPARAGUS STANDARD          11LB
   120100   3  CS          ASPARAGUS JUMBO 1/2 CASE    11LB
   120150   1  CS          BROCCOLI                    14CT
   120410   1  CS          CARROTS JUMBO               50LB
   120930   1  CS          CUCUMBERS SELECT            BUSHEL
   120950   2  CS          CUCUMBERS HYDROPONIC 12EA.  12CT
   120960   1  CS          LEEKS                       12CT
   121550   1  CS          MUSHROOMS OYSTER WHITE 3#    3LB
   121575   2  CS          MUSHROOMS SHITAKE 3#         3LB
   121580   4  CS          MUSHROOMS PORTABELLA 5#      5LB

   All claims must be made immediately upon receipt of goods, pay from invoice, this is your statement.  Subtotal    Tax    Inv Total   Ext Ret Total
                                                                                                                                       CONTINUED
   The perishable agriculture commodities listed on this invoice are sold subject to the statutory trust authorized by Section 5C
   of the Perishable Agriculture Commodities Act, 1930 (7 U.S.C. 499(e)(c)). The seller of these commodities retains a trust claim
   over these commodities, all inventories of food or other products derived from these commodities, and any receivables or     Return
   proceeds from the sale of these commodities until full payment is received.
   All products must be washed and/or cooked before serving.                                                                    Corr Amount
   In the event action is necessary for the collection of this invoice,
   customer agrees to pay all costs, including reasonable attorney's fees.   X
   If this invoice is not paid according to its terms, you will be charged
   interest at a rate of 18%, compounded weekly, as provided by law.
```

FIGURE 12.4 Sample invoice.
Courtesy of Phoenix Wholesale Food Service

■ Delivery Arrives

When arriving at a large operation, the driver must usually indicate arrival, sometimes by ringing a doorbell and asking the receiver for access. These procedures are, of course, less formal in a small operation, but they represent good security precautions.

The receiver opens the receiving area and, using the invoice and, perhaps, a copy of the original purchase order, checks immediately for the proper quantities. The receiver's first step, then, is to check each item's weight, count, and/or volume as quickly and efficiently as possible and compare them to the invoice and the original purchase order, or some other purchase record. The comparisons should match.

Next, where applicable, the receiver checks for the proper quality. Unfortunately, except for a check of the packers' brand names, this is the most difficult kind of check to make and, in some cases, is almost impossible to complete. For example, it is difficult to determine the overall quality of lobster tails. A receiver might be able to tell whether they have been refrozen, but he or she can never be sure if any particular tail is bad until it has been cooked; a bad lobster tail crumbles after it is cooked.

Some establishments expect the receiver to check for quantities only and to call someone else to inspect for quality. In these situations, the receiver calls the chef, housekeeper, maitre d', or whatever department head is appropriate to come check the quality of the items that will eventually be used by the department. The big drawback of this procedure is the potential time lag in waiting for the department head to arrive. Another problem is the possibility of the items, especially frozen ones, deteriorating while waiting for a quality check.

quality control Systems and procedures used by managers to ensure that the actual quality of finished items is consistent with the expected quality.

quality assurance Another term for quality control.

price extension The as-purchased [AP] price per unit of that product times the number of units purchased.

sales tax Taxes a company must pay to state and local governments for things purchased, such as cleaning chemicals, that will not be resold to customers.

use tax Tax charged by the state where the buyer's hospitality operation is located (i.e., home state) on products purchased from out of state. Similar to the sales tax charged by the home state. Charged by the home state to prevent companies from going elsewhere to avoid paying sales tax to their home states.

Large operations, particularly commissaries, usually engage **quality control**, or **quality assurance**, inspectors who check deliveries, as well as the products prepared in the commissary. These inspectors do not normally work for the purchasing agent. In fact, they act as a check on the purchasing agent by keeping tabs on the quality that the purchasing agent procures.

If a quality discrepancy is present, the buyer should be notified as soon as possible to perform the customary duty of dealing with suppliers and salespersons. Moreover, the buyer may want occasionally to be on hand in the receiving area to gain a firsthand impression of the types of items that are actually delivered as compared to what was ordered.

After the quality inspection—unless the entire order has been rejected—the receiver in some operations checks all prices and **price extensions**. (A price extension for a particular item on the invoice is the as-purchased [AP] price per unit of that product times the number of units purchased.) The receiver might also check all **sales tax** and other **use taxes** that are noted on the invoice to ensure accuracy. For instance, in most states, a hospitality operator must pay sales tax for merchandise not to be resold, such as cleaning chemicals, but not for products earmarked for resale to consumers, such as meats and produce.

Unfortunately, checking all of these figures can take too long, usually because a receiver must compare the prices on the invoice with those that the supplier quoted prior to ordering the merchandise. It is necessary for the receiver to compare the invoice with the purchase order, or some other written purchase record, both to check the prices and to note whether the merchandise delivered actually was ordered in the first place. To save time, many operations have the accountant or bookkeeper check invoices later, before paying the bill.

It is probably a good idea to handle any AP price discrepancies as soon as possible. Waiting too long can produce confusion and distrust among business partners. Also, an honest supplier would want to know immediately if, for instance, a driver has altered the prices on the invoice. The opposite can also be true; that is, the supplier, for example, may have quoted a much lower AP price over the telephone than the one now written on the invoice. If so, the receiver should notify the driver so that he or she will be a witness to this discrepancy.

■ Rejection of Delivery

request for credit memo A note sent by the buyer or the receiving clerk to the supplier requesting that the hospitality operation's account be credited because all or part of a shipment was unacceptable.

In some cases, a receiver may merely note a discrepancy regarding prices or taxes listed on the invoice. In other cases all or part of an order may be rejected. When this occurs, the receiver might send to the supplier a **request for credit memo**, which is a written statement attesting to the fact that the particular item or items did not meet quality, quantity, or price standards (see Figure 12.5 for a typical request for credit memo). The driver's signature

Sheldon's Meats   2336
100 MAIN ST.   LAS VEGAS, NEVADA 89123   CREDIT REQUEST
555-1212
Federal Inspected Meat Plant Est. 1000

DATE

P.O. NUMBER

INVOICE NUMBER	DATE	WEIGHT	ITEM	PRICE	CREDIT AMOUNT	REASON NUMBER

AUTHORIZATION

CODE KEY

1 - REFUSED   5 - NOT ON TRUCK
2 - WRONG PRODUCT   6 - PRICE ERROR
3 - SPOILED   7 - INVOICE ERROR
4 - SHORT WEIGHT   8 - OTHER

FIGURE 12.5 A request for credit memo used by Sheldon's Meats.

shows that a representative of the supplier has agreed that the hospitality operation's account must be credited. The objective of this memo is to ensure that your account is credited and that all costs are accurate. Today, drivers typically use handheld smart devices to submit requests for credit instead of using paper forms.

A receiver also may need to prepare a request for credit memo if receiving credit for product substitutions, such as when a less-expensive item than the one ordered is delivered. Also, the invoice might contain arithmetic errors that require adjustment. A back order may have been charged to the hospitality operator, in which case the receiver might want to ensure that the firm does not pay for the items, thereby tying up its money unnecessarily, until it receives them.

When the accounting office pays the invoices, it will reduce the invoice total by the amount indicated on the credit memo itself, which comes from the supplier after the receiver sends a copy of the request for credit memo. Alternately, the supplier will give credit to the operator on the next delivery.

Some operations eliminate the request for credit memo if the supplier gives authority to drivers to "reprice" the invoice on the spot or prepare a **credit memo** or **credit slip** right then and there and give it to the receiver. However, if a **common carrier** (i.e., an independent trucking firm) delivers the shipment, the receiver must complete a request for credit memo because the driver will have no authority to alter the delivery.

credit memo When a shipment, or partial shipment is unsatisfactory, the supplier will send one of these to the hospitality operation, signifying the amount of credit that will be applied to its account.

credit slip When a shipment, or partial shipment, is unsatisfactory, the driver will give a credit slip to the receiving clerk, signifying the amount of credit that will be applied to the restaurant's account. It eliminates the need for the restaurant to prepare a request for credit memo.

common carrier An independent delivery service hired by the vendor to deliver goods to the restaurant operation. UPS is an example of a common carrier.

When credit paperwork is prepared, the original copy is usually sent to the supplier. In addition, the receiver or buyer might call the supplier; this serves as a check on the drivers, who, for example, may have stolen the original item and substituted an inferior product. Another copy usually goes to whoever pays the bills. Some receivers might want to keep a copy as a reminder to be especially careful of any future deliveries from this particular supplier. In addition, the buyer may want a copy to keep up to date on the supplier's performance.

Whenever rejection is contemplated, the owner–manager must not act too hastily. It may not be a good idea to reject a product that deviates only slightly from the hospitality operation's standard, for at least two reasons: (1) suppliers may not like to do business with a customer who focuses on small details, particularly one who sends back a reasonable substitute that the supplier sent because the ordered item was unavailable; and (2) in many cases, a rejection leaves a receiver short. It might be good business occasionally to accept some slight deviation because the potential ill will generated among suppliers and customers by hasty rejections may be detrimental.

■ Returning Merchandise

pick-up memo   Gives the delivery driver permission to pick up something from you. Typically used when you want to return a product to the vendor and you arrange to have it picked up when the driver makes the next regularly scheduled delivery of things you purchased. May also be used when a driver is delivering a substitute piece of equipment (such as a coffee urn) and needs to pick up the one you have so that it can be taken back to the shop and repaired.

returned merchandise Items that do not meet the buyer's and receiving clerk's expectation, and therefore are returned to the supplier.

invoice stamp   Information placed on the receiving agent's copy of the invoice that indicates all appropriate checks were made and that the shipment was accepted.

The receiver may have something from a previous delivery that the driver must return to the company's warehouse. For example, say the buyer has arranged to send back an unintentional overbuy of canned pears from the preceding week. Usually, in this situation, the supplier has given the driver a **pick-up memo**, authorizing a return of the merchandise (see Figure 12.6).

Whenever a belated return must be arranged, a copy of the pick-up memo is left with the receiver. This copy serves as a receipt for the returned goods. The supplier will issue a credit memo later on, once the **returned merchandise** is inspected and the return is deemed justified.

■ Acceptance of Delivery

When an order has been accepted, the receiver normally initials some paperwork attesting to the fact that everything is correct. A delivery sheet or a copy of the invoice is given to the receiver to sign.

Unless the items are definitely substandard, the receiver accepts most deliveries. Even if only part of a shipment is acceptable, the customary practice is to keep what is good and return the rest along with a request for credit memo. For the most part, an owner–manager is reluctant to send back everything because the resultant shortages can, as we said, lead to dissatisfied customers.

Upon acceptance of the deliveries, the receiver usually places the items in the proper storage location or, in some cases, delivers them to a production department. To ensure that all pertinent checks have been made, the receiver normally applies an ink stamp with a predetermined format to the invoice (see Figure 12.7 for a typical **invoice stamp** format stamped on incoming invoices). This format notes all checks that must be performed and provides a space for those responsible to affix their initials. The receiver normally initials the first three entries; the accountant or bookkeeper, number 4; the buyer, number 5; and the owner–manager, number 6.

Sheldon's Meats

100 MAIN ST.   LAS VEGAS, NEVADA 89123
555-1212
Federal Inspected Meat Plant Est. 1000

CUSTOMER NAME

PICK-UP MEMO

DATE	DRIVER	CUST NO	PICK-UP MEMO NO	

QTY	GRADE	PROD CODE	DESCRIPTION	WEIGHT	PRICE

THIS IS NOT AN INVOICE OR CREDIT MEMO. IT IS A RECEIPT FOR MERCHANDISE RETURNED TO OUR PLANT FOR INSPECTION. YOU WILL BE ADVISED OF OUR FINDINGS AND DECISION AT THE COMPLETION OF THE INSPECTION.

DISPOSITION	DATE

FIGURE 12.6 A typical pick-up memo.

1. Date received
2. Received by
3. Prices checked by
4. Extensions checked by
5. Buyer's approval
6. Payment approval

FIGURE 12.7 An invoice stamp example.

After processing the invoice, the receiver may record the delivery on a **receiving sheet,** or "receiving log." This sheet is nothing more than a running account of deliveries (see Figure 12.8 for a typical receiving sheet).

To a certain extent, the receiving sheet is a redundant exercise: it contains a good deal of information already on the invoice or affixed to the invoice

receiving sheet A running account of deliveries maintained by the receiving agent.

DATE	TIME DELIVERED	QUANTITY	INVOICE NO.	PURVEYOR	DESCRIPTION OF ITEM(S)	UNIT PRICE	EXTENSION	*DIRECT			†STORES			OTHER INFORMATION?
								FOOD	BEVERAGE	NONFOOD	FOOD	BEVERAGE	NONFOOD	

* The receiver notes in this column the amount of food, beverage, and nonfood items that go directly to the production department, bypassing the main storage area. In other words, these items go directly into the in-process inventory.

† The receiver notes in this column the amount of food, beverage, and nonfood items that go into main storage.

FIGURE 12.8 A receiving sheet.

via one or more invoice stamps. Large hospitality operations traditionally use the sheet, but the whole process may be avoided without any significant loss of control by merely photocopying invoices or scanning them into the computer for the buyer's and receiver's files.

One reason many operators like the receiving sheet is that it forces the receiver to record information, however redundant. Thus, mistakes previously overlooked sometimes come to light. Also, a copy of the receiving sheet usually stays in the receiver's files, which makes it handy for the receiver to evaluate a certain supplier's past performance. Furthermore, the sheet is useful to cost accountants who prepare daily food, beverage, and nonfood cost reports. Because the receiving sheet notes the deliveries on one page, it is convenient. In addition, the "Other Information" column can contain several comments that are not easily recorded on the incoming invoices. Such elements as the driver's attitude and the cleanliness of the delivery truck may be important to the buyer in future negotiations with that particular supplier.

Another reason for some managers' continuing desire for the receiving sheet is that it can be treated as the receiver's daily report of activities. This type of report is particularly attractive to the accountant in a large hotel who is responsible for the receiver's actions.

Overall, however, it is far more economical to record all such information on the incoming invoices or on invoice copies, or to attach a small Post-it note to these invoices if space is insufficient, and then make a copy of this completed invoice for the receiver's files.

After making the necessary entries to the records, the receiver normally sends the incoming invoices, any credit slips, and a copy of the receiving sheet, if one is used, to the accountant or bookkeeper. If a **bill of lading**, which is a piece of paper that represents title to the goods, comes with the delivered items, he or she sends this along also.

> **bill of lading** Document that conveys title to the goods purchased.

If the storage areas are supervised and controlled by someone other than the receiver, this person may want a copy of the receiving sheet to compare what is on the sheet with what has been put in storage. This is yet another type of control serving as a check on the receiver, although the buyer's and the accountant's copies can serve as more than sufficient control.

At this point, the receiver normally has stored the items or delivered them to production departments, completed the necessary paperwork, and sent the appropriate paperwork to the right office(s), along with any bills of lading that may have arrived at the receiving dock that day. The receiver also keeps a copy of the receiving sheet.

ADDITIONAL RECEIVING DUTIES

As a general rule, the receiving procedure is now complete, but the receiver may have other, less-routine duties to perform. The following are typical duties.

■ Date the Delivered Items

If it is too costly or time consuming to do this, the usual compromise is to date only the perishable items. This dating is usually done with colored tags or with an ink stamp. This can facilitate proper **stock rotation**, a process by which older products are used first.

> **stock rotation** A system of using older products first. When a shipment arrives, the older stock is moved to the front of the shelf and the newer stock is placed behind it.

■ Price All the Delivered Items

dot system   Color-coded, stick-on dots (usually a different color for each day) usually attached to inventories when they are received. They have enough blank space to pencil in dates, times, AP prices, and other pertinent information.

meat tag   Used to control the usage of expensive items, such as meat, fish, and poultry. It contains two duplicate parts. One part is attached to the item when it is received and placed into storage, the other one goes to the controller's office. When an item is taken from storage and issued to production, the part on the item is removed and sent to the controller, who matches it with the other part. The item is then removed from the inventory file. At that point, the storage supervisor (storeroom manager) is no longer responsible for the item, the chef is.

Like dating delivered items, this pricing may also be too costly, but it can have such benefits as costing of inventories for accounting purposes and providing an easy cost reference. Some operators like to price the items for the psychological effect it supposedly provides. Items that an operator has priced are no longer just merchandise to employees, but articles of value to be treated accordingly.

Many properties use the **dot system** to date and price inventories. These are color-coded, stick-on dots (usually a different color for each day) that have sufficient space to pencil in dates, times, and prices. Incidentally, this procedure is also used to identify and code stored products that the kitchen staff has made. For instance, grated cheese to be used later on can be coded so that all cooks use older grated cheese first (see Figure 12.9).

■ Create Bar Codes

In some large hospitality operations, the receiving agent may need to create bar codes and apply them to incoming products that do not have them on their package labels. This is usually done to enhance the inventory management and control process, in that it makes it very easy to track inventories and their AP prices throughout the operation. Although investing in the technology needed to adopt this procedure can be very expensive, in the long run it could prove very cost effective.

■ Apply "Meat Tags"

A **meat tag** contains information similar to that on an invoice stamp. The major difference between the two is that the typical meat tag contains two duplicate parts (see Figure 12.10). During the receiving procedure, one part of the tag is put on an item, and the other part goes to the accountant or

FIGURE 12.9 An example of a dot system.
©2016 Ecolab Food Safety Solutions, photographs by Matt Shannon

No. 100

Date rec'd _____

Item _____

Grade _____

Wt. _____

Purveyor _____

Date issued _____

Date used _____

No. 100

Date rec'd _____

Item _____

Grade _____

Wt. _____

Purveyor _____

Date issued _____

Date used _____

FIGURE 12.10 A meat tag.

bookkeeper for control purposes. When an item moves from the storage area to production, the tag on the item is removed and sent to the accountant or bookkeeper, who matches it with its mate and removes it from the inventory file.

Specifically, meat tags are used as a check on the overall use of an item. For instance, comparisons are made between meat tags and **stock requisitions** (requests from a production department for items that are held in storage). Also, meat tags are sometimes compared with the service department's record of guest services. For example, with steak items, the meat tags can be compared with the sales of steaks to customers, thereby producing a check on the waitstaff. If everything goes right, all these comparisons will reveal that what was used from storage actually went to the paying customer, with no loss of product along the way. The units recorded on the meat tags should correspond exactly to the amounts used in production and the amounts sold to customers.

> **stock requisition** A formal request made by an employee for items needed to carry out necessary tasks. It is given to the person managing the storage facilities. A typical control document used by large hotels.

The meat tag control is, however, cumbersome, unless it can be computerized and/or bar coded. And, like the receiving sheet, it tends to be redundant as well. If meat tags are used, they tend to be used only for high-cost products. Nevertheless, both meat tags and receiving sheets are used in operations that desire close control over their stock.

■ Cleaning and Maintenance

Management usually requires the receiver to maintain a clean, efficient workplace. Also, he or she usually ensures that all equipment and facilities are kept in good working order (see Figure 12.11).

■ Update AP Prices

> **management information system (MIS)**   Method of organizing, analyzing, and reporting information to manage a business effectively.

Hospitality operations that use a **management information system (MIS)** normally maintain updated AP prices for all merchandise they buy. They also might maintain updated portion factors, portion dividers, and EP costs for all the ingredients they currently serve, as well as all the ingredients they might serve in the future. Furthermore, most hospitality operations also tend to maintain costed recipes in a recipe file for those menu items that are currently being offered to customers, as well as those that may be offered at a future date.

An MIS includes the formulas and databases to make the necessary calculations quickly. Because AP prices tend to vary from day to day in our industry, someone must continually "load the computer" with the new, current AP prices. In some operations, this task falls on the receiving agent. After performing the other required receiving duties, the agent must follow the procedures needed to enter the new AP prices and to remove the old, outdated AP prices. The buyer or someone in the accounting department might just as easily do this task, but a receiving agent may be deemed the best person to do this work, especially if the task involves scanning the bar codes or RFID tags of all incoming products.

■ Backhaul Recyclables

Some operations save their recyclables, such as corrugated cardboard, glass bottles, metal cans, and fry oil, and hold them until a common carrier hired by a primary source to deliver a product shipment uses the emptied truck to **backhaul** the recyclables on the return trip

FIGURE 12.11 A modern food storage area.
©Dmitry Kalinovsky/Shutterstock

FIGURE 12.12 A recycling area of a warehouse.
© DreamPictures/Shannon Faulk/GettyImages

(see Figure 12.12 for a picture of a recycling area). In this case, the receiving agent usually needs to help the driver load the truck and see to it that the driver has the necessary paperwork and authorizations. Some companies charge for fry oil pick-up, whereas others will pick it up for free due to higher demand for the oil. The fry oil has become a popular ingredient in environment-friendly fuels for all types of vehicles. Larger hospitality operations, such as Disney and McDonald's, collect their own fry oil and convert it to fuel for company vehicles.[3]

ALTERNATIVE RECEIVING METHODS

Occasionally, other receiving procedures are used. For the most part, though, they are variations of invoice receiving. Some of these alternate approaches are described next.

■ Standing-Order Receiving

This receiving procedure may not differ at all from invoice receiving. But receivers sometimes tend to "relax" a bit when checking items received on a **standing-order** basis. Also, **delivery tickets** rather than priced invoices may accompany the delivery because the operation may make a regular, periodic payment to the supplier in exchange for the same amounts delivered at regular intervals.

It is really best to use invoice receiving to receive standing orders. Otherwise, drivers, receivers, and bill payers can grow careless. In addition, deliveries may begin to "shrink" in both quantity and quality if strict receiving principles are not maintained.

backhaul   Occurs when a driver delivers a shipment to a hospitality operation and then refills the empty truck with items (such as recyclable materials) that need to be delivered to another location. The purpose is to gain maximum efficiency by seeing to it that the truck is always full when it is on the road.

standing-order   Under this procedure, a driver (usually referred to as a route salesperson) shows up, takes inventory of what you have, then takes off the truck enough product to bring you up to some predetermined par stock, enough to last until he or she visits you the next time. The driver writes up a delivery ticket after it's determined what you need and the products are placed in your storage facility.

delivery ticket   Written receipt summarizing what was ordered and delivered. It is typically written up by route salespersons when they are finished restocking the hospitality operation. Similar to an invoice.

■ Blind Receiving

blind receiving When the invoice accompanying a delivery contains only the names of the items delivered. Quantity and price information is missing. The receiving clerk is required to count everything and record it. An expensive way of controlling the receiving clerk's work.

goods received without invoice slip Created by the receiving agent to record a shipment when no invoice or delivery document accompanies the shipment. Without a record of shipments received, a hospitality operation wouldn't be able to calculate actual costs.

mailed deliveries Shipment that is delivered by the U.S. Postal Service, FedEx, DHL, UPS, or other similar delivery services.

The only difference between **blind receiving** and invoice receiving is that the invoice accompanying the delivery contains only the names of the items delivered, and no information about quantity and price. A duplicate invoice, which contains all the necessary information, is usually sent to the accountant or bookkeeper one day before delivery.

Another form of blind receiving involves the need for the receiver to complete a **goods received without invoice slip** whenever a shipment comes in that does not have an invoice or delivery slip. For instance, a **mailed delivery** or shipment delivered by a messenger service may not have accompanying paperwork. When this happens, the receiver must check with management and, if the shipment is legitimate, inspect the products and complete the in-house invoice slip.

The whole idea behind blind receiving is to increase the margin of control. The receiver is forced to weigh and count everything and then record this information. Such a procedure effectively prohibits the receiver from stealing part of the delivery and altering the invoice. Also, the procedure precludes any fraudulent relationship between the receiver and the driver.

A good deal of disagreement exists regarding the benefits of blind receiving. The general feeling in the industry is that the receiving agent should have some idea of what to expect; otherwise, he or she might receive the wrong product, too much product, too little product, and so forth. Such unintentional errors can destroy an operation's production planning.

Blind receiving is a time-consuming, costly method of receiving and processing deliveries. Operations can employ technology to speed up the process, but it normally is too expensive to be used for only a short period each day or in a small operation. Furthermore, drivers do not like to wait for a receiver to record every last detail of information.

Although we can appreciate the control benefits of blind receiving, we consider it an archaic method, similar to receiving sheets and meat tags. We know of few establishments that still use it. It is too expensive; besides, a receiver under suspicion can be checked up on with the accountant's copy of the original purchase order. The invoice should look just like the original purchase order; if they look different, management should ask for a good explanation—or look for a new receiver.

■ Odd-Hours Receiving

odd-hours receiving Receiving activities that are performed when examining an odd-hours delivery.

The major difference with the **odd-hours receiving** method is that the regular receiver is not on hand to accept the delivery. In most cases, an assistant manager is then entrusted with this duty. Although the invoice method may be applied during odd hours, an inadequate receiving job may result. The stand-in receiver usually has other pressing duties and, as a result, tends to rush the receiving process. Usually, the owner–manager recognizes this potential danger and tries to arrange for deliveries when the regular receiver is on duty, but some deliveries must be made at odd hours. As a result, it may be a good idea for the owner–manager to print the regular receiving procedure on a poster and hang it in the receiving area to aid the stand-in receiver.

■ Drop-Shipment Receiving

When a buyer purchases products from a primary source, that source usually hires a common carrier to drop ship the merchandise to the hospitality operation. Remember, the common carrier is typically an independent trucker hired to provide only the transportation function.

When a common carrier delivers a **drop shipment**, the receiving procedure used is very similar to the standard invoice receiving process. The major difference is that the driver is not involved with any disputes that may arise between the buyer and the primary source, unless he or she is directly responsible for the problem. For instance, if the driver damages the goods along the way, the buyer must deal with the driver or the driver's employer. But, as is more often the case, if the products do not meet the buyer's specifications, the receiver usually must take the shipment from the driver and hold it until the problems are rectified. Ordinarily, the driver is not in a position to take back returned merchandise.

> **drop shipment** Typical shipping procedure used when engaging in direct buying. The shipment is delivered to the back door of the restaurant, usually by a common carrier.

When disagreements arise between the buyer and the supplier in this situation, it is difficult to resolve them. For example, the buyer may have to arrange for another common carrier to return the shipment or may have to wait for the supplier's representative to arrive and check the items personally before a settlement can be reached. In addition, if the shipment is insured by an independent insurance company, its representative may need to inspect the claim and monitor the negotiations. When hospitality operators buy directly from primary sources, especially unfamiliar ones on the Web, seemingly little problems can add a great deal of stress to the transaction before they are cured.

■ Mailed Deliveries

When orders are delivered by mail, or by similar means, such as United Parcel Service (UPS) or FedEx, the invoices that come with them are normally referred to as **packing slips**. These slips are treated like any other invoice except when the order does not match the packing slip's description. In this instance, a request for credit memo or some similar record must be completed, but usually management, not the receiver, does this. The receiver notes any discrepancy and then turns the shipment over to a supervisor.

> **packing slip** Typically accompanies a shipment delivered by a common carrier.

■ Cash-on-Delivery (COD) Deliveries

Under this system, the receiver has the added duty of paying the driver or, more commonly, sending the driver to the office for the payment check. It is also possible that the receiver accompanies the driver to the office to attest to the adequacy of the delivered items.

GOOD RECEIVING PRACTICES

Receivers should follow a number of sound procedures. Most of them fall mainly under the security category:

tare weight Weight of all material, such as cardboard, wrapping paper, and ice, used to pack and ship the product that is not part of the product itself. Subtracted from gross weight to compute net weight.

gross weight Weight of product plus the tare weight.

net weight Gross weight less the tare weight.

equal to the facing layer A receiving standard that requires all layers of a product packed in a case to look the same as the layer on top. You want all the layers to look just like the top (facing) one. You don't want the junk hidden underneath the facing layer.

water damage Products that have been injured by moisture and, therefore, are not usable.

expiration date The date after which a product should not be sold because of an expected decline in quality or effectiveness.

incomplete shipments Deliveries that do not have all of the items ordered by the buyer. The missing items may be back ordered, or the supplier may have forgotten to include them with the shipments.

1. Receivers should beware of excess ice, watered-down products, wrapping paper, and packaging that can add dead weight to the delivered items. Receivers must subtract the amount of this dead weight, which is sometimes referred to as the **tare weight**, from the **gross weight** to compute the **net weight** of the merchandise.

2. Receivers should always check the quality under the top layer. Make sure that all succeeding layers are **equal to the facing layer**.

3. Receivers should always examine packages for leakage or other forms of **water damage**. This could indicate that the package contents are unusable. If the packages, especially cans, are swollen, the contents are probably spoiled, and receivers should reject the shipment.

4. If a package label carries an **expiration date**, receivers should ensure that it is within acceptable limits. Receivers should also make sure that the dating codes are correct.

5. Receivers should not weigh everything together. For example, they should separate hamburger from steak and weigh each product by itself. If they weigh these items together, they might begin to buy hamburger at a steak price.

6. Receivers should be wary of drivers eager to help them carry the items to their storage areas. Trust is not the issue. The big problems with letting people on the premises are the distraction they cause among employees and the possibility that liability insurance premiums will increase.

7. Receivers should watch for **incomplete shipments**, as well as for the driver who asks the receiver to sign for a complete order after telling them that the rest of the order will arrive later. Later may never come.

8. Receivers should spot-check portioned products for portion weights. For example, if receivers buy portioned sausage patties by the pound and sell them by the piece, a 2-ounce sausage patty that is consistently 1/4 ounce overweight will inflate the food cost. But operators will not reflect this in their sales because their menu price will still reflect a 2-ounce portion. It is equally troubling if the sausage patties are underweight and are purchased by the piece; a short weight of as little as 1/8 ounce can cost quite a bit of money in the long run.

9. Receivers should be careful of closed shipping containers with preprinted dates, weights, counts, or quality standards. Someone may have repacked these cartons with inferior merchandise. It might be wise to occasionally weigh flour sacks, rice sacks, potato sacks, and even open a box of paper napkins to count them.

10. Receivers should also be careful that they do not receive merchandise that has been refrozen. In addition, they should be on the lookout for supposedly fresh merchandise that is actually **slacked out** (i.e., has been frozen, thawed, and made to appear as if it is fresh).

> **slacked out** A food item that is thought to be fresh but has actually been frozen, thawed, and passed off as fresh.

11. At times, receivers may confuse brand names and/or packers' brand names. This is easy to do when receivers are in a hurry.

12. When receiving some fresh merchandise, such as meats, fish, and poultry, receivers normally give suppliers a "shrink" allowance. The product specification normally indicates the minimum weight per case that receivers will accept, but in some circumstances, they may not be able to judge the delivery as closely as they would like.

13. In general, receivers are concerned about any product that they receive that does not live up to their specifications. It is absolutely essential to prepare adequate specifications because this is the only way receivers can ensure that they have the appropriate standard on which to judge incoming merchandise.

We do not intend to criticize suppliers or drivers. A good rule in business is to maintain a cautious optimism when receiving, but remember that it is possible to get "stung" in at least four ways: (1) the unintentional error, (2) the dishonest supplier with an honest driver, (3) the honest supplier with a dishonest driver, and (4) a dishonest supplier with a dishonest driver. Keep in mind that once receivers sign for a delivery, the items are theirs, so receivers must verify that they receive the right quantity, quality, and AP price.

REDUCING RECEIVING COSTS

Receivers can reduce receiving costs a few ways without losing a proportionate amount of control. Some common cost-saving methods are described in the following list.

1. **Field inspectors.** Large firms sometimes use **field inspectors**, which saves some time for receivers in that they do not have to check for quality and quantity. This is because the inspector often seals the packages to be delivered. The overall cost, though, may not decrease; field inspectors, like receivers, must be paid.

2. **Night and early-morning deliveries.** These odd-hour deliveries (night and **early-morning deliveries**) are often the rule in the downtown sections of many large cities to avoid daytime traffic congestion. With fewer distractions, drivers can make more deliveries, and part of the lower transportation cost per delivery may be passed on to hospitality operations. A variation of this procedure is the **night drop**, in which a driver uses a key to get in, places the items inside the door, locks up, and leaves. Opinion varies among operators regarding the degree of trust required for this practice.

> **field inspector** A person hired by a company to inspect products before they are shipped to the company. Typically done when purchasing large amounts of fresh produce directly from the farmer.

> **early-morning deliveries** A form of odd-hours delivery.

> **night drop** When the delivery driver has a key to the facility, enters it when closed for business, leaves the shipment, locks up, and goes. The shipment is put away the next morning. Intended to reduce costs due to the efficiency of deliveries at off-hours (e.g., late-night or early-morning) and not having to pay a receiving agent.

one-stop shopping
Buying everything you need from one vendor. Alternately, buying everything you need from the fewest possible purveyors.

3. One-stop shopping. One-stop shopping is, perhaps, the most common method of reducing receiving costs. Although some people are not enthusiastic about this buying method, everyone agrees that it can reduce receiving costs.

In trying to reduce receiving costs, receivers must be careful that they do not simply shift the costs around. For instance, low receiving costs accompany one-stop shopping, but the savings from reducing the number of potential suppliers may be wiped out by higher AP prices from a single supplier.

Certain inescapable costs must be incurred if receivers expect to meet the objectives of the purchasing and receiving functions. It is absolutely essential not to negate the effective job the buyer may have done. In the end, the receiving function affords few cost-cutting possibilities unless receivers are willing to give up a certain amount of control.

 ## Key Words and Concepts

Accepting a delivery	Meat tag
Backhaul	Net weight
Bar code	Night drop
Bill of lading	Odd-hours receiving
Blind receiving	One-stop shopping
Common carrier	Packing slip
Credit memo	Pick-up memo
Credit slip	Price extension
Cycle of control	Quality assurance
Delivery ticket	Quality control
Dot system	Receiving objectives
Drop shipment	Receiving sheet
Early-morning deliveries	Request for credit memo
Equal to the facing layer	Returned merchandise
Expiration date	Route salesperson
Field inspector	Sales tax
Goods received without invoice slip	Slacked out
Gross weight	Standing-order
Incomplete shipments	Stock requisition
Invoice	Stock rotation
Invoice receiving	Tare weight
Invoice stamp	Use tax
Mailed deliveries	Water damage
Management information system (MIS)	

Questions and Problems

1. You hear that your competitors are using a control device called "blind receiving." What is blind receiving? Under what conditions would you use this procedure?

2. Explain how one-stop shopping can reduce your overall receiving costs.

3. At 10 A.M. on September 27, the A & H Foods Company delivered the following items:

Unit	Quantity	Item Description	Unit Price	Extension
Pound	80	T-bone steaks	$6.85	$548.00
Pound	18	Sliced bacon	$2.80	$50.40
Pound	20	Flank steak	$4.25	$85.00
Case	2	Floor wax, gallon cans	$28.00	$56.00
Case	2	Boston lettuce	$16.50	$33.00
Case	1	Canned green beans, No. 10 cans	$17.50	$17.50
Total				$789.90

Upon inspection, you determine that the sliced bacon is inferior and that you must return it to the supplier.

(a) Using Figure 12.5 as a guide, prepare a request for credit memo for the bacon.

(b) Using Figure 12.7 as a guide, complete the information on the invoice stamp that the receiver usually completes.

(c) Using Figure 12.8 as a guide, transfer the acceptable items to the receiving sheet. Note: The flank steak goes directly into the in-process inventory.

4. What type of information would you like to have in the "other information" column on the receiving sheet? Why?

5. Many operators feel that the receiving sheet is useful in calculating daily food, beverage, and nonfood costs. How do you think the receiving sheet is helpful in this matter?

6. What should a receiver do when a question arises regarding the quality of merchandise received?

7. What should a receiver do if a delivery is made without an accompanying invoice?

8. A receiver will prepare a request for credit memo when:
    (a)
    (b)
    (c)

9. List some objectives of the receiving function.

10. List the primary essentials that are needed for proper receiving.

11. What is the primary difference between invoice receiving and blind receiving?

12. Briefly describe the computation of price extensions.

13. Describe one purpose of using an invoice stamp.

14. What is the primary reason for using meat tags?

Questions and Problems (continued)

15. Briefly describe the concept of stock rotation.

16. What is a bill of lading?

17. What does it mean when we say that a food item has been "slacked out"?

18. Why should you separate meat items before weighing them?

19. What is the primary purpose of the pick-up memo?

20. Assume you must pay sales tax for all nonfood items you purchase. If the sales tax rate is 6 percent, recalculate the invoice total for Question 3.

21. What is the significance of the expiration date placed on the package label of some food products?

22. Assume you are checking in a shipment of canned goods. You notice some dried water spots on the bottom of one of the cases. You open the case and notice nothing leaking from the cans. Should you accept the shipment? Why or why not?

23. What are the advantages and disadvantages of the standing-order receiving procedure?

Experiential Exercises

1. Visit a local supplier and arrange to ride with a driver on his or her route. Compare and contrast the receiving procedures you see in each hospitality operation. In addition, take the time to examine how the supplier processes his or her copy of the invoice.

2. Arrange to spend one day in the receiving area of a hotel or restaurant. Evaluate the receiving procedures the receiver uses. In addition, try to follow the paperwork, from invoice processing, receiving-sheet completion, and so on, up to the end of the receiver's paperwork duties.

References

1. Howard Riell, "On the Receiving End," *Food Service Director*, 19, no. 5 (May 15, 2006): 58–61; See also Jorge Hernandez, "Supplier Relationships Are Key to Safe Food Receiving," *Restaurant Hospitality*, May 2006, http://food-management.com/business_topics/food_safety/fm_imp_11629/; Bill Schwartz, "Receiving: The First Line of Defense Against High F&B Costs." *Indian Gaming*, 15, no. 12 (December 2005):20–21.

2. Paul R. Dittmer and J. Desmond Keefe III, *Principles of Food, Beverage, and Labor Cost Controls*, 8th ed. (Hoboken, NJ: John Wiley & Sons, 2008).

3. Fry oil references: For McDonald's, see www.crmcdonalds.com/publish/csr/home/report/environmental_responsibility/packaging_and_waste/recycling.html. For Disneyland fry oil reference, see www.environmentalleader.com/2009/02/02/disneyland-powers-steam-trains-with-recycled-cooking-oil/.

CHAPTER 13

TYPICAL STORAGE MANAGEMENT PROCEDURES

The Purpose of This Chapter

After reading this chapter, you should be able to:

- Explain the objectives of storage.

- Describe the factors needed to achieve storage objectives.

- Illustrate the process of managing inventory and storage facilities.

- Analyze the value of exercising tight control over the stock and storage management procedures.

THE OBJECTIVES OF STORAGE

Storage is an activity typically performed in conjunction with receiving. As soon as receivers inspect incoming merchandise, they ensure that it is put in the proper storage facility. In some instances, receivers may send some items directly to a production department. For example, steaks scheduled for tonight's banquet should go directly to the kitchen. (Items sent directly to the production departments are usually referred to as **direct purchases** or "directs" when an internal issues system is used.)

Often, the same person who receives also stores. Large operations may divide this responsibility by assigning, for example, the receiving function to a receiving supervisor and the storage function to a storeroom manager. Typically, however, the receiver and storeroom manager are the same person. In small operations, the user–buyer or the chef might receive and store products and even manage the storage facilities. Good control, however, implies some separation of responsibilities.

The basic goal of storage management is to prevent loss of merchandise due to: (1) theft, (2) pilferage, and (3) spoilage.

Theft is premeditated burglary. It occurs when someone drives a truck up to the back door of an operation and steals all the expensive foods, beverages, and equipment. Generally, storage facilities are not designed to prevent this. Management would need a citadel to eliminate theft. Storage security is normally designed to discourage employee theft by keeping honest employees honest. In some parts of the United States, and the rest of the world, theft is common. Thus, hospitality operators must see to it that storage facilities are designed to make theft more difficult, generally by some combination of clear visibility of general access storage and very tight security on locked, limited-access storage located elsewhere. Locking storage areas when not in use and minimizing the number of persons who have access to the keys are good practices.

Pilferage is a serious problem in the hospitality industry and centers on the employee who sneaks off with a bottle of mustard or ketchup. Eating on the job is another form of pilferage, unless the owner–manager allows it. Shoplifting also falls in this category.

Pilferage is sometimes referred to as **inventory shrinkage** or **skimming**. The dollar losses resulting from pilferage in all retail segments are estimated to be as high as 40–50 billion dollars per year. The most commonly quoted statistics for the restaurant industry are that 4 percent of sales are lost due to pilferage and more than 75 percent of employees have stolen from their employer.[1] Several potential ways to control pilferage exist, some of which we discuss in the next chapter. Unfortunately, in some cases, the cure may be more expensive than the disease.

Spoilage can be controlled a little more easily than either theft or pilferage. Generally, spoilage can be minimized by adhering to rigid sanitation practices, rotating the stock so that old items are used first, and providing the proper environmental conditions for each item in storage.

---

direct purchase   Refers to a purchased product (usually a perishable food) that, once received, will bypass the main storage facility, go straight to production, and be charged to cost on the day it's received. A perishable food item, such as fresh pastry, is an example of a direct purchase.

theft   Premeditated burglary.

pilferage   Refers to minor theft. For instance, employees snatching a drink while on-the-clock, or guests swiping a wine glass.

inventory shrinkage and **skimming**   Other terms for pilferage.

spoilage   Deterioration of food by microbial and/or chemical action.

Rigid sanitation is, in fact, a must in all storage facilities. This involves two quite different kinds of steps. First, products that might induce spoilage in others through migration of odors or chemicals must be separated properly. For example, fresh fish is not stored with butter, and cleaning agents are segregated from food products. A second and more obvious sanitation activity involves keeping the storage facility clean, for instance, by mopping the floor daily.

Any sanitation slipup not only hastens spoilage but also increases the risk of customer or employee sickness. Some states and local municipalities have legislation that requires hospitality management personnel to successfully pass some sort of a sanitation test or to satisfactorily complete an approved sanitation course. There is also discussion suggesting that eventually all hospitality employees will have to pass some type of sanitation certification exam.

The proper environmental conditions for storage seem easy enough to achieve. However, the expense of providing for all the various temperature and humidity requirements for an entire spectrum of food products can be burdensome for small restaurants. Nonfood storage is not so large a problem, but a good deal of valuable space may be required.

Freezers; separate produce, dairy, and meat refrigerators; and separate dry storage areas for groceries, beverages, and cleaning supplies can all add up to a large investment. This can be so large, in fact, that small operations often try to make do with outdated facilities, which can get them into trouble with the local health department.

The benefits of proper environmental conditions are definite but sometimes not readily apparent. The prevention of food-borne illness does not carry a price tag. Moreover, improper storage can cause a significant loss of nutritional value and taste. The value here is difficult to quantify. Lost nutrition does not necessarily concern restaurant customers, but school foodservice operations might consider this loss unacceptable. Fortunately, even though a hospitality operation may maintain an old, erratic refrigerator, proper stock rotation and a reasonably quick stock turnover can minimize quality loss.

It would probably be enlightening for operators to monitor the losses attributable directly to improper environmental conditions. For example, how much cheese has to be discarded because it absorbed onion flavors? How much flour attracts excessive moisture? Most operations experience some losses because of complete spoilage or because products, although technically not spoiled, have passed their peak of culinary quality and are not suitable for guest service. But when these losses are compared with the cost associated with providing the proper environment, they may seem insignificant.

They are not insignificant, however, when operators go beyond mere dollars and cents. Operators must be very concerned, for example, with the loss of their operation's reputation should a customer get sick after eating in their establishment. How do they compare this reputation loss with the cost of proper environmental conditions?

There is an old saying in the hospitality industry: "The most important asset a hospitality company has is its reputation." This asset should be protected first. Clearly, a few thousand dollars pales in comparison with a loss of goodwill. But how many operators are able to make this connection? We see the few thousand dollars easily, but we do not necessarily see the loss of goodwill as the primary concern.

WHAT IS NEEDED TO ACHIEVE STORAGE OBJECTIVES?

The major factors needed to achieve the storage objectives are discussed in the following sections.

■ Adequate Space

Of all requirements, this is probably the hardest for hospitality operators to comply with. Usually, they must accept what they have to work with unless they are willing to remodel or add more floor space to the building.

If hospitality operators are constructing the building from the ground up, designers can plan for optimal **storage space**, for today and for the future. When building costs must be cut somewhere, however, the storage area is vulnerable. This is unfortunate because it not only hampers current storage demands but also limits the types of products operators can store in the future. Also, this more or less permanently limits what they can offer customers.

storage space The amount of room, for example, the number of cubic feet, devoted to storeroom and warehouse facilities.

health district storage requirements Regulations established by a community's health department outlining the sanitation and food safety standards that must be maintained by foodservice operations.

Generally, the space needed for all storage is between 5 square feet per dining room seat and 15 square feet per hotel room, depending on the amount of sales, types of items sold, the quantity of nonfood items held in storage, and the local **health district storage requirements**. A well-managed facility usually allocates about 10 to 12 percent of the total property for the storage function.[2] Typically, owner–managers do try to minimize the storage space so that they can add more dining room seats or sleeping rooms. Real estate is expensive, and no one can blame owner–managers if they prefer tables and chairs that generate sales to storage shelves whose direct relation to sales is not so clear. But the smaller the storage space is today, usually the more limited are an operator's offerings tomorrow.

■ Adequate Temperature and Humidity

A hospitality operation that houses one or more foodservice facilities will need to follow its local health district temperature requirements and space requirements. In general, the health district mandates that all potentially hazardous food—such as meats, seafood, and poultry—must be stored at 40°F, or below, or at 135°F, or above. Nonhazardous food and nonfood items usually have no temperature requirements. Furthermore, they usually have no mandated humidity requirements.

A local health district typically mandates certain space requirements, so that good housekeeping practices can be performed. For instance, merchandise usually must be stored several inches from the walls, ceiling, and floor. Food items usually must be stored on shelving that is not solid, so that proper ventilation can be maintained. Food cannot be stored under any exposed or unprotected sewer lines or water lines, or in rooms with toilet or garbage facilities. Furthermore, such material as soaps, chemicals, and pest control supplies must be stored in a separate storage area so that they can neither contaminate food and beverage products, nor be picked up by accident by someone obtaining food supplies. Although health district requirements are important, they represent minimum standards of sanitation and wholesomeness. Wise hospitality operators will go beyond these requirements to ensure that the shelf life of all stored merchandise is maximized. You can accomplish this objective by following the temperature guidelines presented by the **National Restaurant Association Educational Foundation (NRAEF)**.[3] Its recommendations are

- Meat and poultry: 41°F or lower

- Fresh fish: 41°F or lower

- Live shellfish: 45°F or lower

- Processed crustaceans: 41°F or lower

- Eggs: 45°F or lower

- Dairy products: 41°F or lower

- Fruits and vegetables: ranging from 41°F to 70°F, depending on the item

- **Reduced oxygen packaged (ROP) foods**: 41°F or lower unless otherwise specified by the manufacturer

- Potentially hazardous, ready-to-eat food that has been prepared in-house: up to 7 days at 41°F or lower

- Dry and canned food: 50°F to 70°F

- Freezer storage: 0°F to 10°F

To maintain these suggested temperature requirements, hospitality operators must invest in a considerable amount of expensive storage facilities. For instance, in large hotels, it is common to find several walk-in refrigerators and freezers, each one serving a particular environmental need. Typical hospitality operators cannot afford this investment. Consequently, they must ensure rapid inventory turnover, so that product quality does not deteriorate to the extent that customer dissatisfaction would result.

■ Adequate Equipment

A proper storage area requires at least three major types of equipment: shelving/racks, trucks, and covered containers. Shelving, wall racks, and floor racks (i.e., "dunnage racks" or "pallets") are essential because you cannot store anything directly on the floor. Motorized and/or nonmotorized trucks are needed to transport products into and out of storage. Furthermore, covered containers, including see-through plastic buckets and pans, are needed to hold products, such as cored lettuce, that you may want to remove from shipping crates before placing into storage.

■ Proximity of Storage Area to Receiving and Production Areas

To the extent possible, you should install the storage facilities close to the receiving dock and to the production departments. In addition, it is desirable to place the receiving, storage, and production areas on the same floor level. This saves time and ensures that products are not out of their storage environments for excessive periods.

National Restaurant Association Educational Foundation (NRAEF) Agency of the National Restaurant Association (NRA) that provides educational resources, materials, and programs that address recruitment, development, and retention of the industry's workforce. It is dedicated to fulfilling the NRA's educational mission.

reduced oxygen packaging (ROP) Another term for controlled atmosphere packaging (CAP).

■ Access to Proper Maintenance

Depending on the size of the operation, thousands, tens of thousands, even hundreds of thousands of dollars' worth of inventory can be on hand at any one time. One freezer breakdown can ruin a considerable amount of frozen food. A leaking water pipe can damage huge amounts of food in the dry storage areas. The maintenance to make sure this does not happen is expensive. The 2016 HOST Almanac published by STR, Inc. states that the average property operations and maintenance expenses for all types of United States hotels represent 4.3% of total sales, $2,705 per available room, and $10.09 per occupied room night.[4]

A maintenance contract is, therefore, useful, even though it carries no guarantee that the serviceperson can get there precisely when needed. Some operations hire their own maintenance personnel to ensure that service is available at a moment's notice. Unfortunately, small operations cannot afford this luxury. Their best bet is to purchase good equipment in the first place. In addition, the use of preventive maintenance or service checks can help reduce breakdowns and increase the life of existing equipment.[5]

■ Proper Security

Chapter 14 contains a discussion of relevant security considerations, not only for storage, but also for other aspects of the selection and procurement function.

■ Competent Personnel to Supervise and Manage the Storage Function

In some operations, one person receives, stores, and issues items to production departments. It is even more common for one person to buy, receive, store, and eventually use the items in production. A working chef, for example, may perform all these tasks.

Large firms usually impose some separation of responsibility; small firms often have to rely on whoever is available at the time to receive and store incoming merchandise. When a production department needs an item, quite often someone just goes into an unsecured storage area to get it.

Experts agree that proper receiving, storage, and **issuing procedures** are a key to reducing employee theft. It is difficult, however, to quantify that savings. Because no actual cost studies are available, it is hard to assert a hard-and-fast rule beyond saying that good procedures in this area of logistics are important.

Any savings a hospitality operation achieves in this area will correspond closely with the competence of the person(s) performing these functions. Having a rule that states that nothing leaves the storeroom without permission is one thing; implementing and enforcing this rule is something else again. Hence, the ability of people working in these areas is critical. The best-designed receiving and storage facilities and receiving, storing, and issuing procedures are useless if the right person is not on the job.

Finally, we have to realize that ideal circumstances do not always occur. Sales volume may not be large enough to permit the operation to "follow the book" and have people available for each function. Conversely, volume may

> **issuing procedure** There are two types: formal and informal. The formal procedure requires a product user, such as a chef, to requisition products from a central warehouse or storage facility. The chef signs for the items and is responsible for them. An informal procedure allows the product user to request from the manager what is needed, with the manager getting the products and handling the paperwork later on. Another informal process allows any product user to enter the warehouse or storage facility and take what's needed for production and/or service.

be large enough to afford proper support staff, but the labor market may be too tight and the kind of people you want for the function may be unavailable. Developing ways to secure goods under these less-than-ideal conditions is challenging.

■ Sufficient Time to Perform the Necessary Duties

Adequate time is just as important as employee talent. Receiving, storing, and issuing involve more than just weighing food and putting it into storage. Hospitality operations have many other tasks, such as monitoring the necessary control procedures, maintaining sanitation, rotating the stock, keeping track of usage patterns, and so on.

Small operations cannot always afford the time to do all of these tasks. But even large companies tend to load down the receiver–storeroom clerk with such extraneous duties as sorting mail.

It is unfortunate when hotels, restaurants, institutions, and clubs go to the expense of hiring good people and designing excellent receiving, storing, and issuing procedures, but then stop short at providing enough time to discharge these functions adequately.

■ Storeroom Regulations

Regulations dictate who is allowed to enter storage areas and who is allowed to obtain items from storage. Also specified is the required procedure to use to obtain these items. In some cases, the senior management determines these guidelines. However, large firms that set broad guidelines often expect the storeroom manager to work out the day-to-day details necessary for a smooth-running operation.

MANAGING THE STORAGE FACILITIES

Small operations usually hope that the storage facilities will manage themselves. An idle food server, for example, might be sent into the storeroom now and then to clean up. Similarly, the chef may have a few moments to rotate the stock. Often, though, the storage areas of small operations are not managed systematically. There are many different techniques for **managing storage facilities**.

> **managing storage facilities** Procedures used to ensure stored merchandise is managed effectively and that losses due to spoilage, theft, and pilferage are minimized.

The one exception seems to be the liquor storeroom. An owner–manager keeps this area locked at the very least and may personally receive these items. And because the liquor control commission requires bars to maintain records of their liquor purchases, considerably more bookkeeping and record keeping is done here than elsewhere. Liquor storage tends, then, to be well organized almost everywhere, but the same cannot be said for soap, paper towels, and lightbulbs.

Larger operations that can afford the luxury of a receiver–storeroom manager assign him or her several activities. The major ones are discussed here.

1. Inventories must be classified and organized in a systematic fashion (see Figure 13.1). This procedure simplifies general control and also helps with the preparation of reports that deal with inventories and their costs.

FIGURE 13.1 Classifying food items in inventory by date using Daydots system.
©Daydots

Some storeroom managers label the shelf location with the name of the item that occupies that spot; they take this step in dry, refrigerated, and frozen storage. Furthermore, a diagram of a storage facility, complete with a guide noting where each particular item is located, is often displayed on the doorway of the facility. If a bar code or RFID system is used, areas may be labeled with the proper code or number as well as the name of the products. See the sidebar for a detailed example of how a storage system may be organized. Other operators, however, take a considerably more flexible approach to control the use of storage space.

It is important for operators to organize and classify their inventories in a manner that satisfies the local legal requirements. For instance, normally the local health district stipulates that toxic materials must be housed in a separate storage facility and that this location must be kept locked. It is conceivable that in your locale, alcoholic beverages must be kept in a separate area because underage employees must not be exposed to this merchandise.

inventory usage rates
When referring to food and beverages, it is the rate at which the products are produced and served to customers. When referring to nonfood and nonbeverage supplies, it is the rate at which the products have been exhausted and are no longer available.

2. **Inventory usage rates** must be determined for all inventories. Storeroom managers must keep track of the usage patterns so that they can revise and help improve ordering procedures and par stock levels. Using computerized purchasing and inventory systems greatly enhances the efficiency and accuracy of these calculations. In addition, this information can help determine the optimal reorder point.

3. Storeroom managers must occasionally make an emergency order or travel to the supplier's location to pick up extra items, particularly if a stock-out threatens. The storeroom manager may also need to pick up an order right away rather than wait for the scheduled delivery. In smaller establishments, having the manager pick up items at a warehouse store such as Costco or Sam's Club may be part of the standard operating procedures if one needs small quantities of product or the cost is less expensive than having a supplier delivery.

4. Storeroom managers also keep track of accumulating surpluses. These may occur if the buyer does not know that the chef has taken certain items off the menu or their sales have decreased.

5. Storeroom managers may be responsible for disposing of items that the hospitality operation no longer uses. Buyers may want to do this personally, but often storeroom managers may arrange to return merchandise to the supplier, trade it, or otherwise get rid of it.

6. Storeroom managers may need to make transfers of merchandise to other company outlets. For instance, if another unit in the restaurant chain needs frozen french fries, the manager may need to send some of his or her stock of french fries. Storeroom managers might also do this if they are overstocked and another unit is understocked. Whatever the case, when doing this, storeroom managers usually must complete a **transfer slip** (which is similar to an invoice) so that the stock is controlled and accounted for properly.

7. Storeroom managers may keep track of all inventories and their corresponding dollar value.

Some companies want to keep a **perpetual inventory** system; that is, they want to know what is on hand in the storeroom at all times. These firms might even keep track of all in-process inventories in addition to the storeroom inventories. As a rule, however, this kind of control requires a considerable amount of computer technology.

Because such a system costs a good deal of time and money, it is sometimes used, usually without a computer, for only a few items. In such cases, it is generally used for the most expensive items, especially liquor.

Because storeroom managers must keep records of liquor purchases, it is only a bit more trouble to keep a perpetual inventory by keeping a **bin card** next to each type of liquor in storage (see Figure 13.2).

transfer slip Document used to control and account for products moved from one unit to another one within the same company. For instance, if you run a Red Lobster and you send food product over to another Red Lobster on the other side of town because it's running low, the transfer slip will credit your food cost while debiting the other unit's food cost.

perpetual inventory Keeping a running balance of an inventory item so that you always know what you have on hand. When a shipment is received you add to the balance, and every time you use some of it you deduct that amount. Similar to keeping an up-to-date cash balance in your personal checkbook.

bin card A perpetual inventory record. It includes all items delivered to the restaurant's storeroom, all items issued out of the storeroom, all items returned to the storeroom, and the current balance of all items held in the storeroom.

Perpetual inventory for period _____							
Name of item _____							
1	2	3	4	5	6	7	8
Date Delivered	No. of Units	Unit Price	Date Issued	No. of Units	To Whom Issued	Returns to Storeroom	Balance

FIGURE 13.2 A bin card.

A bin card is a record of all liquor, or other items, delivered, all liquor sent to the production areas—bars, kitchen, and service areas—and, in some cases, all liquor sent back to storage from the production areas.

At one time, many large hotels and clubs kept no inventories in the production areas when these areas were closed. That is, at the beginning of a shift, a bartender, for example, would pick up and sign for a complete par stock of all the items needed during the shift. Any necessary replenishment was usually handled by an assistant manager. At the end of the shift, the bartender would send everything back to storage. Storeroom managers then would determine what had been used during the shift, and this amount should correspond to the bar sales amount. This type of procedure is no longer in widespread use in the industry, but it is still followed for banquet bars.

stock requisition A formal request made by an employee for items needed to carry out necessary tasks. It is given to the person managing the storage facilities. A typical control document used by large hotels.

in-process inventory Products located at employee workstations; most or all will be used during the shift.

management information system (MIS) Method of organizing, analyzing, and reporting information to manage a business effectively. It typically involves the use of computerized record keeping.

physical inventory An actual counting and valuing of all products kept in your hospitality operation.

Such a procedure is time consuming and requires someone in the storeroom to set up the par stocks for each user. However, this approach does eliminate the need for **stock requisitions**—a concept we address in our discussion of issuing later in this chapter. Some operations do insist that at least the more expensive items be treated this way. For instance, a chef may follow this procedure with meat and fish. Also, a bartender may have to follow it for some liquors. In other words, storeroom managers closely monitor the costly items and require users to pick up and return them; it is unacceptable to keep any of them in the **in-process inventory** except during working hours.

The perpetual inventory has some advantages, such as providing for a tight degree of control. Moreover, many operators believe that if they continually monitor inventory levels, they will remain close to the optimal levels because they will have accurate par stocks.

Today, the cost of maintaining a perpetual inventory "by hand" for more than a few items is almost prohibitive. Not only does the labor cost loom large, but also experience teaches that hand-posted records often contain a good deal of human error, often to the point of making their value questionable. Consequently, the greatest use of perpetual inventory for a total inventory is found in hospitality operations in which all departments are integrated into a **management information system (MIS)**.

Operators who once swore by the perpetual inventory system now tend to take a complete **physical inventory** once weekly, every 10 days, semimonthly, or monthly. In this way, they keep track of their overall performance.

A physical inventory, in contrast to a perpetual inventory, is an actual counting and valuing of all of the items in storage and, in some cases, of all of the items in the in-process inventory. Three good reasons exist for taking a physical inventory: (1) It is useful for operators to have this information before calculating order sizes and preparing purchase orders. (2) It is necessary for accountants who must calculate product costs. For example, they might want to compute the actual food cost for the month (see Figure 13.3). (3) Assuming some type of perpetual inventory is used, the physical-inventory count can be compared with the "theoretical inventory" count

The cost equations are:

$$P - EI = C$$
$$C/S = C\%$$

where BI = beginning inventory
P = purchases for the month
EI = ending inventory
S = sales
C = food cost
C% = food cost percentage

Note that in the example below, some operations may make other adjustments, such as granting a credit for employee meals, in order to determine the actual food cost for food sold to guests.

BI (which is last month's EI).....................$12,000

P...+20,000
EI...−14,000
Credit for employee meals........................ −2,000

C... $16,000
If S = $49,000, C% = $16,000/$49,000 = 32.6%

FIGURE 13.3 The calculation of this month's actual food cost.

shown on bin card records. In this case, if the actual inventory does not equal the **theoretical inventory value**, an inventory control problem may exist.

Taking a physical inventory is time consuming, but the hospitality operation usually performs it at least once a month. The monthly profit-and-loss statement for the operation must be prepared. This cannot be done unless the operator knows his or her cost of goods sold, and the operator cannot compute this expense unless he or she takes a physical inventory.

Several ways exist to take the inventory. One method requires two persons, one calling and the other writing. The inventory sheets are preprinted with the items' names and spaces where the writer can record the numerical entries. In a computerized operation, the sheets can be printed from the computer or the writer may enter the quantities directly on a laptop or tablet. Those operators without computers must prepare these sheets in some other way.

Another inventory-taking method that has become popular is to use a handheld bar code scanner to record stock levels. In a hospitality operation that has a fully integrated MIS, such a procedure is a natural addition to the overall inventory management process.

Operators who do not have access to the latest technology can adopt shortcuts that speed the inventory-taking process with only minor sacrifices of accuracy. These shortcuts include: (1) Operators count everything in the storage areas and then add on a certain predetermined percentage to represent the amount of items in the in-process inventory. (2) They count only full-case equivalents. That is, operators do not add in half a can of baking powder; they just count full cases, boxes, or cans. (3) Operators combine inventory taking with the ordering

theoretical inventory value What the inventory value is supposed to be, based on what you sold. For instance, if you had 100 steaks in inventory and the POS system says you sold 50, then there should be 50 steaks left. An actual count, though, may reveal that you have more or less than 50.

procedure. If the storage manager's count is sufficiently accurate, correct purchase orders can be prepared. This does, however, have a drawback: it offers the storeroom manager the opportunity to manipulate the count, a risk that must be judged acceptable if this procedure is to be followed. (4) Operators use a digital recorder to recite units and dollar values, and later, someone transcribes the information. (5) Operators may use a laptop or tablet to encode their inventories, and later on, this electronically gathered information can be processed and printed.

Some operators do not want their storeroom manager taking inventory, at least not all the time. They would rather have someone else do it periodically to serve as a check on the storeroom manager. For instance, the storeroom manager may keep some type of perpetual inventory, and a representative of, for example, the accounting department or controller's office may take a physical inventory once or twice a month both to check on the storeroom manager's accuracy and to calculate various product costs so that financial statements and reports can be prepared.

Sometimes, small operators do something similar. For example, they might ask the head bartender to take a physical inventory of the food-storage areas while the chef or head housekeeper inventories the liquor. Alternately, the owner–manager might do the actual physical counting once or twice a month, while the department heads keep some sort of a perpetual inventory for some or all items. Finally, some member of management who is not attached to any one department may assist the department representative with this inventory.

In some cases, especially for liquor, an owner–manager may periodically hire an outside service that specializes in the hospitality industry to take a physical inventory. This is sometimes done to get an absolutely unbiased inventory report. It is also traditionally done as part of the audit of the entire operation by someone who wants to buy the business.

STOREROOM ORGANIZATION
Daniel Celeste, University of Nevada, Las Vegas

Courtesy of DC Photography, Las Vegas, Nevada

Daniel Celeste is an adjunct lecturer at the University of Nevada, Las Vegas. He is a retired hospitality executive with more than 40 years' experience in Cost Control, Purchasing, Food & Beverage Management, and Casino Administration. He is also an owner/investor in a local casino and a national chain restaurant.

Purpose

Storeroom organization is paramount in order to maintain cleanliness and order, ease placement and retrieval of merchandise, and achieve increased accuracy for the business. The premise of storeroom organization is that each stored item has its own home address or specifically identified location to make it easier for all personnel to be operating with the same procedure. The importance of this cataloging process is particularly noticeable in larger organizations when in all likelihood there are several employees handling merchandise while placing it after receipt, rotating it, and retrieving the merchandise for issue. The employee putting away the merchandise and another employee retrieving the same merchandise, say tomatoes, for issue some time later, will have to go to the *same* place: for instance, specific address. This address for each item should to be decided on in advance by management. There should be no confusion or guessing as to where any merchandise is to be placed for storage once each item has a single, specifically defined address. Simply put, utilizing the best concept for storeroom organization, there must be "*a place for everything and everything in its place.*"

In addition to eliminating unnecessary clutter, which could lead to safety and health concerns, the benefit of the specific address is that inventory count sheets, be they for purposes of merchandise reorder or costing, can be organized in same order as the items are found on storage shelves. Thus the "*sheet to shelf and shelf to sheet*" concept will aid in timely, more accurate recording of the inventory count no matter the purpose of the inventory.

By utilizing the storeroom organizational criteria of *area [room], section [column], shelf [row],* and *bin [slot]* an individually defined address location can be created. Although this organizational structure is particularly useful in larger hospitality organizations, the same criteria can be adapted for midsized and even the smallest of operations as well. Furthermore, with computerized inventory-purchasing systems the storeroom location address can be programmed to print on receiving documents so that receiving and/or storeroom personnel can know exactly where merchandise is to be placed at the time of or soon after receipt without any question. Also a label with the address location identification and the specific item information can be printed and positioned at the storage address location to create (reserve) the individual home address.

Creating the Location Identification

For explanation purposes, the following six-digit combination of numbers and letters is just one example of how this address or location identification number code could be created.

To set up the framework for addresses and make the storage process functional, the following suggested guidelines or ground rules should be established for all to operate by:

1. The room or storage area must have its own number or letter to identify it from other storerooms.

2. Sections of any storeroom or storage area must be numbered or lettered by section (sometimes referred to as columns or column area) from the point one enters the room or storage area moving to the left around the perimeter of the room back to the same point of entry, and if necessary in the center of the room or storage area, then continuing from the left-most aisle from the front to the back, then continuing again to the next aisle from the back to the front, in this fashion until all storage places have been mapped and none have been skipped or duplicated. (See Sidebar Figure 1 on page 16.)

3. Shelves (sometimes referred to as rows) must be numbered or lettered from the lowest shelf, the one closest to the floor, first, to the highest shelf, the one closest to the ceiling, last.

4. Bins on shelves (sometimes referred to as slots) must be numbered or lettered from the left to the right within each individual section.

5. At the time of the initial layout of any storage area, careful thought must be given to the overall

bulk of the merchandise to be placed on a shelf. The overall dimensions of the merchandise: its height, width, length, and weight are important considerations. Another consideration is the volume of usage during the storage time and how that volume affects the maximum quantity to be stored. This is necessary to allow enough height between shelves and enough width for bins on a given shelf so the merchandise will fit properly and will allow easy maneuvering during the rotation process. The strength, in terms of weight load capacity and durability, of the shelving is another very important consideration.

6. Once the areas, sections, shelves, and bins have been decided on, they must be documented on a "map" of each area and posted as a reference for storage personnel.

7. Once created, each address must be labeled with its location address description and the description of the specific merchandise belonging in this address.

Typical storage areas in a large foodservice organization could be: **P**roduce, **D**airy, **M**eat, **F**reezer, **G**rocery (Dry Storage), **B**eer, **W**ine, **L**iquor (Spirits), and General **S**upplies, and **C**leaning Chemicals, etc. Each storage area name can then have its own letter distinguishable from the others and yet have individual meaning without duplication (e.g., **P** for **P**roduce).

Sections or column areas are usually distinguishable by the upright support structure that supports the shelves of a storage unit and can serve as a natural division point to establish the identification of one section or column area from another.

The importance of shelves being numbered sequentially from the lowest shelf starting with number one to the highest shelf having the highest number is in case more storage shelves are added in some future point in time, the logical numbering sequence will be intact.

Each bin on a shelf must be labeled with its number or letter and must also have the additional location address label with the complete address location as well as the description of the specific merchandise that is to be placed there (in its home location) for storage.

The Identification Legend

Given a six-digit combination of numbers and letters for the code, alternating between letters and numbers, and setting up divisions using a dash to separate the components of area/room, section/column, shelf/row, and bin/slot, an identifying address location description would look like this: **P-01-A-01** (**P** the area/room, **01** the section/column, **A** the shelf/row, and **01** the bin/slot) To explain: **P** the storage area [room] for **P**roduce occupies the first position, and this position has the defined total potential of 26 lettered storage areas. **01** in the section [column] position represents the first section to the left as one enters the storage area for produce and there can be up to 99 numbered section/columns in each of the storage areas. **A** in the shelf [row] position represents the first or lowest shelf in section/column A in the produce storage area and there can be up to 26 lettered shelves/rows in each section/column. **01** in the bin [slot] position represents the first position on the shelf starting from the left (within the section) to the right, and there are up to 99 numbered bin/slot positions available on each shelf.

STOREROOM ORGANIZATION (continued)

Address Location Coding Examples:

Area/Room	(letters used—26 available)	**P**roduce	**G**rocery
Section/Column	(numbers used—99 available)	Section **01**	Section **21**
Shelf/Row	(letters used—26 available)	Shelf **A**	Shelf **D**
Bin/Slot	(numbers used—99 available)	Bin **01**	Bin **03**
Code Format:	**X – XX – X – XX**	**P – 01 – A – 01**	**G – 21 – D – 03**

Labels posted at an address location would look something like this:

P – 01 – A – 01   **G – 21 – D – 03**

Tomatoes 6 × 5 × 240 – 42# Avg / cs   or   **Catsup HEINZ, Plst Btls 24 / 12oz / cs**

P-01-A-01 is the first position in the Produce storage area. Under the sheet to shelf and shelf to sheet concept, it would be the first item listed on the inventory count sheets. If *Tomatoes 6 x 5 x 2 40-42#Avg/cs* were to be stored there then the printed inventory count sheet might look like this:

Line	Location	Item Description	Count
1	**P – 01 – A – 01**	**Tomatoes 6 × 5 × 240 – 42# Avg / cs**	_____
2	**P – 01 – A – 02**	**Cantaloupe 6 count 10 – 12# / cs**	_____

P – 01 – A – 02 would be the next position and also listed next on the printed inventory count sheets along with the specific item description belonging to this address, and so on.

The Individual Storage Area Map and Route

For training and reference purposes, a map with the route, or path, documented on it must be conspicuously posted on the entry door or near the entry of the Area/Room. There must be individual maps for each Area/Room as not all will be the same. The route, or path that is taken, is to ensure that all items have been counted, that no items have been missed, and that no items have been duplicated during the inventory process. The documentation of the route or path is important for others who are not familiar with the starting point and ending point. In larger storage areas there may be several subsections of the process where there is stop and restart before the final end point. Sidebar Figure 1 shows the route that would be followed to help ensure the accurate documentation of an inventory.

The Product Rotation Process (Date, Vendor Code, Face, Rotate, and Place)

For the purposes of proper product rotation, and to effectively aid in using the first in, first out concept so important with food products, storeroom employees must be trained to **date** the product and ideally put a **vendor code** on the product as well. For best results, the date the product was received should be documented, using a marker, on or near the product label of the item, along with a vendor code. When the product is placed on the shelf in its home address the label with the date and vendor code must be facing outward in full view. Before actually placing the product, employees should be trained to observe the dates of any existing product on the shelf. The older dated product should be moved out of the way, placing the newer dated product on the bottom or in back and then replace the older dated product in front of or on top of the newer dated product so that it will be retrieved first at the time of issue thus enforcing in the utilization of the first in, first out concept.

STOREROOM ORGANIZATION (continued)

With the "*Date, Vendor Code, Face, Rotate, and Place*" concept, each organization must develop its own code system for their individual vendor codes. Great care should be exercised when deciding on the codes to make them brief and to avoid possible duplication. Also a legend of the codes must be posted as a referral and for training purposes. The purpose of the vendor code on the product is to aid in communication back to a given vendor. Should there be any concern or challenge with the product, management will know which vendor organization to communicate with as not all the products may have been purchased from the same vendor. Also, should there be a product recall from a vendor, the correct product from the correct vendor can be easily identified and removed. Examples of vendor coding might be **GFS** for **G**et **F**resh **S**ales, **USF** for **U.S. F**oodservice, **GBB** for **G**reat **B**uns **B**akery, **AD** for **A**nderson **D**airy and so on.

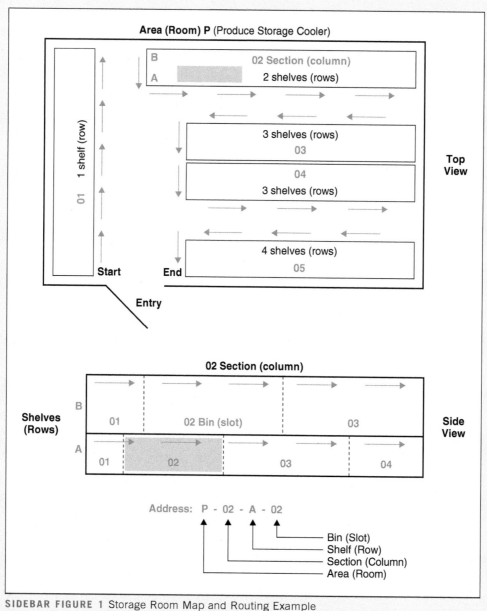

SIDEBAR FIGURE 1 Storage Room Map and Routing Example

EXERCISING TIGHT CONTROL OVER THE STOCK AND ANALYZING THE VALUE OF STORAGE MANAGEMENT PROCEDURES

■ Tight Control Over the Stock

Tight control exists when only a few persons are authorized to withdraw items from the store-room. It also exists when effective and efficient security precautions prevail. These **inventory control** and **security** aspects are, perhaps, the most important parts of the storeroom manager's job. Unfortunately, many operations neglect them. It is also true that many operations do not have storeroom managers.

Some operations with no specific storeroom person manage to have excellent product costs with **open storerooms**. These firms, however, limit storeroom entry to persons who are under close, continuous supervision. Commonly, these firms also maintain minimal stocks so that pilferage is more noticeable to supervisors. In some cases, only small **working storerooms** are open to employees, and large storerooms that are used to stock the working storerooms are accessible only to a limited number of management personnel.

Ideally, when a storeroom manager is present, he or she issues items only to authorized persons and only when they present an official stock requisition. A stock requisition is a formal request made by a user for the items needed to carry out necessary tasks (see Figures 13.4 and 13.5). The primary purposes of stock requisitions are to control who gets the items and to record how much of an item is issued and when it is issued.

The control is not over the storage stock alone, but also extends, to some degree, to the in-process inventories. For example, if the requisitioner (the user) has to note how much of an item is currently held in the in-process inventory, he or she would hesitate to requisition too much, thereby preventing in-process items from slipping to the back of the shelf, eventually to spoil (see Figure 13.5).

The accountant or bookkeeper might use the requisitions to calculate product costs by adding up all the food requisitions and direct purchases for the week and using this computation as the week's food cost. This procedure can be reasonably accurate if operators set strict par stocks on all items in the in-process inventory.

Some operators hold the accountant responsible for issues, not only for the purpose of calculating product costs, but also for serving as an additional check on the receiver or storeroom manager. This approach is impractical for small firms, even though it is theoretically sound to have a separate person responsible for each operating activity.

The issuing activity is, as you can imagine, time consuming, especially if requisitioners can drop in any time. Some operations allow the storeroom to issue goods only at certain times during the day. In some operations, the users must prepare their requisitions in the morning, send them electronically to the storeroom manager's computer or put them in the storeroom manager's mailbox, and then wait for the storeroom manager to deliver the items

> **inventory control** and **security** Procedures used by hospitality operators to ensure that the quality and cost of all items in storage areas are maintained according to company standards. Usually involves environmental controls such as proper temperature, humidity, and ventilation as well as the use of security methods such as web cams, physical barriers, and strict accounting procedures.
>
> **open storeroom** An unlocked storage facility that can be accessed by employees as needed. Usually contains the less-expensive foods, beverages, and nonfood supplies.
>
> **working storeroom** Refers to a storage area that is kept open during the shift to allow employees to enter as needed to retrieve products.

	No. 873

Date _____   Page _____ of _____

Department _____

Requested by _____

1	2	3	4	5
Item	Amount Requested (in units)	Unit Cost	Extended Value	Other Information
			col. 2 × col. 3	such as: How much of the item is in process? What's the forecasted usage of the item?

Signature of
requisitioner _____

Requisition
filled by _____

FIGURE 13.4 A stock requisition.

on a predetermined schedule. If users run out of items during their shift, some member of management may enter the locked storage facilities; complete a stock requisition, time permitting; and take the necessary items to the users. If time is precious, the manager may complete the necessary forms a little later.

In the rare situations, in which each user picks up a complete par stock from the storeroom manager at the beginning of the shift and then returns what is left at the end of the shift, the time spent filling out and processing forms might be reduced considerably.

Additional control is achieved when the storeroom manager issues exact amounts of ingredients needed for either one day or one shift. For instance, a storeroom employee may weigh out the ingredients according to the recipes to be prepared during the shift. (When this is common practice, the storeroom usually houses an area referred to as the **ingredient room** to do this type of work.)

ingredient room Area set aside in the main storeroom where an employee measures out all the ingredients needed for all the recipes to be prepared during the shift, and then issues them to the appropriate kitchen locations.

FIGURE 13.5 Stock requisitions by type.

■ A Value Analysis of Storage Management Procedures

Proper storage management has never been a hallmark of the hospitality industry. This has resulted in unnecessary merchandise loss. Nevertheless, we can sympathize with managers faced with potentially large storage management costs.

It costs a great deal of money, time, and effort to adequately manage inventories. In most large operations, receiving, inspecting, storing, tracking, and properly issuing merchandise constitute a full-time job. However, when you compare an easily noticed cost with a relatively hazy benefit, it is no wonder that most operators have forgone systematic storage management techniques. The issue becomes cloudier when we add the customer dissatisfaction that can arise because of stale or spoiled products resulting from improper storage management.

Large operations have more to gain by employing a full-time receiver–storeroom manager. They can usually afford more personnel, and the potential savings can translate into many dollars for them. Small operators, in contrast, face a bigger dilemma. No one can really blame them for refusing to spend several hundred dollars per month managing the storage function. Clearly, these operators need control as much as anyone, but what they truly need is some sort of truncated method of storage management that is reasonably effective yet fairly economical.

Our suggestions for these small operators follow: (1) Use one-stop shopping to significantly reduce the number of deliveries. (2) Have the owner–manager, or assistant, receive and inspect all incoming merchandise; send expensive items to the main storage facilities and less expensive items to the production areas—that is, to the in-process inventory. (3) Have the owner–manager, or assistant, issue par stocks of the expensive items to the users—the cooks, housekeepers, bartenders, and servers—at the beginning of their shifts. (4) Lock the main storage facilities. (5) If additional expensive items are needed during the shift, have the owner–manager, or assistant, retrieve them. (6) At the end of the shift, have the owner–manager, or assistant, open the main storage facilities to accept the expensive items that were not used during the shift. (7) Have the owner–manager, or assistant, record the number of expensive items used during the shift, and pass this information along to the bookkeeper, who will compare what was used during the shift with what was sold. This comparison procedure is sometimes

critical-item inventory analysis Reconciling the critical-item inventory daily usage with the daily sales recorded in the POS system. Discrepancies between what was used and what was sold must be resolved.

product analysis Evaluating various products to determine which one represents the best value. Alternately, another term for critical-item inventory analysis.

auditing the inventory sales Process whereby a supervisor or manager compares inventory that has been used in production to the sales records. Ideally, the amount missing would be recorded as sold to customers.

referred to as a **critical-item inventory analysis** or **product analysis**. It is also sometimes referred to as **auditing the inventory sales**, that is, calculating the amount of sales that should have been recorded and collected for based on the amount of inventory that is missing. If the comparison reveals a significant difference between what is missing and what was sold, the owner–manager, or assistant, must diagnose the cause of this problem and correct it as soon as possible.

Operators will have to devote some time to these procedures, but much less than more complete inventory control methods. This system can be very useful, assuming that management supports and enforces it. Moreover, we see no reason why it would not work for every operator. It should grant small operators an additional element of control because it is certainly a constructive alternative to leaving storage facilities open and unattended most of the time.

Of course, this system has a couple of disadvantages: (1) it must be done regularly; that is, you cannot miss a day, and (2) it requires adequate physical space, refrigerators, and freezers to hold in-process inventories; otherwise, the owner–manager must run back and forth to the locked storage facilities too frequently. This can create stress, so that, in time, he or she may leave the main storeroom open.

We have not directly addressed the cost-benefit analysis of storage management procedures. Any such analysis ultimately rests on the analyst's interpretation of relevant costs and benefits, however, as does every other economic analysis. Unfortunately, the analysis fails to incorporate such noncash benefits as smooth operations and a no-nonsense image that investors and employees appreciate. In the end, management must decide the appropriateness of accepted storage management principles. It is not an easy decision, but few important managerial decisions are.

Key Words and Concepts

Auditing the inventory sales	Open storeroom
Bin card	Perpetual inventory
Critical-item inventory analysis	Physical inventory
Direct purchase	Pilferage
Health district storage requirements	Product analysis
Ingredient room	Reduced oxygen packaged (ROP)
In-process inventory	foods
Inventory control and security	Skimming
Inventory shrinkage	Spoilage
Inventory usage rates	Stock requisition
Issuing procedure	Storage space
Management information system (MIS)	Theft
Managing storage facilities	Theoretical inventory value
National Restaurant Association	Transfer slip
Educational Foundation (NRAEF)	Working storeroom

Questions and Problems

1. List the objectives of storage management. What is normally needed to achieve these objectives?

2. What are the typical storeroom manager's activities? Which one do you feel is most important? Why?

3. Briefly describe how a perpetual-inventory system works.

4. In most operations, it is too expensive to maintain a perpetual inventory for all items. Note an item you think would be very beneficial to keep on a perpetual-inventory basis. Explain your reasoning.

5. What is one of the main purposes of taking a month-end physical inventory?

6. What are some ways of shortening the inventory-taking procedure? Which seems best? Which seems worst? Why?

7. Assume that you own a small table-service restaurant. Annual sales are approximately $1.2 million. Should you hire a separate receiver–storeroom manager? What are the potential costs and benefits? If you do not have a specific employee for this job, which other employee(s) could normally perform the receiving and storage duties?

8. Assume that a storeroom manager notices that a shipment received by the receiving agent had an accompanying invoice with the notation "Direct Purchase" stamped on it. What should the storeroom manager do with this shipment?

Questions and Problems (continued)

9. What is the main difference between theft and pilferage?

10. Match the following list of products to their proper storage temperatures. Temperatures can be used more than once.

    Products   Temperatures

    1. Meat and Poultry   a. 41° F

    2. Canned Goods   b. 41–70° F

    3. ROP Foods   c. 50–70°F

    4. Fresh Fruit   d. 45°F

    5. Shellfish

11. What are the advantages and disadvantages of computerized inventory management procedures?

12. Define or briefly explain the following terms:

    a. Skimming   i. Working storeroom
    b. Bin card   j. Health district storage requirements
    c. Theoretical inventory value   k. In-process inventory
    d. Full-case inventory-taking procedure   l. Credit for employee meals
    e. Stock requisition   m. Open storeroom
    f. Ingredient room   n. Par stocks
    g. Inventory sales   o. Authorized access to storage areas
    h. Shoplifting   p. Critical-item inventory analysis

13. If the beginning food inventory is $12,500, the food purchases are $40,000, and the food cost is $47,500, what is the ending food inventory (dollar amount)?

14. Given the following data, compute the food cost percentage:

    Total sales: $500,000
    Food sales: 75 percent of total sales
    Beverage sales: 25 percent of total sales
    Beginning food inventory: $25,000
    Ending food inventory: $30,000
    Total food purchases: $200,000
    Employee meal cost: $6,000

Experiential Exercises

1. Contact a hotel manager, and ask permission to observe a physical-inventory procedure. Ask the manager to discuss the inventory-taking process, its purposes, and how the information is used. Prepare a one-page report that includes your observations and the manager's comments.

2. Ask the manager of a local hospitality operation if you can evaluate the storage areas and prepare a draft report that evaluates the operation's storage areas based on the following criteria. If possible, have the manager review your draft, and include his/her comments in your report.
   a. Adequate space
   b. Adequate temperature and humidity
   c. Adequate equipment
   d. Proximity of storage area to receiving and production areas
   e. Proper maintenance
   f. Proper security
   g. Competent personnel
   h. Sufficient time given to storeroom employees to perform the necessary duties
   i. Proper storeroom regulations

3. Ask the manager of a local hospitality operation if you can evaluate the storage areas to develop a recommendation for a storeroom organization system as described in the sidebar by Daniel Celeste. Design the organization system. Present the manager with your ideas and get his/her feedback on it.

 ## References

1. NCR Hospitality, "12 Days of Improved Restaurant Operations—Day 9: Theft," December 19, 2011, http://blogs.ncr.com/hospitality/hospitality/12-days-of-improved -restaurant-operations-day-9-theft/. See also Jill Poulston, "Rationales for Employee Theft in the Hospitality Industry," *Journal of Hospitality and Tourism Management*, January 1, 2008, www.thefreelibrary.com/_/print/PrintArticle.aspx?id=196382606. See also Statistic Brain, "Employee Theft Statistics," September 8, 2012, www.statisticbrain .com/employee-theft-statistics/.

2. M. C. Warfel and Marion L. Cremer, *Purchasing for Food Service Managers*, 5th ed. (Berkeley, CA: McCutchan Publishing, 2005). See also Anonymous, "Hotel Design and Space Allocation," April 16, 2011, http://facilityplanning.wordpress.com/2011/04/16/ hotel-design-and-space-allocation/. See also, Anonymous, "Design Guide for Hotels," www.scribd.com/doc/7151503/Design-Guide-for-Hotels.

References (continued)

3. *ServSafe® Coursebook*, 6th ed. (Chicago, IL: National Restaurant Association, 2013).

4. STR, Inc., "HOST Almanac 2016 for the year 2015," Retrieved from https://www.str.com/Media/Default/Samples/HOSTAlmanac_Highlights.pdf

5. B. Hagar, "The Importance of Scheduled Maintenance," *Foodservice Equipment & Supplies*, 63, no. 1 (2010):36, http://ezproxy.library.unlv.edu/login?url=http://search.proquest.com/docview/235171515?accountid=3611.

SECURITY IN THE PURCHASING FUNCTION

The Purpose of This Chapter

After reading this chapter, you should be able to:

- Discuss why security is important in the hospitality industry.

- Describe the security problems associated with the purchasing function.

- Identify methods used to prevent security problems related to suppliers.

- Identify methods used to prevent security problems related to employees.

- Examine methods used to prevent security problems related to facilities and the owner–manager's role in the security process.

THE NEED FOR SECURITY

Several years ago, many hospitality operators considered theft and pilferage manageable costs of doing business and routinely added a slight markup to menu and room prices to compensate for these losses. In fact, credit card companies supposedly continue these practices today. Because of increased competitive pressure and shrinking profit margins, however, the hospitality industry has become more concerned about these problems.

This concern with security should come as no surprise. After all, it is estimated that employees steal as much as $40 billion a year from their employers.[1] More startling facts of employee theft include the following:

- It is estimated that nearly one-third of all bankruptcies are caused by employee theft.[2]

- Hospitality businesses are said to lose $142.49 per guest theft incident and $737.31 per employee theft incident.[3]

- The National Restaurant Association estimates that employee theft costs about $218 per employee per year.[3]

- The 20/20/60 rule applies to employee theft: 20 percent will never steal, 20 percent will always steal, and 60 percent will steal given the right opportunity.[3]

- Nearly 47 percent of all missing inventory is a result of employee theft.[4]

- The National Restaurant Association estimates 3 percent of annual sales are lost to employee theft.[4]

- According to the National Restaurant Association, employee theft costs the industry roughly $8.5 billion per year.[5]

- Seventy-five percent of inventory missing in restaurants is from theft.[6]

The heightened interest in security found in the foodservice industry can be attributed to at least four factors: (1) hospitality operators find it increasingly difficult to pass on security losses to the consumer in the form of higher menu and room prices; (2) in general, the public has become more security conscious; (3) the cost of insurance coverage has skyrocketed; and (4) a good deal of unfavorable publicity has focused on the hospitality purchasing function.

> **accept gifts**   Usually refers to buyers accepting something of value from suppliers for their personal use.

Much of this unfavorable publicity centers on the willingness of purchasing agents to **accept gifts** and other economic favors. For example, a former executive of the largest Dunkin' Donut franchise group was arrested for taking nearly $400,000 in an elaborate kickback scheme.[7] A federal undercover agent was sentenced to two years in prison after accepting $30,000 in kickbacks.[8] A former manager for Kraft Foods, Inc. pled guilty to taking bribes totaling $158,000 from a tomato processor.[9] And in case you think today's employees are the only ones who steal, two well-known celebrities of the nineteenth century, César Ritz (said to be the greatest hotelman ever) and Auguste Escoffier (said to be the "king of chefs, and the chef to kings"), "were sacked for stealing from the hotel larder and taking kickbacks from food purveyors, to the tune of roughly $20,000."[10]

Theft and pilferage are probably no more common today than they were in the past, but they certainly have been more widely publicized. This notoriety has forced hospitality operators to reexamine their attitudes toward security. Management is no longer willing to dismiss theft, fraud, pilferage, and shoplifting as minor problems.

Security has, of course, always been important in the hospitality business. However, it can be difficult to provide adequate security, particularly in the service areas and those areas that customers frequent because physical facilities are not always designed with security in mind. Security can be more of a consideration during the designing of storage areas, but it often must take a back seat in dining rooms, lounges, front offices, and other public areas.

In many respects, however, buyers can enforce a good measure of security in their realm of responsibility. The activities and duties of buyers, receivers, and storeroom managers, among others, are hidden from public view. If desired, management can set policies that go so far as to resemble an armed-camp atmosphere in the receiving and storage areas of the hospitality operation.

SECURITY PROBLEMS

Several potential **security problems** arise in connection with purchasing, receiving, storing, and issuing, and an owner–manager must be on guard against them. The major ones are discussed next.

■ Kickbacks

A buyer, or user–buyer, could easily collude with a supplier, salesperson, or driver. The operation could, thus, pay for a superior product but receive inferior merchandise, while the buyer and accomplices pocket the difference between the as-purchased (AP) prices. This difference is referred to as a **kickback**.

Sometimes two or more conspirators "pad an invoice," that is, add on a phony charge. This is a form of kickback that requires the cooperative efforts of at least two thieves.

A form of kickback also occurs when a conspirator sends an invoice that has already been paid to the bookkeeper, who pays it again. The thieves then pocket the payment.[11]

Another form of kickback happens when supposedly defective incoming merchandise is "returned" (returned to the thieves, that is, who hope that the bookkeeper will forget or ignore this transaction).

Much the same kind of kickback occurs when **short orders** or **incomplete shipments** are delivered or when half of an order is delivered in the morning, with the other half promised in the afternoon—the afternoon that never comes. Again, the thieves depend on the bookkeeper or management to overlook the shortage.

security problems
Challenges that make it difficult to safeguard people and property. The major ones relevant to the selection and procurement function include kickbacks, invoice scams, supplier and receiver error, inventory theft, inventory padding, inventory substitutions, telephone and e-mail scams, inability to segregate operating activities, and suspicious behavior.

kickback An illegal gift given by a vendor or sales rep to someone if he or she will agree to help defraud the hospitality operation.

short orders See incomplete shipments.

incomplete shipments Deliveries that do not have all of the items ordered by the buyer. The missing items may be back ordered, or the supplier may have forgotten to include them with the shipments.

Perhaps the most common type of kickback happens when the buyer agrees to pay a slightly higher AP price than necessary and, unknown to the owner–manager, receives an under-the-table payment from the supplier. The payment sometimes comes in the form of merchandise, such as a new watch, or may be in the form of tickets to a basketball game or concert. This collusion is extremely difficult to detect, especially when, overall, the product costs appear to be in line.

Keep in mind one important point about kickbacks: although the hospitality operator usually loses, the honest supplier also loses if salespersons or drivers conspire with receivers, buyers, or bookkeepers. It is difficult, however, for continuing theft to go undetected if the supplier is honest, being constantly alert to these practices. Thus, the supplier's management and the buyer's management have the same interests at heart.

■ Invoice Scams

A problem related to kickbacks occurs when someone diverts a bill payment to a fictitious company or a fictitious account. The conspirators then pocket the payment. Similarly, someone

fictitious invoices
Fraudulent bill sent to a company with the hope that the company will not check it closely and just pay it along with all the other bills it receives. May be part of a kickback scheme.

invoice scams Using fraudulent invoices to steal from a company.

might present a **fictitious invoice** to the bookkeeper, which the bookkeeper pays—and mails directly to the thief's post office box.

At first glance, it would seem difficult for a buyer to set up an **invoice scam**. However, even the largest hospitality companies are not immune to this type of fraud. For instance, a school superintendent used fake invoices and vendors to steal almost $300,000 from the school district. He solicited the money from school boosters during fundraisers.[12]

The Better Business Bureau and "Lectric Law Library" provide considerable information on phony invoice schemes, including invoice scams, solicitations as invoices, phony ad solicitations, and bogus yellow page bills.

■ Supplier and Receiver Error

Incoming invoices must be checked for arithmetic errors. It is surprising how many unintentional mistakes occur, but intentional mistakes are also possible. These could be a form of kickback. Either way, the loss is the same.

Several other more or less unintentional mistakes can occur. Most of them are relatively minor, but in the long run, little losses add up. Some of the typical errors are (1) losing credit for container deposits or returned merchandise; (2) receiving a substitute item of a slightly lower quality than that ordered and failing to issue a request for credit memo, or otherwise ensuring that the cost difference is corrected; (3) receiving the wrong items unintentionally (such as receiving bulk butter instead of butter pats); and (4) weighing items with an inaccurate scale.

■ Inventory Theft

To prevent inventory theft, operators should restrict access to all storage areas and receiving facilities. Only authorized persons should be allowed to enter these areas. Furthermore, these areas should be locked when not in use.

The most common type of **inventory shrinkage** is pilferage by employees. Restricted access can reduce pilferage opportunities. Adequate supervision in the production and service areas of the hospitality operation also can reduce or eliminate pilferage and shoplifting opportunities.

inventory shrinkage
The inappropriate loss or removal of supplies.

■ Inventory Padding

Recall from Chapter 13 our discussion of the physical-inventory-taking process, and that one of the reasons for doing this was to compute various product costs. For example, the formula used to compute the actual food cost for the month is

> **Beginning inventory**
> + **Purchases**
> = **Food available for sale**
> − **Ending inventory**
> − **Other credit (e.g., food used for employee meals)**
> = **Cost of food sold**

If the beginning inventory is $12,000, the purchases are $20,000, the ending inventory is $14,000, and the other credit is $2,000, the actual food cost is $16,000:

$$\$12,000 + \$20,000 - \$14,000 - \$2,000 = \$16,000$$

Suppose a food supervisor wants to reduce this food-cost figure to earn a greater performance bonus. An easy way, but an illegal way, is to increase the ending inventory amount, that is, to "pad" the inventory so that top management believes that the supervisor produced a highly favorable food cost for the month. (Notice that, in this example, if the ending inventory were artificially inflated to $15,000, the cost of food sold would drop to $15,000 from $16,000.) Unless management supervises the inventories carefully, a person could easily steal the merchandise and alter the inventory records, and no one would ever uncover the **inventory padding** unless an independent audit was conducted.[13]

inventory padding
Reporting a false inventory amount by indicating that there is more inventory on hand. A fraud that is usually committed to make the actual cost of food sold appear to be less than it is.

■ Inventory Substitutions

In hospitality operations with an open-storeroom policy, it is relatively easy for an employee to remove high-quality merchandise and substitute inferior goods. The employee can consume the stolen merchandise or can sell it on the black market. The potential security problem of **inventory substitution** is similar to inventory padding in that an independent audit may be needed to uncover it.

inventory substitution
Occurs when someone takes a product and leaves behind a different one. Typically done by persons who steal a high-quality item and substitute a low-quality one in its place.

■ Telephone and E-Mail Sales Scams

All companies are susceptible to telephone solicitors who use illegal tactics and high-pressure selling techniques to defraud buyers. Salespersons may attempt **backdoor selling** and offer free gifts and other inducements to clinch a sale.

backdoor selling   This happens when a sales rep bypasses the regular buyer and goes to some other employee, such as the lead line cook, to make a sales pitch. The cook then exerts pressure on the buyer to make the purchase.

A common type of telephone fraud involves offers of sweet deals on replacement toner used for copying machines and laser printers. These telephone solicitors, sometimes referred to as

toner-phoner   Term used to identify a scam artist who contacts people and misleads them into purchasing junk merchandise for a high price. A typical scam is to call and offer to sell printer toner for a bargain-basement price, hence the term toner-phoner.

toner-phoners, typically portray themselves as representing major supply houses offering once-in-a-lifetime low prices, although the unsuspecting buyer usually receives watered-down merchandise and high service charges. Another version of this scam involves convincing an employee to accept a "free promotional item" as a gift. Along with this gift the supplier would also send unordered product and an invoice asking for payment for the product. According to the Federal Trade Commission, "If you receive supplies or bills for services you didn't order, you don't have to pay, and you don't have to return the unordered merchandise. You may treat unordered merchandise as a gift."[14] The buyer must make sure to communicate with the accounting department whenever an unauthorized and unordered shipment arrives at the buyer's doorstep to let it know not to pay the invoice. If this shipment is paid for, it is unlikely that the buyer will ever get the money back.

E-mail is certainly the ideal medium for perpetrating these same types of sales scams on unsuspecting hospitality operators. The rapid growth of e-mail scams can be attributed to the fact that sending large quantities of unsolicited e-mail is relatively inexpensive. It is also much more difficult for authorities to trace these e-mail solicitors, as many of them operate overseas and use sophisticated programming techniques to mask their true identities.

More information on common scams that are being perpetrated against small businesses can be seen at the National Fraud Information Center and Internet Scambusters.

■ Inability to Segregate Operating Activities

segregate operating activities   Separating activities and assigning them to different persons and/or departments. For instance, it is common to separate the buyer from the person authorized to pay the bills. A security measure enacted to minimize the ability of employees to engage in fraudulent activities at the expense of their employers and/or customers.

Ideally, a hospitality operation separates the buying, receiving, storing, and bill-paying procedures. Usually, a separate person pays the bills, but this is not always the case with the other operating activities. This is known as **segregate operating activities**.

The most common potential problem is the buyer, or user–buyer, who both orders and receives the products. There is nothing inherently wrong with this practice, but it can enable buyers to order one item and receive another, which may be inferior. Even worse, buyers can substitute inferior merchandise for the ordered products, converting the better products for their own use.

Nevertheless, buyers who receive are common in the hospitality industry, usually because: (1) they are the only ones who can recognize the various product quality standards (this is especially true of buyers who command an expertise in an area in which the rest of the staff has little knowledge, such as wine stewards); (2) the buyer must do other things to justify time spent on the job (buying may not be enough work); and (3) management just cannot afford to hire a separate receiver.

■ Suspicious Behavior

A variety of employee behaviors call for management scrutiny. The owner–manager should be wary of employees who: (1) seem unduly friendly with suppliers, salespersons, or drivers;

(2) hang around storage areas for no reason; (3) needlessly handle keys or locks; (4) make too many trips to the garbage area, bathroom, locker room, or parking lot (perhaps to move stolen merchandise); (5) requisition abnormally large amounts of supplies; (6) make frequent trips to the storage areas for no apparent good reason; (7) have relatives working for the suppliers; (8) stray from their assigned workstations too frequently; (9) are seen passing packages to guests; (10) are seen stuffing boxes or packages under a couch in a public area, which a conspirator may pick up later; (11) permit drivers to loiter in unauthorized areas; and (12) have visitors on the work site. The list could go on. Because many employees cannot be restricted to one work area, theft and pilferage opportunities are always a part of the workplace.

In general, an owner–manager can take three main steps to prevent security breaches: (1) select honest suppliers, (2) employ honest employees, and (3) design the physical facilities so that tight, effective security conditions can be maintained. In most cases, hospitality operators fall short in attempting to arm themselves with these three basic weapons in the fight against crime. Operators must learn to work, instead, with the resources available to them. Nevertheless, all operators can take several specific steps to prevent theft and pilferage.

PREVENTING SECURITY PROBLEMS—SUPPLIERS AND ACCOUNTING AND INVENTORY PROCEDURES

It is difficult to assess the honesty of potential suppliers. Even if they are willing to talk about dishonesty, the most that they usually say is, "We don't do anything like that." The dishonest suppliers, salespersons, or drivers would hardly be willing to admit it. It is useful, though, to ask other hospitality operators for their advice. Whatever report an owner–manager receives on a supplier, it must be remembered that bad practices may have been corrected. As with so much else, management's own informed judgment must be the guide.

1. The owner–manager should **document cash paid-outs** carefully. Be certain that the driver receiving them initials the copy of the invoice properly. A canceled check always is the preferred receipt, but the convenience of paid-outs is important to many small operators. Nevertheless, operators must be certain that their accounts are credited properly.

   > **document cash paid-outs**
   > Maintaining a record of all cash removed from petty cash or from a cash register.

2. The owner–manager should never pay an invoice that shows a post office box number as the supplier's address without checking further. For that matter, do not pay a bill unless the supplier's name and address are familiar, but it is the box number that is more suspicious. If employees are trying to cheat by sending fraudulent invoices to the bookkeeper, a box number can be the tip-off.

3. Those who buy should never pay the bills. A buyer who pays may be tempted to pay himself or herself once in a while.[15] Most large companies require the manager to verify all invoices for payment and then forward them to the central accounting office at company headquarters. Someone at headquarters then pays. Small firms can copy this practice to some degree by separating the buying and paying functions.

4. The owner–manager should cancel paperwork on all completed transactions. At the very least, operators should mark an invoice paid or punch a series of holes in the invoice as soon as they pay it so that this same invoice will not be paid again.

In addition to canceling all documentation, make sure it has been completed. For example, if part of a delivery must be returned, see to it that a request for credit memo is prepared or that credit for the return has been otherwise received.

As an added precaution, bill payers should compare the invoice with the original purchase order or other ordering record to ensure that they do not pay for nonexistent merchandise. If no purchase order copies exist, take steps to remedy this situation; it is just too easy to pay a fraudulent or padded invoice, particularly if the amount involved is relatively small.

Furthermore, be especially careful to compare the AP prices, delivery charges, and other costs noted on the invoice with those that were quoted earlier. The number of times the quotations are less than the prices noted on the invoices is surprising. In most instances, this probably represents an innocent mistake. However, if operators are not diligent in their comparisons, an unscrupulous supplier can earn a bit of extra income by bidding one price and charging another.

5. The owner–manager should arrange, now and then, for an independent audit of the hospitality organization's operating procedures. If done on a random, unannounced basis, an audit can be an excellent deterrent to theft and pilferage. The independent auditor should: (1) analyze invoices and payment checks to determine their accuracy, completeness, and consistency; (2) check the receiving routine and equipment; (3) inspect the storage facilities, taking a **physical inventory** and noting how consistent it is with the inventory figures recorded on accounting records; the physical inventory should also be consistent with the sales volume and purchase expenditures; (4) check receiving sheets and **stock requisitions** for consistency with invoices, purchase orders, and payment checks; (5) check consumption against reported units of sales—for example, compare the stock requisitions of steaks with guest checks in the dining room and the in-process inventory in the kitchen; and (6) if your company accepts coupons from guests (such as buy one, get one free), be sure to audit them as well. Managers of large operations could easily enter into the accounting system sales at the regular prices as coupon sales to adjust the inventory counts in their favor.

physical inventory An actual counting and valuing of all products kept in your hospitality operation.

stock requisition A formal request made by an employee for items needed to carry out necessary tasks. It is given to the person managing the storage facilities. A typical control document used by large hotels.

surprise audit A security strategy intended to deter theft and pilferage by hiring an outside firm to make unannounced inspections.

Surprise audits are used successfully in such other enterprises as banks, in which the audit team enters the premises, shuts down some teller windows, and begins the audit procedure. Operators cannot always shut down a hospitality facility, but a surprise audit can be performed during slow periods.

The surprise audit is undoubtedly a powerful control in terms of theft and pilferage. It can easily have the same effect on employees as a surprise integrity test. In addition, it is not unduly expensive. Most operations can easily afford such audits.

6. The owner–manager should try to eliminate collusion opportunities by separating the buying, receiving, storing, and issuing activities, even going as far as to separate the bookkeeping and bill-paying functions. This is good control, but it may be impractical for all but the largest firms.

   Some separation is, however, possible. For example, an owner–manager might ask an assistant manager to help the receiver–storeroom manager or the chef–buyer–receiver to inspect incoming merchandise. In addition, a surprise audit can go a long way toward achieving the type of control a complete separation of these operating activities usually affords.

7. An owner–manager should compare what is being paid to current suppliers with AP prices available from other suppliers for the same type of merchandise. It would, of course, be more reliable to compare edible-portion (EP) costs whenever possible because a premium AP price can be, as we have said, entirely justifiable under certain circumstances. An owner–manager must make the effort to compare AP prices periodically, however, because it is just too easy for buyers, or user–buyers, to pay just a little bit more for a kickback. This practice is extremely hard to discover, but it is essential not to overlook this all-too-tempting opportunity within the reach of most buyers.

8. The owner–manager should make sure that whoever pays the bills checks them over carefully. Sometimes a phony invoice gets slipped in. This is especially true with bills for regularly scheduled periodic services, such as waste removal. Another potential problem is receiving a solicitation that looks just like an invoice from a company. If the owner–manager is not careful, someone might honor the solicitation, thinking that it is just another bill that must be paid.

   If possible, the owner–manager should develop an **approved-payee list**, which is a list of names of individuals or companies eligible to receive payments from that firm. If a bill pops up and the supplier's name is not on the approved-payee list, the bill should not be paid unless management personally approves.

   > **approved-payee list**
   > A list of all persons and companies that are allowed to receive any sort of payment from you. An excellent security precaution.

9. As much as possible (and without compromising quality), an owner–manager should take everything out of its shipping container before storing it. This practice minimizes the problem of inventory shrinkage due to theft.

   In addition, when an owner–manager takes a physical inventory, it should include actually lifting a few containers to make sure there is something inside. It is possible for someone to take a full one and leave an empty one or to substitute an inferior product.

10. The owner–manager should be leery of paying cash deposits. A supplier or, more commonly, someone who does remodeling work or other types of service will sometimes request a deposit. The owner–manager must be careful that this person does not take the deposit and skip town. This does not happen too often in the hospitality industry, but it does occur now and then with people who, for example, do some remodeling work and need some cash up front to buy their materials. Also, an owner–manager

could get stung sending away for something advertised in a trade paper: the sales advertisement may be disguising some sort of sham operation. Unless the owner–manager knows the suppliers and other vendors, payment should probably be avoided until the purchase is received.

> **house account** Term used by a vendor to identify a very loyal customer. A customer who continually buys from a vendor and is not interested in buying from competing vendors.

11. A hospitality operation might find it worthwhile to become a **house account** for one or more suppliers whose integrity it trusts completely. Although being a house account usually increases the AP prices a firm must pay, at least for some items, the operation is assured that its friends will not conspire with others to defraud the establishment.

12. Management must develop a procedure to prevent the possibility of unrecorded merchandise getting into the storage facilities or into the in-process inventory. For instance, nothing should be received unless an invoice accompanies it or unless the receiver records it somehow. If this is not done, there will be more stock in inventory than that recorded. Employees could somehow pilfer this excess inventory, and no one would be able to detect the problem. An old bartender's trick is to deliver personal bottles to the establishment, sell drinks made with the contents of these bottles, and pocket the cash.

13. When ordering merchandise, the owner–manager should make certain not to rush into purchasing products without researching the opportunity further. For instance, it is possible that a telephone salesperson can call unexpectedly, offering what at first might appear to be sterling goods. Some telephone solicitors may resort to deceptive practices.

    An owner–manager also might misinterpret, for example, an advertisement and end up ordering something through the mail not wanted. For instance, it is easy to mistakenly order an off-brand artificial sweetener packaged in blue-colored, individual packets, assuming the product is the nationally recognized Equal® brand merchandise.

14. The owner–manager should develop an **approved-supplier list** and instruct all persons who have ordering responsibilities to use the suppliers on the list. Of course, there are

> **approved-supplier list** A list of all vendors who buyers are allowed to purchase from. An excellent security precaution.

exceptions to any rule, but management must be informed if, for example, someone in the operation wishes to purchase something from an unfamiliar supplier. The owner–manager would want to investigate this supplier, utilizing the procedures discussed in Chapter 10, and then make a final decision regarding the admissibility of this supplier to the approved-supplier list.

    Using an approved-supplier list appears to be one of the most effective controls for such problems as kickbacks and other forms of skullduggery. The vast majority of large hospitality operations follow this practice.

15. The hospitality operator should avoid purchasing merchandise in small, single-service packages. These items are very easy to pilfer, although their convenience in terms of customer service may override the requisite need for greater security.

16. One of the most effective deterrents to theft and pilferage is to restrict access to all high-cost products. Although it is not always feasible to lock up everything, management must maintain close control over those items that represent the bulk of the purchase dollar.

17. The owner–manager should maintain close tabs on all expensive items throughout the production and service cycles. For instance, each day a manager should conduct a **critical-item inventory analysis** to balance the use of key, expensive ingredients with the stock requisitions and guest checks. The actual usage of these items and their expected (i.e., "standard") usage should be the same.

18. If affordable, management should adopt technology available to calculate the **theoretical-inventory value**, which is sometimes referred to as the **inventory "book" value**, so that it can be compared with the value determined by a physical-inventory count. Unlike hand-posted records, this type of software facilitates a quick, convenient compilation of bin card balances that, when compared with the physical-inventory count, will immediately highlight inventory control problems.

19. Management must ensure that access to all records is restricted to only those individuals who are authorized to make entries in those records or to those persons who must analyze them.

20. The owner–manager should not allow drivers to enter the premises or loiter in unauthorized areas unless their presence is necessary, such as for standing orders. Some of these agents merely want to be helpful by putting items in storage, but some may have sticky fingers. Furthermore, they tend to distract employees.

21. The owner–manager should not rush receivers. They should take their time and inspect all deliveries adequately, keeping in mind some of the common receiving problems we discussed in Chapter 12.

PREVENTING SECURITY PROBLEMS— EMPLOYEES

Ensuring employee honesty is no simple matter. Hospitality operators have trouble with pilferage for two reasons. First, many of the products they use can easily be converted into cash. Second, few hospitality operators do anything more than simply firing a dishonest employee. Having petty thieves arrested is uncommon, and as a result, except for getting fired, a thief has little to lose if caught.

Lately, however, more employers are beginning to prosecute dishonest employees and dishonest customers. If this becomes the rule, this type of swift, stern action should help minimize the number of dishonest people who are employed by hospitality enterprises.

1. An effective personnel recruiting and selection procedure is a hospitality operator's main weapon in the fight against employee theft and pilferage. One aspect of personnel selection that represents a highly controversial issue is the use of **background check** investigation,

---

critical-item inventory analysis Reconciling the critical item inventory daily usage with the daily sales recorded in the POS system. Discrepancies between what was used and what was sold must be resolved.

theoretical-inventory value What the inventory value is supposed to be, based on what you sold. For instance, if you had 100 steaks in inventory and the POS system says you sold 50, then there should be 50 steaks left. An actual count, though, may reveal that you have more or less than 50.

inventory "book" value The value of inventory that is supposed to be in storage, as recorded on inventory records, such as a bin card. The value is based primarily on perpetual inventory calculations.

background check Researching personal or company history, checking for things such as reliability, unethical behavior, criminal convictions, and so forth.

integrity testing Controversial method used to determine if a person is honest.

reference check Confirming the veracity of information and personal accomplishments provided by vendors and job candidates.

undercover agent or **spotter** A person hired to go undercover in a business to detect fraudulent actions perpetrated by employees. Sometimes referred to as a shopper, even though the two perform different services.

shoppers Persons whose jobs involve checking performance and service at retail and other businesses. These persons usually work for independent companies that provide mystery shopper services or secret shopper services.

quick response (QR) code A type of 2-D bar code used to provide easy access to information through a smart device. The device's owner points it at a QR code and opens a barcode reader app, which works in conjunction with the device's camera. The reader interprets the code, which typically contains a call to action such as an invitation to download a mobile application, a link to view a video, or an SMS message inviting the viewer to respond to a poll.

pre-employment testing Another term for pre-employment screening.

pre-employment screening Initial evaluation of job applicants to determine which one(s) should advance to the next step of the recruiting and hiring process. Alternately, determining which job applicants should be granted a job interview.

particularly the investigation involving the use of "integrity"—that is, "honesty"—tests or other similar reference-checking techniques. These tests are thought to be the most effective weapons in the war against theft and pilferage.

Integrity testing has become more popular primarily because employers cannot use polygraph machines or other similar devices to determine employee honesty during the recruiting and hiring stages. Any type of honesty testing, though, will be controversial because these types of tests are not completely accurate. Furthermore, many people feel that these tests, as well as pre-employment drug tests, are invasions of privacy.

Being certain that a new employee is honest is no simple or sure matter. **Reference checks** can tell what a previous employer knows—or what that employer wants to reveal—about past behavior. Stresses and strains could convert an honest employee to a dishonest one, however. Probably the best rule here is a cautious optimism about people, combined with a set of controls that make dishonesty difficult to engage in and relatively easy to check.[16]

These controls could involve the use of drug testing. A study by the Substance Abuse Mental Health Services Administration reported that in the hospitality industry, 9.3 percent of employees admitted to using illicit drugs in the past month, 17 percent admitted to using illicit drugs during the past year, and nearly 10 percent admitted to heavy alcohol use. Substance abuse is seen across all areas of the hospitality industry but is most frequently attributed to food preparers, groundskeepers, maids, waitstaff, and cleaning crews.[17] This growing problem can lead to important security and safety concerns that directly impact the staff, guests, and property.

An increasingly important security concern is the use and protection of employee, supplier, and guest information. Information technology, such as mobile and cloud-based systems, is particularly vulnerable to leaks. To provide maximum protection, employee policies and procedures should be updated to include changing technology.[18]

2. Hospitality employers do not use **undercover agents** as a rule in the back of the house. But **spotters**, or **shoppers**, are quite often used in the front of the house.[19] For instance, many bars pay a shopping service to periodically send around someone who, posing as a customer, observes all pertinent activities. This person then prepares a report for management, commenting on such factors as product quality, service, and an employee appearing to pocket cash illegally. A shopping service is relatively inexpensive and, like the surprise audit, represents a powerful crime deterrent.

Recently, some major multiunit foodservice operations supplemented mystery shoppers with customer survey systems. A few years ago, Red Lobster and Burger King introduced toll-free numbers listed on the receipts to allow customers to call and rate the establishment. Today, restaurants can solicit feedback through online surveys, smart device apps, and social media. A 2012 study found that quick service restaurants had a

25 percent increase in online surveys in just one year. Major chains such as Panda Express, McDonald's, Applebee's, and Pizza Hut offer discounts or free food for completing the surveys. Some, like Jason's Deli, may have iPads that guests can use for that purpose, whereas others encourage their customers to download an app or use a **quick response (QR) code**, a type of 2-D bar code used to access information from a smart device. Guests can write reviews of the restaurant or hotel in real-time through Facebook, Twitter, Yelp, TripAdvisor, Urbanspoon, and many other websites. These all generate much-needed feedback and can assist operators with finding out about security problems and other operating issues.[20]

3. If operators do not relish **pre-employment testing** (sometimes referred to as **pre-employment screening** or background checks) and are not satisfied with a surprise audit now and then, they can resort to a fidelity bonding company. A **bonding** company insures a hospitality operator against employee theft of cash. Not all employees are bonded, but cashiers usually are. The bonding company performs a thorough background check of all employees it insures. However, operators can conceivably bond everyone for the sole purpose of investigating each applicant (though this might prove a fairly expensive way of getting thorough background checks). In lieu of bonding, an operator could employ a less-expensive background-checking firm, which is sometimes referred to as a **résumé-checking service**, as an alternative.[21] Many major **payroll service companies** and **professional employer organizations (PEO)**—such as Automated Data Processing (ADP; and Paychex—also offer pre-employment screening services to their customers. These services typically include multiple types of employee testing and background checks.

Bonding is expensive. In addition, it tells you only about the past, not the future. Also, if a thief has never been caught, that person will obviously receive a clean bill of health from the bonding company. Moreover, you must first determine the legality of this activity. Some states and municipalities restrict background investigations of this type.

4. As much as possible, the operator should not let anyone who has no business being there remain in the back of the house. Friends of employees should be kept out of these areas. Salespersons and drivers cannot always be barred, but they can be restricted to certain places in the back of the house.

The owner–manager should restrict these people because, not only do they distract employees, but they also might try to establish some sort of pilfering arrangement with an unscrupulous employee. Moreover, the seeds of backdoor selling could find fertile ground.

5. If possible, an owner–manager should try not to hire employees who have relatives working for suppliers. Better to eliminate this and other similar conflicts of interest from the start.

bonding An insurance policy covering cash-handling employees. Alternately, refers to a performance bond, which is insurance taken out by a construction contractor that guarantees work will be done by a certain date or else the client will collect damages.

résumé-checking service Company that specializes in checking employment job applicants' references and verifying information provided by them. Employers, not job applicants, typically pay the fees for this service.

payroll service company Company that provides payroll processing and related activities for businesses that do not want to do this type of work themselves, preferring to outsource it to a firm that specializes in completing the tedious tasks associated with the payroll administrative function. This type of service is very popular with small hospitality operations.

professional employer organization (PEO) Firm that, for a fee, manages the human resources function for client companies. In addition, these types of firms typically join with client companies to become a co-employer. In effect, the client's employees become the employees of the PEO. This allows small clients, such as the typical hospitality operation, to enjoy relief from HR administrative tasks, improved employee benefits, increased employee productivity, and enhanced liability management services.

PREVENTING SECURITY PROBLEMS—FACILITIES AND THE OWNER–MANAGER'S ROLE

■ Facilities

Designing the physical facilities to ensure proper security is relatively easy in back-of-the-house storage facilities if the operation is being built from the ground up, or if the operation is undergoing extensive remodeling and the owner–manager can spare the necessary funds. Unfortunately, many existing operations have flaws that prevent tight security. These flaws are often impossible to correct or, if correctable, require large expenditures.

1. The owner–manager might consider investing in a trash compactor. A lot of stolen items are removed from the operation in trash cans, to be retrieved later by an off-duty employee or an accomplice. A compactor minimizes this opportunity.

2. Whenever possible, employees should be allowed to enter or leave the premises through only one door. This door should not be used to receive deliveries, unless there is some sure way of guarding and controlling access to it. If necessary, it is better to insist that employees use the front door; the same door customers use. As irritating as this requirement might sound, it helps to minimize theft and pilferage.

3. Employees should not be allowed to park their cars close to the building or near a doorway or large window that can be opened. This prevents employees from sneaking out quickly with merchandise, stashing it in the car, and returning to the workplace.

   A related difficulty involves an outside area with hiding places such as tall shrubs, storage or garbage bins, and other nooks and crannies. Whenever possible, eliminate these potential repositories or limit employee access to them.

4. If possible, employee locker rooms and restrooms should be within a reasonable distance so that the operator can check them once in a while. They should not be too close, however. An employee can use either complete isolation or quick access to hide stolen items.

   If the owner–manager cannot place these facilities in an optimal place in the building, the best alternative is to equip the employee lockers with heavy see-through screens instead of solid doors (see Figure 14.1). This eliminates an attractive hiding place for stolen items. Also, these facilities should not be too close to an exit or large window that can be opened.

FIGURE 14.1 Mesh lockers.
Courtesy of Penco Products, Inc.

5. The owner–manager should invest in some cost-effective **physical barriers**.

These include: (1) locks that can be opened only at certain times by certain persons; Saflok offers a variety of locking systems that provide reports indicating who accessed an area and when; (2) heavy-duty locks that are rotated occasionally, with the keys or key cards entrusted only to those who absolutely must have them; Medeco locks (or an equivalent) are good choices as they are very secure[22]; (3) adequate lighting in the storage areas so that thieves cannot hide; (4) reasonably priced **closed-circuit television (CCTV)**; video can be stored on a **digital video recorder (DVR)** and/or accessed remotely online[22] (see Figure 14.2); (5) uniformed guards, who may inspect employees, their packages, and their time cards when they leave work; (6) see-through screens on all storage facility doors—heavy screens can keep thieves out, while allowing a supervisor to spot-check the storage areas quickly; and (7) perimeter and interior **alarm systems**; a sound control system is especially useful for areas in the property that are not continuously open.

FIGURE 14.2 A closed-circuit TV system
©*Alistair Scott/Shutterstock*

> **physical barrier** Device, such as a lock, used to control access to a facility or storage area.
>
> **closed-circuit television (CCTV)** System that allows supervision of a specific area through the use of television monitors.
>
> **digital video recorder (DVR)** Electronic device that plays and copies video streams from a video source.
>
> **alarm system** Security device that alerts when something is wrong. Examples are burglary, fire, and refrigerator/freezer alarms.

■ The Owner–Manager's Role

An owner–manager must also be concerned with additional security precautions in other parts of the operation. We have discussed the principal ones associated with the back of the house, that is, those that are pertinent to the purchasing function. Several security considerations are, of course, relevant to the front of the house. An owner–manager should take the time to review some of the excellent materials dealing with these concerns.[23]

Control and security have become popular terms in the hospitality industry. They are increasingly becoming the subjects of books, seminars, newspaper features, and magazine articles. But some of these often omit a crucial factor: employee supervision.

The best systems fail without proper supervision. Physical barriers, audits, separation of responsibilities, and so on are the machines, but supervision is the grease. Without it, security cannot operate. The owner–manager should use his or her two eyes instead of depending too much on indirect control and security systems.

An owner–manager may well slip into one of two camps: (1) security will become an obsession, and the person will use everything possible to protect the property; or (2) security will occupy a low position on the priority list: visiting with guests, for instance, may be more important to some managers than overseeing production. Control, security, and supervision go hand in hand. Successful operators find the time to supervise properly. Unfortunately, these operators seem to be in short supply; otherwise, the losses due to employee theft and pilferage would not increase as they seem to do every year.

The glamour of the hospitality industry sometimes tempts people to forget the mundane aspects of employee supervision and motivation. Many buyers are no different. They would much rather write specifications, test new food products, and bargain with salespersons than supervise employees. Effective supervision may not guarantee success, but inadequate supervisory attention practically guarantees failure.

Who watches over the manager, especially if the operation has an absentee owner? Also, who watches the chef while the chef is watching someone else? We have to draw the line somewhere and eventually trust someone. It is virtually impossible to have a complete set of checks and balances. An adequate management information system (MIS), however, should help monitor the operating results in a way that will indicate where, if at all, problems may exist in the purchasing–receiving–storage cycle.

REMOTE BAR? KEEPING THE LIQUOR SECURE

Special events held in a hotel or large restaurant often require a remote bar in a banquet or meeting room or at some outdoor location, such as the pool or garden. It is important to maintain control over the liquor inventory in such a setting because failure to do so can result in pilfering on the part of employees and guests. Also, it is critical that accurate records be kept for billing purposes, especially if the host of the event is to be charged by the drink or by the bottle for any alcohol consumed.

Sometime before the event, the required liquor is checked out of the storeroom and placed in a rolling, locked cage. The request from catering might be for anything from a full bar setup with house and call brands, to specialty drinks, such as daiquiris or margaritas, to a simple selection of wines and beer. The catering department will know how many guests are expected and will have a formula for calculating how many drinks will be served, so the request will be very specific, down to the number of bottles of liquor to include.

When the bartender is ready to take up his or her position, the cart is rolled to the event location, and the liquor is unloaded with the bartender and perhaps a manager making sure that everything on the list is in fact on the cart. After the event is over, the remaining liquor is placed back on the cart and the new "inventory" notes the quantity of liquor that is being returned. In some operations, the bartender will be required to save the empty bottles to send back to the storeroom to further deter any theft.

The storeroom manager will do a final review of the liquor on the cart and return it to the general inventory. The catering department will be informed of the amount of liquor that was used, and the client will be billed accordingly.

Key Words and Concepts

Accept gifts	Kickback
Alarm system	Payroll service company
Approved-payee list	Physical barrier
Approved-supplier list	Physical inventory
Backdoor selling	Pre-employment screening
Background check	Pre-employment testing
Bonding	Professional employer organization (PEO)
Closed-circuit television (CCTV)	Quick response (QR) code
Critical-item inventory analysis	Reference check
Digital video recorder (DVR)	Résumé-checking service
Document cash paid-outs	Security problems
Fictitious invoices	Segregate operating activities
House account	Shoppers
Incomplete shipments	Short orders
Integrity testing	Spotter
Inventory "book" value	Stock requisition
Inventory padding	Surprise audit
Inventory shrinkage	Theoretical-inventory value
Inventory substitution	Toner-phoner
Invoice scams	Undercover agent

Questions and Problems

1. What security problems do you risk when you allow the buyer to receive deliveries? When you allow buyers to pay for the items they order?

2. Is employee supervision the best deterrent to theft and pilferage? Why or why not? If possible, ask a hotel manager or restaurant manager to comment on your answer.

3. What are some of the relatively inexpensive physical barriers that an owner–manager can use to deter theft and pilferage?

4. What are some of the reasons that hospitality companies would want to drug test potential employees? Are there any disadvantages to using drug tests?

5. Why is an owner–manager generally reluctant to put up a cash deposit?

6. Why is paying with a check preferable to using a cash paid-out?

7. List three examples of kickbacks. Why are kickbacks unethical?

8. Why does a buyer often double as the receiving agent? Identify at least two reasons.

9. What is the primary purpose of using an approved-payee list as part of the overall bill-paying procedure?

Questions and Problems (continued)

10. The approved-supplier list represents a major security precaution that is popular among large hospitality companies. Explain some of the reasons for its popularity.

11. Why would a hospitality operator use a shopping service?

12. Why would a hospitality operator require employees to be bonded? What purpose does bonding serve?

13. What is inventory padding? What can you do to avoid it?

14. What are the major advantages and disadvantages of becoming a house account?

15. What is the primary reason for not hiring an employee who has a relative working for one of your suppliers?

16. Why would you be reluctant to purchase an item from a telephone salesperson?

17. What is the most common type of kickback arrangement?

18. What can a hospitality operator do to protect the company from being defrauded by an invoice scam?

19. What can you do to prevent shoplifting?

20. When should a hospitality operator use undercover agents in the operation?

21. What are inventory substitutions? What can you do to prevent them?

Experiential Exercises

1. Assuming that it is legal, should a hospitality operator use a drug test during employee selection? Why or why not? What are the potential advantages and disadvantages of the test?
    a. Speak to an operator who likes to use drug testing and one who does not.
    b. Write a one-page report comparing and contrasting their thoughts.

2. Are there any benefits associated with independent, random audits? Do you think they are worth the time and expense?
    a. Ask a local accounting firm what it would charge for an independent, random audit of a small restaurant.
    b. Ask a representative of this company to comment on the costs and benefits of surprise audits.
    c. Write a one-page report detailing your findings.

3. Assume that your buyer is purchasing all meat items from one purveyor. You notice, however, that other meat purveyors offer the same type of meat products, and that their AP

Experiential Exercises (continued)

prices are consistently 2 to 3 percent lower than what you are paying. You decide to talk to the buyer about this situation. What questions would you ask? Why? If possible, ask a hotel or restaurant manager to comment on your answer. Prepare a report that includes the questions you would ask and the manager's comments.

4. Watch a television show such as *Restaurant Impossible*, *Hotel Impossible*, *Restaurant Stakeout*, or *Undercover Boss*.

   Were any security issues featured in the show? If so,
   a. What kind of issues were found?
   b. How did the consultant or boss handle the problem?
   c. Is there anything else that you would do to prevent or solve the problem?
   d. Write a one- to two-page report detailing your findings.

 References

1. Anonymous, "Ernst & Young Estimates Retailers Lose $46 Billion Annually to Inventory Shrinkage: Employee Theft Is Biggest Problem," May 13, 2003, http://hire-safe.com/Retailers_Lose__46_Billion_Annually_to_Inventory_Shrinkage__Employee_Theft.pdf. See also Patricia Bathurst, "Employee Fraud, Theft Cost Firms $40 Billion a Year," *The Arizona Republic*, December 18, 2008, www.azcentral.com/community/phoenix/articles/2008/12/18/20081218phx-fraud1219.html.

2. Natt O. Reifler, "Employee Theft: What You Don't Know Can't Hurt You," *Franchising World*, 40, no. 10 (October 2008):26–29.

3. G. L. Krippel, L. R. Henderson, M. A. Keene, M. Levi, and K. Converse, "Employee Theft and the Coastal South Carolina Hospitality Industry: Incidence, Detection, and Response (Survey Results 2000, 2005)," *Tourism and Hospitality Research*, 8, no. 3 (2008):226–238. doi:10.1057/thr.2008.22.

4. Kevin Lynch, "Stopping Employee Theft a Fast, Cheap Way to Boost Profit," *Nation's Restaurant News*, 42, no. 36 (September 15, 2008):32, 66. See also Ron Ruggless, "Preventing Employee Theft Safeguards Bottom Line, Ensures a Stronger Staff," *Nation's Restaurant News*, 42, no. 46 (November 24, 2008):38.

5. Stephen Shuck, "Catch Me if You Can," *Nation's Restaurant News*, 42, no. 4 (January 28, 2008):76. See also John R. Walker, *The Restaurant: From Concept to Operation*, 5th ed. (Hoboken, NJ: John Wiley & Sons, 2007).

6. No Author, "Bar Scams," *Restaurant Business*, 107, no. 2 (February 2008):74.

References (continued)

7. No Author, "Dunkin Operators Seek Ad Fund Fix after Kickback Flap," *Nation's Restaurant News*, 42, no. 36 (September 15, 2008):3. See also Richard Martin, "Franchisee Sentenced amid Dunkin' Lawsuit Barrage," *Nation's Restaurant News*, April 28, 2003, pp. 4, 111. More information on kickbacks and other white-collar crimes can be found at www.whitecollarcrimefyi.com/.

8. Jay Weaver, "Kickback Scheme Lands ICE Agent in Jail," *Miami Herald*, July 28, 2009, www.miamiherald.com/news/miami-dade/story/1160226.html.

9. No author, "2 Plead Guilty in SK Foods Kickback Scheme," January 27, 2009, www.ksbw.com/news/18576687/detail.html. See also "Man Sentenced to Prison in Tomato Industry Corruption Case," United States Department of Justice: Antitrust Department, August 11, 2009, www.usdoj.gov/usao/cae/press_releases/docs/2009/08 -11-09WatsonSentencing.pdf.

10. Paul Levy, "Skimming at the Savoy: Britain's Foodiegate," *The Wall Street Journal*, May 30, 1985, p. 28. See also Anonymous, "Taking Aim at Crime: Crime Concerns: Polling the Restaurateurs," *Nation's Restaurant News*, May 22, 2000, p. 120.

11. Cinda Becker, "Partners in Crime?" *Modern Healthcare*, 33, no. 23 (June 9, 2003):8–9. See also Carrie Johnson, "7 Plead Guilty in U.S. Foodservice Case: Suppliers Also Settle SEC Charges Related to Earnings Inflation," *The Washington Post*, November 3, 2005, www.washingtonpost.com/wp-dyn/content/article/2005/11/02/AR2005110202867 .html.

12. Meghan Gilbert, "State Audit Outlines Scheme by School Chief: Boosters Target of Alleged Fraud," *The Blade*, August 5, 2009. See also Anonymous, "Rite Aid Sues Man over Invoice Scam," *Las Vegas Review Journal*, June 16, 2000, p. 6B; Susan Todd, "Former J & J Worker Gets Jail Time for Invoice Scam," *New Jersey News*, March 26, 2009, www.nj.com/news/ledger/jersey/index.ssf?/base/news13/1238040932161050 .xml&coll=1.

13. Office of Internal Audit, Northwestern University, "Fraud Awareness," http:// internalaudit.nsula.edu/fraud-awareness/. See also James Scarpa, "Operators Acquiring a Taste for Beverage Management Technology," *Nation's Restaurant News*, 43, no. 1 (January 5, 2009):20.

14. Christina Wood, "The Toner Phoner Scam: Know Your Rights When It Comes to Office Supply Fraud," *InfoWorld*, October 14, 2008, www.infoworld.com/d/adventures -in-it/toner-phoner-scam-552. See also Lucy Komisar, "Cafeteria Kickbacks," *In These Times*, March 3, 2009, www.inthesetimes.com/article/4282/cafeteria_kickbacks/. Scott Cullen, "Buyer Beware: Avoiding Office Scams," *Office Solutions*, 18, no. 9 (October 2001):14–7; See also "Five Steps to Avoiding Office Supply Scams," Federal Trade Commission for the Consumer, March 2000, www.ftc.gov/bcp/edu/pubs/business/ alerts/alt065.shtm.

References (continued)

15. Joseph T. Wells, "The Case of the Pilfering Purchasing Manager," *The Fraud Beat*, American Institute of Certified Public Accountants, May 2004, www.aicpa.org/pubs/ jofa/may2004/wells.htm); "Four New York Archdiocese Purchasing Representatives Indicted on Fraud, Tax and Obstruction of Justice Charges," United States Department of Justice, January 5, 2006, www.usdoj.gov/atr/public/press_releases/2006/ 214014.htm).

16. Michael C. Sturman and David Sherwyn, "The Truth about Integrity Tests: The Validity and Utility of Integrity Testing for the Hospitality Industry," *The Center Hospitality Research*, No Date, www.hotelschool.cornell.edu/research/chr/pubs/reports/ abstract-14602.html. See also Betsy Cummings, "Can Personality Tests Solve Your Employee Problems?" *Restaurant Business*, 104, no. 16 (December 2005):11–12; Saul Fine, Ishayau Horowitz, Hanoch Weigler, and Liat Basis, "Is Good Character Good Enough? The Effects of Situational Variables on the Relationship between Integrity and Counterproductive Work Behaviors," *Human Resource Management Review*, 20, no. 1 (March 2010):73–84. David Arnold and John Jones, "Who the Devil Is Applying Now?" *Security Management*, 46, no. 3 (March 2002):85–88. Joan Axelrod-Contrada, "Personality Assessments' Value Draws Some Debate," *Boston Globe*, October 20, 2002, p. 10.

17. "The Need for Drug Testing in Hospitality Industry," *EDPM*, October 7, 2011, www. edpm.com/blog/the-need-for-drug-testing-in-hospitality-industry/.

18. Patrick Mayock, "5 Pressing Hotel Security Concerns for 2012," *Hotel News Now*, January 4, 2012, www.hotelnewsnow.com/Article/7229/5-pressing-hotel-security -concerns-for-2012.

19. Adam Cunningham, "Mystery Shop Yourself," *Hospitality*, 44, no. 5 (May 2008):12. See also Shirley Wang, "Health Care Taps Mystery Shoppers," *Wall Street Journal*, August 8, 2006, p. D1. Phil Baty, "Mystery Callers Will Shop Statt," *The Times Higher Education Supplement*, January 5, 2007, 1775, p. 2; D. Silver, "Hidden Agenda," *Restaurants & Institutions*, June 15, 2000, pp. 63–64; Bob Krummert, "Show Them the Money," *Restaurant Hospitality*, 87, no. 5 (May 2003):14; Ed Watkins, "The Road to Five Diamonds," *Lodging Hospitality*, 59, no. 3 (March 1, 2003):12; Betty Lin-Fisher, "Mystery Shopping a Hard Sell: Columnist Finds It's Not as Easy as it Sounds," *Akron Beacon Journal*, May 13, 2007.

20. Keith Loria, "Next Level Feedback: Restaurants Make the Change from Paper to Digital," *QSR*, September 2013, www.qsrmagazine.com/technology/next-level-feedback. See also, "Restaurants up Their Use of Social, Mobile," *E-marketer*, September 19, 2013, www.emarketer.com/Article/Restaurants-Up-Their-Use-of-Social-Mobile/ 1010229. See also Susan Spielberg, "Pennies for Their Thoughts: Customers Rewarded for Feedback," *Nation's Restaurant News*, 39, no. 13 (March 238, 2005):1, 6.

References (continued)

21. Julia Levashina and Michael Campion, "Expected Practices in Background Checking: Review of the Human Resource Management Literature," *Employee Responsibilities and Rights Journal*, 21, no. 3 (September 2009):231–249. See also Christine Blank, "Interviews, Screening Help in Hiring," *Hotel & Motel Management*, 222, no. 2 (February 5, 2007):28; Karen Morris, "Don't Forget the Background Check," *Hotel & Motel Management*, 223, no. 10 (June 2, 2008):8; Kevin Conrad, "Employee Background Checks Help Prevent Headaches," *Club Management*, March/April 2008, pp. 16–18; Dina Berta, "Nadell: Background Checks a Smart Step," *Nation's Restaurant News*, 39, no. 33 (August 15, 2005):18; William Hauswirth, "Know Your Employees," *Restaurant Hospitality*, 93, no. 1 (January 2009):20; Kim Kerr, "Don't Skimp on Background Check," *Restaurant Hospitality*, 90, no. 10 (October 2006):42; Bob Sullivan, "Criminal Background Checks Incomplete: How Convicted Felons Can Slip through Safety Net," MSNBC.com, April 12, 2005, www.msnbc.msn.com/id/7467732/).

22. Guy Pithie, "Operators Can Shield Their Businesses from Theft with Updated, Cost-Effective Security Technology," *Nation's Restaurant News*, 42, no. 39 (October 6, 2008):22–24. See also Carol Casper, "Running a Tight Shift," *Beverage World*, 127, no. 4 (April 15, 2008):100–101; Anonymous, "Ipswitch WS_FTP Server Puts CCTV Solution under Surveillance," *Market Wire*, April 3, 2006; Joel Roth, "Security in the Fast (Food) Lane," *Access Control & Security Systems Magazine*, February 1, 2005, http://securitysolutions.com/mag/security_security_fast_food/index.html. For more information on video surveillance in the restaurant industry, see the Video Surveillance blog at www.videosurveillance. com/blog/restaurants/.

23. See, for example, Rudolph Kimiecik and Chris Thomas, *Loss Prevention in the Retail Business* (Hoboken, NJ: John Wiley & Sons, 2006); Thomas N. Monson, Sarah Kaip, and Jerry Antoon, *Loss Prevention Threats and Strategies: How People Steal from Your Business and What You Can Do to Stop It* (Advantage Source, July 2004); Bill Copeland, *Absolutely Complete Retail Loss Prevention Guide* (Phoenix, AZ: Absolutely Zero Loss Inc., 2000); Anthony D. Manley, *The Retail Loss Prevention Officer: The Law and the Fundamental Elements of Retail Security* (Upper Saddle River, NJ: Prentice Hall, 2003); Robert J. Fischer and Richard Janoski, *Loss Prevention and Security Procedures: Practical Applications for Contemporary Problems* (Woburn, MA: Butterworth-Heinemann, 2006); See also Security Management, American Society for Industrial Security (ASIS), www.asisonline.org/, and *Loss Prevention Magazine*, www.losspreventionmagazine.com/index.html.

CHAPTER 15

FRESH PRODUCE

The Purpose of This Chapter

After reading this chapter, you should be able to:

- Discuss the importance and challenges of purchasing fresh produce.

- Choose appropriate fresh produce items based on primary selection factors, including government grades.

- Categorize fresh produce according to product size, form, and packaging and related characteristics.

- Create a specification for fresh produce that can be used in the purchasing process.

- Describe procedures for receiving, storing, and issuing fresh produce.

THE IMPORTANCE AND CHALLENGES OF PURCHASING FRESH PRODUCE

Purchasing fresh produce is a very important component of the buyer's job for most hospitality operations. Even if they do not have a full restaurant operation, many hotels, spas, bars, and entertainment establishments may offer fresh fruit to their guests or serve beverages with fresh juices and fruit and vegetable garnishes. For many restaurants, fresh produce accounts for around 12 percent of all purchases. And there could be a **P.L.O.T.** involved. Potatoes, Lettuce, Onions, and Tomatoes purchases average 40 percent of that total (see Figure 15.1). When you think of your average quick-service restaurant, those four versatile items could make up closer to 75 to 80 percent of the total.[1]

> **P.L.O.T.** Acronym for potatoes, lettuce, onions, and tomatoes. These four vegetables are an average of 40 percent of all fresh produce purchases.

Purchasing fresh produce calls for a great deal of skill and knowledge. Next to fresh-meat procurement, fresh-produce buying is, perhaps, the most difficult purchasing task the hospitality buyer faces.[2] In fact, it can be so difficult that some operators hire professional produce buyers to select and procure these products for them.[3] Fresh-produce buyers must have the wherewithal to purchase products that fluctuate in quality, quantity, and price on a daily basis. The real mark of an amateur in this area is to insist on top quality when none is available anywhere or to accept poor quality when good quality is available.

Fresh-produce buyers, especially those who work for supply houses, are extremely well paid. This fact alone indicates the difficulty and huge responsibility associated with the job. Even

P.L.O.T vegetables

Potatoes

Lettuce

Onions

Tomatoes

FIGURE 15.1 Picture of P.L.O.T. vegetables.

Potatoes: herreid14/Getty Images; Lettuce, clockwise from left: Rob Lawson/Getty Images; Rimglow/Getty Images; Dole08/Getty Images; Kai_Wong/Getty Images; Floortje/Getty Images; Sjo/Getty Images; Isabelle Rozenbaum/Getty Images; AndreaAstes/Getty Images; Onions, clockwise from left: Yvdavyd/Getty Images; Brand X Pictures/Getty Images; Floortje/Getty Images; Amero/Shutterstock; Chengyuzheng/Getty Images; Tomatoes: Anze Buh/EyeEm/Getty Images assistant fresh-produce buyers for a supply house require about two years of on-the-job training (OJT) before being allowed to make major purchasing decisions.

When a buyer purchases fresh, natural food products, several quality variations within the same product line can appear daily. Soil and climatic conditions can affect the quality of the product received. Different geographical areas favor different plant varieties and can have a significant impact on the quality of the crop. Seasonal changes, natural or manmade disasters, or changes in demand have effects on the availability of quality product as well. As a result of variations in quality and quantity, the buyer should expect as-purchased (AP) prices to fluctuate throughout the year for produce, both within a given grade and among grades. For this reason, a single year-round price is unrealistic.

To stay abreast of these changes, the savvy buyer subscribes to trade publications that include information on both price and quality. The *Fruit & Vegetable Market News* (FVMN) website is a major resource for produce pricing, quality, and availability information. Other subscription services, such as *The Packer* and *The Produce News*, published since 1897, are additional sources of current fresh-produce data. Information on produce, as well as meats, poultry, seafood, dairy and other items can also be found in *Perishable News* (see Figure 15.2).

In addition to the natural variations in products, another difficulty in buying fresh produce is choosing from the tremendous number of varieties and sources. Several hundred varieties of fresh-produce items are regularly available at any given time from various primary sources and intermediaries. Without research, it is difficult to decide which variety to use for a particular purpose. Decisions about whether to use and how to source organic and natural products have added another dimension to produce purchasing. More information about that will be discussed later in this chapter under the specification considerations and in the sidebar by Robert Hartman.

Another major problem that the buyer may face is a lack of acceptable sources of fresh produce. Different varieties of produce grown in different regions or countries come to market

FIGURE 15.2 The *Perishable News*.
Courtesy Phoenix Media Network

throughout the growing season. The United States imports almost 10 billion tons of fresh fruit, of which 26 percent comes from Mexico, followed closely by Guatemala at 19 percent, and Costa Rica at 17 percent. For vegetables, more than 74 percent of the 5.6 billion tons imported is sourced from Mexico.[4] Even with these large quantities from other countries, at times, it may be impossible to find suppliers that can obtain the quality the buyer wants, the quantity needed, or both. On the other hand, it may be fortuitous if the buyer is near an orchard or farm where the produce is harvested to obtain fruits and vegetables at the peak of freshness.[5]

PRIMARY SELECTION FACTORS

The owner–manager usually specifies the quality levels of fresh produce desired. The buyer normally carries out these specifications, as much as possible. Management personnel, often in concert with other individuals in the hospitality operation, usually consider one or more of the following fresh-produce selection factors when determining the quality standards as well as the preferred supplier(s).

> **intended use** Refers to the performance requirement of a product or service, which is noted on the specification. Considered to be the most important piece of information on a specification.
>
> **genetically altered food** Food modified by bioengineering techniques. Typically done to enhance flavor, appearance, and/or uniformity of size and to increase shelf life.
>
> **heirloom plants** Plants that are open-pollinated—meaning that unlike hybrids, seeds you collect from one year will produce plants with most of the characteristics of the parent plant. Most date from 1951, the year that the first hybrid seeds were developed, or earlier, and some varieties may be 100–150 years old.
>
> **exact name** Indication of a product or service's specific type, quality, and style.

■ Intended Use

As with any product or service a buyer plans to purchase, it is very important to identify exactly its performance requirement or **intended use**. This could save money in the long run because the buyer will not purchase, say, a superb-quality product to be used for a menu item if a lower-quality, lower-priced product will suffice. For instance, apples that must be on display should be very attractive, and the buyer would probably pay a premium price for this appearance. But if apples were to be used in a pie, where their appearance would be camouflaged to some degree, perhaps lesser-quality apples would be adequate.

■ Exact Name

With the development of so many new types and varieties of fruit and vegetables and the advent of **genetically altered foods**,[6] or the alternative of **heirloom plants** that are grown from open-pollinated, unaltered seeds, the fresh-produce market is filled with a lot of terminology (see Figure 15.3). Keeping track of the types, varieties, and styles of fresh produce can be a challenge. However, understanding this terminology is an absolute necessity for foodservice operations that prepare many menu items from raw ingredients because each item serves a specific culinary purpose. Therefore, a buyer must stay carefully and closely in tune with the **exact name** of products and the

FIGURE 15.3 Heirloom tomatoes.
©Jeannette Lambert/Shutterstock

needs of the hospitality operation and must find a supplier who is likewise aware of both.

It is not sufficient for a buyer to specify only the type of fresh produce required, but must also specify its variety. If a particular foodservice operation requires figs, then the variety must be known (e.g., Brown Turkey, Kadota, Calimyrna, or Black Mission). The same is true for potatoes (e.g., White, White Creamer, Red, Red Creamer, Purple, or Purple Creamer), Oranges (e.g., Cara Cara, Navel, or Blood oranges), and so forth (see Figures 15.4 and 15.5).

FIGURE 15.4 Potatoes, from left to right: White, White Creamer, Red, Red Creamer, Purple, or Purple Creamer.
Source: Cathy Thomas, Melissa's Great Book of Produce. Reprinted with permission of John Wiley and Sons, Inc.

Organic food products have become very popular in the United States. Organic foods account for more than $43.3 billion in sales as of 2015 and have shown consistent year-after-year growth.[7] Therefore, the U.S. Department of Agriculture (USDA) set up stringent guidelines and standards for products to be called organic. These guidelines lay out the organic standards specified by the Agricultural Marketing Service (AMS) to address issues regarding regulations and guidance for certification, production and handling of food, and labeling products that have been certified as organic by the USDA. Organic foods are raised without synthetic fertilizers, pesticides, herbicides, or hormones. They also cannot be genetically modified, exposed to radiation, or grown in sewage sludge.[8] You can review these guidelines on the website of the USDA National Organic Program.

Buyers can also purchase fresh produce that has been grown in nutrient-rich water instead of chemically treated soil. This **hydroponic** fresh produce is especially popular with fine-dining establishments because they can grow it in the foodservice operation and serve it almost immediately after harvest. If, however, buyers purchase organic or hydroponic produce, they can expect to pay a premium AP price.

FIGURE 15.5 Oranges, from left to right: Cara Cara, Blood, or Navel oranges.
Source: Cathy Thomas, Melissa's Great Book of Produce. Reprinted with permission of John Wiley and Sons, Inc.

> **organic food**   Natural food grown, produced, packaged, and delivered without the use of synthetic chemicals and fertilizers. Primary sources and distributors must adhere to the organic guidelines and standards published by the USDA.
>
> **hydroponic**   Method of growing plants in nutrient-rich water instead of chemically treated soil.

■ U.S. Government Inspection and Grades (or Equivalent)

Grade standards were developed out of the necessity for common terminology of quality and condition in the produce industry (see the USDA website for more discussion on this topic). The first U.S. grade standard for fresh produce was established for potatoes in 1917. "U.S. No. 1" was the term given to the highest grade. It covered the majority of the crop and meant that the product was of good quality. "U.S. No. 2" represented the remainder of the crop that was worth packing for sale under normal marketing conditions.

Perishable Agricultural Commodities Act (PACA) Legislation prohibiting unfair and fraudulent practices in the sale of fresh and frozen produce.

Agricultural Marketing Service (AMS) Agency of the USDA that establishes federal grading standards for several food products, under authority of the Agricultural Marketing Act.

To enforce these standards, the U.S. Inspection Service for fresh produce was established that same year. In 1930, the **Perishable Agricultural Commodities Act (PACA)** was signed; it prohibited unfair and fraudulent practices in the interstate commerce of fruits and vegetables.[9] By 1946, the Agricultural Marketing Act was signed into law and provided for the integrated administration of marketing programs. This act also gave the **Agricultural Marketing Service (AMS)** basic authority for major functions, including federal standards, grading and inspection services, market news services, market expansion, and consumer education. Currently, the USDA, through its AMS, Fruit and Vegetables Division, has approximately 166 grading standards for 86 types of fruits, vegetables, and nuts.[10]

Although government grades are used as a quality guideline, the buyer should be aware that each vegetable or fruit might have a different grading schedule. For example, there is only one grade for blueberries, which is U.S. No. 1, but there are multiple grades for topped carrots—U.S. Extra No. 1, U.S. No. 1, U.S. No. 1 Jumbo, and U.S. No. 2; and the grades for apples are U.S. Extra Fancy, U.S. Fancy, U.S. No. 1, U.S. Utility, and Combination grades (see Figure 15.6).

Because most specifications for fresh produce include some reference to federal grades, buyers need to know where to find this information. In addition to the USDA,

FIGURE 15.6 A federal grade stamp used for fresh produce. *Courtesy of United States Department of Agriculture*

they can locate grading data in *Melissa's Great Book of Produce* (see Figure 15.7). The Produce Marketing Association also provides online vegetable and fruit reference information to its membership.

The U.S. government grader considers several factors when grading fresh produce, but appearance is the most important factor. The critical appearance factors include size, size uniformity, maturity, shape, color, texture, and freedom from disease, decay, cuts, and bruises. Other factors sometimes come into play. For example, if produce is to be shipped long distances, say from California to Chicago, a more stringent examination may be applied to ensure that it represents the grade stated at the delivery point (as opposed to the shipping point). The wise buyer is aware of the potential product change during transit and will insist that the fresh produce meet the specified grade at the time of delivery, not at the time the products were shipped from the supplier's warehouse.

Several grading terms exist in the marketplace for fresh-produce items. The most commonly used terminology for fresh fruit, vegetables, and nuts are as follows:

- Fancy—the top quality produced; represents about 1 percent of all produce
- No. 1—the bulk of the items produced; the grade that most retailers purchase
- Commercial—slightly lower quality than U.S. No. 1

microgreens

BULLS BLOOD
MIZUNA
POPCORN
RAINBOW
RED BEET
TATSOI

MICROGREENS, IMMATURE SALAD GREENS, are the new darlings of the chef set. Some are mild, some are spicy; some buttery, some peppery.

Often they're tossed together to make a crisp, colorful garnish, then used atop or beneath appetizers or entrées. They can also be added to lettuces to make a stunning salad potpourri—a balance of color, texture, and flavor that can be napped with a wide variety of dressings.

Most of these infant greens are harvested when they are only 14–20 days old. Baby greens are more mature 35-day-old toddlers.

BUYING AND STORING

Look for greens that look crisp and fresh; avoid any that look damp or wilted. Refrigerate unwashed 2–3 days wrapped loosely in plastic bag.

Domestic: *year-round*
Global: *none*

PREP

Wash in cold water; pat dry.

USE

Combine with baby greens (such as baby spinach, baby oak-leaf lettuce and small pea shoots and leaves) to make a tasty mesclun mix for salads. Use as garnish, with one type of microgreen, or combine with others to make a colorful mixture.

NUTRITIONAL INFO

1 cup is generally a significant source of vitamins C and A, but varieties vary in nutritional content.

CLOCKWISE FROM BOTTOM LEFT:
Tatsoi, Popcorn, Red Beet, Mizuna, Rainbow, Bull's Blood

BULLS BLOOD
Bright magenta and teal leaves ▪ *Perky, peppery taste.*

MIZUNA
Elongated feathery green leaves that are notched on both sides (similar appearance to chrysanthemum leaves). ▪ *Pleasant, earthy cabbage, mustard-like taste; crisp texture.*

POPCORN
Long slender greenish-yellow shoots. Leaf portion is elongated and gently cups. ▪ *Subtle popcorn flavor; crisp texture.*

RAINBOW
Mixture of most popular varieties of microgreens for the season. ▪ *Combination of flavors, often a blend that includes mizuna, tatsoi, and red beet.*

RED BEET
Elongated feathery green leaves with red stem. ▪ *A pleasant earthy flavor with a mustard-like edge.*

TATSOI
Infant cabbage leaf looks like a little green spoon. ▪ *Sweet with mild pepper edge.*

SERVING SUGGESTIONS

Crab cake balance: Often warm crab cakes are accompanied by a rich sauce, such as a creamy aioli. Use microgreens to add texture and flavor balance to the dish, either on top of the crab cakes or next to them. If desired, microgreens can be tossed with just enough extra-virgin olive oil to lightly coat leaves.

Salad heaven: Make mixed green salad using baby greens and microgreens. Add thin apple wedges or seedless red grapes (halved). Toss with Simple Vinaigrette (page 310) and some minced fresh tarragon. Top servings with crumbled blue cheese and a small bundle of microgreens.

Grilled chicken with green babies: Brush boned chicken breasts with mixture of 3 tablespoons olive oil, 2 tablespoons lemon juice, and 1 tablespoon chopped fresh rosemary leaves, plus salt and pepper to taste. Grill until completely cooked. Let cool 5 minutes; cut into ½-inch-thick crosswise slices. Fan chicken breasts on plates and top with microgreens. Drizzle with smidgen of extra-virgin olive oil.

FIGURE 15.7 Example of the type of information included in the book, *Melissa's Great Book of Produce.*

Source: Cathy Thomas, Melissa's Great Book of Produce. Reprinted with permission of John Wiley and Sons, Inc.

field run Refers to fresh produce items that have not been graded. They may be low-quality items intended to be used by food processors to make things such as juice, jam, jelly, and so forth.

shelf life The amount of time a product can remain in storage before it loses quality and cannot be used.

- No. 2—much lower quality than U.S. No. 1; very superior to U.S. No. 3
- Combination—usually a mixture of U.S. No. 1 and U.S. No. 2 products
- No. 3—low-quality products just barely acceptable for packing under normal packing conditions
- **Field run**—ungraded products

The grades most commonly used in food service are the top grades because the low grades yield less, require additional labor for trimming, and often have a shorter **shelf life**. Thus, they are not generally a good buy, even at a low price.

The grade most often ordered is the high end of U.S. No. 1, or the equivalent. Clubs, hotels, and restaurants normally order the high end of U.S. No. 1 or the U.S. Fancy grade; the low end of U.S. No. 1 usually is reserved for supermarkets and grocery stores. The few items that fall into the lower-grade categories may not make it to market in any fresh form. Typically, they find their way to some of the food-processing plants that produce juices, jams, and generic-brand canned fruit and vegetables.

Generally, purveyors are knowledgeable about the grading system. If a buyer expresses interest in U.S. No. 1, they will know what is wanted. However, grades are sometimes unavailable for some fresh produce because: (1) the buyer may be purchasing an item for which there is no grading standard; (2) the suppliers refuse to have an item graded; or (3) more commonly, the produce may come from a foreign country that may not carry a grade, though it must be inspected before it is allowed to enter the United States.

Because considerable problems exist regarding variation in quality due to several seasonal factors, the use of government grades in buying fresh produce typically is not the sole selection criterion. The grade is just one of many factors that influence buyers' purchasing decisions. However, if they bid buy and U.S. grades are a major criterion in their specifications, they must be sure to use the appropriate grade terms.

packers' brand name Very specific indication of product quality. More precise than a brand name. A packer's personal grading system. Usually intended to take the place of federal government grades.

■ Packers' Brands (or Equivalent)

Because branded fresh produce is not as commonplace as branded canned and frozen goods, some buyers commonly use both U.S. government grades and **packers' brand names** when developing their fresh-produce buying procedures. Perhaps the most familiar brands are the Sunkist® brand used for citrus fruits, the Chiquita® brand used for several high-quality fruits, especially bananas, and Dole® for pineapple.

With fresh produce, a packer's brand may also indicate that a particular packing process has been used or that a particular cleaning and cooling process has been followed in the field (see Figure 15.8). U.S. grades may or may not indicate these attributes, depending on the area of the country the products come from.

Consistency, which should be a hallmark of packers' brands, is particularly important with fresh produce. It can result in a much more predictable edible-portion (EP) cost, which is always difficult to calculate for fresh produce in the best of situations. Consistency helps to minimize

FIGURE 15.8 Flats of packer's brand strawberries.
Courtesy of Andrew Feinstein

the variation both between and within case packs. For example, many products, such as whole lettuce, are sold by the case. Some types of lettuce are firm and weighty; others have a lot of space between the leaves. Citrus fruit varies in juice content from one crop to the next; fruits carrying a packer's brand may be more consistent. Asparagus may be old and woody or young and pleasantly crisp, but a packer's brand usually is consistently sound.

Even though a packer may not purchase the U.S. government grading service, government inspections, which consist of random visits by an official inspector, are mandatory. In addition, if a packer wants to use a brand name, most states require that this name be registered with the state's department of agriculture.

Packers' brands exist for many varieties of fresh produce. Packers' fresh-produce brands that do not include some reference to federal grades make up only a small portion of the fresh-produce business, and they are not widely known in most parts of the country. In most situations, packers use the brand name in conjunction with the U.S. grade designation (e.g., U.S. No. 1). Beware of a stencil on the box with the designation "No. 1." This sign indicates that the product is not under continual government inspection, nor has it been graded by a federal government inspector; however, in the opinion of that packer, the product meets all U.S. requirements for U.S. No. 1 graded products.

A major problem found with packers' brands for produce is that packers sometimes put out two categories of the same brand. For example, some packers have been accused of putting the same brand name on demonstrably different qualities of the same product—and trying to imply that the qualities are the same because they both carry the same name. For instance, on a high No. 1 and on a low No. 1, the high No. 1 produce typically goes to hospitality operations, whereas the low No. 1 produce goes primarily to supermarkets. The possibility of a switch should disturb and alert hospitality buyers.

point of origin Refers to the part of the world where a product originates. Important selection factor for some food items, as the point of origin can have a significant impact on their culinary quality.

color A substance, such as a dye, pigment, or paint that imparts a hue.

■ Point of Origin

If buyers shop around, they must be careful that they understand the differences in quality, texture, appearance, and taste that will accompany products from different areas of the world (see Figure 15.9). If buyers do business with only one or two purveyors, generally these suppliers will try to provide fresh produce whose characteristics are somewhat consistent. This may not be the case, however, if buyers wish to deal with multiple purveyors.

Another dimension of this selection factor is the problem associated with noting on the menu the **point of origin** for certain menu offerings. For instance, if a hospitality operation indicates that it serves Idaho potatoes, the operator must be certain that its potatoes actually come from Idaho or it will be in violation of truth-in-menu legislation. Also, if the restaurant promotes that it uses local produce, it must be aware of its guests' perceptions of what is considered local. Although there is no official definition of local produce, many people believe that it applies to items grown within the state or within a 100- to 200-mile radius.

FIGURE 15.9 This ad for sweet potatoes focuses on the point of origin.
Courtesy of North Carolina Sweet Potato Commission,
www.ncsweetpotatoes.com

FIGURE 15.10 Red, green, yellow, and orange peppers.
Source: Gisslen, Professional Cooking, 7th Edition, Copyright 2011.
Reprinted with permission of John Wiley and Sons, Inc.

■ Color

Generally, when buyers specify the type or variety of merchandise desired, that in itself will indicate **color**. However, with the growing number of varieties of fruits and vegetables available, buyers may need to specify the color preferred. For example, bell peppers come in many colors, including green, red, yellow, and orange (see Figure 15.10).

GOING GREEN: COSTS AND BENEFITS OF LOCAL, SEASONAL, AND ORGANIC INGREDIENTS
Robert Hartman, Principal, Robert Hartman Food & Beverage Management and Consulting.

Going green appears to be an idea whose time has come. In recent years the number of new "sustainable" product introductions has doubled or even tripled over previous years. Sales of organic foods and environmentally friendly brands are also increasing despite economic ups and downs.[1] The majority of customers who "go green" do so for a variety of reasons. Some are concerned about their health, others with the health of the environment. And although these concerns influence their choices to varying degrees,[2] many customers remain loyal to brands they recognize as "green."

Purchasers who are aware of these trends try to obtain the freshest, most appealing, and most highly nutritious products from the most sustainable sources. However, weighing the advantages and costs of green alternatives can sometimes be confusing. Is it enough to offer an organic menu option or two? Are the "green" claims of suppliers reliable? Do organic, local, and seasonal products provide real value to customers, or have their benefits been oversold?

Since the first chemical fertilizer was invented in 1842,[3] modern agriculture has increasingly relied on technology to create improvements in yield. During and after World War II, scientific or "conventional" farming methods have revolutionized agricultural productivity in the United States and around the world.[4] Even so, critics complain that these higher yields have come at the cost of severe ecological impacts[5] and the degradation of food quality. Because of the large amounts of fossil fuels required to produce artificial fertilizers and other agricultural chemicals, as well as the risks to farm workers from chemical residues, proponents of organic farming raise concerns that conventional farming methods might not be sustainable.[6] By some estimates, 10 to15 calories of energy are currently used to deliver each calorie of nutrition within the commercial food system.[7] For their part, advocates of scientific farming claim that organic methods cannot provide the yields required to sustain the population.[8]

For the purchasing agent, choosing between the alternatives can depend on the preferences of the market segment being served, as well as the relative availability and price of particular food products. The standards for organic foods have already been discussed in the text. The extra care that organic production requires adds value in the eyes of many consumers, which can increase the appeal of your offerings and make the often-higher AP price of these items more acceptable. Even so, it can be difficult to distinguish organic from conventional products on the basis of quality alone. There are many high-quality producers whose products, although more sustainably produced, are not certified as organic. Thus, although organic certification is one indication of sustainability, it is not the only one.

Another indicator of quality and sustainability is "food miles," the distance between harvest and consumption. In the United States, fruits and vegetables travel an average distance of between 1,300 and 2,000 miles before being served.[9] There are also delays of up to two weeks in transit and storage that can degrade their flavor and reduce their nutritional value.[10]

Locally grown produce, picked at the peak of ripeness and served as quickly as possible after picking, has the highest nutrient content.[11] Fresh, local produce can also have superior taste, appearance, and variety because commercially produced varieties of fruits and vegetables are often selected for yield, ease of large-scale cultivation, and their ability to withstand the rigors of shipping. By contrast, local producers can select primarily for taste, appearance, and nutritional content.[12] When it comes to energy impacts, taking delivery of local produce can minimize fuel costs. However, products transported by ship or rail can have lower energy impacts than equivalent items shipped by truck, even when the trucked items are produced much closer to the point of sale.[13]

To ensure that your organization achieves the best return on investment with respect to sustainability, it is helpful to build relationships with local, reliable producers. Many institutions, such as colleges and hospitals, enter into "farm-to-school" or "farm-to-hospital" arrangements with local producers or producer co-ops, who guarantee delivery of a reliable supply of fresh, high-quality produce in exchange for a commitment to purchase in quantity. The Community Alliance with Family Farmers has developed guidelines for implementing local food programs that can complement an organization's current purchasing system.[14]

To aid purchasers in understanding the trade-offs, the Sustainable Food Laboratory has developed a booklet called "The Changing Vocabulary of Food Purchasing," which can help you to stay current by defining terms such as "local," "seasonal," "sustainable," and "food miles."[15]

■ REFERENCES

1. Jack Neff, "Green-Marketing Revolution Defies Economic Downturn," *Advertising Age* (Midwest edition), 80, no. 14 (April 20, 2009):1.

2. Green America, *Guide to the Green Marketplace*, www.greenamericatoday.org/cabn/resources/greenmarketplace.

3. Rothamstead Research, "The Origins of Rothamsted Research," www.rothamsted.ac.uk/corporate/Origins.html.

4. Wright State University, "Conventional Agriculture," *The Bahn Lab Wiki*, Dayton, Ohio, http://bahn.pbworks.com/Conventional-agriculture.

5. David Pimentel, Paul Hepperly, James Hanson, Rita Seidel, and David Douds, "Organic and Conventional Farming Systems: Environmental and Economic Issues," http://ecommons.library.cornell.edu/bitstream/1813/2101/1/pimentel_report_05-1.pdf.

6. Michael Pollan, "Our Decrepit Food Factories," *The New York Times Magazine*, December 16, 2007, www.michaelpollan.com/article.php?id=91.

7. Kristen Markley and Marion Kalb, "Linking Farms with Colleges," *UW Madison Center for Integrated Agricultural Systems*, April, 2005, p. 4, www.farmtocollege.org/Resources/LinkingFarmstoColleges.pdf.

8. Stephan Dabbert, Anna Maria Häring, and Raffaele Zanoli, *Organic Farming: Policies and Prospects* (London: Zed Books, 2004), ISBN 1842773275, p. 7.

9. ATTRA, National Sustainable Agriculture Information Service, "Reducing Food Miles," http://attra.ncat.org/farm_energy/food_miles.html.

10. Diane M. Barrett, "Maximizing the Nutritional Value of Fruits and Vegetables," *Food Technology*, 61, no. 4 (April 2007), http://postharvest.ucdavis.edu/datastorefiles/234-780.pdf.

GOING GREEN: COSTS AND BENEFITS OF LOCAL, SEASONAL, AND ORGANIC INGREDIENTS (continued)

11. Ibid.

12. British Society of Plant Breeders, *Plant Breeding: The Business and Science of Crop Improvement*, www.bspb.co.uk/BSPB%20Handbook.pdf, pg. 4.

13. James E. McWilliams, "Food that Travels Well," *The New York Times*, Opinion, August 6, 2007, www.nytimes.com/2007/08/06/opinion/06mcwilliams.html.

14. Community Alliance with Family Farmers, *Building a Successful Local Food Program: Tips for Institutional Buyers*, pp. 1–2, www.caff.org/publications/TipsforInstitutional Buyers.pdf.

15. Karen Karp, John Turenne, Susan Sweitzer, and Shayna Cohen, *The Changing Vocabulary of Food Purchasing: A Guide for Foodservice Professionals*, Sustainable Food Laboratory, pp. 1–35, www.sustainablefoodlab.org.

SIZE, FORM, PACKAGING, AND RELATED CONSIDERATIONS

■ Product size

Product size is a very critical selection factor for at least two reasons. First, it would be embarrassing to serve guests items of varying sizes. Second, if the products were sold by the piece rather than by weight, buyers would find it impossible to achieve effective cost control if varying sizes are served.

Many buyers, especially novices, are unaware of the many fresh-produce sizes available. Indicating this selection factor is sometimes overlooked when buyers purchase fruits and vegetables. Buyers should not merely order a box of lemons; they should indicate the size of the lemon wanted by specifying the count per box—the lower the count, the larger the lemon. A great many types and varieties of fresh fruits are sold this way.

Still another common way to indicate product size is to indicate the desired number of pieces per layer of the **lug**, or box. This is particularly true when you buy a lug of tomatoes. For example, a "4 by 5" preference indicates a specific tomato size: the lug has layers of tomatoes with 4 on one side and 5 on the other, or 20 tomatoes per layer.

Some products carry a unique nomenclature. For instance, a packer may classify onions into four product sizes: pre-pack, large medium, jumbo, and colossal.

Furthermore, buyers may find that some produce sold in their area is sized according to the approximate number of pieces per pound. For example, a "3 to 1" item size indicates that there are approximately three items per pound. Moreover, agribusiness has advanced to the point where several sizes exist within narrow product lines; for instance, Idaho potatoes come in 12 sizes, ranging from 4 to 18 ounces each.

> **product size** Refers to the buyer's specified weight, or volume, of a particular item he or she wants to purchase. Examples would be a 10-ounce steak or a 4-ounce hamburger.
>
> **lug** Container that has two layers of product. Term typically used in the fresh produce trade.

■ Size of Container

Foodservice buyers prefer to purchase the size of container that is consistent with the needs of the operation. Generally, most fresh-produce items are packed in at least two, sometimes more, container sizes, and buyers usually find one of these sizes more suitable for their operation's needs. For instance, if buyers do not require a particular type of produce in large quantities, it would be appropriate for them to purchase it in small containers so that waste and spoilage are minimized.

As with many other types of foods and beverages, the fresh-produce product line has uni-

> **flat**   Refers to one layer of a product. Term typically used in the fresh produce trade.

form container sizes. For instance, avocados typically come in a **flat** which is one layer of product, or a lug, which consists of two layers of product (see Figure 15.11). Some suppliers may be willing to "break" a case. However, chances are that you will need to pay for this added supplier service.

■ Type of Packaging Material

Several standardized types of packaging materials are available in the fresh-produce product line. However, these materials vary quite a bit in terms of quality and price. The AP price variation for some fresh produce is related solely to the quality of packaging; less-expensive merchandise may be scantily packed, and more expensive products may be wrapped in high-quality packaging. Certain assurances come with the type of packaging material used. For instance, high-quality fiberboard costs more than thin brown-paper wrappings. With the former, the merchandise will be protected, whereas with the latter, you will probably lose some of it to damage during shipping and handling.

FIGURE 15.11 Lug of tomatoes.
Courtesy of Phoenix Wholesale Food Service

■ Packaging Procedure

Packing generally takes two forms: **layered** and **slab-packed** merchandise. With the layered style, the product is arranged nicely, usually between sheets of paper or cardboard. With the slab-packed style, the product is randomly placed into a container with no additional packaging. If it is important to preserve the edible yield of an item, buyers should probably purchase better packaging arrangements, or the savings associated with slab packing will be illusory.

For some products, buyers can request each item to be individually wrapped and layered in the case. One example of this is Asian or Korean pears, which are sometimes individually wrapped in a plastic net.[11] They may also be able to purchase products that are layered in a **cell pack**, which is a cardboard or plastic sheet with depressions in it; the items can sit in the depressions and not touch each other. Some apples and pears are packed this way. These procedures are expensive, but if this process is necessary to preserve appearance, probably no better way exists for buyers to accomplish their goal than to insist that cell packs are used.

■ Minimum Weight per Case

Because so much fresh produce is purchased by the case, or by the container, the case weight can vary considerably. This has implications on the bid price because the weight will vary from case to case. Therefore, buyers should indicate the minimum acceptable weight during the bidding process and write it in the specifications. Also, fresh produce tends to "shrink," or dehydrate, while in transit. Thus, specifying a **minimum weight per case** enables buyers to receive the appropriate amount while giving suppliers some **shrink allowance**. In some cases, buyers might also indicate a **decay allowance** on a fresh-produce product specification. For example, when buyers purchase ripe plums, slab-packed, a few unusable ones are bound to be in the lot. Buyers and suppliers should agree on the number of bad pieces that will be acceptable.

Another dimension of this selection factor is the possibility that buyers might wish to indicate a weight range per case of produce they order. This gives suppliers a bit more flexibility and ensures that, once in a while, buyers might receive more weight, and, therefore, more usable servings of product than they would if they indicated only a minimum weight required on the specification.

■ Product Yield

Some of the fresh produce that buyers purchase will be subject to a certain amount of **trim**, or unavoidable waste. For example, when purchasing whole, fresh turnips, buyers should note on the product specification the minimum

layered   Products packed between sheets of paper, plastic, or cardboard. Intended to protect products so that they do not break or otherwise lose quality.

slab-packed   Refers to items tossed into a container in no particular order or style. An inexpensive packing procedure, though it can cause breakage and other quality deterioration for some products.

cell pack   Products layered in a cardboard or plastic sheet that has depressions in it so that the items sit in them and do not touch one another. Typically used to pack high-quality fresh fruit.

minimum weight per case   Important selection factor when purchasing products that may vary in weight from one vendor to another, or because of other factors, such as seasonal variations. Helps ensure that the buyer receives a predictable amount of product.

shrink allowance   The amount of weight loss the buyer will accept in a shipment. The weight loss is due to unavoidable moisture loss during transit.

decay allowance   The expected amount of a purchased product that will be unusable, yet will be acceptable to the buyer when it is shipped to the hospitality operation. The typical situation involves the purchase of fresh produce where the buyer will expect, and accept, a few broken and/or spoiled pieces in the lot.

trim   Another term for waste.

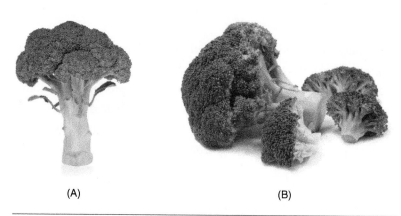

FIGURE 15.12 (A) Broccoli versus (B) broccoli crowns.
Broccoli: ©Dizzy/iStockphoto; Broccoli crowns: ©MarenWischnewski/iStockphoto.com

product yield   The same as edible yield.

product form   Refers to the degree of processing, or lack thereof, a product has when you purchase it. For instance, a buyer can purchase whole chickens or selected chicken parts. The parts typically would cost more than the whole birds.

ready-to-serve product   Convenience food that can be served right out of the container, with no additional preparation other than perhaps thawing and/or reheating.

value-added product   Another term for convenience food. Alternately, it could also refer to a non-food item that has many upgraded features, such as a kitchen ventilation system that is self-cleaning as opposed to one that has to be cleaned by hand.

precut fresh produce   Refers to fresh produce that has been chopped or otherwise cut, and packaged in cello wrap or other similar type of packaging material.

prewashed   Produce that has been washed or rinsed with water during processing.

degree of ripeness   A measure of a food or beverage product's maturity and readiness to be used in production, or to eat or drink.

product yield expected or, alternatively, the maximum amount of acceptable trim loss. This can be an important consideration when determining how much processing you would like done to the product. For example, deciding whether to buy whole bunches of broccoli or broccoli crowns may be affected by whether you can specify the amount of trim for the crowns (see Figure 15.12).

■ Product Form

Buyers can purchase fresh produce in many **product forms**. From the whole "fresh-off-the-vine" items, to the **ready-to-serve products**, to anything in between, buyers must determine which product best meets the requirements of their operations. When they purchase an item in anything other than its original form, varying degrees of value have been added: different degrees of economic "form" have given value to the item. These **value-added products** are more expensive, but in the long run may be more economical than whole products that require considerable labor and handling before service.[12] Today, many operators prefer purchasing value-added, **precut fresh produce** that has been subjected to additional cleaning, chopping, and so forth. For example, buyers can purchase peeled and chopped onions, potatoes, garlic, and other similar items. For spinach, lettuces, and herbs, the buyer may want to specify if they would like the items **prewashed**.

■ Degree of Ripeness

Buyers can purchase some fresh produce at varying **degrees of ripeness**. Usually, buyers will purchase mature, fully ripened produce. However, immature, green produce can also be found. For some items, such as bananas and tomatoes, several stages of ripening can be ordered; these options may be quite suitable for an operation that wants to ripen some of its own fresh produce so that it is at its peak of quality when served.

■ Ripening Process Used

Buyers should be aware of the types of **ripening processes**. Some produce is naturally ripened on the plant. These items are a bit more expensive because of the difficulty of handling and the loss producers experience; they often end up with some rotting merchandise in their fields. The taste of the item, though, may be so desirable that buyers are willing to pay for it.

Some produce is ripened in a **ripening room**. In this situation, the produce is picked when it is green and then is placed in a room, train car, or truck. **Ethylene gas** is then introduced into the "room." When some types of produce ripen naturally, they emit ethylene gas, so the introduction of this gas into the "room" speeds up the ripening process.[13] Unfortunately, if the process is hastened too much, the fresh-produce item will not mature properly. Bananas, for example, will turn bright yellow, but the fruit under the skin will not have kept pace (i.e., it will not be very flavorful because it has not ripened fully, even though the skin color suggests that it has).

■ Preservation Method

Fresh produce is not considered a potentially hazardous food; consequently, the federal government does not require any type of **preservation**. Nonetheless, storage conditions throughout the fresh-produce channel of distribution affect culinary quality and availability of produce. These conditions may also create unsanitary conditions that can cause a food-borne illness outbreak. However, this problem is typically the result of contaminants present in the soil or water. The food itself is not usually the issue.

Some fresh produce items are refrigerated, whereas others can be left unrefrigerated. The channel for items that must be refrigerated is often referred to as the **cold chain** and is an important part of the logistics of purchasing produce. The cold chain refers to maintaining the temperature of the produce during transportation from the producer to the supplier to the foodservice operation, and ultimately to the guest. The **Sanitary Food Transportation Act of 2005** transferred responsibility for safe transportation of food from the Department of Transportation to the Food and Drug Administration. It contains the names and types of products that must be refrigerated and appropriate sanitation standards to ensure the quality and integrity of the product.[14]

Buyers must note on their specification their refrigeration requirement, if any. However, even if it is not required as is the case for items such as bananas, potatoes, and most onions, they still should be kept in a cool environment so that they do not overripen or rot.

Refrigeration is expensive, so operations expect to pay more for refrigerated fresh produce. But unrefrigerated or uncooled product can rapidly deteriorate. As a result, the EP cost for such produce will usually be much greater than the EP cost associated with refrigerated produce.

If buyers are purchasing precut, convenience fresh produce, refrigeration is mandatory. The supplier must preserve the appropriate "pulp" temperature; otherwise, the produce will quickly

ripening process   Can be natural or artificial ripening. Important selection factor when purchasing some fresh produce products.

ripening room   Closed storage area used to ripen some fresh produce products, such as bananas. The storage area is sealed, and ethylene gas is introduced to induce and hasten the ripening process.

ethylene gas   Used to induce and hasten the ripening of fresh produce.

preservation   A procedure, such as refrigeration, freezing, canning, drying, or chemical additives, used to maintain a product's shelf life and quality and, in some cases, impart additional flavorings.

cold chain   Keeping product refrigerated from the producer to the supplier to the buyer and ultimately to the guest.

Sanitary Food Transportation Act of 2005   Federal regulation related to the transportation of human and animal food.

pulp temperature
Internal temperature of precut, convenience fresh produce products, such as chopped salad greens.

deteriorate. For instance, chopped salad greens should be delivered at a **pulp temperature** of approximately 34°F to 36°F to preserve their culinary quality.

Waxing is another method used to preserve some produce. The wax prevents moisture loss and also contributes to the appearance of the produce. Mother Nature uses this process for such foods as peppers and cucumbers. Producers are also allowed to apply wax to some items, especially when they remove the natural wax when cleaning the product. Some items are traditionally waxed, and operators will receive them in this state unless they specify otherwise. Fresh-produce items most likely to be waxed by producers are apples, avocados, bell peppers, cantaloupes, cucumbers, eggplant, grapefruit, lemons, limes, melons, oranges, parsnips, passion fruit, peaches, pineapples, pumpkins, rutabagas, squash, sweet potatoes, tomatoes, and turnips.

Some fresh produce is preserved in **controlled atmosphere storage**. The produce is put into a room, and the room then is sealed. Oxygen is removed, and a variety of other gases are intro-

controlled atmosphere storage   Similar to controlled atmosphere packaging (CAP). However, it can also refer to a controlled atmosphere that exists in other types of storage environments, such as controlled atmosphere warehouses.

duced. The lack of oxygen reduces the rate of respiration, hence retarding spoilage. The produce held in atmosphere-controlled chambers will remain as is for a considerable period of time. Unfortunately, when this produce is removed from this environment, it deteriorates very rapidly. Generally, suppliers do not sell this type of merchandise to hospitality operators; rather, they sell it to the retail trade. However, when buyers shop around, they should note on their specification that they prefer merchandise that has not been stored in a controlled environment.

Another controlled atmosphere storage technique is to oxidize or remove the ethylene gas that naturally occurs in ripening fruit and vegetables. Ethylene "scrubbers" (i.e., pellets) that react to the ethylene gas can be introduced to the storage facilities to substantially reduce this gas and thereby slow down the ripening process of fruits and vegetables.

Some of the fresh produce that comes to market has been chemically treated to preserve its shelf life and palatability. If buyers do not want this type of merchandise, they can opt to purchase fresh produce that has been organically grown—that is, grown without the use of synthetic chemicals and fertilizers.[15]

PURCHASING FRESH PRODUCE

Produce Marketing Association (PMA)   Trade association representing members who market fresh fruits, vegetables, and related products worldwide. Its members are involved in the production, distribution, retail, and foodservice sectors of the industry.

The first step in purchasing fresh produce is to access the **Produce Marketing Association (PMA)** website. This site contains information on many fresh-produce items. It also includes information on receiving, storing, and handling techniques, as well as food safety information.

The next step is to decide on the exact type of produce and quality wanted. Buyers may not be the ones to make this decision, unless they are user–buyers or owner–user–buyers. Once the decision on the type and quality of produce to be ordered has been made, the buyer should prepare specifications for each item. These specifications should be as complete as necessary and should include all pertinent information, especially if the buyer intends to engage in bid buying. (See the guidelines noted in Chapter 7. For examples of fresh-produce product specifications and a product specification outline, see Figures 15.13 and 15.14, respectively.)

Red Delicious apples
Used for fruit plate item
U.S. Fancy
Washington State
72 count
30- to 42-pound crate
Moisture-proof fiberboard
Layered arrangement,
cell carton
Whole apples
Fresh, refrigerated
Fully ripened

Cauliflower, white
Used for side dish for all
entrées
U.S. No. 1 (high)
12 count
18- to 25-pound carton
Moisture-proof fiberboard
Loose pack (slab pack)
Pretrimmed heads
Fresh, refrigerated
Fully ripened

Sweet Spanish, yellow
globe onion
Used for onion rings
U.S. No. 1 (high)
Jumbo size
50-pound plastic
mesh bag
Whole onions
Fresh, unrefrigerated
Fully ripened

Iceberg lettuce
Used for tossed salad
U.S. No. 1 (high)
10-pound poly bag
Loose pack (slab pack)
Chopped lettuce
Fresh, refrigerated
Fully ripened

FIGURE 15.13 An example of fresh-produce specification.

Intended use:

Exact name:

U.S. grade (or equivalent):

Packer's brand name (or equivalent):

Product size:

Size of container:

Type of packaging material:

Packaging procedure:

Minimum weight per case:

Product yield:

Point of origin:

Color:

Product form:

Degree of ripeness:

Ripening process used:

Preservation method:

FIGURE 15.14 An example of a product specification outline for fresh produce.

After buyers prepare the specifications, the next step is to consider the suppliers likely to satisfy their needs. Here, again, they can become a house account, use bid buying, or settle on some procedure in between. (Again, note that bid buying is not as prevalent in the fresh-produce trade as it is for processed foods and nonfoods, although it is used in some situations.)

Over the years, several fresh-produce buying groups and trade associations have evolved. This, in turn, has made such products more readily available in the local markets. Buyers may also find several suppliers handling a few fresh-produce items as a sideline to their regular business of canned goods, frozen foods, and various nonfood items. Generally, though, it is difficult to find more than one or two consistently capable full-line, fresh-produce suppliers. Because of this, buyers may find it difficult to engage in bid buying.

■ Buying Direct

farmers' market Area where local farmers, growers, and other merchants come together to sell their own products directly to consumers.

An added attraction in the fresh-produce area is the independent farmers. These small businesspersons may occasionally want to sell buyers "farm-fresh produce." Some may sell on the roadside. Others may allow customers to come in and "pick their own." Still others may gather together one or two days a week in what is referred to as a **farmers' market**.

Over the years, farmers' markets have become more visible, numerous, and popular. In some instances, the small, local farmer will be a wise choice. For example, as part of a college project, some students were required to compare an independent farmer's AP prices and supplier services to the same products and supplier services offered by other fresh-produce suppliers. The results of the study indicated that the restaurant's management was paying the farmer about 7 percent more per month. However, it was the opinion of the class that the quality of the farmer's fresh produce was far superior. In addition, the farmer delivered daily. Unfortunately, he could not supply all the needs of this restaurant, but for what he did supply, the class judged it to be the best overall value.

If you wish to deal with farmers' markets, you need to realize that their sales and marketing procedures differ greatly from the typical suppliers you patronize. For instance: many of these folks can't come to you, you must go to them; most have a very limited selection and quantities; because their products are almost always organic, product shelf lives are very short; credit terms are rarely available, you have to pay cash; you will need to adjust to packaging that varies from the standardized ones you are used to; and it may be difficult to prepare accurate product specifications for many of the foods due to the typical independent farmer's inability to guarantee consistency.

localvore Person who is dedicated to eating food grown and produced locally or grown and produced personally; localvores typically are not motivated strictly by a profit motive.

One way to overcome this issue is to work directly with multiple growers and farmers to ensure sufficient quantities and qualities of these products. The use of locally produced items involves the use of coordinated efforts on the part of the restaurant and the grower/farmer. This relationship, however, can have benefits for the restaurateur/chef and also be appealing to customers.[16]

Generally speaking, you will be dealing with vendors who are not businesspersons; they prefer a personal relationship, not a business one. You may also be dealing with **localvores**—that is, persons who are dedicated to eating food grown and produced locally or grown and produced personally; they typically are not motivated strictly by a profit motive.

One chef/owner sums it up nicely: "If one of my (other) purveyors sends me something sub-par, I can call and curse at them. It's a different ethos with farmers. You have to tread more carefully. It's a personal relationship, really, rather than a business one. And they have tremendous pride in their product."[17]

■ Growing your own

Adventurous operators might consider developing their own fresh-produce gardens. Lately, several restaurant chefs have taken this unique step.[18] Gardens located on the premises ensure freshness (see Figure 15.15). They can also be excellent marketing and promotional tools used to attract guests. Mario Batali, Rick Bayless, and Alice Waters are all examples of chefs who have aided in bringing a voice to the farm-to-table movement. Each of these chefs/owners utilize local produce and other food stuffs as their preference. Some even have gone so far as to have a farm located at or near their restaurant. Success in using their own produce comes with the ability for restaurants like these to use daily menus that ensure the highest-quality products.[19]

FIGURE 15.15 A restaurant garden.
©JBryson/Getty Images

■ Trusting the Supplier

Specifying U.S. grades, packers' brands, and one particular supplier can make you a "house account" of the highest order, which may or may not be in accord with company policy. However, building a trusting relationship with suppliers may be the key to the success of an operation. This is because suppliers are linked to several crucial factors associated with operating an establishment. These may include delivery schedules, seasonal changes, weather factors, the suppliers' buying capabilities, the transportation and storage facilities, and the speed with which the suppliers rotate products.

With fresh produce, and to a lesser extent with processed items, suppliers must assure buyers that they will get the quality they need and want, and that this will be as good on the table as it was in the field. If buyers do not work closely with a fresh produce supplier, they take some risks. For instance, just because you specify Sunkist and U.S. No. 1, there is no guarantee that you will receive them. The box might note U.S. No. 1, but it can easily have been repacked with lower-quality product.

In addition, fresh-produce buying does not lend itself easily to bid buying. Buyers have many points to consider, and in some parts of the United States, there are few suppliers to bid for their business. Consequently, this is an area in which they may wish to rely on the suppliers' highly developed expertise.

PROCEDURES FOR RECEIVING, STORING, AND ISSUING FRESH PRODUCE

■ Receiving

Taking delivery of the correct amount of produce of the specified quality is a major challenge. Some receivers may merely look at the box of lettuce, read "24 heads," and take it for granted that 24 heads of lettuce are in the carton. A skillful receiver resists the temptation to examine only the printing on the containers and cartons and to look at only the top layer of merchandise.

Before accepting a produce shipment, the receiver should conduct a visual inspection of the top layer and check the weight of the entire carton. This inspection provides a quick and accurate idea of the quantity and quality of the shipment. The receiver should also conduct a random sampling of a proportion of the containers. Here, a receiver carefully unpacks a box of produce to check the count, size, and quality throughout the carton. A good place for this inspection is in refrigerated quarters, such as a walk-in refrigerator, so that the produce does not become too warm, thus decreasing its shelf life.

Although receiving fresh produce can be a daunting task, we are not suggesting that receivers break open every carton to see whether it really contains full count. This undertaking can cause extensive damage to fragile fruit and vegetables, particularly if they are packaged in special protective films designed to extend their shelf life (see Figures 15.16 and 15.17 for signs of acceptable and unacceptable quality in some fresh-produce items). However, buyers can make the task less stressful by establishing a partner-like relationship with vendors. If buyers have concerns about trusting their suppliers and receivers completely, it will be in their best interest to continually review their receiving practices very carefully. At the very least, they should verify that the produce is acceptable by checking to see that the quality is equal throughout and to make certain that no repacking has occurred. The receiver may also need to check the temperature of items for which maintaining the cold chain is important, as discussed earlier.

After checking quality and quantity, receivers should check the prices and complete the appropriate accounting documents.

■ Storing

To prevent rapid quality degradation and loss of some nutritional value, it is imperative that hospitality operations properly store fresh fruits and vegetables. If buyers can arrange for frequent deliveries from their fresh-produce supplier and move the produce rapidly through production, they can be a little more flexible with their storage duties. Because many suppliers are not equipped to provide daily delivery, however, operators should plan for a suitable storage facility.

Fresh produce must be stored immediately at the proper temperature and humidity (see Figure 15.18 for requirements for some vegetables). Large foodservice operations usually have a separate cool area or refrigerator for these items, but any cool temperature is better than none. Hospitality operations must avoid all delays in getting produce to a cool place: most fresh produce deteriorates considerably when it is left at room temperature. In fact, most fully ripened produce becomes inedible quite quickly if it is held in the wrong storage environment. For example, fresh corn loses about 50 percent of its sugar in the first 24 hours after it is picked; proper refrigeration, however, can slow this deterioration.

	SIGNS OF GOOD QUALITY	SIGNS OF BAD QUALITY, SPOILAGE
Apples	Firmness; crispness; bright color	Softness; bruises (irregularly shaped brown or tan areas do not usually affect quality).
Apricots	Bright, uniform color; plumpness	Dull color; shriveled appearance
Bananas	Firmness; brightness of color	Grayish or dull appearance (indicates exposure to cold and inability to ripen properly)
Blueberries	Dark blue color with silvery bloom	Moist berries
Cantaloupes (muskmelons)	Stem should be gone; netting or veining should be coarse; skin should be yellow-gray or pale yellow	Bright yellow color; mold; large bruises
Cherries	Very dark color; plumpness	Dry stems; soft flesh; gray mold
Cranberries	Plumpness; firmness. Ripe cranberries should bounce.	Leaky berries
Grapefruit	Should be heavy for its size	Soft areas; dull color
Grapes	Should be firmly attached to stems. Bright color and plumpness are good signs.	Drying stems; leaking berries
Honeydew melon	Soft skin; faint aroma; yellowish white to creamy rind color	White or greenish color; bruises or water-soaked areas; cuts or punctures in rind
Lemons	Firmness; heaviness; should have rich yellow color	Dull color; shriveled skin
Limes	Glossy skin; heavy weight	Dry skin; molds
Oranges	Firmness; heaviness; bright color	Dry skin; spongy texture; blue mold
Peaches	Slightly soft flesh	A pale tan spot (indicates beginning of decay); very hard or very soft flesh
Pears	Firmness	Dull skin; shriveling; spots on the sides
Pineapples	"Spike" at top should separate easily from flesh	Mold; large bruises; unpleasant odor; brown leaves
Plums	Fairly firm to slightly soft flesh	Leaking; brownish discoloration
Raspberries, boysenberries	Stem caps should be absent; flesh should be plump and tender	Mushiness; wet spots on containers (sign of possible decay of berries)
Strawberries	Stem cap should be attached; berries should have rich red color	Gray mold; large uncolored areas
Tangerines	Bright orange or deep yellow color; loose skin	Punctured skin; mold
Watermelon	Smooth surface; creamy underside; bright red flesh	Stringy or mealy flesh (spoilage difficult to see on outside)

FIGURE 15.16 Signs of acceptable and unacceptable quality in some fresh fruit items.
Reprinted with permission from Applied Foodservice Sanitation Certification Coursebook, *4th edition. Copyright 1992 by the National Restaurant Association Educational Foundation. All rights reserved.*

To extend the shelf life of fresh produce, buyers must research the best possible storage environment for each fruit and vegetable. This includes knowing how the produce is packaged because some packages are designed to extend shelf life. Some fruits and vegetables, packed in a box, carton, or cello wrap, are best stored by merely placing them in the refrigerator. On the other hand, some produce arrives in crates that are not designed to extend shelf life. Celery, for example,

	SIGNS OF GOOD QUALITY	SIGNS OF POOR QUALITY, SPOILAGE
Artichokes	Plumpness; green scales; clinging leaves	Brown scales; grayish-black discoloration; mold
Asparagus	Closed tips; round spears	Spread-out tips; spears with ridges; spears that are not round
Beans (snap)	Firm, crisp pods	Extensive discoloration; tough pods
Beets	Firmness; roundness; deep red color	Gray mold; wilting; flabbiness
Brussels Sprouts	Bright color; Tight-fitting leaves	Loose, yellow-green outer leaves; ragged leaves (may indicate worm damage)
Cabbage	Firmness; heaviness for size	Wilted or decayed outer leaves (leaves should not separate easily from base.)
Carrots	Smoothness; firmness	Soft spots
Cauliflower	Clean, white curd; bright green leaves	Speckled curd; severe wilting; loose flower clusters
Celery	Firmnessl crispness; smooth stems	Flabby leaves; brown-black interior discoloration
Cucumber	Green color; firmness	Yellowish color; softness
Eggplant	Uniform, dark purple color	Softness; irregular dark brown spots
Greens	Tender leaves free of blemishes	Yellow-green leaves; evidence of insect decay
Lettuce	Crisp leaves; bright color	Tip burn on edges of leaves (slight discoloration of outer leaves is not harmful).
Mushrooms	White, creamy, or tan color on tops of caps	Dark color on underside of cap; withering veil
Onions	Hardness; firmness; small necks; papery outer scales	Wet or soft necks
Onions (green)	Crisp, green tops; white portion two to three inches in length	Yellowing; wilting
Peppers (green)	Glossy appearance; dark green color	Thin walls; cuts, punctures
Potatoes	Firmness; relative smoothness	Green rot or mold; large cuts; sprouts
Radishes	Plumpness; roundness; red color	Yellowing of tops (sign of aging); softness
Squash (summer)	Glossy skin	Dull appearance tough surface
Squash (winter)	Hard rind	Mold; softness
Sweet potatoes	Bright skins	Wetness; shriveling; sunken and discolored areas on sides of potato (sweet potatoes are extremely susceptible to decay.)
Tomatoes	Smoothness; redness (tomatoes that are pink or slightly green will ripen in a warm place.)	Bruises; deep cracks around the stem scar
Watercress	Crispness; bright green color	Yellowing, wilting; decaying of leaves

FIGURE 15.17 Signs of acceptable and unacceptable quality in some fresh vegetable items.

Reprinted with permission from Applied Foodservice Sanitation Certification Coursebook, *4th edition. Copyright 1992 by the National Restaurant Association Educational Foundation. All rights reserved.*

Commodity	Storage Temperature (F)	Relative Humidity (%)	Maximum Total Storage Period
Asparagus	32–36	95	2–3 weeks
Apples	32	90	2–6 months
Broccoli	32	95	10–14 days
Carrots, mature	32	95	4–5 months
Cauliflower	32	95	2–4 weeks
Celery	32	95	2–3 months
Cucumbers	45–50	95	10–14 days
Lettuce	32	95	2–3 weeks
Onions	32	65–70	6–7 months
Parsley	32	95	1–2 month
Peppers, sweet	45–50	95	2–3 weeks
Potatoes, early	50	90	1–3 weeks
Squash, winter	50–55	50–60	2–6 months
Sweet Potato	55–60	80–85	4–6 months
Tomatoes, ripe	45–50	90	4–7 days

FIGURE 15.18 Recommended storage requirements for some fresh vegetables.
Courtesy of Restaurants & Institutions *magazine, a Cahners publication*

usually arrives in a crate and rapidly loses moisture and becomes limp if not repacked. Cello bags or plastic, reusable, see-through tubs are excellent for repacking. Contrary to popular opinion, produce should not be washed before it is stored. Moisture enhances the growth of soft-rot microorganisms and invariably decreases the shelf life of the fruit or vegetable. Washing may also remove protective wax coating designed to extend the shelf life of vegetables such as green peppers and cucumbers. Products should be washed, if necessary, when they enter the production cycle.

Operators also should expect to extend fresh-produce shelf life if they practice proper fresh-produce handling techniques. The techniques are quite simple. The general rule is to handle the merchandise only when it is absolutely necessary. Employees should not pick it up, move it around, bend it, or bounce it because this will cause unnecessary bruising that will manifest itself in excessive spoilage and waste.

■ Issuing

Fresh-produce purchases often bypass the central-storage facility and go directly to the food production department. If employees first move the fresh produce to a central-storage facility and issue it later to the food production department, they may want to issue these items as ready-to-go. That is, they may consider issuing cleaned, chopped onions instead of whole onions; sliced tomatoes instead of whole tomatoes; or topped, peeled, and cut carrots instead of whole carrots (see Figure 15.19 for preparation waste of some fresh fruit and vegetables). By doing this, they may be able to save labor costs or extract better value from higher-paid cooks and chefs.

Employees should follow proper stock rotation when issuing produce (see Figure 15.20 for storage times for some fresh-produce items). Because these items spoil quickly, make sure that the requisitioner takes no more than necessary. It may be wise to ask him or her to note the **in-process inventory** before asking for more stock.

in-process inventory
Products located at employee workstations; most or all will be used during the shift.

Item	Trimmed/ Cleaned Ounce Weight per AP Pound	Yield Percent	Trimmed/Cleaned Weight (EP) ounces per cup
Apples, Red Delicious	14.38	89.9%	4.3 peeled, cored, diced
Asparagus	9.13	57.1%	4.75 trimmed
Bananas	10.6	66.3%	5.3 sliced
Beans, green	14.1	88.1%	3.9 trimmed
Blueberries	14.3	89.4%	5.1 whole
Broccoli	10.1	62.8%	2.5 florets
Brussels sprouts	14.2	88.8%	3.2 trimmed
Cabbage	12.8	80.0%	3.3 shredded
Cantaloupe	9.3	58.1%	5.65 cubed
Carrots	13.0	81.3%	5.0 diced
Cauliflower, whole	9.6	60.0%	4.7 florets
Celery, whole stalk	11.0	68.8%	4.0 diced
Cucumbers	15.2	95.0%	4.8 sliced
Eggplant, whole	13.5	84.2%	2.9 peeled/cubed
Grapefruit	8.4	52.6%	7.4 sectioned
Honeydew	9.2	57.5%	5.9 cubed
Kale	9.6	60.0%	2.4 chopped
Lettuce, Iceberg	11.7	73.1%	2.0 chopped
Lettuce, Romaine	12.0	75.0%	2.0 choppeOd
Mushrooms, white	15	93.8%	2.5 sliced
Onions, green	13.3	82.9%	2.0 sliced
Onions, large	14.6	91.2%	3.9 diced
Oranges	5.5	34.4%	6.1 sectioned
Parsnips	13.5	84.4%	4.7 sliced
Peas, snap	15	93.8%	2.2 trimmed
Peaches	12.5	78.1%	6.0 sliced
Pears	13.1	81.6%	5.1 diced
Peppers, green	13	81.3%	5.2 chopped
Peppers, jalapeno	14.9	93.5%	3.8 chopped
Pineapple	7.75	45.5%	5.9 cubed
Potatoes, Russet	12.5	78.1%	5.0 peeled/diced
Shallots	14.5	90.6%	5.2 peeled
Squash, butternut	13.5	84.4%	4.6 cubed
Squash, yellow	15.2	95.0%	3.9 sliced
Squash, zucchini	15	93.8%	3.8 sliced
Strawberries	14.7	91.9%	5.36 sliced
Tomatoes, 5 x 6	12.55	78.4%	5.9 peeled, seeded, chopped
Turnips	13	81.3%	4.5 diced
Watermelon	7.9	49.4%	5.4 cubed

FIGURE 15.19 The preparation waste of some fresh-produce items.

STORAGE TIMES FOR FRUITS AND VEGETABLES

APPLES, Fresh	Store in fruit or vegetable box three weeks to a month. Inspect daily to remove rotten fruit so that the balance will not be contaminated. Watch for blue mold or black rot.
APRICOTS	Easily stored for one to two weeks.
ASPARAGUS	Can be kept for two weeks but must be crated with the heels packed in moss.
AVOCADO	May be kept in refrigerator one week after ripening.
BANANAS	May be kept at 50 to 60 degrees and used within two to three days after ripening. Do not store in the cooler at any time.
BERRIES	All fresh berries can be kept for a week to 10 days. However, it is recommended that these be used as quickly as possible for best flavor.
BROCCOLI	Can be stored for 8 to 10 days.
CABBAGE	EARLY VARIETY will keep about two weeks. LATE VARIETY is much sturdier—will last two months.
CANTALOUPE	Inspect daily for ripeness. When ripe, may be held in the cooler for one week.
CARROTS	If in good condition, they may be kept in the storeroom for a few days. Under refrigeration, they will last three months.
CAULIFLOWER	May be kept for two weeks if the leaves are not cut away. After the leaves are removed, it deteriorates rapidly.
CELERY	Should not be kept longer than a few days. If it is wilted, placing in water will freshen it.
CORN	Corn is one of the most sensitive of vegetables and should be used within 24 hours after arrival.
CRANBERRIES	May be stored in a vegetable box for as long as two months.
CUCUMBERS	These are not sturdy and should be used within a week.
EGGPLANT	Should not remain in storage more than a week.
GARLIC	Can be kept for about two months at temperatures from 55 to 65 degrees. In a vegetable cooler at temperatures 32 to 36 degrees, garlic will last four months.
GRAPEFRUIT	Will last six weeks at 32 to 36 degrees.
GRAPES	White seedless or red Tokay grapes will keep for four weeks. Red Emperor, obtainable in late fall, will keep for two months.
KALE	In temperatures from 32 to 36 degrees, kale will remain in good condition for three weeks.
LEMONS	May be kept from one to two months at 50 to 60 degrees.
LETTUCE, Iceberg	If in good condition and inspected regularly, iceberg lettuce may be kept for four weeks. The leaves should not be removed until the lettuce is to be used, unless they have begun to rot. However, to obtain a maximum quality, lettuce should be used as soon as possible after arrival.
LIMES	Will not last in storage over two weeks.
MELONS	May be stored a maximum of three weeks. However, it is recommended that they be used as soon as the proper degree of softness is achieved.
MUSHROOMS	Fresh, should not be kept more than one or two days.
ONIONS, Green	If kept under refrigeration, they will last a week or 10 days.
ONIONS, Yellow	If stored in a cool, dry place, unrefrigerated, they will last three months.
ORANGES	Should be used within a week if possible. If necessary, they may be held in a reasonably good condition for a month or six weeks.
PARSNIPS	Can be stored two to three months at 32 to 36 degrees.
PARSLEY	A week is about the time limit for parsley. Keep it well iced.

FIGURE 15.20 Storage times for some fresh-produce items.
Reprinted from Lodging *magazine*

■ In-Process Inventories

Buyers will discover that control of purchasing, receiving, storing, and issuing fresh produce is easier than control of produce production and service. For instance, a great deal of supervision is required to ensure that salad greens do not sit out at room temperature too long. Generally, once the fresh produce is issued to a user, buyers are relieved of their responsibility.

We have known several restaurants that undertook considerable expense to purchase fresh produce efficiently, only to see the savings disappear because an inexperienced manager did not, or could not, supervise its use. Many operations are careful to protect the AP price, or back-door cost, but the EP cost, or front-door cost, does not often enjoy equal consideration. Figure 15.19 shows that considerable unavoidable loss is associated with fresh produce; the chances for excessive loss increase if proper supervision is absent.

Key Words and Concepts

Agricultural Marketing Service (AMS)

Cell pack

Cold chain

Color

Controlled atmosphere storage

Decay allowance

Degree of ripeness

Ethylene gas

Exact name

Farmers' market

Field run

Flat

Genetically altered food

Heirloom plants

Hydroponic

In-process inventory

Intended use

Layered

Localvore

Lug

Minimum weight per case

Organic food

Packers' brand names

Perishable Agricultural Commodities
    Act (PACA)

P.L.O.T.

Point of origin

Precut fresh produce

Prewashed

Preservation

Produce Marketing Association (PMA)

Product form

Product size

Product yield

Pulp temperature

Ready-to-serve product

Ripening process

Ripening room

Sanitary Food Transportation Act of 2005

Shelf life

Shrink allowance

Slab-packed

Trim

Value-added product

Questions and Problems

1. Name the U.S. grades for fresh produce.

2. What is the most frequently ordered grade of fresh produce in the hospitality industry?

3. A product specification for fresh lemons could include the following information:
    a.
    b.
    c.
    d.
    e.

4. Why does the foodservice operator normally not care for fresh produce that has been in controlled atmosphere storage?

5. Why should buyers note the minimum weight per case on their specifications for fresh produce?

6. Why is the point of origin for fresh produce very important?

7. What is an appropriate intended use for:
    a. green tomatoes
    b. U.S. No. 2 grade tomatoes
    c. roma or plum tomatoes
    d. "field-run" fresh produce

8. When would a buyer use a packer's brand in lieu of a U.S. grade when preparing a product specification for fresh tomatoes?

9. What are some advantages and disadvantages of buying fresh produce from a farmers' market?

10. Assume that you manage a cafeteria and have run out of salad greens at 7:30 P.M. on a Saturday night. What do you do?

11. Why is it important to note the exact variety of fresh produce desired, instead of merely noting the type of item needed?

12. What does the notation "3 to 1" indicate to a buyer?

13. Precut fresh produce usually carries an AP price that is much higher than that of raw fresh produce. Identify some of the reasons for this difference.

14. What are some of the methods fresh-produce suppliers can use to extend the shelf life of fruits and vegetables?

15. When would a buyer specify organically grown fresh produce on a product specification for fresh produce?

16. What is a decay allowance?

Questions and Problems (continued)

17. What critical information is missing from the following product specification for onions?

    Onions
    Used to make onion rings
    U.S. No. 1 Grade (or equivalent)
    Packed in 50-pound mesh bags

18. What are the differences between genetically altered tomatoes and heirloom tomatoes?

19. For which types of products is "pulp temperature" an important selection factor?

20. What are the P.L.O.T. vegetables? Why are they important for operators to be familiar with?

21. Supplier A offers lettuce at $16.75 per case, and Supplier B offers it at $18.50 per case. The yield for Supplier A is 88 percent; for Supplier B, 94 percent. Supplier A expects a COD payment; Supplier B gives seven days' credit terms. Which supplier should a buyer purchase from? Why?

Experiential Exercises

1. Why might it be difficult to engage in bid buying when purchasing fresh produce? When and why would a buyer bid buy? Speak with a buyer for a hotel or chain restaurant. Ask him/her whether the company uses bid buying. Prepare a one-page report with your findings.

2. Outline the specific procedures a buyer would use to purchase, receive, store, and issue salad greens—lettuce, red cabbage, and carrots—and baking potatoes. Assume that these products will be used in a steakhouse. Ask a steak-house manager to comment on your answer. Write a one-page report on your findings

3. Prepare product specifications for the products noted in Experiential Exercise 2.

4. Visit a local farmers' market. Speak with the farmers and make observations about:
    a. the number of farmers/booths
    b. how many different types of products each carries
    c. whether the products are labeled with terms such as organic, natural, or locally grown
    d. whether the patrons are mostly ultimate consumers or restaurant chefs/buyers

    Write a one-two page report about what you learned.

References

1. "The Sysco Produce Product Catalog," http://syscoezine.com/12Produce/docs/book.pdf.

2. Patt Patterson, "A Hard Sell: Buying Produce Is No Day in the Park," *Nation's Restaurant News*, January 25, 1993, p. 23. See also Caroline Perkins, "De La Cruz Sows Knowledge of Fresh Produce," *Nation's Restaurant News*, 40, no. 6 (February 6, 2006):16.

3. Thomas M. Burton, "Buying Fine Produce for Finicky Chefs Is No Bowl of Cherries," *The Wall Street Journal*, August 6, 1991, p. A1.

4. Produce Marketing Association, (December 2013). "Foodservice Overview," www.pma.com/system/files/2014%20Foodservcie%20overview%20Final_1.pdf.

5. Dana Tanyeri, "Local, on a Large Scale," *Restaurant Business*, 107, no. 5 (May 2008): 13–14. See also Karen Herzog, "Buyer Helps Local Produce Find Its Way to Area Restaurants," *Journal Sentinel*, September 8, 2009, www.jsonline.com/features/food/57742052.html.

6. Anonymous, "What Are Genetically Modified (GM) Foods?" Genome Programs of the U.S. Department of Energy Office of Science, www.ornl.gov/sci/techresources/Human_Genome/elsi/gmfood.shtml. See also Rick Charnes, "Genetically Altered Food: Myths and Realities," *EarthSave*, www.earthsave.org/ge.htm; Anonymous, "What Are Genetically Modified Foods?" www.howstuffworks.com/question148.htm. See also John Lang and Susanna Priest, "Understanding Receptivity to Genetically Modified Foods," *Gastronomica*, 7, no. 3 (Summer 2007):88–92.

7. Barbara Haumann, "U.S. Organic Sales Post New Record of $43.3 billion in 2015," by *Maggie MacNeill*, May 19, 2016, https://www.ota.com/news/press-releases/19031.

8. Betsy Spethmann, "Planting the Seed," *Promo*, 15, no. 9 (August 2002):26–28. See also Stephanie Salkin, "USDA Unveils Final Organics Rules," *ID: The Information Source for Managers & DSRS*, 37, no. 2 (February 2001):20.

9. Anonymous, "Frequently Asked Questions," *Produce Law*, www.producelaw.com.

10. Agricultural Marketing Service, "Grading, Certification, and Verification," www.ams.usda.gov/.

11. Naomi Imatome-Yun, "All About the Korean Pear (Bae) AKA Apple Pear and Asian Pear," http://koreanfood.about.com/od/koreanfoodbasics/p/Bae.htm. See also Fred Wilkinson "Retailers are Warming to Asian Pears," August 17, 2011, http://www.thepacker.com/fruit-vegetable-news/Retailers-warrm-to-Asian-pears-127968588.html.

12. Meg Major, "Produce Perspectives 2000," *Supermarket Business*, October 15, 2000, pp. 89–94. See also Food Spectrum, "Retail Prepared Refrigerated Foods: The Market and Technologies Mini Study on Value-added Produce," www.foodspectrum.com/produce; Karen Weisbert, "Speed Prep Smarts," *FoodService Director*, 20, no. 9 (September 15,

References (continued)

2007):48–50. Sofo Foods, "Fresh Pre-Cut Vegetable Guide," www.sofofoods.com/pdf/ sofofreshcutproduce.pdf. More information on value-added produce can be found at www.freshcut.com.

13. Steve Harrison, "Picasso of Bananas Says His Art Is a Gas," *The Miami Herald*, April 13, 2006. More information about ethylene gas can be found at www.ethylene control.com.

14. Lara Sowinski, "Maintaining Cold Chain Integrity," *Food Logistics*, December 14, 2011, www.foodlogistics.com/article/10525032/maintaining-cold-chain-integrity. See also, Riëtte van Laack, "FDA Releases Proposed Sanitary Food Transportation Regulations," February 9, 2014, www.fdalawblog.net/fda_law_blog_hyman_phelps/2014/02/fda -releases-proposed-sanitary-food-transportation-regulations.html.

15. "Frequently Asked Questions about Organic Food and Farming," *Organic Farming Research Foundation*, http://ofrf.org/resources/organicfaqs.html. See also Monica Eng, "Line Between Natural and Organic Becoming Blurred for Consumers," *The Chicago Tribune*, July 10, 2009; Mayo Clinic Staff, "Organic Foods: Are they Safer? More Nutritious?" www.mayoclinic.com/health/organic-food/NU00255. Jennifer Febbraro, "Organic Panic," *Foodservice & Hospitality*, 38, no. 12 (February 2006):16–22.

16. Catherine A. Strohbehn, "Local Food Connections: From Farms to Restaurants," *Iowa State University Extension*. http://lib.dr.iastate.edu/cgi/viewcontent.cgi?article=122 0&context=leopold_grantreports.

17. Katie Ayoub, "Field Notes on Farmer/Chef Relationships," *The National Culinary Review*, August 2008, p. 17.

18. Dina Berta, "From the Frying Pan to the Garden," *Nation's Restaurant News*, 39, no. 36 (September 5, 2003):41–42. See also Michael Nagrent, "More Chefs Tending to Own Produce," *Chicago Sun Times*, July 9, 2008, www.suntimes.com/ lifestyles/ food/1045996,FOO-News-garden09.article. Mary Landers, "Downtown Savannah Restaurant Growing Its Own Food," *Savannah Morning News*, August 9, 2009, http://savannahnow.com/node/765092. Ken Macqueen, "Kitchen Garden," *Maclean's*, 116, no. 26/27 (July 1, 2003):77. See also Amy Zuber, "On the Menu: Foodlife, Chicago," *Nation's Restaurant News*, September 4, 2000, p. 38.

19. Twilight Greenaway, "Celebrity Chefs and Food Movement Leaders Tell Congress: 'This Farm Bill Stinks'," *Grist*, http://grist.org/farm-bill/celebrity-chefs-and-food -movement-leaders-tell-congress-this-farm-bill-stinks/.

CHAPTER 16

PROCESSED PRODUCE AND OTHER GROCERY ITEMS

The Purpose of This Chapter

After reading this chapter, you should be able to:

- Explain management considerations surrounding the selection and procurement of processed produce and other grocery items.

- Choose appropriate processed produce and other grocery items based on primary selection factors, including government grades.

- Categorize processed produce and other grocery items according to product size, form, and packaging and related characteristics.

- Consider supplier and AP price factors when purchasing processed produce and other grocery items.

- Create a specification for processed produce and other grocery items that can be used in the purchasing process.

- Describe procedures for receiving, storing, and issuing processed produce and other grocery items.

MANAGEMENT CONSIDERATIONS

The purchasing procedures for convenience items, such as processed fruit and vegetables, and for other grocery items, such as spices, pastas, fats, and oils, are more routine than those required for fresh products. In general, the qualities are more predictable, and the as-purchased (AP) prices do not fluctuate so widely as those for fresh products.

To prevent the mistaken idea that this area of purchasing does not present difficulties, we must stress that purchasing processed items requires several management considerations. As is almost always the case, these considerations center on the determination of what a hospitality operation wants, what type of product is best suited for its needs, and which supplier can accommodate these needs.

It is probably impractical to imagine any storeroom without a few cans of tomatoes on its shelves. Thus, the decision here is not an either/or proposition. It is more a question of which products should be fresh and which should be processed. In addition, some methods used to cook certain fruits and vegetables do not produce food that tastes substantially different from its processed counterpart. For example, a tomato sauce made with canned tomatoes may taste about the same as one made with fresh tomatoes. Finally, you can combine some fresh products with processed ones. For instance, a Japanese salad can be made with frozen edamame, reconstituted, dried shitake mushrooms, and fresh scallions or canned corn can be mixed with fresh onions and peppers.

Food processors process produce for many reasons in addition to preserving them. Food processors seek to smooth out seasonal fluctuations and to capture items at their peak of flavor while adding value to the items. In doing so, food processors transfer some work from the foodservice kitchen to the food-processing plant. Thus, processing fruits and vegetables can be viewed as the procedure of extending the availability of perishable items.

One of the ironies about processed produce is that most items are processed to increase **shelf life**.

shelf life   The amount of time a product can remain in storage before it loses quality and cannot be used.

When these items are lost because of mishandling in the foodservice operation, one of the main reasons why they were processed in the first place is defeated. Many processed products, once thawed, opened, or heated, have extremely short in-process shelf lives. In addition, reheating or reusing many of these items usually results in inferior finished products. Processed produce shares this problem with most convenience products.

Consequently, a major management decision involving processed produce items is whether to use them at all. (Hospitality operations usually have little choice for other grocery items, although some properties make their own pasta, prepare their own sauces, bake their own breads, and blend their own condiments.) Taking into consideration the current interest in "natural, whole foods," operators cannot take this decision lightly. Some make a point of reminding their patrons that all vegetables on their menus are cooked from the fresh state. Whether this approach has marketing value may be a matter of opinion.

Once hospitality operators realize that at least some processed produce and other grocery items will be used in preparing menu items, they face the question of which processing method to choose. For some products, they have little choice. For example, if buyers decided to purchase plain pasta, they must keep in mind that it is usually a dried product, though some fresh refrigerated and some precooked frozen pastas are available. Other processing techniques include pickling and other fermentation methods. Buyers almost exclusively purchase foods processed in these ways for the taste the processing imparts and not necessarily for convenience, AP price considerations, or other reasons. Also, some other preservation methods, such as adding chemical preservatives and refrigerating some soup bases, have become standard. Unless buyers specify otherwise, they will receive the product this way. The buyers' selection of a processing method, then, is affected by: (1) food quality, (2) AP price, and (3) the need for convenience. Although the standards of quality vary within each processing method, by and large, the processing method itself predetermines the taste, AP prices, and convenience.

If buyers opt for canned goods or **shelf-stable products** packed in **aseptic packaging**, they will receive the benefits of standardized packaging, longer shelf life, and less-expensive storage costs (see Figure 16.1). The buyers may also get a distinctive "canned" taste, however. For some items, such as tomato sauce, cans or aseptic packages may be the only choices. For others, such as white asparagus spears, buyers may have to settle for a can or a bottle.

When buyers choose frozen processing, they have the benefit of fresher flavor, or at least a taste as close as possible to natural flavor. Moreover, purveyors claim that only products picked at their peak of flavor are frozen. Some processed items are usually sold only in the frozen state. For example, corn on the cob and french fries are normally available only fresh or fresh-frozen.

Unfortunately, frozen-fruit and frozen-vegetable packaging is not quite as standardized as the cans. Buyers also take greater risks with frozen items: the chances of thawing and refreezing, of a freezer breakdown, and of **freezer burn**. The shelf life of many frozen items is not as long as that of canned and bottled items. The AP prices tend to be higher, and a higher storage cost is associated with frozen products.

One of the biggest difficulties with any frozen product is the possibility of thawing a larger amount than is needed. The excess cannot be refrozen without a considerable loss of quality. Usually, the item is then wasted entirely. Frozen products are just too costly to throw out, however; consequently, a hospitality operator may try to work them into the menu somehow at the risk of alienating customers.

When choosing dried products, buyers are obviously going to save on storage. In addition, if buyers care for the items properly, they will have a long shelf life. Also, because the food is lightweight and does not require refrigeration, its transportation costs remain low, which, in turn, reduces AP prices. On the other hand, the AP prices of many dried

shelf-stable product A food item that is processed and packaged in such a way that it can maintain its quality for long periods of time at room temperature.

aseptic packaging A form of controlled atmosphere packaging (CAP). Sterile foods placed in an airtight, sterilized package. The package contains a hygienic environment that prolongs shelf life and makes the foods shelf-stable.

freezer burn The loss of moisture from a food product while it is held in frozen storage. Typically causes dry (i.e., "burned") spots on the product as well as an unpleasant odor.

FIGURE 16.1 Aseptic packaging.
©Rosanne Tackaberry/Alamy Stock Photo

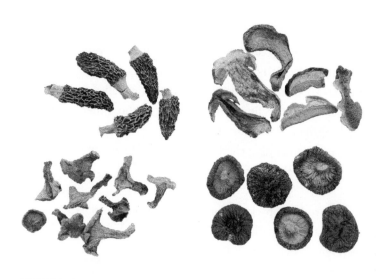

FIGURE 16.2 Dried mushrooms, clockwise from top left: morels, porcini, shiitake, chanterelles.

Source: Gisslen, Professional Cooking, 7th Edition, Copyright 2011. Reprinted with permission of John Wiley and Sons, Inc.

items may still be high because of the amount of time and energy used to process them. Unfortunately, buyers cannot purchase very many food items in a dried state. However, some processed items, including instant mashed potatoes, dried onion flakes, and dried spices, are usually sold only in a dried state.

Many dehydrated foods are expensive. For example, dried fruit requires very ripe fruit with a high concentration of natural sugar. These qualities are costly; however, they make such fruit particularly desirable. For example, dried pineapple rings used in making upside-down cakes probably have an AP price that exceeds that of the canned counterpart, but the taste is different—dried pineapple is extremely sweet and strong. The same culinary characteristics are inherent in dried vegetables, such as dried mushrooms (see Figure 16.2).

A major difficulty with some dried items is the need to reconstitute them. A mistake here, even a tiny one, can ruin the product. Another difficulty is the style of packaging. For instance, macaroni products come in all sorts of packaging materials and package sizes. Dried fruit is sometimes nicely layered on waxed paper and lined up neatly in a box. However, it may also be slab-packed, or tossed in randomly and pushed together so that by the time buyers get it, some of it may be damaged.

In addition to deciding which processing method best suits the needs of the operation, management must make another major decision regarding processed products, which centers on the question of substitution. For example, a recipe for mixed vegetables could include some fresh product, to use leftovers; some frozen product, bought at bargain prices; and some dried product, to take advantage of the excess sweetness. Consider the problem of inertia, however: because these purchases do not usually represent a large percentage of the purchase dollar, few operators devote much effort to determining the least-expensive recipe unless they have access to a management information system (MIS). Although this area may not seem to offer a great deal of money-saving potential, some money can, nevertheless, be saved.

When buyers purchase processed food, they usually obtain what they want. They name it, and somebody will make it if the purchase volume is large enough. For instance, fats and oils can be manufactured almost according to individual specifications, but operators must pay for this service. Nevertheless, when buyers purchase these products, it is good to know that they can get what they need.

There are several other management considerations involving processed food that may also need to evaluated.

1. Some buyers tend to neglect generally accepted purchasing principles when it comes to some processed produce and grocery items. This is probably because only a small amount of the total purchase dollar is involved, as the majority goes toward meat, fish, poultry, alcoholic

beverages, and some desserts. For example, the temptation is strong for buyers to set the par stock for condiments and let it go at that. Manufacturers and suppliers who rely heavily on "pull strategies" for some of these items further foster this tendency. Some products that grace a dining room table, such as Heinz® ketchup and A-1® steak sauce, seem almost traditional. To a lesser extent, other condiments, such as olives, pickles, and relishes, fall into this category.

2. The neglect mentioned earlier might also be nurtured by the cavalier attitude with which some employees approach inventory. For instance, some managers allow service personnel to bypass the normal issuing system when they need steak sauce, hot sauce, or similar condiments. In many small operations, service staff walk into the storeroom and take what they need. If a bottle or two spills or disappears, few supervisors get upset.

3. Numerous **impulse purchases** flood the market. For example, buyers can purchase devices to: drain near-empty catsup bottles, check the pressure in canned goods, and determine whether a product has been thawed and refrozen. These may be used once or twice and then tossed into the back of a drawer.

4. For one reason or another, several new products are introduced each year in grocery product lines. Of course, many food products are not really new, just new variations of existing foodstuffs. For example, buyers can find all sorts of new vegetable combinations and sauce variations. The same is true for rice and pasta concoctions. Taking the time to examine all these "new" ideas can cause buyers to neglect other more important business.

5. Sometimes buying one processed item entails buying something else. For instance, if buyers purchase semolina flour to make their own pasta, they must also buy the pasta machine. Similarly, if they buy corn flour to make their own tortillas and taco shells, they may need a special basket to hold the shells in the fryer.

6. Processed foods present several **opportunity buys**, such as **introductory offers**, **quantity discounts**, **volume discounts**, **salvage buys**,[1] and other hospitality operations' **going-out-of-business sales**. For operators who control a lot of purchase money, long-term contracts may also be available. These opportunities usually require a bit of extra analysis. Buyers must decide whether they are going to buy these items on a day-to-day basis or be persuaded by a salesperson who comes in with a flamboyant special offer.

7. Buyers must decide which container size they should buy. Smaller packages have higher AP prices per unit, but they sometimes provide the best edible-portion (EP) cost. A related concern exists: Should buyers purchase individual, filled catsup bottles, or should they keep the empty bottles and refill them with catsup from a No. 10 can or some other bulk pack? The latter choice may entail some waste and labor, but it may also produce the best EP cost.

impulse purchase An unplanned or otherwise spontaneous purchase.

opportunity buy A purchase intended to save a great deal of money. The products are price discounted. A quantity discount is an example of an opportunity buy.

introductory offers A price reduction for buying a new product or one that a distributor has just started selling.

quantity discount A price reduction for buying a large amount of one specific type of merchandise.

volume discount Similar to a quantity discount. The buyer agrees to purchase a huge volume of goods; however, unlike a quantity discount, he or she buys more than one type of merchandise.

salvage buy Buying a deep-discounted item. Usually the AP price is very low because the item is damaged.

going-out-of-business sale Held to dispose of all remaining inventory and in some cases, all the existing furniture, fixtures, and equipment (FFE). Everything is typically sold at heavily discounted prices.

push strategy Refers to vendors who will do whatever is necessary, and legal, to entice buyers to purchase their products, usually by providing discounts and/or very generous supplier services.

8. A final major consideration relates to Point 6. Should buyers accept an offer that looks appealing but that would involve changing the form of the product they usually purchase? For instance, they may be offered a bargain in canned green beans, but they normally use the frozen form. Buyers should not take this temptation lightly. If profits are running a little low for the business, or if a particular buyer is just naturally conservative with money, it's surprising how big a few pennies can look. (This problem also arises with introductory offers or other types of **push strategies**. Suppliers often try to switch a buyer from one item to another by temporarily manipulating the AP price.)

YOU SAY POTATO . . .
Don Odiorne, aka "Dr. Potato," is the Vice President of Foodservice, Idaho Potato Commission

Courtesy of Idaho Potato Commission

Potatoes are one of the most important vegetables for the foodservice industry. In 2012, more than 46.7 billion pounds were grown in the United States with 12.1 billion pounds used as table stock or whole potatoes and 16.8 billion pounds for frozen french fries.[1] Idaho was the top producing state with 14.3 billion pounds of potatoes. In 2010, nearly 8 billion servings of french fries were sold in U.S. restaurants representing 15.5 percent of all restaurant orders.[2]

Don Odiorne joined the Idaho Potato Commission in 1989. He is now Vice President of Foodservice for the organization. He knows so much about potatoes that he writes a foodservice blog under the name of "Dr. Potato." He works with corporate and high-volume unit chefs on a daily basis, cultivating the usage of Idaho potatoes in their operations. He encourages them to decide which types of potato items to sell in their restaurants, which form to buy, and how to market the potatoes on the menu.

One of the most important points Don emphasizes is that cheaper is not necessarily better. Restaurant operators definitely have to evaluate edible-portion (EP) costs rather than as-purchased (AP) prices. He gives the example that serving longer french fries is generally better than shorter fries. A restaurant needs more of the shorter fries to fill up a plate or container than the longer fries. Although decorative baskets or cones may have an initial equipment cost, a restaurant can serve less and charge more than just putting the fries on a regular plate. A sprinkle of a house-made spice blend or a side of a specialty sauce can increase the value even more.

A big consideration for a restaurant is whether to use fresh or frozen french fries. Although some chains like In-N-Out Burger, Five Guys, and high-volume fine dining restaurants may have fresh fries as a signature menu item, Don says that frozen fries are generally the better value. Frozen have a more consistent EP weight than fresh because fresh lose water weight when they go through the typical two-step method for making fries of blanching them once in oil and then re-frying them. Frozen fries have already been through the blanching process so their EP weight is the same (or even higher due to absorbing some fat) than their AP weight. Of course, with fresh there is also weight loss if the restaurant peels the potatoes or discards any for defects. Frozen fries have lower labor costs due to several factors; they take less time to prep, can be made by cooks who are not as skilled and may make lower

YOU SAY POTATO . . . (continued)

wages, and training costs are minimal. Frozen fries generally can be held and stay crisper longer, minimizing the chance that they will lose quality and have to be thrown out if they are not served within a certain time. The final factor is that restaurants using fresh potatoes must be aware that their quality varies due to their source, the variety, the time of year, and the amount of water to solids ratio, so extra care must be taken when writing product specifications, locating sources, and purchasing them.

Don says that it is very important for buyers to know the intended use of the potatoes they purchase so that costs per portion can be calculated. He gives an example of using russet potatoes for baked potatoes. They are sold by count, per 50-lb carton. At $15 per case, each 80-count potato will cost $0.19 but a 60-count potato at the same carton price will cost $0.25 each. It may be $0.06 more, but if the larger size will give a better plate presentation and increase the guests' perceived value of the dish, the restaurant may be able to charge a higher price for the menu item. Don expects that as beef and pork prices rise over the next few years, many restaurants could reduce the portion price of the protein and increase the size of the potato serving to maintain an acceptable plate cost. If the culinary staff ensures that they always serve the correct portion size and utilize all parts of the potato, such as julienning peels for a potato straw garnish, the potatoes can be even more cost effective.

When purchasing the potatoes, it is important to visit the location of the supplier to see how the potatoes are stored and handled.

A restaurant can buy from a full-service distributor that carries produce or a produce specialist. Although it is feasible that a large chain such as McDonald's could buy whole fields of potatoes from the grower–shipper or specify one to three preferred suppliers, the trend is to match the source and the supplier to lock in availability year-round. The final pricing needs to consider transportation costs. It may not be economical for a chain to purchase all its processed potatoes from the West if it has high concentrations of restaurants in the Northeast or North Central regions where it could be cheaper to source the potatoes from Canada or Wisconsin. On the other hand, an operator can specify a source of origin, such as Idaho for better consistency of the end product.

Who would think there was this much to know about buying and using potatoes? Fortunately, the Idaho Potato Commission provides many resources for buyers, chefs, students, and educators. A few of its most popular tools and information sites are the following:

Cost and size guide:

> https://idahopotato.com/foodservice/cost-and-size

Nutrition information

> https://idahopotato.com/uploads/media/nutrition-infographic.pdf

Potato harvest information

> https://idahopotato.com/uploads/media/15-1005%20Harvest%20Infographic.pdf

■ REFERENCES

1. National Potato Council (May, 2013), *2013 Potato Statistical Yearbook*,
   http://nationalpotatocouncil.org/files/4613/6940/5509/2013_NPCyearbook_Web_FINAL.pdf.

2. Barney Wolf, November 2010, "These Spuds Aren't Duds," *QSR Menu Innovations*,
   www.qsrmagazine.com/menu-innovations/these-spuds-aren-t-duds.

PRIMARY SELECTION FACTORS

Management, either alone or in conjunction with others, decides the quality, type, and style of food wanted for each processed item. During this decision-making process, the owner–manager should evaluate the selection factors in the following sections.

■ Intended Use

As always, owner–managers want to determine exactly the **intended use** of the item so that they will be able to prepare the appropriate, relevant specification. For example, canned fruit used in a recipe that has several other ingredients need not be as attractive as that used alone in a pie filling.

> **intended use** Refers to the performance requirement of a product or service, which is noted on the specification. Considered to be the most important piece of information on a specification.

■ Exact Name

Confusing terminology clutters the market, especially the processed-produce market. For instance, buyers cannot simply order pickles; they must order Polish pickles, kosher pickles, sweet pickles, and so on. Similarly, they must specify canned Bartlett pear halves if that is what they desire, or extra virgin olive oil if they want olive oil from the first pressing with the lowest possible acidity.

The list of these designations can grow incredibly long, and more esoteric terms seem to exist in the area of processed produce and other grocery items than in most other areas. Nonetheless, buyers must become familiar with the market terminology and know the **exact name**.

> **exact name** Indication of a product or service's specific type, quality, and style.

The federal government has provided some assistance to buyers who are responsible for ordering many processed foods. Recall from Chapter 4 that it has issued several "standards of identity" that essentially establish what a food product is (e.g., what a food product must be in order to be labeled "strawberry preserves"). Some standards set specific processing requirements, such as heating at very high temperatures in hermetically sealed containers. This is necessary to ensure the wholesomeness and safety of the finished product. Other standards are related to composition. For instance, any food that purports to be organic or to contain organically produced food ingredients—that is, the product label or labeling bears the term "organic" or makes any direct or indirect representation that the food is organic—must meet a particular set of standards. For example, canned organic vegetables must contain at least 95 percent organic ingredients, which are ingredients that are grown without added hormones, pesticides, herbicides, or synthetic fertilizers. If a can of soup, for instance, simply states "made with organic vegetables," then the percentage of organically produced ingredients in the soup must be stated on the label as "Contains _____ percent organic ingredients" (with the blank filled in with the actual total percentage of organically produced ingredients in the soup). In retail foodservice, such as a grocery store, manufacturers can voluntarily use the USDA Organic seal (Figure 16.3) as long as their product is at least 95 percent organic.

FIGURE 16.3 USDA Organic Seal. *Courtesy of United States Department of Agriculture*

These types of standards, however, do not keep different companies from making distinctive recipes. For example, the U.S. Department of Agriculture (USDA) content requirement for beef stew specifies only the minimum percentage of beef (25 percent) that the stew must contain. The USDA requirement does not prevent a manufacturer from using its own combinations of other ingredients or increasing the amount of beef to make the product unique. Therefore, all brands of stew probably will taste somewhat different, which makes it risky for buyers to rely only on standards of identity when selecting processed produce and other grocery items, as well as some meat, dairy, fish, and poultry items.

Standards of identity are available for approximately 300 items if you care to use them. The USDA has established standards for meat and poultry products, and the Food and Drug Administration (FDA) has set them for cocoa products; cereal, flour, and related products; macaroni and noodle products; bakery products; milk and cream products; cheese and cheese products; frozen desserts; sweeteners and table syrups; food flavorings; dressings for food; canned fruits and fruit juices; fruit butters, jellies, preserves, and related products; soda water; canned and frozen fish and shellfish; eggs and egg products; oleomargarine; nut products; canned and frozen vegetables; and tomato products.

For some items, buyers may be able to make do with only a **standard of identity**. For instance, although all types and brands of frozen orange juice are not the same, most of them are close. This is true of other frozen juices, too. Thus, buyers might be governed primarily by the AP price for these products.

■ U.S. Government Inspection and Grades (or Equivalent)

The **USDA's Agricultural Marketing Service (AMS)** Fruit and Vegetables Division and the FDA conduct mandatory inspections of processors' facilities. If any meat is incorporated in a product or if any items require egg breaking, the inspection falls under the jurisdiction of the USDA's Food Safety and Inspection Service (FSIS). Recall that continuous federal inspection or equivalent state inspection exists for any type of meat product that is sold. If no meat is involved, the foodstuffs are, nonetheless, inspected for wholesomeness, though less frequently. Of course, some state and local inspection may also be involved.

Government inspection is mandatory, but the U.S. grading service is voluntary, and food processors must pay for it. However, they have the option to pay for continuous inspection with or without a grade. Many buyers include federal-government grades in their specifications to ensure that the products are produced and **packed under continuous government inspection**. Understandably, bid buyers also seek out the relevant grading standards for their specifications.

Buyers can also specify that the products desired must carry the federal government inspection shield. This shield indicates that the product was "packed under continuous inspection of the U.S. Dept. of Agriculture." The USDA provides this fee-based service to those primary sources who want inspection only and who do not want to purchase the federal-government grading service.

standard of identity A U.S. government regulation that establishes what a food product must be to carry a certain name. For example, what a food product must be to be labeled "strawberry preserves."

USDA Agricultural Marketing Service (AMS) Agency that establishes federal grading standards for several food products, under authority of the Agricultural Marketing Act.

packed under continuous government inspection Selection factor some buyers may specify when purchasing food products (such as fresh produce and fish) that are not legally required to be produced under continuous government inspection.

FIGURE 16.4 Federal grade and inspection stamps used for processed produce and other grocery items.
Courtesy of United States Department of Agriculture

grading factors
Characteristics of food or beverage products examined by grading inspectors. Used to judge and rank products.

packing medium The type of liquid used to pack foods. Especially relevant when purchasing canned goods.

drained weight Refers to the weight of the product (such as canned sliced peaches) less its juice or other packing medium. It is computed by draining the product in a specific sieve for a certain amount of time. Sometimes referred to as the edible weight.

Federal grades have been established for canned, bottled, frozen, and dried produce and grocery items (see Figure 16.4).[2] Specific **grading factors** exist for different items. For instance, the grading factors for canned and bottled foods include the color, the uniformity of size and shape, the number of defects and blemishes, and the "character," which refers to the texture, tenderness, and aroma. Also, the quality of the **packing medium**—the water, brine, or syrup—may be important for some products. For some items, such as canned, whole tomatoes, during the evaluation process the grader considers the **drained weight**, which is the servable weight that remains after the juice is removed.

Grading factors for frozen foods include the uniformity of size and shape, maturity, quality, color, and number of defects and blemishes.

Grading factors for dried foods include the uniformity of size and shape, color, number of blemishes and defects, moisture content,[3] and the way the products are packed—are they carefully layered or packed tightly together in a container, thus distorting their natural shape?

As with fresh produce, no single categorization of grading nomenclature exists for processed foods. As a matter of convenience, buyers could rely on the following grading categories for canned, bottled, and frozen items:

1. Grade A. The very best product with excellent color, uniform size, weight, and shape, and few blemishes.

2. Grade B. Slightly less perfect than Grade A.

3. Grade C. May contain some broken and uneven pieces, perhaps some odd-shaped pieces; the flavor usually falls below Grades A and B, and the color is not so attractive.

Again, for convenience, you could rely on the same nomenclature for dried foods:

1. Grade A. The most attractive and most flavorful product.

2. Grade B. Not quite as attractive as Grade A.

3. Grade C. More variations in taste and appearance, and usually broken pieces.

Although this convenient grading system for canned, bottled, frozen, and dried products might be ideal, it is not reality. Not all these types of foods use the grading system A, B, and C. For example, canned mushrooms, frozen apples, and several dried foods carry Grades A, B, and Substandard. Frozen apricots carry the Grades A, B, C, and Substandard. Sometimes you hear the terms "Fancy," "Choice," or "Extra standard." These are alternate terms for U.S. grades that several people in the channel of distribution use. For example, many buyers use the following U.S. grade designations when purchasing canned fruit and canned vegetables:

Canned Fruit	Canned Vegetables
Fancy	Fancy
Choice	Extra standard
Standard	Standard

More difficulties in differentiating between these standards can arise based on the displayed product label. **"U. S. Grade A" versus "Grade A"** shows the buyer that the Grade A product has not been graded by a federal inspector. It should be noted that many times, food processors are allowed to use the word "Grade" on their labels as long as that label is not using the "U.S." prefix. Because some discrepancy exists between these terms, to avoid any potential confusion, buyers should carefully note whether U.S. Grade A or Grade A is listed on the package label. (As we noted in Chapter 15, buyers usually can communicate with a purveyor and make their desires known.)

> **U.S. Grade A versus Grade A** The former grade designation indicates that a federal government inspector has graded the product, whereas the latter indicates that the product was not graded by a federal government inspector.

■ Packers' Brands (or Equivalent)

We noted in Chapter 10 that a bit of **pull strategy** is inherent in certain product lines. As such, buyers can sometimes be "coerced" into purchasing Heinz ketchup, A-1 steak sauce, Del Monte® relish, and so on by tradition or customer demand.

> **pull strategy** Refers to vendors trying to influence their buyers' customers to demand the vendors' products in their favorite restaurants or hotels. The buyers, then, will have to purchase these products to satisfy their guests.

In addition, many processed items come and go. So, if buyers want a very special combination of fruit, they might find only one producer who handles it.

Also, because packaging may not be standardized, buyers may seek out brands that meet their particular packaging requirements. (Recall that a brand normally implies more than just product quality.)

For some items, particularly something like frozen peas in cream sauce, a packer's brand may be the most important indication of quality and flavor. The quality of a fruit or vegetable varies from year to year and from place to place. The top-of-the-line brands make an effort to smooth out these annual fluctuations.

Packers' brand names may be desirable, therefore, if only because subtle differences occur between, for example, tomato packers. After all, canned tomatoes can vary tremendously, not only in appearance, but in taste as well. Consequently, some buyers may be wary about trading Heinz for Del Monte simply because they detect a slightly different flavor.

> **packers' brand names** Very specific indication of product quality. More precise than a brand name. A packer's personal grading system. Usually intended to take the place of federal government grades.
>
> **packers' grades** Another term for packers' brand names.

A tremendous variety of brands is available to buyers. For instance, some companies package only the best-quality merchandise and will pack lower-quality products only if these items carry some other brand name.

These firms refer to themselves as "premium" brands. Recall from Chapter 7 that some companies prepare several qualities under the same brand-name heading; that is, they carry several **packers' grades** (i.e., packers'

> **generic brand** The package label typically does not refer directly to the company that processed the item. Rather, the label generally highlights only the name of the item while downplaying other information. Its quality is very unpredictable. Typically, it is low-quality merchandise that is sold to economy-minded buyers.
>
> **single-ingredient, generic-brand food** A product that does not carry a "name" brand label, but because it has only one ingredient, is likely to be of uniform quality and may also be equivalent to the quality of a name-brand product.

brands). For instance, buyers can sometimes purchase a specific producer's brand of carrots, but they will notice that different-colored labels exist for each quality of carrots that specific producer packs. These different-colored labels represent the packers' grades produced by the company.

Buyers can also opt for **generic brands**. These brands are not as plentiful in the wholesale-distribution channels as they are in retail grocery stores and supermarkets, probably because if buyers desire this type of quality, a packer's brand already exists to satisfy their needs. If they insist on purchasing generic brands, they probably will need to shop at the numerous warehouse wholesale clubs that cater to small businesses.

Generic brands can be very economical. Generally speaking, they typically are offered at very low AP prices for at least three reasons: (1) lower, or non-existent, selling and advertising costs; (2) lower packaging costs; and (3) in some cases, lower quality. Keep in mind that lower quality does not necessarily imply lower nutritional value. Also, buyers are apt to receive a more uniform quality when ordering **single-ingredient, generic-brand food**. For instance, canned sliced peaches would tend to have better and more consistent quality than, say, mayonnaise, which includes several ingredients and involves relatively complicated processing.

SIZE, FORM, PACKAGING, AND RELATED CONSIDERATIONS

■ Product Size

> **product size** Refers to the buyer's specified weight, or volume, of a particular item he or she wants to purchase. Examples would be a 10-ounce steak or a 4-ounce hamburger.

A very important consideration is the question of **product size**, or count. For example, when buyers order pitted green olives in a No. 10 can, they should also indicate the olive size they want. They can do this by stating a specific count, which, in turn, implies a number, or count, of olives in a particular can. The higher the count, the higher the number of olives in the can and the smaller the olives. Sometimes, too, buyers can specify the approximate number of product pieces they would like in a can. They will, however, usually be limited in the count that they can have. Only a few choices are available.

In lieu of specifying the count, buyers could use other marketing terms that essentially serve the same purpose. For instance, although it is true that buyers can indicate olive sizes by stating the count desired, they can also use such terms as "large," "extra large," "jumbo," or another appropriate marketing term to convey the necessary size information to their suppliers.

Buyers also may want to know how many cups they can get from a can or a frozen pack. Although these volume measurements appear on consumer products' package labels, buyers must be careful with volumes listed on commercial labels; they are sometimes misleading. For instance, on an instant mashed potato can label, there could be a reconstituted, or ready-to-serve, volume of 3 gallons stated—a volume that may be attainable only if you whip the potatoes long enough to incorporate a great deal of air.

Can Size	Weight	Volume (fl oz)	Volume (cups)	Uses
6 oz.	6 oz.	6	.75	Frozen concentrated juices, individual portion juices, tomato paste
8 oz.	8 oz.	8	1	Fruits, vegetables, specialty items
No. 1 (Picnic)	10.5 oz.	9.5	1.25	Condensed soups, some fruits, vegetables, meats, poultry products
No. 300	15.5 oz.	13.5	1.75	Specialty items, such as spaghetti, macaroni, chili con carne, a variety of fruits, including cranberry sauce and blueberries
No. 303	1 lb.	15	2	Vegetables, fruits
No. 2	1.25 lbs.	18	2.5	Juices, ready-to-serve soups, pineapple slices
No. 2 ½	1.75 lbs.	26	3.5	Fruits, tomatoes, sauerkraut, pumpkin
46 oz.	2.9 lbs.	46	5.75	Juices, whole chickens
No. 5	3.5 lbs.	56	7	Tuna, Asian sauces and vegetables
No. 10	6.5 lbs.	96	12	The "Institutional" can size. Vegetables, fruits, sauces, nuts, olives. Normally six cans per case.

FIGURE 16.5 Average can sizes.

Courtesy of American Can Company, Greenwich, Connecticut

■ Size of Container

Buyers must indicate on the specification the exact size of the container that they wish to buy (see Figure 16.5). To do this, they should determine whether the size of each package meets their needs. It costs more per ounce to buy dried oregano in a little bottle than in a much larger container. If hospitality operations do not use much dried oregano, however, some product in the big container will go to waste. So the EP cost becomes the buyers' main consideration when they evaluate appropriate container sizes.

■ Type of Packaging Material

For frozen and dried products, especially frozen, the packaging materials are not nearly so standardized as those for cans and bottles. If buyers purchase large amounts of these products, such as an annual supply, they should examine the packaging very carefully. Will it hold up for a few weeks or a few months in the freezer? Also, especially for dried products, can moisture seep into the containers?

Another packaging consideration that emerges occasionally is ease of opening. Also, can the package be reclosed tightly enough to save the rest of the contents for later? Sometimes an item comes in an inconvenient package, which can lead to waste. In this case, the EP cost goes up. A more convenient package generally costs more. But as long as the EP cost is acceptable, it may be worth it.

We should address the need to use **environmentally safe packaging** whenever possible. When buyers purchase cans or bottles, these items may not be as convenient as, say, plastic pouches or aseptic containers. However, buyers can recycle them. This helps protect the environment, and in some parts of the United States, buyers may even be able to earn a small amount of income from recycling plants that purchase these materials.

> **environmentally safe packaging** Packaging materials that do not harm the natural surroundings during their production, use, and disposal.

FIGURE 16.6 Individually quick frozen blueberries in a resealable bag.
©*Dole Packaged Foods, LLC.*

Another packaging consideration is the issue of "personalized" packaging. For some processed items, such as sugar packets, buyers can order packaging that contains the hospitality operation's logo or another form of advertisement. Sometimes these options will increase the AP price of the underlying food item; however, the advertising value may more than offset the added expense.

■ Packaging Procedure

This is an important consideration for some processed produce and other grocery items. As a general rule, packing usually has two styles: slab-packed merchandise and layered merchandise.

Most processed produce and other grocery items are necessarily slab packed—that is, they are poured into the container and the container is then sealed. Some products, though, such as dried fruit, can be slab packed or neatly layered between sheets of paper or cardboard. Furthermore, some layered merchandise, such as frozen, double-baked, stuffed potatoes, might be individually wrapped.

As usual, the layered and/or individually wrapped products cost more, at least in terms of higher AP prices. However, because better packaging and a more careful packing style minimize product breakage and other forms of product loss, the resulting EP costs may be quite acceptable.

> **pouch packaging**
> Another term for aseptic packaging.

Recently, many multiunit companies have started utilizing **pouch packaging**[4] (see Figure 16.6) for processed foodservice items.

These pouches offer greater flexibility than the standard No. 10 can, bucket, carton, or tub. Some advantages of these pouches include:

Labor Savings

- Easier to handle product (smaller package sizes)
- Less time spent on disposal
- Less time spent on product evacuation

Food Safety

- Sanitary, hermetic, barrier packaging
- Only open what you need

- Reduced product loss due to spoilage
- Reduced cross-contamination

  Convenience
- Custom sizes (right size pouch for the job)
- Storage efficiency (less space required)
- Empty pouches take up less space
- Reheat in package for hot serve items
- Easy open capability with limited tools required

■ Drained Weight (Servable Weight)

Considering weights instead of volumes is usually a good idea. For instance, the weight of the contents of a can may vary. It is good practice for buyers to calculate drained weight (servable weight) when purchasing canned items; this is the weight of the product less its juice. To compute this figure, buyers drain a product in a specific strainer for a certain amount of time. Some packers' brands offer a great deal of fruit and little juice. Other brands could have more juice and less fruit. Buyers must confirm portions per can and drained weights—and calculate EP costs, to be sure.

Recall that food processors need to note on consumer package labels the serving size and number of servings in the package. Processors may eventually be required to list the weight of the fruit and, separately, the weight of the juice, water, or syrup. To a certain extent, buyers can estimate the amount of juice by the absence or presence of the words **heavy pack** or **solid pack**. If these words do not appear, buyers should expect a lot of liquid—for example, about 5 1/2 ounces of liquid in a typical 16-ounce can of fruit. The term *solid pack* means no juice added; heavy pack means some juice added, but not much.

> **heavy pack** Packing product with very little added juice or water.
>
> **solid pack** Packing product in a container with no added juice or water.

Best of all, however, buyers should measure the drained weight. It is more reliable than estimating weight by looking at a can's label.

When buyers compare the weights of two or more packers' brands of frozen products, they should thaw frozen fruit and cook frozen vegetables from the frozen state before weighing them. Buyers should also do the same with dried products: weigh them only after reconstituting them.

Buyers should be wary of purchasing anything after considering only the volume. Remember from Chapter 4 the standard of fill, which protects buyers from a packer who fills a can only halfway and pretends to give a lot for the money. Remember, too, the possibility that an unscrupulous supplier may pump air into a product or lower the **specific gravity** of a product (by decreasing the product's density to make it lighter). Some possible examples here include ready-to-serve potato puffs. (Should buyers purchase them by count or by weight?) Similarly, tomato puree can vary in density; it can weigh about as much as an equal amount of water, which has a specific gravity of 1.00. Alternately, the puree can have a specific gravity of 1.06 or even a little more, and, thus, a greater weight.

> **specific gravity** A comparison of a product's density to that of water.

■ Type of Processing

Buyers must indicate the type of processing desired. The type of processing implies certain flavor and texture characteristics, as well as specific product-preservation techniques. Generally, buyers will purchase canned, bottled, frozen, and/or dried merchandise.

---

product form Refers to the degree of processing, or lack thereof, a product has when you purchase it. For instance, a buyer can purchase whole chickens or selected chicken parts. The parts typically would cost more than the whole birds.

Brix level A higher Brix denotes a higher sugar content, and vice versa.

additives Chemicals added or used to upgrade product quality and/or help a product resist spoilage.

preservatives See additives.

packing date Date that a product was packaged. May be written in code or in the plain dominant language.

■ Color

In some cases, buyers will need to specify a preferred color. Some common examples include whether a buyer wants green or black olives; red, green, or yellow roasted peppers; or yellow or red onions. Generally, when buyers specify the exact name of the item wanted, they indicate the color required. If the exact name of a product does not include this notation, buyers must be sure to point it out elsewhere on the specification if it is relevant.

■ Product Form

At times, buyers will need to indicate the specialized **product form** of the merchandise they want. Usually this is not necessary if they are purchasing common, ordinary processed produce and grocery items. However, if buyers are purchasing, say, a particular vegetable medley, they may want to note the amounts and types of vegetables desired such as 40 percent broccoli and 30 percent each carrots and cauliflower. Alternately, buyers may find it necessary to point out that they want a minimum number of almonds in the frozen green beans almandine they want to procure for their establishment.

FIGURE 16.7 Pineapples packaged in heavy syrup and in pineapple juice.
©*Dole Packaged Foods, LLC.*

■ Packing Medium

For some products, several packing mediums are available. For example, for canned fruit, buyers can select fruit packed in water, in syrup, or with juice. They also can specify the syrup density desired by noting the minimum **Brix level**. Thick syrup has a higher Brix (i.e., more sugar) than light syrup (see Figure 16.7). The federal government sets minimum Brix levels for some products, yet buyers may want higher levels. For instance, a higher Brix carries a higher AP price, but because fruits packed in heavy syrup do not break easily, the resulting EP cost may be quite satisfactory.

When purchasing vegetable products, buyers may be able to specify the type and amount of sauce desired. For instance, frozen broccoli could be packed with butter sauce, cheese sauce, or some other specialized sauce.

■ The Use of Additives and Preservatives

The concern some hospitality operators show regarding the issue of preservatives in canned, bottled, frozen, and dried items appears to be less than they exhibit regarding dairy and meat products. Operators could not get the products they need if they had to settle for "fresh" produce all the time. Moreover, they could not store fresh produce efficiently and would probably waste a great deal of it. Some processors are more discreet with their use of **additives** and **preservatives** than others, however.

If the thought of additives and preservatives bothers buyers, they may need to specify "organic," or "natural" foods. However, although the supply of these items is increasing, they may be more expensive or carried only by specialty suppliers. Furthermore, shelf life might be shorter, resulting in greater handling costs and subsequently more spoilage loss.

FIGURE 16.8 A Nutrition Facts label.
©Kathy Burns-Millyard/Alamy Stock Photo

■ Other Information That May Appear on a Package Label

The federal government requires a great deal of information to be displayed on consumer product labels, such as nutrition information (see Figure 16.8). However, required label information aside, typical hospitality operators would be much more interested in other kinds of information that may or may not appear on a package label. Many operators would like to see **packing dates**, **freshness dates** (or shelf lives), and serving cost data noted on package labels.

Many also would like to see the **lot number** on a package label. (Because the quality of product shifts, it would be nice to be able to reorder, for instance, corn of not only the same packer's brand but also from the same batch as the previously ordered corn.) Instructions for cooking the product and serving suggestions can also be very useful. School foodservice buyers seek out products that carry **Child Nutrition (CN) labels**, which indicate how the products conform to the nutritional requirements of the USDA. When food processors put these details on their package labels, buyers must expect to pay a bit for this added information value.

freshness date Another term for pull date.

lot number An indication that packaged goods originated from a particular group, or lot. Important if, for example, you are purchasing canned goods; products coming from the same batch will have similar culinary quality whereas those from different lots may be slightly different.

Child Nutrition (CN) label Indicates that the product conforms to the children's nutritional requirements of the USDA. Typically found on product containers sold to school foodservice operations.

PACKAGING CONTAMINANTS: BISPHENOL A AND PHTHALATES
Robert Hartman, Principal, Food and Beverage Management & Consulting

Bisphenol A (BPA) is a component of plastics and resins that are used for food containers and the interior coatings of metal cans. It recently made the news when a *Consumer Reports* study found that it could leach from those containers into food, particularly when the contents of those containers are heated. BPA is also found in the heat-activated inks used for many store receipts.

According to the National Institutes of Health, exposure to BPA is widespread, with 93 percent of people over six years old testing positive. When ingested, BPA mimics the effects of the reproductive hormone estrogen. Studies have shown that BPA can cause reproductive harm in animals. Concern about exposure to infants led the FDA to ban its use in baby bottles and spill-proof cups.[1] Although a 2014 study showed no effects in lab animals at low levels of exposure, higher doses did produce reduced fertility. Other studies have linked BPA to various chronic conditions. It is banned in Canada and other countries.

Phthalates are another class of chemicals that make hard plastics more flexible, particularly in polyvinyl chloride (PVC) products. These additives are also found in sunscreens and other cosmetics. Like BPA, phthalates mimic estrogen. Exposure to phthalates (as well as phenols and phytoestrogens in cosmetics and medicinal tablet coatings) has been linked to birth defects and very early onset of puberty in girls.[2]

In most cosmetic and container uses, neither BPA nor phthalates are listed on product labels. Unless the label indicates that a product is free of these plasticizers, it is safer to assume that they are there. Another concern is that BPA substitutes are often related compounds that are either untested or possibly of even greater toxicity when ingested.

Although there is no clear consensus on just how damaging these additives are to human health, there is enough concern to cause the FDA to restrict their use in products used by children.[3] You can play it safe by eliminating these contaminants from the foods you serve by following these guidelines:

- Do not microwave in plastic or polycarbonate containers.

- Reduce or eliminate your use of canned items, especially acidic products such as tomatoes (which are pasteurized in their cans)—items preserved in glass jars are okay (although some BPA is likely to be present in the lids).

- Store food in nonreactive glass, porcelain, or stainless steel containers.

■ REFERENCES

1. National Institutes of Health, National Institute of Environmental Sciences, Bisphenol A (BPA), *Questions and Answers about Bisphenol A,* www.niehs.nih.gov/health/topics/agents/sya-bpa.

2. Science Daily, Featured Research, *Exposure to three classes of common chemicals may affect female development, study finds,* April 5, 2010.

3. Federal Register Volume 77, Number 137 (Tuesday, July 17, 2012), Department of Health and Human Services, Food and Drug Administration, 21 CFR Part 177, Docket No. FDA-2012-F-0031, *Indirect Food Additives: Polymers,* www.gpo.gov/fdsys/pkg/FR-2012-07-17/html/2012-17366.htm.

SUPPLIER AND AP PRICE FACTORS

■ One-Stop-Shopping Opportunities

Small operations tend to prefer **one-stop shopping** for many items, including processed products. To capitalize in this area, some national corporations carry extensive lines of processed produce and other grocery items and compete directly with local and regional distributors. For instance, General Mills, Green Giant, Pillsbury, and McCormick produce, market, and distribute wide varieties of processed products. These companies normally offer only one level of product quality, and they usually control all aspects of production and distribution. As a result, their products are often referred to as **controlled brands**.

Some national corporations carry extensive lines as well as extensive qualities of processed produce and other grocery items. For instance, Sysco distributes many types of products, as well as many different "packer's grades" (i.e., packer's brands) in most product lines.[5] Sysco uses the name "Supreme®" on its signature brand line of canned fruits.

As the typical hospitality operation grows, it shows less and less of a tendency to use one-stop shopping for processed produce. Too many opportunity buys and long-term contracts at a good savings are available, but they can usually be exploited only if buyers shop around. Large firms usually have the time to do such shopping around. In addition, as its menu gets larger and incorporates more variety, an operation has less opportunity to satisfy its needs with the one-stop-shopping method.

However, one-stop shopping for processed produce, other grocery items, and meat products provides a subtle advantage. Shortages sometimes occur for these items, and being a good customer may ensure a buyer a continual supply. In fact, some suppliers "allocate" certain product lines; that is, they predetermine how much a buyer can purchase. This amount is referred to as the buyer's **allocation**.

> **one-stop shopping**
> Buying everything you need from one vendor. Alternately, buying everything you need from the fewest possible purveyors.
>
> **controlled brand**
> Products produced by a company that typically offers only one level of quality (usually a high quality). The company controls all aspects of production and distribution.

> **allocation** Process whereby a distributor and/or primary source determines how much of a product you are allowed to purchase. Usually done with high-quality wines so that all restaurants have a chance to buy at least some of it.

■ AP Price

The EP cost is the only relevant concern for a buyer. The EP cost includes not only the cost of the product, but, indirectly, the cost of the labor it takes to prepare and serve it, the cost of the energy needed to work with it, and other overhead expenses. Making these judgments is difficult, but a buyer must look beyond, for example, the drained weight of canned mushrooms.

Because an interminable number of varieties, styles, and packaging methods exist for processed foods, there are correspondingly different AP prices. It is not easy to tell whether it is advantageous to take a Grade C instead of a Grade B for a savings of, perhaps, 5 cents a can. In most cases, the trade-off here would be a matter of opinion. Because lower grades are perfectly acceptable in some recipes, lower qualities can save money without reducing a recipe's acceptability.

new pack time Time of the year when products intended for sale the following year (or other period of time) are packed. For instance, canned fruits and vegetables are usually processed and packed right after harvest. Vendors then work off of this inventory until the next new pack time rolls around.

For similar items, a buyer usually pays similar AP prices, but some suppliers may give better quantity discounts and volume discounts than others. Typically, these discounts are quite lucrative. Therefore, bid buying can save money, but only if a buyer is willing to accept a large supply, put the cash up front, and make the buy at **new pack times**, that is, when packers process that year's products.

Unfortunately, there may not be enough bidders for a buyer's business, especially if the local supplier cannot find enough of a product to satisfy company requirements. Even if the buyer finds only one supplier, however, a large buy can be valuable: a substantial savings may result if a large supply can be stored and protected. However, this has subtle disadvantages: if a buyer is "locked in" for a year, the menu is somewhat set. Also, if AP prices for similar items fall, the buyer cannot easily take advantage of them when the storage area is full.

■ Supplier Services

Normally, canned products require only nominal **supplier service**. Most of these items are not readily perishable, so buyers are not likely to be concerned with how quickly the supplier moves them. This cannot be said of frozen items, however. If buyers doubt the capability of a supplier to maintain frozen products at 0°F or below, they should avoid this person. Frozen food costs more because it maintains a better culinary quality, but this quality rapidly deteriorates when storage temperatures are above zero or if they fluctuate; in addition, these problems reduce shelf life drastically.

supplier service Service, such as free delivery or, generous credit terms, provided by vendors to buyers who purchase their products.

forward buying When a buyer purchases a large amount of product (for example, a three-month supply) and takes delivery of the entire shipment.

break point The point at which a vendor will accept a lower price. For instance, if you buy from 1 to 50 cases, the AP price may be $5 per case. If you purchase more than 50 cases, however, the AP price may be $4.75 per case. In this example, the break point is 50.

Occasionally, buyers may want to obtain a stockless purchasing deal, in which they protect an AP price for six months to a year. This tactic rarely saves as much as traditional **forward buying**, in which buyers take delivery of a large amount. Now and then, however, it can produce a reasonable savings.

Buyers would also like to receive reasonable **break points**. They may not want to buy, for example, 100 cases before they get a price break or quantity discount. Fifty cases may be more acceptable. We have noticed that break points are somewhat standard among suppliers.

Sometimes an AP price shoots up dramatically. Buyers like to be warned about this beforehand, if possible. If buyers use bid buying exclusively, they may not receive that warning. If buyers are house accounts, chances are they will.

Together with fluctuating AP prices, which really are not as common with processed products as they are with fresh foods, comes the potential for shortages. A rainstorm can reduce the canned-peaches supply. Only certain buyers may be on the list of those slated to get some of that supply. Again, bid buyers may be left behind. They always take a chance that nobody will answer their solicitations for bids. House accounts may be better serviced.

Buyers should consider another supplier service: If they want a low grade, can they get it? Low-grade products, generally, are not in plentiful supply. Here again, house accounts find themselves in a better position than bid buyers.

Yet another service is the delivery schedule. Realistically, though, most buyers can live with one delivery every week, or even one every two weeks. If, however, buyers have only a limited storage area, they might want other arrangements.

■ Local Supplier or National Source?

Buyers can easily go to the primary source for a direct purchase and have the carload of canned tomatoes "drop-shipped" (which means that they will be delivered straight to the back door). Buyers can also buy direct and arrange for a local supplier to distribute the merchandise.

We have already expressed our views on buying directly and bypassing the local supplier. Still, buyers must do what they believe is best given their circumstances.

PURCHASING PROCESSED PRODUCE AND OTHER GROCERY ITEMS

A buyer's first step in purchasing processed produce and other grocery items is to obtain copies of reference materials that contain useful information that they can use to prepare specifications. Most suppliers publish several in-house materials, particularly individual brochures that detail their major product lines. They also have very informative websites. These references usually include considerable product information, as well as detailed descriptions of grading factors used by U.S. government graders.

The buyer's next step is to determine precisely what to order. This may not be an easy task because several management decisions are involved. Some items are traditionally purchased canned or bottled, some frozen, others dried, but the tradition does not hold true for all products.

Once buyers know what they want, they can make the actual purchase simple or difficult. It will be relatively simple if they buy on a day-to-day basis. If they become dissatisfied with a particular packer's brand, they can just switch to another brand. It is, however, a little more adventurous to enter the bid-buying route, especially when buyers seek to lock up a six-month or one-year supply.

If buyers enter into a long-term contract on a bid basis, they will need detailed specifications. They may find it beneficial to prepare these detailed specs even if they do not use bid buying; it is good discipline for buyers to put their ideas on paper before they actually commit to any type of purchase. (See Figure 16.9 for some example product specifications and Figure 16.10 for an example product specification outline for processed produce and other grocery items.)

If buyers go the long-term route, which is usually available in this product area even for small operations, they will have a bit of work ahead of them. Before they sign a long-term contract, they should examine the bidders' products very carefully. A mistake in this area can be extremely costly, and unintentional mistakes happen easily. For example, buyers may examine three brands of canned tomatoes. They may perform all sorts of tests—comparing drained weights, looking for tomato skins, noting the clearness of the juice—but they may discover too late that one brand has slightly less acid, which may be unsuitable for some recipes. These tests are called **can-cutting tests**. If competing salespersons or suppliers are in attendance, the testing is sometimes referred to as **holding court**. Buyers usually complete a checklist for each brand and then compare each brand's scores (see Figure 16.11). If buyers are purchasing for large commissary production, a little oversight

> **can-cutting test**
> Examining the characteristics of two or more similar products to determine which one represents the best value. Alternately, an examination of all relevant characteristics of a product the buyer is thinking about purchasing.
>
> **holding court**   Refers to a buyer analyzing several competing products while the competing vendors are in attendance.

Pineapple slices
Used for salad bar
Dole® brand (or equivalent)
66 count
No. 10 can
Unsweetened clarified pineapple juice

White cake mix
Used to prepare cupcakes
Pillsbury® Food Service brand
5 pounds
Cardboard box

Whole canned onions
Used for plate granish
U.S. Fancy
350 count
No. 10 can
Water pack

Confectioners' powdered sugar
Used for baking
C & H® brand
1-pound cardboard box
Packed 24-pound boxes per case

FIGURE 16.9 An example of processed produce and other grocery items product specification.

Intended use:

Exact name:

U.S. grade (or equivalent):

Packer's brand name (or equivalent):

Product size:

Size of container:

Type of packaging material:

Packaging procedure:

Drained weight:

Type of processing:

Color:

Product form:

Packing medium:

FIGURE 16.10 An example of a product specification outline for processed produce and other grocery items.

like insufficient acid in a recipe can significantly impair the culinary quality of the finished product.

Another problem can occur through purchasing errors. How do buyers return a year's supply of canned tomatoes to a supplier if they make an error? Buyers should consider a

SAMPLE	1	2	3
Vendor/brand			
Drained weight			
Color			
Size			
Uniformity of size			
Defects			
Clearness of syrup			
Grade			
Flavor			
Case price			
Unit price			
Serving size			
EP cost/serving			

FIGURE 16.11 A checklist for canned sliced peaches.

related problem: If they buy a year's supply and later notice that the product is not quite as good as what they contracted for, they must protect themselves by retaining a few unopened packages that were available for their can-cutting test just prior to signing the contract. Buyers then have on hand a standard of quality they can use to prove that they actually contracted for something better.

Buyers should consider other suggestions for can-cutting tests: (1) Always check frozen fruit after it has thawed; in particular, check the fruit's texture, which tends to suffer in the freezing process. (2) Be sure to cook frozen vegetables from the frozen state before testing them. (3) Check all canned goods immediately after opening them, especially their odor; a foul odor indicates that the product is contaminated. Canned products are cooked during the canning process to kill harmful bacteria so that the products will stay wholesome and not deteriorate. Thus, they are ready to eat. (4) Conduct tests of dried and concentrated products, such as soup, on the reconstituted product.

Generally, then, buyers should test products after they have been prepared for customer service. In some instances, buyers may even want to prepare a full recipe with each one of the competing bidder's products and then perform their tests.

Unless buyers are invited to a supplier's headquarters for some type of product introduction or abbreviated can-cutting test, these tests can take time and effort. However, it is normal practice in large organizations to spend a great deal of effort when considering a quantity buy.

Once buyers enter into a long-term contract, salespersons carrying similar products will still undoubtedly approach them. For instance, each competing supplier with its new brand of spaghetti sauce will bring it to a buyer's attention. Alternately, thanks to backdoor selling, a cook may urge the buyer to purchase a new type of soup base.

Actually, buyers will not see too many revolutionary products, but they may see subtle changes, such as different packaging. For instance, they may buy a new packer's brand of soup base if it is similar to the one they currently use simply because it comes in a 30-pound pack instead of the 1-pound packs they usually buy. If buyers purchase the new product, their old supplier may come out with a 22-pound pack, so testing tends to be a continuing process.

A very complicated test arises when buyers want to evaluate, say, canned peas and frozen peas by using each in two versions of the same recipe, and when buyers want to try other combinations of canned, frozen, and dried. For instance, one stew recipe might be made three ways, with frozen onions, canned onions, and fresh onions. Buyers have to decide which meets their criteria the best.

We have not seen very many local small producers in the processed produce area, but suppose somebody in the family has won a state fair blue ribbon for canned pears and now wants to sell them. We do not consider it a good idea to buy these items. Indeed, recall that most states prohibit the use of home-cooked products in foodservice operations because they come from unapproved sources.

Having struggled successfully with all these details, buyers will find the actual buying, at last, relatively easy. The ordering procedures themselves rarely present any burdensome difficulties.

PROCEDURES FOR RECEIVING, STORING, AND ISSUING PROCESSED PRODUCE AND OTHER GROCERY ITEMS

■ Receiving

Generally accepted procedures for inspecting the quality of delivered processed produce and other grocery items have been established:

1. Canned, bottled, and pouched products. Check the containers for any swelling, leaks, rust, dents, or broken seals. These characteristics, especially swelling, indicate contamination problems. Refuse damaged containers, as well as those that are dirty, greasy, or generally unkempt.

2. Dried products. Check the condition of the containers. If the dried foods are visible, look for mold, broken pieces, and odd appearance.

3. Frozen products. Check the condition of the container, looking for any indication of thawing and refreezing; stained packaging indicates this. Check the food temperature. Look for −10°F, but 0°F is acceptable. If the frozen foods are visible, check for freezer burn, the excessive, often brownish dryness that occurs if food has not been protected properly in frozen storage.

Occasional problems occur with quantity checks. Most of these processed products come in cases, and when the cases are full, buyers may assume that these cases are full of exactly what they ordered. Repacking is rare, but it can happen. In any event, buyers should open at least some cases when they are receiving these items. This is particularly true when receiving a large quantity.

Carefully check incoming products against the invoice and a copy of the purchase order. Some packers' brands resemble one another. Also, be careful of supplier substitutions, which can occur from time to time, especially for these types of products.

Quality checks are not always easy, mainly because what you can actually see is limited. Rarely will a chef, for example, come to the receiving dock to check the quality of processed products unless a large quantity is being delivered.

After checking the quality and quantity, check the prices, and complete the appropriate accounting documents.

■ Storing

Generally accepted procedures for storing processed products have also been established:

1. Canned and bottled products (and some pouched products). Store these products in a dry area at approximately 50°F to 70°F. Avoid any wide fluctuation in temperature and humidity. Heat can be especially damaging. For instance, it robs spices of their flavor; it hastens the oxidation of frying fats, which means that these fats will not retain flavor or last as long in the deep fryer; and it hastens the chemical changes in canned items, which means taste changes. Avoid dampness, too, which causes rust and attracts dust and dirt. In hot climates, consider refrigerating such items as spices and fats. Keep all canned and bottled products tightly covered, opening only what is necessary; otherwise, they will lose some shelf life.

2. Dried products (and some pouched products). Be especially careful of dampness, as it can hasten the growth of mold, thereby ruining the products. Try to keep these products a little cooler than canned items so that insects are not attracted to them.

3. Frozen products (and some pouched products). If at all possible, store these products at −10°F or lower. This temperature will preserve the maximum flavor, especially if the other distribution channel members have maintained this temperature. Be careful not to damage any packages because that will eventually lead to freezer burn. Also, avoid fluctuations in temperature, which reduce shelf life drastically.

Perhaps the most unfortunate aspect of storing processed produce and other grocery items is that so many of them require slightly different storage environments. As a practical matter, we can hardly satisfy each requirement, so we try to reach a happy medium by paying especially close attention to proper **stock rotation**.

However, it is not always easy to ensure proper rotation because many employees grow complacent in their handling of processed items, thinking they will hold forever. Theoretically, canned, bottled, and dried food will last a long time, but no one would try to keep them very long. Nor will frozen food last forever; freezing merely slows, but does not eliminate, deterioration.

Other storage considerations include the following: (1) keeping the items off the floor, where they can attract dirt; and (2) when filling flour bins, and

> **stock rotation** A system of using older products first. When a shipment arrives the older stock is moved to the front of the shelf and the newer stock is placed behind it.

other such storage bins, trying not to mix the new flour with old. If possible, use bins that load from the top and unload from the bottom.

■ Issuing

Hospitality operators often find a good deal of neglect for many processed items. Such products as individual containers of catsup, salt, and sugar—usually food that goes to the service personnel stations—are not always controlled closely. The best way to avoid this waste is to ensure that written stock requisitions exist for every item and that no requisitioner asks for more than necessary. Buyers can control a requisitioner by asking that notes be taken of the **in-process inventory** prior to asking for additional stock.

> **in-process inventory**
> Products located at employee workstations; most or all will be used during the shift.

Buyers need to consider how they would issue half-cans or some similar amount. The fact is, if this problem arises frequently, they might be better off with smaller containers.

Finally, the EP cost is more vulnerable to attack in the area of in-process inventories. Here, as elsewhere, supervision is the key. Without effective and efficient supervision, it is futile to spend time and effort to save money in purchasing.

Key Words and Concepts

Additives	Impulse purchase
Allocation	In-process inventory
Aseptic packaging	Intended use
Break point	Lot number
Brix level	New pack time
Can-cutting test	One-stop shopping
Child Nutrition (CN) label	Opportunity buy
Controlled brand	Packed under continuous government
Drained weight	inspection
Environmentally safe packaging	Packers' grades
Exact name	Packers' brand names
Forward buying	Packing date
Freezer burn	Packing medium
Freshness date	Pouch packaging
Generic brand	Preservatives
Going-out-of-business sale	Product form
Grading factors	Product size
Heavy pack	Pull strategy
Holding court	Push strategy
Introductory offers	Quantity discount

Key Words and Concepts (continued)

Salvage buy	Standard of identity
Shelf life	Stock rotation
Shelf-stable product	Supplier service
Single-ingredient, generic-brand food	USDA Agricultural Marketing Service (AMS)
Solid pack	U.S. Grade A versus Grade A
Specific gravity	Volume discount

Questions and Problems

1. What are the U.S. grades and grading factors for canned, bottled, frozen, and dried items?

2. What is the primary difference between U.S. Grade B and U.S. Grade C products?

3. Give an example of optional information a packer could note on a package label.

4. What is an appropriate intended use for:

   a. canned peas

   b. dried apricots

   c. Dijon mustard

   d. frozen asparagus spears

5. Give an example of the pull strategy in the processed produce and other grocery items channel of distribution.

6. What are the recommended storage temperatures for canned and bottled products and for frozen products?

7. What critical information is missing from the following product specification for canned peach halves?

   Peach halves
   Packed in light syrup
   CODE brand, red label (or equivalent)
   Packed in No. 10 cans, 6 cans per case

8. Your supplier calls to say that the price of tomato paste is due to rise soon and suggests that you purchase at least 2,500 cases immediately. Assuming that you find your supplier completely trustworthy, what specifically should you consider before making your decision about this potential purchase?

Questions and Problems (continued)

9. Why is organic processed produce more expensive than the nonorganic variety?

10. Note three examples of grocery products that you have seen in a restaurant operation that carry personalized packaging. What are some of the advantages and disadvantages of personalized packaging?

11. A product specification for frozen corn could include the following information:

    a.

    b.

    c.

    d.

    e.

12. The choice of which food-processing method a buyer selects is usually affected by three major criteria. Identify these three criteria.

13. Why would a canned tomato puree with a high specific gravity usually be more expensive than one with a lower specific gravity?

14. What is the difference between the designations "U.S. Grade A" and "Grade A"?

15. Define or explain the following terms:

    a. AMS

    b. CN label

    c. Standard of identity

    d. Stock rotation

    e. Break point

    f. Drained weight

    g. Heavy pack

    h. Specific gravity

    i. New pack time

    j. Can-cutting test

    k. Holding court

    l. Freezer burn

    m. Solid pack

    n. Premium brand

    o. Generic brand

    p. Packer's grade

16. Assume that you manage a burger restaurant. You have been using individually wrapped half-ounce portions of catsup. One Saturday afternoon, you notice that you have very few of these packets left because the previous night's business was especially brisk. At first glance, you do not believe you can get a delivery from the commissary—the burger restaurant is part of a national chain—until Monday morning. However, you are open tonight until 9 P.M. and all day tomorrow, 11 A.M. to 9 P.M. What course of action do you take?

Questions and Problems (continued)

17. Assume that you own a small family restaurant and that you have no franchise affiliation. Your annual sales volume (open 24 hours, every day) is $825,000. You sell hamburgers, and you are currently using Heinz individual catsup bottles. You can save about 8 percent of your $438-a-year catsup expense (i.e., 0.08 × $438 = $35.04 per year) if you buy a different brand of bulk-pack catsup and plastic containers and fill these containers from the pack. What course do you recommend?

18. Assume that you normally purchase 1,200 cases of canned peaches every three months. (You order once every three months.) The AP price per case is $8.75. Your supplier offers you a one-year supply for $8.60 per case, cash on delivery (COD). (You currently have 30 days in which to pay your invoices from this supplier.) Assume you are the purchasing director for a 400-room hotel that does excellent restaurant and banquet business. What course of action do you suggest?

19. Assume that you are the purchasing director for a university food-service with 15 campus housing buildings, 8 snack bars, a large dining commons, and an unpredictable catering business. Currently, you operate a central commissary and a central distribution center. Outline the specific procedures you would use for the purchasing, receiving, storing, and issuing of canned peach halves.

20. Assume that you manage a college foodservice facility. You want to purchase your annual requirement of canned tomatoes. You have four brands of tomatoes from which to choose, three reasonably well-known brands and one generic brand. The AP prices vary only slightly among the three name brands, but the generic brand offers a 22 percent savings. Unfortunately, the generic brand contains mostly broken pieces and has a drained weight that is 15 percent less than the name-brand merchandise. In addition, the supplier warns you that the quality of the generic brand is not predictable from year to year. Which type of merchandise would you purchase? Why?

21. A recipe for chicken pot-pie calls for a mixed vegetable medley that includes carrots, peas, and corn. Conduct a make-or-buy analysis to determine if it would be more cost effective to purchase a frozen vegetable medley or prepare your own from fresh ingredients. For one full recipe, you will need 3 lbs of vegetable medley (one pound of each vegetable). Use the following information to assist in making this decision.

Frozen Vegetable Medley: $0.99/lb

Fresh Carrots (Diced):	$0.88/lb	75% Yield	Labor Cost: $1.45/lb
Fresh Green Peas:	$1.10/lb	38% Yield	Labor Cost: $2.00/lb
Fresh Yellow Corn:	$1.30/lb	46% Yield	Labor Cost: $1.60/lb

Experiential Exercises

1. Visit a storeroom in a hotel, restaurant, or even a cafeteria. Note the types of products that can be found on the shelves and their use in the facility. Meet with a manager to discuss how the decision to purchase these items as fresh or processed is made. Write a one-page summary of your findings.

2. Organize a can-cutting for Marinara Sauce. Purchase two to three different brands. Evaluate the sauces for flavor (served cold and hot), consistency, and AP price versus EP cost. Write a one-page summary of how you conducted the test and the results.

References

1. Recall that these purchases may be outlawed by local health authorities. At any rate, these are questionable opportunities because buyers cannot be sure that the products have not been exposed to prolonged heat, chemicals, or other contamination.

2. For a detailed discussion of processed fruits and vegetables grades, see www.ams.usda .gov/AMSv1.0/Grading.

3. No federal standard exists for moisture content. The usual dried item has at least 75 percent of its moisture removed, but this is not enough to make the product last for an extended period. The term "sun-dried" implies high moisture residual, about 25 percent, whereas foods dehydrated in other ways usually contain 5 percent moisture.

4. For more information on pouch packaging, see www.cryovac.com.

5. For a list of Sysco's signature brands, see www.sysco.com/customer-solutions/products .html.

CHAPTER 17

DAIRY PRODUCTS

The Purpose of This Chapter

After reading this chapter, you should be able to:

- Discuss the management considerations when purchasing dairy products.

- Choose appropriate dairy products based on primary selection factors, including government grades.

- Categorize dairy products according to product size, form, and packaging, and related characteristics.

- Create a specification for dairy products that can be used in the purchasing process.

- Describe procedures for receiving, storing, and issuing dairy products.

MANAGEMENT CONSIDERATIONS

Purchasing dairy products can be an arduous task. Foodservice buyers are inundated with numerous varieties and forms of these products, including milk, cheeses, and frozen concoctions. Whether the product is fresh, aged, dried, or fermented, the savvy buyer is knowledgeable in the distinguishing factors that characterize each product. The most noted component of dairy products is butterfat. The **butterfat content** affects quality, including flavor and mouthfeel. Because it is such a key component, the amount of butterfat in a dairy product has a direct correlation with the as-purchased (AP) price.

> **butterfat content** The amount of fat in a dairy product.

Buyers may ask what the difference is between one whole-milk brand and another. There should be little, because most dairies use fairly standardized management techniques. However, dairies may vary somewhat in their quality control programs and their processing methods, so that, perhaps, a taste comparison between dairies is not a wasted effort. The type of feed, seasonal variation, and the stage of lactation of the dairy herds can also cause slight flavor variations.

Chances are that even though little difference in flavor may exist between one brand of whole milk and another, the same cannot be said of other dairy products. The taste of many of these products, especially cheese, tends to be unique to each producer. Once buyers settle on a particular brand—for example, a specific cheese—especially if the cheese is served alone, they may find it difficult to discontinue it in favor of another brand. If they do, their customers probably will notice any change. Thus, for these items, there is a good possibility that buyers will inevitably become a house account with the supplier of the chosen brand.

As mentioned, butterfat is an important component in dairy products, and it is considered an expensive fat. Because butterfat content is almost directly related to the AP price of a dairy item, many products have been manufactured in which the butterfat has been either reduced or replaced. These types of substitutions can be cost-effective. For that reason, the owner–manager should evaluate the types of **substitution possibilities**. Will it be butter or margarine; half-and-half or a nondairy creamer; and natural cheese or cheese food made with vegetable fat? The type of foodservice establishment will help answer these questions on the number and types of allowable substitution possibilities. For example, margarine chips are not a suitable substitute for butter pats in a gourmet dinner house.

> **substitution possibilities** Opportunities for using substitute ingredients in recipes that will not compromise the culinary quality of the food and beverage items made with those recipes. Alternately, opportunities for using substitute nonfood and nonbeverage products, such as cleaners, equipment, and utensils, to accomplish the same purposes.

Buyers face another series of substitution issues: one dairy item may be substituted for another in food-production recipes. More possibilities exist for dairy products than for other ingredients because any time an item contains fat, at least one substitution is a possibility: for example, yogurt for sour cream, skim milk for whole milk, and pasteurized processed cheese for natural cheese. These factors can complicate the decision-making process for buyers. For example, they do not have to use sour cream on the baked potato; they have at least two alternatives: a cultured dressing, which is like a low-fat sour cream, or an imitation nondairy product.

Food service operations may also offer substitutes for dairy products to accommodate the growing number of guests with dietary concerns and preferences. Some examples are people with lactose intolerance, on low-fat or low cholesterol diets, following religious practices that forbid products from cows or mixing meat and dairy products, and vegans. There is more variety than ever of dairy substitutes made from soybeans, almonds, and other foods, and a buyer must be familiar with all of them.

Whatever the decision, if hospitality operations use a suitable dairy substitute product, the possible flavor and nutrition alterations in the final product must be addressed. To a certain extent, it is a matter of opinion whether these flavors are different. Whenever operators combine two or more ingredients in a recipe, the possibility of recipe change always exists. So it is to the firm's benefit to experiment (see Figure 17.1, which notes some dairy product substitutions).

Proper representation of substitute products is critical. **Truth-in-menu** legislation in some parts of the country prohibits misrepresentation—plus, it is unethical. In addition, operators must be careful not to serve one product and imply that it is another; for example, they cannot serve half-and-half and imply that it is cream, a richer product that has more butterfat and is more expensive.

> **truth-in-menu** Guidelines menu planners use to avoid unintentionally misleading the customer by ensuring accurate descriptions and prices of all menu offerings. Alternately, refers to legislation prohibiting misrepresentations on the menu.

Once operators decide what dairy products they want, they must then determine the exact products and supplier(s) they would like to use. The typical foodservice operation can use one supplier for its dairy products—a sort of built-in one-stop buying strategy. Most broad-line distributors and many

1 cup butter	1 cup margarine ⅞ to 1 cup hydrogenated fat plus ½ teaspoon salt ⅞ cup lard plus ½ teaspoon salt ⅞ rendered fat plus ½ teaspoon salt 1 cup dairy free butter spread plus ½ teaspoon salt 1 cup coconut butter
1 cup coffee cream (20 percent)	3 tablespoons butter plus about ⅞ cup milk
1 cup heavy cream	⅓ butter plus about ¾ cup milk 1 cup Non-dairy cream (soy based)
1 cup whole milk	1 cup reconstituted nonfat dry milk plus 2 ½ teaspoons butter or margarine 1 cup soy milk (full fat) 1 cup coconut milk (full fat)
1 cup milk	3 tablespoons sifted nonfat dry milk powder plus 1 cup water 6 tablespoons sifted nonfat dry milk crystals plus 1 cup water 1 cup almond mink 1 cup rice milk
1 cup buttermilk or sour milk	1 tablespoon vinegar or lemon juice plus enough sweet milk to make 1 cup (let stand 5 minutes) 1 ¾ teaspoons cream of tartar plus 1 cup sweet milk 1 tablespoon white vinegar or lemon juice to 1 cup soy milk (let stand 5 minutes)

FIGURE 17.1 Some dairy product substitutions.

produce suppliers now carry dairy products, which might eliminate the need to have a separate dairy supplier. Alternately, a buyer can take the time to evaluate the wide variety of suppliers available for each type of dairy product.[1]

one-stop shopping
Buying everything you need from one vendor. Alternately, buying everything you need from the fewest possible purveyors.

Small operators may prefer **one-stop shopping** for the majority of their dairy products. If buyers can use a standing order system and get a supplier to bring their current stock of dairy items just up to par, this supplier service is an added plus. However, the supplier then controls the inventory level. But because dairies often provide frequent deliveries, this reduces the amount of inventory of perishable items hospitality operations must carry.

However, a single supplier may not have everything needed. Consequently, the decision sometimes involves a choice between one or two suppliers, who may not always have exactly what the firm wants and who make fewer deliveries, versus several suppliers who carry what the firm needs and who make more frequent deliveries.

This decision is not easy to make. On the one hand, dairy products do not usually represent a great deal of the purchase dollar. Hence, hospitality operators could argue that little potential gain is associated with evaluating every available brand and supplier. Conversely, the substitution possibilities can be lucrative. A single sure way of an operation knowing whether it has examined all the substitution possibilities is to plow through every available brand and supplier. To complicate matters, many new products come and go. In some cases, it is preferable to procure the desired dairy products from one or two suppliers. But bear in mind that in many instances, a more careful search of the possibilities may pay for itself.

PRIMARY SELECTION FACTORS

Management personnel usually determine the varieties and qualities of dairy products to be included on the menu. They may or may not work in concert with other company personnel in making these decisions. Regardless, they usually consider many of the selection factors outlined here.

intended use   Refers to the performance requirement of a product or service, which is noted on the specification. Considered to be the most important piece of information on a specification.

exact name   Indication of a product or service's specific type, quality, and style.

standard of identity
A U.S. government regulation that establishes what a food product must be to carry a certain name. For example, what a food product must be to be labeled "strawberry preserves."

■ Intended Use

As always, buyers want to determine exactly the **intended use** of the item so that they will be able to prepare the appropriate, relevant specification. For instance, if a cheese may be needed primarily for flavor, such as cheddar for a cheese sauce, appearance is not important, and potential labor cost and prep time savings may make buying shredded more practical. Therefore, the specification should reflect this.

■ Exact Name

It is very important for buyers to note the specific, **exact name** of the item they want. The majority of dairy products carry a **standard of identity** established by the federal government. This standard is based primarily on the minimum amount of butterfat content. For some products, the standards of identity also prescribe minimum or maximum amounts of milk solids allowed (see Figure 17.2 for some dairy products' legally defined minimum fat contents).

ITEM	MINIMUM PERCENTAGE FAT
Cheddar cheese	30.5%
Cottage cheese, creamed	4.0%
Cottage cheese, dry curd	0.5% (Maximum)
Cottage cheese, low fat	0.5% to 2.0%
Cream cheese	33.0%
Ice cream	10.0%
Ice milk	2.0% to 7.0%
Milk, evaporated	7.9%
Milk, low fat	1.0% to 2.0%
Milk, skim	0.1% to 0.5%
Milk, whole	3.25%
Mozzarella cheese	18.0% to 21.6%
Mozzarella cheese, part skim	12.0% to 18.0%
Neufchatel cheese	20.0% to 33.0%
Pasteurized process American cheese	26.8%
Pasteurized process American cheese food	23.0%
Pasteurized process American cheese spread	20.0%
Ricotta cheese	11.0%
Ricotta cheese, part skim	6.0% to 11.0%
Sour cream	18.0%
Whipping cream	30.0%

FIGURE 17.2 Some dairy products' legally defined minimum fat contents.

FIGURE 17.3 Organic milk.
©2009 Organic Valley Family of Farms

If an operation can use these minimum governmental standards, it may find bid buying the easiest procedure. Assuming that everything else is equal, the buyer could write the specifications with just a few words, for example, "vanilla-flavored ice cream." So, assuming that every bidder meets the required standard, a buyer could save money when one supplier bids lower than the rest.

■ Organic Dairy Products

In recent years, more people are requesting organic milk as an alternative to processed versions that are currently available. To that end, in 2015, organic milk retails sales rose to more than six billion dollars in the United States, an increase of more than 10 percent over the previous year. According to the Organic Trade Association, dairy accounts for 15 percent of total organic food sales. In Wisconsin alone, organic milk sales increased by 30 percent from 2008 to 2014.[2] The USDA's Agricultural Marketing Service reports that sales would be even stronger if availability could keep up with consumer demand.[3] In addition, 75 percent of Americans believe that diet is a better influence on their health than medicine, and 60 percent feel that lowering their exposure to chemicals will result in better health. With this public opinion, it seems that **organic dairy products** may become even more popular, and guests may request organic dairy items more frequently in the future (see Figure 17.3).

organic dairy products Products produced from milk obtained from cows that were: fed organic feed raised on land certified as meeting national organic growing standards; raised in conditions that limit stress and promote health; cared for as individuals by dairy professionals who value animal health; and not given routine treatments of antibiotics or growth hormones.

■ Nondairy Products

Many operators may use nondairy items for several reasons, including: (1) AP prices may be lower; (2) nondairy products, being less perishable, save on storage costs and reduce waste; and (3) weight watchers and those people who cannot tolerate lactose (milk sugar) may represent a clientele worth accommodating. **Lactose-free milk** is made when the producer introduces lactase, a natural enzyme to the milk that breaks down the lactose that naturally occurs. This product comes in a variety of forms, including whole, 2 percent, 1 percent, and nonfat milk. It is also available in organic and nonorganic forms in a variety of brands. Lactose-free is not something that you would see designated on a cheese product because the process of making cheese sufficiently breaks down the naturally occurring lactose.[4]

lactose Sugar that is found most notably in milk. It makes up around 2 to 8 percent of milk (by weight).

lactose-free milk Milk that has the lactase enzyme added to break down the lactose in it.

Other varieties of milk available include **soy milk, almond milk,** and **rice milk** (see Figures 17.4 and 17.5). All are considered milk alternatives and are produced by first cooking their originating products and then pressing to extract the juice. The juice is then pasteurized and left plain or sweetened and flavored.[5] In addition to these milk alternatives, there are also other dairy alternatives such as soy cheese, soy cream cheese, soy yogurt, almond cheese, and ice cream and chocolate products made from soy, almond, and rice milk.

FIGURE 17.5 Almond milk.
©ValeStock/Shutterstock

soy milk The liquid obtained by suspending soy bean flour in water.

almond milk A beverage made from ground almonds. It is a cholesterol- and lactose-free substitute for whole milk.

rice milk A grain milk processed from rice. It is normally made from brown rice and unsweetened.

Agricultural Marketing Service (AMS) Agency that oversees and regulates the marketing of agricultural and meat products.

Unfortunately, most imitation items contain some chemical additives and usually are not nutritionally equivalent to the products they imitate; consequently, some customers may refuse to use them. The fat substitutes being marketed today do not impress many nutritionists, who doubt very much that these products will make people healthier or slimmer. Furthermore, nondairy products, such as butter substitutes, will not work in some recipes that call for dairy ingredients.

■ U.S. Government Grades (or Equivalent)

The **Agricultural Marketing Service (AMS)** of the U.S. Department of Agriculture's (USDA's) Poultry and Dairy Division has set federal grading standards for poultry, eggs, and dairy products. U.S. grades, however, do not

FIGURE 17.6 Federal grade and inspection stamps used for dairy products.
Courtesy of United States Department of Agriculture.

exist for every type of dairy product.[6] However, milk, which is the base for all natural dairy products, usually is graded. As is true with most foods, the grading of milk and milk products is voluntary; however, many states require milk to be graded by the federal government (see Figure 17.6).

Like most foods high in protein, milk is a good medium for harmful bacteria. Consequently, most states and local municipalities have stringent health codes covering milk production. As such, milk must be produced and bottled under government-prescribed conditions. The U.S. Public Health Service's milk sanitation program (termed the Grade "A" **Pasteurized Milk Ordinance** [Grade "A" PMO], 2011 Revision) contains provisions covering such activities as the approved care and feeding of dairy cows, the handling of the milk, the **pasteurization** requirement, and the holding temperature of the milk.[7]

Because of these safety controls, dairies have little influence regarding milk production. They do, however, have the option of **homogenization**. This is the dividing of the butterfat globules so that they stay suspended in the milk and do not rise to the top. The dairies can also dictate what to do with their milk: sell it to ice cream makers, sell it to dry-milk producers, market it to households, and so on.

Fluid milk grades are based primarily on the finished product's bacterial count. There are two federal-government grading designations for fluid milk:

1. **Grade A.** This is the milk the government considers to be fluid milk, to be sold in retail stores and delivered to consumers.

2. **Manufacturing Grade.** This milk is sometimes called Grade B. More bacteria are allowed in **manufacturing grade** milk than in Grade A; this milk is used for manufacturing milk products, such as butter, cheese, and ice cream.

Some **spoilage bacteria** always exist in pasteurized milk, but they are harmless. In addition to the number of bacteria, the grader also considers the milk's odor, taste, and appearance.

Milk can be **fortified** with vitamins A and D, and some states allow other types of nutrient additives.

Pasteurized Milk Ordinance (PMO) Another term for U.S. Public Health Service's Milk Ordinance and Code.

pasteurization Heating foods to the point where it kills most bacteria and harmful enzymes. (Raw milk is milk that has not been pasteurized.)

homogenization Process of breaking up fat globules in liquid milk in such a way that they remain suspended in the milk and do not separate out and float to the top of the milk container.

manufacturing grade A very low grade given to food products that are not intended to be sold as fresh items but are meant to be used by processors to produce a finished item. For example, low-grade beef usually is purchased by a processor who makes things such as canned chili or canned beef stew.

spoilage bacteria Micro-organisms that do not necessarily cause food-borne illness but do cause product decay.

fortified milk Milk to which vitamins, such as vitamin A and vitamin D, have been added.

As we noted previously, few dairy products are graded; this is primarily because the fluid milk used to produce them is usually graded and produced under continuous government inspection. Furthermore, the federal government has not established grading standards for most dairy products. In addition to fluid milk, U.S. grading standards have been determined for dry milk, Cheddar, Swiss, Colby, and Monterey Jack cheeses, and butter.

The federal grades for dry nonfat and dry whole milk are

1. U.S. Extra

2. U.S. Standard

grading factors
Characteristics of food or beverage products examined by grading inspectors. Used to judge and rank products.

The **grading factors** for dry milk that the grader evaluates include the product's color, odor, flavor, and bacterial counts; how scorched the milk is; how lumpy it is; how well it will go into solution; and how much moisture it contains.

The federal grades for Cheddar cheese (see Figure 17.7) are

1. U.S. Grade AA

2. U.S. Grade A

3. U.S. Grade B

4. U.S. Grade C

There are also federal standards for grades of Swiss and Emmentaler, Colby, Monterey Jack, and bulk American cheese. Each federal standard for grades varies slightly. For detailed information on cheese grades, see the USDA AMS website. The grading factors for cheeses that the grader evaluates include the product's color, odor, appearance, flavor, texture, finish, and plasticity (i.e., body).

FIGURE 17.7 Cheddar cheese.
Source: Gisslen, Professional Cooking, 7th Edition, Copyright 2011. Reprinted with permission of John Wiley and Sons, Inc.

The federal grades for butter are

1. U.S. Grade AA

2. U.S. Grade A

3. U.S. Grade B

U.S. Grade A versus Grade A The former grade designation indicates that a federal government inspector has graded the product, whereas the latter indicates that the product was not graded by a federal government inspector.

The grading factors for butter include the product's flavor, odor, freshness, texture, and plasticity.

Some states use their own grading systems. For example, Wisconsin imposes grades for cheese and butter (see Figure 17.8). Also, the **U.S. Grade A** designation on a package label indicates that the federal government graded the dairy product,

FIGURE 17.8 Wisconsin-graded butter.
©LunaseeStudios/Shutterstock

whereas the notation **Grade A** on the package label signifies that the dairy product meets specific criteria that a state, county, and/or local government agency established.

Additional terminology sometimes appears in the dairy products market, but this terminology does not necessarily represent governmental grades. Instead, this terminology tends to comprise terms and designations that, for one reason or another, have become popular. For example, ice cream carries several designations. It can be called "premium," "regular," or "competitive" (premium has 15 to 18 percent butterfat, regular has about 12 percent, and competitive has 10 percent). Alternately, ice cream might be called "French," which means that eggs have typically been used as a thickening agent.

Another type of terminology especially prevalent on dairy product package labels is dating information. In some states, "pull" dates must be listed on dairy products' package labels. These dates tell supermarket managers, suppliers, and consumers the last day that the products can be sold. If states do not require pull dates to be listed, they usually require some sort of coded dates, or "blind" dates, to be noted on the package labels.

Typically, foodservice buyers opt for Grade A milk and a comparable quality for all the other dairy products. In fact, it is very rare that suppliers will offer anything of a lesser grade. If they do, it should raise a red flag about the quality of the supplier. Because several dairy products differ in taste as one goes from one supplier to the next, it is not difficult to understand why U.S. grades, and even local government grades, are not the major selection criterion.

■ Packers' Brands (or Equivalent)

The difference in taste between one supplier and another can be remarkable for cheese, yogurt, ice cream, sherbet, and dry milk. It is, in fact, amazing how different the taste can be between two brands of apparently equal merchandise.

> **packers' brands** Very specific indication of product quality. More precise than a brand name. A packer's personal grading system. Usually intended to take the place of federal government grades.

Consequently, **packers' brands** tend to become important to buyers. Foodservice managers cannot be easily persuaded to drop their current ice cream for competing products. Of course, the bid buyer, or the buyer who has the time, occasionally checks out different brands of dairy products. New dairy items enter the market periodically, and some of them may be deemed to be good substitutes. Some of these new products may even save hospitality operators a bit of money.

■ Point of Origin

Point of origin can be important for some types of dairy products, in particular butter and cheese. For instance, many chefs prefer to use Kerrygold butter, which is produced in Ireland with milk from grass-fed cows. In contrast, Challenge and Plugra make "European-style" butters that are made in the United States. With cheeses, it can be very important whether a Brie is from France or the United States or whether a blue cheese comes from France, Denmark, Italy, or the United States. Where buyers used to assume that they could order Gorgonzola or Mozzarella and it would be from Italy, today high-quality domestic brands are widely available.

SIZE, FORM, PACKAGING, AND RELATED CONSIDERATIONS

product size Refers to the buyer's specified weight, or volume, of a particular item he or she wants to purchase. Examples would be a 10-ounce steak or a 4-ounce hamburger.

■ Product Size

A few dairy products require **product size** designations. For instance, butter could be ordered in 1-pound prints, 50-pound blocks, or one or more "chip" sizes. Cheese slices usually come in two or more sizes; for example, you might order a 1-ounce size for the cheeseburger platter and a 2-ounce size for the grilled cheese sandwich plate.

■ Size of Container

Dairy products are sold in various package sizes. Because of the highly perishable nature of dairy items, experience shows that the size of the container is very important. Buyers should purchase only the necessary amount to minimize leftovers and reduce waste.

Naturally, the smaller the package size unit—for example, half-pint milk containers in contrast to half-gallons—the higher the AP price. The edible-portion (EP) cost could, however, be lower. For instance, bartenders use cream in some drinks. A small package could carry a premium AP price, but if the cream drink volume is low, bartenders may waste cream if you use large containers. In this case, the EP cost would jump to an unacceptable level.

Not every supplier carries the package sizes buyers want. For example, a buyer may be satisfied with a particular brand but find that the supplier does not stock that brand in the individual portion packs the buyer desires.

■ Type of Packaging Material

In general, packaging materials for dairy products are quite standardized throughout the hospitality industry. One of the major reasons for this is that dairy regulations usually specify minimum packaging requirements that protect the culinary quality and wholesomeness of the products.

This standardization does not mean, however, that all dairy products are packaged alike. Buyers usually can select from a wide variety of packaging materials. There are plastic, fiberboard, metal, glass, and aseptic containers. Typically, two or more choices are available for many products.

Custom-packaging options may also be available for some dairy products. For instance, some dairies will include an operation's name and/or logo on individual half-pint containers of milk, individually wrapped butter chips, and single-serve creamers. Of course, the buyer must be prepared to pay a bit more in exchange for this added value.

■ Packaging Procedure

This can be an important consideration, especially for the single-serve dairy product items many restaurant operators purchase. For instance, buyers can purchase butter chips that are layered in a 5-pound container and separated by pieces of waxed paper. Alternately, buyers can obtain individually wrapped butter chips (which, by the way, the local health district may require to protect the wholesomeness and cleanliness of the butter).

As mentioned several times, the layered and/or individually wrapped products will carry premium AP prices. However, the end result—that is, the EP costs—may be quite acceptable if buyers purchase premium packaging and packaging procedures that tend to protect the shelf life of the merchandise.

■ Product Yield

For some dairy products, buyers may need to indicate the maximum waste they will accept (or the minimum **yield** acceptable). For instance, they might need to indicate whether they would accept rind on the cheese they want to buy. Similarly, buyers should note on the specification that, for example, they will not accept more than two broken cheese slices per hundred.

> **yield** The net weight or volume of a food item after it has been processed and made ready for sale to the guest.

■ Product Form

For some dairy items, buyers may need to note the exact **product form**. For example, they might need to note sliced, whole, grated, shredded, or crumbled cheese. Similarly, they might need to note whipped butter, if applicable, instead of just butter.

> **product form** Refers to the degree of processing, or lack thereof, a product has when you purchase it. For instance, a buyer can purchase whole chickens or selected chicken parts. The parts typically would cost more than the whole birds.

■ Preservation Method

Most dairy items are kept under continuous refrigeration. Although refrigeration is not required for some items, such as certain cheeses, if buyers want these types of items kept under refrigerated conditions, they need to note this on the specification. Some dairy items are frozen. The obvious ones are ice creams and frozen yogurts. However, some suppliers freeze the cheeses and butter they sell. So if buyers do not want frozen dairy items, they may have to specify this for some items that they purchase.

A few dairy items are traditionally canned. Evaporated milk, sweetened condensed milk, and canned whole milk are usually marketed in metal containers. Whole milk also comes in aseptic packages and can be kept at room temperature for months. This **shelf-stable product** is pasteurized using **ultra-high temperatures** (UHT), and its taste is very similar to fresh, refrigerated, whole, fluid milk and coffee creamers. This technique is sometimes referred to as **ultra-pasteurized** (UP). Although individual UP coffee creamers are used extensively in foodservice operations, the whole-milk UP product has yet to gain widespread popularity in the United States.

When considering **preservation methods**, wise buyers also take the time to specify the maximum pull date allowed at time of delivery. If stored correctly, dairy products will remain safe to consume for a few days after the pull date; however, their culinary quality could be compromised to the point where these products should not be served to guests. Furthermore, the local health district may not allow the use of outdated products.

> **shelf-stable product**
> A food item that is processed and packaged in such a way that it can maintain its quality for long periods of time at room temperature.
>
> **ultra-high temperature (UHT)** Ultra-high temperatures sterilize food by heating it above 135 °C (275 °F)—the temperature required to kill spores in milk—for 1 to 2 seconds.
>
> **ultra-pasteurized (UP)** Pasteurization process using ultra-high temperatures (UHT). Used to produce a shelf-stable product that is packed in aseptic packages.
>
> **preservation method** A procedure, such as refrigeration, freezing, canning, drying, or chemical additives, used to maintain a product's shelf life and quality and in some cases, impart additional flavorings.

■ Butterfat Content

In general, as the butterfat increases, so does the AP price, but more butterfat also makes for a richer product. Moreover, producers tend to treat dairy products with high butterfat content with more respect. For example, a premium ice cream typically contains high-quality flavoring, such as fresh fruits rather than fruit syrups.

If buyers are satisfied with the amount of butterfat mandated by the federal government's standard of identity, they can ignore this selection factor. However, if they want a product that is more or less "creamy," they must note this requirement on the specification.

■ Milk Solids Content

The federal government also mandates the maximum amount of nonfat, dried milk solids that some dairy products can have. If these standards are acceptable, this selection factor is irrelevant. However, if buyers desire fewer solids than the maximum allowed, they must indicate their exact requirement on the specification.

■ Overrun

overrun The amount of air whipped into a frozen product.

The amount of air whipped into a frozen dairy product is referred to as **overrun**. Most people in the foodservice industry consider overrun to be the amount of air incorporated into any type of dairy product. Some dairy products contain a good deal of air. When a chef whips butterfat, it incorporates air. Also, butterfat holds the air for quite a while, and even longer when the product is frozen or contains some added emulsifiers.

The air content is crucial to the flavor of such items as ready whipped cream in an aerosol can and ice cream.

Whipped cream is usually sold by the number of ounces in the can, but it can also be sold by volume, which is a typical measure of quantity for many types of dairy products. If buyers start to compare AP prices on the basis of volume, they must keep in mind that air costs nothing. So they could be buying more volume but less solid product.

The federal government standard of identity for ice cream dictates that 1 gallon must weigh at least 4 1/2 pounds and contain at least 1.6 pounds of total food solids. Therefore, for this type of product, buyers are protected to some extent. But this is not the case for such items as whipped topping. For these types of products, buyers must be ever mindful of the exact value of the purchase.

■ Chemical Additives

chemical additives Substances added to food and beverages to preserve flavor, maintain shelf life, and/or improve taste and appearance.

Because milk is a food for babies, it has been kept natural for many decades. However, a few dairy products contain **chemical additives** that stabilize, emulsify, and preserve them, and at times, the dairy industry has been unjustly criticized for this. It is easy to assume that all dairy items include several chemical additives, but this is just not the case. The products that typically contain chemicals are nondairy items. All things considered, dairy products in their natural form, processed or relatively unprocessed (pasteurized), have significantly fewer chemical additives than other processed foods.

■ Untreated Cows

In this age of biotechnology, dairies are able to treat their herds with naturally occurring and **synthetic hormones**—such as **bovine somatotropin (bST)** and **recombinant bovine growth hormone (rBGH or rBST)**—designed to increase milk production. Buyers, who do not want to purchase products made from this type of milk need to note on the specification that they will accept only products coming from cows that have not been treated with these synthetic horomones.[8]

Since 2009, due to consumer demand for more wholesome products, many dairies and retailers are dropping the use of synthetic hormones from their products. These include consumer brands such as Dannon, General Mills, and WalMart.[9]

■ How the Product Is Processed

Dairy processing methods usually fall under government inspection. However, these inspections ensure only wholesomeness, not flavor, convenience, or packaging.

The type of processing can be very important for some dairy products. For example, all Swiss cheeses are a bit different. Although they all meet a minimum standard of identity, substantial differences in aging methods and aging times can exist. The packer's brand usually indicates these processes.

Buyers may want to know whether or not the process is "natural." For example, some cottage cheeses contain an absolute minimum of additives; others may contain extra acid, such as phosphoric acid to set the curd, and artificial flavorings. If buyers want all of the dairy items they purchase to be natural, they will have to search out the appropriate brand.

> **synthetic hormone** Man-made chemical used as a substitute for the natural hormone produced by animals' glands. Given to animals to increase weight, milk production, speed up weight gain, and so forth.
>
> **bovine somatotropin (bST)** Chemical injected into lactating cows to increase their milk production.
>
> **recombinant bovine growth hormone (rBGH or rBST)** Chemical injected into lactating cows to increase their milk production.

PURCHASING DAIRY PRODUCTS

Because most dairy products are highly perishable, the buyers' first purchasing steps are to determine precisely what they want and then to determine the delivery schedule they think will be appropriate. Buyers prefer daily delivery; however, they should negotiate for and follow any supplier service or purchasing tactic that helps control the quality of these items.

Preparing elaborate specifications for dairy products usually is not necessary unless the buyer is a bid buyer or is expecting to enter into a long-term contractual arrangement with the supplier. As always, it might be good discipline for a buyer to reduce general ideas to detailed written specifications before committing to purchasing any item. (See Figure 17.9 for some example product specifications and Figure 17.10 for an example product specification outline for dairy products.)

Dairy buyers must also understand that supply and payment for milk has been primarily controlled by the federal government for more than 100 years. The last major revision to the Federal Milk Marketing Orders, which established this control, was in 2010. The federal regulations covered approximately 60 percent of the milk in the United States in 2010. In 2012, about 19 percent of milk was from unregulated free-market areas,[10] where some opportunities may exist to reduce the AP price for dairy products.

Butter
Used for customer service
U.S. Grade AA
Butter chips
90 count
Layered arrangement, easily separated
5-pound box
Waxed, moisture-proof, vapor-proof
Refrigerated

Nondairy coffee whitener, liquid
Used for customer service
House brand
3/8-ounce portion, single serve
400 servings per case
Loose pack (slab pack)
Moisture-proof carton
Unrefrigerated

Bleu cheese
Used for tossed salad
Frigo® brand
Crumbles
5-pound poly bag
4 bags per case
Moisture-proof, vapor-proof
Frozen

Half-and-half
Used for customer service
U.S. Grade A
3/8-ounce portion, single serve
400 servings per case
Loose pack (slab pack)
Moisture-proof carton
Refrigerated

FIGURE 17.9 An example of dairy product specifications.

price control Refers to government agencies dictating the minimum price that must be charged for a product. This type of control is fairly common in the dairy and beverage alcohol distribution channels.

credit control Refers to government agencies dictating the credit terms that can be extended to buyers. This type of control is fairly common in the dairy and beverage alcohol distribution channels.

Control states can also specify that you must legally pay at least the minimum AP price. Most states have a variety of price control and credit control policies; that is, the local governments regulate the price and the type and amount of credit a dairy can extend to its customers. Periodically, someone starts a drive to eliminate the local government and the federal government's power in this area. The **price** and **credit controls** seem to weather these attacks very well, however.

Also, some dairy products, especially cheese, are imported. Import taxes tend to add up, thereby increasing AP prices.

If a hospitality operation uses the ordinary types of dairy products and is located in a noncontrolled state, bid buying might be profitable, but as a percentage of total purchase dollars, these savings are liable to be small. However, if operators can live with some variations, their savings can add up through the optimal selection of many suppliers and packers' brands.

If buyers can live with variations and/or purchase a large quantity of dairy products, they should take the time to evaluate some of the substitution possibilities. Several products are capable of providing comparable culinary quality in a recipe, and a few minutes of cost calculation might indicate that a particular recipe

Intended use:
Exact name:
U.S. grade (or equivalent):
Packer's brand name (or equivalent):
Product size:
Size of container:
Type of packaging material:
Packaging procedure:
Product yield:
Product form:
Preservation method:

FIGURE 17.10 An example of a product specification outline for dairy products.

is much less expensive to produce with one product rather than another. For instance, if buyers use large quantities of fresh milk to prepare breads, a switch to dry milk may yield a comparable-quality finished product at a lower EP cost.

Dairy products may be sold through a number of channels. Many products may be available through distributors, but it may be advantageous to purchase through a local dairy for such items as fresh milk, some cheeses (see Figure 17.11), and even ice cream. This is especially the case if the dairy is known for a particular product—ice cream,

FIGURE 17.11 Clockwise from top left: Morbier, Cheddar, Fontina, Tilsit, Baby Gouda, Emmentaler.
Source: Gisslen, Professional Cooking, 7th Edition, Copyright 2011. Reprinted with permission of John Wiley and Sons, Inc.

for example—and as discussed earlier in Chapter 5, it is always a good idea to support the local economy whenever possible. For instance, sometimes independent farmers and local artisan cheese producers seek to do business with hospitality operations. Be careful when considering this option because their products might not come under the rigid quality control standards the federal and state governments have established.

PROCEDURES FOR RECEIVING, STORING, AND ISSUING DAIRY PRODUCTS

■ Receiving

When receivers get dairy products, they should take the time to carefully examine them for dirt, broken containers, and faulty wrapping. Milk cartons can get dented, and cheese wrappings sometimes crack or split. Because these products deteriorate quickly, receivers should be reluctant to accept anything that does not look clean and properly packaged.

Receivers also must check to see that they receive everything that was ordered. This check can be difficult for at least two reasons. First, with so many dairy items on one invoice, either the receivers or the suppliers may miss something. Second, some dairy items are delivered on a standing-order basis. This is typical with ice cream and sherbet, and it may allow the delivery agent to work alone stocking an operation's freezers. When leaving, the agent may present an invoice for the receiver to sign. A busy receiver may not thoroughly check what has been delivered. Alternately, an unscrupulous delivery agent may tell a receiver that a container that already was in the dairy box was delivered that day.

A related problem centers on supplier substitutions. For example, a supplier may be out of Roquefort cheese and send a house brand blue cheese instead, not wanting to see the operation serve guests without at least a similar item. Some substitutes in the dairy line do not always match well, however, especially among cheeses (see Figure 17.12). A house brand blue cheese, for example, would not be acceptable if a restaurant's menu calls for Roquefort. Though similar cheeses are produced elsewhere, European cheese law dictates that only those cheeses aged in the natural Combalou caves of Roquefort-sur-Soulzon may bear the name Roquefort, as it is a recognized geographical indication, or has a protected designation of origin.

Although receivers do not often take the time to make planned but random taste tests, they should. This may not be necessary if buyers purchase a proprietary brand; they will then have some assurance of quality.

Because most dairy items are perishable, receivers might consider moving everything into a refrigerated area before they make their inspection. After checking qualities and quantities, receivers should check the invoice arithmetic and complete the appropriate accounting procedures.

FIGURE 17.12 Clockwise from left: Stilton, Cabrales, Roquefort, and Bleu d'Aurvergne. *Source: Gisslen, Professional Cooking, 7th Edition, Copyright 2011. Reprinted with permission of John Wiley and Sons, Inc.*

■ Storing

Most dairy products should be stored in a refrigerator or freezer as soon as possible. Dried, canned, and bottled items can go to the storeroom, as can, possibly, some nondairy products.

If chefs are going to serve a certain dairy product—for example, if they plan on presenting a cheese platter on that evening's menu—they should bring the cheese to the correct serving temperature by leaving it out at room temperature before serving. If they are going to serve the cheese later in the week, it should be refrigerated because room temperatures cause most cheeses to age. This will have a detrimental effect on the cheese by causing it to quickly change in odor, flavor, and appearance.

Most dairy items readily pick up odors. Therefore, maintaining a separate dairy refrigerator is recommended. If that is impossible, hospitality operators should keep dairy products tightly covered, in a segregated area in the common refrigerator, and away from odorous foods.

As much as possible, operators should also keep dairy products, particularly cheeses, in their original packaging. When they store these items, they should try not to nick or cut the packaging. This is easy to do and hastens spoilage and waste.

When storing dairy products, operators should take a bit of extra time to ensure that they rotate the products on the shelves properly. They cannot take a chance that a customer will get sour milk. It is not easy to tell whether the food is rotated properly unless they take the extra time to check the pull dates many dairies put on their products. Dairy products are not like lettuce: if a head of lettuce is bad, you know it, but whole milk in individual half-pints is harder to monitor.

■ Issuing

Hospitality operators should issue older dairy products first. Many of these items, especially ice cream, go straight from receiving to a production area. If they are issued from a central storeroom, make sure that the requisitioner receives the correct product. For example, if the requisitioner wants milk for a cake recipe, make sure that the appropriate dry milk is provided.

Because most dairy products deteriorate rapidly, hospitality operators should try not to handle them any more than necessary. Also, they should make sure that requisitioners do not take more than they need for any one particular work shift or job. Operators might consider asking the requisitioner to make a note of the **in-process inventory** before asking for more stock.

> **in-process inventory**
> Products located at employee workstations; most or all will be used during the shift.

■ In-Process Inventories

Dairy products fall victim to spoilage, waste, and pilferage whenever they stay in-process for any extended period. They spoil because butter, cheese slices, and coffee cream, for example, are often left at room temperature too long. Also, employees waste dairy products by failing to empty milk containers and cans of whipped cream completely. Pilferage is particularly common. For instance, employees may help themselves to a quick glass of milk once in a while.

As usual, supervision is the key. It helps both to head off waste and pilferage and to prevent, as well, such embarrassing situations as a customer tasting curdled coffee cream or rancid butter.

RESTAURANT CHEESE PROGRAMS

General Charles De Gaulle, President of France from 1958 to 1969 is famous for saying, "How can one govern a country that has 246 different kinds of cheeses?" In the United States, cheese production and consumption are growing annually. In 2013, more than 300 companies and cooperatives operated 524 cheese-making plants. According to the USDA 2013 Dairy Products Annual Summary, more than 11.1 billion pounds were produced in the United States, of which 25.7 percent was made in Wisconsin and 20.8 percent was made in California. Cheese consumption has more than doubled over the past 35 years. In 1975, it was 15 pounds per person and in 2012 it was 33.5 pounds.[1]

Just about every foodservice operation uses some type of cheese. But many fine dining restaurants are known for their cheese programs and the cheese courses offered on their menus. Cheese courses can be offered at the beginning of the meal, mid-meal as an alternative to a sorbet or other intermezzo, or at the end of the meal. Because it takes extensive dedication and knowledge to know how to select, purchase, store, age, and sell premium and artisan cheeses, some restaurants even have their own "fromager," a cheese merchant or an "affineur," a person who ages and ripens cheeses.

One premier American restaurant that was known for its pioneering cheese program was Picholine in New York City. It was opened by chef–restaurateur Terence Brennan in 1993 and recently closed. He served flights of three cheeses with appropriate wines. The cheeses were stored in a portion of the wine cellar known as the Cheese Cave. Brennan continued his emphasis on cheese at his Artisanal Fromagerie, Bistro and Wine Bar, which has a cellar that stocks more than 200 cheeses available both in the restaurant and for retail sale.[2]

Restaurants located in wine-producing and agricultural areas are naturals for having cheese programs. At the Herbfarm in Woodinville, Washington, culinary director Ron Zimmerman and executive

RESTAURANT CHEESE PROGRAMS (continued)

chef Chris Weber include cheese courses in their eight- to nine-course theme dinners, which change seasonally. Prior to the restaurant's closing in November 2013, "Top Chef Master" Douglas Keene was known for his cheese courses at Cyrus Restaurant in Healdsburg, California, in the heart of the Sonoma Valley vineyards. More than 70 percent of the restaurant guests ordered at least one of the 15 to 20 cheeses available nightly.[3] Chef Patrick O'Connell serves a selection of up to 25 cheeses from "Faira," a fiberglass cow that moos as it is wheeled through the dining room at his award-winning restaurant at The Inn at Little Washington in Washington, Virginia. As the sample menu says on its website under desserts, for "Our Fromager's Cheese Selections, just ask for Faira the Cow or Cameron—'Resident Cheese Whiz.'"

Both the Wisconsin Milk Marketing Board (WMMB) and the California Milk Advisory Board (CMAB) offer extensive resources for restaurateurs and chefs who would like to establish cheese programs. The WMMB has a free online Cheesecyclopedia® Self-Study Course, which provides practical information about how to profit from your investment in Wisconsin cheeses. Course objectives include understanding the process of cheese, identifying cheese categories, following proper guidelines for storing and handling cheese, and using this knowledge to menu and merchandise cheese. "The Cheese Course" brochure emphasizes training for the waitstaff; explains considerations when selecting cheeses, including flavor, texture, aging, and color; and stresses the importance of attention to service details, such as size of the course in terms of number of cheeses and weights, proper temperature for each type of cheese, and presentation. Other WMMB resources on the training website include a cheese storage brochure, a foodservice merchandising guide, and a beer and food pairing guide. It also has an online magazine called *Grate. Pair. Share.*

The CMAB publishes the *Professionals Guide to Real California Cheese*. It offers many of the same guidelines as the WMMB materials but features more details on merchandising the cheese programs. Some of its suggestions for written menus are numbering the cheeses, printing phonetic spellings, and including the origin, name of the cheesemaker, and flavor profile of each cheese. For suggestive selling, it recommends displaying the cheeses on cloth-covered ice to keep them somewhat cool, under a glass or plastic dome to keep them from drying out, and in small quantities replenished frequently to minimize waste. If a restaurant does not have a separate fromager, the CMAB suggests that the sommelier be trained in cheese service because it is so often paired with wine.

Restaurants can also hire consultants to assist with establishing their cheese programs. For instance, Artisanal restaurant sells wholesale cheeses and has culinary advisors who will work with executive chefs to recommend cheese selections that complement the restaurant's cuisine, customers, and property goals, share presentation and display guidelines, train staff, and monitor performance of the program. Fromager Carolyn Stromberg worked for one of the first nationally known artisan cheese producers, Cowgirl Creamery, and developed the cheese program for the Gaylord National Resort and Convention Center in Washington, D.C., before starting her own company, The Cheese Course, which does restaurant and retail consulting. Like Artisanal, she works with both back of the house and front of the house managers and staff to develop the program and ensure that all the cheeses are being stored and merchandised properly.

And in today's world, if a restaurateur or chef wants to learn about something, there are always videos available. Cheese even has its own "Channel Cheese TV" on YouTube. One segment shows Fromager Dimitri Saad explaining his cheese program at Casellula Restaurant in New York City.

■ REFERENCES

1. U.S. Department of Agriculture, April 2014, "2013 Dairy Products Annual Summary," http://usda.mannlib.cornell.edu/usda/current/DairProdSu/DairProdSu-04-29-2014.pdf. See also, Wisconsin Milk Marketing Board, "Cheese Statistics," www.wisconsincheesefoodservice.com/media/statistics/cheeseStatistics.aspx.

2. John Mariani, "America's Cheesiest Restaurants," *Luxury Travel on NBC News.com*, August 28, 2008, www.nbcnews.com/id/26350141/ns/travel-luxury_travel/t/americas-cheesiest-restaurants/.

3. Ibid. See also, Tara Dugan, "Douglas Keane Tastes Life after Cyrus," www.sfgate.com/restaurants/article/Douglas-Keane-tastes-life-after-Cyrus-4062470.php.

Key Words and Concepts

Agricultural Marketing Service (AMS)	Pasteurization
Almond milk	Pasteurized Milk Ordinance (PMO)
Bovine somatotropin (bST)	Preservation method
Butterfat content	Price control
Chemical additives	Product form
Credit control	Product size
Exact name	Recombinant bovine growth hormone
Fortified milk	(rBGH or rBST)
Grading factors	Rice milk
Homogenization	Shelf-stable product
In-process inventory	Soy milk
Intended use	Spoilage bacteria
Lactose	Standard of identity
Lactose-free milk	Substitution possibilities
Manufacturing grade	Synthetic hormone
Organic dairy products	Truth-in-menu
One-stop shopping	Ultra-high temperature (UHT)
Overrun	Ultra-pasteurized (UP)
Packers' brands	U.S. Grade A versus Grade A Yield

Questions and Problems

1. What are the U.S. grades for these items?

    a. Fresh fluid milk
    b. Butter
    c. Nonfat dry milk

2. What is the minimum weight of a gallon of ice cream?

3. What is the minimum butterfat content for ice cream?

4. What is an appropriate intended use for these items?

    a. Nondairy creamer
    b. Dry nonfat milk
    c. Soy milk

5. What is the primary purpose of pasteurization?

6. What is the primary purpose of homogenization?

7. What are the U.S. grading factors for Cheddar, Swiss, Colby, and Monterey Jack cheeses?

8. What critical information is missing from this product specification for milk?

    Milk, fluid
    U.S. Grade A
    Used for cooking and baking
    Bulk container

9. What is the primary difference between premium ice cream and competitive ice cream?

10. Explain why dairy products should not be stored with fresh produce.

11. A product specification for an ice cream bar could include this information:

    a.
    b.
    c.
    d.
    e.

12. One-stop dairy product shopping is especially popular among small operators. Why do you think this is the case? What advantages are there? What disadvantages are there?

13. Define or explain these terms:

    a. Pull dates
    b. Fortified milk

Questions and Problems (continued)

    c. Lactose

    d. Minimum butterfat content

    e. Overrun

    f. Controlled AP prices

    g. UHT pasteurization

    h. Custom packaging

    i. Product form

    j. Aseptic container

    k. Nondairy products

    l. Product yield

    m. Standard of identity

    n. U.S. Grade A versus Grade A

14. Describe the alternative dairy products that restaurants can use to make menu items that their lactose-intolerant guests are able to eat.

15. For which types of dairy products is "point of origin" a possible selection factor?

Experiential Exercises

1. Assume that you operate the food service in a senior living community with assisted living and long-term care facilities. You serve approximately 400 residents and 50 staff members a day, three meals and various snacks. You have a severely tight food budget but must also adhere to federal nutrition regulations and be able to accommodate many specialty diets. Outline the specific procedures you might use to purchase, receive, store, and issue milk and other dairy products for use in cooking and as a beverage.

    a. Ask a registered dietician or culinary director at a facility for information on this topic.

    b. Write a one- to two-page paper on this topic.

2. Price and supply controls, whether raw milk should be sold in the United States, and availability and inspection of imported dairy products are all controversial issues. Research one of these topics and write a one-page paper about your findings.

3. Visit a restaurant in your area that has a specialty cheese program. Interview a manager or chef about the program. Ask him or her:

    a. Do they have a special employee who oversees it?

    b. How many cheeses do they serve? Are all available at all times?

    c. How do they merchandise the cheeses?

    d. Write a one- or two-page paper about your findings

References

1. "Purchasing Dairy Products," www.hotelmule.com/html/10/n-1910-2.html.

2. International Dairy Foods Association, "Organic Dairy Products: U.S. Organic Sales Post New Record Driven by Produce and Dairy," www.idfa.org/resource-center/industry-facts/organic-dairy-products.

3. Dairy Herd Management, "Whole, Organic Milk Trends Continue," October 26, 2015, www.dairyherd.com/news/whole-organic-milk-sales-trends-continue.

4. Organic Valley, "Lactose Free Products," www.organicvalley.coop/products/milk/lactose-free/lactose-free-whole-ultra-pasteurized-64-oz/.

5. Merriam-Webster, "Soy Milk," www.merriam-webster.com/dictionary/soy%20milk; Merriam-Webster, "Almond Milk," www.merriam-webster.com/dictionary/almond%20 milk; Fitday, "Soy Milk vs. Rice Milk: Which is Better for You?," www.fitday.com/fitness-articles/nutrition/healthy-eating/soy-milk-vs-rice-milk-which-is-better-for-you.html#b.

6. For a detailed discussion of dairy grades, see www.ams.usda.gov/AMSv1.0/dairy.

7. See, for example, Anonymous, "Pasteurized Milk Ordinance 2011," U.S. Food and Drug Administration, www.fda.gov/downloads/Food/GuidanceRegulation/UCM291757.pdf. See also the website of the National Dairy Council, which reports on nutrition, dairy safety, and research: www.nationaldairycouncil.org. See also Dairy Reporter.com, www.dairyreporter.com.

8. See, for example, "Milk and Hormone Fact Sheet," National Dairy Council Website, www.nationaldairycouncil.org/SiteCollectionDocuments/footer/FAQ/food_safety/MilkandHormonesFactSheetAugust2008.pdf. "POSILAC(r) bovine somatotropin," Monsanto Dairy website, www.monsantodairy.com/. See also Stonyfield Organic, "How Do Artificial Hormones and Antibiotics Figure into Milk Making," August, 2013, www.stonyfield.com/blog/no-artificial-hormones-and-antibiotics/; John T. Barone, "Declining Growth Hormone Usage Likely to Hurt Milk Output, *Nation's Restaurant News*, 41, no. 29 (July 23, 2007):54–55; Mitch Lipka, "Is Organic Milk Worth Its Higher Price?," February, 2012, www.reuters.com/article/2012/02/17/us-yourmoney-milk-idUSTRE81G1MR20120217.

9. Bruce Horovitz, "Companies Cut Synthetic Hormone from Dairy Products," *USA Today*, March 16, 2009, http://usatoday30.usatoday.com/money/industries/food/2009-03-15-dairy-growth-hormone-ban_n.htm.

10. John Guess, "The US Milk Payment System . . . How Do They Control the Mooooovements?", *Dairy Reporter*, August 9, 2013, www.dairyreporter.com/Commodities/The-US-milk-payment-system-How-do-they-control-the-mooooovements.

EGGS

The Purpose of This Chapter

After reading this chapter, you should be able to:

- Choose appropriate eggs based on primary selection factors, including government grades.

- Categorize eggs according to product size, form, and packaging, and related characteristics.

- Create a specification for eggs that can be used in the purchasing process.

- Describe procedures for receiving, storing, and issuing eggs.

PRIMARY SELECTION FACTORS

The most important egg purchasing considerations center on determining what hospitality operations want and which type of product is best suited to their needs. Purchasing fresh shell eggs is a relatively easy task. Buying processed eggs, whether frozen, refrigerated, dried, or precooked egg products, requires first identifying how you will use the egg product and, if necessary, note specific functional needs. The egg products industry offers a variety of egg products, often processed to meet buyers' specific requirements.

As with all products, management personnel, either alone or in cooperation with others, normally decide in advance the quality of eggs the operation needs. They use the following selection factors to evaluate the standards of egg quality and, to a certain extent, the egg suppliers.

■ Intended Use

As always, buyers want to determine exactly the **intended use** of an item, so that they will be able to prepare the appropriate, relevant specification. For instance, an egg product may be needed primarily for flavor and only secondarily for appearance. If so, the specification should reflect this.

> **intended use**   Refers to the performance requirement of a product or service, which is noted on the specification. Considered to be the most important piece of information on a specification.
>
> **fresh shell egg**   Product that is less than 30 days old.

■ Exact Name

Generally, this selection factor causes very little difficulty. Fresh eggs are chicken eggs, so if buyers use the term "eggs," they will receive chicken eggs (see Figure 18.1). The term **fresh shell eggs** refers to eggs that are fewer than 30 days old.

Today, most shell eggs are processed and distributed within a few hours to a few days after lay.

FIGURE 18.1 A flat of chicken eggs.
©Qizhi He/iStockphoto

FIGURE 18.2 Processed egg products.
Courtesy of Michael Foods, Inc.

The term "egg products" refers to eggs that have been removed from their shells for processing at facilities called **breaker plants**. Whole eggs, whites, yolks, and various blends—with or without added ingredients—that are processed and pasteurized, are basic types of egg products (see Figure 18.2). These products are available in refrigerated, refrigerated extended shelf-life, frozen, and dried forms. Because of the different combinations of types and forms, buyers need to carefully consider their selection factors when ordering **processed egg** products. Buyers must be absolutely certain that they indicate the **exact name** of the desired item to ensure receipt of a product that will meet the buyer's needs.

> **breaker plant** Facility that removes eggs from their shells and processes them further.
>
> **processed eggs** Eggs that have been removed from their shells for processing at facilities called "breaker plants."
>
> **exact name** Indication of a product or service's specific type, quality, and style.

■ U.S. Government Inspection and Grades (or Equivalent)

Unlike most foods produced in the United States, both the U.S. Food and Drug Administration (FDA) and the U.S. Department of Agriculture (USDA) regulate shell eggs. The two agencies share responsibility for the safety of eggs, regulating the production, processing, transportation, and holding of shell eggs. Regulations promulgated by the FDA in 2009 place strict biosecurity, pest control, testing, and refrigeration requirements on farms producing shell eggs for human food. In addition, under authority provided by the Federal Food, Drug, and Cosmetic Act and the Fair Packaging and Labeling Act, the FDA has overall jurisdiction of shell egg processing and packing. The **Egg Products Inspection Act (EPIA)** of 1970 requires the USDA to ensure that eggs and egg products are safe, wholesome, unadulterated, and accurately labeled, for the protection of the health

> **Egg Products Inspection Act (EPIA)** Applies to shell eggs that are removed from the shell and processed. Sets standards for sanitation and wholesomeness. Also mandates the pasteurization of egg products and requires egg production to be inspected by the USDA.

and welfare of consumers. The original impetus for this act was driven by industry and government concerns regarding the contamination risk present with eggs and egg products. The USDA is responsible for the Shell Egg Surveillance Program to ensure that eggs in the marketplace contain no more restricted eggs than the amount permitted in the U.S. Consumer Grade B quality standards. Shell egg processing is also subject to individual state egg laws. In most states, an egg producer is subject to inspections by federal and state inspectors.

Under the EPIA, egg breaking and processing plants producing liquid, frozen, and dried egg products must submit to continuous government inspection. A USDA **Food Safety and Inspection Service (FSIS)** inspector must be on duty when these plants are operating. Only red meat, poultry, and egg products are subject to this level of inspection. (The USDA is currently working on regulations that will subject catfish processing to similar inspections.)

> **Food Safety and Inspection Service (FSIS)**   Division of the U.S. Department of Agriculture (USDA). Also oversees meat inspection.

USDA also administers a voluntary grading service for shell eggs and poultry. Shell egg plants that elect to contract with the USDA's Agricultural Marketing Service (AMS) for the egg quality grading program may place the USDA grade shield on product packaging when eggs are graded for quality and checked for weight (size) under the supervision of a trained USDA grader. Producers that do not use this service may label their eggs Grade A, but not USDA Grade A. About 30 percent of eggs sold in the United States carry the USDA Grade mark.

Three federal government consumer grades for fresh shell eggs have become familiar quality guidelines (see Figure 18.3 and Figure 18.4).

USDA A GRADE

FIGURE 18.3
Federal grade and inspection stamp used for eggs.
Courtesy of U.S. Department of Agriculture.

1. **U.S. Grade AA.** These eggs have whites that are thick and firm; yolks that are high, round, and practically free from defects; and clean, unbroken shells. Because these eggs are the top quality produced, only the freshest products earn this grade.

2. **U.S. Grade A.** These eggs have characteristics of Grade AA eggs except that the whites are "reasonably" firm. This is indicative of slightly lower quality. As eggs age, they may fall into this grade category. This product's white and yolk are not quite as firm as those found in

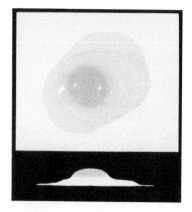

FIGURE 18.4a Grade AA.
Courtesy of United States Department of Agriculture

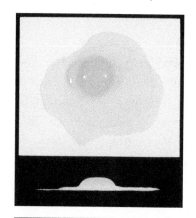

FIGURE 18.4b Grade A.
Courtesy of United States Department of Agriculture

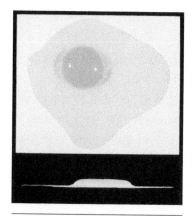

FIGURE 18.4c Grade B.
Courtesy of United States Department of Agriculture

Grade AA merchandise. Driven in part by consumer preferences, in some areas of the country, you may not see eggs marked Grade AA. However, both Grade A and Grade AA eggs are suitable for all finished menu products, including those where appearance is important. In fact, there is often a high percentage of individual AA eggs in packages labeled Grade A.

3. **U.S. Grade B.** You may not see any eggs labeled Grade B. With modern production, animal husbandry, and processing practices, there are few eggs that fall into this category. These eggs have whites that may be thinner and yolks that may be wider and flatter than eggs of higher grades. The yolks may be susceptible to breaking under slight pressure. The shells must be unbroken but may show slight stains. Therefore, because of these appearance problems, Grade B merchandise is suitable only for finished menu products in which eggs are used as an ingredient or as scrambled eggs (or omelets).

Fresh eggs are graded on interior and exterior quality factors. Interior quality, such as the firmness of the egg yolk and egg white, is determined primarily by freshness. The exterior quality factors, such as shape, cleanliness, and soundness, are determined by the age of the hen, the feed eaten, and the general management of the flock and of the egg-laying facilities. The fresher an egg, the higher the quality, assuming that the laying hen is the right age (from 6 months to 1 1/2 years old), is eating a proper diet, and is living in an appropriate environment.

The USDA grader and/or company quality assurance personnel use a process called **candling** to check the interior quality of fresh eggs. This involves passing the egg over a light source, which reveals the yolk (a yolk in the center of the thick and thin white implies freshness), the size of the air space (which gets larger as the egg becomes older), impurities, and cracks. The grader may also crack open randomly selected eggs to determine the height and firmness of the egg white and might also evaluate the condition of the shell, especially if the laying hens are relatively old. Older hens produce eggs that have rougher and thinner shells.

> **candling** Looking inside a shell egg by passing it over a light to determine its quality. Part of the egg-grading process.

The use of U.S. grades for fresh-egg purchasing is widespread, although an unwary buyer might see a significant difference in quality between different sources of eggs labeled with the same grade. A major advantage of USDA-graded shell eggs is that they have been produced under continuous government inspection. It is a good idea for buyers to insist on this type of inspection because shell eggs are on the FDA's list of **potentially hazardous foods**, as are other high-protein foods. Fresh shell eggs, even those that appear to be sound, can be contaminated with salmonella bacteria by the hens on rare occasions. Continuous government inspection, as well as buyers insisting on constant refrigeration at 45°F, should help mitigate this problem.

> **potentially hazardous food** Food, especially protein-based food (such as meat, fish, and poultry), that can cause food-borne illness if not handled properly.

Foodservice buyers usually purchase Grade A eggs. Grade AA eggs are difficult to obtain. In addition, Grade A eggs normally suffice, particularly for fried and scrambled eggs and omelets.

■ Packers' Brands (or Equivalent)

Supermarkets today may stock eggs co-packed for them under their brand name along with producer brands or national brands. But foodservice buyers do not show a great deal of brand loyalty for fresh shell eggs. For them, the federal grade is the most common quality indicator.

However, packers' brands can be extremely important when buyers purchase processed and convenience forms of eggs, such as frozen, refrigerated, and dried egg products. Processed egg products, although produced under continuous government inspection, do not have established grading standards. As a result, buyers often use past success with a particular brand or processor to help ensure consistent quality. Most egg product processors will work with the buyer to develop a specification that fits the buyer's needs.

SIZE, FORM, PACKAGING, AND RELATED CONSIDERATIONS

■ Product Size

> **product size**   Refers to the buyer's specified weight, or volume, of a particular item he or she wants to purchase. Examples would be a 10-ounce steak or a 4-ounce hamburger.

Buyers are normally interested in the size and uniformity of the shell eggs they purchase. The U.S. government helps in this area because graded eggs must meet quality and size standards. Producers are required to indicate the egg size somewhere on the container. Buyers should choose the **product size** most useful and economical. Shell eggs are available in six sizes (see Figure 18.5).

Peewee eggs, sometimes called "pullet eggs," come from younger hens, usually at the beginning of their laying life. Jumbo eggs come from relatively

SIZE OR WEIGHT CLASS	MINIMUM NET WEIGHT PER DOZEN (OUNCES)
Jumbo	30
Extra large	27
Large	24
Medium	21
Small	18
Peewee	15

18.5a

U.S. Weight Classes–Minimum Weight Per Dozen Eggs

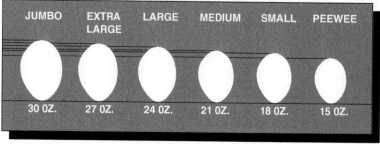

18.5b

FIGURE 18.5 U.S. weight classes for shell eggs.
Courtesy of United States Department of Agriculture

FIGURE 18.6 Huevos Rancheros.
Source: Gisslen, Professional Cooking, 7th Edition, Copyright 2011. Reprinted with permission of John Wiley and Sons, Inc.

older hens, usually at the end of their laying life. These extreme sizes are not common in the fresh-egg trade. If buyers want these sizes, normally they must make arrangements with the producer to check for availability.

When choosing eggs to be fried, scrambled, poached, or prepared in omelets, buyers usually prefer the large size. These eggs have a very acceptable appearance and show up well on the plate (see Figure 18.6). Also, those who purchase fresh eggs for use in baking recipes tend to choose **large eggs** because most quantity recipes, as well as recipes found in most cookbooks and Internet sources, assume a 2-ounce (large) egg.

Buyers who keep close track of the as-purchased (AP) prices for each size might be able to save a few pennies when purchasing fresh shell eggs. For instance, in a recipe calling for eggs by weight, if large eggs cost $1.20 per dozen and medium eggs cost $1 per dozen, buyers could determine the best price per ounce in the following manner:

> **large egg** Common fresh shell egg size purchased and used by the hospitality industry. It weighs approximately 2 ounces. The typical standard recipe requiring fresh shell eggs assumes the cook will use this size.

$1.20 per dozen / 24 ounces per dozen = $0.05 per ounce

$1.00 per dozen / 21 ounces per dozen = $0.0476 per ounce

So, medium eggs represent a slightly better buy.

We do not normally see buyers use this procedure; it is probably more helpful to homemakers than to commercial buyers, who are often restricted to the large-size egg. But if buyers want to purchase a large volume of shell eggs (instead of buying huge containers of liquid shell eggs) for use in various recipes and the labor is available to process them, such a procedure might save money.

■ Size of Container

For shell eggs, the normal package size is a 15-dozen or 30-dozen case. At times, buyers might order one or more "flats"; a flat contains 2 1/2 dozen fresh eggs. It is unusual to purchase eggs in 1-dozen or 1 1/2-dozen containers.

Processed egg products offer a bit more variety in package sizes, so buyers must be prepared to describe the exact packaging characteristics that best suit their needs.

■ Type of Packaging Material

For fresh shell eggs, the packaging is standardized. Buyers probably will not need to consider this selection factor if they order only fresh eggs. The most common material used and the one recommended by the American Egg Board (AEB) is shell eggs packed in snug-fitting fiberboard boxes.

The same may not be true with processed egg products because a considerable variation in packaging quality can exist. Buyers must be concerned with this selection factor because improperly packaged products can result in quality deterioration or even food safety issues. This is especially true if hospitality operators must store the processed egg products on their premises for a reasonably long period of time.

Usually, frozen egg products are packaged in moisture-proof, vapor-proof containers. In most instances, a processed product, such as frozen, precooked scrambled eggs, normally is packaged in a heavy plastic pouch; these pouches are sometimes referred to as **Cryovac®** bags, or "Cryovac packaging." (Cryovac is a brand name. It is the company that developed the vacuum **shrink-wrap** technology that enables food processors to store products for considerable lengths of time.)

Cryovac® The company that pioneered shrink-wrap technology.

shrink-wrap Product is packed in plastic, and a vacuum is pulled through it so that air is removed and the wrapping collapses to fit snugly around the product. A type of controlled atmosphere packaging (CAP).

Some frozen items are also packed in metal or plastic containers. For instance, frozen eggs, frozen egg yolks, and frozen egg whites are shelled and typically packaged in 30-pound plastic containers. Liquid egg products are available in cartons, 10- and 30-pound containers, poly-lined drums, self-contained refrigerated tanks, and tank trucks. Dried egg products—which are becoming less frequently used in the hospitality industry—are sold in a variety of larger package sizes, commonly a fiberboard box lined with airtight, plastic bags. Some of these products are also packaged in metal or plastic containers.

■ Packaging Procedure

The packaging process is not a concern for most egg products that the typical hospitality buyer purchases. The types of packaging and packaging procedures for fresh shell eggs are very standardized, as they are for most processed products.

In a few instances, buyers may need to specify a desired packaging procedure. For example, if they want to purchase frozen, precooked, plain omelets, they could purchase them individually wrapped and stacked neatly in the case, or in a layered arrangement, where they are separated by sheets of waxed paper. In some cases, it is possible for buyers to specify a combination of inner wrapping and outer wrapping that meets their needs.

■ Color

The breed of the hen determines the color of an egg shell. White-feathered chickens, such as the Leghorn, White Rock, and Cornish chickens, lay white eggs. Chickens with red feathers, such as the Rhode Island Red, New Hampshire, and Plymouth Rock chickens, lay brown eggs (see Figure 18.7). Although no differences in flavor and nutrition have been proved, in some parts of the United States, such as New England, consumers request brown eggs. So, in addition to a potential price difference between brown- and white-shell eggs, buyers must keep this customer preference in mind.

FIGURE 18.7 Brown eggs.
©gosphotodesign/Shutterstock

■ Product Form

In some instances, buyers may wish to purchase one or more convenience egg products. For example, they may want to buy precooked, refrigerated, whole, peeled eggs and use them as a breakfast buffet offering. Alternately, buyers might wish to purchase cheese-stuffed, frozen, precooked omelets. As always, the added value of the desired form will increase the AP prices, but the ultimate edible-portion (EP) costs may be quite affordable.

■ Refrigeration

This is the most common **preservation** method for fresh shell eggs. As fresh eggs get older, they lose quality: moisture dissipates, the white gets thinner, and the yolk becomes weaker. Refrigeration is the best deterrent to this quality loss. FDA and USDA regulations require that fresh shell eggs be received and stored at no greater than 45°F ambient air in order to minimize food-borne illnesses that can result if the eggs are contaminated with small amounts of salmonella bacteria. The USDA also requires that shell eggs (1) be held under refrigeration at an ambient temperature of no greater than 45°F after packing, and (2) contain

> **preservation** A procedure, such as refrigeration, freezing, canning, drying, or chemical additives, used to maintain a product's shelf life and quality and in some cases, impart additional flavorings.

labeling that indicates that refrigeration is required. Wise buyers do not jump to the conclusion that the fresh shell eggs they have purchased have been kept under constant refrigeration.

■ The Processing Method

When buyers purchase processed egg products, they are actually purchasing homogenized egg meat that has been removed from the shell under USDA inspection. Among the most common forms of processed eggs are frozen or refrigerated whole eggs, egg yolks, and egg whites (albumen). Large bakeries and food manufacturers primarily used these products in the past. However, over time, food service operators have expanded their use of these egg products. In addition to the labor savings associated with these products, they are convenient to use and are pasteurized to ensure the destruction of harmful microorganisms. When food-service operations do use processed eggs, it is most common that they rely on refrigerated products.

Problems can be associated with these egg products, however, particularly when frozen. Frozen products are convenient for long-term storage. Be aware that frozen yolks will become thickened or gelatinous if sugar or salt is not added to them before freezing and if they are not frozen correctly. The thawing process for frozen eggs must be done in a controlled refrigerated temperature or under cold running water. (Operators should allow time for defrosting frozen eggs, but not in excess of 48 hours.) Unsupervised employees may not be patient enough to wait out this relatively long thawing procedure. If frozen eggs are thawed at room temperature, harmful bacteria can multiply rapidly.

Other familiar forms of processed eggs used in foodservice operations and large bakeries are dried eggs, dried egg yolks, and dried egg whites. Because reconstitution may be problematic, dried eggs are not normally used for scrambling. They tend to be used most often in breads, pastries, and other baked goods. Spray drying, or spraying the liquid egg mixture into a heated environment, is a superior method. Freeze-drying, or freezing liquid eggs and going from the frozen state directly to the dried state, is also successful.

Buyers can purchase other types of processed egg products. For instance, they can order frozen deviled eggs and frozen, cooked scrambled eggs. These items can be expensive because of the convenience they offer, but the potential labor savings might more than offset the high AP price.

A DAY IN THE LIFE
John Howeth, Vice President of Foodservice & Egg Product Marketing
American Egg Board, Park Ridge, Illinois

©Courtesy of John Howeth,
American Egg Board

For John Howeth, it's all about The Incredible Edible Egg™. It is his job as VP of Foodservice & Egg Product Marketing for American Egg Board (AEB) to promote egg use to the away-from-home segment of the food industry. Otherwise known as foodservice, this segment includes commercial establishments such as national and regional chains, fine dining, and independent restaurateurs as well as noncommercial operators such as schools, colleges, and healthcare providers.

Now, Howeth doesn't sell eggs. He markets them for the egg producers across the country who financially support the AEB. To help create demand for The Incredible Edible Egg™, AEB conducts programs, promotions, and research.

"We produce information for use in publications, we work with our corporate chef to develop recipe cards, and we distribute a newsletter Breakfast Beat which goes to over 100,000 recipients," said Howeth. "AEB has an egg safety program to teach foodservice operators how to safely store and cook eggs to prevent spoilage. We also provide restaurants with new egg menu ideas. In our consumer program we have advertising in both radio and digital formats and print ads in popular magazines about the egg," he added.

Howeth works with an extremely efficient staff in his 20-person office as well as an advertising agency and three consultants who specialize in various industry segments to develop marketing ideas and materials. With the increase in digital focus, the team has to be very well versed in communicating through this new medium as so many people are moving to the Internet for their business-to-business communication needs.

AEB promotes only chicken eggs in a white or brown shell and egg products including dried eggs, egg yolks, egg whites, eggs with added sugar for baking, and liquid eggs. In addition, AEB concentrates on generic promotion of eggs and doesn't make distinctions among free range, natural, organic, or other specific types of eggs.

Howeth travels throughout the country, making contacts and giving presentations on eggs.

"In foodservice, we concentrate on profitability," he said. "Eggs have such a low food cost, that the operator can turn around and have a reasonable menu price, and the profit margin is still good. We also talk about the versatility of eggs and encourage food service operators to use eggs for all meal occasions and for many menu applications. In today's environment a tremendous amount of attention is placed on protein, as all demographics are looking to increase their protein intake."

Eighty-five percent of all breakfasts eaten away-from-home are eaten at Quick Serve Restaurants. For Howeth, the most fun is engaging chains and increasing their usage. "You can imagine the excitement and impact when you educate chains about eggs, especially since billions are sold every day of the week."

PURCHASING EGGS

As usual, the first step in egg purchasing is for hospitality operators to determine precisely what they want. As noted earlier, fresh shell eggs present few problems. The problem with buying eggs is not so much selecting the quality: buyers will rarely go wrong if they stipulate U.S. grades for fresh shell eggs or if they settle on a particularly desirable brand name for a processed egg product. The most widely used quality is U.S. Grade A, and the normal size is large. However, considerably more combinations of qualities and sizes are available. As a result, management, either alone or in conjunction with other key employees, must determine the efficacy and usefulness of these combinations as they relate to a particular operation.

The qualities and styles of processed egg products are not so easily chosen. If buyers purchase these items, their best bet is to consider a reliable supplier that meets the guidelines of the Egg Products Inspection Act[1] and specify that the processed product be prepared with fresh eggs of a

packer's brand Very specific indication of product quality. More precise than a brand name. A packer's personal grading system. Usually intended to take the place of federal government grades.

Global Food Safety Initiative (GFSI) Launched in 2000, the GFSI seeks to ensure confidence in the delivery of safe food to consumers through continuous improvement of food safety management systems. GFSI provides a platform for collaboration between some of the world's leading food safety experts from all levels of food companies, international organizations, educators, and government.

certain U.S. grade. More often, the convenience and reliability of the **packer's brand** name eventually become the overriding factors in selecting processed egg products. The AEB website has names of all companies that produce egg products.

Once buyers make their decision, they need to prepare a complete specification that includes all pertinent information, whether or not they use it in bid buying. If nothing else, the discipline of preparing this document will help to ensure that buyers have considered all the relevant factors and are, indeed, purchasing the egg product that suits their needs (see Figure 18.8 for some example product specifications and Figure 18.9 for an example of a product specification outline for egg products).

After determining what they need and when they need it, buyers must evaluate potential suppliers. Buyers will find a reasonable number of potential suppliers in the fresh-egg trade, which is good news for those who like the bid-buying strategy. A visit to the suppliers to view their operation and handling of eggs can be a good idea. Many shell egg packers and egg products companies operate under food safety schemes recognized by the **Global Food Safety Initiative (GFSI)**. Use of the Safe Quality Food Initiative, a GFSI recognized program administered by the Food Marketing Institute, is commonly used in these industries.

Buyers must make sure that a supplier can meet specifications and delivery requirements. Also, if buyers expect that fresh eggs be refrigerated, they may need to check that the supplier maintains the specific storage environment.

The processed-egg trade does not offer as many suppliers or brands. If buyers want dried eggs, the limited number of purveyors stocking them may

Fresh shell eggs
Used for fried, poached, scrambled eggs
U.S. Grade AA
Large
30 dozen per shipping case
Cartons labeled with an expiration date not to exceed 28 days from date of packaging
Eggs delivered within 7 days of official grading
White shell

Scrambled egg mix
Used for scrambled eggs on buffet
Fresh Start® brand
2-pound carton
Moisture-proof, vapor-proof carton
6 cartons per case
Refrigerated liquid

Meringue powder
Used to prepare dessert topping bakery products
R & H® brand
6-pound container
Plastic, resealable container
Unrefrigerated

Frozen, whole, shelled eggs
Used to prepare bakery products
McAnally® brand
30-pound container
Metal can

Intended use:

Exact name:

U.S. grade (or equivalent):

Packer's brand name (or equivalent):

Product size:

Size of container:

Type of packaging material:

Packaging procedure:

Color:

Product form:

Preservation method:

FIGURE 18.8 An example of egg product specifications.

FIGURE 18.9 An example of product specification outline for egg products.

be a surprise. Furthermore, if buyers want reduced-cholesterol eggs, they may find even fewer suppliers. Similarly, not too many producers carry such specialty items as frozen deviled eggs.

Before purchasing any egg product, buyers should take some time to evaluate the substitution possibilities. Several processed items substitute nicely for fresh eggs, and vice versa. If buyers purchase a lot of eggs, it may pay for them to have recipes printed several ways to include various forms of eggs and egg substitutions. For example, cake recipes might be written to incorporate fresh eggs, dried eggs, or frozen eggs. If the AP prices vary favorably, a few minutes of cost calculation might signal that one of these recipes is demonstrably more economical than the others.

In addition to supplier services, buyers must consider purchasing options. Bid buying and becoming a house account are two alternatives. Both have their advantages and disadvantages, and buyers must make their choice.

PROCEDURES FOR RECEIVING, STORING, AND ISSUING EGGS

■ Receiving

When receiving fresh shell eggs, receivers should take the time to examine them carefully for cracks, dirt, and lack of uniformity. They should also check the temperature to see if the eggs were transported at an ambient temperature of 45°F or lower without being frozen. In addition, receivers should make sure that all the eggs are there. Weighing the containers might be the easiest quantity check.

It is difficult for receiving personnel to determine the age of fresh eggs. The American Egg Board recommends that receivers randomly break a few eggs and inspect them to determine if they meet the guidelines of their given grade.[2] The delivery drivers may think that the receivers have lost their mind if they expect them to wait around while they conduct this ritual. A little skepticism never hurt a buyer, however.

It is becoming more common for egg cartons to display a **Julian date**. This is the date the eggs were packed. An expiration date on the egg itself may also be done, particularly for retail use. Egg cartons that have a USDA grademark are required to display the Julian date.

Processed liquid, frozen, and dried egg products must bear the USDA mark of inspection.

Similar to shell eggs, peeled hard-cooked eggs and precooked eggs are not required to bear a USDA inspection shield. Assuming that all the products ordered have been delivered, receivers then need to assess the quality of the items. This is not very easy. Receivers can check frozen egg products to see whether any crystallization has occurred; this is an indication of refreezing. They can also use a temperature probe to test frozen egg products.

> **Julian date** The interval of time in days and fractions of a day since January 1, 4713 BC Greenwich noon. The system was introduced by astronomers to provide a single system of dates that could be used when working with different calendars and to unify different historical chronologies.

If receivers do not take or make the time to check egg quality, they must trust their supplier and delivery agent. Because processed-egg quality is always difficult to determine, we suppose that a certain degree of trust is inherent here in any case.

After checking the quality and quantity, receivers should check the prices and complete the appropriate accounting procedures.

■ Storing

Fresh eggs should be refrigerated as soon as possible at 45°F or below, but do not freeze them. Eggs stored at 45°F or below will retain their quality for weeks. Move them rapidly from the transport vehicle into the cooler. Never allow them to sit in warm or extremely cold weather. In addition, because these items pick up odors quickly, they should be kept in their original containers. Some large operations maintain a dairy refrigerator to keep fresh eggs away from particularly odorous products, such as onions, fish, cabbage, and apples. Processed eggs also require a specific storage environment, either frozen, refrigerated, or dry storage, suggested by the form in which they come.

■ Issuing

Hospitality operators should properly rotate stock, so that the oldest items are issued first (first in, first out [FIFO]). This may be accomplished by dating containers as they are received. In some cases, the egg purchases go straight into production. If operators issue eggs from a central storeroom, they must make sure, for example, that the requisitioner who wants eggs for a cake recipe gets the frozen or dried eggs, if applicable.

> **in-process inventory**
> Products located at employee workstations; most or all will be used during the shift.

Because fresh shell eggs deteriorate rapidly once they leave refrigeration, operators must ensure that the requisitioner takes no more than needed for any one particular work shift or job. Eggs should not be left unrefrigerated in excess of 2 hours. Operators might consider asking the requisitioner to take note of the **in-process inventory** before asking for additional stock.

■ In-Process Inventories

The benefit of good purchasing effectiveness can be immediately offset if hospitality operators do not control in-process inventories. For example, if breakfast cooks leave fresh shell eggs out at room temperature all day, the egg quality could drop a grade. The same is true of processed eggs. As always, supervision is the key. Without it, there is little sense in buyers taking care to purchase the proper items for the production staff. The best a supervisor can do is insist that all eggs be kept in the recommended environment at all times and removed from this environment only when necessary.

Key Words and Concepts

Breaker plant	Intended use
Candling	Julian date
Cryovac®	Large egg
Egg Products Inspection Act (EPIA)	Packer's brand
Exact name	Potentially hazardous food
Food Safety and Inspection Service (FSIS)	Preservation
Fresh shell egg	Processed eggs
Global Food Safety Initiative (GFSI)	Product size
In-process inventory	Shrink-wrap

Questions and Problems

1. What are the U.S. grades for fresh shell eggs?

2. List the sizes for fresh shell eggs.

3. What procedure can receivers follow to determine the freshness of shell eggs?

4. Eggs are regulated by both the USDA and FDA. What are the responsibilities of and regulations enforced by each agency in regard to eggs?

5. What is an appropriate intended use for:
   a. frozen whole eggs
   b. dried egg whites
   c. USDA Grade B shell eggs

6. A product specification for dried eggs could include this information:
   a.
   b.
   c.
   d.
   e.

7. A foodservice buyer normally specifies the large-size fresh egg because:
   a.
   b.

8. What are the two typical package sizes for fresh shell eggs?

9. What happens to a fresh shell egg as it becomes older?

10. What is the preferred preservation method for fresh shell eggs?

11. A "flat" contains _____ dozen fresh shell eggs.

12. What are the primary grading factors for fresh shell egg grades?

13. What is the primary indication of quality of a processed egg product?

14. What is the difference between the designations "U.S. Grade A" and "Grade A"?

15. When would buyers purchase reduced-cholesterol egg products?

16. A product specification for frozen omelets could include this information:
   a.
   b.
   c.
   d.
   e.

Questions and Problems (continued)

17. What critical information is missing from this product specification for a frozen egg mix?
    Frozen egg mix
    Used for low-fat entrées
    EggBeaters® brand

18. What will be the AP price per ounce of a large shell egg at $1.25 per dozen?

 Experiential Exercises

1. Assume that you are the manager of an employee food service. Outline the specific procedures you would use for the purchasing, receiving, storing, and issuing of fresh shell eggs that will be used for eggs over easy. Ask an employee foodservice manager to comment on your answer. Write a one-page paper on your findings.

2. Assume that you are the kitchen supervisor for a resort hotel. Your Sunday brunch normally includes scrambled eggs. You are trying to decide whether to scramble them a few at a time to order, scramble fresh eggs in advance and cook them in large batches, or to use frozen scrambled eggs packed in 5-pound Cryovac® bags that need only to be steam-heated for 20 minutes. What would be the advantages and disadvantages of each method? Ask a resort hotel's food and beverage director or kitchen supervisor to comment on your answers. Write a one-page paper about your findings, and include a recommendation for which type of egg you would purchase and how you would cook them.

 References

1. USDA FSIS Egg Products Inspection Act, www.fsis.usda.gov/regulations/Egg_Products_Inspection_Act/index.asp.

2. American Egg Board, *The Incredible Edible Egg: A Natural for Any Foodservice Operation* (Park Ridge, IL: American Egg Board, 2003). See also American Egg Board, *Egg Handling and Care Guide*, 2nd ed. (Park Ridge, IL: American Egg Board, 2000); American Egg Board, Eggcyclopedia, www.aeb.org/LearnMore/Eggcyclopedia.htm. Da-Wen Sun, ed., *Handbook of Frozen Food Packaging and Processing* (Boca Raton, FL, Taylor & Francis, 2006), which covers frozen eggs but also a wide range of other foods.
    For a summary of safe egg handling, see "Shell Eggs From Farm to Table,"
U.S. Department of Agriculture Food Safety and Inspection Service, www.fsis.usda.gov/Fact_Sheets/Focus_On_Shell_Eggs/index.asp. For more information about eggs, visit www.aeb.org.

POULTRY

The Purpose of This Chapter

After reading this chapter, you should be able to:

- Choose appropriate poultry items based on primary selection factors, including government grades.

- Categorize poultry according to product size, form, and packaging, and related characteristics.

- Consider supplier and AP price factors when purchasing poultry.

- Describe procedures for purchasing, creating specifications for, receiving, storing, and issuing poultry.

PRIMARY SELECTION FACTORS

poultry A term applied to all domesticated birds used for food.

commodity A basic, raw food ingredient. It is considered by buyers to be the same regardless of which vendor sells it. For instance, all-purpose flour is often considered a commodity product, whereby any processor's product is acceptable.

ratite A family of flightless birds with small wings and flat breastbones. Ostrich and emu are the two most common types sold in the United States. The meat tastes like beef and has less calories and fat than beef, chicken, or turkey.

Poultry is a term applied to all domesticated birds used for food. Poultry is not an especially difficult item to purchase, unless you are in the market for certain types of processed items. Generally, raw poultry is still considered to be a **commodity**, which means the typical buyer does not perceive a great deal of difference between one frying chicken and another.

The poultry that foodservices typically buy are chicken, turkey, and duckling. On occasion, some might also purchase goose, squab, and quail (see Figure 19.1). Some restaurants may serve ostrich and emu, which are classified as **ratites** or flightless birds.

For the most part, a specific class of bird is raised the same way all over the country. For example, frying chickens are raised in about eight weeks. They consume a relatively standardized diet—standardized, at least, according to nutritional needs—and are slaughtered, cleaned, and packed with similar production line techniques. In short, raising any bird these days is a standard, scientific undertaking. Hospitality operators find very few small-scale producers, although a few independent farmers here and there may seek their business.

As with other products, the operators' major problem is deciding exactly what they want. If they want fresh or fresh-frozen poultry, they will have several suppliers from which to choose. Also, unless the buyers include packers' brands of fresh poultry, the as-purchased (AP) price will be about the same among the suppliers, provided, of course, that these suppliers offer the same quality and supplier services.

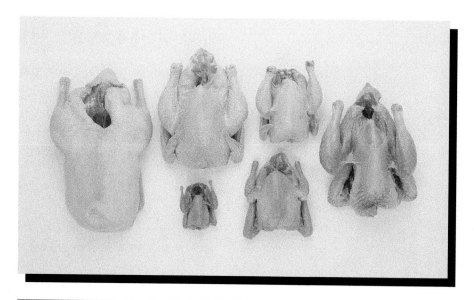

FIGURE 19.1 Clockwise from left: duckling, free-range chicken, poussin, guinea fowl, squab, quail.
Source: Gisslen, Professional Cooking, *7th Edition, Copyright 2011. Reprinted with permission of John Wiley and Sons, Inc.*

If buyers want other types of processed poultry, they obviously face the question of the degree of convenience they would like built into the products. They can usually purchase whole, dressed birds (it is not easy to purchase live birds today); cut-up birds; and precooked, prebreaded, presliced, and prerolled poultry. Numerous processed poultry products, as well as some imitation items, are available.

Only a few food processors undertake some types of processing. For instance, buyers can purchase cut-up frying chickens from a variety of sources, but they can purchase canned, cooked whole chickens from only a few suppliers.

In general, buyers will encounter little difficulty when purchasing poultry items. Numerous suppliers exist, and numerous varieties of poultry items are available in the market.

As with all products, the owner–manager normally decides the quality, type, and style of poultry products desired. Either alone or in cooperation with other employees, the owner–manager usually evaluates the following selection factors when determining the desired standards of quality and, to a certain degree, the supplier for poultry items.

■ Intended Use

As always, buyers want to determine exactly the **intended use** of the items so that they will be able to prepare appropriate, relevant specifications. For example, poultry used for soup will differ from that needed for a deep-fried menu item.

Fresh, whole chickens may have the lowest AP price. If foodservice operations have a variety of poultry items on the menu, for example fried chicken wings, a grilled chicken breast sandwich, and a stir-fry with the dark meat, buying whole may be the best option. However, the buyer must be aware that poultry has a short **shelf life**, especially if it is fresh, and the fresh poultry inventory should be turned quickly. If the operation only has one or two specific intended uses, buying the particular item best for that use is more practical.

If buyers purchase a lot of poultry, they should examine the **substitution possibilities** because bargains may await them. They might, for instance, substitute turkey rolls for turkey breasts or for whole turkeys. They could also substitute canned poultry for fresh; purchase precooked, chopped chicken pieces if the intended use is for chicken salad; and use precooked sliced turkey breast instead of cooking their own.

Substitutions can disrupt the production and service functions, however. In addition, buyers must, of course, keep track of the distinctive culinary differences between these items. The culinary quality varies for at least two reasons: (1) for different menu items, food processors use poultry of different ages, and (2) the processing method itself could rob or add favorable qualities.

A major issue with any processed product centers on the substitution possibilities and on how much convenience buyers want built into it. Whatever type of processing they want, they have a generous number of suppliers from which to choose, giving them additional flexibility. Poultry products encourage bid buying.

intended use Refers to the performance requirement of a product or service, which is noted on the specification. Considered to be the most important piece of information on a specification.

shelf life The amount of time a product can remain in storage before it loses quality and cannot be used.

substitution possibilities Opportunities for using other ingredients in recipes that will not compromise the culinary quality of the food and beverage items made with those recipes. Alternately, opportunities for using other nonfood and non-beverage products, such as cleaners, equipment, and utensils, to accomplish the same purposes.

exact name Indication of a product or service's specific type, quality, and style.

standard of identity A U.S. government regulation that establishes what a food product must be to carry a certain name. For example, what a food product must be to be labeled "strawberry preserves."

age at time of slaughter Characteristic that affects the flavor, tenderness, and other culinary characteristics of poultry.

conversion weight Another term for yield.

■ Exact Name

The **exact name** is an important consideration because the federal government has established **standards of identity** for many poultry items. For example, some fresh products are standardized according to the birds' sex and/or **age at the time of slaughter** (see Figure 19.2). Exact descriptions of the kinds of poultry available and other items included on the specification such as packaging and preservation are available from the USDA.[1]

Age can affect the intended use of the poultry. Poultry to be cooked with dry heat such as roasting or grilling, should be young if buyers want a tender product. (As poultry ages, it becomes less tender. However, it also develops more fat, which carries flavor.) If chefs want to simmer a chicken for chicken soup, buyers will probably opt for an old bird. It will have more flavor, and moist heat will ensure tenderness. As a bonus, an old bird tends to have a high **conversion weight**, that is, a high edible yield. If a bird gets too old, though, much of the weight begins to collect in the abdominal fat. This fat can be collected and used for, perhaps, a roux for a chicken gravy. However, the yield of cooked meat per pound of raw chicken may be less than expected because of the extra fat.

The sex of young birds is not particularly relevant to their cooking style or usage, but in older birds, the differences in taste, texture, and yield diverge dramatically between the sexes. Females tend to be tastier, be juicier, and have higher conversion weights than males. So, if buyers purchase mature poultry, they should consider the cooking implications of sex, especially if they are bid buying.

In lieu of using standards of identity, buyers can use the numbering system for poultry products that is now contained in the latest edition of *The Meat Buyer's Guide* (MBG) published by the North American Meat Institute (NAMI), 2014©. These numbers take the place of part of

CHICKEN
Young (tender) birds
Broiler/fryer—9 to 12 weeks old; $1\frac{1}{2}$ to $3\frac{1}{2}$ pounds; either sex
Roaster—3 to 5 months old; $3\frac{1}{2}$ to 6 pounds; either sex
Capon—less than 8 months old; 6 to 10 pounds; desexed male bird
Cornish game hen—5 to 7 weeks old; 1 to $1\frac{1}{2}$ pounds; immature bird
Old (less tender) birds
Stewing hen—more than 10 months old; 3 to 7 pounds; mature female bird
Stag—more than 10 months old; 3 to 7 pounds; mature male bird
TURKEY
Fryer/roaster—less than 16 weeks old; 4 to 8 pounds; either sex
Young hen—5 to 7 months old; 8 to 14 pounds; female bird
Young tom—5 to 7 months old; over 12 pounds; male bird
Yearling hen—under 15 months old; up to 30 pounds; mature female bird
Yearling tom—under 15 months old; up to 30 pounds; mature male bird
DUCK
Duckling—under 8 weeks old; under 4 pounds; either sex
Duck—over 16 weeks old; 4 to 6 pounds; either sex

FIGURE 19.2 Definitions of different poultry products.

a poultry specification. For instance, if buyers order a number P1015 chicken broiler breast half without ribs, they will get a particular style and trim.

As with other product lines, buyers occasionally encounter market terminology that defines very specifically what a poultry product is. For instance, **"free-range" chickens** are allowed to roam free instead of spending their lives in cages. **Kosher chickens**, prepared according to Jewish dietary laws, are frequently allowed to roam free and tend to be a little older at the time of slaughter in order to promote flavor development. Further, because the chickens are soaked and salted to comply with kosher regulations, the meat is more tender. Because these types of poultry products are usually much more expensive than those raised in the traditional way, buyers must not use this terminology carelessly.

If buyers purchase processed poultry products, merely noting the exact name may not be enough because even though standards of identity exist for such products as chicken pot pies, the producers of these items need to meet only some minimum standard. Also, even though buyers may not be averse to a producer's particular formula, they must keep in mind that chicken pot pies can come with several onion varieties and potato varieties. If buyers are dealing with fresh poultry, either whole birds or standardized parts, using the exact name is normally adequate because these fresh items are more consistent among producers. The same cannot be said for processed products, however. These items can and will vary significantly among producers, so overreliance on standards of identity can be a bit chancy.

■ U.S. Government Grades (or Equivalent)

Poultry inspection became mandatory with the 1957 **Poultry Products Inspection Act**.[2] This law applies to all raw poultry sold in interstate commerce, as well as to ratites, squab, and such processed products as canned and frozen items.

Some states conduct their own poultry inspection programs, and the 1968 **Wholesome Poultry Products Act** requires state programs to be at least equal to the federal inspection program. Poultry inspected under a state program, however, can be sold only within that state. Any poultry product transported across state lines or exported to another country must be produced under continuous federal inspection. In states that do not conduct inspection programs, all plants are required to be under continuous federal government inspection (see Figure 19.3).

The **Food Safety and Inspection Service (FSIS)** of the U.S. Department of Agriculture (USDA) performs federal inspection for wholesomeness and federal grading. Assuming that the product is wholesome, a poultry producer can elect to

> **free-range chicken** Poultry that is not confined to a cage during its life cycle. Furthermore, it is not fed unnatural foods, nor is it injected with hormones or other chemicals.
>
> **Kosher chicken** Chicken that fulfills the requirements of Jewish dietary law.
>
> **Poultry Products Inspection Act** Legislation mandating federal government inspection of poultry products sold interstate.
>
> **Wholesome Poultry Products Act** Enhances the USDA's authority to regulate safety in the poultry industry. Requires state inspection of poultry production to be at least equal to the federal inspection program.
>
> **Food Safety and Inspection Service (FSIS)** Division of the U.S. Department of Agriculture (USDA). It oversees meat, poultry, and egg products inspection.

FIGURE 19.3 Federal grade and inspection stamps used for poultry products.

Courtesy of U.S. Department of Agriculture

purchase the grading service. Some states, such as Utah, are licensed to have their own employees perform the inspection and grading processes.[3]

Some states leave poultry producers no choice: they must have their products federally graded after they are inspected. In others, because most poultry product specifications contain a U.S. grade designation, producers have their poultry graded.

grading factors
Characteristics of food or beverage products examined by grading inspectors. Used to judge and rank products.

Federal inspectors grade poultry according to several **grading factors**. Inspectors, or graders, consider: (1) conformation (Does the bird have good form?), (2) fleshing (Does the bird have a well-developed covering of flesh?), (3) fat covering (Does any flesh show through the skin—that is, is it a "thin-skinned" bird?), and (4) other factors (Does the bird have any bruises, excessive pin feathers left after cleaning, broken bones, missing parts, or discoloration?).[4]

Several poultry grades exist. The consumer grades are as follows:

1. Grade A. This is the top poultry quality produced. It indicates a full-fleshed bird that is well finished and has an attractive appearance.

2. Grade B. This bird usually has some dressing defects, such as a torn skin. Also, the bird is, generally, less attractive. For example, it might be slightly lacking in fleshing, and the breast bone may be very visible.

3. Grade C. This bird resembles a Grade B bird, but it lacks even more in appearance. Also, parts of its carcass might be missing. Grade C poultry would not be sold to consumers. All of it is used by food processors.

packer's brand name
Very specific indication of product quality. More precise than a brand name. A packer's personal grading system. Usually intended to take the place of federal government grades.

organic poultry Poultry that meets standards set forth by the USDA, which requires that the poultry must be raised under organic management no later than the second day of life.

natural poultry Poultry that must have no preservatives, have no artificial ingredients, and be minimally processed.

A specification for poultry products usually contains some grade reference. This is especially true when buyers purchase fresh or fresh-frozen whole birds or parts. Buyers usually opt for U.S. Grade A products when appearance is very important. For instance, chefs would most often prepare a fried-chicken entrée with the highest-quality raw products. When appearance is not as important to a hospitality operation, such as when poultry is used to prepare chicken salads, turkey casseroles, or pot pies in the operation's kitchen, Grade B may be adequate. If buyers purchase processed products, such as prebreaded, precooked chicken patties, they are more apt to rely on a **packer's brand name** to specify the desired quality.

More information on grading regulations and standards of poultry is available on the USDA Agricultural Marketing Service website.

■ Organic and Natural Poultry

Organic poultry is a relatively small market, whereas **natural poultry** has made incredible gains over the past years. Natural poultry, the labeling of which is completely voluntary, must have no preservatives, have no artificial ingredients or added color, and be minimally processed. The label must then include a statement that explains the meaning of the term natural, such as "No Artificial Ingredients" or "Minimally Processed"[5] (see Figure 19.4). Organic poultry must meet standards set forth by the USDA, which requires that the poultry must be raised under organic management no later than the second day of life.[6] Whether purchasing natural, or organic, poultry, it is important to consider the AP price and EP cost differentiations between the two as compared to conventional poultry.[7]

FIGURE 19.4 An organic chicken label.
©*Blackwing Quality Meats*

■ Packers' Brands (or Equivalent)

For fresh and fresh-frozen poultry, brand loyalty rarely comes into play. Buyers seem to rely a little more on specific brands of raw turkey or duck. However, this does not seem to be the case with raw chicken, which is usually viewed as a basic commodity.

Some manufacturers attempt to take poultry out of the commodity class and instill brand loyalty in consumers, who have several brands from which to choose. For instance, Perdue®, Tyson®, and Foster Farms® are some of the brand labels buyers can specify for fresh chicken.

Some value, as well as a higher AP price, is associated with proprietary chicken brand names. For example, producers generally slow down the assembly line to use a "soft-scald" procedure, which removes feathers at a lower temperature, thereby significantly increasing the tenderness of the birds. Some producers use a **chill pack** preservation procedure for their finished products. This maintains the chickens' temperature at about 28°F to 29°F (they freeze at about 27°F to 28°F), which extends the products' shelf life without freezing them. Mary's® is a popular brand of free-range, air-chilled chicken.

Furthermore, these brand name items are usually produced in exceptionally clean environments. Very high levels of sanitation will increase the products' shelf life because it is directly related to the numbers of bacteria found on the skin of the birds.

The brand-name campaign seems aimed primarily at homemakers, however. Hospitality operations that list a lot of poultry **signature items** on their menus strive to ensure that their customers identify such poultry

> **chill pack** Preservation method whereby the temperature is held at approximately 28°F to 29°F, just above the product's freezing point. Usually done for fresh meat and poultry. Intended to increase the product's shelf life.
>
> **signature item** A menu item that is very popular; the restaurant is known for it.

with the operations that prepare it, and not with a particular packer's brand name. Generally, packers' brands are important to hospitality buyers only when they purchase processed poultry products.

SIZE, FORM, PACKAGING, AND RELATED CONSIDERATIONS

■ Product Size

> **product size** Refers to the buyer's specified weight, or volume, of a particular item he or she wants to purchase. Examples would be a 10-ounce steak or a 4-ounce hamburger.
>
> **weight range** Indication of the approximate size of a product the buyer wishes to purchase. Used when it is impossible or impractical to specify an exact weight.

When purchasing raw poultry products, buyers usually cannot specify an exact **product size**. Instead, they must indicate the acceptable **weight range**. For example, they need to indicate a weight range for whole birds and, to some extent, for raw poultry parts, such as chicken thighs and turkey breasts.

As a general rule, the larger the bird, the higher its edible yield. Buyers might find it helpful—and interesting—to know that, for example, a turkey's bone structure stops developing when it reaches about 20 pounds. Turkeys that weigh more than 20 pounds have more fat and a bit more meat on the same-size skeleton as "thinner" birds. If the operations' intended use allows, their buyers should purchase large birds because these may be the most economical choice.

Buyers also must note the product size of any processed products that their operations need. Fortunately, they normally can specify an exact size for these items and do not have to rely on weight ranges. Many sizes are available for such products as precooked, breaded chicken breasts; chicken patties; and turkey pot pies.

■ Product Yield

> **product yield** The same thing as edible yield.

For some poultry products, such as frozen, breaded chicken patties, buyers may want to indicate the maximum **product yield**, or the minimum trim, expected. For example, they may want to note on the specification that they will accept no more than two broken pieces in a 48-piece container of chicken patties.

■ Size of Container

As always, buyers must indicate the package size that they prefer. If necessary, they would need to note the size of any inner packs. For instance, buyers may want a 25.5-pound case with 120 pieces (30 legs, thighs, wings, and breasts) or a 30-pound case of frozen chicken breast strips, with six 5-pound plastic pouches per case.

■ Type of Packaging Material

A reasonable variety of packaging quality is available, so buyers would do well to consider this selection factor when preparing their specifications. The variety is considerable for fresh product—for instance, fresh poultry may arrive at your back door wrapped in butcher paper; packed in cardboard or wooden crates; packed in shrink wrap, or packed in large, reusable plastic containers that the suppliers will pick up when they deliver the next shipment. The relatively brief shelf life of fresh items makes it necessary for buyers to reject packaging that would do anything to shorten a product's shelf life drastically.

When buyers purchase several types of processed products, they will experience a greater variety of packaging qualities. Normally, processed items used in the hospitality industry are packed in moisture-proof, vapor-proof materials that are designed to withstand freezer temperatures. Buyers must be certain that the items they purchase in this manner are packaged properly so that they can avoid any unnecessary loss of product.

■ Packaging Procedure

Like most products, poultry is packaged in many different ways. For instance, most raw, refrigerated items are slab-packed, whereas their frozen counterparts are usually layered. Whole birds, typically, are individually wrapped if they are frozen, whereas fresh, refrigerated birds may not be; in fact, fresh birds may be slab-packed with crushed ice covering them, which is sometimes referred to as an **ice pack procedure**.

Fresh or frozen boneless poultry products are sometimes packaged in **cello packs**. Products packed this way usually come in a 5-pound box that has six cello-wrapped portions, each of which contains two to four poultry pieces.

Fresh birds or bird parts can also come in **gas-flushed packs**. In this arrangement, the poultry is placed in plastic bags, and the air is "flushed" out of the bag and replaced with carbon dioxide. This packaging procedure, which is a type of controlled-atmosphere or modified atmosphere packaging, is done primarily to extend the fresh poultry's shelf life.

Some fresh, refrigerated products can be purchased in a **marinade pack**. Here, suppliers pack individual poultry parts, for example, chicken wings, in a reusable plastic tub and pour a specific marinade solution over them. The chicken wings then absorb the requvired flavor as they journey through the channel of distribution, so that by the time they are delivered to the hospitality operation's back door, they can be put directly into production.

Most processed poultry products that the typical hospitality operation purchases are frozen and layered. These items are usually referred to as **individually quick frozen (IQF)**. This designation indicates that the products are flash-frozen and layered in the case. In some instances, they may even be individually wrapped.

---

ice pack procedure
Foods packed in crushed ice. Intended to increase shelf life. A typical packing procedure used for things like fresh chicken and fish.

cello pack   Products completely surrounded by clear plastic film. Typical packing procedure for things like ready-to-serve salad greens. Also commonly used as an inner wrap. For instance, if you purchase a 5-pound box of frozen fish fillets, usually there will be six cello-wrapped packages inside, each containing approximately two to four pieces of fish.

gas-flushed pack   A type of controlled atmosphere packaging (CAP).

marinade pack   A packing medium intended to impart flavor, and sometimes tenderness, to foods. For instance, if you feature spicy wings on your menu, you may decide to purchase fresh wings marinated in a special sauce. When they arrive at your restaurant they are ready-to-cook; you do not need to marinate them yourself.

individually quick frozen (IQF)   Process whereby products are quick frozen and individually layered in the case. Typical packing procedure for things like portion-cut boneless, skinless chicken breasts.

snap pack   Another term for individually quick frozen (IQF). When you remove a layer of frozen items from a case and drop it onto a counter, the IQF portions should snap apart easily. If they do not come apart easily and cleanly, it usually means that they have been thawed a bit and refrozen.

shatter pack   Another term for individually quick frozen (IQF).

product form   Refers to the degree of processing, or lack thereof, a product has when you purchase it. For instance, a buyer can purchase whole chickens or selected chicken parts. The parts typically would cost more than the whole birds.

number of pieces per bird   Selection factor that may be important when purchasing poultry. Refers directly to the number of parts to be cut from a bird carcass, and indirectly to the style of cut that will be used.

IQF is sometimes referred to as a **snap pack** or **shatter pack** (see Figure 19.5). When you remove a layer of product and drop it onto a counter top, the pieces should snap apart cleanly. If they don't, it's likely the products have been refrozen.

■ Product Form

One of the amazing aspects of the poultry trade is the seemingly endless number of products available and the **product forms** in which buyers can purchase them. At one extreme are the raw products, while at the other extreme several artificial meat items, such as "ham" and "hot dogs," are sometimes made using poultry ingredients. The most common processed product forms are items like frozen chicken strips and seasoned chicken wings (see Figure 19.6).

If buyers purchase whole birds, they will have the option of receiving them whole or they can request that the birds be cut into a specific **number of pieces per bird** (see Figure 19.7). Buyers also may be able to specify a particular cutting pattern, although the standards of identity the federal government has established address this issue fairly well; hence, it is often unnecessary to dwell on this aspect.

When purchasing whole birds, buyers can opt to have the **variety meats** included or excluded. These are the organ meats, such as the liver and heart. Because they are not usually included with whole birds intended for use by foodservice establishments, if buyers want them, they normally will need to indicate this desire on the specification. Ordinarily, if foodservice operators need to purchase variety meats, they will buy them separately; for example,

FIGURE 19.5 An IQF chicken product.
©Westend61 GmbH/Alamy Stock Photo

FIGURE 19.6 A processed chicken product.
©Keith Homan/Alamy Stock Photo

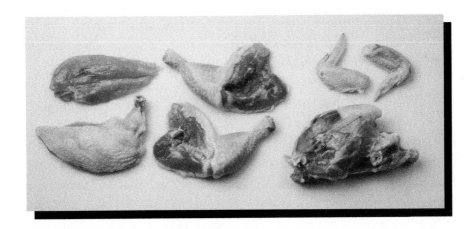

FIGURE 19.7 Cut-up chicken. From left: Breast portions without and with wing bone, leg portions without and with thigh bone, wing sections, and carcass.
Source: Gisslen, Professional Cooking, 7th Edition, Copyright 2011. Reprinted with permission of John Wiley and Sons, Inc.

chicken livers are normally purchased separately, packed in a 5-pound Cryovac® bag.

> **variety meat** Refers to organ meat, such as liver, kidney, and so forth.

Sometimes raw poultry, especially raw-poultry parts, includes a bit of cutting and trimming that adds to the AP price of the items but enhances their convenience. For example, buyers can order boneless, skinless chicken breasts. This convenience, although initially a costly alternative, could, in the long run, result in the most economic edible-portion (EP) costs.

If buyers need to purchase a good deal of highly processed poultry products, such as pre-cooked turkey breast or frozen, prepared chicken egg rolls, and are not satisfied with the federal government minimum standards of identity, they will need to do something to indicate the particular type of formula they want. For example, they may find it necessary to specify in great detail a chicken patty's proportion of white and dark meat, the amount and type of breading, and so forth. Buyers might be able to utilize a packer's brand, one that resembles what they want, but this convenience may not always be available.

■ Preservation Method

Most poultry purchased for use in the hospitality industry is preserved in one of two **preservation methods**: refrigerated or frozen. Many refrigerated products are packed at chill pack temperatures. If suppliers do not provide the chill pack alternative, usually they will provide the ice pack method, which tends to accomplish the same effect as the chill pack—namely, the reduction of the storage temperature to just above freezing. Both chill packs and ice packs maintain temperatures of about 28°F to 29°F.

> **preservation method** A procedure, such as refrigeration, freezing, canning, drying, or chemical additives, used to maintain a product's shelf life and quality and in some cases, impart additional flavorings.

Foodservice operations that strive for a good poultry reputation usually purchase fresh, ice-packed, or chill-packed poultry. For instance, if fried chicken is an operation's signature item, it is very unlikely that the firm will use a frozen item because it can cause several problems. Frozen items can, for example, very easily thaw just a bit during the receiving cycle and

irradiation Controversial product preservation procedure that can reduce or eliminate harmful bacteria. It is used to extend a product's shelf life.

become freezer-burned when they refreeze in storage. In addition, frozen poultry products get a red tinge around the bones when they are cooked. Furthermore, frozen items lose flavor and moisture when they are thawed too long before cooking.

Some fresh poultry (as well as fresh meat, fish, and produce) may be preserved with **irradiation**. Irradiation removes almost all traces of harmful bacteria in meat and fish, and spoilage bacteria in fresh produce. However, many critics maintain that nutrients are lost during the irradiation process and that not enough information is known about the safety of this procedure. As a result, many foodservice operations are not eager to embrace this technology.

Generally, buyers purchase processed poultry products in the frozen state. Some canned products exist, but the typical hospitality operation seldom uses them. For instance, buyers could purchase either frozen or canned chicken noodle soup. The canned item is usually less expensive, but many foodservice operators opt for the frozen variety because the culinary quality is superior.

SUPPLIER AND AP PRICE FACTORS

■ AP Price

Raw-poultry products offer little spread in AP price from one supplier to another. The distance that a finished poultry item must travel to get to a hospitality operation's back door, does, however, make a difference. For example, Colorado free-range chicken for a foodservice operator in New York usually costs more than a similar item raised closer to home. However, given the same style of poultry, the same quality, and the same supplier services, the AP prices are pretty much identical.

In addition, AP prices for raw products tend to be more predictable because farmers can produce poultry much more easily and quickly than many other foods. For instance, it takes about two years to bring a steer from birth to the dining room table. With a frying chicken, this process takes only a few weeks. Also, fresh-poultry AP prices reflect the standardized, scientific management used in raising poultry. For instance, suppliers use pretty much the same feeding formulas and environments so that the poultry looks the same, tastes the same, and has the same conversion weight. Because AP prices vary little, the EP costs, theoretically, should also be similar between competing suppliers' raw products.

AP prices vary quite a bit for processed items, however, and this requires buyers to estimate EP costs as well as customer acceptance of these processed products. If buyers purchase a lot of chicken, they should consider entering into long-term contracts or, at least, using the hedging technique discussed in Chapter 9. Buyers may be able to maintain an AP price that they can live with by hedging in the commodity futures market. In addition, quantity buys offer reasonably good savings.

■ Trust the Supplier

No matter what type of poultry buyers purchase—fresh or processed—they can find several potential suppliers in the marketplace. Hospitality operations do not need to become house accounts unless they want to.

The AP prices of raw poultry do not vary significantly among suppliers. Consequently, bid buying these items may not be as profitable as it is for processed products, unless, of course, buyers can get some additional service. For instance, if they purchase fresh poultry, they will want to keep it at a temperature of at least about 30°F to 35°F. Also, they might want the supplier or processor to cut up the poultry and put it into a marinade. Alternately, they might want a whole chicken cut into eight, nine, or ten parts, depending on the intended use. Not every supplier can provide these services. If two or three have these capabilities, however, buyers might consider bidding out their business once in a while.

In our experience, buyers tend, eventually, to become fresh-poultry house accounts; that is, they tend to purchase from one trusted supplier. This product requires at least a 30°F to 35°F temperature environment, as well as one that is very sanitary. We have known buyers whose only evaluation of a fresh-poultry supplier centered on the odor emanating from the supplier's poultry storage refrigerator. To these buyers, a clean refrigerator meant a reliable supplier.

Several suppliers sell various processed poultry items. The exact one buyers want, though, may be available from only one purveyor.

If buyers are very particular, they may find that they have to cast their lot with one supplier. If they are satisfied with a variety of choices, bid buying and extra negotiating might generate rewards.

PROCEDURES FOR PURCHASING, RECEIVING, STORING, AND ISSUING POULTRY

■ Purchasing

As always, the first step in purchasing is for buyers to decide on the quality and type of product they want. For fresh poultry, and even for some processed poultry, they may find few suppliers who can provide exactly what they want, particularly if they have special requirements. As we have noted, though, usually enough potential suppliers exist to satisfy bid buyers.

Buyers normally use U.S. Grade A quality for poultry, especially when appearance is important. Of course, they can buy several combinations when other grades are available. However, buyers cannot always assume that Grade B is available for every item because most producers strive to achieve the Grade A.

Once buyers know what they want, it is usually beneficial for them to prepare a complete specification. Guides such as the poultry section of the *Meat Buyer's Guide* and online resources such as The Poultry Site can be very useful in determining what information to include in the specification. It should include all pertinent information, whether or not they use it in bid buying, simply because the discipline of preparing this written document helps to ensure that buyers have considered all relevant factors and are, indeed, purchasing the right quality and quantity (see Figure 19.8 for some example product specifications, and Figure 19.9 for an example product specification outline for poultry products).

Broiler/fryer, raw
Used for fried chicken lunch entrée
U.S. Grade A
Quarter chicken parts, cut from
   whole birds weighing between
   $2\frac{1}{2}$ to $3\frac{1}{4}$ lb. dressed weight
No variety meats
Ice packed in reusable plastic tubs
Approximately 30 lb. per tub

Boneless chicken breast, raw
Used for dinner entrée
Tyson® brand
4-oz. portions
48, 4-oz. portions packed per case
Moisture-proof, vapor-proof case
   with plastic "cell-pack" inserts;
   products layered in cell packs
Frozen

Chicken base
Used to prepare soups and sauces
Minor's® brand
16-oz. resealable plastic containers
12 containers packed per case
Refrigerated

Turkey breast, raw
Used for sandwiches
U.S. Grade A
Bone in, skin on
Under 8 lbs.
Wrapped in Cryovac® (or equivalent)
Refrigerated

FIGURE 19.8 An example of poultry product specifications.

After preparing the specs, buyers must evaluate potential suppliers. Keep in mind that for raw poultry, the important consideration probably is supplier services because quality and AP prices usually vary only a little. Buyers need to consider such matters as freshness, delivery capabilities, temperature control, and plant appearance. Buyers usually can find many processed poultry product suppliers, but not too many if they have strict requirements. For example, if buyers want turkey or chicken cold cuts, they will not find many suppliers.

As in the fresh-produce and fresh-egg trades, independent farmers can probably supply poultry. We do not recommend this, however, unless a farmer's products and plant are under continuous inspection.

Intended use:
Exact name:
U.S. grade (or equivalent):
Packer's brand name (or equivalent):
Product size:
Product yield:
Size of container:
Type of packaging material:
Packaging procedure:
Product form:
Preservation method:

FIGURE 19.9 An example of product specification outline for poultry products.

■ Receiving

First, when accepting poultry, receivers must make the customary quality and quantity checks. Because harmful bacteria can multiply rapidly on poultry, especially at room temperatures, many hospitality operations receive and inspect poultry in refrigerated storage. The delivery agent and the receiver go straight to this area.

The raw-poultry quality check is not difficult. The grade shield is usually displayed prominently on the carton, and with whole poultry, on the wing of each bird. However, receivers must be careful that the boxes have not been repacked. They can never be quite sure of what is in the boxes, regardless of the grade noted on the carton. A trustworthy supplier is the best insurance.

The quality check can cause some trouble if receivers are concerned with the age of the poultry. For instance, buyers might purchase hens to get the flavorful meat, but how do receivers know whether the hens are as old as they should be? Receivers can look at their size and amount of abdominal fat. To the trained eye, this check is routine, but some receiving agents lack this skill.

Processed products usually require other types of quality checks. Receivers must perform the normal checks of frozen products—looking for proper temperature, signs of thawing and refreezing, and inadequate packaging—and of canned products—looking for leaks, rust, and swollen cans.

Once receivers are satisfied with the quality, they must check quantity. Normally, buyers purchase poultry by the pound or by the bird. Also, some poultry comes packed in ice, which tends to make weighing difficult. Receivers might have to weigh enough birds to see whether they are within the weight range that the buyers have specified. Thus, they may have to dig around in the ice a little or weigh the poultry with the ice on it. It is preferable, however, to temporarily remove the ice before weighing the poultry. Another option is to weigh the packer's brand, prepackaged, chill pack chicken to compare it with the weight stated on the label.

Receiving agents also need to check the types of parts, variety meats, and processed items they get. Sometimes, buyers order legs and receivers get wings, buyers order chicken livers and receivers get gizzards, or buyers order chicken franks and receivers get turkey franks. These are usually honest mistakes, but they can ruin a production schedule.

Receiving agents can streamline the poultry-receiving process by using the **USDA's Acceptance Service**. This service is popular among large food-service operators for meat and poultry items. Remember also that buyers can hire an inspector to help them write specifications. Also, under the Acceptance Service, the federal inspector, or the state counterpart, will accept or reject the product according to what the buyers specify.

> **USDA's Acceptance Service** Agency that, for a fee, will help buyers prepare meat specifications and oversee the purchase and delivery of meat.

Finally, after making quality and quantity checks, receivers must check the prices and complete the appropriate accounting procedures.

■ Storing

Hospitality operators should store fresh and frozen poultry immediately and at the proper temperatures and humidity in the environment its form suggests.

Fresh poultry has a short shelf life. Following proper storage practices can extend this shelf life from three to four days to up to a week. For example, if chickens are received in an ice pack, they should be stored as is, but in such a way that any melted ice runs out of the storage package and does not soak into the birds. As the ice melts, operators should add more ice. When receivers get poultry items packed without ice, they can increase the shelf life by placing them in a perforated pan, layering in ice, and refrigerating them. This maintains the temperature at approximately 28°F to 29°F.

Some operations may wish to marinate their poultry to lengthen the shelf life; this imparts a distinctive flavor as well. They can also extend poultry's shelf life by precooking it, although this could hamper their standard production schedule. Whatever storage procedures they follow, operators should not handle poultry any more than is absolutely necessary. If improperly handled, it will become contaminated.

Because poultry is expensive, operators might consider keeping a perpetual poultry inventory. To do this, they need to enter the appropriate information into their inventory management system.

◾ Issuing

If hospitality operators use a perpetual inventory system, they must deduct the quantity issued. If applicable, they will need to make the following decision: Should they issue the item as is, or should they issue it as ready-to-go (for example, cut-up and breaded, or precut)? Recall that any choice involves several advantages and disadvantages.

> **in-process inventory**
> Products located at
> employee workstations;
> most or all will be used
> during the shift.

Operators should follow proper stock rotation guidelines when issuing these items. Also, because these products, especially fresh ones, deteriorate rapidly and are expensive, operators must make sure that the requisitioner does not take more than is absolutely necessary. If they can, they should make it mandatory for this person to note the **in-process inventory** before asking for more poultry.

◾ In-Process Inventories

Depending on the type of poultry product, several types of waste are possible. For example, it is easy for a chef to burn a breaded poultry item on the outside while failing to cook it thoroughly on the inside. Similarly, if a chef is carving a whole roast turkey, a lot of usable meat can stick to the bones. Also, leaving a roast turkey under a glow lamp too long can make a once beautiful bird collapse into charred rubble.

If hospitality operators use several types of poultry, they need to keep them separated and clearly labeled. For example, a cook might unknowingly use the chopped, cooked chicken slated for chicken salad in the soup.

Probably the biggest consideration with in-process poultry inventory is the sanitation problem. Staphylococcus and salmonella bacteria should not be present on cooked poultry products. However, when poultry items are contaminated after cooking, usually by a human handler or by being placed on a contaminated surface, bacteria grow very quickly at warm temperatures (41°F to 135°F). For example, a finished chicken soup kept in a warm instead of a hot steam table for four or five hours can become sufficiently contaminated to cause an outbreak of food-borne illness.

WHEN ALL YOU SERVE IS CHICKEN . . .
Joe Micatrotto, Jr., President and Chief Executive Officer
MRG Marketing and Management, Inc., Las Vegas, Nevada

Courtesy of MRG Marketing & Management Inc.

MRG Marketing and Management, Inc. (MRG), founded in 2005, is a franchisor for a quick-service restaurant (QSR) chain. By 2015, it grew to having franchised 20 restaurants in the Southwestern United States, employing more than 1,000 crew members. With a limited menu based on selling fresh chicken tenders, poultry procurement is an essential part of its business model. Forecasting usage and availability along with a sensible pricing model are constant business practices. In this sidebar, Joe Micatrotto, Jr., President and Chief Executive Officer, explains the company's procurement procedures and challenges.

Kristina Dollard, Director of Operations Services, is responsible for procurement management. The first step is forecasting annual usage by weight, based on the specification focused on a weight range and an average number of chicken tenders within that range. These variations make affect her ability to determine exactly how many cases she will need and the food cost. To combat this challenge, forecasting is also based on individual restaurant sales' historical usage patterns provided by the distributor. In addition, potential sales increases at existing restaurants and the growth of new restaurants are also considered. In 2014, MRG purchased more than 10 million pounds of tenders.

The second step is to submit the annual forecast to the franchisor. The franchisor and franchisee then work together to ensure supply and demand are adequately met and determine which national producer is best positioned to support the operations and development. The goal would be to regionally position restaurants to have similar distribution channels and suppliers.

The continual process of negotiating the price and specifying how much is needed at particular times begins. Ordering for fresh chicken is much more complex than that of frozen, and prices are more volatile. Urner Barry reports and other forecasts are used to monitor prices. Prices move on a rolling 30-day basis. The price for the last 30 days will dictate the price for the next 30 days.

Within a target tender range, producers must work to find a target total chicken weight as well. A chicken's weight then dictates the weight of the items that are sold to distributors and restaurant companies. It takes 60–65 days for the chickens to grow to that weight.

Remember the sidebar in Chapter 4 about the effects of weather on beef supply and prices? Weather also affects the chicken business. If it is too hot or humid, the chickens will not eat, and then it takes longer for them to reach the desired weight. In 2014, there were horrible ice storms impacting the largest chicken-producing regions, electricity was cut off to some farms, and many chickens were lost. Transportation in certain areas was impossible, impacting all aspects of the poultry industry. This in turn had a severe impact on supply, which in turn had an impact on pricing and recovery for many distribution systems.

As in all industries, ensuring that all of your production is adequately planned so that all of it is sold to the market is most important. With commodities like poultry, producers must find a use for as much of the chicken as possible to ensure they adequately cover overhead and properly price their product on the market. Certain quick-service restaurants (QSRs) and fast-casual restaurants primarily

WHEN ALL YOU SERVE IS CHICKEN . . . (continued)

purchase chicken breasts and/or wings. Global politics is another factor that can affect the prices. Imports and exports of commodities always have a major effect on pricing agreements.

The next step in the poultry procurement is MRG ordering the exact amounts for each week from the chicken producer. There is a seven-day lag between when the chicken is ordered from the vendor and when it is delivered to the distributor in the city where it will be used. Then the chicken must be used within one week. Therefore, MRG must evaluate its forecasted sales over a 14-day period to order the right amount of product

Once the weight of tenders needed for a one-week time period is determined and ordered by MRG, the chicken producer delivers it to a specific broadline distributor that services each city with MRG franchisees. MRG has a separate agreement with the distributor detailing the markup added to the price negotiated with the chicken producer. The managers of each restaurant then place the order for the exact quantity they need from the distributor by phone or email. They have to take into account that the tenders need to be marinated for a day before cooking when determining how much to purchase. Between being concerned with the weather, possible transportation delays and breakdowns, and the accuracy of their ordering, MRG is constantly checking on the distributor to make sure that deliveries will be on time.

When the chicken is delivered to the restaurant, a manager checks the use-by date and the weight. The manager spot checks the weight of the tenders in every single case. The tenders have a 14-day shelf life from the time the chicken is killed. They will not accept any product that does not have at least 5 days left on the use-by date. MRG's president says the most useful technology for them is the barcodes on the cases of chicken. If anything is wrong with the product, they can trace it back to the exact time, date, and details from when it was processed.

Because MRG's restaurants have a limited menu and they do not buy that many other food, beverage, and supply products, the stores carry minimal inventory and turn over the entire inventory of all products approximately every 72 hours.

 ## Key Words and Concepts

Age of bird at time of slaughter	Gas-flushed pack
Cello pack	Grading factors
Chill pack	Ice pack procedure
Commodity	Individually quick frozen (IQF)
Conversion weight	In-process inventory
Exact name	Intended use
Food Safety and Inspection Service (FSIS)	Irradiation
Free-range chicken	Kosher chicken

Key Words and Concepts (continued)

Marinade pack	Ratite
Natural poultry	Shatter pack
Number of pieces per bird	Shelf life
Organic poultry	Signature item
Packer's brand name	Snap pack
Poultry	Standard of identity
Poultry Products Inspection Act	Substitution possibilities
Preservation method	USDA's Acceptance Service
Product form	Variety meat
Product size	Weight range
Product yield	Wholesome Poultry Products Act

Questions and Problems

1. What are the U.S. consumer grades for poultry? What are some of the differences between the grades?

2. Why is the age of a bird at the time of slaughter an important selection factor?

3. Why do hen turkeys generally have a higher AP price than tom turkeys?

4. What is an appropriate intended use for:
    a. a broiler-fryer
    b. a frozen chicken breast
    c. a duckling

5. What are lower-quality poultry products generally used for?

6. Which type of poultry product would buyers purchase if they were planning to prepare chicken and dumplings and wanted to use fresh chicken? Why? What type of information would you need on a product specification for this item?

7. When hospitality operators serve turkey and dressing, they could use fresh turkey or a processed turkey product, such as a turkey roll. What are the potential advantages and disadvantages of using the fresh product? What are the potential advantages and disadvantages of using the processed product?

8. What is another name for the term "conversion weight"?

9. Why is the weight range of a fresh, whole bird an important selection factor?

Questions and Problems (continued)

10. What critical information is missing from the following product specification for sliced, cooked chicken breast?

> Sliced, cooked chicken breast
> Used for deli sandwiches
> Country Pride® brand (or equivalent)
> Packed in Cryovac® bags
> Refrigerated

11. Describe the necessary storage conditions for fresh and processed poultry.

12. Why are free-range and kosher chickens more expensive than chickens raised in the typical way?

13. Why are frozen chicken parts, such as breasts and thighs, unacceptable to many foodservice operators?

14. What method can hospitality operators use to extend the shelf life of fresh poultry?

15. Explain why chicken is referred to as a commodity item.

16. A product specification for turkey hot dogs could include the following information:
    a.
    b.
    c.
    d.
    e.

17. What are the major advantages of the chill pack procedure?

18. When would buyers substitute a processed chicken patty for a boneless, skinless chicken breast?

19. Prepare a product specification for the following poultry products:
    a. Chicken wing
    b. Turkey
    c. Chicken egg roll
    d. Duckling
    e. Chicken patty

20. What is the difference between the ice pack procedure and the marinade pack procedure?

21. When purchasing chicken for an item like chicken salad, buyers must often determine whether it is more cost effective to purchase Bone-in, Skin-on Chicken Breasts and to take off the skin and bone themselves or just to purchase Boneless, Skinless Chicken

Questions and Problems (continued)

Breasts. You will need 5 pounds of edible portion chicken breast. Use the following information to make your determination.

	Bone-in, Skin-on	Boneless, Skinless
Yield Percent:	68%	95%
AP Cost:	$1.98	$3.49

22. Other than the overall EP price, what other considerations would a buyer have in deciding whether to use the bone-in or boneless product?

Experiential Exercises

1. Outline the specific procedures hospitality operators should use for purchasing, receiving, storing, and issuing frozen, prebreaded broiler-fryer parts. Assume that these parts will be used for a buffet restaurant in a large resort. Ask a food and beverage director or chef to comment on your answer. Write a one-page report of your findings.

2. Assume that you manage a school foodservice. You serve lunch only—5,000 lunches per day, five days a week. A poultry purveyor calls to tell you that he is going out of business. He has about 7,500 pounds of frozen, cut-up broiler-fryers. He will sell you this stock for 50 percent of the current AP price. You have to let him know your decision tomorrow. What do you do? Ask a school foodservice manager to comment on your answer. Write a one-page report about what your decision would be and why.

3. Purchase three different types/brands of frozen, breaded, flavored chicken wings or frozen chicken pot pie. Perform a cooking and tasting test of the items. Compare their ease of cooking, taste, yield, and appearance. Write a one-page report about the results of your comparison.

References

1. U.S. Trade Descriptions for Poultry, www.ams.usda.gov/AMSv1.0/getfile?dDocName =STELDEV3004362.

2. USDA Food Safety and Inspection Service, "Poultry Products Inspection Act," www.fsis.usda.gov/Regulations/PPIA/.

References (continued)

3. Utah Department of Agriculture and Food, *Meat and Poultry Inspection*, www.ag.utah. gov/food-safety-consumers/meat-and-poultry-inspection.html. See also Minnesota Department of Agriculture, *Meat, Poultry, and Egg Inspection in Minnesota*, www.mda. state.mn.us/licensing/inspections/meatpoultryegg.aspx.

4. USDA, "Poultry-Grading Manual," www.ams.usda.gov/AMSv1.0/getfile?dDocName=S TELDEV3002393.

5. USDA Food Safety and Inspection Service, "Meat and Poultry Labeling Terms," www.fsis .usda.gov/wps/portal/fsis/topics/food-safety-education/get-answers/food-safety-fact -sheets/food-labeling/meat-and-poultry-labeling-terms/meat-and-poultry-labeling-terms/. See also "FSIS Issues Advance Notice of Proposed Rulemaking on Use of the Voluntary Claim 'Natural' in the Labeling of Meat and Poultry Products," Food Safety and Inspection Service, USDA, www.fsis.usda.gov/News_&_Events/NR_091109_01/index .asp; Natalie Russell, "What Food Labels Really Mean," *USA Weekend*, October 5, 2008, www.usaweekend.com/08_issues/081005/081005food-label-language.html.

6. "Organic Production and Handling Standards," National Organic Program, USDA AMS, April, 2008, p. 1, www.ams.usda.gov/AMSv1.0/getfile?dDocName=STELDEV 3004445&acct=nopgeninfo. See also "Using the Claim 'Certified Organic By . . .' on Meat and Poultry Product Labeling," National Organic Program, USDA, www.fsis. usda.gov/Regulations_&_Policies/Certified_Organic/index.asp.

7. Lydia Oberholtzer, Catherine Greene, and Enrique Lopez, "Organic Poultry and Eggs Capture High Price Premiums and Growing Share of Specialty Markets," Economic Research Service, USDA, December 2006, www.ers.usda. gov/Publications/ LDP/2006/12Dec/LDPM15001/ldpm15001.pdf. See also "Organic Prices Overview," Economic Research Service, USDA, www.ers.usda.gov/Data/OrganicPrices/.

CHAPTER 20

FISH

The Purpose of This Chapter

After reading this chapter, you should be able to:

- Discuss the importance and challenges of purchasing fish.

- Choose appropriate fish based on primary selection factors, including government grades.

- Categorize fish according to product size, form, and packaging, and related characteristics.

- Consider supplier factors when purchasing fish.

- Create a specification for fish that can be used in the purchasing process.

- Describe procedures for receiving, storing, and issuing fish.

THE IMPORTANCE AND CHALLENGES OF PURCHASING FRESH FISH

Buying fresh fish can be one of the most frustrating jobs in all of purchasing. Processed—that is, canned, salted, and frozen—fish is easier to buy. With fresh items, not only will buyers find fewer suppliers, but they may also have to take whatever fresh fish is available. If hospitality operations want fresh fish on the menu, they might have to offer whatever their supplier has in stock. At times, however, the supplier may have nothing.

Obtaining a wide variety of fresh fish and maintaining consistent culinary quality is very difficult unless operators are willing to deal with and maintain good working relationships with all potential suppliers. It is not unusual for a foodservice operator to purchase only one type of fresh fish from as many seafood suppliers as possible to obtain a steady supply and consistent quality.

One nice feature of fish is that operators can usually get by with processed products, unless they want to advertise fresh items. If they insist on fresh fish, it is not particularly difficult to buy something fresh; it is just that, as we said earlier, they have few suppliers from which to choose.

Moreover, fresh fish can cause other challenges. Unless operators are close to a major transportation hub, the "fresh" fish can be in tired condition; its as-purchased (AP) prices can fluctuate, which can force operators to price their menu almost every day; once they get the fish, production employees may not be able to handle it properly unless they are highly skilled in this area, and some choice items, such as Dover sole, Maine lobster, and Alaska king crab, cannot always be purchased fresh. So, unless operators can obtain a reasonably steady supply, they might want to reconsider any decision to feature fresh fish on the menu.

Some companies take the guesswork and the difficulty out of the selection and procurement of fresh fish by "growing their own," or by purchasing products that suppliers grow under controlled conditions. Although not as common as growing herbs or other produce items, some restaurants practice **aquaculture**, or fish farming, which serves to produce fish items of consistent size and culinary quality.[1] Any foodservice operation, though, can purchase farm-raised fish from suppliers who provide this option.

Aquaculture is not a new development; in fact, its roots go back to China, where the Chinese people have farmed fish for more than 2,000 years. However, the procedures have become very popular only within the last few years. Each year sees an increase in the amount of farm-raised fish purchased in the United States. According to the World Agriculture Network, farm-raised catfish is the largest segment of the aquaculture industry in the United States. Other popular farm-raised fish are trout, tilapia, salmon, oysters, mussels, clams, scallops, abalone, crawfish, and shrimp. Although aquaculture, technically, can be expanded to include other fish species, such as halibut and flounder, the technology needed to do it effectively and efficiently is still being refined.[2]

There are benefits and drawbacks to both farm-raised and **wild-caught** fish. The Environmental Working Group found that farmed salmon raised in the United States had the highest levels of **polychlorinated biphenyls (PCBs)**. PCBs are a toxic grouping of manmade chemicals that were

aquaculture The controlled farming of plants and animals, such as fish, shellfish, and algae, in a water environment.

wild-caught Refers to any seafood caught from its natural environment or fishery, rather than from a controlled farm.

polychlorinated biphenyls (PCBs) Any of a family of toxic chemicals containing chlorine and benzene. PCBs have been found to cause some skin cancers and can become concentrated in animal flesh.

commonly found in the food that farm-raised fish were eating. Other studies have confirmed that wild-caught salmon were less likely to be exposed to toxins like PCBs but they had lower levels of beneficial Omega-3 fatty acids than their farm-raised counterparts.[3] Quality wise, many believe that wild-caught fish is more flavorful and may have a better texture and color. It must also be noted that although a natural product, wild-caught fish cannot be classified as organic.[4]

Many buyers are fond of farm-raised fish because it eliminates a lot of the risk from the fish-purchasing process. It also ensures stable quality and a consistent supply. Increasing the overall supply of seafood through aquaculture is important because it is estimated that 30 percent of all wild marine fish populations are being killed faster than they reproduce.[5] **Sustainability**, the condition where the fish population does not decline over time because of fishing practices, may be an important concern for seafood buyers. At times, certain fish may not be available if they have been over-fished. Groups such as the Marine Stewardship Council, Seafood Watch, and the Blue Ocean Institute provide excellent resources on all topics related to seafood sustainability. Some chefs such as Rick Moonen of RM Seafood and RX Boiler Room in Las Vegas are known as advocates for sustainable seafood.[6]

> **sustainability** For sea-food, the condition where the fish population does not decline over time due to fishing practices.

Fresh-fish buyers must be very knowledgeable about the fish products they purchase. These items are not very standardized, and unlike other fresh products, such as fresh produce and fresh meats, few market guidelines are available for most items. So operators who are responsible for purchasing fresh-fish products can never know too much about them.

PRIMARY SELECTION FACTORS

Management must determine the varieties and qualities of fish they want on the menu. Remember, they usually make this type of decision in cooperation with other company personnel. Management usually considers several of these selection factors.

■ Intended Use

As always, hospitality operators want to precisely determine the **intended use** of an item so that they will be able to prepare the appropriate, relevant speci-fication. For example, a whitefish that will be broiled needs a more attractive appearance than a whitefish that will be used in breaded fish patties.

■ Exact Name

Many varieties of fish exist in the world. In the United States more than 200 varieties are sold. Obviously, then, buyers must be especially careful and indicate the precise name of the item they want (see Figures 20.1 and 20.2 for some of the more popular varieties of fish products used in the foodservice industry).

Unfortunately, even if buyers indicate an **exact name**, they could receive an unwanted item because the fish industry is fond of **renaming fish**.

> **intended use** Refers to the performance require-ment of a product or ser-vice, which is noted on the specification. Considered to be the most important piece of information on a specification.
>
> **exact name** Indication of a product or service's specific type, quality, and style.
>
> **renaming fish** A method used in the fish industry to change a seafood product's name if that name is con-sidered a detriment to its sales potential.

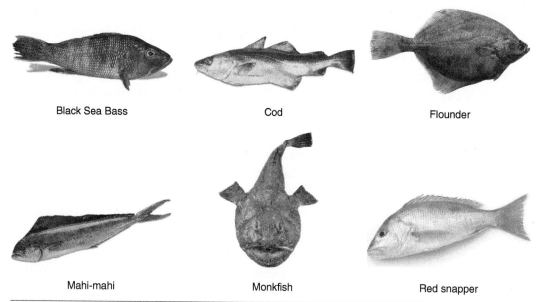

Black Sea Bass   Cod   Flounder

Mahi-mahi   Monkfish   Red snapper

FIGURE 20.1 Popular varieties of fish the food-service industry uses.
Clockwise from top left: Black Sea Bass: Mike Focus/Shutterstock; Cod: ©2011 Professional Cooking, 7th Edition, John Wiley and Sons; Flounder: Arsty/Getty Images; Mahi-mahi: ©2011 Professional Cooking, 7th Edition, John Wiley and Sons; Monkfish: Arsty/Getty Images; Red snapper: fcafotodigital/Getty Images

Acceptable Market Name	Common Name	Scientific Name
Bass, Sea	Argentine Sea Bass	Acanthistius brasilianus
Catfish	White Cat Fish	Ameiurus catus
Clam, Littleneck	Pacific Littleneck Clam	Protothaca staminea
Cod	Atlantic Cod	Gadus ogac
Lobster	American Loster	Homarus gammarus
Monkfish	Anglerfish	Lophius piscatorius
Mussel	California Mussel	Mytilus californianus
Oyster	Pacific Oyster	Crassostrea gigas
Perch, Ocean or Rockfish	Pacific Ocean Perch	Sebastes alutus
Pollock	Pollock	Pollachius virens
Roughy, Orange	Orange Roughy	Hoplostethus atlanticus
Salmon, Atlantic	Atlantic Salmon	Salmo salar
Scallop or Bay Scallop	Bay Scallop	Argopecten irradians
Shrimp	Common Shrimp	Crangon crangon
Snapper or Red Snapper	Red Snapper	Lutjanus campechanus
Tuna	Albacore	Thunnus alalunga
Trout, Rainbow or Steelhead	Rainbow Trout	Oncorhynchus mykiss
Whitefish	Round Whitefish	Prosopium cylindraceum

FIGURE 20.2 Varieties of fish.

For example, on the East Coast of the United States, the name "lemon sole" refers to a particular size of flounder, whereas on the West Coast and in Europe, it refers to another fish species. A similar problem occurs with the name "snapper." It sometimes seems that almost every fish under the sea is called a snapper.

The federal government actually encourages renaming fish because it would like to see the public eat products that are quite good, yet suffer from an image problem because they have unappealing names. Many perfectly delicious and nutritious fish species abound primarily because they are protected by repugnant names. Lately, though, several "trash" fish have become more popular.

Renaming fish is also done as an attempt to increase its marketability and profitability. For example, we recall that years ago a fish product called "slimeheads" or "Australian perch" was on the market. There was little demand for it. However, once Australians renamed it "orange roughy," sales skyrocketed. And, we might add, so did its price.

Another example of fish renaming occurred for the "toothfish," which is more widely known as Chilean Seabass. For years, this fish was primarily purchased by cat food manufacturers due to its unappealing name. Since the name change, Chilean Seabass has become quite popular.

Renaming fish is a particularly sensitive issue in the hospitality industry. Receivers must be careful to get only those products that buyers actually order. If customers are adventurous and accept more exotic species, then buyers will order them. If not, buyers must be certain to select only those suppliers who will help them achieve their purchase objectives.

In addition to the exact name of the product, operators must be careful to use, where applicable, the appropriate market terminology in their particular area that further identifies what they want. Although some market terms are common, each growing and harvesting area tends to adopt its own peculiar nomenclature to identify some items (see Figures 20.3 and 20.4 for some of the most common marketing terms).

Block—a solid cube of raw fish; usually skinless; normally weighs about 10 to 20 pounds.
Breaded/battered—fish product coated with a seasoned crumb or batter mixture.
Butterfly fillet—two small fillets held together by a small, thin piece of skin.
Chunk—cross-section of a large, dressed fish. It contains the cross-section of the backbone. It is similar to a bone in beef pot roast.
Drawn—whole fish that has been eviscerated.
Dressed—a completely clean fish; can be cooked as is or processed into steaks, fillets, portions.
Fillet—boneless fish, cut away from the backbone.
Fin fish—fish that has fins and a backbone. There are "fat" fin fish and "lean" fin fish. There are saltwater and freshwater species.
Green, headless—usually refers to a raw, unprocessed shrimp.
Peeled and deveined (P&D)—a shrimp without its shell or black vein.
Portion—a piece of fish cut from a block of fish. It is similar to a fillet, but it does not meet the exact definition of the fillet.
Shellfish—fish products that are completely or partially covered by a shell. There are crustaceans, whose shells are soft (e.g., shrimp), and mollusks, which have hard shells (e.g., oysters).
Shucked—fish that has been removed from its shell. Normally used when ordering shell-less mollusks.
Steak—a cross-section of a large fish that has been cut from a dressed fish carcass.
Stick—a cross section of fillets; alternately, small, processed item that has been battered or breaded.
Whole (round)—fish right out of the water; nothing has been done to it.

FIGURE 20.3 Common marketing terms for fish products.

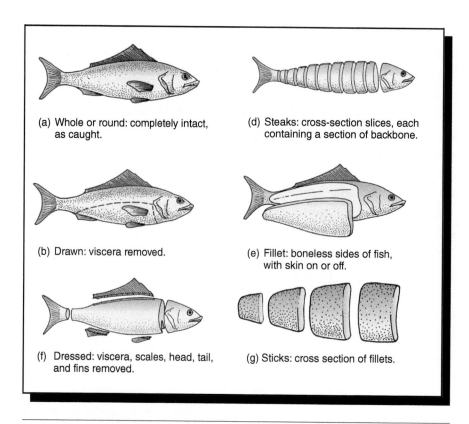

(a) Whole or round: completely intact, as caught.

(b) Drawn: viscera removed.

(f) Dressed: viscera, scales, head, tail, and fins removed.

(d) Steaks: cross-section slices, each containing a section of backbone.

(e) Fillet: boneless sides of fish, with skin on or off.

(g) Sticks: cross section of fillets.

FIGURE 20.4 Market forms of fish.

Source: Gisslen, Professional Cooking, *8th Edition, Copyright 2015. Reprinted with permission of John Wiley and Sons, Inc.*

A few fish products meet federal government standards of identity. For instance, a "lightly breaded" shrimp product must contain at least 65 percent shrimp, whereas a "breaded" shrimp product must contain at least 50 percent shrimp. As with all standards of identity, though, the figures represent minimal requirements. Furthermore, in the fish trade, only a handful of processed products are subject to the **standard of identity** regulations. Consequently, wise buyers usually do not rely on standards of identity when preparing specifications for fish products.

standard of identity A U.S. government regulation that establishes what a food product must be to carry a certain name. For example, what a food product must be to be labeled "strawberry preserves."

National Oceanic and Atmospheric Administration (NOAA) Agency of the U.S. Department of Commerce (USDC) that, for a fee, will provide continuous inspection of a fish processor's plant.

■ U.S. Government Grades (or Equivalent)

The U.S. Department of Commerce's (USDC) **National Oceanic and Atmospheric Administration (NOAA)**, under the Seafood Protection Program, publishes grade standards and offers grading services for fishery products (fresh and frozen) similar to those that the U.S. Department of Agriculture (USDA) established for other foods. The USDC's grading program also provides for official inspection of the edibility and wholesomeness of fishery products, and many of its grade standards specify the amount of fish component required in a processed product.

The U.S. government grades a few fish items. They have established standards for grades of fish forms, such as whole, dressed, and fillets. They have also established standards for particular species and forms of fresh or frozen fish, including halibut, salmon, whiting, cod, flounder, sole, haddock, and perch and for canned tuna and salmon. Grades have also been established for shrimp and scallops.

Fish grades are based on several **grading factors**. Normally, the grader evaluates the fish's appearance, odor, size, uniformity, color, defects, flavor, and texture, as well as its **point of origin**.

The federal grades for whole or dressed fish, frozen halibut or salmon steaks are as follows:

1. **Grade A.** This is the best quality produced. The appearance and culinary quality are superior. Grade A products have a uniform appearance, possess good flavor and odor, and are practically devoid of blemishes or other defects.

2. **Grade B.** This is good quality and, generally, is suitable for many food-service applications. Grade B items possess reasonability good flavor and odor but have significantly more blemishes and/or defects than Grade A products.

3. **Substandard.** Substandard fish fail to meet the requirements of the "U.S. Grade B." The product does not have reasonably good flavor and odor and/or has considerable defects. Types of physical defects are categorized as "abnormal condition," "appearance defects," "discoloration," "dehydration," "surface defects," "cutting and trimming defects," and "texture defects."

The federal grades for most fish fillets and fish products are as follows:

1. **Grade A.** This is the best quality produced. The appearance and culinary quality are superior. Grade A products have a uniform appearance, practically devoid of blemishes or other defects, and possess good flavor and odor characteristic of the species.

2. **Grade B.** This is good quality and, generally, is suitable for many foodservice applications. Grade B items have significantly more blemishes and/or defects than Grade A products. The product possesses reasonably good flavor and odor characteristic of the species.

3. **Grade C.** This grade resembles Grade B, but it is lacking in appearance and possesses minimal acceptable flavor and odor characteristic of the species. It must have no objectionable off-flavors or off-odors.

4. **Substandard.** Substandard fish fail to meet the requirements of the "U.S. Grade C." The product does not have reasonably good flavor and odor and/or has considerable defects.

Standards for grades of fishery products vary. Specific details for each type of fish and fish product graded by the NOAA can be found on its website.

When buyers use U.S. grades as one of their selection factors, normally, only the U.S. Grade A designation is specified (see Figure 20.5). Lower grades usually do not carry a federal grade shield; rather,

> **grading factors**
> Characteristics of food or beverage products examined by grading inspectors. Used to judge and rank products.
>
> **point of origin** Refers to the part of the world where a product originates. Important selection factor for some food items, as the point of origin can have a significant impact on their culinary quality.

FIGURE 20.5 Federal grade stamps used for fish.
Courtesy of United States Department of Agriculture

manufacturing grade
A very low grade given to food products that are not intended to be sold as fresh items but are meant to be used by processors to produce a finished item. For example, low-grade beef usually is purchased by a processor who makes things such as canned chili or canned beef stew.

Hazard Analysis Critical Control Point (HACCP) system Process used by food processors and others in the foodservice industry to ensure food safety. It identifies the areas at which foods are most susceptible to contamination and recommends procedures that can be used to prevent it from occurring.

these **manufacturing grades** are left unmarked and are usually sold to food processors who will process them into several types of convenience fish products.

■ Packed Under Federal Inspection Seal

Recall from Chapter 4 that fish products are not subject to mandatory, continuous, federal government inspection. The Food and Drug Administration (FDA) provides periodic inspections for all food-fabricating plants, monitors imported and interstate fish shipments, and requires fish processors to adopt the **Hazard Analysis Critical Control Point (HACCP) system** to increase food safety. Also, a cooperative agreement exists between federal and state agencies that monitor the farm beds where oysters, clams, and mussels are raised. However, these inspections fall far short of those the USDA uses to monitor meat-packing, poultry-packing, and egg-breaking plants.

Fish are cold-blooded animals; hence, the diseases afflicting them supposedly do not threaten the human beings who eat them. However, fish can be exposed to many toxins, bacteria, and parasites that can be harmful to human beings. Even though properly prepared and served fish causes no more health problems than meat products and fewer problems than poultry items, many fish buyers seem to be reluctant to purchase fish that has not been produced under continuous government inspection.

One way for buyers to ensure this type of inspection is to demand that all fish products they purchase carry a U.S. grade designation. Fish products that are produced and graded under the USDC inspection program may carry the USDC "Federal Inspection" mark or the U.S. grade shield. Unfortunately, grading designations, as mentioned earlier, are available only for a few fish items.

Another problem is that only fish produced in the United States can carry the federal government's grade or inspection shield. In 2015, the United States imported about 91 percent of the seafood consumed here. That seafood comes from approximately 120 other countries. These countries include Norway, Chile, Canada, China, Ecuador, Indonesia, and Honduras to name a few.[7]

Packed Under Federal Inspection (PUFI)
Seal placed on the product labels of fish items that have been produced and packed under continuous government inspection by the U.S. Department of Commerce (USDC).

An alternative to requiring a U.S. grade designation or federal inspection is to purchase only those fish products that are produced under the continuous inspection of a state or local government agency. However, these agencies normally do not provide an extensive array of inspection services, and the ones they do provide usually are not very comprehensive.

The only sure way to obtain fish items that are produced under continuous government inspection is to demand that any fish product purchased carry the **Packed Under Federal Inspection (PUFI)** seal (see Figure 20.6). This

FIGURE 20.6 PUFI seal.
Courtesy of United States Department of Commerce

seal indicates that the product is clean, safe, and wholesome, and that it has been produced in an establishment that meets all the sanitary guidelines of NOAA. The product is not graded for quality, but it meets the acceptable commercial quality standards the federal inspection agency has set.

Specifying that all of the fish buyers purchase must carry the PUFI seal probably will significantly reduce the potential number of suppliers who can bid for their business. Continuous fish inspection is a voluntary program, and not many fish-processing plants participate. Furthermore, time-consuming inspection is not easily adaptable to many fish suppliers who sell fresh fish products; in many instances, the products are caught in the morning and sent via air express to a foodservice operation, where they will be used on the menu that evening.

■ Packers' Brands (or Equivalent)

Because most fresh fish does not carry a brand name, this criterion is not a useful selection factor for fresh items. But packers' brands for **processed fish** items, especially canned fish, abound. In fact, a brand name, as well as the reputation of the item's producer and distributing suppliers, is very important to many buyers. For example, we probably could safely assume that StarKist® and Chicken of the Sea® brands instill a good deal of confidence in the marketplace.

> **processed fish**   Fish that are marketed in many forms, except the whole form.

In some instances, a brand name may be the only guide to seafood consistency. In addition, the type of processed product you want may be available from only one company. For example, not too many firms are producing marinated baby sardines.

Few beginning purchasers are familiar with the brand names in the seafood area. As a result, these brands may not be very useful until a buyer has studied the brands and experimented with them for awhile.

Some brand-name, processed fish products carry the U.S. Grade A designation. Items such as fish sticks and raw breaded shrimp usually carry this type of grading mark. The brand is indicative of a certain culinary quality, and the grade shield ensures wholesomeness.

■ Point of Origin

A lobster is not simply a lobster. If a lobster comes from the Gulf of Mexico, it is not the same type as the lobster that comes from Australia. This is true of any other type of fish, fresh or processed: the area it comes from influences its distinctive character, flavor, and texture. Hence, buyers sometimes carefully specify the origin of the fish they buy, especially if they purchase a great deal of fresh fish.

Many foodservice operators note on their menus the points of origin for some menu offerings. This seems to be a very popular practice for fish products. For instance, it is quite common to see menus that advertise Lake Superior whitefish, Alaskan salmon and crab legs, Australian lobster tails, and Chilean sea bass (see Figure 20.7). This menu nomenclature forces buyers to purchase fish products that originate from these locales. In addition to where the product is from, as discussed at the beginning of the chapter, restaurants may also want their menu to tell guests whether the fish was farm-raised or wild-caught. Using substitute items cheats the customer. Furthermore, in some parts of the United States, any substitutes would violate **truth-in-menu** legislation.

> **truth-in-menu**   Guidelines menu planners use to avoid unintentionally misleading the customer by ensuring accurate descriptions and prices of all menu offerings. Alternately, refers to legislation prohibiting misrepresentations on the menu.

FIGURE 20.7 Point of origin ad.
Courtesy of Maine Lobster Council

A DAY IN THE LIFE

Lisa Hogan, Regional Vice-President of Sales, Santa Monica Seafood, Rancho Dominguez, California

Lisa Hogan is the regional vice-president of sales for Santa Monica Seafood (SMS) in Rancho Dominguez, California. In other words, she sells fish. She sells fish to chef-owned, 40-seat restaurants, multistar restaurants in hotels, and national food distributors. She sells fish to country clubs and caterers through all of San Diego and Orange County. She is knowledgeable about kinds, sources, cooking, and sustainability of fish.

©Santa Monica Seafood Company

When Hogan was at Cal Poly Pomona she was in the hospitality program and worked as the purchasing agent for the school's foodservice department. Santa Monica Seafood was one of Hogan's vendors, and later her employer when she graduated from school.

"I think one thing that has helped me is my restaurant management background," Hogan said. "I know the stresses and constraints that many of my customers experience, and it helps me anticipate their needs and provide better service."

A DAY IN THE LIFE (continued)

When Hogan first started with the company, she spent three months on the warehouse floor, literally learning the seafood business from the ground up. She scaled, weighed, and packaged fish. She created a personal resource manual covering the 260 products the company carried starting with "A" for "albacore" and ending with "W" for "wolf fish." The manual contained information on product sources, tastes, textures, profiles, cooking methods, and countries of origin.

"It probably took me three years before I was really comfortable with my knowledge base," Hogan said. "The seafood industry is ever-changing. I still learn something new every week," she added. "I am very fortunate to work for a family-owned business where my job description is always evolving. The Cigliano family is committed to continuous education of its customers and employees. We have a great team dynamic at SMSF so there is always something I am jumping into."

©Santa Monica Seafood Company

Hogan oversees a staff of four to five account executives and helps manage the company's customer relations. She ensures that her team has the tools they need to give the best customer service they can offer to their customers. She assists them with opening new accounts and conducting Front of the House and Back of the House staff trainings with current customers.

Hogan is also the direct liaison between her sales team to ensure their needs are being met from SMSF's other departments, such as production, logistics, and marketing. She emphasizes that managing hundreds of receiving time requests while making a route profitable and ensuring the best carbon footprint can be more challenging than you think.

About 35 percent of her time is spent on administrative duties and 65 percent on personal sales. Most of her clients send their orders through email, which has a staff that monitors it 24 hours a day, but many new-generation chefs also like texting their orders. SMSF also offers online ordering.

Hogan performs business reviews with the SMSF customers, showing them where their seafood dollars are being spent, assisting with developing new menu items, ensuring they are buying the correct specification for their menu application, and addressing food cost issues. When necessary, she can suggest alternatives when certain seafood items have major market swings or become unavailable. "Key points the sales executives need to let the customers know about are our Food Safety System Certification (FSSC) 22000 and International Organization for Standardization (ISO) 14001 certifications—making us the only food distributor in the world (yes, world!) to have both." FSSC 22000 defines requirements for integrated processes that work together to control and minimize food safety hazards, whereas ISO 14001 addresses various aspects of environmental management.

©Santa Monica Seafood Company

People in the seafood industry are not just interested in appearance or accuracy of weights. The overriding issue today is responsible sourcing of seafood items. Overfishing and pollution and destruction of fish habitats are threatening fish throughout the world. Hogan is very proud of SMSF's Responsible Sourcing Vendor Partner (RSVP) program. SMSF applies a percentage of its purchases to funding projects it believes in as a company. It gives 100 percent of these monies back to seafood initiatives with the help of a third-party partner. One important use of RSVP funds is to invest in identifying, qualifying, and verifying new (and existing) suppliers and to confirm that they share SMSF's commitment to food safety, supply integrity, and sustainable practices. Some of the RSVP program achievements in 2013 are 3.2 million animals protected by removing derelict fishing nets and crab pots in Puget Sound, 170,000 white seabass released throughout Southern California for restocking, and 27,000 low-income students taught marine science with the Heal the Bay organization. Hogan says, "We want our customers to know that by spending their seafood purchasing dollars with us, they are a partner in making changes for a better seafood world in the future, and it is important to give back!"

"We put an emphasis on educating our customers about responsible sourcing issues, and in turn, they educate the consumers," Hogan said. "We try to introduce our customers to new fish that will meet their needs. Hoki from New Zealand is an example of an easy menu change instead of orange roughy. Hoki is certified by the Marine Stewardship Council and not endangered."

In addition, the company has a formal partnership with the Monterey Bay Aquarium. It includes a grading system (0–4), with 4.0 being an A like in school. 4's are green, 3's and 2's are yellow, and so on based off their color chart rating system. SMSF can run reports for its customers that have a weighted average to show how they are doing in the responsible sourcing/sustainability department. Hogan says, "We teach our customers if this is important to them, it is also important not to 'sustain' themselves out of business! For example, if ahi tuna is their #1 signature seafood seller on the menu, would it make sense to change it to albacore or remove it from the menu entirely?"

Hogan's job responsibilities also include working with the company's purchasing department to help evaluate new products being brought to market and if they would be a fit for SMSF and its customer base. To show the emphasis the company has on responsible sourcing, Hogan mentions that Logan Kock's title, formerly the director of purchasing, has been retitled as VP of Strategic Sourcing. Hogan explains that SMSF's buyers travel the globe looking for new products being brought to market; these items are evaluated by the company's top sales people, and they decide if it is something they should market. Availability has a lot to do with what the company carries and stocks on a regular basis, but customers of course travel to different areas and ask about getting some of those seafood items in SMSF's marketplace, which has expanded to Monterey, California, down to San Diego and east to the greater Phoenix and Tucson, Arizona, and Las Vegas markets. SMSF writes its own specifications with vendors in the supply chain for items such as calamari and scallops. For example, it buys calamari steaks that are tenderized with needles (no chemicals), and not bleached and has its own scallop sources on the East Coast.

A DAY IN THE LIFE (continued)

Hogan says that one of the largest concerns with all the products they carry and particularly new ones is adhering to the federal seafood labeling standards. *The Seafood List* is the FDA's Guide to Acceptable Market Names for Seafood sold in Interstate Commerce. Foodservice operations must ensure that when they name a fish on their menu, they must use the acceptable market name from the list, which is not necessarily the common name people are familiar with.

In addition to juggling the demands of her clients and staff, Hogan teaches at the Disney Culinary Institute, taking her fish cutter for filleting demonstrations. She also works with the Art Institutes and Cypress Culinary College and does front and back of the house training for seafood education. She works in the community by being active with Surfrider, assisting with beach cleanups, and guest speaking at Slow Food movement events.

Related Links:

Fishwatch—www.nmfs.noaa.gov/fishwatch

Fishwise—www.fishwise.org

Marine Stewardship Council—www.msc.org

Monterey Bay Aquarium—www.montereybayaquarium.org

Santa Monica Seafood—www.smseafood.com

The Seafood List—http://www.accessdata.fda.gov/scripts/fdcc/?set=seafoodlist

SIZE, FORM, PACKAGING, AND RELATED CONSIDERATIONS

■ Product Size

As usual, **product size** information is a very important selection factor. Fish products come in so many sizes that a specification without this type of information is seriously deficient.

> **product size** Refers to the buyer's specified weight, or volume, of a particular item he or she wants to purchase. Examples would be a 10-ounce steak or a 4-ounce hamburger.

Some shellfish items, such as crab legs and lobster tails, are usually sized by count. For these two products, the count is based on 10 pounds. For example, if lobster tails are sized "10/12," a 10-pound lot comprises approximately 10 to 12 pieces.

For many fresh fish products, buyers may be able to specify a weight range only. For example, if buyers are purchasing large salmon fillets, the supplier may be unable to accommodate an exact size.

If buyers are purchasing whole-fish products, they will also need to settle for a weight range. For instance, they cannot specify an exact size for whole lobsters. They must be satisfied with one of the five traditional sizes available: "chickens" (approximately 1 pound), "quarters" (1 to 1½ pounds), "selects" (1½ to 2½ pounds), "jumbos" (2½ to 5 pounds), and "monsters" (more than 5 pounds).

For processed products, buyers are normally able to indicate the exact desired weight per item. For example, when purchasing breaded fish sticks, they usually can choose among several available sizes.

product yield The same as edible yield.

ice pack Foods packed in crushed ice. Intended to increase shelf life. A typical packing procedure used for things such as fresh chicken and fish.

live-in-shell Refers to shellfish that are still alive when delivered.

chill packed Preservation method whereby the temperature is held at approximately 28 to 29°F, just above the product's freezing point. Usually done for fresh meat and poultry. Intended to increase the product's shelf life.

cello packed Products completely surrounded by clear plastic film. Typical packing procedure for things such as ready-to-serve salad greens. Also commonly used as an inner wrap. For instance, if you purchase a 5-pound box of frozen fish fillets, usually there will be six cello-wrapped packages, each containing approximately two to four pieces of fish.

Individually quick frozen (IQF) Process whereby products are quick frozen and individually layered in the case. Typical packing procedure for things such as portion-cut boneless, skinless chicken breasts.

marinade pack A packing medium intended to impart flavor, and sometimes tenderness, to foods. For instance, if you feature spicy wings on your menu, you may decide to purchase fresh wings marinated in a special sauce. When they arrive at your restaurant they are ready-to-cook; you do not need to marinate them yourself.

The sizing system is an informal procedure that has developed over the years. No federal government standards deal with this issue. Furthermore, many producers attach their own type of size designation to their items. When this happens, buyers will need to determine the exact nomenclature so that their specifications are adequate.

■ Product Yield

Buyers may need to indicate the minimum **product yield** they will accept, or the maximum trim they will allow, for the fish products they receive. For example, buyers could note on their specification that they will accept no more than, perhaps, 2 percent broken fish sticks in every 20-pound case purchased. Alternately, the buyer will accept no more than 2 percent dead oysters for each barrel purchased.

■ Size of Container

When considering the size of individual fish products, buyers must also give some thought to the size of the container they would prefer. Container sizes vary sufficiently to satisfy most buyer preferences. Generally speaking, the size and type of packages available for fish products are very similar to those used to package poultry products.

■ Type of Packaging Material

Fresh fish often is delivered in reusable plastic tubs or foam containers. The products normally also are packed in crushed ice—that is, fresh product is often **ice packed**.

Processed fish items usually are packaged in cans, bottles, or moisture-proof, vapor-proof materials designed to withstand freezer temperatures.

Live-in-shell fish items usually are packaged in moisture-proof materials. These products also may be packed in seaweed, or some other similar material designed to prevent dehydration. Usually, these products are not packed in ice or in fresh water because these packing media reduce their shelf lives.

As mentioned, fish products are generally packaged in the same type and variety of materials used to package poultry products. Buyers, therefore, have several choices.

■ Packaging Procedure

Once again, we note the similarity between poultry and fish products. As with poultry, fish items are slab-packed, layered, **chill packed**, ice packed, **cello packed**, and **individually quick frozen (IQF)**. Some items are also available in a **marinade pack**; for example, buyers may be able to purchase Cajun-seasoned tilapia fillets.

Fresh **shellfish** are, typically, slab-packed. Fresh **fin fish** normally are ice packed to preserve their culinary quality and extend the shipment's **shelf life**. Some fresh fin fish are placed in **modified-atmosphere packaging (MAP)**, which is a type of controlled-atmosphere packaging that involves chilling freshly harvested fish; placing it in plastic wrap; and pumping a combination of carbon dioxide, oxygen, and nitrogen into the wrap. The shelf life of fresh fish packaged this way can be as long as three weeks.

Fresh-frozen fish products are usually trimmed, cut, IQF, and packaged on board a fish-factory ship. These items are often cello wrapped and placed in moisture-proof, vapor-proof containers.

Processed frozen-fish items are most often processed, IQF, layered on plastic or waxed sheets or plastic "cell packs," and placed in moisture-proof, vapor-proof containers. As with similarly processed frozen poultry products, this type of packaging procedure is sometimes referred to as a **snap pack** or **shatter pack**.

■ Product Form

Fish is processed into many **product forms**. Foodservice operations that strive for a high-quality seafood reputation normally need to use dressed fresh fish and, if further processing is necessary, to perform these tasks in the operation's kitchen. High-quality processed convenience items, though, are usually available. For example, breaded/battered, portion-control products are very popular, as are portion-control stuffed, marinated, and other preseasoned fish products.

Many unique types of convenience fish products are available. For example, "flaked and re-formed" "shrimp" items, which consist of odd scraps of shrimp material shaped to look like whole shrimp, are available. Also, several imitation fish products, such as imitation shrimp and seafood salad,

FIGURE 20.8 A processed surimi product.
©Patty Orly/Shutterstock

shellfish   Exoskeleton-bearing aquatic invertebrates used as food. They are filter-feeding mollusks such as clams, mussels, and oysters.

fin fish   A typical fish used in food service operations. In its whole form, this fish is ectothermic, has a streamlined body for rapid swimming, extracts oxygen from water using gills or uses an accessory breathing organ to breathe atmospheric oxygen, has two sets of paired fins, usually one or two (rarely three) dorsal fins, an anal fin, and a tail fin, has jaws, has skin that is usually covered with scales, and lays eggs.

shelf life   The amount of time a product can remain in storage before it loses quality and cannot be used.

modified-atmosphere packaging (MAP)   Another term for controlled atmosphere packaging (CAP).

snap pack   Another term for individually quick frozen (IQF). When you remove a layer of frozen items from a case and drop it onto a counter, the IQF portions should snap apart easily. If they do not come apart easily and cleanly, it usually means that they have been thawed a bit and refrozen.

shatter pack   Another term for individually quick frozen (IQF).

product form   Refers to the degree of processing, or lack thereof, a product has when you purchase it. For instance, a buyer can purchase whole chickens or selected chicken parts. The parts typically would cost more than the whole birds.

surimi Fish-based paste used to produce imitation lobster, crab, and other shellfish items.

are made with a fish-based paste called **surimi** (see Figure 20.8). Surimi is also used to produce various "meat" products—such as imitation frankfurters and bacon bits. Although these items do not necessarily provide the same health benefits as the real products, some of these low-cost substitutes are very attractive to budget-conscious restaurant operators.

If buyers purchase a good deal of processed fish, they may need to rely exclusively on packers' brands as an indication of quality and other desired product characteristics. If buyers do not use brand name identification and are purchasing, say, a frozen-fish patty, they need to note on the specification the types of fish and other food matter that must be used to process these items. Buyers also would need to note the proportion of these materials desired. If they do not note

packer's brand name Very specific indication of product quality. More precise than a brand name. A packer's personal grading system. Usually intended to take the place of federal government grades.

substitution possibilities Opportunities for using substitute ingredients in recipes that will not compromise the culinary quality of the food and beverage items made with those recipes. Alternately, opportunities for using substitute nonfood and nonbeverage products, such as cleaners, equipment, and utensils, to accomplish the same purposes.

these characteristics and do not wish to specify a particular **packer's brand name**, they cannot expect to maintain quality control. Although federal standards of identity exist for some fish products, hospitality operators cannot rely on them exclusively because they represent only minimum guidelines to which commercial fish processors must adhere.

Usually, the major issues that need to be resolved when contemplating the purchase of processed fish products are: (1) what are the **substitution possibilities**, and (2) what degree of convenience do you want?

Several substitution possibilities exist. Processed fish products come in many forms. For example, buyers can substitute fillets for steaks, butterfly shrimp for headless shrimp, and imitation crab for real crab. These alternatives are limited because, as buyers go from one item to the next, the culinary quality changes. Managers must not risk alienating their customers.

The degree of convenience desired usually is related to the labor skill, equipment, and utensils available to produce menu items, and the size of the kitchen and storage facilities. Today, the economics of the foodservice industry tend to favor the use of many convenience products, and as long as the culinary quality is acceptable, managers will seriously consider using them.

Whatever the degree of processing buyers' desire, they will, typically, have more than one supplier from which to choose. Fresh fish may be scarce, but buyers usually have two or more brands of processed fish from which to choose. This makes it easier for buyers who like to shop around and bid buy. It also makes it convenient for hospitality operators who want to move fish items around on their menus. This gives buyers a great deal of flexibility.

■ Preservation Method

Fish is preserved in many ways: frozen, dried, smoked, refrigerated, ice packed, cello packed, chill packed, live, live-in-shell, and canned.

preservation method A procedure, such as refrigeration, freezing, canning, drying, or chemical additives, used to maintain a product's shelf life and quality and in some cases, impart additional flavorings.

The operation that offers fish signature menu items prefers live, live-in-shell, and/or ice packed or chill packed dressed fresh fish. If fresh product is unavailable, the frozen item is normally the preferred **preservation method** because at least it ensures a steady, year-round supply.

For restaurants that serve raw fish items such as sushi, sashimi, and tartares, health department regulations may require that the fish be frozen to prevent the growth of microorganisms. The FDA Model Food Code states that freezing and storing at –4°F (–20°C) or below for 7 days (total time), or freezing at –31°F (–35°C) or below until solid and storing at –31°F (–35°C) or below for 15 hours, or freezing at –31°F (–35°C) or below until solid and storing at –4°F (–20°C) or below for 24 hours are methods sufficient to kill parasites. This process is intended for retailers who provide fish intended for raw consumption.[8]

For some products, canned is the preferred choice. For example, snails and sardines are usually purchased in cans or bottles. Indeed, Americans buy more canned fish than any other type.

Packing Medium

In some instances, buyers need to indicate the specific **packing medium** desired. For example, canned tuna is packed with water or with several varieties of oil. The same is true for other canned fish products. Because the packing medium significantly affects a product's culinary quality, buyers must be careful to include this selection factor on the specification.

> **packing medium** The type of liquid used to pack foods. Especially relevant when purchasing canned goods.

Supplier Factors

When buyers use a great deal of fresh fish, they may have to cast their lot with one primary supplier, assuming that they are satisfied with that supplier's capability. Together, a buyer and a supplier take what they can get from several sources, usually dictated by season, from the various seafood-producing areas of the world.

For instance, if a buyer purchases fresh, live-in-shell lobsters, the typical scenario may go something like this. The buyers will either go through a local supplier or purchase directly from a supplier on the East Coast and order what is wanted for the next two or three days. The lobsters will be shipped FedEx air freight. At the airport in the buyer's city or a nearby city, the lobsters will be put into a local FedEx van, and brought right to the buyer's back door. The buyer will pay the East Coast fish supplier the going rate for that day, usually on a cost-plus basis. Alternately, the buyer may pay a local supplier, who will then take care of all the details. Scenarios like this often take place for other types of fresh fish as well, but with other types, buyers may need to accept what is available.

The cost-plus purchasing procedure will influence an operator's menu pricing procedures. When buyers purchase fresh-fish products, they may wish to set a different menu price every day or every week. In the live-lobster example, a typical price-setting strategy is as follows: Pay for the lobsters. Throw out any dead ones, perhaps 2 out of 24. Divide the total as-purchased (AP) price plus any freight cost by 22. Add a markup to cover labor, overhead, and profit, and use this figure as the live-lobster menu price for today or for however long it takes to sell this batch of lobsters. Another way for a restaurant to handle price fluctuations in fresh fish and other products is to present those food offerings as "specials of the day." These specials are not normally printed in the menu and have prices that reflect the daily cost of the ingredients plus the appropriate markup.

It is a good idea for buyers to deal consistently with trusted suppliers when they purchase a great deal of fresh fish. The items are not standardized, the quality is variable, the supply is erratic, and the prices change continuously. Buyers need the supplier's expertise. Also, they must be confident that the buyer will charge the correct market price for the items and not try to take advantage of the buyers' inability to track the fresh-seafood market on a daily basis. Furthermore, the suppliers must ensure that the products they distribute are wholesome and safe for human consumption. Fresh fish are very difficult items to move successfully through the distribution channels; several contamination opportunities exist. The competent fresh-fish supplier deserves the buyer's respect.

new pack time Time of the year when products intended for sale the following year (or other period of time) are packed. For instance, canned fruits and vegetables are usually processed and packed right after harvest. Vendors then work off of this inventory until the next new pack time rolls around.

When buyers purchase processed fish, they do not need to become a house account. Processed-fish buying, like most other processed-food purchasing, lends itself nicely to bid buying. Buyers learn, in time, the qualities associated with particular brand names. They can also learn to specify the type of processing they want and the area from which the fish should come.

Bear in mind, too, that there is a **new pack time** for canned and frozen fish, similar to the new pack time for canned fruits and vegetables. If hospitality operators have the money and the expertise, and large firms often have both, bid buying for a six-month or one-year supply can be rewarding.

PURCHASING FISH

The first step in purchasing fish is to acquire some of the indispensable reference materials available. For instance, fish buyers might want to have a copy of *The Seafood Handbook*, Second Edition (Hoboken NJ: John Wiley and Sons, 2010; see Figure 20.9). They should also consult some of the leading trade journals, such as *SeaFood Business* or *Seafood Choices Alliance*.

Food and Drug Administration (FDA) Office of Seafood Safety Agency that, among other things, will provide buyers with a list of approved interstate fish suppliers operating in their areas.

health district Local regulator that is responsible for preventing food-borne illness and other related safety problems.

statement of quality Information regarding standards buyers would like to have, such as product size and preservation method, when dealing with vendors who sell and distribute fresh food items that are hard to define and can vary significantly in quality from one delivery to the next. Examples of these types of products are fresh fish and organic produce.

Buyers should also consider subscribing to the *Seafood Price-Current* published by Urner Barry. This report contains twice-weekly market prices for many fish products from various regions of the United States. The Web also has a large amount of current seafood information. For instance, the websites Seafood News and Sea-Ex provide daily price information and news regarding the seafood industry. The Monterey Bay Aquarium Seafood Watch™ website has up-to-date information and recommendations on which fish to purchase if sustainability is a concern.

The next step is for buyers to contact the **FDA Office of Seafood Safety** and ask for a list of approved interstate fish suppliers operating in their area. The local **health district** can provide a list of suppliers who operate only in their local markets.

Next, buyers and other management personnel need to decide the exact type of product and quality they want. Once they determine what they want to include on the menu and what quality they want, the buyers should take the time to prepare a specification for each product. However, we do not think that specs are very valuable for fresh fish because buyers usually have to take what is available or go someplace else. They might prepare a **statement of quality** and give it to their suppliers, who then might call them when something meeting their standard comes in. A statement of quality might include the area the fish is to come from, as well as its size, form, and preservation method. If the fish is grown under controlled conditions, buyers might be able to specify its feed and nurturing techniques.

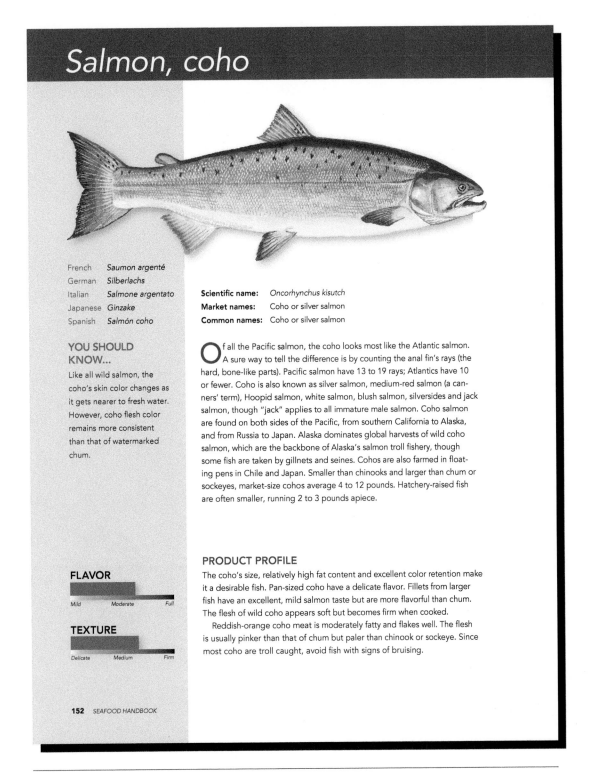

Salmon, coho

French	*Saumon argenté*
German	*Silberlachs*
Italian	*Salmone argentato*
Japanese	*Ginzake*
Spanish	*Salmón coho*

Scientific name: *Oncorhynchus kisutch*
Market names: Coho or silver salmon
Common names: Coho or silver salmon

YOU SHOULD KNOW...

Like all wild salmon, the coho's skin color changes as it gets nearer to fresh water. However, coho flesh color remains more consistent than that of watermarked chum.

Of all the Pacific salmon, the coho looks most like the Atlantic salmon. A sure way to tell the difference is by counting the anal fin's rays (the hard, bone-like parts). Pacific salmon have 13 to 19 rays; Atlantics have 10 or fewer. Coho is also known as silver salmon, medium-red salmon (a canners' term), Hoopid salmon, white salmon, blush salmon, silversides and jack salmon, though "jack" applies to all immature male salmon. Coho salmon are found on both sides of the Pacific, from southern California to Alaska, and from Russia to Japan. Alaska dominates global harvests of wild coho salmon, which are the backbone of Alaska's salmon troll fishery, though some fish are taken by gillnets and seines. Cohos are also farmed in floating pens in Chile and Japan. Smaller than chinooks and larger than chum or sockeyes, market-size cohos average 4 to 12 pounds. Hatchery-raised fish are often smaller, running 2 to 3 pounds apiece.

PRODUCT PROFILE

The coho's size, relatively high fat content and excellent color retention make it a desirable fish. Pan-sized coho have a delicate flavor. Fillets from larger fish have an excellent, mild salmon taste but are more flavorful than chum. The flesh of wild coho appears soft but becomes firm when cooked.

Reddish-orange coho meat is moderately fatty and flakes well. The flesh is usually pinker than that of chum but paler than chinook or sockeye. Since most coho are troll caught, avoid fish with signs of bruising.

FLAVOR

Mild — Moderate — Full

TEXTURE

Delicate — Medium — Firm

152 *SEAFOOD HANDBOOK*

FIGURE 20.9 The *Seafood Handbook* is a useful reference for fish buyers.
Copyright Diversified Business Communications, www.seafoodhandbook.com. Reprinted with permission of John Wiley and Sons, Inc.

If buyers purchase processed fish, they should prepare detailed specifications so that they compile ideas on exactly what they want. The specs must include all pertinent information, especially if buyers will use them in bid buying (see Figure 20.10 for some examples of product specifications and Figure 20.11 for an example product specification outline for fish products).

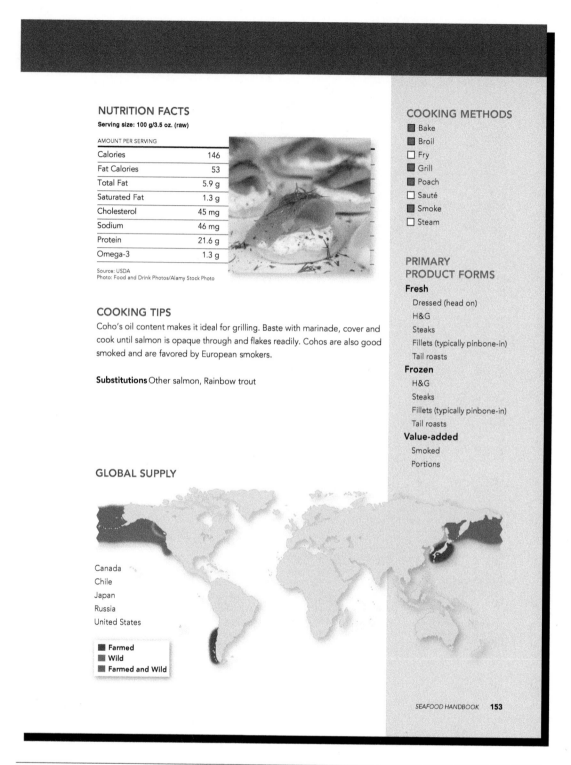

NUTRITION FACTS

Serving size: 100 g/3.5 oz. (raw)

AMOUNT PER SERVING

Calories	146
Fat Calories	53
Total Fat	5.9 g
Saturated Fat	1.3 g
Cholesterol	45 mg
Sodium	46 mg
Protein	21.6 g
Omega-3	1.3 g

Source: USDA
Photo: Food and Drink Photos/Alamy Stock Photo

COOKING TIPS

Coho's oil content makes it ideal for grilling. Baste with marinade, cover and cook until salmon is opaque through and flakes readily. Cohos are also good smoked and are favored by European smokers.

Substitutions Other salmon, Rainbow trout

COOKING METHODS

- ☑ Bake
- ☑ Broil
- ☐ Fry
- ☑ Grill
- ☑ Poach
- ☐ Sauté
- ☑ Smoke
- ☐ Steam

PRIMARY PRODUCT FORMS

Fresh
  Dressed (head on)
  H&G
  Steaks
  Fillets (typically pinbone-in)
  Tail roasts
Frozen
  H&G
  Steaks
  Fillets (typically pinbone-in)
  Tail roasts
Value-added
  Smoked
  Portions

GLOBAL SUPPLY

Canada
Chile
Japan
Russia
United States

- ■ Farmed
- ■ Wild
- ■ Farmed and Wild

SEAFOOD HANDBOOK **153**

FIGURE 20.9 Continued

If buyers purchase processed fish in quantity, it might be worth a little trouble for them to shop around. For instance, purchasing a lot of frozen fish, such as a six-month supply, can save buyers a bit of money, as long as the storage costs are reasonable. Many frozen-fish suppliers will

Tuna, solid white, albacore
Used to prepare tuna salad
Chicken of the Sea® brand
Water pack
66.5-ounce can
6 cans per case
Moisture-proof case

Australian lobster tails
Used for dinner entrée
U.S. Grade A (or equivalent)
16/20 count
25-pound moisture-proof, vapor-
   proof container
Layered pack, frozen

Seafood Newburg
Used for banquet service
Overhill® brand
6-ounce individual portion pack
48 portions per case
Packaged in moisture-proof, vapor-
   proof material
To be reconstituted in its package
Frozen

Clam juice (ocean)
Used for beverage service
Nugget® brand
46-ounce can
12 cans per case
Moisture-proof case

FIGURE 20.10 An example of fish product specifications.

Intended use:

Exact name:

U.S. grade (or equivalent):

PUFI seal:

Packer's brand name (or equivalent):

Product size:

Product yield:

Size of container:

Type of packaging material:

Packaging procedure:

Product form:

Preservation method:

Packing medium:

Point of origin:

FIGURE 20.11 An example of a product specification outline for fish products.

set up a **stockless purchasing plan** for you or will provide the same type of supplier service for a slight carrying charge.

Another interesting aspect of buying processed fish is the reasonable spread in the AP prices between one brand name and another. Naturally, when the AP price is lower, buyers usually suspect a lower quality. Although this conclusion is typically true when buyers purchase other processed

stockless purchasing plan When a buyer purchases a large amount of product, for example, a three-month supply, and arranges for the vendor to store it and deliver a little at a time.

products, especially canned fruits and vegetables, it is not always the case with processed fish. For example, buyers will see a big difference in AP price between canned dark-meat tuna and white-meat tuna. Some people care very little about this color differential. Another example is the processed fish stick: a little more cod and a little less haddock may yield a fine-tasting product at a more economical AP price. Similarly, different formulas for fish patties, fish stews, and other processed entrées can yield substantially different AP prices while maintaining acceptable quality standards.

Minimum-order requirements may trouble buyers. If they buy fresh fish, but only a little, they might find that a high minimum-order requirement and freight cost hinder their desire to serve a high-quality fish entrée.

Sometimes, buyers may be tempted to purchase fish from a neighbor who has just returned from a fishing trip. No mandatory federal-inspection requirement exists for the neighbor, and the fish may be perfectly good. The state or local health district, however, may have some regulations prohibiting the sale of this fish. We believe that buyers should avoid this practice because they never really know where the fish came from or, more important, how it has been handled.

Because fish availability can be somewhat unpredictable, buyers can sometimes find real seafood bargains. For example, a supplier may have some merchandise on a **move list**. Perhaps more shrimp has suddenly shown up on the market and its AP price has gone down, or the tuna industry has a larger promotional effort. Before buyers jump at these bargains, though, they need to consider four factors: (1) Can their employees handle the item properly if it is a new item to them? (2) Do they have the proper equipment to prepare and serve the new item? (3) If the item is currently on their menu, should they drop its menu price? (4) Should they use this bargain as a **loss leader** on their menu? That is, would they be willing, for instance, to serve bargain shrimp in their lounge at a very inexpensive menu price to attract customers who supposedly will then order more profitable merchandise from them during a subsequent visit to the restaurant? This type of promotion may establish a trend whereby buyers would be forced to continue it well after the AP price of shrimp soars.

Management and buyers must decide what fish they want. Then they must engage the supplier who can handle their needs. For processed fish, bid buying may be the answer, but this is not always possible when purchasing fresh merchandise.

> **move list** A list of products that need to be sold ASAP. For instance, they may be on the verge of spoilage, or they might be discontinued items. If vendors have items on a move list they may call you to see if you're interested in any of them. Usually the AP prices of these items are deeply discounted.

> **loss leader** Product sold at a much lower profit margin to attract customers who will purchase it as well as other more profitable items.

PROCEDURES FOR RECEIVING, STORING, AND ISSUING FISH

■ Receiving

> **shucked shellfish** Shellfish that have had their protective shells removed.

When a fish shipment is delivered, the receivers' first step is to check its quality. When they examine fresh fin fish or fresh, **shucked shellfish**, the product should have a mild, not fishy, scent. Its flesh should be firm, and it should spring back when slight pressure is applied. The product should be slime-free. Gills should be bright pink or red. If the head is attached, the eyes should be clear and bright. To ensure quality and maximum shelf life, the product should be ice packed or chill packed.

Sometimes, suppliers will send **slacked-out** fish, that is, thawed fish, instead of the fresh product ordered. Usually, this product looks a little dry, or it has **ice spots**, which are dried areas on its flesh.

When examining live fish, receivers should see a product that is very active. They do not want live fish that seem sluggish or tired. Also, the product should be heavy for its size.

Live-in-shell **crustaceans**, upon examination, should also be very active and feel heavy for their size (see Figure 20.12).

When receivers evaluate live-in-shell **mollusks**, the shells should be closed, or they should at least close when tapped with fingers. Open shells indicate that the products are dead and are past their peak of culinary quality. Live-in-shell mollusks also should feel heavy for their size (see Figures 20.13–20.15).

Frozen fish should be frozen solid. They should be packaged in moisture-proof, vapor-proof material. No signs of thawing or refreezing, such as crystallization, dryness, items stuck together, or water damage on the carton, should be visible. Also, if applicable, the amount of **glaze** on the items—a protective coating of ice on the frozen items that the producer adds to prevent dehydration—should not be excessive.

Canned merchandise should show no signs of rust, dents, dirt, or swelling. Canned fish is especially dangerous if it is contaminated, so the receiving agent can never be too careful when evaluating the containers.

One problem receivers have when checking the quality of fresh fish is knowing whether or not they have received the right species—the item they ordered. Many fish products look similar to the untrained eye. For example, it is not easy to distinguish bay scallops from shark meat cubes, red snapper from Pacific rockfish, or cod fillets from haddock fillets. Having a copy of *The Seafood Handbook* or other references available at the receiving dock can be helpful in knowing the characteristics of each fish to look for.

Here is a corollary problem: What represents good quality to one nose may be offensive to another. We have seen receivers try to send back fresh-fish items because these items did not "look right" or "smell

FIGURE 20.12 Dungeness crab.
Source: Gisslen, Professional Cooking, 7th Edition, Copyright 2011. Reprinted with permission of John Wiley and Sons, Inc.

slacked out A food item that is thought to be fresh, but has actually been frozen, thawed, and passed off as fresh.

ice spot A dry spot on a food product that has been previously frozen. An indication that an item that is thought to be fresh has actually been frozen, thawed, and passed off as fresh.

crustacean Shellfish with a soft shell (e.g., shrimp).

mollusk Shellfish with a hard shell (e.g., oysters).

glaze A thin coating of ice applied to frozen products, such as boneless, skinless chicken breasts. Done to provide protection from freezer burn.

FIGURE 20.13 St. James River Oysters.
Source: Gisslen, Professional Cooking, 7th Edition, Copyright 2011. Reprinted with permission of John Wiley and Sons, Inc.

right." They had to be convinced that the slipperiness or ocean aroma was natural.

Another problem with receiving fresh fish arises when receiving agents need to return it. Suppose that the driver made a mistake and must take the fish back. Chances are that the product will go bad before the supplier can resell it. Also, operators are left without a fresh-fish item they may need that very night. Consequently, they might keep it and use it if the quality is acceptable despite its being the wrong variety. Receivers then would complete a Request for Credit memorandum or make some mutually agreeable settlement with the supplier.

FIGURE 20.14 Clams: clockwise from top left: steamers, littlenecks, cherrystones, chowder clams.
Source: Gisslen, Professional Cooking, 7th Edition, Copyright 2011. Reprinted with permission of John Wiley and Sons, Inc.

An unfortunate problem with some processed fish is that it is hard to tell whether they will be acceptable once they are prepared for customer service. For instance, chefs may not know whether a frozen lobster tail is bad until they cook it and it falls apart. With a fresh lobster tail, experienced chefs can usually judge its quality before cooking it.

After satisfying their nose and eyes, receiving agents should go on to weigh, preferably without the ice, or count the merchandise and then get it into the proper storage environment as quickly as possible. Fresh fish will deteriorate right before agents' eyes if they fail to keep it refrigerated. Whatever receivers do, they should not let fresh and frozen fish stay on the receiving platform any longer than is absolutely necessary. Some companies put scales and checking equipment in the walk-in refrigerator to receive fish, poultry, and meat. Others temporarily roll the scale into the refrigerator.

If receivers are getting a shipment of shellfish from a supplier on the FDA's **Interstate Certified Shellfish Shippers List**, a tag in the container will note the number of the bed where the shellfish were grown and harvested. Operators are required to keep this tag on file for 90 days if the products are fresh and two years if they are frozen (see Figure 20.16). If an outbreak of food-borne illness is traced to the shellfish, health officials must be able to determine the **lot number** of the offending products so that any as-yet-unused parts of that batch can be removed from the channel of distribution.

Interstate Certified Shellfish Shippers List Agency within the Food and Drug Administration (FDA) that approves the areas where shellfish are grown and harvested. When a buyer purchases these shellfish, the container will include a tag (that must be kept on hand for at least 90 days) that shows the number of the bed of water where the products were grown and harvested.

lot number An indication that packaged goods originated from a particular group, or lot. Important if, for example, you are purchasing canned goods; products coming from the same batch will have similar culinary quality, whereas those from different lots may be slightly different.

FIGURE 20.15 Mussels. From left: green, blue (wild), blue (farm-raised).
Source: Gisslen, Professional Cooking, 7th Edition, Copyright 2011. Reprinted with permission of John Wiley and Sons, Inc.

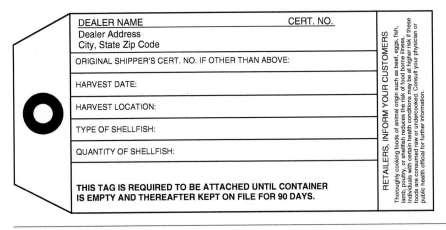

FIGURE 20.16 A shellfish tag.

In some areas, other tags may accompany a fish shipment. For instance, some parts of the United States do not allow the importation of fish from other areas unless they carry identifying tags. These tags are usually issued to indicate that the products are acceptable to the local **Fish and Game Office** and the local health district, and that they have not been purchased from unapproved local sources.

After doing the quality and quantity checks, receivers must verify the prices and complete the appropriate accounting documents.

> **Fish and Game Office**
> Local agency that certifies that fish and game products from other areas have not been purchased from unapproved sources and are acceptable to use and resell to customers.

■ Storing

Fresh fin fish and fresh, shucked shellfish should be maintained at approximately 32°F and at no less than 65 percent relative humidity. These products are best stored on a bed of crushed ice and covered with waxed paper to prevent dehydration. If hospitality operators cannot use crushed ice, they should wrap the products tightly in plastic wrap, aluminum foil, or some other suitable container and store them in the coldest part of the refrigerator. The maximum shelf life for these items is about two days.

Operators must store live fin fish in tanks specifically designed to hold the particular types of products they are purchasing. Operators can also store live-in-shell fish in the appropriate water tanks, although they could be kept in their original containers and covered with damp cloths. Generally, these shellfish items should not be stored in fresh water or crushed ice. This is especially true for mollusks because the fresh water can kill them.

Hospitality operators should store frozen fish at or below 0°F. Ideally, these fish should be stored at −10°F or lower[9] because these temperatures are conducive to maximum shelf life, which is about three months. If the products have the correct amount of glaze on them, they could maintain acceptable culinary quality for up to one year.

Operators should keep canned or bottled fish products in a dry storeroom. The ideal temperature of this storeroom would be 50°F, though 70°F is acceptable. The storeroom's relative humidity should not exceed 60 percent.

■ Issuing

Most fresh fish goes directly into production, but if fish enters an issue-controlled storage area, hospitality operators will need to prepare issue documents when it goes to production. Just as when operators issue most items, they have a choice: Should they issue the product as is, or should they issue it as ready to go? For example, oysters can be shucked ahead of time. Similarly, escargot can be pre-prepared, and someone might portion a fresh snapper, put it in pie pans, and season it, so that all the cook has to do is pop it into the oven.

Operators should try to avoid the temptation of pre-preparing the snapper and then storing the portions in a freezer. On the one hand, this practice allows the cook to take the pre-prepared snapper out of the in-process freezer and put it in the oven. This is convenient; it also reduces left-overs, which usually go straight into the garbage can. On the other hand, some of the flavor is lost when fish are frozen this way. Besides, if operations have fresh fish on their menu, they have to risk some loss; they will also have to price these menu items to take into account these probable losses.

> **in-process inventory**
> Products located at employee workstations; most or all will be used during the shift.

Of course, it is absolutely essential for operators to follow proper stock rotation when issuing fish products. Also, because these items deteriorate rapidly and are expensive, operators must make sure that requisitioners do not take more than is absolutely necessary. Management should ask them to note the **in-process inventory** before requisitioning more fish.

■ In-Process Inventories

A great deal of risk—spoilage, especially—is associated with fish, particularly fresh fish. This risk increases dramatically when fish is not handled properly at this step. Merely listing fish on the menu probably places hospitality operators in a high "risk category."

Operators must try to reduce losses in the in-process inventories; typically, however, some loss occurs, particularly if several fresh fish items appear on the menu. But two rules are paramount: (1) Employees should not handle the product needlessly because this spreads bacteria and hastens the deterioration of fish quality. (2) Do not pre-prepare any more fish than chefs can use during the shift. Conservative pre-preparing can cause production problems later on if the operation gets an unexpected rush, but it is necessary if the firm wants to avoid excessive leftovers.

Key Words and Concepts

Aquaculture	Grading factors
Cello packed	Hazard Analysis Critical Control Point system (HACCP system)
Chill packed	
Crustacean	Health district
Exact name	Ice packed
Fin fish	Ice spot
Fish and Game Office	Individually quick frozen (IQF)
Food and Drug Administration (FDA) Office of Seafood Safety	In-process inventory
	Intended use
Glaze	Interstate Certified Shellfish Shippers List

Key Words and Concepts (continued)

Live-in-shell

Loss leader

Lot number

Manufacturing grade

Marinade pack

Modified-atmosphere
    packaging (MAP)

Mollusk

Move list

National Oceanic and Atmospheric
    Administration (NOAA)

New pack time

Packed Under Federal Inspection
    (PUFI) seal

Packer's brand name

Packing medium

Point of origin

Polychlorinated biphenyls (PCBs)

Preservation method

Processed fish

Product form

Product size

Product yield

Renaming fish

Shatter pack

Shelf life

Shellfish

Shucked shellfish

Slacked out

Snap pack

Standard of identity

Statement of quality

Stockless purchasing plan

Substitution possibilities

Sustainability

Surimi

Truth-in-menu

Wild-caught

 Questions and Problems

1. List the U.S. grades for fish and the grading factors.

2. A product specification for frozen, breaded shrimp could include this information:

    a.

    b.

    c.

    d.

    e.

3. Briefly describe the necessary storage environments for fresh-fish products.

4. What is the difference between farm-raised and wild-caught seafood?

5. Why is sustainability a concern when purchasing seafood items?

6. What is an appropriate intended use for

    a. canned, dark-meat tuna?

    b. shucked, fresh scallops?

    c. frozen crabmeat?

Questions and Problems (continued)

7. What does the acronym PUFI stand for?

8. What are the differences between fin fish and shellfish?

9. What are the two main types of shellfish?

10. What is the difference between a fish fillet and a fish portion?

11. Why is the point of origin of a fish product an important selection factor?

12. What does the term "14/16 crab legs" indicate to a foodservice buyer?

13. What is the primary difference between "round" fish and "drawn" fish?

14. A supplier calls to tell a buyer that he has just gotten a good buy on frozen ocean perch. The hospitality operation has never used this item before on its menu, but with the low AP price the supplier quoted, the buyer is tempted. She has to buy 500 pounds to get the deal. What would be some of the advantages and disadvantages of buying the ocean perch?

15. What critical information is missing from this product specification for shrimp?

> Whole, raw, headless shrimp
> Used for shrimp cocktail
> U.S. Grade A (or equivalent)
> Packed in 5-pound laminated cardboard containers

16. Under what conditions would buyers purchase an imitation fish product?

17. What is the purpose of the tagging system that is in effect for shellfish products?

18. When would buyers purchase a flaked and re-formed fish product?

19. Why is fish that will be used for sushi and other raw preparations commonly frozen? What are some of the guidelines for freezing fish for consumption as a raw product?

20. KWG Enterprises sells a frozen, breaded shrimp, 8 to a pound, for $7.69 per pound. Its fresh, raw shrimp, 14 to a pound, sell for $6.24 per pound. A restaurant normally sells about 24 orders of fried shrimp with 6 pieces per order each day. Perform a make-or-buy analysis assuming that the cost of the breading ingredients is $0.02 per shrimp and a prep cook paid $10 per hour can bread 24 orders in one-half hour.

Experiential Exercises

1. Outline the specific procedures hospitality operators should use for purchasing, receiving, storing, and issuing frozen lobster tails. Assume that the tails will be used in a steakhouse for a steak and lobster tail entrée. Ask a steakhouse manager to comment on your answer. Write a one-page report on your findings.

Experiential Exercises (continued)

2. Visit a fresh seafood restaurant, and speak to the manager or chef. Ask him/her these questions:
   a. How do you determine what seafood items to sell?
   b. How often do you change your menu and your prices?
   c. How is the menu influenced by the availability of the product?
   d. How is the menu influenced by your relationship with the suppliers?
   e. What do you do if the product is not available and the supplier sends a substitute item?

   Write a two-page report of your findings.

3. Visit a seafood supplier. Ask a manager or buyer to show you their facility and explain their buying, receiving, storage, and delivery systems. Write a one-page report on what you learn from the visit.

References

1. Steve Coomes, "Ouita Michel Opens Smithtown Seafood in Lexington, Kentucky's First Sustainable Fish Restaurant," September 17, 2013, http://insiderlouisville.com/lifestyle_culture/dining/ouita-michel-opens-smithtown-seafood-ky-s-first-sustainable-fish-restaurant/. See also Multi Aquaculture Systems Inc., Funky Fish Farm, http://fishfarmamagansett.com/index.htm. See also Anton's Taproom Restaurant, Kansas City, http://antonskc.com/about-antons/.

2. Beth Panitz, "A Modern-Day Fish Story," *Restaurants USA*, June/July 2000, www.restaurant.org/tools/magazines/rusa/magArchive/year/article/?ArticleID=545. Connie Barclay, "NOAA to Pursue National Policy for Sustainable Marine Aquaculture," National Oceanic and Atmospheric Association, USDC, Sept. 3, 2009, www.nmfs.noaa.gov/fishwatch/. See also Roy Eccleston, "Sashimi on Demand?" *Time*, August 25, 2008, 8, p. GB1; Sasha Chapman, "Where'd That Salmon Come From?" *Maclean's*, 120, no. 24 (June 25, 2007):56.; David Brown, "Aquaculture in America," http://worldagnetwork.com/aquaculture-in-america/. For more information on aquaculture, see the Aquaculture Network Information Center (aquanic.org).

3. Elizabeth Landau, "Farmed or Wild Fish: Which Is Healthier?," CNN Health, www.cnn.com/2010/HEALTH/01/13/salmon.farmed.fresh/.

4. "Organic Seafood: Fact or Fiction," Food & Water Watch, www.foodandwaterwatch.org/fish/seafood/labeling/organic-seafood-fact-or-fiction/. For more information on organic seafood see: The Organic Seafood Council, "Comment to the National Organic Standards Board Aquaculture Working Group Interim Final Report,"

References (continued)

www.ams.usda.gov/AMSv1.0/getfile?dDocName= STELPRD 3413354; "URI Sustainable Seafood Initiative," http://seagrant.gso.uri.edu/sustainable_seafood/index.html.

5. Ted Williams, "Gone Fish," *Audubon Magazine*, www.audubonmagazine.org/articles/conservation/gone-fish.

6. "Rick Moonen—Chef, Author, Educator," www.rickmoonen.com.

7. Anonymous, "The Surprising Sources of Your Favorite Seafoods," *FishWatch: U.S. Seafood Facts*, www.fishwatch.gov/sustainable-seafood/the-global-picture.

8. "Seafood Safety: Seafood Safety Topics," Seafood Health Facts: Making Smart Choices, http://seafoodhealthfacts.org/seafood_safety/practitioners/parasites.php.

9. "A Foodservice Guide to Seafood Quality: Basic Tips on Handling Fresh and Frozen Alaska Seafood," Alaska Seafood Marketing Institute, www.alaskaseafood.org/fishingprocessing/fsgsq.htm. See also "Seafood Quality Information," Seafood Network Information Center, Sea Grant Extension Program, http://seafood.ucdavis.edu/pubs/qualityinfo.htm.

MEAT

The Purpose of This Chapter

After reading this chapter, you should be able to:

- Identify the management considerations surrounding the selection and procurement of meat.

- Choose appropriate meats based on primary selection factors.

- Explain the USDA's inspection process for evaluating meat wholesomeness.

- Select appropriate meats based on the type of quality grade, yield grade, and/or packer's brand.

- Categorize meat according to product size, form, and packaging, and related characteristics.

- Create a specification for meat that can be used in the purchasing process.

- Describe procedures for receiving, storing, and issuing meat.

MANAGEMENT CONSIDERATIONS

Meat represents a major portion of the foodservice purchase dollar. Consequently, buyers tend to be especially careful when making meat-purchasing decisions. Although the meat industry and the federal government provide buying guidelines, purchasing meat is a time-consuming experience.

■ Types of Meat Items Purchased

Many foodservice operations purchase some type of beef, veal, pork, or lamb in addition to many types of processed meats, such as cold cuts, sausages, ham, and bacon. Operations use pre-prepared meat entrées, such as meatballs and barbecue pork or beef, and other less familiar products to a lesser extent (see Figure 21.1 for some of the more popular types of meat products the foodservice industry uses).

As a rule, deficient supervision is not an issue in the purchasing, receiving, storing, and issuing of meat, nor is it an issue in production, but management finds that deciding on the quality they want and the cuts they prefer is not easy. They must seek suppliers who can provide what they want on a continuous basis. Managers who are responsible for the ordering, expediting, and receiving of meat products can attest that this is no simple task.

Some of the major managerial meat-purchasing decisions are discussed in the following sections.

■ Should Management Offer Meat on the Menu?

Or should you minimize the amount of meat items that you offer? The question usually is how much of your brand image do you want to be associated with meat? Although some operations, such as vegetarian restaurants, exclude meat on the menu, realistically, almost all operations offer meat entrées. It is difficult to alter an image of the establishment when the concept is tied to meat. This is evident in theme or specialty restaurants, such as a steak house, where meat represents the **signature item**.

signature item A menu item that is very popular; the restaurant is known for it.

grain-fed beef Beef from cattle that have been fed a grain-based diet, typically featuring corn.

grass-fed beef Beef from cattle that have a low percentage of body fat. Tends to be less flavorful than corn-fed beef.

concentrated agricultural feeding operations (CAFOs) Facilities in which livestock undergo intensive feeding or finishing before being slaughtered.

In addition to the possibility of featuring organic meats, restaurants may also consider whether to serve **grain-fed beef** versus **grass-fed beef** (see Figure 21.2). Most meats come from animals finished in **concentrated agricultural feeding operations (CAFOs)**. However, there are some environmental concerns with this practice, which are discussed in the sidebar by Robert Hartman. Alternatively, some restaurants feature meats from small farms and often include the name of the farm on the menu. Regardless of the type of meats purchased you must stay with your specialty, regardless of availability or increases in the as-purchased (AP) price.

Given the high cost of meats in relation to that of other foods, the restaurateur's goal is to utilize every edible morsel. Therefore, meat may appear as menu items in discrete ways. What is intended to be served once sometimes blossoms into an unwieldy number of meat-related menu items: the luncheon chef's special created from the preceding night's leftovers, a soup or stir-fry prepared from the trimmings from a large piece of meat, and new menu selections based on customer request.

Beef	Cured Meat and Sausage	Pork	Veal
Brisket	Bacon	Back rib	Breast
Bottom sirloin butt	Bologna	Boston butt	Cubed steak
Chuck	Bratwurst	Center-cut chop	Cutlet
Cubed steak	Breakfast sausage	Cutlet	Crown roast
Eye of round	Breseaola	Fat back	Hotel rack
Flank steak	Capicola	Fresh ham	Ground veal
Filet mignon	Corned beef	Ground pork	Leg
Ground beef	Frankfurter	Leg hocks	Loin chop
Inside round	Ham	Loin	Osso buco
London broil	Italian sausage	Loin chop	(Foreshank/Hindshank)
Outside round	Knockwurst	Loin steak	Rib Chop
Porterhouse steak	Liver sausage	Pigs feet	Round steak
Rib	(Braunschweiger)	Rib chop	Shank
Ribeye roll	Mortadella	Salt pork	Tenderloin
Ribeye steak	Pastrami	Shoulder hocks	
Sirloin tip	Pepperoni	Spare rib	
Short loin	Polish sausage	Tenderloin	
Short ribs	Prosciutto		
Skirt steak	Salami	**Variety Meat**	
Strip loin steak	Smoked sausage	Beef honeycomb	
Swiss steak		tripe	
T-bone steak	**Lamb**	Beef oxtail	
Tenderloin		Beef tongue	
Tenderloin steak	Breast	Calf liver	
Top blade steak	Ground lamb	Steer liver	
(Flatiron)	Hotel rack	Sweetbread	
Top sirloin butt	Leg	Veal brains	
Top sirloin steak	Loin	Veal heart	
Tri-tip steak	Loin chop	Veal liver	
	Rib chop	Veal kidney	
	Rump	Veal tail	
	Shank		
	Shoulder		

FIGURE 21.1 Popular types of meat products the foodservice industry uses.

FIGURE 21.2 Grass-fed cows.
©R. Hamilton Smith/GettyImages

■ Alternatives

Many alternatives for conventional meat items exist. Fish and poultry are excellent substitutes. Also, hospitality operators can take a chance on exotic types of meat dishes, such as buffalo, bison, and venison. In addition, they can experiment with different grades of meat. For instance, operators can use a lower meat grade from an older, tougher, but more flavorful animal when a moist cooking method is employed. Otherwise, they can purchase lower grades of meat and tenderize them chemically or mechanically. Meat recipes that contain several ingredients make good candidates for lower-cost substitutions. Meat loaves, stews, and pasta sauces and fillings can be manipulated by including or excluding certain fats, qualities of meat, and fillers. Also, meat alternatives, such as soybean extender, can be incorporated into certain recipes.

Although the list of meat alternatives is seemingly endless, operators always take a chance when they make substitutions. This is especially true when customers are used to one item and taste a substitute product that is unfamiliar, or when the replacements are visible to consumers, such as when a low-quality steak that has been mechanically or chemically tenderized is substituted for a naturally tender steak of higher quality.

■ The Quality Desired

As always, the quality hospitality operators need reflects the intended use of the product and the image they wish to project. Spending considerable time determining the quality of the product they want does not guarantee that the desired item is readily available.

One reason for this is that differences exist from animal to animal, and because many meat items come fresh, quality variations result. To minimize this phenomenon, most livestock farmers have standardized the care and feeding of their animals. In addition, this variability is generally less of a problem with processed meats. For example, pork that is cured for ham and bacon offers a great deal of predictability.

A second reason buyers cannot always find desired items is that meat of the highest (or lowest) quality grade may be in short supply. Because this can also thwart the operators' plans, buyers may need to rethink their strategies.

A third challenge relates to bid buying. Obtaining consistent quality should be a concern when purchasing in this manner. When bids are accepted, they often cover a long period. Changes in quality may become evident over time. The problems associated with finding consistent quality and a continuous supply of meat may drive buyers to stay with one supplier.

■ Type of Processing

Although buyers can still purchase a **side** of beef, which is half of an animal **carcass**, most buy fresh meat items that are butchered to some extent. Although many dining establishments prefer only fresh cuts of meats, numerous foodservice operations rely on frozen meat products to operate efficiently. Also, when it comes to some processed-meat items, such as bacon, ham, and bologna, most operations would never consider purchasing fresh meat and processing it in-house. Ultimately, buyers must decide on what type and amount of processing is most economical for the meat's intended use.

side   A lengthwise half of a carcass.

carcass   The whole body of a dead animal.

A key factor used in making this decision is the AP price; usually, it has a direct correlation with the degree of fabrication. A considerable spread may exist between the AP price per pound for "portion-cut" meat that needs nothing more than some cooking or heating, such as ready-to-cook sirloin steak, and the AP price per pound for a **wholesale cut** of meat, such as a whole loin, which can be butchered into sirloin steaks. An even greater AP-price-per-pound spread may exist between a portion-cut steak and a side of beef.

> **wholesale cut** Refers to a large cut of meat used to produce several retail cuts. It is smaller than a forequarter or hindquarter but larger than a retail cut.

Many restaurants find it more economical to let suppliers wield the cutting tools because it is too expensive to devote a great deal of space to a butcher shop. They prefer to concentrate on devoting as much space as possible to a revenue-generating dining room and lounge.

Still, some foodservice operations perform a great deal of fabrication in-house. They may have determined that in-house processing is more economical or that it enables them to have better control of the quality. Some may even use this feature in their marketing efforts. In any case, the hospitality industry generally thinks that in-house meat fabrication presents four major problems:

1. This practice requires additional labor hours and skilled laborers, which may lead to increased operating expenses, especially labor costs.

2. This practice tends to increase the level of pilferage; it is easy to steal items that are being pre-prepared, usually in a remote area of the kitchen.

3. Avoidable waste also tends to increase whenever hospitality operators engage in major production efforts.

4. Meat production creates a considerable amount of "working" dirt and waste products that must be removed continuously to prevent contamination. As such, an operation's sanitation needs increase substantially. The typical restaurant kitchen does not have the equipment, time, and skill needed to perform these duties adequately.

Conversely, some disadvantages exist with **portion-cut meats**. These drawbacks include the following:

> **portion-cut meat** Equal to one serving. Typically refers to precut steaks and chops that are all the same weight.

1. A premium may be charged for uniform weight, shape, and thickness. (This uniformity, however, may be very useful to relatively inexperienced cooks.)

2. Pilferage may increase with portion cuts of meat; they are easy to steal, especially because they usually come in convenient packages.

3. Sometimes, a case of precut steaks contains one or two steaks of demonstrably lower quality. Can the receiver catch this problem or will the cook notice the difference?

When purchasing in large quantities, some buyers may find it advantageous to choose frozen-meat items. With today's processing technology, freezing does not harm the products. Proper freezing, thawing, and cooking methods can make any quality differences in taste or texture almost imperceptible. Quality problems are usually due to improper handling.

Another option buyers can consider is convenience foods. Frozen-meat entrées, including fajitas, meatballs, and barbecue beef or pork, may not be popular in some hospitality operations, but college, hospital, and other off-site foodservices use these products readily. These prepared, portion-controlled items are sometimes used for large banquets and employee meals, too.

■ Reducing the AP Price and the EP Cost

Meat purchasers can find all sorts of ways to reduce the AP price while keeping the edible-portion (EP) cost, profit margins, and dollar profits acceptable. Some opt for substitutions, such as replacing meat with fish, offering casseroles instead of sandwich steaks, and widening the menu to include lower-cost products. This latter tactic, though, reduces both AP prices and menu prices. The food cost as a percentage of menu sales prices may decrease, but the sales revenue may also decline and cut into the number of dollars left to cover labor, overhead, and profits.

Buyers can also substitute meat of lower quality and tenderize it; purchase some "formed-meat" products, which are less expensive cuts of meat that have been "flaked," then, for instance, re-formed and sliced to resemble a steak; or add soybean extenders, as long as chefs follow the legal requirements. (For example, soybean-extended ground beef cannot be called "hamburger.")

Furthermore, hospitality operations can reduce the AP price and the EP cost by shrinking portion sizes. Alternately, instead of including a baked potato with the steak, they can charge extra for it. (This reduces the EP cost of the steak dinner, not the EP cost of the steak itself.) Yet another option is to consider serving coleslaw as a substitute for tossed salad. Remember, these substitution strategies always carry a certain amount of risk.

One way to protect the AP price and EP cost is to enter into a long-term contract with the supplier. This arrangement can help operators retain their standards of quality while considerably reducing the risk of both blurring their image and annoying their customers—a risk that may accompany the other cost-cutting strategies just noted. Buyers may realize a saving if they contract for, perhaps, a six-month supply of beef. Of course, they must have the wherewithal to procure the huge quantities that are necessary to interest a supplier. Consequently, only large chains regularly use this method. Not everyone in the hospitality industry thinks that firms can save money this way. For instance, the daily cash price for meat may drop considerably at any time during the contractual period.

hedging Attempting to reduce or avoid the risk of fluctuating AP prices by taking a position in the commodity futures market.

The **hedging** procedure (see Chapter 9) may be a viable way of maintaining a relatively stable AP price. Large foodservice companies that have the resources and skills needed to practice this procedure may save money in the long run.

As a practical matter, small operators may have to make do on a day-to-day basis. If they try to spend too much time concentrating on the AP price, they may neglect the EP cost. It may be better for small operators to concentrate on the EP cost, especially on ways of reducing it that represent little or no risk. For instance, they should ensure that there is minimal waste in production and service, minimal shrinkage, zero pilferage, and so forth.

Every once in a while, buyers may find a bargain. Unfortunately, most bargains come from new suppliers in the form of temporary introductory offers. In addition, bargains may force buyers to purchase a new convenience entrée at a special AP price or to take fresh-frozen meat in lieu of fresh-refrigerated meat.

Normal quantity buy opportunities do appear. Aside from items on a move list, however, fewer meat bargains are available in comparison to those offered in other product areas. Furthermore, buyers do not shift suppliers or meat specifications quickly. Meat is a major purchase, so meat buyers practice discretion more widely.

ENVIRONMENTAL IMPACTS OF MEAT PRODUCTION
Robert Hartman, Principal, Robert Hartman Food and Beverage Management & Consulting

The scientific consensus about the effect of human activity on the global climate raises concerns for consumers. They want to know about the environmental impacts of the foods that they consume, and meat is no exception.

Most livestock production involves a blend of open grazing for extended periods, followed by an intensive feeding or "finishing" process. While grazing in open fields, livestock animals consume mostly grasses, seeds, and other forms of roughage and protein. During the finishing phase, animals are penned and given high-calorie, grain-based feeds to bring them up to market weight or maximize their production of milk or eggs. Facilities in which finishing occurs are referred to as concentrated agricultural feeding operations (CAFOs). The relative periods of open grazing and finishing differ widely depending on the type of animal, the availability of CAFOs, and what the animal produces (that is, meat, milk, eggs, and/or leather).

Critics of modern livestock production raise a number of concerns about the environmental impacts of CAFOs and their role in meat production.

- **Greenhouse gas emissions (GHGs).** According to the United Nations Environmental Programme, "the livestock sector [accounts] for a 10–25 percent share of greenhouse gas emissions worldwide."[1] These gases trap heat in the atmosphere and include the methane and nitrous oxide that are released by the animals themselves and the decomposition of their manures, as well as the production of fertilizers used in the grain they consume.

- **Groundwater and air pollution.** The large quantities of animal manures produced by CAFOs can cause toxic runoff and pollute water sources. Manures also generate noxious odors and provide habitat for microbial pathogens that can infect people and animals.[2]

- **Consumption of grain that people could eat.** According to Stanford University's School of Earth Sciences, and Worldwatch Institute, it takes approximately seven pounds of grain to produce one pound of beef.[3] Although feed-grain is raised for animal consumption, it is also suitable for milling into flours and other products that might better sustain a growing human population.

- **Water consumption.** Stanford also cites a figure of 12,000 gallons for every pound of beef, or enough water for 250 showers—more than 60 showers for every quarter-pound burger

- **Concentrated use of antibiotics and the risk of antibiotic resistance.** The close confinement of large numbers of animals together raises the risks of contagious illness spreading among them. To prevent this, and to increase growth rates, CAFOs typically rely on low-level doses of antibiotic drugs. Physicians for Social Responsibility estimates that 80 percent of antibiotics used in the United States are for this purpose, which provides an environment for antibiotic-resistant bacteria to emerge. According to the Centers for Disease Control and Prevention, as of 2013, approximately 23,000 people die from antibiotic-resistant bacteria annually in the United States.[4]

ENVIRONMENTAL IMPACTS OF MEAT PRODUCTION   (continued)

■ REFERENCES

1. United Nations Environmental Programme, Global Environmental Alert Service, "Growing Greenhouse Gas Emissions Due to Meat Production," October 12, 2012, http://na.unep.net/geas/getUNEPPageWithArticleIDScript.php?article_id=92.

2. United States Environmental Protection Agency, "Ag 101, Beef Production," www.epa.gov/oecaagct/ag101/printbeef.html.

3. Stanford University School of Earth Sciences, Earth Systems Program, Sustainable Choices, "Reduce Meat Consumption," http://sustainablechoices.stanford.edu/actions/at_the_store/reducemeat.html.

4. Centers for Disease Control and Prevention, "Antibiotic Resistance Threats in the United States, 2013," www.cdc.gov/drugresistance/threat-report-2013/

PRIMARY SELECTION FACTORS

As with all products, management decides on the quality and style of meat desired. Then, either alone or in concert with other personnel, management evaluates several of these selection factors when determining standards of quality desired and suppliers.

■ Intended Use

As always, buyers must determine the exact intended use of an item to be able to prepare the appropriate, relevant specification. For example, if a restaurant is serving roast prime rib, it would need to purchase a form of the whole rib. However, if it serves ribeye steaks, it would have the option of buying the wholesale cut and cutting the steaks or buying portion cut steaks. For ground beef, the quality and exact type needed might be different if it is going to be used for a signature hamburger versus as an ingredient in an Italian meat sauce.

■ Exact Name

As with all other products, it is very important for hospitality operators to note the **exact name** of the meat items they want so they do not receive unsuitable products. To some extent, identifying the exact product that they prefer is a bit easier in this channel of distribution than it is in some other product lines. Over the years, a great deal of standardization has evolved, spurred by the meat industry, meat users, and the U.S. Department of Agriculture (USDA).

> **exact name**   Indication of a product or service's specific type, quality, and style.

The federal government has set several **standards of identity** for meat products. For instance, if buyers specify that they want hamburger, they will get a mixture that is 70 percent lean meat and 30 percent fat. Of course, as with all standards of identity, a producer is free to improve on the government definition. In this example, the producer can use beef from just about any part of the animal. So, if buyers expect to receive a specific type of meat in their hamburger, they must include this information in their specification.

Using standards of identity, therefore, is a bit risky unless buyers include additional appropriate information on the specification. They will be able to reduce this amount of information considerably if they use the Institutional Meat Purchase Specifications (IMPS) numbering system in their specification. These numbers take the place of part of a meat specification. For example, if buyers order a 1112 ribeye steak, they will get a particular style and trim.

The IMPS numbers evolved from a cooperative effort by the **North American Meat Institute (NAMI** [formerly National Association of Meat Purveyors]), the **National Livestock and Meat Board**, foodservice purchasing agents, and the USDA's **Agricultural Marketing Service (AMS)** Livestock Division. These numbers are included in **The Meat Buyer's Guide (MBG)**, published by NAMI. In addition to the numbers, a description and a picture of each item are included. This is very desirable to buyers who can then "order by the numbers" and be assured of receiving the exact cut of meat they want (see Figure 21.3).

standard of identity
A U.S. government regulation that establishes what a food product must be to carry a certain name. For example, what a food product must be to be labeled "strawberry preserves."

North American Meat Institute (NAMI) Trade organization representing meat processing companies and associates who share a continuing commitment to provide their customers with safe, reliable, and consistent meat, poultry, seafood, game, and other related products.

National Livestock and Meat Board Group made up of representatives from all areas of the meat industry. Its primary objective is the promotion of all red meats (beef, lamb, and pork) through research, education, and information sharing.

Agricultural Marketing Service (AMS) Agency of the USDA that establishes federal grading standards for several food products, under authority of the Agricultural Marketing Act.

The Meat Buyers Guide (MBG) Another term for Institutional Meat Purchase Specification (IMPS) number.

Series Number	Series Name
100	Fresh Beef
200	Fresh Lamb and Mutton
300	Fresh Veal
400	Fresh Pork
500	Cured, Cured and Smoked, and Fully-Cooked Pork Products
600	Cured, Dried, Cooked, and Smoked Beef Products
700	Variety Meats and Edible Byproducts
800	Sausage Products
900	Fresh Goat

FIGURE 21.3 Institutional Meat Purchase Specifications (IMPS) Categories.

IMPS/NAMI number
Another term for
Institutional Meat Purchase
Specification (IMPS) num-
ber.

retail cut   A small
meat item produced
from a wholesale cut.
Alternately, another term
for portion cut.

variety meat   Refers to
organ meat, such as liver,
kidney, and so forth.

edible byproduct
Trimmings of food items,
such as meat and seafood,
that can be processed into
another type of menu
item. For instance, meat
trimmings left over from
cutting steaks may be
processed into sausages or
hamburgers.

The IMPS numbers, sometimes referred to as the **IMPS/NAMI numbers** or the MBG numbers, provide a considerable degree of convenience. Typical buyers would never think of preparing meat product specifications without first consulting this major reference book. IMPS numbers are indexed according to product category. The first digit of the number refers to the type of product; the remaining digits indicate a specific cut and trim (see Figure 21.4 for the IMPS numbers for some meat cuts).

If, for some reason, buyers do not wish to use the IMPS numbers when preparing specifications, they must at least be able to indicate the exact cut of meat they want or the exact type of processed item they need. Fresh meat comes in five basic cuts: (1) the whole carcass; (2) a side, essentially half a carcass; (3) a forequarter or hindquarter, essentially one quarter of a carcass; (4) a wholesale (primal) cut; and (5) a **retail cut**. Numerous other cutting terms, such as hotel-sliced bacon, Spencer-cut prime rib of beef, and square-cut chuck, are involved, too. Buyers are responsible for becoming familiar with these cuts and related terminology, especially if they decide to forgo the use of IMPS numbers.

In addition to cuts of meat, buyers need to be knowledgeable about other commonly used trade terms. Two major ones are **variety meats** and other **edible byproducts**, such as liver, tongue, heart, hams, and sausages, which are preserved, usually dried or salted, chunked or chopped meat and spices shaped into tubes. Some sausages have skins; some do not. Some are cooked; some are not.

The federal government and trade associations can modify current terminology via additions or deletions. The government can also modify definitions of the terms used in its grading practices and grading standards. Buyers should stay abreast of these changes if they purchase a great deal of meat. You can get more information on terminology and standards by consulting the websites of the American Association of Meat Processors (AAMP), the National Cattleman's Beef Association (NCBA), and the North American Meat Institute (NAMI).

If buyers need a great deal of processed meat products, they must be concerned with the exact name, specific form, and culinary quality of these items. Standards of identity exist for some products; for example, a minimum formula exists for pre-prepared beef stew. Generally, though, these identity formulas are not very useful as a major selection factor for processed-meat products.

■ Point of Origin

truth-in-menu   Guidelines menu planners use
to avoid unintentionally
misleading the customer
by ensuring accurate
descriptions and prices
of all menu offerings.
Alternately, refers to legislation prohibiting misrepresentations on the menu.

Occasionally, a foodservice operator notes on the menu the point of origin for a meat entrée. For example, guests may see "Iowa Corn-Fed Beef," "West Virginia Ham," "Wisconsin Veal," "Colorado Lamb," or "Belgian Blue Cattle" (a rare, costly, imported breed that is exceptionally low in fat and calories) listed on a menu. If hospitality operations want to use this form of advertising, they must purchase the appropriate product or else they will be violating any relevant **truth-in-menu** legislation.

Beef rib steak (IMPS/NAMPS 1103).

Beef porterhouse steak
(IMPS/NAMPS 1173).

Lamb loin chop (IMPS/NAMPS
1232A).

Lamb, boneless shoulder, rolled
and tied (IMPS/NAMPS 208).

Pork loin chops (IMPS/NAMPS 1410).

Pork tenderloin (IMPS/NAMPS 415).

FIGURE 21.4 IMPS numbers for some meat products.
Source: Gisslen, Professional Cooking, 7th Edition, Copyright 2011. Reprinted with permission of John Wiley and Sons, Inc.

■ Imitation Meat Products

imitation meat products
Products that approximate the aesthetic qualities (primarily texture, flavor, and appearance) and/or chemical characteristics of specific types of meat. Also referred to as meat analogues, meat substitutes, mock meats, and faux meats.

Several **imitation meat products** are available. For instance, hospitality operators can use soybean and oat bran as meat extenders. Alternately, they can use these products to create such items as "bacon bits." Many meat producers sell "ham," "hot dogs," and other similar items that are made with chicken, fish, and/or turkey.

Imitation meat products seem to be very popular in the on-site segment of the foodservice industry. However, there is no reason why they cannot enjoy success in any type of foodservice operation. If operators introduce them as a new "alternative" menu item or emphasize their nutritional value, they may sell briskly.

Some foodservice operators like imitation meat products because they can manipulate the fat content. This generally translates into a lower AP price; however, a low-fat product may sometimes be more expensive than the traditional item. Imitation meats may even have positive health implications. Reducing the fat content and/or substituting polyunsaturated oils can lead to an imitation meat product that is lower in calories and cholesterol compared to the real item.

■ U.S. Government Inspection

Federal Meat Inspection Act Establishes the ability of the federal government to inspect and label meats before and after slaughter.

The inspection of meat for wholesomeness has been mandatory since the passage of the **Federal Meat Inspection Act** in 1907. This law applies to all raw meat sold in interstate commerce, as well as meat exported to other countries. Processed products, such as sausages, frozen dinners, canned meats, and soups made with meat, must also be inspected. An exception is rabbit meat; it is not required to be federally inspected. However, the rabbit industry has a voluntary program that requires rabbit meat packers to pay for inspection.

Federal inspection falls under the jurisdiction of the USDA's Food Safety and Inspection Service (FSIS). The principal inspection system the FSIS uses for most meat-slaughtering and -processing facilities is the Hazard Analysis Critical Control Point (HACCP). The food industry instituted HACCP to ensure that food safety and nonfood safety conditions exist in all critical stages of food handling by reducing and eliminating defects that pass through traditional inspection. FSIS inspectors conduct online carcass inspection and verification inspection to make certain that plants are meeting the FSIS's performance standards for food safety or nonfood safety defects.

Wholesale Meat Act
Enhances the USDA's authority to regulate safety in the meat industry. Requires state inspection of meat production to be at least equal to the federal inspection program.

States with companies that sell meats solely through intrastate commerce channels have the discretion of conducting their own meat-inspection programs. Under the 1967 **Wholesale Meat Act**, these state inspection programs are required to be at least equal to the federal inspection programs. For more information on the Federal Meat Inspection Act, see the Regulatory Information and Legislation section of the FDA website.

The federal inspection program begins with the approval of plans for a slaughtering or processing plant to ensure that the facilities, equipment, and procedures can adequately provide for safe and sanitary operations. Facilities and equipment in plants must be easy to clean and to keep clean. The floor plan, water supply, waste disposal methods, and lighting must be approved for each plant facility. Each day before operations begin, the inspector checks the plant and continues the inspection throughout the day to ensure that sanitary conditions are maintained. If, at any time, it is determined that the equipment is not properly cleaned or an unsanitary condition is present, slaughtering or processing operations are stopped until corrective steps have been taken.

The inspection of animals is done both before and after slaughtering. Before slaughter, USDA inspectors examine all livestock for signs of disease, and any animal appearing sick undergoes a special examination. No dead or dying animal is allowed to enter the slaughtering plant. After slaughter, the inspectors examine each carcass and its internal organs for signs of disease or contamination that would make all or part of the carcass unfit as human food. To ensure uniformity in the inspection process, veterinary supervisors regularly monitor the inspectors' procedures and work.

Meat that passes the rigorous USDA inspection is marked with a federal-inspection stamp (see Figure 21.5). This stamp indicates the number of the meat-processing plant where the meat was slaughtered and packed. The stamp does not appear on all meat cuts; usually, it is visible only on wholesale cuts of meat. Some retail cuts, however, may include remnants of an inspection stamp unless it is completely removed during the cutting and trimming process.

FIGURE 21.5 Federal inspection stamps used for meat products.
Courtesy of U.S. Department of Agriculture

The inspection program the USDA provides is the most trusted inspection program available. The program the United States military uses to inspect its meat products before use in troop feeding is comparable to the USDA's procedures.[1] Although several types of inspection programs exist, they are not the same as USDA inspection for wholesomeness. For instance, religious inspections are performed in some meat plants. These inspections certify only that the meat items satisfy the religious codes, not that they have met a certain standard of quality.

In addition to its meat inspections, the federal government also prepares guidelines on such topics as humane slaughter techniques, animal husbandry, and transportation techniques.

■ Other Inspection Factors

Some buyers may be concerned with the various chemicals and additives that suppliers can use to enhance meat production. If buyers are worried, they should seek out meat producers who do not use these methods. Alternately, buyers can hire private inspectors, such as the **USDA Acceptance Service**, to ensure that meat products meet their standards. The USDA also has an inspection program for which buyers can contract that guarantees that the meat they purchase is free of pesticides and pesticide residues.

> **USDA Acceptance Service** Agency that, for a fee, will help buyers prepare meat specifications and oversee the purchase and delivery of meat.

The organic meat program ensures that organic livestock be given access to the outdoors, fresh air and water, sunshine, grass, and pasture and are fed 100 percent organic feed, which is also a vegetarian diet. The organic label is one that is overseen by the USDA by way of certifying agencies that inspect and audit facilities for compliance.[2]

If buyers purchase meat that comes from another country, its inspection for wholesomeness may not be as demanding as the one U.S. meat must undergo. For instance, many U.S. foodservice operations purchase large quantities of beef from other countries. The federal government must inspect these meat products before they are allowed to enter the United States, but the inspection is hampered somewhat because some exporting countries use additives and chemicals that U.S. regulations do not cover. As far as we can determine, this practice has not caused any health hazards. Again, however, if buyers are very concerned with product safety, they should indicate on the specification that they want considerably more inspection than is normally provided.

Agricultural Marketing Act   Law that regulates the marketing of agricultural and meat products.

Agricultural Marketing Service (AMS), Live Stock & Feed Division   Agency that oversees and regulates the marketing of meat products.

U.S. quality grades   Rating system used by the federal government to indicate the quality of food products. Not all foods have established federal government quality grading standards.

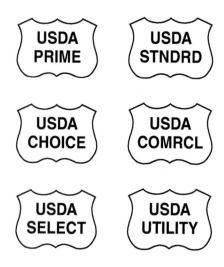

FIGURE 21.6 Federal grade stamps used for meat items.
Courtesy of United States Department of Agriculture

U.S. GOVERNMENT GRADES AND PACKER'S BRANDS

■ Quality Grades

In addition to mandatory inspection, the USDA offers voluntary grading programs. It has long recognized the importance of a uniform system of grading slaughter animals to facilitate the production, marketing, and distribution of livestock and meats. These grading programs also provide an objective evaluation of the culinary quality and edible yield of fresh meat items. The initial U.S. standards for grades of beef were formulated in 1916, with the official standards adopted in 1928. Today, these services are conducted under the regulations of the **Agricultural Marketing Act** of 1946. The **Agricultural Marketing Service (AMS), Live Stock & Feed Division** publishes the grades (see Figure 21.6).

Quality grading systems exist for beef, lamb, pork, and veal; voluntary yield grading systems are available for beef and lamb. Although no formal yield-grading system exists for pork, these items' **U.S. quality grades** are based primarily on yield; other culinary characteristics play a lesser role. Veal is not graded for yield.

Because grading services are not mandated, they must be purchased. Nonetheless, purchasing such services is popular with many meat processors, distribution intermediaries, and retailers because it is quite common for buyers to use government grades as one selection factor when they purchase meat. However, some cattle breeders and meat packers feel that grading is too capricious and inconsistent, and some people are not happy with the changes and proposed changes (usually done for health and nutrition concerns) in the grading systems that have occurred over the years. Nevertheless, approximately 50 percent of the meat sold in the United States is graded for quality. Despite the problems associated with federal grades, those mentioned earlier among others, buyers have not been deterred from using those systems. Buyers may not rely so heavily on the grades as they once did, but most meat specifications contain some reference to a U.S. grade.

Quality grades for slaughter cattle are based on an evaluation of factors related to the palatability of the meat. Federal graders primarily evaluate beef quality by the amount and distribution of **finish**, that is, the degree of fatness; the firmness of muscling; and the physical characteristics of the animal that are associated with maturity. Other grading factors the federal grader evaluates include the age of the animal at the time of slaughter, the sex of the animal, the color of the flesh, the amount of external finish, the shape and form of the carcass, the amount of **marbling**, or the little streams of fat that run through the meat, and the number of defects and blemishes.

U.S. quality grades for beef also are subject to several **limiting rules**. The USDA grading system strictly defines some, whereas others grant some discretion to the federal grader. The most severe limiting rule, and the one that normally causes a great deal of anxiety among meat producers, is the regulation associated with the beef animals' **maturity class**. These animals are divided into five maturity classes:

> finish   Refers primarily to the fat cover on a carcass.
>
> marbling   Fat within the muscle tissue. Important grading factor for beef items.
>
> limiting rule   Federal regulation that stipulates if a product to be graded scores very low on one grading factor, it cannot receive a high grade regardless of its total score for all grading factors.
>
> maturity class   Used to categorize an animal's age at time of slaughter. Important grading and selection factor for beef.

Class A: Age at the time of slaughter is 9 to 30 months.
Class B: Age at the time of slaughter is 30 to 42 months.
Class C: Age at the time of slaughter is 42 to 72 months
Class D: Age at the time of slaughter is 72 to 96 months
Class E: Age at the time of slaughter is greater than 96 months.

It is the grader's responsibility to determine an animal's physiological age at the time of slaughter. The grader does this by examining the color and texture of the lean meat, the condition of the bones, and the amount of hardening, or ossification, of the cartilage.

Beef animals' quality grades are affected by their maturity class. For instance, regardless of the quality present in Class C cattle, it cannot be graded Prime. In general, any beef animal older than 42 months at time of slaughter cannot receive the highest-quality grade regardless of the score it received on the other factors the grader considers.

The federal quality grades for beef are

1. **Prime.** This is the best product available. Tender and very juicy, Prime beef contains 8 to 10 percent fat. Usually, the animal has been grain-fed for at least 180 days to develop the exceptionally large amount of firm, white fat. The meat is extremely flavorful.

2. **Choice.** Choice grade beef contains at least 5 percent fat. Three levels exist: High U.S. Choice, Average U.S. Choice, and U.S. Choice. High Choice is similar to Prime, although the animal has been grain-fed for only about 150 days. Average Choice indicates that the animal has been grain-fed about 120 days; U.S. Choice, for about 90 days. Foodservice operators normally purchase one of the Choice grades of meat.

3. **Select.** This beef is a very lean product, containing 4 percent fat. The fat on this product usually is not very white, nor very firm. This grade is popular in supermarkets. It is a low-cost item and is more healthful than higher-quality grades, but it lacks flavor and tenderness. Select is typically sold through supermarkets and grocery stores.

4. **Standard.** Although similar to Select, Standard beef is even less juicy and tender. It has a very mild flavor. This product also tends to be referred to as "grass-fed beef."

5. **Commercial.** Beef from older cattle, Commercial grade is especially lacking in tenderness. Usually, dairy cows receive this quality grade. Because of the animals' age at the time of slaughter, some of this meat may be quite flavorful.

6, 7, 8. **Utility, Cutter, and Canner.** No age limitation exists for these quality grades. Old breeding stock (older cows and bulls) is usually classified into one of these three quality grade categories. Generally, these products are not available as fresh meat. Rather, these grades are intended for use by commercial food processors.

> **feathering**   Amount of fat streaks in an animal's ribs and inside flank muscles.

Lamb quality grades are based primarily on the color, texture, and firmness of the flesh; quality and firmness of the finish; the proportion of meat to bone; and the amount and quality of the **feathering**, which is the fat streaking in the ribs and the fat streaking in the inside flank muscles.

The federal quality grades for lamb are

- Prime
- Choice
- Good
- Utility

> **manufacturing grade**
> A very low grade given to food products that are not intended to be sold as fresh items, but are meant to be used by processors to produce a finished item. For example, low-grade beef usually is purchased by a processor who makes things such as canned chili or canned beef stew.

If a foodservice operation offers fresh lamb on the menu, the Prime and Choice quality grades are normally used. Lower-graded products are not intended for use as fresh meat items. As is typically the case in the hospitality industry, commercial food processors primarily use **manufacturing grades** to prepare convenience food items.

Pork quality grades are based almost exclusively on yield. The most important consideration is the amount of finish, especially as it relates to color, firmness, and texture. Feathering is also an important consideration. Grain-fed pork makes better-quality products, which are far superior to those animals that are given other types of feeds.

The federal quality grades for pork are

- No. 1
- No. 2
- No. 3
- No. 4
- U.S. Utility

Most pork is used by commercial food processors to fabricate a variety of convenience and processed items, such as ham and bacon. As a result of this and the fact that most pork is separated into small cuts before it leaves the meat-packing plant, very few pork carcasses are graded for quality. Meat packers and purchasing agents rely on the various packers' brands (i.e., packers' "grades") that are available.

If fresh pork is included on the menu, the typical foodservice operation necessarily must use the No. 1 or No. 2 quality grade, or equivalent packers' brands. Lower-quality items will shrink too much during the cooking process, resulting in an unacceptable finished menu item.

Veal quality grades are based on the color, texture, and firmness of the flesh; the proportion of meat to bone; the quality and firmness of the finish; and the amount and quality of the feathering. High-quality veal will have a pink color and smooth flesh.

The federal quality grades for veal are

- Prime
- Choice
- Good
- Standard
- Utility
- Cull

The Prime and Choice quality grades are intended for use as fresh products. The lower-quality products tend to be tough and, therefore, are more commonly used to fabricate convenience items.

For more information on U.S. government inspection and grades, see the website of the USDA Agricultural Marketing Service.

Whether certain types of meats are graded evolves as products become more popular in the marketplace. For example, the USDA is investigating whether to establish voluntary grading standards for goat meat, which is very common in some cuisines, such as Mexican and Indian.[3] More restaurants are serving game meats such as bison and elk, which are not graded in the United States. Because a large part of the grading is based on marbling and these animals have very minimal fat levels, the grading criteria would be limited.[4] However, in countries such as Canada, Australia, and New Zealand, some farm-raised game, such as venison, is graded.[5]

> **U.S. yield grades** Rating system used by the federal government to indicate the yield of meat products. Not all meats have established federal government yield grading standards.

■ Product Yield

The federal government provides a voluntary yield grading service for beef and lamb (see figure 21.7). **U.S. yield grades** are numbered 1 through 5, with Yield Grade 1 representing the highest yield of cuts and Yield Grade 5, the lowest. Grading criteria are based on these factors: (1) thickness of fat over ribeye; (2) area of ribeye; (3) percent of kidney, pelvic, and heart fat; and (4) carcass weight. Some limiting rules apply. For instance, USDA Prime beef cannot earn a Yield Grade of 1 or 2 because of its high percentage of fat, which reduces its edible yield.

Prime beef has a great deal of marbling—and, hence, flavor—and the amount of muscle is considerably reduced for this quality grade. For similar

FIGURE 21.7 A federal yield grade stamp used to indicate the yield of a carcass.
Courtesy of United States Department of Agriculture

reasons, USDA Choice beef also cannot earn a Yield Grade 1. So, to a certain degree, quality and yield grades are interrelated.

Buyers who purchase beef sides, quarters, or wholesale cuts want to specify a desired yield grade, but with such large cuts of beef, an exact yield grade cannot always be specified. Instead, a yield range must be denoted. For example, a buyer may purchase a USDA Commercial beef brisket, with a U.S. Yield Grade 1–2, or its equivalent.

Buyers who purchase only retail cuts can use the federal government standards to specify an exact yield grade. For example, a specification for sirloin strip steak can state that it must be cut from a beef carcass that carries U.S. Yield Grade 1, or its equivalent.

If buyers use the IMPS system and/or the USDA yield grades, they can be assured of standardized edible yields for the fresh products they purchase. If, however, they do not utilize these systems, they will need to indicate on the specification the minimum yield, or the maximum trim, they will accept.

No formal yield grading system is available for pork and veal. Recall, though, that the U.S. quality grades for pork are based primarily on yield. The pork grades are sometimes referred to as "yield standards." The U.S. No. 1 pork grade represents the leanest, meatiest product, whereas the U.S. No. 4 product has about twice as much fat and one-third less muscle.

■ Packers' Brands (or Equivalent)

Many meat producers have developed their own grading procedures for branding their fresh meat. As mentioned earlier, this branding system is sometimes referred to as "packers' grades." For instance, JBS® USA sells 5 Star® and 5 Star Reserve® meats and Showcase® ground beef. A significant number of foodservice buyers find this procedure quite acceptable. Although packers' grades are similar to federal grades, they may not reflect an objective viewpoint.

Some meat producers sell "certified organic" products. A qualifying entity must have: (1) standards for what constitutes an agricultural product that is "organically" produced, and (2) a system for ensuring that the product meets those standards. Once the associated animal husbandry and production methods meet USDA standards, the meat items can be labeled as "certified organic by [the certifying entity]."

Any type of processed meat, other than fresh-frozen or portion-cut, is often purchased on the strength of a brand name. Most pork products, particularly those that are cured, are purchased this way. In almost every instance, these brand names are the only indication of quality. We have seen few specifications for cold cuts that did not rely on a brand name or its equivalent. (It is possible to detail the material used in these items. For a product like breakfast sausage, it would be easy to specify the amount of pork, fat, seasonings, water, and type of grind. For most other types of products in this area, it would not be this simple.)

Packers' brands are sometimes used when purchasing portion-cut meats. Buyers should be concerned with uniformity. Although portion-cut items have a standardized weight, not all packers necessarily supply the same shape. Second, the packaging can differ drastically; steaks may be individually wrapped and neatly stacked, or tossed together in a box. In addition, equal weights are not necessarily an indicator of uniform appearance; some items may be sloppily cut, with excess nicks and tears.

Other forms of brand name identification exist in the meat channel of distribution. For instance, the SYSCO brand Supreme Angus Beef products include only young beef of predominantly Angus breed that fall within the upper two-thirds of the USDA Choice grade. Also, if a meat packer's products meet the quality standards that the popular **Certified Angus Beef® Program** mandates, they are allowed to carry the certification seal. The program, developed by the **American Angus Association**, stipulates that a beef product must meet 10 stringent guidelines, including having at least modest marbling, being in the youngest maturity class, and qualifying for U.S. Yield Grade 1, 2, or 3.[6]

The list of packer/processor members of the NAMI is a good reference to find the names of meat brands.

> **Certified Angus Beef® Program** Group that monitors and regulates the sale of Angus meat that has met its mandated quality standards.
>
> **American Angus Association** An organization that serves the beef cattle industry. Its primary objective is to help the industry increase the production of consistently high-quality beef that will satisfy consumers throughout the world.

SIZE, FORM, PACKAGING, AND RELATED CONSIDERATIONS

■ Product Size

Invariably, buyers must indicate the size of the particular piece of meat they order. This task is made easy because the MBG notes **weight ranges** for wholesale cuts of meat, as well as standardized portion sizes for retail cuts. For example, all large cuts are categorized into four weight ranges: A, B, C, and D. Small retail cuts can be purchased in several sizes. For instance, the IMPS regulations stipulate that portion cuts of beef specified less than 6 ounces must be accurate within ¼ ounce; those specified between 6 to 12 ounces must be accurate to within ½ ounce; those specified between 12 to 24 ounces must be accurate to within ¾ ounce, and those specified more than 24 ounces must be accurate to within 1 ounce. There are also tolerance limits for fat limitations and thickness of beef portion cuts.

> **weight range** Indication of the approximate size of a product the buyer wishes to purchase. Used when it is impossible or impractical to specify an exact weight.

If buyers purchase processed convenience items, such as frozen, prepared, stuffed pork chops, a size indication may also be required. Usually, a particular packer's brand carries only one size, so if buyers consistently indicate the same brand on their specification, they will not need to specify product size information.

■ Size of Container

Container sizes are standardized in the meat channel of distribution. Processed products come in package sizes that normally range from about 5 pounds to more than 50 pounds. For instance, frozen, pre-prepared barbecue beef may be packed in a 5-pound Cryovac® bag, packed six bags to a case. Alternately, the beef may be packed in a 5-pound, oven-ready, foil tray, which is sometimes referred to as a **steam-table pack**, packed six trays to a case.

> **steam-table pack** Convenience food items packed in a container that can be popped into an oven or combi-steamer to reheat the food inside. When hot, the top of the container is removed and the container is then placed directly into a steam table or chaffing dish and kept warm for service. The typical container is usually made out of aluminum.

FIGURE 21.8 Shrink-wrapped beef.
©*kcline/Getty Images*

catch weight The approximate weight in a case of product. Used when it is not possible to specify an exact weight. For instance, if you purchase a case of whole, fresh fish, you usually cannot specify the exact total weight of all pieces of fish, but you can ask for an approximate total weight of the case.

shrink-wrap Product is packed in plastic and a vacuum is pulled through it so that air is removed and the wrapping collapses to fit snugly around the product. A type of controlled atmosphere packaging (CAP).

Fresh, portion-cut meat products are usually packed in 10-pound cases. Some, such as ground beef, normally come in 5-pound and 10-pound Cryovac® bags. Fresh, wholesale cuts of meat are typically packed in a container that is big enough to accommodate them. For example, if buyers order beef rib, IMPS number 109, weight range C (9 to 22 pounds each), the items will usually be packed three to a case. In such instances, buyers would not specify the size of the container if an accurate size could not be determined. Another option is to specify a **catch weight** (approximate weight) of 60 pounds per case.

If buyers purchase canned or bottled merchandise, they must specify the appropriate can number or volume designation. For instance, they can purchase canned chili in a No. 10 can and beef jerky in a 1-gallon jar.

■ Type of Packaging Material

Packaging materials play an integral role in maintaining product quality by minimizing the degree of product deterioration. As a result, meat buyers should specify materials that optimize product quality in accordance with intended use. The typical packaging used in the industry comprises moisture- and vapor-proof materials. Cryovac® plastic, or its equivalent, is particularly popular because it is ideal when a meat packer wants to **shrink-wrap** the product; this involves packing the meat in plastic and pulling a vacuum through the parcel so that air is removed and the wrapping collapses to fit snugly around the product (see Figure 21.8).

Packaging quality has a significant effect on a meat product's AP price. Most suppliers adhere to standardized materials. However, a supplier who seeks to undercut a competitor could easily do so by using inferior packaging materials. This is false economy because buyers must be concerned with protecting meat properly, especially if it is or will be frozen.

■ Packaging Procedure

The packaging procedure for meat items parallels those procedures used in the poultry and fish channels of distribution, except that meat is not normally ice packed. The choice of packaging procedures varies. Large cuts of meat are necessarily slab-packed in containers that are big enough to hold them. Portion cuts are usually layered, but if buyers prefer, the packer will wrap each portion cut individually and then layer them in the case. Bacon comes in a **shingle pack**, which is the way it normally appears in a supermarket; a **layout pack**, in which several bacon strips are placed on oven paper and the cook can then conveniently place a layer of this bacon on a sheet pan and pop it into the oven; or a **bulk pack**, which is a type of slab-packing procedure. Not every supplier offers a wide range of packaging options because this practice adds to the cost of doing business. However, most suppliers will accommodate buyers' needs if they are willing to pay for these services.

■ Product Form

Once again, we note the usefulness of the MBG. If buyers use the IMPS numbers when specifying meat cuts and sellers follow them, the meat will be cut and trimmed according to the standards that exist for those items. If buyers are purchasing processed items, they can rely, to some extent, on the MBG because it contains IMPS numbers for several convenience items. However, many more items are available in the meat channel of distribution that are not noted in this reference book. Buyers must be very careful to indicate the exact product desired; usually, the best way for buyers to ensure that they obtain a suitable convenience product is to rely on a packer's brand name.

■ Preservation Method

Most meat products that foodservice buyers purchase are preserved in one of two ways: refrigerated or frozen. Canned, dehydrated, and pickled products are also available. For example, buyers can purchase canned soups and canned chili products; however, many operators tend to favor the frozen varieties.

Meat is also preserved by **curing** and/or **smoking**. Curing is accomplished when the meat is subjected to a combination of salt, sugar, **sodium nitrite**, and other ingredients. Smoking preserves the meat and, in most instances, cooks it as well. Many cured items are also smoked. Foodservice buyers purchase a good deal of these products. The primary factors used for the selection of cured and smoked meats are the unique flavor, texture, and aroma that these **preservation methods** create. Usually, these products are refrigerated when delivered to a hospitality operation, though many of them could be frozen. For instance, bacon, which is a cured and smoked product, may be refrigerated or frozen.

The hospitality industry has witnessed a great deal of controversy concerning the use of nitrites. Sodium nitrite combines with certain amino acids to form nitrosamine, a carcinogenic substance. Nitrites continue to be used, though in lesser amounts than before, because of their superior preservation qualities and because they can control the growth of *Clostridium botulinum*, the deadly bacterium that causes **botulism** food poisoning. Nitrites also are responsible for the characteristic color and flavor of cured meat products.

---

shingle pack Layering product in such a way that the pieces overlap and do not completely cover one another. May be done for things like sliced bacon.

layout pack Products are packed in layers that can be lifted from the case and placed in other containers for storage or production. For example, layout sliced bacon may be layered on baking sheets that can be placed on sheet pans and cooked off in the oven.

bulk pack Package containing a large amount of product. Unit cost for products packed this way is typically much less than individually wrapped products, or products purchased in small packages.

curing A preservation process involving the use of ingredients such as salt, sugar, and sodium nitrite. The process also imparts flavor.

smoking Technique used to extend the shelf life of food, particularly meat. Alternately, technique used to add flavor and tenderization to meat.

sodium nitrite Preservative used in meat that helps prevent botulism. Also imparts a characteristic color, flavor, and texture to the meat.

preservation method A procedure, such as refrigeration, freezing, canning, drying, or chemical additives, used to maintain a product's shelf life and quality and in some cases, impart additional flavorings.

botulism A form of foodborne illness, oftentimes fatal. Caused by improper and/or inadequate food preservation methods.

If operators use cured and/or smoked products, they must ensure consistent culinary quality by specifying very clearly the types of products they desire. Ordinarily, the only way to obtain consistency is to specify a particular packer's brand. The many combinations of curing and/or smoking procedures that can be used almost force buyers to select one desired packer's brand for each item purchased. Product substitutions are inadvisable because customers would notice them very quickly.

■ Tenderization Procedure

If buyers purchase meat to be used for steaks and chops—meat that will be broiled or fried—it has to have a certain degree of tenderness. High-quality meats come with a good measure of natural tenderness. In other cases, it may be necessary for someone in the channel of distribution to introduce a bit of "artificial" tenderization. And, usually, a primary source or an intermediary contributes this.

> **dry aging** An expensive method used to tenderize meat and to enhance its flavor.

The natural tenderization process is referred to as "aging" the meat. Beef and lamb can be aged. Pork and veal usually are not. One of several aging methods may be employed. The first is called **dry aging** (Figure 21.9). This method tenderizes the meat and adds flavor. Only high-quality grades of meat

FIGURE 21.9 Dry-aged beef.
©NightAndDayImages/GettyImages

can be dry aged successfully. Although a very old animal would be flavorful, no amount of aging would tenderize it. Conversely, young meat that is aged goes through a rushed maturation process. In fact, a couple of weeks of dry aging may produce as much flavor as an extra year of life. USDA Prime beef and USDA Choice beef (High U.S. Choice, and Average U.S. Choice, not U.S. Choice) are good candidates for dry aging.

Dry aging is expensive. This method requires the meat to be held for about 14 days in carefully controlled temperature and humidity. As a result, the meat loses moisture. So it weighs less after aging, which forces up its AP price. Also, dry aging requires an additional investment in facilities and inventories, which forces up the AP price even more. Buyers should never assume that the meat they purchase has been dry aged. They must request this expensive procedure—and must be prepared to pay for it.

Another type of aging done in the trade is called **wet aging**, also referred to as **Cryovac aging**. This method is less expensive than the conventional dry-aging process and causes no weight loss. This method involves shrink-wrapping the meat cuts and keeping them refrigerated for about 10 to 14 days. The wrapped meat can be in transit, aging, while it is trucked to the restaurant. Unfortunately, wet aging causes very little flavor development. Also, wet-aged meat seems to be much drier than dry-aged meat if it is cooked past the medium state. The wet-aging process is the most common form of aging available. If buyers do not specify a tenderization procedure, they can expect that the fresh meat they purchase will undergo this wet-aging process. The NCBA provides an excellent executive summary guide to aging meats, which includes results of research studies comparing the results of dry and wet aging.

The biggest disadvantage of using aged meat is that it quickly cooks to the well-done state. However, if hospitality operators are going to roast large wholesale cuts, they can do a bit of aging themselves. By cooking these items in a slow oven, say, at between 200°F and 225°F, they actually simulate aging. They do not add much flavor, but at these temperatures the meat tenderizes somewhat while it cooks. Whatever the method used, aging usually provides a good meat product.

Some people are under the impression that they can purchase unaged meat, which is sometimes referred to as "green" meat, and successfully age the product themselves in the refrigerator or freezer. Certainly, purchasing **green meat** is tempting because the AP price would be significantly lower than that of a properly aged product. Unfortunately, meat will not age in the typical refrigerator. Meat also will not age if it is frozen or once it is cooked. It will age properly only if its storage environment has the required temperature and humidity.

Meat can also be "chemically" or "mechanically" treated to tenderize it. **Chemical tenderization** involves adding an enzyme to the meat that changes the protein structure. Meat packers can inject enzymes into live animals just before slaughter. They also can give postmortem injections. Alternately, after dressing the meat and, usually, cutting it into no more than 1/2-inch-thick pieces, packers can dip the meat into an enzyme solution and allow it to remain there for about 30 minutes. This dipping method, however, prevents the enzyme from penetrating the muscles too deeply.

wet aging Shrink-wrapping meat, which allows the release of meat enzymes that soften the connective tissues.

Cryovac aging Another term for wet aging.

green meat Product that has not had a chance to age. In some cases its use will result in an unacceptable finished product that cannot be served to guests.

chemical tenderization Adding an enzyme to meat to change the protein structure.

FIGURE 21.10 Manual meat tenderizer.
©Jaccard Corporation

mechanical tenderization
A physical tenderization technique. Usually takes the form of grinding, chopping, cubing, flaking, or needling. May change the shape of the product being tenderized.

needling   A tenderization procedure. Submitting a large cut of meat (or fish) to a machine with several tiny needles. The needles penetrate the item, tenderizing it without altering its shape. The needle marks are usually invisible once the product has been cooked.

comminuting   Process of reducing a substance into smaller, random-shaped pieces. Typical method used to produce things such as processed chicken patties.

Restaurants may use the dipping tenderization procedure in their own kitchens when they offer a low-priced steak dinner. The steaks probably came from a low-quality animal. The operations want it tender, though, and chemical aging is a way of achieving this.

These chemical procedures are not as popular today as they once were in the hospitality industry. A major problem concerns the possibility that the enzymes used will continue to attack the muscles and connective tissues of the meat if the meat product is kept at a temperature range of approximately 120°F to 140°F. This could easily result in a product that is very mushy and, hence, unacceptable to customers. Mechanical methods, such as grinding and cubing, alter the shape of the product, but not so much the taste. Tenderizing via physical techniques may be preferable to chemical means. However, if not applied properly, mechanical methods can ruin the product.

Mechanical tenderization can be accomplished using the **needling** method (see Figure 21.10). This procedure involves submitting the meat to a machine with several tiny needles. The needles penetrate the meat, tenderizing it without altering its shape. Chefs have to look carefully to see the needle marks, and once the meat is cooked, they are not visible. This method can be used on boneless or bone-in wholesale cuts. Most often, operators use it on wholesale cuts that will be served as steaks or roasts.

Inexpensive, tough pieces of meat can also be tenderized by **comminuting**, which is a flaking and re-forming process. These pieces are flaked, not ground, and then pressed together to resemble, for example, a loin of beef. "Steaks" are then cut from this "loin."

Hospitality operators can accomplish mechanical tenderization themselves; they can even buy an expensive needling machine if they wish. For that matter, they can age their own meat and apply a dipping chemical bath. The question is: Who can provide these services less expensively—the buyer or the supplier?

Usually, the tenderization question arises only when buyers purchase fresh beef products. If veal is tenderized at all, the mechanical method is used. More typically, veal can be tenderized if it is roasted very slowly. Also, operators rarely experience a tenderness problem with pork. Lamb is aged, but only about half as long as beef.

PURCHASING MEAT

A buyer's first step in purchasing meat is obtaining a current copy of the MBG. This unique publication is an indispensable reference source that every meat buyer should have. Other good meat reference books are available, but the MBG is the only source that addresses the purchasing function exclusively.

The buyer's next step is to determine precisely what meat is needed. As noted earlier, fresh meats are usually selected on the basis of U.S. grades and IMPS numbers, whereas processed convenience items are typically selected on the basis of packers' brands. Supplier selection may be based on numerous criteria, including availability, reliability, accountability, shipping, and price.

After determining the meat products the operation requires, it is always wise to prepare specifications for each item, whether or not the buyer uses them in bid buying (see Figure 21.11 for example product specifications, and Figure 21.12 for an example of a product specification outline for meat products).

Beef loin, strip loin steak, boneless
Used for dinner entrée
IMPS number 1180
USDA Choice (High U.S. Choice)
Cut from USDA Yield Grade 2 carcass
Dry aged 14 to 21 days
12-ounce portion cut
Individually wrapped in plastic film
Layered pack
10- to 12-pound case
Refrigerated

Beef flank, flank steak (IM)
Used for London broil entrée
IMPS number 193
Sipco® brand
Weight range B (1 to 2 pounds)
Packed 8 pieces per Cryovac® bag
Packed 6 bags per case
Case weight, approximately 70
    pounds (catch weight)
Refrigerated

Beef base
Used to prepare soups and sauces
LeGout® brand
16-ounce resealable plastic containers
Packed 12 containers per case
Refrigerated

Vegetable beef soup
Used for lunch appetizer
Campbell's® brand
51-ounce can
Packed 12 cans per case
Unrefrigerated

FIGURE 21.11 An example of meat product specifications.

Intended use:
Exact name:
U.S. grade (or equivalent):
Product yield:
Packer's brand name (or equivalent):
Product size:
Size of container:
Type of packaging material:
Packaging procedure:
Product form:
Preservation method:
Tenderization procedure:
Point of origin:

FIGURE 21.12 An example of a product specification outline for meat products.

After writing the specifications, the buyer must evaluate potential suppliers, determine order sizes, determine order times, and so on. Many suppliers work in the fresh- and processed-meat areas. Most parts of the United States are a bid buyer's paradise. Purchasing meat, therefore, can be as easy or as difficult as the buyer wants to make it. In fact, as long as the buyer avoids obscure meat items or highly processed convenience items, one-stop-shopping opportunities can often be found. In general, the more processing hospitality operations want, the more suppliers they need. Buyers must ask themselves a question: "Should I tailor my menu around one or two suppliers, or should I write the menu and take my chances with a lot of suppliers?" Buyers should not take this issue lightly. On one hand, buyers like to make deals and bid buy because of the potential savings, but, on the other hand, they do not enjoy taking risks with signature items. Conversely, the buyer can shop around or practice trade relations.

Because meat represents such a large part of the foodservice purchase dollar, buyers are mindful of AP prices. AP prices vary for meat items, types of packaging, and any other value-added feature in a rather predictable way. However, some buyers are concerned about how the meat industry sets contract prices. In some cases, large meat contracts are prepared in such a way that the eventual AP price is not known until the day the hospitality operation takes delivery. On that

HRI Buyer's Guide An e-mail subscription service that notes current commodities prices being paid to wholesalers and purveyors by foodservice operations for eggs, poultry, meat, and seafood.

day, the price reported on the **HRI Buyer's Guide**, or in some comparable market pricing report, may be the one the buyer must pay the supplier.

The HRI Buyer's Guide is published each Thursday. It is an e-mail subscription service that notes current commodities prices being paid to wholesalers and purveyors by foodservice operations for eggs, poultry, meat, and seafood. You can also subscribe to the Beef Retail Marketing Wholesale Price update. Although it is true that with this type of pricing mechanism, the eventual AP price may be lower than expected, it is also true that it could be much higher. This is a risk some buyers do not want to take—or it may be a risk that some foodservice firms forbid their buyers to take.

One way to keep AP prices down is to bid buy among acceptable suppliers. The time involved, as well as the inconvenience, may be worthwhile. Good savings can accrue by this method, but switching suppliers indiscriminately, especially for signature items, can be risky. Different delivery times, supplier capabilities, and product form may be trivial concerns for other items, but they are usually crucial for meat.

If buyers have adequate cash reserves, they may do well with quantity buys once or twice a year for fresh meat and many processed-meat items. On the cash market, purchasing day to day, buyers take their chances. Although a good deal represents potentially great savings, a miscalculation represents potentially serious losses. Several companies keep statistics on both AP prices and the availability of meat supplies. By tracking the supply and demand over time, buyers can develop models to predict the optimal times to purchase meat in large quantity.

Even though meat buying is a bid buyer's dream, most buyers approach it cautiously. We may see some long-term contract bidding, perhaps three or six months, but we rarely see indiscriminate shopping around. Most meat buyers seem to be concerned with supplier services, especially dependability. A good reputation helps meat suppliers tremendously. After all, their customers must have their signature items. Stockouts are intolerable to buyers; they must have the right item at the right time.

Naturally, cautious buyer attitudes make it difficult for new meat suppliers to establish themselves. In theory, no difference in items should exist for the same grade and cut of meat, but suppliers' item handling, delivery service, and dependability tend to overshadow this fact. Consequently, new suppliers must resort either to offering low AP prices, at least on an introductory basis, or to offering exceptionally attractive supplier services.

The quality and style of processed-meat items are not easily decided. So packers' brands and suppliers' capabilities tend to weigh heavily in these decisions. The owner–manager, either alone or in consultation with others, determines the requirements. Of course, if the hospitality operation needs exotic meats, it will have more trouble finding suppliers. Packers' brands are important guides, but the brand the owner–manager wants may not be available in the local community, or, more likely, only one supplier will stock that brand. We have often noticed such items available on a cost-plus basis only.

Of course, the independent farmer is ever-present. Some independent farmers sell fresh meat, but many sell products like homemade sausage. We suggest staying away from all uninspected meat.

Before purchasing any meat item, and usually before or during the writing of specifications, buyers should take the time to evaluate the multitude of substitution possibilities.

Meat buying does not have to be difficult, but it certainly is not easy, especially if the buyer is responsible for procuring a wide variety of meat products. In general, the minimum knowledge the buyer needs can be summarized as: the different types of meat, the U.S. grades, the appropriate brand names, the various cuts, and the intended uses for the meat items (see Figure 21.13).

PROCEDURES FOR RECEIVING, STORING, AND ISSUING MEAT

■ Receiving

When meat products reach a hospitality operation, many owner–managers insist that all inspection be done in the walk-in refrigerator. This practice minimizes spoilage opportunities, but it may be too cautious for some. However, it drives home the fact that an operation cannot take chances with meat—it is too expensive to treat carelessly.

The chef, or someone else in the operation who is also knowledgeable about meat quality, should handle the quality check. This receiver must be able to determine that what the buyer ordered matches what is being received. For instance, suppose a purchase order is for top round, but the item received is bottom round. This mistake could lead to a stockout and potential disgruntled customers at the dinner hour.

The receiver should check the condition of the meat. For example, all meats have a characteristic color. Fresh beef is a bright, cherry red. If it is not, it could be old. Also, it could be vacuum packed, such as the Cryovac®-packaged meat, so that it is not exposed to oxygen to give it the bright, cherry red color, or "bloom," as it is sometimes called. If the characteristic color does not appear to be correct, the receiver should double-check the meat.

Odor is another sign of bad meat. If meat has an unpleasant odor, refuse it. (Fresh pork is difficult to check for odor because it deteriorates from the inside out, not the outside in.)

Pork's Most Popular Cuts

SHOULDER

Shoulder Steak;
bone-in

Shoulder Roast;
bone-in

Shoulder
Country-Style Ribs;
bone-in

LOIN

New York Chop

Porterhouse Chop

Ribeye Chop

Sirloin Chop;
boneless

Loin Back Ribs

Loin Country-Style Ribs;
bone-in

Loin Country Style Ribs;
boneless

New York Roast

Tenderloin

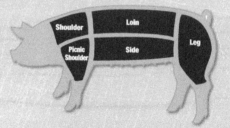

SIDE

Spareribs

St. Louis-Style Ribs

For recipe ideas visit:
www.PorkBeInspired.com

Be inspired

FIGURE 21.13 Retail pork cuts.
Courtesy of the National Pork Board

If meat products have a slimy appearance and are slimy to the touch, the receiver should refuse them. This slime consists of spoilage bacteria.

The receiver should also check the packaging. It should be appropriate for the item purchased. Proper packaging is essential for reducing loss in quality, especially for frozen meats. For instance, frozen meats whose packaging is split should be refused.

The receiver should also consider the temperature of the item. It should be about 40 °F, minimally, for refrigerated meat, and 0 °F, minimally, for frozen meat. Other processed items—those that are preserved with chemicals, like some sausages—could be less chilled. But a receiver should not make a habit of accepting even these products when warm because this could imply a certain degree of general carelessness on the part of the supplier or a willingness on the part of the operation to relax standards.

Making these kinds of checks on fresh meat and some processed items is not difficult. However, checking frozen meat can be problematic because detecting spoilage in frozen items is more difficult.

Next, the receiver should check quantities and not rely completely on what is printed on the meat packages. Repacking is not impossible for an unscrupulous supplier or a larcenous employee. The receiver should look for such specifications as weight, count, and sizes. If all of the meat the buyer ordered is in one container, the receiver should separate and weigh the contents individually, also making sure to deduct the weight of the carton and the packaging.

After checking the quality and quantity, the receiver should move to the prices. As might be expected, meat requires a strong emphasis on record keeping. The receiver should devote a reasonable amount of attention to recording the deliveries. Receiving sheets, bin cards, and meat tags are all methods that can be used to protect expensive meat items. Before a purchase, most buyers express considerable concern with suppliers regarding the actions needed to correct any potential problems. And, a supplier, out of stock on the buyers' regular orders, often quickly adjusts any agreements in the policies regarding returns, credit terms, and substitute meat items to maintain the buyers' loyalty.

Hospitality operators can streamline the meat-receiving process by using the USDA's Acceptance Service. This practice is popular in meat purchasing, even though it is expensive. Using this service, a hospitality operator can pay a meat expert to write meat specifications and to ensure that the specified products are actually delivered. Acceptance buying is sometimes referred to in the meat trade as **certified buying** or "certification" (see Figure 21.14).

A related program the USDA offers that may also interest meat buyers is called the **USDA Product Examination Service**. With this service, a federal inspector examines the purchased meat while it is in transit. The primary purpose of this service is to ensure that product quality does not deteriorate during shipment.

certified buying
Another term for USDA Acceptance Service.

USDA Product Examination Service
Agency that provides inspection of purchased meat by a federal inspector while the products are in transit.

FIGURE 21.14 USDA Acceptance purchasing stamps. *Courtesy of U.S. Department of Agriculture*

■ Storing

Mandatory government inspection ensures that most meat is very clean when it is delivered. The onus is on the foodservice operation to receive and store meat in the correct environment. Whether fresh or frozen, meat must be kept clean and cold. In addition, the stock must be rotated properly.

Meat products are susceptible to bacterial contamination; keeping them clean and sanitary is a big challenge. A dirty storage refrigerator can contaminate good meat. Therefore, it is important for hospitality operations to perform the necessary housekeeping chores to minimize contamination.

Operators should store fresh meat in a meat refrigerator apart from cooked-meat items, at a temperature of 35 °F to 40 °F. If this is not possible, operators should designate a segregated area of the refrigerator for meat storage. To prevent contamination from raw-meat drippings, operators should place cooked items above the raw meats. Also, they should not wrap fresh meat too tightly or stack it too tightly. Both of these practices tend to cut down on the beneficial cold-air circulation around the pieces of meat.

Operators should store frozen products at −10 °F or lower. If they must freeze some chilled meat, they must be careful to wrap it correctly and to store it in a freezer no longer than suggested. (It is not a good idea to freeze fresh meat because the typical hospitality operation's freezer (and the typical home freezer) is designed to hold frozen foods, not to freeze fresh products.)

■ Issuing

Operators should properly rotate the stock so that the oldest items are issued first. Meat is rarely received and sent straight to production; an employee typically needs a stock requisition to get it. More control of meat items tends to exist at the requisition stage. In many cases, operators add to a perpetual inventory when the meat is delivered. Also, the stock requisition is commonplace. The requisitioner should return any unused meat at the end of the work shift. The meat consumed should be consistent with the guest checks, that is, the number of meat items sold during that shift. Managing these controls may be somewhat time-consuming, but the practice is quite common in hospitality operations for meat and other expensive items.

By all means, operators must make sure that the requisitioner gets the right item and the right quantity, and must make sure that the in-process inventory does not get so large that it encourages waste or pilferage.

■ In-Process Inventories

Surprisingly, in-process meats cause relatively little trouble. These items receive the bulk of the supervisory efforts; moreover, the penalties for pilferage and waste are normally quite severe.

Some employees will make "mistakes." For example, they may burn a steak, accidentally on purpose, and give it to a friend or eat it themselves. Operators can reduce the number of these "errors" by demanding that the mistake, along with the rest of the leftover meat, be turned in to the storeroom at the end of the shift so that it can be accounted for at that time.

Meat also provides some opportunity for shortchanging customers. For example, a server might slice the beef a little thin and keep the extra few ounces handy to trade for a few ounces of gin that the bartender saved in a similar fashion. As is usually the case, effective supervision is the best answer.

A DAY IN THE LIFE
Seth Larson, Sales Representative
Newport Meat Company, Irvine CA

Bob Beresh Photograph

It's early morning, and Seth Larson is standing on the loading dock of his newest customer. He waits patiently for the Newport Meat Company delivery truck, and when it arrives, he carefully helps unload and weighs each and every item. Larson doesn't do this with every delivery, but he does this for the first delivery to make a point: he provides good service and the products are 100 percent reliable and as-ordered.

"When you are working with people who themselves offer stellar service, you have to do likewise," said Larson. "I try to anticipate my customers' needs and allay any concerns they might have before they even surface."

Newport Meat Company is located in Irvine, California, but its "white tablecloth" restaurant customers are on both coasts and points in between. Thomas Keller's restaurants, Per Se in New York and The French Laundry in San Francisco, are just two on an impressive list of customers that include the West Coast Ruth's Chris Steak House restaurants, the Wolfgang Puck restaurants, and Lawry's Restaurants, Inc. The company has more than 1,400 customers and serves a California area from the San Diego/Mexican border north to Santa Barbara and east to Palm Springs, with daily deliveries to Las Vegas, San Francisco, Monterey Bay, and the Napa Valley.

Larson's day begins at 6 A.M. when he checks his voicemail to make sure everything went as planned when the delivery trucks were loaded. More than once he has had to call and make sure that a replacement item *wasn't* delivered to a customer—knowing that the customer in question would want something different or perhaps no replacement item at all. One could say that most of the time he just "drives around," but in a day he visits 8 to 10 customers and puts more than 100 miles on his car. He checks voicemail (hopefully for the last time) around 10 P.M.

Larson works from his car, using his Android phone and iPad as his contact with the world. His contact at the office is an assistant who enters orders into a computer, handles most of the paperwork, and is also allowed to take orders over the phone. Larson averages $140,000 in sales a week, sometimes spiking to more than $175,000. Larson has only been in the business for seven years. He currently serves a client list with more than 50 restaurants, hotels, and clubs.

"One of the things that we do to streamline the ordering process is provide our customers with a customized list of products that meets their specific needs," said Larson. "We have over one thousand items available, and it helps the customer—and us—to have a smaller order list, that changes with their menus and features any new items."

Some of Larson's new customers come from referrals, but many come from driving around and noting the names of new restaurants in the area. Larson researches the new restaurant, any history it might have in another location, and information on the chef or its owners. When he makes his first sales call, he's prepared with information. He makes the sale because of his company's reputation, the products it offers, and his presentation and personality. He keeps the new customer by providing unexpected service.

"Once I had a long-standing restaurant customer where a new chef came on board who had worked with one of my customers," Larson said. "I talked to him early in the week about our products and appeared in his office on Wednesday. 'You pick up your orders in person?' he asked. 'As often as possible,' I replied. That impressed him, and he is still one of my customers."

The company's offerings range from Japanese Kobe beef to air-chilled game hens. It includes rattlesnake, every kind of game bird, buffalo, elk, and seafood. One of Larson's customers wanted turtle meat—something he had never sold and that wasn't on the product list. After just a few phone calls, Larson's customer had a 5-pound bucket of turtle meat for a dish to serve at a wine dinner.

Although he works long, hard hours, there are some perks to the job. Every Thanksgiving, Larson delivers a large Diestel turkey, free-range grown in California, to the family of one of his college friends. He now spends holidays with his own family, but is still able to be part of the traditions he established earlier.

"It's a job that I love," said Larson. "I'm directly rewarded for my efforts, I'm developing lasting relationships with my customers, and I'm happy working in the dynamic, growing hospitality industry. Admittedly, it's a balancing act between work and my personal life, but it's worth it for me."

Key Words and Concepts

Agricultural Marketing Act

Agricultural Marketing Service (AMS)
  Live Stock & Feed Division

American Angus Association

Botulism

Bulk pack

Carcass

Catch weight

Certified Angus Beef® Program

Certified buying

Chemical tenderization

Comminuting

Concentrated Agricultural Feeding
  Operations (CAFOs)

Cryovac™ aging

Curing

Dry aging

Edible byproduct

Exact name

Feathering

Federal Meat Inspection Act

Finish

Grain-fed beef

Grass-fed beef

Green meat

Hedging

HRI Buyers' Guide

Imitation meat products

IMPS/NAMI numbers

Layout pack

Limiting rule

Manufacturing grade

Key Words and Concepts (continued)

Marbling	Signature item
Maturity class	Smoking
Meat Buyer's Guide numbers (MBG numbers)	Sodium nitrite
	Standard of identity
Mechanical tenderization	Steam-table pack
National Livestock and Meat Board	Truth-in-menu
Needling	USDA Acceptance Service
North American Meat Institute (NAMI)	USDA Product Examination Service
	U.S. quality grades
Portion-cut meat	U.S. yield grades
Preservation method	Variety meat
Retail cut	Weight range
Shingle pack	Wet aging
Shrink-wrap	Wholesale cut
Side	Wholesale Meat Act

 Questions and Problems

1. On what are the quality grades for beef primarily based?

2. All meat must be inspected during production in the United States except _____ meat.

3. Design a table showing the USDA quality grades for beef, pork, veal, and lamb.

4. What are lower-quality grades of meat typically used for?

5. What is the primary reason food buyers use the IMPS numbering system when preparing meat specifications?

6. On what are USDA yield grades primarily based?

7. A product specification for fresh pork chops could include this information:

    a.

    b.

    c.

    d.

    e.

Questions and Problems (continued)

8. Briefly describe the maturity classes for beef.

9. What is the primary purpose of using the USDA's Product Examination Service?

10. What critical information is missing from this product specification for lamb loin chops?

> Lamb loin chops
> Used for dinner entrée
> IMPS number 1232A
> 6-ounce portion cut
> Packed in 10- to 12-pound containers

11. List some differences between dry aging and wet aging.

12. Give an appropriate intended use for hamburger that has been extended with soybean.

13. Prepare a product specification for these meat products:

> Veal cutlet
> Skirt steak
> Prepared chili with beans
> Breakfast sausage
> Ham

14. When would a buyer purchase an imitation meat product or a flaked and re-formed meat product?

15. What is the difference between grain- and grass-fed meats? How does this relate to concentrated agricultural feedlots?

16. What benefit would a restaurant owner gain by listing on the menu the point of origin for the meat offerings?

17. What benefit would a buyer gain from buying a packer's brand meat product?

18. Briefly describe one type of meat product you might purchase that would be a good candidate for the needling tenderization procedure.

19. What are the quality grading factors for veal and lamb?

20. Define or explain briefly these terms:

a. Variety meat	g. Curing
b. Wholesale cut	h. Feathering
c. Retail cut	i. Certified buying
d. Marbling	j. Layout pack
e. Product examination service	k. Bloom
f. NAMI	l. Shrink-wrap

Questions and Problems (continued)

21. The AP price of lean hamburger is $1.89 per pound. The AP price of regular hamburger is $1.09 per pound. The lean meat shrinks 10 percent when cooked; the regular meat shrinks 30 percent.

    a. At what AP price must the lean hamburger sell at to make it equal in value to the regular hamburger?

    b. Assume that the EP cost of both the lean and regular meat is equal. What other specific considerations should you examine before purchasing either the lean or the regular?

22. Would it be more cost effective to purchase beef tenderloin and cut filet mignon (8 oz) from it or to purchase individually packaged filet mignon (8 oz)? Use the following information to make your determination.

AP price per pound	Labor Cost		Yield
Individually Packaged Tenderloin:	$13.65		100%
Beef Tenderloin:	$12.42	$12/hr	91%

Experiential Exercises

1. Contact a local steakhouse and set a meeting with the manager. Determine the amount of product that this location uses on a weekly basis. Ask for information regarding the meat supplier and its ordering procedures, including how often it delivers, the type of meat purchased, and how much it goes through in a week (average order size). Write a report where you summarize your findings. Present to the manager if possible for comments and review.

2. Meet with a local hospital foodservice manager. Determine the approximate cost of feeding a patient per day. Determine the percentage of that which is used for meat. Ask questions regarding food cost percentage, how to reduce costs, and ways in which he or she keeps food costs low despite an overall increase in food cost. Write a one-page report where you outline this information. If possible, present the report to the foodservice manager for feedback.

3. Search the Internet for information regarding packers' brands of meats. Select one company. Research information about the company's location, history, corporate structure, products, distribution and marketing strategies, and sustainability practices. Write a two-page report of your findings.

References

1. Minnie Jones, (June 2013, 2008) "Military food inspectors are on the frontline of defence," www.army.mil: The Official Homepage of the U.S. Army, www.army.mil/article/9970/Food_Inspection_Specialists_Are_On_Frontline_Of_Defense/.

2. USDA, "What Is Organic?," www.ams.usda.gov/AMSv1.0/getfile?dDocName=STELPRDC5103286.

3. U.S. Department of Agriculture, "Request for Information to Develop Voluntary Standards for Meat Goat Carcasses and Cuts," December 2010, www.ams.usda.gov/AMSv1.0/getfile?dDocName=STELPRDC5088274.

4. "Bison—Frequently Asked Questions," www.bisonbasics.com.

5. Deer and Elk Farmer's Information Network, "Venison Grading and Certification," www.deerfarmer.org/index.php?option=com_content&view=article&id=192:venison-grading-and-classification&catid=31:venison.

6. American Angus Association, "Our 10 Quality Standards," www.certifiedangusbeef.com/brand/specs.php.

CHAPTER 22

BEVERAGES

The Purpose of This Chapter

After reading this chapter, you should be able to:

- Discuss the management considerations when purchasing beverage alcohols.

- Choose appropriate beverage alcohols based on various selection factors.

- Consider AP price and supplier factors when purchasing beverage alcohols.

- Create a specification for beverage alcohols that can be used in the purchasing process.

- Describe procedures for receiving, storing, and issuing beverage alcohols.

- Discuss the management considerations when purchasing nonalcoholic beverages.

- Choose appropriate nonalcoholic beverages based on various selection factors.

- Describe procedures for purchasing, receiving, storing, and issuing nonalcoholic beverages.

MANAGEMENT CONSIDERATIONS FOR BEVERAGE ALCOHOLS

Beverage alcohols (also referred to as "liquor" and "alcoholic beverages") include wines, beers, and spirits. Wines result from the fermentation of sugars in fruits or berries (most commonly grapes), various plants or their saps, honey, and even milk. Beers are produced by the fermentation of grains after the starch in them is converted to sugar. Spirits are distilled from fermented fruit, grain, or vegetables.

Beverage alcohol products are often the easiest items a buyer can purchase. These are standardized products that are manufactured under controlled conditions resulting in consistent quality. Although most beverage alcohols will not spoil, some products, such as canned and bottled beer, and some wines, tend to lose their quality over a period of time. Beer and wine are sensitive to changes in temperature, humidity, light, and vibration. Generally, however, when hospitality operators store beverage alcohols under controlled conditions, buyers do not have to worry about an oversupply spoiling before they can serve it to customers.

Another favorable factor relating to beverage alcohols is that many customers tend to order a preferred, or "call," brand. For instance, typical customers would not ask a restaurant operator for Heinz® catsup; they would take the one the establishment offers and, usually, not give it a second thought. However, these customers may specify an exact **brand name** when ordering a favorite beverage alcohol. This type of "pull" strategy in the beverage alcohols distribution channel can facilitate the buyers' job.

> **brand name** Indication of product quality. A typical selection factor for purchased items, especially when purchasing beverage alcohols.
>
> **exclusive distributor** A vendor who has the exclusive right to sell a particular product or product line. For instance, if you want Sara Lee brand pastries, there may be only one vendor in your area that sells it; this eliminates your ability to shop around for these items.
>
> **control state** A state that sells beverage alcohols. It is the only purveyor of beverage alcohols in that state.
>
> **license state** A state that grants licenses to importers–wholesalers, distributors, and retailers, who then handle the distribution and sale of beverage alcohols.

In some instances, selected suppliers are exclusive distributors for one or more products in a given market area. Under such conditions, if bar operators want specific brands, they will have only one source of supply. Because only a small number of **exclusive distributorships** exist in the beverage alcohol trade, buyers do not have the opportunity to shop around very much.

In 17 states, state governments (and some counties, such as Montgomery county in Maryland) regulate and control the manufacturing, possession, sales, transportation, and delivery of beverage alcohols (see Figure 22.1). In these "control" states, the buyers must follow the states' specific ordering and bill-paying procedures. This makes the buying job easier; however, the excessive regulation found in **control states** tends to increase the edible-portion (EP) costs of beverage alcohols. The National Alcoholic Beverage Control Association (NABCA), headquartered in Washington, DC, represents and supports the control states in their mission to protect public health and safety and ensure proper and efficient systems for beverage alcohol distribution and sales.

Alternately, some states regulate beverage alcohol commerce through the issuance of "licenses." These **license states** also simplify the buyers' job. For instance, a certain amount of price control exists in some areas; the state or local government agency stipulates that beverage alcohols must be sold at minimum wholesale prices and minimum retail prices. Although as-purchased

Alabama Alcoholic Beverage Control Board
Idaho State Liquor Dispensary
Iowa Alcoholic Beverages Division
Maine Bureau of Alcoholic Beverages
Montgomery County Department of Liquor Control, Maryland
Michigan Liquor Control Commission
Mississippi State Tax Commission, ABC Division
Montana Department of Revenue
New Hampshire State Liquor Commission
North Carolina Alcoholic Beverage Control Commission
Ohio Department of Commerce Division of Liquor Control
Oregon Liquor Control Commission
Pennsylvania Liquor Control Board
State of Utah Department of Beverage Alcohol Control
Vermont Department of Liquor Control
Virginia Beverage Alcohol Control Board
West Virginia Beverage Alcohol Control Administration
Wyoming Department of Revenue Liquor Division

FIGURE 22.1 Control state agencies.
Courtesy of National Alcohol Beverage Control Association,
www.nabca.org

(AP) price discount opportunities and other sorts of "deals" are available in license states, buyers do not have that many to evaluate, which implies less work for buyers.

License states are slightly more liberal than control states in terms of liquor-ordering and bill-paying procedures. For example, licensed distributors are able to deliver products, whereas in control states, buyers usually must pick up the order at a state liquor warehouse. License states are also allowed to offer credit terms, whereas in control states, buyers usually must pay cash when they pick up their order. License states tend to restrict the amount and types of **supplier services** that can be provided, much more than other types of suppliers. Consequently, even in a state where two or more suppliers carry some of the same brands, buyers may not be able to exploit the situation.

The problems associated with beverage alcohols rarely center on purchasing procedures. Rather the hospitality operator must consider these fundamental questions.

> **supplier services**
> Services, such as free delivery, generous credit terms, and so forth, provided by vendors to buyers who purchase their products.

■ Should We Offer Beverage Alcohol Service to Guests?

This is not an easy decision. On one hand, many foodservice operations rely on both food and beverage alcohol sales to achieve profit. When compared, food sales are generally less profitable than beverage alcohol sales. Not only are liquor sales more profitable, but beverage alcohols are also easier to produce and serve. Yet hospitality operators must be aware of the steady decline in U.S. liquor consumption. The basis for this decline may be attributed to increased health and

driving while intoxicated (DWI) The criminal offense of operating and/or driving a motor vehicle while under the influence of alcohol and/or drugs to the degree that mental and motor skills are impaired. In some states the offense is called driving under the influence (DUI), operating while impaired (OWI), or operating a vehicle under the influence (OVI).

Mothers Against Drunk Driving (MADD) A nonprofit organization that seeks to stop drunk driving, support those affected by drunk driving, prevent underage drinking, and encourage legislation that establishes stricter alcohol policies.

Center for Science in the Public Interest Organization that advocates for nutrition and health, food safety, alcohol policy, and sound science.

Center on Alcohol Marketing and Youth A research organization located at the Johns Hopkins Center for Public Health, which is funded by the Centers for Disease Control and Prevention.

dram shop Legal term for bars, restaurants, taverns, inns, and the like, where beverage alcohol is sold by the drink. A "dram" is a small measure of liquid, hence the term "dram shop."

liquor license Granted by a government agency. Gives the licensee the authority to purchase and sell beverage alcohols.

nutrition concerns, laws prohibiting happy hours, and tougher **driving while intoxicated (DWI)** or driving under the influence (DUI) laws. Also, the pressures created by such groups as **Mothers Against Drunk Driving (MADD)**, the **Center for Science in the Public Interest**, and the **Center for Alcohol Marketing and Youth** have had an impact on the consumption rate. The website of the Alcohol Problems and Solutions organization contains a listing of anti-alcohol activist organizations and leaders along with descriptions of alcohol policies throughout the United States. Furthermore, when hospitality operations want to cultivate a family image, serving beverage alcohols may compromise this perception.

In addition to all these considerations, 30 states have **dram shop** laws. Although the exact regulations vary, these laws basically provide rules on who can be held liable for an alcohol-related accident. In effect, if a guest becomes intoxicated at your establishment, dram shop laws may allocate some of the liability to the servers and hold the establishment responsible for any injuries caused after the guest leaves. In a non-dram-shop state, the establishment cannot be held responsible.[1]

Once operations decide to sell beverage alcohols, they must obtain a **liquor license**, or permit. This can be an arduous process. The paperwork, legal proceedings, and hearings can quickly drain the operations' resources. Sometimes, even if operators want to serve liquor, they may not be able to secure a retail liquor license from the appropriate government agency. In most parts of the United States, liquor licenses are restricted in number. For instance, only one liquor license may be available for every 2,000 to 3,000 residents of an area. If the allotment of licenses that the government agency issues is depleted, operators must try to obtain one by purchasing it from an establishment that has one. This can be very expensive, particularly when the demand for these licenses far exceeds the restricted supply. However, if operations serve only beer and wine, the procedure usually will not be as difficult. The average cost of a license depends on the city and state of application as well as the type of beverage alcohols to be served. For example, in Illinois the cost of a retail license to sell any type of beverage alcohol is $750,[2] but in Pennsylvania the cost to transfer an existing liquor license to a new owner of a bar or restaurant is $550–$700 and a license for a new establishment may cost as much as $25,000, as the number of new licenses is very limited.[3] It is important to note that the cost of a liquor license is governed by the marketplace and therefore can vary greatly.

Other major expenses associated with liquor service include increased liability insurance premiums and license renewal costs. Currently 47 states[4] require that all servers of alcohol obtain alcohol awareness certification, creating more work for managers and human resources departments to ensure verification. Compliance with those laws and other government-mandated record-keeping procedures, participation in a safe-driver program and/or a designated-driver program, and employment of floorpersons, or bouncers, to restrict minors may substantially increase operating expenses.

Some hospitality operations try to maintain their beverage profit margins by altering their marketing policies to capitalize on the consumer trend toward drinking more wine, beer, and nonalcoholic beverages. For instance, in states where the law allows, some bar operators have opened **brew pubs**, which combine food service and a small, in-house minibrewery. Other operators offer wine bars, whereas others may publish a wine list, a cocktail list, and a specialty water list.

brew pub   Retail establishment that brews draft beer on-site and sells it to retail customers. The typical brew pub also serves food and other beverage alcohols.

well brand   Term used in the bar business to refer to a drink that customers order by type of liquor and not by brand name. Opposite of call brand.

call brand   Term used in the bar business to refer to a drink that customers order by brand name. Opposite of well brand.

house brand   Another term for well brand. Alternately, another term for proprietary brand.

■ What Quality of Beverage Alcohols Should We Serve?

An age-old argument centers on the value of premium brands versus nonpremium brands. This decision is further complicated because operations usually serve **well brands**; **call brands**, such as Absolut® vodka, Sauza® tequila, and Bombay® gin; and "premium brands," such as Belvedere® vodka, Hennessy XO® cognac, and Lagavulin® single malt Scotch whiskey. Well liquor, sometimes called the **house brand**, is served when a patron asks for a shot of Scotch without specifying a particular brand. The term *well* derives its name from where this type of liquor is located, typically being stored in a well located just below the bar top. Call liquor refers to specific brand names, as when a patron asks for a Jack and Coke (the cocktail that contains Jack Daniels® and Coca-Cola®) or a shot of Crown Royal®. A premium brand would be an expensive call liquor that commands a high price, such as a glass of Grey Goose® vodka, Mount Gay® rum, or Pappy Van Winkle® bourbon (see Figure 22.2).

Generally, the AP price difference at wholesale between a call brand and a well brand is not too significant. If operations sell a considerable quantity of liquor, however, the savings from even a modest difference can amount to a considerable sum. The question, then, becomes, "Should we save a few pennies on each drink, or should we influence our customers by pouring only recognized brand names?" This question generates wildly differing opinions and should not be taken lightly.

FIGURE 22.2 A premium brand liquor.
©*BRENDAN MCDERMID/REUTERS/Newscom*

> **proof** Measure of the amount of alcohol in a beverage. Equal to twice the percentage of alcohol in a beverage. For example, if a beverage is 50 percent alcohol, its proof is 100.
>
> **pouring cost** The cost of beverage alcohol sold.
>
> **premium well brand** A well brand that is higher quality than the typical well brand poured by most bars.

Part of this controversy can be attributed to another difference between seemingly comparable liquor brands. This difference is the **proof**. The proof number is an indication of alcoholic strength. It correlates to twice the percent alcohol present in the liquor. For example, "100 proof" bourbon contains 50 percent alcohol.

Some equally well-known brands have different proofs. Some have 80; some, 86; some, 90; and some, 100 or more. If a hospitality operation serves a nonpremium brand with a low proof, the dilution factor in a mixed drink may need adjustment. Premium-brand advocates point out that the EP cost per serving, sometimes referred to in bars as the **pouring cost**, for lower-proof brands may not be significantly less than that of a higher-proof brand.

Many foodservice and bar operations serve premium brands as their well brands. This is sometimes referred to as the **premium well brand**, which may include items such as Original Baileys Irish Cream®, Cointreau® triple sec, Wild Turkey® bourbon, Absolut® vodka, and Bombay Sapphire® gin. Apparently, these operators are willing to forgo the extra profit per drink to satisfy their customers. Through the creation of a positive image, this approach may have an overall favorable impact on the net profit of the entire hospitality operation.

■ Should We Serve Draft Beer, Bottled Beer, or Both?

Many guests prefer draft beer (see Figure 22.3). It is something they cannot normally get at home. Unfortunately, draft beer is difficult to serve properly. In addition to sanitation concerns, new kegs must be tapped, tap pressure must be monitored, and the lines must be kept clean and flowing. Nevertheless, draft beer is a good merchandising tool, and it can attract considerable business. Also, draft beer can yield a lower pouring cost than bottled beer, even when operators take into account the additional labor and other costs involved.

Even if operations want to serve draft beer, acquiring the preferred brand may not be possible. Beer distributors sometimes want to restrict the number of retail outlets for their product. This is especially true of small, regional breweries seeking exclusivity for their products.

FIGURE 22.3 Draft beer.
©*zoom-zoom/iStockphoto*

■ Which Wines Should We Serve?

> **house wine** Refers to the "well brand" of wine used when customers ordering wine do not specify a particular brand name.
>
> **vintage** Refers to the year of production. Important selection factor for some wines.

Which wine should hospitality operators use as their **house wine**? House wine, like well liquor, is served when someone orders a glass or carafe of wine without specifying any particular brand or **vintage**.

Buying wines is trickier than buying other beverage alcohols. Because restaurant patrons do not always have one or two preferred brands of wines in mind, as they often do for beer and distilled spirits, the buyer or the owner–manager is required to have considerable product knowledge. The sommelier, wine steward, or other service personnel may have to suggest wines, and it is important that they provide correct choices that will complement the customers' dining experience. This requires solid training and knowledgeable supervision.

Perhaps the major concerns are how many varieties and types of wines to carry. With increased complexities of the wine list come increased complexities of the operation. Some operational challenges are (1) wine is difficult to store properly, (2) it requires considerable storage space, (3) it may be in storage a long time before it sells, (4) service personnel must be trained to sell and serve it correctly, and (5) a variety of wines may require several suppliers.

A substantial wine inventory can also mean tying up large amounts of capital. The **capital costs**—the interest on borrowed money or the loss of interest on alternate investments; that is, an opportunity cost—of a large wine cellar can be a major consideration in wine list design.

A well-stocked wine cellar can, however, offer many potential advantages. The main ones include (1) prestige, (2) indulging and pleasing patrons, (3) a marketing edge, and (4) bigger profits. This is evident in such operations as Charlie Palmer's Aureole Restaurant inside Mandalay Bay Hotel and Casino in Las Vegas (see Figure 22.4). The four-story "Cellar in the Sky" wine tower has 1800 wines where the wine stewards, wearing virtually invisible safety harnesses, float up and down within the tower to make their selections. Here the "performance" of the selection is almost as important as the wine itself.

On the other hand, some fast casual restaurants or family restaurants may have guests who will be satisfied with a small number of choices, in which case, an emphasis on wine can lead to

> **capital cost** The rate of return (e.g., interest income) that capital could be expected to earn in an alternative investment of equivalent risk. Alternately, cost incurred when purchasing land, buildings, construction/remodeling, and equipment to be used in the production of goods and/or services to be sold to consumers.

FIGURE 22.4 Aureole's wine cellar.
©Gail Mooney-Kelly/Alamy Stock Photo

wine speculating The act of investing in wine for a profit-making purpose. The speculator does not consume the product; rather, he or she treats it as a valuable collectible that may increase significantly in value.

a misallocation of dollars and effort. Furthermore, some styles of operations are in between. For instance, a steak house could have a minimal or a broad wine list, depending on the clientele.

Some operators like to speculate in wine. They buy wine and wait for its value to significantly increase for the purpose of selling it at a high profit. For these operators, **wine speculating** is like playing the stock market. This sort of "investing" goes beyond the responsibility of ordinary buyers.

■ What Is the Appropriate Number of Brands of Distilled Spirits and Beer to Carry?

Guests can be annoyed when they cannot get their favorite brand of beer or distilled spirit. However, if the operator decided to opt for a wide variety of brands, the same difficulties and potential advantages that we noted for wines may result.

Deciding what to carry is not easy. Management must determine what is optimal for the operation. It is not feasible to stock everything, but where does an owner–manager draw the line? Past experience indicates that the added investment between a restricted stock and more variety is not substantial, especially when the initial investment in the hospitality operation is taken into consideration. For example, it can cost more than $200,000 to erect one first-class hotel room. What, then, are a few more bottles of liquor and the space needed to store them? Nevertheless, in striking a balance, the owner–manager cannot ignore the costs and benefits of holding inventory as discussed earlier in this text.

■ What Is the Appropriate Menu Price for Beverage Alcohols?

Customers are very sensitive to menu prices for beverage alcohols because they usually have a good idea of the retail price of these items in their local liquor store. As such, a bar operator must emphasize service and other value-added features. A pricing policy can be a reflection of the type of operation. For example, if a restaurant or bar is rather plain and does not offer guests a unique experience, the pricing system must take that into account. In contrast, a fine-dining or drinking establishment should have more flexibility in its menu-pricing procedures. Alcohol pricing may also vary significantly based on geographic location, especially in tourist destinations, and then whether the establishment is marketed toward tourists or locals. For example, New York City, San Francisco, and Las Vegas are known for having high drink prices, whereas Chicago is considered a lower-price market. Owners/managers of nightclubs may

bottle service Service, typically in an upscale nightclub, where guests pay a high price for a bottle of alcohol and receive VIP service and seating.

want to offer **bottle service**. They may charge $300 or more for a bottle of Jack Daniels® or Ketel 1® vodka but guests receive VIP service from a dedicated cocktail server, their choice of mixers, and access to seating or better areas of the establishment.

Today, many customers are switching from distilled spirits to wine, beer, and nonalcoholic beverages. So, operators must consider a pricing strategy that takes into account this shift in customer preference. Otherwise, a potential loss in net profit may result. This is why a bottle of Fiji® water is commonly priced as high as a Dewar's® and soda; an operation cannot survive unless it achieves a certain profit margin per drink, regardless of the type of drink a customer demands.

A DAY AT AN ALCOHOLIC BEVERAGE DISTRIBUTION COMPANY

John Smith, Director of Trade Relations and Business Development
Drew Levinson, Director of Strategic Activation
Wirtz Beverage Nevada, Las Vegas, Nevada, part of Wirtz Beverage Group, Chicago, Illinois

Courtesy of John Smith

Courtesy of Drew Levison

There is never a quiet time at Wirtz Beverage Nevada (WBN) in Las Vegas. A phone call in the morning results in a wine tasting that afternoon with the head chefs of a multiproperty casino group. A salesperson may rush off to deliver a rare $10,000 bottle of wine to a high-roller's plane—a special service for a good casino customer. The Venetian calls on Wednesday and needs 15 Grand Cru wines by Friday.

"Las Vegas has become the beverage, wine, and food epicenter of the world," said John Smith, WBN's director of trade relations and business development. "This is one of the most exciting places to be if you're in the wine industry." It is part of Smith's job to work with wine buyers throughout southern Nevada, helping track down obscure wines and providing education. Smith knows wines, having attended wine seminars around the world. As a former restaurant owner, he also knows food, a valuable asset when working with chefs and food and beverage managers. Smith's focus reflects that of WBN's business philosophy that reads in part, "to improve our distribution and market penetration while providing excellent services to our customers." As Smith says, "My definition of a good wine and liquor distributor is one who makes his or her customers look good."

WBN's main Nevada distribution center in northeastern Las Vegas is a tribute to organization and ultimate customer service.

Here the offices of the multi-million-dollar operation are utilitarian and no-nonsense. The accounting department is clean and neat—no towering stacks of backlogged orders, invoices, or change requests (something to look for when seeking a new supplier). The sales team is equipped with notebook computers and smart devices, so orders can be sent to the main office as they are being received out in the field. The wine-tasting room is tastefully appointed but not opulent. The entire atmosphere says, "Business is being conducted here."

The warehouse area is awe-inspiring, both in its size and in its organization. There are more than 8 acres of air-conditioned warehouse space with 47-foot ceilings—high enough for five stories of shelving. The warehouse is spotless. The floors gleam, and there is not a piece of trash or dust bunny in sight. The provenance, arrival date, and warehouse location of every single bottle and keg can be pulled up on the computer at a moment's notice. This is important information when product arrives daily from the world's thousands of distilleries, vineyards, and breweries.

Loading of the company's fleet of 50 refrigerated delivery trucks is accomplished with the help of a computer and a labyrinth of conveyor belts that move product at a thunderous pace. Automatic barcode readers confirm the accuracy of each shipment. Las Vegas, with its high summer temperatures and low humidity, poses several challenges to a wine and liquor distributor. To counter these adverse conditions, much of WBN's warehouse space is refrigerated; kept at the perfect 58 degrees for wine storage or 32 degrees for beer. Food and beverage managers and chefs visiting the facility know that the products they receive from WBN have been cared for properly. As a result of the success of WBN's operation in Las Vegas, Wirtz Beverage Group (WBG) opened an even larger facility in Chicago. That warehouse uses all robotic pickers to restock beverages and fill orders. The company has seen big advantages because they are more accurate than human employees and never call in sick.

Drew Levinson is WBN's director of strategic activation. Both John and Drew make the comparison that "Wirtz is no longer just a distribution company than one of the casino resorts like Bellagio or Cosmopolitan is just a gambling hall. We are now a beverage consulting company." It was no longer working to rely on brand managers who represent all the products of a company, which may include all types of spirits and wines. They "turned the model sideways" and now employ category experts that specialize in a single product such as whiskey, tequila, sake, boutique wines, craft beers, and cocktail development. And even that is not enough. Originally, those specialists were working individually. Now they are all supervised by Drew as part of the "Strategic Activation Team." By serving as a one-stop consultant for all aspects of beverage, the team can bring the most value to its customers. Drew sums it up as that we have "agility, capability, and a consulting mind-set."

Katie Prindl serves in a relatively new position for the team of new accounts manager. When a client is opening a new restaurant or bar she can work with them to set up the proper licenses and credit processes. After an assessment of the client's goals, she acts as the "quarterback" along with Drew to determine who from the team will help and how many types of alcoholic products and drink recipes the establishment should serve. For example, the tequila expert would get more involved in a new Latin American restaurant and the whisky/scotch expert would have more of a role for a classic steakhouse. But the whole team would most likely contribute in some way.

Master Sommelier Thomas Burke is another member of the team. As the director of category education—wine—he teaches both beginner and intermediate classes for all WBN employees, in addition to providing training for restaurant personnel and aspiring master sommelier students. Eric Swanson, director of sake, is one of the two recognized sake experts whose native language is English. Fluent in Japanese, Swanson conducts numerous trade and charitable events nationwide featuring Wirtz's vast portfolio of sakes. Products such as sake, soju, and Asian beers are now so popular that WBN added Aya Namamoto to the Strategic Activation Team as category director for their Asian portfolio.

One way the team helps determine the needs of a new beverage program or how to revise an existing one to achieve higher sales and be more profitable is to find out how the actual or projected sales compare to national statistics. Drew consults Beverage Information Group's digital resources and statistics constantly, in particular national and statewide consumption patterns. He also reviews alcohol categories in terms of total sales volumes and a category's percent of those volumes. For example, nationally tequila is 6 percent of alcohol sales, but Las Vegas is "overindexed" because tequila is 13 percent of sales for Las Vegas. Therefore, it would be beneficial for a restaurant that only has tequila sales of 5 percent to evaluate whether it is serving the right brands and types of tequila cocktails and how it can increase its average.

While working as master mixologist and beverage director at Bellagio Hotel and Casino, Drew saw the flaws in the frontline hotel and restaurant training and development for new beverage programs and menus. In the kitchen, you can find space to prepare new menu items, perform tastings, and train staff. But for the bar, you do not want to disturb the employees or guests by working at the front bars,

A DAY AT AN ALCOHOLIC BEVERAGE DISTRIBUTION COMPANY (continued)

there is not enough room at service bars in the back of the house, and portable banquet bars are not set up the same way as restaurant bars.

When he started working at WBN, he had the opportunity to build a training facility that was as exact a replica of a working restaurant or hotel bar as possible. Thus, the Alchemy Room, a cutting-edge beverage education and lab was born. The first-class facility is known industry-wide for hosting special events, trainings, demonstrations, recipe tastings, educational seminars, cocktail competitions, product kick-offs, and much more. It even includes overhead cameras that look straight down on the bar so clients can see how a drink is made from the bartender's perspective. The room has been so successful that WBN now hosts an average of 7–9 training sessions per week topping more than 300 classes per year. Like the warehouse, the Alchemy Room has now been duplicated and enhanced at the Chicago location. That one includes a demonstration kitchen too.

The WBN team also adds value by participating in special events with its suppliers. Sponsoring wine, beer, and spirits dinners can educate guests and create a market for their products. The company is very active in the community, assisting such events as the Nevada Restaurant Association Epicurean Affair; the Life is Beautiful music, food, and art festival; and many more. These also keep the WBN name in the front of people's minds.

The next evolution in WBN's services will be using a new sales force automation system. WBG recently purchased an Enterprise Resource Planning (ERP) software system. It had a multi-million-dollar cost, but the cloud-based system, accessible from any device, will integrate all aspects of inventory, ordering, sales, and consulting. Just some of the items that the staff will have instantaneous access to are live inventories, live allocations for certain accounts, sales sheets, national and local competitive data sets, and product information, tasting notes, pictures, videos, and recipes. Buyers will do all ordering through the system. It will even be integrated with the company's human resources processes. By harnessing these new technologies, WBN sales teams are able to enhance their "consultative" approach to the business.

Staying on top of the trends and predicting new ones is always an important part of the job. John says that one of the major ones affecting the beverage business is that national accounts such as Chili's, Applebee's, and MGM Resorts International as well as regional chains are moving toward having corporate purchasing programs. By buying for the whole company, they can build better leverage and get better pricing from the distributors. The negative side is that the homogenous offerings may not reflect the tastes of the local guests, and the quantities needed to supply certain products nationally may not be available. John and Drew both believe that the national accounts also need to leave room for their restaurants to serve items from local suppliers, in particular, craft beers. Consolidations among the large alcoholic beverage suppliers such as Diageo and Anheuser-Busch InBev are also constantly changing the business and the products available.

Wirtz Beverage Group's website (www.wirtzbev.com) states that WBG "is transforming the identity and execution standards of beverage distribution, earning distinction by embracing innovation and aggressively driving top-line growth. Quality and integrity are company hallmarks." John Smith, Drew Levinson, and the rest of the team at Wirtz Beverage Nevada carry out that philosophy every day. By acting as consultants to, and partners with, their clients, they are changing the nature of the beverage distribution industry.

SELECTION FACTORS

For discussion purposes, we assume that the hospitality operation has a full liquor license and is allowed to serve wine, beer, and distilled spirits. Operators must consider a few selection factors.

■ Intended Use

As always, buyers want to determine exactly what the intended use of an item is so that they will be able to prepare the appropriate, relevant specification. For example, a house wine may be packaged differently than wines that will be sold by the bottle.

■ Exact Name

Numerous types and variations of beverage alcohols exist (see Figure 22.5 for some of the more popular products the beverage service industry uses). Therefore, to avoid the risk of receiving something that will not suit their needs, buyers must specify the exact name of the item they want. Usually, this selection factor presents no difficulty because over the years, a great deal of standardization has developed in this channel of distribution. Liquor-producing countries and states typically define several of the alcoholic products made within their borders, as well as part or all of the production processes. Also, standards of identity exist for many items. For example,

Beer	Distilled Spirits	Wine
Altbier	Bourbon Whiskey	Aromatized Wine (e.g., Vermouth)
American Lager	Brandy	Fortified Wine (e.g., Port and Sherry)
American Pale Ale	Cachaca	Dessert Wine (e.g., Eiswein and
Barleywine	Canadian Whiskey	Sauternes)
Belgian Ale	Cordial	Sparkling Wine (e.g., Champagne,
Bitter and English Pale Ale	Corn Whiskey	Cava, Prosecco)
Bock	Grappa	Table Wine (e.g., Chardonnay and
Brown Ale	Gin	Cabernet Sauvignon)
English, Scottish, or Belgian Strong Ale	Irish Whiskey	Red Wine (e.g., Syrah, Merlot, Pinot
European Dark Lager	Liqueur	Noir, Malbec)
European Pale Lager	Ouzo	White Wine (e.g., Sauvignon Blanc,
French Ale	Pisco	Semillon, Pinot Grigio)
Fruit Beer	Raki	Rose Wine (e.g., White Zinfandel,
German Amber Lager	Rum	White Merlot)
Imperial Stout	Rye Whiskey	
India Pale Ale	Scotch Whiskey	
Koelsch	Tequila	
Lambic	Vodka	
Light Ale		
Porter		
Scottish Ale		
Smoked Beer		
Stout		
Wheat Beer		

FIGURE 22.5 Popular types of beverage alcohols.

bourbon must meet a certain formula, as must Tennessee whiskey. Furthermore, vintners who grow their own grapes typically must follow certain pruning processes on the vines; this is especially true in Europe.

■ Brand Name (or Equivalent)

The most fundamental selection factor is the brand name. For the vast majority of beverage alcohols, a brand name tends to be the only characteristic a patron considers. Substituting an "equivalent" brand may be difficult if patrons insist on being served a specific wine, beer, or spirit. Convincing customers to try a different brand of beer or wine instead of the preferred one may be possible. Also, guests may allow the usage of comparable brands under certain situations, such as a banquet, but generally, many guests have specific desires and are not eager to change.

Where the law allows, some hospitality operators can purchase beverage alcohols that carry customized brand labels. Private labeling of wines is common. For instance, hotel guests may find the hotel's name on a bottle of wine that is stocked in their room's minibar refrigerator. This tactic enhances the hotel's advertising and promotion program. It also makes it difficult for guests to compare the hotel's price with comparable wine prices at a local liquor store. For example Wolfgang Puck and Marc Forgione have wines that are available wherever wine is sold and also use this product in their restaurants.

■ Vintage

The vintage, or the year in which the beverage alcohol is produced, is associated most with fine wines. Therefore, the vintage is an essential selection criterion. Also, the year or date of production is important when buyers purchase products that could lose quality. This is especially true of wines with low tannins (i.e., compounds that precipitate proteins and give wines their astringency or "pucker power"), such as Chenin Blanc or Sauvignon Blanc; low-alcohol or lightly hopped beers, such as stouts; and other beverage alcohols that have a limited shelf life. Unfortunately, some wine and beer companies do not indicate production years.

In addition to the vintage, skilled buyers also consider the wine manufacturer. They must also check the production date for nonalcoholic beers. Alcohol acts as a preservative, so old nonalcoholic beers may not have a satisfying taste. Most brewers have realized this and typically date-code these products.

■ Alcohol Content

Beverage alcohols have varying levels of **alcohol content**. In general, the alcohol content in beer products ranges from approximately 3.2 percent to more than 6 percent. Wines contain approximately 12 percent to as much as 20 percent alcohol. Most distilled spirits rate about 70 proof, or 35 percent alcohol, up to 151 proof, or 75.5 percent alcohol.

> **alcohol content** The amount of alcohol in a beverage, expressed as a percentage or as a proof.

Usually, the state or local government agency controls the alcohol content of these beverages. For instance, some areas prohibit the sale of any distilled spirit that exceeds 100 proof. Because of such restrictions, many breweries, wineries, and distilleries manufacture products with varying alcoholic strengths.

Because brands of liquor can have different alcoholic strengths, buyers must be very careful to avoid ordering and receiving products that they cannot use. For example, it is not uncommon for a distiller to sell an 80-proof bourbon and a 100-proof bourbon under the same brand name. In addition to a brand with different proofs, "light" distilled spirits are about 54 proof; that is, they contain approximately one-third less alcohol than a standard 80-proof spirit. Furthermore, nonalcoholic beers and wines are available.

Some buyers are concerned primarily with the alcohol content of a beverage. For instance, brandies used in flaming dishes should have high alcohol content. Buyers may also consider alcohol content when they compare various brands of the same liquor. For example, having decided on a well Scotch, a buyer might opt for a higher-proof beverage even though its brand name may be unfamiliar. Some hospitality operators believe that brand names need not be a major consideration if guests are not likely to see them. Obscure brands of liquor with proofs equal to or greater than premium brands are attractive products that may not differ significantly in taste from the premium brands. So, if purchasing unfamiliar brands is more economical and does not compromise the operations' standard of quality, then operators should at least consider them.

■ Size of Container

Package sizes are standardized in this channel of distribution. As a result, buyers should have little difficulty with this selection factor (see Figure 22.6).

Of course, buyers must determine the size that best fits their needs. For example, generally, the larger the size, the less per milliliter or ounce buyers will pay for the product. However, they may not want to invest in a large package size if the item purchased is a slow mover or is subject to spoilage.

BEER
12-ounce bottle (available in plastic or glass)
12-ounce can
Keg (15.5 gallons)
Keg (13.2 gallons)
1/2 keg (7.75 gallons)
1/4 keg (3.88 gallons)

DISTILLED SPIRITS
750-ml bottle
1-liter bottle
1.75-liter bottle

WINE

1/4 bottle	175 ml	
1/2 bottle	375 ml	Demi-bottle (split)
1 bottle	750 ml	Bottle
2 bottles	1.5 l	Magnum
4 bottles	3.0 l	Jeroboam
6 bottles	4.5 l	Rehoboam
8 bottles	6.0 l	Methuselah
12 bottles	9.0 l	Salmanazar
16 bottles	12.0 l	Balthazar
20 bottles	16.0 l	Nebuchadnezzar

FIGURE 22.6 Popular container sizes for beverage alcohols.

■ Type of Container

Packaging materials are also standardized in the beverage alcohol distribution channel. Generally, products come in cans, kegs, glass bottles, and plastic bottles. Some products, such as a few wines, come in "bag-in-the-box" packages; these are bulk wines packed in a plastic liner and then placed into a cardboard box, similar to the bulk milk containers used in milk-dispensing machines.

It is possible that a company will manufacture a product, such as table wine, and package it in corked bottles and in bottles with screw-top lids. Usually, a distinction in the exact name indicates this type of packaging difference. However, buyers must ensure that they do not accidentally purchase a product that their hospitality operation cannot use.

Some opportunities are available for buyers to personalize their beverage containers. Recall that buyers might consider purchasing beverage alcohols from a supplier who is willing to include their hospitality operation's name and logo on the package label, thereby creating a more impressive merchandising effect and customer experience. **Personalized packaging** for liquor products is especially popular in hotels that use these products for room service and catered events. Personalized items also make excellent additions to complimentary fruit baskets in guest rooms.

> **personalized packaging** Unique packaging produced according to the buyer's specific requirements. Normally includes the buyer's company logo and/or other proprietary marks.
>
> **point of origin** Refers to the part of the world where a product originates. Important selection factor for some food items, as the point of origin can have a significant impact on their culinary quality.

■ Point of Origin

The **point of origin** is a very important selection factor for wines. It implies taste variations. In some cases, as with imported wines, the point of origin denotes the type of government inspection to which the products were submitted.

■ Preservation Method

Although operators normally serve red wines at about 60 °F, and white, rosé, and sparkling wines at refrigerated temperatures, about 40 °F, they and the distributors should maintain all wines at cool temperatures.

Distributors and operators should keep canned and bottled beers cool as well. In addition, they must keep draft beer, which has the shortest shelf life of all beverage alcohols, under constant refrigeration. Otherwise, this type of beer tends to lose its culinary quality very rapidly. To maintain the quality, distributors should ensure that canned, bottled, and draft beers are transported under optimal conditions.

Distributors should store wines and beers in a dark environment. Light has a negative impact on these products. In fact, even a brief exposure to natural light can adversely affect their flavor.

Distributors can, however, keep distilled spirits at any temperature, although excessive heat will tend to cause them to evaporate. Also, products with considerable sugar in them can sour under extreme heat conditions. Generally, though, because distilled spirits are inert products, their shelf lives are virtually unlimited.

Distributors usually do not find it too difficult to maintain proper temperatures, but this is not the case in the control states where buyers must pick up their orders from the state liquor store warehouses. Unless they have an appropriate vehicle, or can hire one, their liquor items will not have the best possible in-transit storage environment.

CRAFT BEERS

Mark Lawson, Craft Brand Manager, Cicerone Certified Beer Server, and MBAA Beer Steward
Bill Leaver, Craft Brand Specialist, Key Account Manager, Cicerone Certified Beer Server
Jeff Bradach, Marketing Coordinator
Nevada Beverage Company, Las Vegas Nevada

Courtesy of Bill Leaver

In 2015, the total beer market in the United States was $105.9 billion and the craft beer segment was $22.3 billion or more than 24 billion barrels of beer. Craft beer production increased 16 percent over the previous year.[1]

Craft beer is produced by a brewery that is small, independent, and traditional as defined by the Brewer's Association. Small means the brewery produces less than six million barrels of beer annually. Independent means that less than 25 percent of the brewery is owned or controlled by an alcoholic beverage entity that is not itself considered a craft brewer. Traditional refers to the techniques and ingredients, like malted barley used to brew and ferment the beverage. However, craft brewers use unique twists and develop new styles of beer. Craft beer breweries have distinctive, individualistic approaches to their beer recipes, brewing procedures, marketing strategies, customers, and communities.[2]

The definition of craft beer based on size and ownership creates paradoxes for breweries wanting to be popular but not becoming too large or affiliating with a large brewing company. At 2.5 million cases per year, Sam Adams is one of the largest producers of craft beer. However, some of the other original craft beer pioneers, such as Widmer Brothers (Oregon) and Redhook (Washington), are no longer considered craft beers because both sold part of the company to Anheuser-Busch (AB) in exchange for distribution rights by the AB wholesaler network.

Nevada Beverage Company (NBC) is one of the 10 largest beer distributors in the United States. Due to craft beer's importance for hospitality and retail sales, NBC has a special craft beer philosophy and craft beer team. The company "is committed to acquiring quality, handcrafted, world-class craft brands that not only provide balance and strength to our current portfolio, but provide the consumer with a unique drinking experience."

Craft Brand Manager Mark Lawson is the face of NBC to craft brand suppliers. He studies market trends locally and nationally and coordinates the craft beer portfolio in regard to inventories, seasonal and limited releases, ordering, pricing, and educating the general sales staff about beer styles and new brands. As a Craft Brand Specialist and Key Account Manager (KAM), Bill Leaver is part of the frontline team, selling and training people about craft beer. Jeff Bradach, Marketing Coordinator, supports the craft team's efforts with marketing and planning all special events for NBC.

NBC sells approximately 2.5 million dollars of craft beer annually from a portfolio of beers from all over the country, from companies such as Abita from Louisiana, Alaskan Brewing, Epic Brewing from Utah, Gordon Biersch Brewing from California, and Kona Brewing from Hawaii.

Although the company has more than 2,900 accounts, only about 50 or 60 are what the team considers "craft-centric" Key Accounts. These include national chains such as Total Wine & More,

CRAFT BEERS (continued)

Yardhouse restaurants, casino restaurants such as The Pub in the Monte Carlo hotel in Las Vegas, and local liquor stores and bars.

Although the KAM job description officially uses the term sales, Jeff emphasizes that it's more about educating, rather than "selling." A KAM's success is based on his or her relationships with accounts, providing them high quality products for their discerning guests, and assisting with 3 Ps—pricing, position, and point of sales (POS) materials. One of the challenges is tailoring what craft beers they pitch to the particular account. Bill explains that because all craft beers are different, you have to sell each separately and meet frequently with owners and managers. Bill does not like to tell the customer what brand to sell; he would rather they choose the specific style of beer they are looking for to fit their customer needs. If they are looking for an IPA or Belgian Wit, he will sample the customer on all of the brands of that style NBC carries and let them decide which to buy.

Establishments that sell craft beers have to know the demographics of their guests. In terms of age, Mark calls the 21- to 25- and the 30-year-old groups who want to try the newest beers "trendsetters" and the 30- to 50-year-old group, who are willing to pay more for higher-quality beer, "the bourbon set." Surprisingly, international visitors to Las Vegas do not drink a lot of craft beer. For example, in many countries, such as Ireland and Japan, brands like Budweiser are expensive "import" beers. Therefore, tourists from those countries order it when they come to the United States because it is more readily available and cheaper than in their home countries.

Once a restaurant or bar selects the craft beers it will serve, its managers may be uncertain of how much they will sell versus the tried-and-true brands. This creates a challenge for Mark of deciding how much of each craft brand NBC needs to buy from its suppliers. Because beer is considered a food product and has a very limited shelf life, he does not want to overorder. But if NBC is out of stock, it may be very difficult to get more beer quickly, especially from smaller brewers with limited production. In addition, unlike wine and spirits, with craft beers there are many seasonal and limited edition beers. The craft beer team has to get product information and start selling these products months in advance of their availability dates.

What's in store for the future of craft beer? One trend that Mark sees is selling more craft beer in cans. Cans maintain beer quality much better than bottles because they let in less light and oxygen. They also are cheaper and easier to recycle. For craft beers, canned beer is a big point of difference, especially when sold in 16-ounce cans. Some breweries, like Golden Road (GR) from Los Angeles, use only cans to package their beers. GR also has one of the few female brewery owners.

The NBC team also sees more segmentation in the market between the top-tier macro craft breweries and regional peers with deep penetration in their markets. One regional example is Ninkasi Brewing Company from Eugene, Oregon which now sells in seven states including Colorado, Idaho, and Nevada, and is ranked as the 30th-largest craft brewery in the United States.

If you want to learn more about beers, in particular craft beers, the NBC Craft Beer Team recommends attending the largest beer festival in the United States—the Great American Beer Festival (GABF) held in Denver each October, as well as craft beer events in your area.

CRAFT BEERS (continued)

■ REFERENCES

1. Watson, B. & Herz, J., "National Beer Sales and Production Data." https://www .brewersassociation.org/statistics/national-beer-sales-production-data/.

2. Brewers Association, "Craft Brewer Defined." https://www.brewersassociation.org/statistics/ craft-brewer-defined/.

AP PRICE AND SUPPLIER FACTORS

■ AP Price

Normally, buyers must pay the going price for the liquor items they stock. The price is controlled directly, as in a control state, or indirectly, as in a state that requires minimum wholesale prices.

> **price maintenance**
> Another term for price control.

Today, **price maintenance** for beverage alcohols is not as restrictive as it once was. Liquor buyers and liquor retailers in some states have more flexibility in setting their prices. Because the largest part of the price can represent tax, however, we may never see a completely free market in beverage alcohols. For example, the 2016 federal tax rate on beer is $18 for a 31 gallon barrel, wine is $1.07/gallon for varieties 14 percent alcohol or lower, and 100 proof spirits is $13.50/gallon.[5]

As with most products hospitality operators purchase, quantity buys for beverage alcohols are available. Because of this, buyers can expect to achieve a quantity discount. However, other ways to attain potential savings exist, so buyers are not required to invest in considerably more of a product than they might be able to use within a reasonable time.

One of these other ways buyers can save on liquor, typically about 10 percent, is by purchasing the largest possible containers, such as the 1.75-liter bottle of distilled spirits. These

> **automatic dispenser**
> A piece of equipment that allots a portion-controlled amount of beverage.
>
> **post-off** Term used for a discount offered by a beverage alcohols vendor.

containers are clumsy, but they are acceptable or even preferable when a bar has **automatic dispensers**. When a bartender uses an automatic dispenser, a push of a button can automatically dispense a portion-controlled amount of beverage into a glass.

States sometimes permit distributors to offer price discounts. These discounts are sometimes referred to as **post-offs** in control states. Distributors can and usually do grant these discounts, which do not always take the form of money. Sometimes buyers receive, for example, a free bottle of liquor for every case or two that they purchase at the regular AP price. Post-offs normally do not require buyers to greatly alter their orders to obtain them. These discounts may, perhaps, require them to slightly increase their order size to achieve a substantial savings.

Buyers must also be concerned with import duty. Taxes and tariffs levied on imported products can have a major impact on the AP price. Some imported products have lower tariffs than others; consequently, a considerable price differential may exist among several similar items. For well items, buyers have an opportunity to at least consider the AP price differences when making a decision in this area.

■ Supplier Services

For well brands, management has a choice about which brands to use; hence, the AP price might be important for these items. Because differences in AP prices among the major brands are slight, however, supplier services may be more important.

One supplier service that distributors provide is the simplification of clerical routines; for example, they may be able to provide paperwork forms, such as blank purchase orders and bin cards, to their customers. These forms can save operators some money, and because they are required to maintain records of their purchases of beverage alcohols, the forms represent a worthwhile supplier service. As we move toward a paperless environment, distributors may improve services by operating in a virtual marketplace. Distributors who are efficiently and seamlessly linked with buyers through online services can further streamline the purchasing process. For example, the automation of the entire request for quote/purchase order (RFQ/PO) process can result in substantial savings of both time and money.

Distributors extend their services by providing classes in understanding and complying with local liquor codes. Others offer personnel training in suggestive selling and merchandising. Some hold tastings of new recipes and conduct seminars on beer, wine, and spirits. The sidebar by John Smith and Drew Levinson of Wirtz Beverage Nevada discussed many of the methods and people involved with educating their clientele. Although most hospitality operators are reluctant to let a supplier plan their food menus, they are usually willing to receive assistance in the preparation of a wine list. Operators who are not very familiar with wines find this service beneficial.

Some distributors allow for reasonable minimum-order requirements. This service is of particular importance when buyers need only one or two bottles of a slow-moving product. Conversely, buyers with extensive wine lists are eager to receive as much product as possible from the best wineries. When primary sources "allocate" product, buyers consider a large **allocation** a much-prized supplier service.

Although liquor distributors do what they can to provide some supplier services, the law severely restricts them in what they can do for their customers. Federal, state, and local governments strictly limit the types of supplier services distributors can give because the governments worry about kickbacks and other illegal temptations these supplier services invite.

> **allocation** Process whereby a distributor and/or primary source determines how much of a product you are allowed to purchase. Usually done with high-quality wines so that all restaurants have a chance to buy at least some of it.

PURCHASING BEVERAGE ALCOHOLS

To assist buyers in the purchase of beverage alcohols, the liquor industry generates a number of publications that note products, distributors, and AP prices. For instance, in Nevada, a monthly publication titled the *Nevada Beverage Analyst* contains this information. Beverage Media Group has a list of all the available state publications on its website. The *Beverage Industry News* has considerable information regarding the promotion and distribution of beverage alcohols in California, whereas Bevnet.com provides reviews of beverage products from around the world. The Beverage Information Group supplies a variety of beverage industry news, consumption trend information, handbooks, and research publications.

Once buyers select suppliers and determine the types of beverages they want, the purchasing procedure follows a fairly routine pattern. Ordering and delivery schedules become precise; buyers rarely have any control over them. In most cases, payment schedules are also predetermined. If buyers purchase product in a control state, the process follows strict regulations. Buyers usually order once a week and pay cash when they pick up their orders. If they buy in a license state, limited credit terms may be available.

Probably the biggest decision that buyers face is how much to order. The typical par stock is set for one week; slow-moving items may be ordered once a month or less often. Normally, buyers purchase in case lots with minimum-order requirements. This may present problems in situations where purchasing case quantities is not feasible. For example, if buyers' needs for a particular premium brand, which takes a year to sell, are less than the minimum-order size, they may be faced with the dilemma to carry it or drop it.

Many distributors may allow buyers to "break" the case. Buying a bottle from a "broken case" is usually more expensive than its **case price**. However, some distributors may permit buyers to combine different items to form a case lot. For instance, they may be able to buy two bottles each of six different brandies and receive a **mixed-case** price. This practice is regarded as an attractive supplier service because this price may be considerably lower than purchasing each bottle separately.

Buyers often face two other major decision points when purchasing beverage alcohols: (1) the post-off opportunity discussed earlier, and (2) the need, perhaps, to purchase a very large supply of one brand. For example, there is only so much vintage Duckhorn Vineyards Napa Valley Merlot® to go around. If customers like this wine, buyers might consider purchasing as much as possible to ensure that they can offer it for as long as possible. However, such a large purchase may require a **stockless purchase**, which would require buyers to pay now for the large order and have partial deliveries sent at specified times.

Once buyers know what they need, it is a good idea for them to prepare specifications for each beverage alcohol product (see Figure 22.7 for some examples of product specifications, and Figure 22.8 for an example of a product specification outline for beverage alcohol products).

The tendency in liquor purchasing exists to downplay the use of specifications, primarily because very few bid-buying opportunities are available. Also, buyers sometimes have the opportunity to evaluate products available only in their local area. This is especially true for fine wines and other specialty products.

Today, it is possible for buyers to contract with a winery, brewery, or distiller to prepare products according to their precise formulas. Some large hospitality operations may consider offering these house brands to customers. As with personalized packaging, the added prestige and merchandising value may more than compensate for the extra cost and effort that operations expend to secure these products.

case price   Equal to the AP price for one case divided by the number of units per case. For instance, if you pay $12 for a six-can case of canned tomatoes, the case price is $2 per can. If a vendor is willing to sell you less than one case, but charges you only $2 per can, he or she is charging the case price and not a premium price for a broken (busted) case.

mixed-case   A case that contains more than one type of item. Usually found in the beverage alcohol trade, where the vendor will allow the buyer to purchase a case of 12 bottles, but each bottle may be a different product. Vendors may allow this for products you purchase that you don't sell very quickly, such as specialty bourbons. Vendors who sell mixed cases are usually willing to charge the appropriate case price for each item.

stockless purchasing
When a buyer purchases a large amount of product, for example, a three-month supply, and arranges for the vendor to store it and deliver a little at a time.

Brandy
Used for drink service at main bar
E & J® brand (Original Extra Smooth)
80 proof
750-ml bottle

Alcohol-free white zinfandel
Used for wine list in main dining room
Sutter Home Fre® brand
Less than 0.5% alcohol by volume
750-ml bottle
Delivered at cool temperature

London dry gin
Used for drink service at main bar
Gilbey's® brand
80 proof
750-ml bottle

Vodka
Used for drink service at service bar
Smirnoff® brand
80 proof
1.75-l bottle

FIGURE 22.7 An example of beverage alcohol product specifications.

Intended use:
Exact name:
Brand name (or equivalent):
Vintage:
Alcohol content:
Size of container:
Type of container:
Point of origin:
Preservation method:

FIGURE 22.8 An example of a product specification outline for beverage alcohol products.

PROCEDURES FOR RECEIVING, STORING, AND ISSUING BEVERAGE ALCOHOLS

■ Receiving

Because alcohol has a high cost and involves extreme exposure to pilferage, hospitality operators spend much care and effort in the receiving area. Generally, the receiver is a supervisor, an owner–manager, or an assistant manager, and much less often a receiving clerk.

If a hospitality operation has an extensive wine list, and few staff members are sufficiently knowledgeable about wines, it is traditional, if not necessary, for a company to employ a sommelier, or wine steward. Contrary to the generally acceptable operating procedure of the separation of duties, the wine expert usually does it all: buys, receives, stores, and sells the wine in the dining room.

Whoever receives the product typically follows the procedures noted in Chapter 12. This individual checks the quantity, sometimes by weighing unopened cases, and compares the invoices against the POs, as well as against the beverage labels. It is crucial for the receiver to check labels very carefully. For example, some liqueurs are made with a brandy base and some are made with a neutral-spirits base; the labels indicate this distinction, but these labels may be unclear to the untrained receiver. Beer kegs can present some receiving difficulty. Some delivery agents want to attach the kegs to the hookups in the operation's refrigerator, or at least deliver them to the refrigerator, which may be against company policy. Another problem is that the kegs may be jostled too much at the receiving area, which can cause quality deterioration.

The receiver must also carefully compute the exact amount of the deposits that the company must put up for bottles and kegs, ascertain that these deposits are correct, and ensure that the company receives the appropriate credit for those kegs and bottles it is returning to the distributor.

After examining the merchandise and being satisfied that everything is correct, the receiver completes any required paperwork. It is important to keep in mind that the federal government requires hospitality operations to maintain liquor invoices and bill-paying records. State and local government agencies may have similar requirements.

■ Storing

Typically, hospitality operations designate a separate storage facility exclusively for beverage alcohols. It is commonplace for operations to inventory all beverage alcohols within the same general area. However, some operations also maintain separate storage facilities for beer and wine.

perpetual inventory
Keeping a running balance of an inventory item so that you always know what you have on hand. When a shipment is received you add to the balance, and every time you use some of it you deduct that amount. Similar to keeping an up-to-date cash balance in your personal checkbook.

Stolen liquor can be easily converted into cash. Therefore, operations should store beverage alcohols in a well-secured facility with as few individuals as possible having access to the keys. For example, the keys to a well-stocked wine cellar might be restricted to the wine steward and, perhaps, one or two other service personnel.

As mentioned previously, many operators maintain a **perpetual inventory** of most beverage alcohols. It is common to add the amount of new product placed in the storeroom to a bin card or to enter this figure into a computerized inventory management system. With beverage alcohols, most operators take the bottles out of their shipping containers. This extra security precaution, although less popular for bottled beer, eliminates the possibility of operators later discovering an empty bottle, or no bottle, in the liquor case.

Distilled spirits, wine, and beer all have somewhat unique storage requirements.

■ Distilled Spirits

This liquor requires little care, and its storage life is usually long. Hospitality operators should place distilled spirits in a dry storage facility devoid of direct sunlight and excessive heat. Some people believe that these spirits improve in flavor when they age a while, but this is not true once they are put in a bottle. In addition, if staff members leave some bottles even slightly open, evaporation can occur. Furthermore, operators should not store spirits that contain sugar for long once they have been opened; not only do they evaporate, but they also develop offensive odors and flavors.

■ Wine

Wines are harder to store than other beverage alcohols. They require specific temperature and humidity conditions. Generally, operators should store red wines in a cool area, whereas they usually should refrigerate white wines and sparkling wines because they are served cold.

Cork-bottled wines are stored on their side. This position enables the cork to remain moist, which facilitates its removal. When bottles are stored standing up for a protracted period, the cork may dry out. A dry cork permits more air to pass through it, and this air, in turn, causes wines to change gradually in flavor and eventually to become a type of vinegar. A final reason for storing wine bottles on their sides relates to old wines that contain sediment. If these wines are properly stored, the sediment will collect in the neck of the bottles, making it easier to remove it at the time of service.

Not all wines need to be stored in this manner. Wines that come in screw-top capped or synthetic corked bottles and fortified wines can be stored upright. Fortified wines, such as Madeira, sherry, and port, are wines to which brandy has been added to increase the alcohol content.

Wine should not be exposed to excessive heat or to widely fluctuating temperatures. Both condi-

FIGURE 22.9 A wine-dispensing unit.
©*VINOTEMP INTERNATIONAL*

tions can activate a chemical reaction that turns the wine into a form of vinegar. Consequently, operators should avoid displaying wines in the dining areas for long periods. In contrast to distilled spirits, some wines improve in flavor as they age in the bottle. In fact, wine has a life cycle: birth, adolescence, maturation, adulthood, and death. Red wines have longer lives than white wines. At times, buyers may have to purchase wine that is immature and wait for it to mature before it can be served.

Most wine sold in large bag-in-the-box bulk containers is sometimes referred to as **jug wine**. This kind of wine is often used for the house wine. Although this type of wine does not improve in flavor as it ages and has a relatively long shelf life, it can spoil if operators keep it too long after opening it.

If a hospitality operation wishes to serve leftover wine or to serve fine wines by the glass, it should consider purchasing a **wine-dispensing unit** specifically designed to store opened bottles of wine. An operator can open a wine bottle, serve one glass, and put the opened bottle in this unit where its quality will be maintained (see Figure 22.9). The unit typically uses a

> **jug wine** Refers to a product typically served as the house wine. Usually packed in large containers, such as bag-in-the-box containers.
>
> **wine-dispensing unit** Mechanical equipment that stores open wine and maintains its quality after opening. It can be programmed to dispense predetermined portion sizes.

nitrogen flush A gas-flushed pack. Using nitrogen to remove air, thereby removing all oxygen from the package. Done to enhance shelf life.

nitrogen-flushing process to eliminate oxygen, which causes quality deterioration; it also maintains the proper storage environment. Such a unit is very expensive; however, if an operation wishes to offer a "wine bar," it is an essential piece of equipment.

If an operation does not have this type of wine-dispensing unit, it can still save the opened wine and serve it later. To do this, the operator must reseal the bottle tightly, refrigerate it, and try to serve it as soon as possible. A bottle-sealing device on the market enables an operator to reseal an opened bottle, attach a hand pump, and physically pump out as much air from the bottle as possible. By pumping out most of the air, the operator extends the leftover wine's shelf life.

If it is impossible, or undesirable, to save opened wine, operations can, perhaps, use it for cooking purposes. They can also use it to make vinegar; for instance, a vinegar-starter kit on the market lets an operator add wine and possibly one or more other ingredients. Eventually, the operator can use the wine vinegar for salad dressings and other vinegar-based food items.

■ Beer

Keg beer is not pasteurized; therefore, hospitality operations must refrigerate it at approximately 36 °F to 38 °F. Otherwise, the active yeasts continue to work, manufacturing more alcohol and carbon dioxide gas. If this process continues long enough, it can negatively affect the beer's flavor. It can also cause a keg to explode.

Operations should not keep kegs more than two weeks. By this time, the quality and fresh taste will have vanished, and patrons will be sure to complain if operators try to serve it. At the very least, companies should plan to properly rotate the kegs and, if possible, to arrange for weekly deliveries.

Usually, operators store beer kegs in a walk-in refrigerator that is very close to the bar. They are tapped in place, and the beer travels through pipelines to the bar. If an operation has more than one bar, it might find it necessary to have a refrigerator for each one.

Operators must be careful when it comes to freezing beer. If it freezes and then thaws, they will find that a quantity of flakes will settle and refuse to go back into the solution. This will change the integrity of the beer, and therefore, it must be discarded.

Unlike keg beer, most canned and bottled beers are pasteurized. They have a longer life as a result of this process. When operators store canned beer in refrigerated conditions, it has a shelf life of approximately four months; bottled beer, on the other hand, has a shelf life that ranges from one to approximately six months. Without refrigeration, these shelf lives shrink to fewer than three months. By no means do canned and bottled beers retain their quality and fresh taste indefinitely.

Canned and bottled beers are often delivered in trucks that are not refrigerated. As a result, some quality deterioration will have already begun before the beer is received. However, operators may be able to retard the process if they immediately place these beers in a refrigerator.

Once an operator opens a can or bottle and pours the beer, there is no way to save any leftovers for later. The operator can use the open beer in some recipes, such as fish batter and cheese soup, but even here, fresh beer is preferable. Consequently, if the beer is not consumed, the operator can do little to preserve it for later use.

■ Issuing

Unlike most other food and nonfood items, beverage alcohols call for the strict scrutiny of owners and managers. In fact, some sort of perpetual inventory implemented in conjunction with tight security on the physical storage facilities is the rule rather than the exception. Many operations may leave food and nonfood storage facilities unattended and unguarded, but not beverage alcohol storage areas. Even if no full- or part-time storeroom manager is on hand, the owner–manager, assistant manager, or head bartender will complete this task. Employees rarely have the authority to get their own beverage alcohols.

Typically, a receiver prepares a stock requisition. An additional requirement may be to turn in an empty bottle for every full one requisitioned. Technically, however, this might be illegal in some states because those states require the empties to be broken as soon as they are drained.

Management also should set fairly strict par stocks for most, if not all, beverage alcohols. This makes it easier for bartenders to requisition only what they need. This practice also ensures that excess stock does not accumulate around the bar areas.

In operations that demand the strictest control, or in those that have several banquet bars or temporary bars, we might encounter a slightly different form of issuing. In these places, the head bartender or assistant manager might stock each bar; that is, bring it up to par. During the shift, if an employee needs additional product, it is obtained from the head bartender or assistant manager.

At the end of the shift, the employee either returns all the remaining stock to the storeroom or locks it up at a liquor station. The head bartender or assistant manager counts what is left and determines the liquor usage. This quantity of liquor should be converted to theoretical sales and should agree with the amount of sales recorded on the point of sale (POS) system and with the amount of cash and/or drink tickets collected from guests. This control procedure represents a little more work, but it is a worthwhile procedure. For places that can afford it, there are private companies, such as Bevinco, that provide this type of inventory-taking service for a modest fee. Other examples include Accubar, BarVision, and Barmaxx.

Before issuing beverage alcohols, especially distilled spirits, management may want to code the bottles with a number or with some other mark that can be seen only with an infrared light. Coding is done so that dishonest employees cannot substitute their own bottles, sell their own beverage to the guest, take the money, and pocket it without ringing up a sale.

If an operation maintains an extensive wine list, it might consider giving the wine steward free access to the wine storage facilities while selling it in the dining room. This may sound like poor management, but it can work out well if operators keep track of what the wine steward buys and sells in the dining room. A physical inventory, performed regularly, can also help to uncover any inexplicable shortages or other problems attributable to the wine steward.

Operations that have an extensive automatic bar system can simplify the issuing process and, in some cases, eliminate it for many beverage items. For example, in a large hotel, several bar areas throughout the property may be connected to a central liquor-dispensing room. This room holds all the liquor, which is fed through pipelines that end at the dispensing heads located at each bar. Bartenders, therefore, do not have to requisition these beverage alcohols because someone, usually an employee of the food and beverage control office, loads the beverages on the system and is responsible for maintaining a constant supply.

■ In-Process Inventories

Purchasing, receiving, storing, and issuing beverage alcohols are not difficult tasks, although selecting and procuring a list of fine wines can be. The real difficulties lie in the preparation and service of these products. The general feeling in the hospitality industry seems to be that when dealing with food, operators must be primarily concerned with quality and product control—for example, with meat shrinkage and excessive trimming losses. Because beverage alcohols do not involve such problems, the primary concern is personnel control.

Certainly, some problems can be associated with beverage alcohol product control, but they are minimal: basically, a bit of over- or underpour, spillage, and an occasional mistake. These problems are easily controlled.

Security considerations are the real problem in bars. Bartenders may begin to pour free drinks for other employees or for their friends. They may take it upon themselves to pour drinks "on the house." In addition, they may overpour for their friends and make up the difference by under-pouring for other patrons or by replenishing the liquor supply with water. This method is a form of **inventory padding**. Alternately, they may charge their friends for less than they actually consumed, making up the difference by overcharging a guest who is not fully aware of what was actually purchased. This is sometimes referred to as **check padding**; that is, an unsuspecting patron's guest check is padded with overcharges. Some bar operators employ a mystery shopping service to help prevent these problems.

So many opportunities for dishonesty exist in the bar business that it can be tiring just to enumerate them. However, hospitality operators cannot ignore them. Operators must practice tight security procedures, and when they do, they need to take note of the most important security measure of all: supervision. Because our primary concern in bars is personnel control, it stands to reason that the most effective tool is employee supervision.

> **inventory padding**
> Reporting a false inventory amount by indicating that there is more inventory on hand. A fraud that is usually committed to make the actual cost of food or beverage sold appear to be less than it is.
>
> **check padding**
> Overcharging a customer to make up for under-charging another customer. Alternately, overcharging a customer to pocket the extra cash.

MANAGEMENT CONSIDERATIONS FOR NONALCOHOLIC BEVERAGES

The growth in the nonalcoholic beverages industry is evident by the expanding number of both traditional and new beverages available in the marketplace. Café latte, green tea, specialty waters, sports drinks, and energy drinks are now commonplace in foodservice operations.

In many respects, the purchasing of nonalcoholic beverages parallels that of beverage alcohols. Of course, operators have more freedom here, mainly because patrons do not seem to have the same brand loyalties as they do for beverage alcohols. For instance, if an operation does not serve Coca-Cola®, only a few customers will balk at Pepsi®. On the other hand, some soft-drink companies are very active in enforcing their rights under copyright law, and so, in listing soft drinks, as on a menu or drink list, operators must take care to be accurate. The terms "Coca-Cola" and "Coke" are proprietary brand names and can be used only when Coca-Cola is served.

Management must make several decisions about nonalcoholic beverages, but the three most important are: (1) How many varieties should the operation carry? Operations could offer several types of soft drinks, juices, teas, and mixers. One brand of coffee and milk is sufficient, but soft drinks represent a major area of decision. (2) Should the operation have soft drinks available in bottles and cans, or should it use dispensing machines that mix concentrate, water, and carbon dioxide? Although canned and bottled products are more convenient, they are less profitable. In addition, some customers prefer soft drinks in a glass or disposable container, with ice, because the beverage stays fresher and colder. (3) Who will supply the coffee? Because of the various types and qualities of products available, selecting the right coffee supplier is critical. Choosing the right coffee supplier is a lesson that most seasoned hospitality operators learn quite early in their careers. With the aid of the supplier, an operator very carefully selects coffees and teas that are appropriate for that particular type of hospitality operation. When compared with the impression coffees and teas leave with customers, the portion cost of coffees and teas is insignificant. A great deal of hand-wringing accompanies a hospitality operator's decision to take a chance with a product that will "save money." So, as in the selection of a meat supplier, it is unusual for operators to switch coffee suppliers capriciously.

SELECTION FACTORS FOR NONALCOHOLIC BEVERAGES

Despite the relative purchasing freedom nonalcoholic beverages permit, buyers must quite carefully consider the selection factors before deciding what to purchase. Once they know what they want, the buying is easy, especially because the same type of exclusive wholesale-distributorship system that exists for many beverage alcohols also exists for many nonalcoholic beverages. The major selection factors are described here.

■ Intended Use

As always, buyers need to determine exactly what the intended use of an item is so that they will be able to prepare the appropriate, relevant specification. For instance, a juice used in an alcoholic punch recipe may be of lower quality than one that will be served straight.

■ Exact Name

Some nonalcoholic beverages have standards of identity that the federal government sets. For instance, the word *juice* on a label or package implies that the product is 100 percent derived from the fruit or vegetable—no water is added.

This is not true for all products, though. For instance, several types of "drinks" are on the market, and buyers need to examine these items very carefully for taste, color, and so forth before determining their suitability.

To some extent, certain types of nonalcoholic beverage producers follow and adhere to trade association standards. For instance, the National Coffee Association (NCA) sets minimum standards for coffee products. NCA works closely with the industry to set those standards.

■ U.S. Government Grades (or Equivalent)

Grades exist for fruit and vegetable juices and milk, as noted in Chapters 16 and 17. Other non-alcoholic beverages carry no grades. For example, tea grades vary all around the world. In the United States, there is a complex lettering system for black teas based more on tea leaf size than quality. There are no standards for green tea, whereas the USDA provides classifications for types of tea mixes, but not grades.[6]

■ Organic, Natural, Fair Trade

As discussed regarding many food product categories, buyers and consumers may look to organic and natural standards as an alternative to quality grades. The use of the organic label on coffee and tea products is subject to USDA third-party federal inspection for compliance. To meet the USDA requirements, organic coffee and tea must be grown using materials that have a low environmental impact. These growing systems must also replenish and maintain the fertility of the soil while not relying on the use of pesticides and fertilizers.[7]

For a product to bear the label of natural, it must be grown and harvested without the use of synthetic pesticides, herbicides, insecticides, and fertilizers. In addition, if coffee is to be sold as decaffeinated, the chemical methylene chloride may not be used in the process.[8]

FIGURE 22.10 A Fair Trade label.

©fairtradeusa.org

> **Fair Trade** Products produced by farmers who are compensated fairly for their work. They have the fair trade logo displayed on their packaging.

As popularized by Starbuck's®, **Fair Trade** is another classification that buyers should be aware of. Products that have the Fair Trade logo displayed on them come from farmers who are compensated fairly for their work (see Figure 22.10). The nonprofit organization, Fair Trade USA, works with farmers and communities directly to teach them how to benefit from using the free market.[9]

■ Brand Name (or Equivalent)

Brand names are important to buyers, who are accustomed, through habit and advertising, to relying on certain products, but many customers are indifferent to brands. One point buyers need to keep in mind about brand names is that they may be able to promote a certain brand, thereby enhancing their business. Some suppliers help buyers by providing some type of promotional discount, customized events, or POS materials. In addition to the choice of soft drinks brand, hospitality operations are increasingly electing to promote their use of a particular coffee brand, such as Starbucks®, Lavazza®, or Illy®.

Other buyers are not tied to a brand. They can shop around, and if the quality and customer acceptance are similar, they will have a reasonable choice among brands. However, buyers must remain mindful of what we said earlier about copyright laws and proprietary rights of suppliers in regard to brand names.

■ Size of Container

A fairly wide array of package sizes is available to buyers of nonalcoholic beverages. Sizes normally range from 6-ounce, single-serve containers to 5-gallon kegs of syrup. In general, in the carbonated-soft-drink trade, the sizes are not as numerous as they are in, say, the fruit and vegetable juices line. Nevertheless, it is very important for buyers to select and procure the package size that suits their needs best.

■ Type of Container

Nonalcoholic beverages come in different sizes and types of containers made of various packaging materials. The quality of these materials is standardized. Consequently, the buyers' major decision is determining which type of material suits their needs most effectively. For some products, such as soft-drink syrup, their choices usually are limited to bottles, kegs, and bag-in-the-box containers. For other items, such as ready-to-serve drinks, additional options are available.

Some suppliers offer unique types of containers, though these ordinarily can be used only in the dispensing equipment that they provide. For instance, some Vitality® brand juices can be purchased in an Express Pak® that fits snugly into the Vitality dispenser. The dispenser releases a programmed portion size at the push of a button.

Buyers might be interested in personalized packaging for some of their nonalcoholic beverages. For instance, some dairies will use private labels on the single-serve containers of milk that operations purchase. A corollary might be the willingness of a soft-drink company to personalize the disposable drink cups sold to operations, along with the syrup.

As a convenient alternative, hospitality companies can purchase some nonalcoholic beverages that are not packaged. For instance, certain soft-drink suppliers can pump syrup from their trucks into the operations' reusable tanks, which are attached to the dispensing machine. This can reduce packaging needs and contribute to a cleaner environment. This process is commonly used in fast-food organizations such as McDonald's and Burger King.

■ Product Form

Buyers can purchase ready-to-serve, or **premix**, beverages. These beverages can be purchased in bottles, plastic cartons, waxed cartons, cans, kegs, and bag-in-the-box containers. Buyers can also purchase **postmix** beverages. Postmix products require someone on the staff of the hospitality operation to do some additional preparation. Buyers purchase these products in forms similar to the containers in which premix products are packed.

With postmix products, buyers anticipate saving a few dollars because they are purchasing concentrates—frozen, dried, or liquid—and are providing the reconstitution needed to make the item ready for service. For instance, most carbonated-soft-drink dispensing units are set up in such a way that a hospitality staff member must hook up a water supply line, a container of concentrate, and a cylinder of carbon dioxide gas. When customers order soft drinks, or help themselves to the soft drink machines located in the dining areas, the ingredients are mixed as they flow through the lines into the glass or disposable drink cup. This procedure also provides a freshly mixed finished product, which is pleasing to the customer.

> **premix**   Refers to a ready-to-serve nonalcoholic beverage, such as a 12-ounce can of Coke.
>
> **postmix**   Refers to a nonalcoholic beverage concentrate, such as frozen juice concentrate or soda pop syrup, that must be reconstituted just before serving it to customers.

Buyers must consider other product characteristics when purchasing nonalcoholic beverages, such as whether the cola is diet or regular and whether the coffee is regular or decaffeinated. Other considerations may include the type of grind desired (or whole bean), roast (light to dark), and growing region (such as Kona in Hawaii) for brewed coffee, also the size and type of crystals for instant coffee.

Buyers can purchase most nonalcoholic beverages with varying degrees of form value. In general, the more convenient the form, the more buyers pay for the item, but a high AP price means nothing if the EP cost and overall value are acceptable. If buyers are concerned about the AP price, though, they can, quite possibly, reduce it considerably by accepting less form value.

■ Preservation Method

Generally, suppliers deliver premix products at room temperature, although there is no reason not to insist that suppliers maintain refrigerated temperatures while the products are in transit. They should, for example, keep some specialty products, such as "natural" apple juice, under constant refrigeration to preserve their quality and extend their shelf lives.

Depending on the type of item, postmix products are held under refrigerated, freezer, or dry-storage temperatures. For instance, liquid coffee concentrates are normally kept at refrigerated temperatures, liquid juice concentrates are normally delivered at freezer temperatures, and powders are normally kept at dry-storage temperatures.

Some products, such as ground coffee and whole coffee beans, are normally kept at dry-storage temperatures, unless something different is specified. However, because refrigerated and freezer temperatures tend to extend these products' shelf lives, buyers may want to consider dealing only with those suppliers who provide that service.

■ AP Price

Quality and AP price appear to be positively correlated. A higher quality seems to imply, within reason, a higher AP price. This may not always be the case, especially when a certain soft-drink company tries to gain a foothold by reducing prices temporarily. The straight-line relationship between AP price and quality holds up reasonably well, however. For example, a less-expensive, premix soft drink implies that the flavorings are artificial; in addition, these products do not hold carbon dioxide gas very long once they are opened. Thus, their overall value is seriously undermined.

EP cost can also rise disproportionately for some nonalcoholic beverages. For instance, several coffees taste somewhat similar, but the type of grind and the type of bean involved can make a difference in how much coffee you need to use to brew a pot.

Many nonalcoholic beverages present opportunity buys, such as quantity and promotional discounts. For example, Coke may help defray a hospitality operation's menu-printing costs if the operation includes Coke's brand name on the menu. Also, price wars can occasionally erupt between the major soft-drink companies.

Buyers can save money by continually switching from one soft-drink brand to another. Pepsi and Coke constantly strive for operators' business. So if a hospitality operation owns its own refrigeration and dispensing and ice-making machinery, the switch is easy. If the supplier owns this equipment, however, it is not convenient to change, even though it may be economical. Another problem: an operation cannot sell Pepsi instead of Coke if it advertises Coke on its menu.

Sometimes, the AP price is irrelevant. For instance, some states require wholesale price maintenance for milk; some even require retail price maintenance for milk. Although suppliers or retailers can charge more than the minimum required under the law, the minimum requirement is the price that all buyers are usually charged.

■ Supplier Services

Supplier services are crucial when buyers purchase nonalcoholic beverages. If buyers have two relatively similar brands from which to choose, they will tend to select the one that carries with it more supplier services. Some manufacturers give away or lend items—anything from menu decals to refrigerators—as long as buyers agree to purchase their products. In general, buyers are not interested in such trinkets as clocks, but their interest surely will be piqued when a "free" refrigerator awaits them. The fact that this refrigerator can be used for items other than those they purchase from that distributor (and that it will be maintained by the distributor free of charge) makes such a "gift" useful indeed.

Some suppliers also lend to buyers for free, or charge only a token amount for, the use of brewing equipment, dispensing equipment, coffee pots, and so forth when buyers purchase beverage products. These **equipment programs** are popular in the hospitality industry. Buyers tend to pay more for the beverage products when they participate in these programs, but the convenience may be worthwhile. Also, if they really want a particular beverage product, they might as well take the equipment program because, unless they work for a very large hospitality company with a great deal of purchasing power, it is unlikely that they will receive a discount if they do not agree to the program.

> **equipment program**
> Process whereby a purveyor allows you the free use of equipment if you purchase other products. For instance, if you purchase all your coffees and teas from a vendor, he or she may offer you the free use of the brewing and serving equipment. In some cases there may be a nominal charge for the equipment; it's not always free.

The types of delivery schedules, ordering procedures, and minimum-order requirements also are important. Moreover, if buyers are participating in an equipment program, they must ascertain how well the distributor will maintain the equipment.

PROCEDURES FOR PURCHASING, RECEIVING, STORING, AND ISSUING NONALCOHOLIC BEVERAGES

■ Purchasing

Once buyers have decided on the types of beverages they want, their purchasing procedure follows a fairly routine pattern. Ordering and delivery schedules are pretty well set, although they are not as restrictive as those for beverage alcohols. In addition, buyers have more payment freedom; the credit terms are subject to more negotiation possibilities than are those for beverage alcohols.

As with beverage alcohols, the buyers' primary decision is how much to order. The par stock for these items usually varies quite a bit from one operation to the next. When buyers purchase soft drinks, a three-day stock is typical. The par stock for coffee and frozen beverages might run a week or more. Buyers should purchase perishable products, such as milk, on a day-to-day, standing-order basis when possible. Usually, buyers can arrange a standing-order agreement for some of these types of items. In such arrangements, it is normal for a **route salesperson** to call on buyers and "bring them up to par."

> **route salesperson**
> The driver who delivers standing orders to the restaurant.

Some suppliers stipulate minimum-order requirements, but this rarely presents a difficulty. Unlike with beverage alcohols, buyers probably would not carry an exceptionally slow-moving nonalcoholic beverage.

Like beverage alcohols, nonalcoholic beverages encourage hospitality operators to follow the par stock approach entirely and to deal with several distributors to obtain the desired variety of beverages. Some distributors carry wide lines of beverages, but most carry only one or two varieties of nonalcoholic beverages.

With the exception of normal quantity and volume discounts, other opportunity buys are infrequent. Those available usually take the form of introductory offers or, more commonly, promotional discounts. Ordinarily, these discounts take the form of menu printing and the provision of other signs. Introductory offers and free samples occur sporadically, such as when soft-drink firms make a concerted effort to increase market share. Sometimes buyers can obtain a cash discount if they pay the route salesperson cash-on-delivery (COD).

As with beverage alcohols, though, detailed specifications usually are not prepared for these items because brand-name merchandise that can fit an operation's particular storage and dispensing machinery tends to be a major consideration. However, some large hospitality enterprises with the resources to shop around might prepare detailed specifications for such products as coffee, tea, and juices (see Figure 22.11 for some examples of product specifications, and Figure 22.12 for an example of a product specification outline for nonalcoholic beverage products).

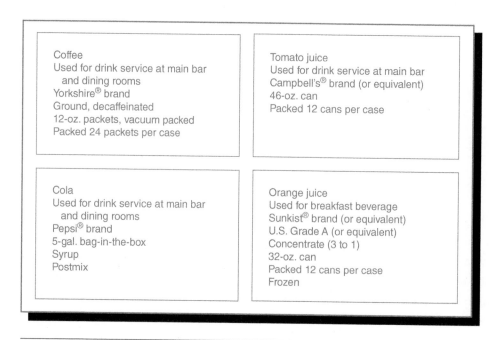

FIGURE 22.11 An example of nonalcoholic beverage product specifications.

Intended use:
Exact name:
U.S. grade (or equivalent):
Brand name (or equivalent):
Size of container:
Type of container:
Product form:
Preservation method:

FIGURE 22.12 An example of a product specification outline for nonalcoholic beverage products.

■ Receiving

Hospitality operations should use the suggested receiving principles noted in Chapter 12. Unfortunately, though, the care operations exercise when receiving beverage alcohols often dissipates when it comes to nonalcoholic beverages.

Receivers normally check the quantity, AP prices, and condition of the delivered goods. Refrozen merchandise, split packages, and broken glass are the major quality checks, along with a careful examination of the labels to see whether the supplier has delivered the correct product. The best quality check is to note the effective age of the product, but this is difficult. For example, time is an enemy of coffee quality; unfortunately, it is hard to tell how old coffee is when it is received unless the package has some type of dating. Some companies, such as PepsiCo, put **freshness dates** on some of their products; for instance, Diet Pepsi package labels contain a **best-if-consumed-by date**.[10]

> **freshness date** Another term for pull date. A pull date is the date beyond which a product (usually food) should not be used, or should not be sold.
>
> **best-if-consumed-by date** Another term for pull date.

Receivers must also be careful to correctly account for any returned merchandise, especially empty returnable containers. Because bottle and keg deposits may exist, receivers should ensure that the appropriate credit is received when the empties are returned. Once receivers examine and approve the merchandise, they must complete any necessary paperwork.

■ Storing

Storing nonalcoholic beverages in the correct environment can retard quality deterioration. Coffee quality, for example, rapidly fades in heat. Many operators keep ground and whole-bean coffee under refrigeration or even in the freezer. Canned and bottled beverages do best in a refrigerator, although some products, such as canned tomato juice, keep well in a dry storeroom.

Operators must store frozen items in a freezer and should not thaw them in advance. For instance, they should not thaw frozen juice concentrate prior to preparation; a hospitality staff member should mix it with water while it is frozen and allow it to thaw in this manner. Ideally, operations should have a dispensing unit that is programmed to mix one glass of juice at a time, using the frozen concentrate stored in the unit. This ensures a high-quality finished product—and satisfied guests.

With frozen beverages, operators should take the time to periodically check the condition of their containers because these tend to crack and split.

▪ Issuing

Some operators do not exert a great deal of control over nonalcoholic beverages. The fact that many of these products go directly to a production department, or sometimes even to self-service dispensing units in the dining room, works against a strict accounting. Ideally, they should control nonalcoholic beverages as much as they do any other product, but because nonalcoholic beverages rarely represent a great portion of the total purchase dollar, they tend to be taken for granted.

Managers and owners slight nonalcoholic beverage control for three major reasons. First, the cost of controlling these items may be much higher than any potential savings. Second, many operators permit employees to drink soft drinks, milk, and coffee for free. If so, why would employees steal them? However, employees may abuse the situation by giving these drinks away to their friends. Furthermore, it is usually impractical to track closely items such as self-serve soft drinks. Third, these beverages may get shifted back and forth between the bar, the kitchen, room service, and poolside service, which makes monitoring difficult. However, when bartenders are responsible for their mixers—the soft drinks, cream, and juices used in the preparation of cocktails—operators pay more attention to them, usually the same consideration that they give beverage alcohols. This is especially true of operations that generate high-volume bar business.

▪ In-Process Inventories

Many problems with nonalcoholic beverages center on the pre-preparation, preparation, and service functions: (1) How much do operators let employees drink on the job? (2) Who makes the coffee: an idle dishwasher? A server who is not busy at the time? (3) Who refills the milk dispenser? (4) Who retrieves the single-service cans of tomato juice? (5) How much coffee should operators make at one time? How much iced tea?

Once again, supervision is the key. Waste can be a problem in this area. Operators who carefully monitor and control the use of these items have the greatest potential to accrue reasonable savings.

 ## Key Words and Concepts

Alcohol content	Dram shop
Allocation	Driving while intoxicated (DWI)
Automatic dispenser	Equipment program
Best-if-consumed-by date	Exclusive distributor
Brand name	Fair Trade
Bottle service	Freshness date
Brew pub	House brand
Call brand	House wine
Capital cost	Inventory padding
Case price	Jug wine
Center for Alcohol Marketing and Youth	License state
Center for Science in the Public Interest	Liquor license
Check padding	Mixed-case
Control state	Mothers Against Drunk Driving (MADD)

Key Words and Concepts (continued)

Nitrogen flush	Price maintenance
Perpetual inventory	Proof
Personalized packaging	Route salesperson
Point of origin	Stockless purchase
Post-off	Supplier services
Postmix	Vintage
Pouring cost	Well brand
Premium well	Wine-dispensing unit
Premix	Wine speculating

Questions and Problems

1. Which type of hospitality operation is most inclined to use a premium well brand? Why?

2. What is the alcoholic content of a spirit of 100 proof?

3. Describe the difference between a dram shop state and a non-dram-shop state.

4. What are some of the differences between a license state and a control state?

5. The consumption of beverage alcohols in the United States has declined over the past few years. What are some of the reasons for this decline?

6. What is the recommended storage procedure for:
   a. white wines?
   b. red wines?
   c. keg beer?

7. Assume that you own a small neighborhood tavern. You employ one bartender and one barback, that is, someone who assists the bartender. You also tend bar. Who should order the items? Why? Who should receive and store them? Why?

8. What are the major advantages and disadvantages of providing your guests with a well-stocked wine cellar?

9. What is the major selection factor for beverage alcohols?

10. Why is the selection factor "point of origin" an important consideration for beverage alcohol products?

11. Why do buyers seldom prepare detailed specifications for beverage alcohol products?

12. Is it a good idea to let a wine steward purchase, receive, store, and sell the wines? Why or why not? Assume that as the owner–manager of the operation, you allow this practice. How would you exercise control over the wine steward?

Questions and Problems (continued)

13. What critical information is missing from this product specification for beer?

> Beer
>
> Used for bar service
>
> Packaged in 12-ounce, nonreturnable bottles
>
> Packed 24 bottles per case

14. A product specification for fruit juice could include this information:

    a.

    b.

    c.

    d.

15. An owner–manager would be interested in a soft-drink company's equipment program because of several advantages this program offers. What are some of these advantages?

16. Identify one major disadvantage of an equipment program.

17. What is the primary difference between a premix beverage and a postmix beverage?

18. When would you specify personalized packaging for a beverage product?

19. Which nonalcoholic beverages typically have quality grades, and which do not?

20. Define or explain briefly these terms:

    a. Liquor license

    b. Inventory padding

    c. Pouring cost

    d. House wine

    e. Jug wine

    f. Post-off

    g. Case price

    h. House brand

    i. Wine steward

    j. Check padding

    k. Price maintenance

    l. Wine speculation

    m. Perpetual inventory

    n. Fair Trade

    o. Bottle service

    p. Craft beer

Experiential Exercises

1. Assume you are a country club manager. You are choosing the well brand you want to use for Scotch. One brand is 86 proof. Its AP price is $12.40 per liter. Another brand, with the same proof, has an AP price of $11.50 per liter. The former brand is fairly well known and is thought to be a respectable product. The latter brand is rather obscure. Which brand would you select? Why? If possible, ask a country club manager to comment on your answer.

2. Call a local liquor distributor, and determine the process by which one would become a customer. Ask about the difficulties associated with delivering to your location, liquor board requirements, brand specifics, and payment terms. Write a short paragraph about your conversation.

3. Visit a local coffee shop. Assess the shop for menu prices (compared to competitors' prices), volume of business, and the varieties of beverages offered. Do you think this coffee shop does a good job of catering to its clientele? Write a brief summary of your visit, and include information that aids in your determination.

References

1. Mothers Against Drunk Driving, "Dram Shop and Social Host Liability," June 2012, www.madd.org/laws/law-overview/Dram_Shop_Overview.pdf; See also, National Council of State Legislatures, "Dram Shop Liability and Criminal Penalty Statues," June 30, 2014, www.ncsl.org/research/financial-services-and-commerce/dram-shop-liability-state-statutes. See also "Dram Shop Rule," Law.com Dictionary, Retrieved September 2010: http://dictionary.law.com/default2.Asp?typed=dram shop rule&type=1. Amy Vitarelli, "Protecting Restaurants in a Tough Environment," *American Agent and Broker*, 80, no. 12 (December 1, 2008):22–24.

2. State of Illinois Liquor Control Commission, "ILCC Form and Application Downloads," www.state.il.us/lcc/viewall.asp.

3. Pennsylvania Liquor Control Board, "Licensing FAQs," www.lcb.state.pa.us/PLCB/Licensees/FAQs/index.htm.

4. National Restaurant Association, "Montana, Virginia Approve ServSafe Alcohol Training Program," www.restaurant.org/News-Research/News/Montana,-Virginia-approve-ServSafe-Alcohol-trainin.

5. Alcohol and Tobacco Tax and Fee Bureau, "Tax and Fee Rates," www.ttb.gov/tax_audit/atftaxes.shtml.

References (continued)

6. Randy Altman, "The Art of Grading Tea," www.tealaden.com/teaweb/articles/art _grading_tea.htm. See also *Types of Tea*," www.frontiercoop.com/learn/tea_grades.php. See also USDA, "Commercial Item Description—Tea Mixes, Instant," www.ams.usda .gov/grades-standards/cid/beverages.

7. Organic Facts, "Organic Coffee," www.organicfacts.net/organic-products/organic-food /organic-coffee.html.

8. Caribou Coffee, "All Natural Decaf," www.cariboucoffee.com/page/1/all-natural-decaf .jsp.

9. Fair Trade USA, "What Is Fair Trade?" http://fairtradeusa.org/what-is-fair-trade.

10. Andrea Petersen, "A Little Secret about Bottled Water; Containers Say It Expires, But Evidence for That Is Scant; Blame It on New Jersey," *The Wall Street Journal*, February 11, 2004, p. D1. See also G. Bruce Knecht, "The Search for Fresh Beer," *The Wall Street Journal*, January 28, 2006, p. P1.

23

NONFOOD EXPENSE ITEMS

The Purpose of This Chapter

After reading this chapter, you should be able to:

- Identify management considerations regarding the types of nonfood expense items used.

- Explain management considerations related to price and supplier factors for nonfood expense items.

- Create a specification for nonfood expense items that can be used in the purchasing process.

- Describe the selection factors for cleaning and maintenance items.

- Analyze the selection factors when deciding whether to purchase permanent or disposable ware and utensils.

- Differentiate the characteristics of fabrics and paper goods that affect the purchasing decision.

MANAGEMENT CONSIDERATIONS—TYPES OF NONFOOD EXPENSE ITEMS

expense item   Relatively inexpensive nonfood item, such as glassware, the cost of which can be written off in the year in which it is incurred. Opposite of a capital item.

operating supplies
Another term for expense items or nonfood expense items.

depreciation   Loss of value over time.

Some operations devote a great amount of money to nonfood **expense items**, which are sometimes referred to as **operating supplies**. (An expense item is one that hospitality operations can write off in the current year's income statement; that is, it is not a "capital" item that must be **depreciated** over a period of years.) However, the attention that operations lavish on food and beverage items typically is greater than what they devote to these types of purchases.

Hospitality operators typically purchase nine categories of nonfood expense items: (1) cleaning supplies, (2) cleaning tools, (3) maintenance supplies, (4) permanent ware, (5) single-service disposable ware, (6) preparation and service utensils, (7) fabrics, (8) other paper products, and (9) miscellaneous items. Buying these items is sometimes a highly routine activity. Buyers usually establish the major guidelines, and department heads are held responsible for ensuring an orderly flow of cleaning agents, stationery, glassware, and so forth. In these instances, operations pay at least some minimal attention to purchasing decisions.

Unfortunately, small operations tend to view these purchases as nuisances and may try to conclude them as speedily as possible, but this can be a serious mistake. Although these purchases often represent a comparatively small portion of the total purchasing dollar, a considerable number of managerial concerns surround them—concerns that can, on closer examination, dramatize the need for careful nonfood procurement procedures.

Buying nonfood expense items sometimes presents difficult decisions. The quality of mops purchased probably will not influence the operation's sales volume, but the quality of guest amenities—such items as individually wrapped or liquid soap, and paper or linen towels in restrooms—definitely help to shape the operation's image. Consequently, buyers should not make purchasing decisions regarding these items lightly. Some of the considerations that can affect these decisions are discussed in the following sections.

■ Personalization of Nonfood Items

The degree of personalization that hospitality operations want in a nonfood item is related to the image they wish to create. How customized do they want their nonfood products to be? Will any old paper napkin do, or should it have their name or, perhaps, some other type of advertising or insignia on it? (See Figure 23.1.) In some cases, nonfood items become advertisements in disguise, and operators should treat them accordingly. (This issue is discussed further in Chapter 24.) This fact makes it difficult for buyers to evaluate the price of nonfood items. Generally, the more personalized these items become, the higher their price.

When buyers consider the price of a personalized bar of soap, for example, they have to divide it into two components: the advertising component and the functional component. They

FIGURE 23.1 Paper products with logos.
©Bloomberg/Contributor/Getty Images

can note the price for a plain bar of soap, to which any increment in price would represent an advertising expenditure.

Sometimes buyers form the habit of staying with a certain style of nonfood guest supplies. Salespersons know this, so it is only natural for them to sell buyers one item, such as a personalized napkin, for a very reasonable price. The idea might be for buyers to work the item into their business, for their customers to become enamored of it, and then for the salesperson to urge the buyers to purchase similar, additional nonfood expense items for perhaps a slightly higher price.

The process may not work quite like this, but image is crucial to the sale of nonfood items, and salespersons know this. They continually remind buyers of this. By doing so, they can place buyers accustomed exclusively to food buying on the defensive. The image phenomenon does complicate some nonfood purchases. Moreover, once buyers have decided what they want, it may be hard to turn back because they cannot necessarily go to another supplier and get exactly the same product.

This is not to say that buyers will be stuck for life with a certain type of napkin, but they may hesitate to change styles too abruptly. They do not make major changes without incurring some risk. For instance, customers really notice when a hotel moves from high-quality guest amenities to lesser-quality items. As such, buyers should make sure that several of their nonfood items will serve their needs for a long time.

■ Nonfood Product Variety

Another major concern involves the many nonfood items available on the market and the numerous suppliers who carry items of this type. This situation favors bid buyers. However, it can also cause confusion and anxiety for typical owner–managers, who may seek relief with a sympathetic one-stop supplier. They must be aware, though, that many of these selection and procurement

bid buying When buyers shop around seeking current AP prices from vendors. The vendors are asked to quote, or bid, the prices they will charge. Intended to give the buyer competitive pricing information that will allow him or her to get the best possible value.

as-used cost Another term for edible-portion (EP) cost.

supplier services Services, such as free delivery, generous credit terms, and so forth, provided by vendors to buyers who purchase their products.

decisions may affect their image for quite some time and that it may be wise to take more time and try **bid buying**.

Bid buying offers a bit more potential benefit in the nonfood area because when buyers purchase in large quantities, they can often get favorable bids from several competing suppliers. In addition, because they may not need to go through the time-consuming bidding procedures too often, the little bit they do endure can lead to impressive savings. Finally, because these items are not perishable, they do not spoil; hence, their **as-used cost** is quite predictable—unless, of course, operators fail to exert the proper supervision over in-process inventory use.

If buyers purchase a lot of standard nonfood items, such as plain napkins, ordinary flatware, and standard drinking glasses, bid buying may be less beneficial. These standard items typically have a small spread in price, quality, and **supplier services** among suppliers. Wider spreads normally occur when buyers purchase personalized items and have varying quality requirements.

■ Nonfood Packers' Brands

The use of packers' brands as a selection factor does not seem to be as prevalent for nonfood expense items as it is for food and beverages. Buyers might rely on a specific producer, especially for personalized items, but not for standard, everyday items. So many producers and varieties of standardized nonfood expense items exist that buyers are often encouraged to shop around.

■ Degree of Product Convenience

An interesting managerial issue is the degree of convenience to specify in certain nonfood items. For example, does the hospitality operation want one all-purpose cleaner, which, according to some people, does not exist, or does it want to spend time selecting individual cleaning agents for specific uses?

In this situation, form economic value comes into play once again. Obviously, the greater the convenience, the greater the form value; hence, buyers can expect a higher as-purchased (AP) price.

disposable versus reusable Disposable refers to single-use products, such as paper napkins, plastic dishes, and paper cups. Reusable refers to similar products; however, they are not single-use. They can be washed and reused many times before being replaced.

Perhaps the touchiest issue associated with nonfood convenience centers on **disposable versus reusable** items—for example, linen napkins and place mats versus their paper or plastic counterparts. The permanent-versus-disposable argument that surrounds permanent dish and silverware and disposables is especially acute. Several studies "prove" the economics of permanent ware.[1] But, as you can imagine, a lot of people consider disposables the wiser choice. Complicating the issue further is the negative environmental impact associated with disposable ware, although some buyers overcome this by purchasing items made with recycled materials.

For some types of hospitality operations, using permanent ware is necessary to maintain the appropriate image. Any operation can work with at least a few disposables, however, and most customers accept some, if only paper towels in the restroom. The convenience of using such items is certainly something we cannot argue with.

We think that permanent ware is the logical choice when operations are concerned with cost savings. With reusable items, they minimize the cost of solid-waste disposal. Moreover, not only is disposable ware expensive, but it is also a waste of natural resources unless operators take the time to send the disposable ware to a recycling plant after use.

■ Safety Considerations

Some nonfood expense items may present a safety hazard. For instance, hospitality operations must be concerned with toxic chemicals, cleaners that impart distasteful odors, and cleaners and similar products that, although safe initially, could, through mishandling, become dangerous.

Operations cannot always refuse to purchase an item because it represents a possible danger, but they should be well prepared to store and use such items properly. Local health districts normally require stringent storage procedures for toxic materials. Operations can also obtain safety regulations regarding such items from the Occupational Safety & Health Administration (OSHA) website. Operations must, however, supplement these legal requirements with stringent operating procedures of their own to ensure that no harm comes to their guests or themselves.

Some operators would rather eliminate the need to store and to use toxic products by purchasing a service to do the work for them. For example, instead of purchasing, storing, and using pest control materials, operators might prefer to hire a pest control company to perform this function.

■ Supervising Nonfood Items

Another problem associated with nonfood items is the hospitality operators' tendency to neglect the supervision of employees when they use them. Although few of these items represent a large portion of the purchase dollar, their continual disappearance and misuse can significantly increase overall operating costs. All too often, for instance, a cook who cleans the steam table pours in a half-gallon of cleaning solution instead of the recommended half-quart, or similarly, might toss out a dirty mop head instead of sending it to the laundry.

Examples of wasted nonfood items are numerous, and small expenses add up. So supervisors should strictly monitor the usage of them. Large operations consider this need for supervision to be a given. However, they, too, can become lax at times. For example, during a rush period, who stops to make sure that only one paper doily, instead of two or three, is under the soup bowl?

Even large operations have a tendency to set flexible par stocks for nonfood items and then to allow the department head to monitor the usage rates and order replacement items that are deemed necessary. In these situations, frequent stockouts of these items can occur because these purchases may not be monitored closely.

ENERGY EFFICIENT LIGHTING
Audrey Alonzo, Adjunct Chef Instructor, and Jean Hertzman University of Nevada, Las Vegas

In 2007, the Energy Independence and Security Act (EISA) was passed to aid in phasing out the use of inefficient light bulbs. It set forth energy targets that were to be enacted in two phases, the first in 2012 and the second in 2020. By 2012, all screw-based light bulbs, including compact fluorescent lighting (CFL), light emitting diodes (LEDs), halogens, and incandescent bulbs, were required to use 25–30 percent less energy. That is, they were required to consume less electricity (measured in watts) for

ENERGY EFFICIENT LIGHTING: (continued)

the amount of light produced (measured in lumens). By 2020, most light bulbs must be 60–70 percent more efficient than the standard incandescent today.[1]

As much as 42 percent of energy usage in hospitality operations can be attributed to lighting.[2] Lighting is very important, as it sets the mood and ambience in both guest and employee areas. Energy efficient lighting in the form of CFL has become an increasingly popular way for the hospitality industry to meet EISA regulations, go green, and save money. CFLs reduce energy use and consumption by up to 75 percent over traditional incandescent lighting.[3] Operators were initially reluctant to use CFLs due to the unnatural light that was produced. Now, one can purchase CFLs in the same forms as incandescent bulbs, including soft white, bright white, and warm white. There were also problems with CFLs not working with dimmable switches; this too has been resolved. One important note for users of these bulbs is that they do contain a small amount of mercury, which means that they cannot be disposed of in the garbage. Many programs for recycling these bulbs are already in place.[4]

LEDs are another lighting choice. These bulbs produce a bright and efficient light. By replacing light sources with LED, a hospitality operator can expect to reduce lighting energy use over the long lifetime of up to 45,000 hours per bulb. This can reduce maintenance and operating costs. And because LED lighting generates little heat, it may be possible to spend less on air-conditioning, too. Hotels such as the Scandic Hotel in Copenhagen and Rafayel Hotel in London, have experienced energy savings of more than 60 percent by switching to LED lighting.[5]

Cold cathode compact fluorescent lamps (CCCFLs), originally used in laptop screens, are another option. They offer reduced energy consumption, dimming ability, flashing, and colored bulbs. They are best used in decorative applications, accent lighting, emergency lighting, signage, and flashing applications. Paul Kuck, www.sustainablefoodservice.com, predicts "Vegas will save millions with these things."

■ REFERENCES

1. "Energy Independence and Security Act of 2007 (EISA): Frequently asked questions," *US EPA Backgrounder*, Spring 2011, www.energystar.gov/ia/products/lighting/cfls/downloads/ EISA_Backgrounder_FINAL_4-11_EPA.pdf. See also, Joseph Truini, "What You Need to Know about the Lightbulb Law," *Popular Mechanics*, November 27, 2012, www.popularmechanics.com/home/improvement/energy-efficient/what-you-need-to-know-about -the-lightbulb-law-14789203.

2. Phillips, "Hospitality: Feel What Light Can Do for Your Guests," www.comm-tec.es/pdf/ Hospitality%20segment.pdf.

3. Solid & Hazardous Waste Education Center, UW Extension. "Saving Energy Is Good for Business," *Focus on Energy*, www3.uwm.edu/Dept/shwec/publications/cabinet/energy/ Lighting1(8-19).pdf.

4. Paul Kuck, "Energy Efficient Lighting," 2013, www.sustainablefoodservice.com/cat/lighting.htm.

5. Philips, "Hospitality: Feel What Light Can Do for Your Guests," www.comm-tec.es/pdf/ Hospitality%20segment.pdf.

MANAGEMENT CONSIDERATIONS—PRICE AND SUPPLIER FACTORS

■ Quantity and Volume Discounts

Whenever possible, buyers should make every attempt to purchase large amounts of these products. Our experience suggests that significant savings are associated with this practice. The discounts available in the nonfood channel of distribution are quite attractive, and if buyers have the money and the storage space necessary to participate in this practice, their as-used costs for the supplies usually will be considerably less than those obtained with small order sizes.

■ Systems Sale

A **systems sale** occurs when buyers purchase a particular product, such as a specific type of point-of-sale (POS) system, that can accept only paper guest checks that one company manufactures, usually the company that also manufactures the system.

An owner–manager must consider a type of trade-off whenever the opportunity arises to participate in a systems sale. On the one hand, the salesperson of the main item, such as a POS, might be willing to sell the POS for a very low price. When buyers need the paper products, parts, and so forth for their operation, however, they could be staring at expensive prices, with no alternatives.

Another example would be soap dispensers in restrooms. Often these dispensers require a specific packaging of the soap. Once those dispensers are on the walls, a buyer must remain with the supplier of the designated soap or pay the costs of having the dispensers removed when deciding to buy a different product. How many times have you seen an empty soap dispenser on a bathroom wall and a filled freestanding soap dispenser sitting on the side of the sink?

> **systems sale** Usually occurs when buying equipment that requires parts made by only one manufacturer, usually the manufacturer that made the equipment in the first place. For example, buying a dish machine that cannot use other companies' dish racks. Over the long run, a systems sale purchase may cost you more money than a nonsystems sale purchase.

■ Operating Supplies Schemes

For one reason or another, hospitality operations are more vulnerable to rip-off artists in the nonfood expense items, **capital items** (furniture, fixtures, and equipment; FFE), and service channels of distribution. The care and diligence buyers exercise in their food and beverage purchasing somehow decline a bit when they buy nonfood products. For example, buyers tend to order nonfood expense items from an online catalog or from some other type of advertising solicitation, such as one that shows up in a trade magazine. Buyers should keep in mind that it is possible that items ordered in such a way may not be satisfactory because the catalog description may be misleading.

> **capital item** Expensive FFE, the cost of which must typically be depreciated over time. Opposite of an expense item.

Another problem many businesspersons encounter is the office supply telephone salesperson. As discussed in Chapter 14, salespersons may offer what appear to be tremendous bargains, but, unfortunately, the merchandise delivered is often inadequate. A quick check with the Better Business Bureau on any potential supplier is often worth the time and effort.

It is important for buyers to follow rigorous selection and procurement procedures for all products and services they must purchase. For instance, in the examples discussed earlier, buyers would not get hurt if they followed an approved-supplier list that restricted their purchasing authority.

■ New Versus Used

Buyers can purchase some nonfood expense items in a used condition. Such products as china, glass, and flatware often are available from secondhand dealers, at auctions, or from other hospitality companies that are liquidating their assets. Buyers can also obtain items by going to **online auction sites**, such as eBay.

Our experience suggests that buyers can save a tremendous amount of money if they are lucky enough to stumble onto a good deal. As with any type of used item, though, they must be willing to take chances. Furthermore, they must be willing to spend considerable time and effort to locate this type of merchandise.

■ Equipment Program

It is possible for buyers to purchase a nonfood expense item and concurrently obtain from the supplier the equipment needed to use it. For instance, if buyers purchase a certain amount of dishwashing machine chemicals, they might be able to rent the machine from the chemical supplier at a very favorable rate.

equipment program
Process whereby a purveyor allows you the free use of equipment if you purchase other products. For instance, if you purchase all your coffees and teas from a vendor, he or she may offer you the free use of the brewing and serving equipment. In some cases, there may be a nominal charge for the equipment; it's not always free.

These **equipment programs** are similar to the ones for nonalcoholic beverages we discussed in Chapter 22. The same advantages and disadvantages apply here. Owner–managers, though, seem to prefer some sort of equipment program because it eliminates the need to invest in equipment and because the equipment generally is maintained free of charge. In the long run, it probably costs more to operate in this fashion; however, in the short run, such a strategy can enhance a hospitality operation's cash flow.

■ Lifetime Cost

lifetime cost A term typically used when analyzing an equipment purchase. Along with the AP price of the item, the buyer might also examine the trade-in value of the old equipment, the cost of the energy needed to operate the new equipment, extra charges for delivery, setup, and training, how much it can sell the new equipment for when it is time to replace it, and so forth.

Some nonfood expense items have a long life. They are not used once and discarded, but remain with an operation for a reasonable period of time. Consequently, when computing their as-used costs, buyers must consider the **lifetime cost**. For long-life items they must be interested in the products' original AP price. They must also be aware of any operating costs that will be associated with the use of these items. For instance, a cleaning tool must be used by someone who receives a wage. Furthermore, if the cleaning tool is less expensive than another one, but requires more time to use, buyers will do the operation a financial disservice in the long run if they purchase such an item.

Similarly, buyers must consider the potential salvage value of a long-life item. For example, somewhere down the line they might be able to trade in a cleaning tool for a new model and receive a very generous trade-in allowance. Buyers can probably best understand this concept via the "new car" example. A very expensive new car can easily cost less to operate and can retain its value much longer than an automobile with a much lower sticker price. Furthermore, a more expensive car may require less routine maintenance and may be more energy efficient.

■ Credit Terms

Sometimes, buyers must purchase a large amount of nonfood expense items. They should consider shopping around for the best **credit terms** if this option is available. They should be especially discerning about the amount, if any, of deposit they must put up before they are allowed to place an order for a customized item. Furthermore, they must consider what will happen if they change their minds about the item later on and they do not wish to purchase the product, even though they ordered it. They need to find out ahead of time what will happen to their deposit: Will they lose all of it or only part of it? Similarly, what is a purveyor's return policy; will a **restocking fee** be charged if an order is returned?

> **credit terms** The type and amount of financing a vendor will provide, along with the prescribed type of bill-paying procedure that must be followed. Also included are things such as a description of late fees, penalties, and so forth.

> **restocking fee** payment a supplier requires if an order is returned.

UNINTENDED CONSEQUENCES
Robert Lindsay, Purchasing and Receiving Manager

■ LIVE NATION ENTERTAINMENT—HOUSE OF BLUES AND FOUNDATION ROOM, MANDALAY BAY HOTEL AND CASINO, LAS VEGAS, NEVADA

Robert Lindsay, purchasing and receiving manager for House of Blues®, who was introduced in Chapter 10, provides a great example of what can happen when a company tries to save money on nonfood expense items. You would think that buying the bar picks used for fruit and garnishing drinks would be easy. However, he learned his lesson that cheaper is not always better when he bought a brand with a lower AP price than what they had been using. The cheaper ones were much thinner and had a sharper point. They broke all the time when the bartenders used them for spearing harder fruits like pineapple, causing a lot of waste. In addition, the bartenders and cocktail servers were none too happy when during the nonstop, fast pace of service they kept stabbing themselves and drawing blood with the sharper pick. Needless to say, everyone was pleased when the stock was used up and they switched back to the original type of pick. Robert emphasizes that this shows how value can be more important than cost savings and that you need to be careful to ensure that a product will work for its intended use.

PURCHASING NONFOOD EXPENSE ITEMS

Buyers can purchase nonfood expense items several ways, although fewer ways exist to buy them than to buy food. However, perhaps because nonfood expense items are not perishable, the various alternatives available can be quite viable and represent a few cost-saving opportunities. Buyers can purchase many of these items on a day-to-day basis. Alternately, they can be purchased as far in advance as the foodservice operation's storage permits.

quantity discount
A price reduction for buying a large amount of one specific type of merchandise.

volume discount
Similar to a quantity discount. The buyer agrees to purchase a huge volume of goods; however, unlike with a quantity discount, he or she buys more than one type of merchandise.

stockless purchase
When a buyer purchases a large amount of product, for example, a three-month supply, and arranges for the vendor to store it and deliver a little at a time.

The major problems are identifying the proper par stock and the appropriate supplier. These are not easy questions because several **quantity discount** and **volume discount** variations exist among suppliers. Also, because nonfood expense items are not perishable, most suppliers will try to accommodate your needs.

Typically, par stocks are large. Furthermore, if buyers want any sort of personalization, usually they must purchase these items in huge quantities from one supplier. Also, it is common to find some sort of **stockless purchase** arrangement. The ability for a supplier to hold items in its warehouse until the establishment needs them may be just as important to some buyers as prices.

Multiunit operations save the most when they exercise their quantity buying power. Franchisees tend to purchase from the company commissary because this usually represents the lowest possible price.

The principal step in purchasing nonfood expense items is for buyers to decide exactly what they require. This is not necessarily an easy task because many potential suppliers and many varieties of items are available. For some products, though, such as cleaning supplies, the quality and as-used cost differences among the suppliers may not be readily apparent.

Once buyers know what products will suit their needs, it is a good idea for them to prepare specifications (see Figure 23.2 for some example product specifications, and Figure 23.3 for an example of a product specification outline for nonfood expense items).

As when purchasing liquor, buyers tend to de-emphasize the use of specifications when buying nonfood expense items. Many times when they need these products, buyers go to the supplier and examine the items in person before placing an order. Alternately, it is common for salespersons to demonstrate and/or show these products to potential buyers before soliciting purchase orders.

Irish coffee mug Used for bar service Standard restaurant logo on white background Libbey® brand (or equivalent) 8½-oz. mug Packed 24 per case	Disposable foam cup Used for hot drinks Plain white color CODE® brand (or equivalent) 6-oz. cup size 25 cups per plastic sleeve Packed 40 sleeves per case

Bar straw
Used for bar service
House brand (or least expensive brand)
Red color
7¾-in. straw
500 straws per box
Packed 10 boxes per case
	Liquid chlorine bleach
	Used for general cleaning purposes
	House brand (or least expensive
	  product)
	1-gal. plastic container with screw-
	  top cap
	Packed 4 to 6 gallons per case

FIGURE 23.2 An example of nonfood expense item specifications.

Intended use:
Exact name:
Safety needs:
Convenience requirement:
Odor limitations:
New versus used options:
Promotional needs:
Maximum as-used cost:
Personalization requirement:
Effectiveness requirement:
Compatibility requirement:
Product form:
Product size:
Size of container:
Type of container:
Brand name (or equivalent):
Color:
Material used to make the item:

FIGURE 23.3 An example of a specification outline for nonfood expense items.

Purchasing nonfood expense items can be as easy or as difficult as buyers want to make it. As we have already noted, it may be to the buyers' benefit to expend a lot of effort to select and procure these products because their work may be rewarded with lower AP prices and, it is hoped, lower as-used costs. Realistically, many hospitality operations use one-stop shopping; perhaps for these operations, the number of dollars that could be saved do not compensate for the extra purchasing efforts.

TYPICAL NONFOOD ITEMS—CLEANING AND MAINTENANCE ITEMS

■ Cleaning Supplies

Hospitality operations normally purchase several types of cleaning supplies: guest supplies, such as moisturizing cream; chemical cleaners; hand soaps; detergents; bleach; and polishes and waxes. The guest supplies usually represent as much advertising as they do guest convenience. For instance, the individually wrapped soap, shampoo, and shoe polish placed in guest rooms normally carry some type of advertising.

When purchasing guest amenities, buyers might be able to bargain for a **promotional discount**. For example, Procter & Gamble might offer a price reduction if a hotel uses its soap in the guest rooms, restaurant restrooms, and lobby restrooms.

Cleaning supplies, other than those purchased for customer needs, are usually selected on the basis of the following factors:

- **As-used cost.** Buyers are concerned with a cleaning agent's efficiency. Efficiency is especially critical because in addition to the cost of the

promotional discount
Price discount awarded to the buyer if he or she allows the vendor to promote the product in the hospitality operation, or if the hospitality operation agrees to personally help promote the sale of the product to its customers.

cleaner, buyers must consider the cost of the labor and energy needed to use it. For example, buyers are concerned with the cost of cleaning a square foot of floor or a square foot of wall tile. When examining various samples of these cleaners, then, buyers often must make several cost computations, but this is necessary if they are concerned with efficiency.

product effectiveness
The extent to which a product lives up to its vendor's claims. A typical example would be the ability of an all-purpose cleaner to clean satisfactorily any type of surface.

product safety Refers to the level of risk incurred when using some products, such as cleaning solutions.

- **Product effectiveness.** Can the product actually get the job done, or are the claims exaggerated?

- **Adaptability.** Can the cleaner be adapted to other cleaning needs? That is, can the operation use one cleaner that can be used for multiple purposes? This may be more convenient, but the buyer must consider whether it will be equally effective for those purposes and whether buying just one item will actually reduce their total inventory of cleaning supplies. Also, it is possible that the AP price of all-purpose cleaners may be less than the combined AP prices of seldom-used, single-purpose cleaners.

- **Product safety.** Will the product harm the item being cleaned? Can it harm the person using it? Does it have the potential to harm the environment? If so, buyers should consider hiring a professional service instead of having employees use it.

- **Ease of use.** Is the product easy to use, or do employees have to undergo extensive training or briefing to master it? Availability of instructions for use and training materials in multiple languages may also be a desirable quality.

- **Odor.** Does the cleaner have a strong, lingering odor sufficient to cause guest and employee discomfort?

- **Container size.** Is the cleaner available only in very large containers? Although they are cheaper per unit than smaller containers, they are harder to handle and can cause waste from spillage. Operators must be very careful to follow all local health department and OSHA safety and labeling regulations when they buy large containers of cleaners and then transfer it to smaller containers or bottles for actual use.

- **Supplier services.** Carefully examine supplier services and the product information. Does the supplier offer employee training for items such as dishwashing-machine chemicals and silver-polish usage? Also, at times, employees may encounter some difficulty when using the products, so it would be helpful to be able to call the supplier or salesperson and ask for help at a moment's notice. A very popular service is the 24-hour maintenance and troubleshooting service that such chemical companies as Ecolab and Swisher Hygiene provide. In some cases, this service can be more important to customers than the products themselves.

Purchasing cleaning supplies is not particularly difficult once buyers select the suppliers they wish to deal with. The supplier may offer a standing order system where the company's route salesperson comes on a regular basis to bring the supply stock up to the set par levels. Similarly, receiving these products poses no more than run-of-the-mill problems.

Storage, though, can present some difficulty. Operators must store these cleaning supplies away from foods and beverages to avoid contamination. Operators will be in violation of the FDA Model Food code and local health department's sanitation regulations if they do not segregate these products.

▪ Cleaning Tools

Food services and lodging operations buy several types of cleaning tools, such as brooms, mops, buckets, vacuum cleaners, floor polishers, pot brushes, and squeegees. Several selection factors affect these purchasing decisions, including the following:

- **Cost.** Determining the long-term cost of a broom is not easy because buyers never know how long a broom will last. Nor do they always know who will be pushing the broom: someone paid specifically to push it or an idle employee whose salary remains the same regardless of assigned duties. Consequently, most buyers consider a broom's purchase price to be a minor selection factor. The general feeling seems to be that it pays to purchase high-quality hand tools because: (1) they withstand the tough punishment that busy employees normally place on the item, (2) the product cost pales in comparison to the cost of the labor needed to wield these tools—high-quality tools should be more efficient, and (3) high-quality tools generally last longer, so the as-used cost should be minimal.

- **Employee skill.** Buyers need to consider the skill of the people using the tools. Low-skill, or low-cost, employees usually need better products and, perhaps, more convenient products to work with. Like the cleaning supplies, the availability of clear, easy-to-follow instructions for use, in multiple languages, will be beneficial in providing training for use of the items for employees of any skill level.

  > **employee skill** Workers' abilities to perform certain tasks.

- **Material used to make the item.** Brushes and brooms, for example, are manufactured from a variety of raw materials. Sponges and scouring pads also come in a range of materials. It is important for buyers to identify the type of material that best suits their needs and budget.

- **Used tools.** It is possible for buyers to purchase used tools at a salvage sale, going-out-of-business sale, auction, or used-products stores. The savings are usually considerable. Buyers agree to take the items on an as-is, where-is basis. Although the savings may be attractive, the quality of the tools may be quite low. In addition, buyers must take the time to shop around for these types of deals. Also, they must usually arrange for delivery themselves.

Cleaning-tool procurement procedures are fairly routine. As usual, buyers first either bid buy or find suppliers who understand what they need and are willing to work with them. Buyers often make impulse purchases in this area. Moreover, many buyers are sometimes tempted to purchase some type of gadget that may carry an exaggerated claim.

Receiving and storing cleaning tools pose no more than the ordinary problems. Their in-process storage and use, however, can create problems. Keeping the tools maintained—that is, the mop heads clean, for example, or the mop buckets empty when not in use—can be difficult. High-quality tools should minimize these difficulties and make cleaning easier and more efficient.

▪ Maintenance Supplies

Hospitality operations purchase several types of maintenance supplies: light bulbs, plumbing parts, and other similar items. The supplies that operations purchase usually depend on the type of service or maintenance contracts they have with a professional service. Generally, for most repair and maintenance needs, operations contact a professional service that provides the necessary parts and labor. These contracts will be discussed in Chapter 24.

All operations buy at least some maintenance supplies, however. Small operations may buy only light bulbs and a few other products, but larger operations, especially the big hotels, may stock everything from light bulbs to water pipes. Buyers use several factors for selecting these items:

- **Cost.** The price of maintenance supplies may or may not be relevant. When buyers purchase items such as circuit breakers or water pipes, they must purchase good-quality merchandise. No inferior-quality products exist because many of these items must pass safety and other building-code standards that federal and local governmental agencies establish.

- **Quality.** If buyers have a choice among a variety of qualities, they need to consider the life of the replacement part. If they do not want to change light bulbs every other month, they should buy high-quality, expensive bulbs. A higher-quality item may also be more energy efficient.

  Buyers also need to consider the length of time their operation will continue to exist in its current form. For example, the owner–manager intending to sell the business next year may not want to splurge for the best maintenance part; perhaps a lower-quality, less expensive item will do.

- **Labor availability.** Buyers should consider the **labor availability** for the maintenance. If they have only a few labor hours for maintenance, they should consider purchasing easy-to-use replacement parts or long-life parts or engaging in a maintenance contract with a professional service. This trade-off is one that operators contemplate quite often. When buyers purchase replacement parts, they also have to think about providing the labor. Labor is quite expensive, and operations want to reduce it. As a result, many small operators learn how to "fix the ice machine" themselves.

- **Used supplies.** These may be available, but buyers must consider whether the trouble to find them and possible lower quality and useful life are worth the cost savings.

- **Product size.** Maintenance supplies come in various sizes, shapes, model numbers, and the like, so buyers must be very careful to purchase the exact product required or it will not serve their needs. For instance, an air-conditioning filter of the wrong size can be used in an air-conditioning system only at the risk of damaging the machinery.

- **Capitalizing expenses.** If operators get tired of replacing parts and maintaining equipment, buyers can **capitalize an expense**; that is, they can buy more expensive capital equipment that does not need much maintenance work. This decision represents a major capital equipment decision, however, that typically only the owner–managers make, not buyers.

labor availability The amount of labor that exists in the hospitality operation's location. Sometimes referred to as the labor pool.

product size Refers to the buyer's specified weight, or volume, of a particular item he or she wants to purchase. Examples would be a 10-ounce steak or a 4-ounce hamburger.

capitalizing an expense Term used to refer to the purchase of an expensive capital item, such as a new heating system, to reduce future operating expenses, such as the cost of energy used to heat a building.

The procurement procedure for these supplies is reasonably straightforward, and receiving and storing them present no more than the average problems. However, two unique issues can occur with these items. First, a hospitality operation can tend to carry a lot of these supplies in stock. This tendency is understandable because an owner–manager can get annoyed very quickly if there are no light bulbs to replace the burned out pool lights. If buyers work at it, they might be able to reduce the stock level, although only the owner–manager can decide how much of a stockout potential to accept.

Second, maintenance schedules can be a headache. For example, should operators replace light bulbs as they burn out, or should they estimate the average life of the bulbs and change all of them at once, thereby saving some labor cost?

TYPICAL NONFOOD ITEMS—PERMANENT AND DISPOSABLE WARE AND UTENSILS

■ Permanent Ware

A hospitality operation's initial investment in permanent ware may be a capital expenditure that has to be depreciated on the income statement. Once an operation buys its original stock, however, the replacements it buys every so often—or has delivered, if it is on a stockless purchase plan—are generally considered "costs of doing business," or expenses that will be written off on the operation's current year's income statement.

Several types of permanent ware enter the typical food service operation: plates, flatware, glasses, ashtrays, vases, salt and pepper shakers, creamers, sugar bowls, and so forth (see Figure 23.4). Operators may, however, have the option of using disposables for some or all of these, depending on their operation.

FIGURE 23.4 A typical permanent ware setup for a food service dining room.
©arsenik/iStockphoto

Comparatively few selection factors exist for permanent ware, but they are very critical. Buyers should consider the following points:

- **Permanent ware needed.** Operators must decide exactly what type of permanent ware they want. If they want standardized items, their buyers could go to just about any supplier and buy them. For run-of-the-mill products, buyers will find very little spread between prices. Determining exactly what operators want depends on how much impact they think these items have on their image. The more personalization required, the more these products cost and, typically, the fewer the suppliers buyers have to choose from. In addition, the greater the degree of personalization, usually the larger the quantity the buyer must purchase, or guarantee to purchase, in order to make the transaction economical for the operation and the supplier.

- **AP price.** The AP price for these items may be a marginal consideration if buyers purchase highly personalized products. For standardized products, however, buyers can reduce the price by opting for lesser quality.

  Buyers can also reduce the price of certain personalized items. For example, manufacturers produce standard shapes to which buyers can ask them to apply certain lettering or other pictorial designs. Typically, buyers receive only a few options, but these may be enough to satisfy their taste and budget.

---

product compatibility
The extent to which a product is able to interact well with other products. A typical example would be purchasing a new piece of equipment because it would fit nicely with the current equipment.

- **The need to match.** How well does the plate the operators selected go with the salt and pepper shaker set, or with the general decor? Operators tend to select all of the permanent items together as one set to ensure **product compatibility** and a standard design and image throughout. If the establishment uses a design consultant, he or she may have a strong influence on what styles and colors the operation should use. Operations that have mismatched permanent ware risk developing a poor image, though in some cases, mismatched items are an integral part of a restaurant's overall theme.

- **Source of supply.** Should buyers purchase these items directly or from local suppliers? As with all direct purchases, operators must be able to provide the missing economic values, which, in many cases, is best left to professionals. If buyers purchase directly, they probably cannot obtain a stockless purchase plan, which is something of great value to most operations with limited storage facilities.

- **Material used to make the item.** A seemingly endless variety of materials can be used to manufacture permanent ware. Vitrified china, cut crystal, plastic, and so forth are available. Prices vary with the type of material, as will the image operators create.

- **Sizes.** Operators must note the specific size of product they require. They must consider, for instance, the volume of glasses and the shape of plates. For glasses and plates they will also have to consider the cost of the proper racks and dollies needed to wash and store them properly.

- **Length of service.** To a certain extent, operators must make a trade-off between price and durability. Durability is not the same as the life of a product in this case because theft is a constant problem that all hospitality operators face; shoplifting, in particular, is a major concern. So when operators pay more for higher-quality and more durable products, ironically, the extended **length of service** might make these items more attractive to thieves.

> | length of service |
> | Amount of time equipment, tools, and utensils can be used before they need to be replaced. Alternately, the amount of time a person has worked for an employer. |

- **Used permanent ware.** Again, operators can purchase used items and incur the advantages and disadvantages noted earlier.

The major purchasing concern, of course, is deciding what products operators need and want. Once they determine this, buyers should shop around a little, at least initially. When buyers settle on a supplier—and they normally settle on one, especially if they purchase highly personalized items—the rest falls easily into place because they stay with this supplier for their replacements. Problems may occur if the supplier discontinues selling the item. It may take time to find an alternative supplier or the buyer may be forced to switch to a different item. However, receiving and storing are not major problems with permanent-ware items.

Difficulties can occur with the in-process inventory, however. Waste, breakage, and pilferage take their toll. In a busy restaurant, the manager may go through a full set of glasses every 3 to 6 months. When they do, operators may be tempted to replace the original item with a cheaper imitation. This practice works for some operations, but it can potentially hurt the image of some companies. Operators must always consider very carefully the decision to reduce quality.

■ Single-Service Disposable Ware

As noted earlier in this chapter, the operators' major decision in this area is whether to use disposable ware exclusively, permanent ware exclusively, or some combination of the two. In some states and local municipalities, the disposables purchase decision is restricted considerably. For instance, some areas outlaw the use of any type of disposable product unless it is biodegradable. Some areas also mandate the use of paper goods made with unbleached materials; for instance, instead of purchasing white paper coffee filters, buyers may be restricted to the brown, unbleached alternative. It may also be necessary for buyers to purchase products made from recycled materials.

One specific example is the city of Santa Cruz, California, which prohibits the use of polystyrene/plastic foam disposable foodservice wares and requires the use of biodegradable, compostable, or recyclable disposable wares. Penalties for noncompliance include fines ranging from $100 for the first violation up to $1,000 for repeated violations.[2] Emeryville, California, has similar ordinances in place. It requires the use of biodegradable/compostable or recyclable disposable foodservice wares by all food vendors who utilize to-go type products. Fines are assessed for each infraction of this ordinance.[3]

Several types of disposable ware are available from a multitude of suppliers. For instance, buyers can purchase single-service plates, platters, bowls, cups, glasses, knives, forks, spoons, and ashtrays. The selection factors for these items are similar to those for permanent ware, with the addition of the following:

- **What do you need?** The operators' decision about precisely what they want and need is critical. A variety of items is available, as are numerous quality variations. Furthermore, operators can make several possible substitutions for permanent ware.

FIGURE 23.5 Disposable ware.
©jannoon028/Shutterstock

Operators can find just about any item they want (see Figure 23.5). They can usually select from among several acceptable degrees of personalization and from among several price and quality combinations. They can choose exceptionally strong, attractive items, or they can opt for very inexpensive, standard items. Once operators figure out what they want, though, the number of potential suppliers diminishes in proportion to the amount of personalization they want.

- **Packaging.** Buyers can purchase some disposable ware packaged together. For example, they can get a single-service package that includes a fork, knife, spoon, napkin, and individual salt and pepper packets. These are expensive, but they are very convenient for some applications, such as take-out meals.

  To save money, and to help protect the environment, many operations try to minimize these packaging alternatives. For instance, they may purchase recyclable, single-service cups packed in cases without plastic wrappers. Plastic saved this way not only helps the environment but can also mean long-term AP price reductions.

Some operations, such as fast-food restaurants with brisk carry-out business, use a good deal of disposable ware. Other operations, however, would never consider these products. The operations of the multitude of properties that fall between these two extremes must do some serious decision making. Again, the operator must balance the potentially high cost and consumer perceptions of disposable ware against its convenience. Operators must keep in mind, though, that the cost of dishwashing machines, their space requirements, and their operation, can be costly as well—not usually as expensive as disposable ware in the long run, but in the short term, disposable ware may be the logical alternative.

When operators decide what they want in the way of disposable ware, it is typical, as noted for some other nonfood expense items, for them to settle on one supplier. They must certainly do so if they want a high degree of personalization.

Once operators have selected their supplier(s), the procurement procedures, receiving, and storing then follow a fairly routine pattern. Issuing and the in-process inventory of disposable ware present few problems, primarily because places that use them can keep track of their usage as an extra control measure. For example, many fast-food operators keep track of the number of single-service clam-shell Styrofoam sandwich containers used during a shift. If 100 are missing, management takes it to mean that 100 sandwiches were sold. So, the amount of sales revenue collected should be consistent with the missing 100 containers.

Finally, waste can become a problem if operators let customers help themselves to disposable ware or permit employees to use these items indiscriminately.

■ Preparation and Service Utensils

A hospitality operation's initial purchase of these items, say, when it first goes into business, may need to be treated as a capital investment. That is, the initial purchase is depreciated. Replacement items can be treated as a current expense, however. Normally, a hospitality operation must keep several preparation and service items on the premises, such as pots, pans, service trays, dish racks, carts, and cutting boards.

Generally, the selection factors noted for permanent ware are the same as those for preparation and service utensils. However, two additional concerns exist. First, operators must be alert to any safety hazards and any unusual sanitation difficulties with such objects as knives and other utensils. Second, the material used to make the item is an important consideration. For example, aluminum, copper, cast iron, and stainless steel can be used to make pots, but each material serves a different purpose and carries a different AP price.

In some situations, operators might consider replacing some of these products with their disposable counterparts. For instance, buyers can purchase single-use steam table pans, which are used for cooking or reheating food and then holding it on a hot steam table for service. Generally, buyers do not have to be especially concerned with the image aspect of these items. However, operations with open kitchens or banquet and catering operations that use many items on buffets may be concerned with the physical appearance and design aspects of the items. The procurement procedure for such products parallels that for permanent ware: in both situations, the owner–manager tends to settle on a particular supplier.

Some utensils lend themselves to only one or two choices of suppliers. Buyers may have to purchase such items as dish racks and refrigerator trays from the equipment dealer(s) who sold them the dishwasher and the refrigerator. Fortunately, a reasonable amount of standardization exists among most equipment, so buyers may be able to avoid this potential problem.

Operators must closely supervise the in-process usage of these items. Our experience suggests that these utensils will yield years of acceptable service if they are not abused; once abused, they tend to deteriorate rapidly.

TYPICAL NONFOOD ITEMS—FABRICS AND PAPER GOODS

■ Fabrics

Hospitality operations may purchase several types of fabrics, such as uniforms, bed and table linen, costumes, drapes, table skirting, and curtains. Three ways exist to procure fabrics: buy them, lease them, or use disposables. If operations buy or lease permanent fabrics, they must then decide whether they will clean and maintain the fabrics themselves or whether they will use some type of laundry service. (See the discussion of laundry and linen supply service in Chapter 24.) It is possible for operations to buy disposable fabrics, such as aprons and hats. Operations can even purchase completely disposable uniforms and costumes.

If operations care to, they can buy uniforms and let the employees clean and maintain these garments. Alternately, some operations require employees to buy their own uniforms and costumes, as well as clean and maintain them. When companies do this, they must be sure that they do not violate the federal and/or state Department of Labor's regulations governing employee compensation.

As with all nonfood expense items, operators must decide precisely what they want. With fabrics, they must be prepared to like what they select because they cannot easily change their minds without incurring some extraordinary added expense.

Many concerns related to permanent ware are also applicable to fabrics, especially the concern about image. However, a few additional considerations exist. These are as follows:

- **Length of service.** Operators must decide how long they want fabrics to last. In addition to being more costly, long-life fabrics may outlast an image and may have to be discarded if operators remodel their facilities, even though they may still be functional.

- **Maintenance.** Operators must determine a maintenance schedule for the fabrics. Large hotels usually employ laundry workers who keep these items in good repair. Smaller hospitality operations usually must decide whether they want to provide these services for themselves or to purchase a professional laundry and linen supply service that will take over these duties. Generally, smaller operations opt for the professional service.

- **Who chooses?** Who should choose the fabrics and fix their specifications? This might be an emotional issue. For example, an owner–manager may buy dust-catching draperies, leaving the housekeeper to clean and maintain them. Perhaps it might be best to have a group of employees involved in the selection process. This way, once the draperies are installed, those responsible for their maintenance will be aware of the reasons for their selection.

  If operators expect employees to clean and maintain their uniforms, they should bear this in mind when selecting the clothes. Likewise, an employer may want to use more than one type of uniform for some job classifications; for instance, cocktail servers may be offered the choice between a contemporary style and one that is more conservative (see Figure 23.6). A little advice from the users will go a long way toward promoting harmonious relations in the future.

FIGURE 23.6 A traditional cocktail server uniform.
©*Chris Ryan/iStockphoto*

- **Fabric types.** Should operators consider easy-care, wash-and-wear types of fabrics? Some people consider them to be of lower quality in terms of feel and appearance than traditional fabrics, such as cotton and silk. They also may be more expensive and have shorter life spans. However, operators must weigh these disadvantages against the convenience and savings associated with less care and maintenance, as well as, if applicable, the savings operators realize by not investing in ironing equipment.

Once operators determine the fabrics they want, as well as how they want to have them cleaned and maintained, their purchase is not particularly difficult. In general, they will not have a large number of suppliers from which to choose, especially if they decide to purchase a laundry and linen supply service. When selecting this type of supplier, operators must keep in mind that some of them will help select uniform styles and give related advice regarding other types of fabrics needed.

Fabric receiving and storage are not particularly difficult, although operations might have some receiving problems if they use a professional laundry and linen supply service. A typical difficulty is that when the service delivers, they also pick up soiled items. Sometimes items that should be in the soiled batch are missing, and this can cause some confusion and delay. It is also costly because many laundry and linen service suppliers require operations to pay for lost items.

In-process care and maintenance can cause some difficulties, too. Large hotels usually do a good job when taking care of these items; these operations have linen rooms, which are analogous to food storerooms with all the proper controls. Smaller operations cannot afford this luxury, however. Furthermore, they are less likely to clean and maintain fabrics on schedule, which, if not done, will shorten their useful life.

■ Other Paper Products

Several types of paper, other than paper cups, plates, and napkins, appear in hospitality operations. These include: guest checks, cash register tape, tissues, doilies, scratch pads, take-out containers, stationery, purchase order forms, and other accounting documents. These items are usually selected according to the following factors:

- **Image.** Once again, operators must consider the operation's image. Patrons, suppliers, and the general public will see most of these paper products.

- **Special requirements.** An operation's product needs might inadvertently restrict the number of potential suppliers from whom buyers can choose. For instance, operations may require a special type of guest check to fit the cash register they have; the tissue must fit the tissue dispenser; and the purchase order records must fit the filing system.

- **Personalization.** Operations may choose to personalize some paper products. Such personalization requirements may reduce the number of suppliers from whom operations can choose. They can, of course, always get what they want, but if they resist a standardized format, they might have to turn to specialized suppliers.

- **AP price.** The price of many of these items is important because operators often encounter considerable waste in usage. Effective supervision can minimize this problem. This problem can be expensive, especially if employees misuse the expensive multipart forms. Some suppliers, as a service, might provide complimentary forms of one type or another. Even though operators may pay for these forms in the long run, chances are that the supplier can get these much more cheaply because of quantity purchasing power.

  Operators may be able to get a promotional discount for some items. For instance, paper towels may carry a brand name, which may justify a lower purchase price for operators.

> **minimum-order requirement** The least amount of an item a buyer needs to purchase before a vendor will agree to sell it. Alternately, the least amount a buyer needs to purchase before he or she can qualify for free delivery.

- **Minimum-order requirement.** Generally, a large order size requirement is common for some of these items. This saves operators quite a bit of money, but they might encounter unforeseeable storage costs. They also might get a stockless purchase plan for such items as personalized stationery or business cards. Alternately, if operators accept a standard type of product that differs only in that it has their name on it instead of someone else's, perhaps they will not have to buy as much at one time.

Once operators decide what they want, the purchasing, receiving, and storing of these products rarely present any particularly troublesome problems. Typically, management sets par stocks, and the users order up to par level as needed or as management dictates.

The in-process inventory may, however, generate some waste. It is probably impossible for operations to avoid it entirely, although good supervision can keep it down to acceptable levels. However, some waste is inevitable with paper products, if only because it is not cost effective to continually monitor the paper tablets hotel guests take. Also, operators cannot completely eliminate employee mistakes.

■ Miscellaneous Items

Such products as pest control supplies and plant food fall into this category. Operators should avoid purchasing many of these items, especially insecticides, and should avoid storing them on their premises as well. Kept on the premises, these materials could contaminate food and injure guests and employees. It is best for operators to hire a professional service to handle these dangerous products.

As with all nonfood expense items, the same selection factors and managerial concerns apply. In particular, image may be a major factor for many of them. Also, depending on the miscellaneous product that hospitality operations are evaluating, most of the other criteria discussed in this chapter will dictate the selection and procurement process.

Key Words and Concepts

As-used cost
Bid buying
Capital item
Capitalizing an expense
Credit terms
Depreciation
Disposable versus reusable
Employee skill
Equipment program
Expense item
Labor availability
Length of service
Lifetime cost
Minimum-order requirement

Online auction site
Operating supplies
Product compatibility
Product effectiveness
Product safety
Product size
Promotional discount
Quantity discount
Restocking fee
Stockless purchase
Supplier services
Systems sale
Volume discount

 Questions and Problems

1. Five typical nonfood expense items that hospitality operators might purchase are:

   a.

   b.

   c.

   d.

   e.

2. A product specification for permanent ware could include this information:

   a.

   b.

   c.

   d.

   e.

3. What is the primary difference between a nonfood expense item and a nonfood capital item?

4. When considering the lifetime cost of some nonfood expense items, operators should compute these costs:

   a.

   b.

   c.

Questions and Problems (continued)

5. What are the primary advantages and disadvantages of purchasing used nonfood expense items?

6. What critical information is missing from this product specification for dinner plates?
   Dinner plates
   Used for entrées and some desserts
   Permanent, vitrified china
   House brand (or least-expensive items)
   Bulk packed

7. Assume these facts: Cleaning agent A costs $1 per quart, cleaning agent B costs $1 per pint, and both agents will do the same cleaning job. What other information would you like to have before deciding which cleaning agent to buy?

8. Outline the specific procedures catering operators would use to purchase, receive, store, and issue disposable ware.

9. The concept of image is central to the selection of many nonfood expense items. Why is this true? What types of operations do you think must be most concerned with this issue? Which do you think must be the least concerned? Why?

10. The "color" selection factor would be an important consideration for these nonfood expense items:
    a.
    b.
    c.

11. Briefly describe the concept of "capitalizing" an expense.

12. Briefly describe the "systems sale" concept.

13. Safety is an important consideration when preparing a product specification for these nonfood expense items:
    a.
    b.
    c.

14. Prepare a specification for these nonfood expense items:
    Water glass
    Silver polish
    Plastic fork
    Mop
    Ounce scale

Questions and Problems (continued)

15. What are some advantages and disadvantages of using disposable ware? Determine which type(s) of disposable products, if any, are outlawed in your local market area. If one or more items are banned, what does the typical foodservice operation use instead?

16. Why is the selection factor "employee skill" an important consideration when operators purchase cleaning supplies and cleaning tools?

17. What are some of the different types of light bulb alternatives available today?

18. Given this data, determine the most economical product.

	CLEANER A	CLEANER B
AP price	$3.25/qt	$4.15/liter
Amount of cleaning solution yield per container	4 qt	4 1/2 liters
Amount of area cleaned per container	100 ft²	125 ft²

19. Assume that you operate the food-service in a 500-bed hospital. You currently use permanent ware, own a dishwashing machine and dishes, and employ seven full-time (40 hours per week) dishwashers with an average wage, including fringe benefits, of $12.65 per hour. You are exploring the possibility of converting to disposable ware. Preliminary estimates suggest an $18,500 per-month expense for the type and amount of disposable ware you need. Calculate the monthly cost of the labor for washing permanent wares. Is this higher or lower than using disposable ware?

Experiential Exercises

1. List five types of food preparation and service utensils or five types of housekeeping equipment. Contact a local supplier to find out the prices. Then look for used prices on the Internet. Write a one-page paper comparing the prices of the new versus used items.

2. Attend a hospitality trade show, such as the National Restaurant Association Show, the International Hotel, Motel, and Restaurant Show, Catersource, or a local/regional trade show. Select one type of nonfood expense item. Speak with the company representatives, and collect information and brochures about that item. Write a two-page paper comparing the products that the companies offer.

References

1. Alice Segal and Katherine Chu, *Reusable Dishes: Economically and Environmentally Sound*, Center on the Environment, Roosevelt Institution at the University of Chicago, http://roosevelt.uchicago.edu/policy/disposables.html. See also Franklin Associate, a division of ERG, "Life Cycle and Environmental Cost Analysis of Disposable and Reusable Ware in School Cafeteria Including Dishwasher Operations," School Nutrition Foundation, November 2009, www.thegreenteam.org/wp-content/uploads/2014/04/Warewash_Study-Summary.pdf.

2. City of Santa Cruz, "Chapter 6.48 Environmentally Acceptable Food Packaging," The Santa Cruz Municipal Code, passed April 8, 2014, www.codepublishing.com/ca/santacruz/html/santacruz06/santacruz0648.html.

3. City of Emeryville, "Ordinance No. 07-004," Effective date January 1, 2008, www.ci.emeryville.ca.us/DocumentCenter/Home/View/333.

CHAPTER 24

SERVICES

The Purpose of This Chapter

After reading this chapter, you should be able to:

- Identify management considerations, including security concerns, surrounding the selection and procurement of services.

- Create a specification outline for services that can be used in the purchasing process.

- Evaluate the major selection factors for cleaning and maintenance-related services.

- Examine selection factors for other facilities-related services.

- Formulate a promotional strategy for a hospitality operation using various types of advertising.

- Review selection factors for consulting, financial, and insurance services.

MANAGEMENT CONSIDERATIONS

In most hospitality operations, managers purchase the services needed. These typically include cleaning and maintenance services such as waste removal, groundskeeping, cleaning, laundry and linen supply, and maintenance and other facilities-related services such as pest control, decorating and remodeling, and vending machines. Other categories of services that will be discussed in this chapter are advertising and consulting, financial, and insurance services. The purchasing directors of large corporations may contract for some services or department heads might purchase one service specifically for their department. However, as a general rule, because local suppliers primarily provide many services, the unit manager, whether employed by an independent operation or part of a chain, tends to have a great deal of input in the selection and procurement process.

When managers buy services, many of them assume that service costs are fixed costs. That is, they believe that they must spend a certain number of dollars per year for services and that they cannot get along without these services.

It is true that some services are unavoidable costs of doing business. Expenditures for such items as legal, accounting, bookkeeping, and insurance services are necessary, although the range in cost and quality can vary considerably. Some other services, though, are more or less discretionary. For example, managers do not necessarily have to purchase menu-design services or cleaning services; in many cases, operators are perfectly capable of using employees to complete these tasks.

Thus, one of the main points that managers must remember about services is that not all of these are fixed costs. Managers do have some discretion. Consequently, they should consider spending as much purchasing time and effort on these services as they would on food, beverages, and supplies.

Perhaps managers should even spend a little extra time. If they receive a load of bad tomatoes, they can correct the mistake or change suppliers without too much difficulty, but if they purchase a service that turns out to be poor, they may well find the first problem creates additional problems. First, managers may not know that a service is being poorly done until the job is completed. Moreover, if they buy a poor service, it is poor—period. No such thing as an in-between service exists. Managers may be able to salvage a few good tomatoes from the bad load delivered to them, but such partial value is usually not the case with services.

Obviously, it may be difficult for managers to judge the quality of a service in advance. For instance, it is difficult to judge a carpenter's ability unless managers have samples of completed work: even then, however, managers have no guarantee that past performance will be replicated. Only when the work is finished will managers really know, but at that point it may be difficult to do much about it if major alterations are needed.

Faced with this problem of evaluating service performance, managers or department heads may find it is easy to neglect inspecting a service provider's performance. Managers who never think of receiving a food item without inspecting it assume that the maintenance crew that comes around once a month performs its assigned tasks.

A typical case might be in purchasing a hood-cleaning service. The crew comes in one night every six weeks to clean the hood required to be over all cooking equipment. No one checks to see what the crew members are accomplishing because it is assumed the crew is conscientious. One night, however, a good-sized fire erupts in the hood. The fire marshal quickly discovers that it had not been cleaned for months and was coated on the inside with several inches of grease.

Thus, another concern with services is whether they are hard to monitor and inspect. Managers' or department heads' inability or unwillingness to inspect can easily lead to completely overlooking poor performance.

Another major service concern for managers and department heads is whether they should buy a service or provide the service themselves. In many cases, the same considerations that determine whether hospitality operations cut their own steaks or purchase portion-cut steaks enter the picture here. Moreover, the same emotional arguments usually surface. One of the major differences, though, is that some services do, in fact, require experts. For example, it is unlikely that managers can provide their own legal and insurance services.

A cost-benefit analysis of managers doing their own service work will probably indicate which pattern is best. Their decision to provide their own economic values and supplier services when they purchase products can be based on previous experience, but there is no clear-cut historical pattern to guide their decision in this situation. In some instances, it is cheaper for businesses to wash their own windows; in some cases, it is not. Contrast this to the readily compiled evidence that shows, for example, that cutting their own steaks from a side of beef may be too expensive for most hospitality operators.

Thus, managers and department heads normally have a little more flexibility when pondering the question of whether to provide some of their own services. A great deal of tradition, however, suggests that operators should buy some services while providing others on their own. Traditionally, hospitality operators purchase a service when one (or more) of the following apply: the service is impossible for them to do, that is, it might require complicated expertise; it is too expensive, that is, it might require costly equipment; or it is very inconvenient to provide it themselves.

Lately, managers more commonly practice what is referred to as **outsourcing**. This involves identifying work that is not central to their hospitality operation's primary mission and contracting with a service provider to do it. For instance, payroll processing is necessary, but it is something guests will never encounter. Thus, it may be a good candidate for outsourcing. **Professional employer organizations (PEOs)** provide even more human resource services to their small business clients. Along with paying wages and taxes in compliance with state and federal laws, they often provide workers with access to 401(k) plans; health, dental, and life insurance; dependent care; and other benefits not typically provided by small businesses.

The number and types of outsourcing opportunities in the hospitality industry have exploded over the past few years. Managers have become more focused on their core businesses and do not wish to be distracted by noncore activities. Some of the functions most likely to be outsourced include laundry, equipment, pool, and elevator maintenance, public relations and marketing, and reservations. Although common for some time for offsite operations like

outsourcing Identifying work that is not central to your hospitality company's primary mission and hiring an outside service to do it for you instead of doing it yourself. Things such as pest control and gardening services are usually outsourced.

professional employer organization (PEO) Firm that, for a fee, manages the human resources function for client companies. In addition, these types of firms typically join with client companies to become a co-employer. In effect, the client's employees become the employees of the PEO. This allows small clients, such as the typical hospitality operation, to enjoy relief from HR administrative tasks, improved employee benefits, increased employee productivity, and enhanced liability management services.

hospitals, employee feeding, and entertainment venues, now many hotels and resorts are outsourcing all or part of their food and beverage operations. A considerable majority of all companies in the United States are thought to outsource one or more functions. However, many do have concerns over the loss of control over outsourced operations and potential declines in service quality.[1]

If hospitality operators are leasing their real estate facilities, the landlord may provide certain services as part of the lease contract. For instance, tenants in a shopping center normally pay a monthly rental fee plus a **common area maintenance (CAM) fee.** The landlord uses this CAM fee to defray the costs of parking lot maintenance, window cleaning, waste removal, restroom maintenance, and other expenses related to the general upkeep of the shopping center's common areas. Usually, the CAM fee is not as negotiable as the monthly rental payment. In this situation, the landlord shoulders the burden of selecting and procuring the necessary services. On one hand, this relieves tenants of this time-consuming activity; on the other hand, however, tenants relinquish the opportunity to do the work themselves or to shop for the best possible prices.

Examining a service provider's background and abilities is another major management consideration. It is necessary, at times, to contact current and/or previous customers and solicit their advice. It is a good idea for managers to ask the **business license** bureau about such particulars as the service provider's status, whether the proper insurance coverage is maintained, and whether customer complaints have been lodged against that service provider. It is also a good idea to contact the local **Better Business Bureau (BBB)** and ask to examine any file that exists on the service provider.

Avoid unlicensed, uninsured service providers. Their mistakes can cost operators a great deal of money. These providers have no insurance to handle any claims for damages operators may sustain. Also, if they install, for example, some electrical wiring incorrectly, and this leads to a fire, the operation's insurance company may not honor any claims the operation makes for damages.

Some unlicensed and uninsured service providers are **moonlighters,** that is, part-time persons who work odd evening hours while holding down another day job, but not all moonlighters are uninsured and/or unlicensed. Unfortunately, moonlighters cannot always provide service exactly when operations need it. Consequently, even though a moonlighter may be a less-expensive choice, whether or not operations can tolerate such delays in service is a major management concern. In some situations, delays are no problem, but they can be devastating at other times.

common area maintenance (CAM) fee Fee charged to tenants. Used by the landlord to pay for facility upkeep, especially of things like the parking lot and landscaping.

business license Authorization issued by local, state, and/or federal governments needed to conduct business.

Better Business Bureau (BBB) Organization that helps protect consumers from shoddy and fraudulent business practices. It also helps consumers resolve complaints they have about businesses they've dealt with.

moonlighter An individual who arranges a second job that is outside the course and scope of his or her first job. Sometimes a person may "moonlight" only with the written approval of his or her primary employer.

■ Security Concerns

Shady characters are always ready to sell hospitality operators a nonexistent product or service or to pretend that they have a real bargain to offer—a bargain that never materializes. Hospitality operators do not usually buy questionable advertised bargains. However, services invite all sorts of ingenious tricks. For instance, purchasing an ad in a soon-to-be-published directory can be costly: the directory may never be printed. Also, donating money to buy ad space in a charitable association's publication may be costly and wasteful unless operators have verified that the charity is a bona fide operation.

Invoices for services usually go directly to the bookkeeper, who might pay them routinely. Therefore, operators should check these bills and initial them because a dishonest company may send an invoice that resembles the ones their bookkeeper always pays.

Dishonest service providers may also try to slip in extra invoices for the service that operators pay for on a regular, periodic basis. Again, if the bookkeeper does not check the bills carefully, operators might pay for the same service twice. In fact, one local restaurant in Las Vegas regularly paid its alarm company twice a month instead of once, for more than a year.

Another insidious problem, to which small operators are particularly vulnerable, is the contractor who demands a deposit before beginning work but then never returns. For example, suppose an operator wants someone to install new cabinets in the room service area of a hotel. A contractor tells the operator that he needs $1,000 to procure the materials required to complete the job. The operator gives him the money—then never sees this contractor again.

Admittedly, this problem occurs more with homeowners than with commercial businesses. This can happen to hospitality operators, however, if they deal with moonlighters and other contractors who are not licensed by the state or city. If operators have any doubts about a contractor, they can contact the Better Business Bureau (BBB). Alternately, they might put their deposit money in an escrow account, from which the materials supplier will receive the money only after delivery of the materials. Another option is for operators to pay the materials supplier directly without giving any money to the contractor. Finally, operators might consider working strictly with their friends, with those with whom they have had positive business dealings, or with members of the local chamber of commerce or other similar civic groups.

In Chapter 14, we discussed the major security problems associated with purchasing, receiving, storing, and issuing. The problems we noted there seem to multiply when operators buy several services, especially services that are difficult to monitor and are paid for on a regularly scheduled basis. Other potential concerns can also plague managers that may become very important under certain circumstances are that: (1) managers may have to permit strangers (i.e., nonemployees) on the premises, (2) managers may have to give strangers access to personal and confidential information, and (3) managers may have to let a third party have direct control over some aspect of their businesses.

Small businesses, rather than large firms, are usually targets for dishonest persons who realize that small operators have less time to examine every detail. As noted in Chapter 14, however, all hospitality operators must force themselves to be careful. Dishonest acts are just too common and too easily perpetrated.

To recap, at least six major concerns come into play when managers or department heads purchase services: (1) they must recognize that services are not fixed costs, (2) they must realize that evaluating a service provider's performance can be difficult, (3) they must decide whether to provide their own service or buy it, (4) they must examine a service provider's background and abilities, (5) they must consider the advantages and disadvantages of using moonlighters, and (6) they must avoid security issues related to services.

GENERAL PROCEDURES IN SERVICE PURCHASING

inspection procedures
An organized examination or formal evaluation exercise. It involves the measurements, tests, and gauges applied to certain characteristics in regard to an object or activity. The results are usually compared to specified requirements and standards for determining whether the item or activity is in line with these targets.

bid buying When buyers shop around seeking current AP prices from vendors. The vendors are asked to quote, or bid, the prices they will charge. Intended to give the buyer competitive pricing information that will allow him or her to get the best possible value.

Once managers or department heads decide which services they intend to purchase, they should prepare a specification for each one, detailing as much as possible the desired criteria (see Figure 24.1 for an example of a specification outline for services).

Preparing some parts of the specification is not particularly difficult. Managers usually can include what they want accomplished and when they want the work completed. Their **inspection procedures**, however, are not as easy to detail. Nevertheless, complete specifications are absolutely essential if managers intend to use a bid-buying strategy.

To bid buy services is just as risky as **bid buying** products. Bid buying services can produce a potentially greater monetary reward because prices for services tend to vary considerably from one provider to another. Also, in many cases, the lowest-price service will still provide acceptable quality. This is true because service providers are more eager to reduce their prices when business is slow. Most service providers are small firms, and if they do not work at that particular service, they do not have sales of other services or product lines to support them until business picks up. A less-acceptable standard of quality may accompany a lower price. Assuming managers can inspect and monitor the service provider's performance, however, they should be able to extract maximum value.

Bid buying, negotiating with service providers, and monitoring the actual work—all of these tasks can be time-consuming. Although it is commendable for hospitality operators to get the most for their purchase dollar, they must get the results they need. Thus, their service-purchasing strategy has to be constructed with this in mind; it is worthless to save a dollar only to find out that the hood is still dirty. Operators must keep in mind that if they pay too much for products, all they really lose is money. If they fail to get the service results they want, however, they will lose whatever they paid and will receive very little in return. If the canned goods are unsatisfactory, they can quickly rectify the error. If a service is unsatisfactory, however, operators are less likely to be as forgiving—and are more apt to dismiss the offending service provider and contact someone else. The delays associated with an inadequate service can be bothersome.

When choosing whether to use bid buying, operators must do what they feel is best, but really, the most important aspect of service purchasing is for operations to get what they want. Perhaps the best way for operators to accomplish this is to settle on one service provider and, together, determine what they need, when they need it, how much it costs to do the job correctly, and what payment arrangements will ensure that they receive the quality of service necessary. While discussing their needs, operators should also evaluate the service provider's past performance by asking for and contacting business references who are former or current clients.

These are general guidelines about service purchasing. Emphases change a little as operators go from one particular service to another. For instance, it seems more appropriate to bid buy a contract cleaning service than to bid buy a lawyer's service. Operators can probably make an

Intended use:
Exact name of service required:
Quality of materials that must be used:
Quality of the finished work:
Completion time:
Required work schedule:
Amount and type of experience required:
Business license:
Other licenses required:
References:
  BBB:
  Licensing division(s):
  Current customers:
  Former customers:
  Other:
Insurance coverage (bonded) for:
  Security:
  Property damage:
  Liability:
  Incomplete work:
  Deposits:
  Other:
Moonlighting restrictions:
Priority restrictions:
Guarantee(s):
Desired bill-paying procedure:
Inspection procedure(s):

FIGURE 24.1 An example of a specification outline for services.

intelligent decision about the buying strategy best for them after considering the services they are most likely to purchase.

CLEANING AND MAINTENANCE-RELATED SERVICES

▪ Waste Removal

Operators will probably need to purchase their own disposal service because few cities and towns provide a tax-supported service for hospitality operations. If they are located in a shopping center or office park, part of their CAM fee may cover the cost of waste removal.

Although most waste removal companies are large firms, some small operators exist in this area; the person who buys a truck and goes into business may be the norm in some areas. Sometimes these small operators are efficient; sometimes they are not.

Operators should make sure that the disposal service: (1) provides on-time collection; (2) does not mangle and destroy containers; (3) does not mangle the containers' enclosed housing area, if any; (4) removes all refuse piled on the ground; (5) replaces containers in the proper locations; (6) provides suitably large and strong containers for their type of business; (7) provides containers with locks, if necessary, to prevent outsiders from dumping on the hospitality operation's premises; and (8) charges a competitive price.

The primary purpose of waste disposal is to maintain a neat and sanitary disposal area. Operators must find a company that will maintain this area in the way that is appropriate for their type of business.

Another detail is the pick-up schedule. Operators do not want a garbage truck driving through their parking lot in the middle of the lunch or dinner hour. Also, if the refuse company's truck looks unkempt, the hospitality operator probably should shy away from that service, although, realistically, they may not have a large selection of potential suppliers in their vicinity from which to choose.

If operators have a grease trap that must be cleaned periodically, they will find it convenient to use a waste removal firm that can provide this additional service. They may be willing to pay a bit more for this one-stop-shopping opportunity. However, recently, there has been an increase in the trend to recycle used restaurant grease. This type of recycling allows government-approved and licensed agencies to recycle used grease by removing it from a grease trap and processing it elsewhere. The used grease is typically converted into animal feed or biodiesel

> **waste removal service**
> Outside contractor that carts away trash and other unwanted items. May also provide clients with trash containers, such as dumpsters.
>
> **groundskeeping service**
> Vendor contracted to maintain all outside landscaped areas.

fuel.[2] In a few parts of the United States, the local government may be the only **waste removal service** available. Alternately, it might mandate that all businesses use a specific waste removal company. In this situation, hospitality operators cannot shop around for the best deal; they must agree to the legislated terms and conditions.

Some waste removal companies may pay companies for their waste. For example, some recycling firms, such as grease salvers and metal salvers, may pay a modest amount for recyclable waste. However, to take advantage of this other-income opportunity, businesses generally need to take the time to segregate their wastes. Furthermore, in some instances, they may even need to deliver their wastes to the recycling plant.

■ Groundskeeping

Few operators are able to provide their own landscaping, snow removal, or parking lot maintenance services. Typically, companies purchase these services from reputable service providers. In addition, a landlord commonly provides these services as part of the CAM-fee arrangement.

Probably the most difficult **groundskeeping service** to purchase is a landscaping service. Small firms are particularly prominent in the landscaping business. Anyone with a little bit of capital and desire can easily enter the business. Operators should avoid anyone who does not have a demonstrated knowledge of this trade, especially in regard to tree service that may involve professional cutting, pruning, or stabilizing.

Landscapers usually undertake snow removal in the winter months to supplement their income and to keep busy all year long. As a result, operators can contract with one firm to handle all of their grounds maintenance.

The operators' objective is clear: they want an attractive exterior (see Figure 24.2). Rather than negotiate a low price, they might economize by minimizing the number of plants, trees, and lawns they nurture—assuming that they are more interested in a price they can afford than in an extravagant outdoor display. Some landscape service providers also maintain indoor decorative plants, although operators often must go to another source when they want to purchase or rent smaller plants and flowers.

FIGURE 24.2 A landscaped entrance to a hotel.
©zhu difeng/Shutterstock

When operators purchase a landscaping service, they must be specific about what they want done and when they want it done. They should resist the temptation to say, "Cut the grass when necessary." Ambiguous instructions like these can lead to conflicts later on. Operators should, instead, say something like, "Cut and edge the lawn, and clean up afterward, every Thursday afternoon after 4 o'clock."

Landscaping services often have a firm rate schedule, unless operators happen to find one whose business is slow. Operators need to keep in mind, though, that a landscaper with few customers may be a poor choice. The good ones often have more business than they can handle.

■ Cleaning

Several specialized contract cleaning services are available. Some of the more typical ones include (1) exhaust hood, (2) degreasing, (3) window, (4) carpet and upholstery, and (5) concrete cleaning.

Unlike many services, cleaning is one that typical hospitality operations conceivably could perform on their own. Consequently, using contract cleaners tends to generate a good deal of discussion, which usually centers on the crucial question: Should I purchase this service, or should I do it myself?

It is probably better for operators to do some cleaning tasks themselves, particularly ones that must be done every day. Monthly or quarterly cleaning tasks that require a great deal of specialized equipment and labor expertise should probably become the responsibility of a contract cleaner. Unfortunately, the distinction between these two types of tasks is not always clear.

Many operations contract for an outside firm to take care of almost all the cleaning. Hospitals often use these services, and some housekeeping contractors sell complete services to hotel properties.

For heavy cleaning, such as carpet shampooing, it seems best for operators to purchase this service. This eliminates the need for expensive equipment, for storing expensive shampoo, and for expensive labor.

Of course, operators must also consider the disadvantages of contract cleaners. One drawback is the lack of complete control over the workers. Another disadvantage is the cost, which may be quite expensive—although it is unlikely that operators could provide some of these services more cheaply.

Contract cleaners are numerous. However, like decorators, they are relatively easy to evaluate. Operators can contact references and ask to examine the cleaners' work.

If contractors do a poor job, usually several others can take their place. The number of competitors in the field helps keep their prices within reasonable limits and their service timely.

A problem with contract cleaners is the laxity with which hospitality operators examine and inspect the work done in their establishments. (Recall the hood story earlier in this chapter.)

Yet another problem is that operators may sometimes want to use less-expensive, unlicensed amateurs. However, the quality of their work probably is not very professional or competent. Furthermore, it is not wise for operators to expose themselves to potential liability.

A final concern is that some contract cleaners have trouble maintaining a complete staff themselves. They are frequently shorthanded and may, as a result, provide operators with poor service. In addition, when operators inspect work that they have done for someone else, the operators do not know whether the same people working for the contract cleaners today were the ones responsible for the job they are checking.

laundry and linen supply service   Outside service that provides cleaning, pressing, and fabric repair. Delivers fabrics to the hospitality operation. May lease its fabrics to the hospitality operation or may maintain those owned by the hospitality operation.

■ Laundry and Linen Supply

No service generates as much disagreement as **laundry and linen supply service**. Some hospitality operators seem to have a good experience with these suppliers, whereas others simply are not satisfied.

If operators use linens and uniforms, they may: (1) buy their own and purchase a laundry service, (2) purchase the laundry service and rent the fabrics, or (3) purchase their own fabrics and laundry machines and do their own work.

The first two options require less work on the operators' part than the third, in that they order just what they need, receive it, store it, and use it. Also, they expend only a minor amount of effort to shop around because, usually, they have only two or three laundry and linen supply services in their area from which to choose.

Large operations are more interested in the third option. They often own an in-house laundry system. Smaller operations might experiment with their own laundry machinery. However, the cost of the space needed to house the machinery, the labor cost, the cost of cleaning chemicals, and other overhead costs usually seem to be too expensive for these properties.

Some operations have gone so far as to eliminate linens and uniforms altogether; these companies use disposable linens and give employees a uniform allowance so that they can provide their own uniforms.

Renting a laundry and linen supply service is more convenient, and operators receive professional service. If operators erect their own laundry, they must be prepared for more responsibility to accompany the savings they may realize. If they eliminate permanent fabrics, they need to be prepared for the high cost of disposables and, possibly, customer resistance to disposable napkins, tablecloths, and bed linens.

If operators decide to rent linen and laundry service, they should evaluate each potential supplier based on the following factors: (1) length of contract; (2) service schedule; (3) how seasonal fluctuations are handled; (4) variety and quality of products offered; (5) overall cost of the service; and (6) cost of lost, damaged, or stolen products for which operators are responsible.

It is possible for operators to have an outside management contractor manage their laundry and their dish- and pot-washing systems in their establishments. Some independent contractors specialize in providing laundry and steward services to hospitality operations. In some cases, they might provide the least-expensive alternative.

■ Maintenance

An almost endless variety of repair and **maintenance services** appears to exist in the hospitality industry. Some of the more typical ones are (1) security; (2) fire and intrusion alarm; (3) locksmith; (4) dishwashing machine; (5) knife sharpening; (6) plumbing; (7) electrical; (8) refrigeration; (9) heating, ventilation, and air conditioning (HVAC); (10) beverage-dispensing equipment; (11) elevator; (12) sign; (13) water systems; (14) office machines; (15) cooking equipment; (16) computers; and (17) transportation services.

Typical hospitality operators tend to purchase one or more maintenance contracts to supplement the service agreements that normally accompany new equipment purchases. Although operators often use the terms **maintenance contract** and **service agreement** interchangeably—along with the more generic term, "service contract"—the actual meanings are different. Whereas a service agreement covers equipment defects and malfunctions during the **warranty** period, a maintenance contract is much more detailed. Usually, for a consistent monthly fee, the maintenance contractor provides routine maintenance, such as periodically changing filters and lubing mechanical parts. Most contracts also cover emergency service when you need it, such as when a freezer suddenly breaks down.

Most new mechanical equipment that operators purchase generally comes with some sort of warranty or service agreement. During the **guarantee** period, usually only major repair problems are covered; operators are responsible for routine maintenance. Many equipment dealers, though, sell **extended warranty coverage** in the form of a maintenance contract, which is designed to relieve operators of all repair and maintenance responsibilities. Also, after this period expires, the dealers usually are willing, for a price, to extend the buyers' coverage once again.

Some operators do not wish to purchase maintenance contracts. They would rather wait until they need service and then pay only for what they need. This may be a good idea because maintenance contracts, especially those that equipment dealers and manufacturers sell, tend to be very lucrative for these primary sources and intermediaries. However, many operators like the "insurance" that maintenance contracts provide and are willing to pay for peace of mind.

maintenance service Outside contractor who provides repair and maintenance service. May involve the purchase of a maintenance contract, or the service may be purchased only when needed.

maintenance contract Type of extended warranty coverage. For a fee, usually paid monthly, the contractor provides routine maintenance as well as emergency service. Typically purchased when the initial warranty period is set to expire.

service agreement Covers the cost of furniture, fixtures, and equipment (FFE) defects and malfunctions during the initial warranty period provided by the FFE vendor.

warranty Another term for guarantee.

guarantee May be expressed or implied. Assurance that a product or service will be provided. Alternately, assurance that a product or service will meet certain specifications. Alternately, assurance that a product or service will be acceptable for a specified period of time or amount of use. Alternately, assurance that parts and/or repairs needed during a specified time period will be paid for by the vendor.

extended warranty coverage Maintenance contract purchased to cover the cost of parts and service over a defined period of time.

Buying a contract is not an easy decision. First, operators are generally asked to pay up front for the following year's service. Also, the price usually is not negotiable. Another major difficulty is the possibility that the service technicians will take care of cash customers before taking care of any of the operators' emergency needs. Now that the maintenance company has the operators' money, it may not be eager to be as punctual as it might be for cash customers, although it should be equally as concerned about the operators' future business once the initial contract expires.

One item that must always be done before signing a maintenance contract: be certain that the service is available as advertised. For example, if the service is supposedly available 24 hours a day, 7 days a week, operators should make sure that this is always the case. They might, for instance, call the service provider at 3 A.M. If no one answers the telephone, operators should forget that maintenance contractor.

OTHER FACILITIES-RELATED SERVICES

■ Pest Control

pest control operator (PCO) Company licensed to handle and apply pesticides that are not available to the general public.

integrated pest management (IPM) Program to systematically prevent pests from entering and surviving in a facility. It features the use of PCOs.

Pest control to eliminate insects and vermin is one of the trickiest control areas in the entire hospitality industry. It is easy for some hospitality operators to feel that they are pest control experts because spraying chemicals appears to be the only necessary action. Pest control is a difficult service to perform, however, and some chemicals are so dangerous that only licensed **pest control operators** (**PCOs**) can legally handle them (see Figure 24.3).

Working with a PCO is an essential part of **integrated pest management (IPM)** programs commonly used by hospitality companies. These put preference on prevention measures to keep pests from entering and also integrate control measures to eradicate any pests that are already present. The three rules to achieve this goal are (1) do not allow pests to enter the facility; (2) make the environment less suitable for pests by denying the basics of food, water, and hiding; and (3) work with a PCO who can get rid of pests that are already in or on the premises.[3] Probably the best strategy is for hospitality operators to contract for a weekly or monthly visit, as well as a price to be charged for emergencies, such as an unanticipated infestation. Calling a pest control service only when an obvious problem arises is bad business. A great deal of damage to the operators' building, as well as to their reputation, may have already occurred.

FIGURE 24.3 A pest control operator (PCO).
©*Huntstock/Getty Images*

Operators will learn that purchasing this service is, generally, preferable to providing it themselves. When they purchase this service, they do not need to store poisonous chemicals on their premises, which is always a risky practice.

The operators' purchasing objective here is obvious: no pests. They must determine what pest control services charge, and they should check various companies' performances by speaking with their customers. Normally, prices among these firms are very competitive. The pest control company that can provide the best service schedule, solid advice on how to correct any building problems that invite infestation, and direction regarding the appropriate sanitation procedures employees should follow probably will be an operator's first choice.

A few national pest control companies exist. Large chain operations might consider negotiating one contract at a lower price that includes every unit in the chain.

The cost of pest control service is small indeed compared with the problems it can prevent and the expenses it can save. This is no area for operators to be sticklers over a few cents difference among service providers.

■ Decorating and Remodeling

These services are almost always purchased, and small contractors dominate these fields. Hospitality operators must be wary of them and be careful if the contractors they hire are moonlighters, who may have trouble meeting a deadline. The smaller the contractor firm, the less likely it can afford the equipment necessary to do an excellent job. Operators should take the time to solicit competitive bids from established contractors who can provide several references and are licensed, insured, and familiar with their needs.

When evaluating these services, operators may be concerned more with time than with money. That is, they certainly do not want to pay outrageous prices, but they must first make sure that they are not unduly inconvenienced or closed down too long. Because time is money, they may be willing to pay a bit more to get the work completed earlier.

It is probably a good idea for operators to see, in person, examples of the contractors' work before they contract for it. They should go to a place where the workers have hung wallpaper and see whether or not they like the job. This is the best part about purchasing these types of services: operators can always see what the contractors have done, and this past work serves as a continuing standard of quality for contractors to maintain in their future work. Operators must watch, though, not to see only the best work, while the contractors' skeletons remain safely in the closet.

When buyers purchase this type of service, they appear to be very concerned and quite fearful about the possibility of incomplete work or work that is shoddy and cannot, or will not, be repaired by the service provider. It would be well worth the operators' extra expense in terms of forcing the service provider to purchase a performance **bond**, which is an insurance policy guaranteeing satisfactory completion of all work.

A related problem with this type of work is the **lien-sale contract** that these service providers normally want clients to sign. This contract stipulates that the service provider can attach a lien to the entire property if clients fail to pay for the

bond An insurance policy covering cash-handling employees. Alternately, refers to a performance bond, which is insurance taken out by a construction contractor that guarantees work will be done by a certain date or else the client will collect damages.

lien-sale contract Allows the service provider, usually some type of construction, decorating, or designer service, to attach a lien to the entire property if he or she is not paid for the work performed.

unconditional lien release
Document verifying that a vendor has been paid in full. Typically used in the construction trades to protect a buyer who has signed a lien-sale contract. Once the vendor signs it, he or she is prevented from placing a lien on the property.

construction management firm
Organization that specializes in managing and controlling the various companies (such as architects, designers, and construction contractors) needed to build a new facility and/or remodel an existing one.

work performed. The logic in this contract suggests that the service provider can hardly "take back" an improvement to a customer's property and that this improvement by itself is worthless. Hence, the service provider must be able to take over the entire property to gain satisfaction. To counteract this problem, operators must insist that they will make installment payments that correspond with the major stages of the project, and that they will pay only when a stage is completed satisfactorily. Once operators pay for the entire project, the service provider must agree to sign an **unconditional lien release**, verifying that payment has been made in full. This can be a difficult and inconvenient process if several persons are working on your place, but it is necessary to avoid any possible loss of your entire property. If operators do not have the time to do this, they can hire a specialized service, such as a **construction management firm**, to oversee these details.

■ Vending Machines

Some operations use coin-operated or smart-card-operated vending machines for both customer and employee convenience. The machines dispense candy, soft drinks, food, and many other items.

In many cases, these machines come with established agreements: the company puts them in the operators' property, the operators agree to provide adequate space and necessary utilities to power the machines, the company takes full responsibility for the maintenance and restocking of the machines, and the operators receive a commission, that is, they get to keep some percentage of the gross sales of the machines.

A major purchasing consideration for operators is whether or not they want such machines on their property. Another major concern is the potential quality differences among competing companies' machines and the products in these machines. Also, one company may service its machines much better than the others, as well as restock them more regularly.

user discount Typical arrangement with vending companies that place machines, such as video games, in your hospitality operation. As part of your compensation, you are allowed to use the machines at no cost, or at a reduced cost.

vending-machine service
Outside contractor that provides and maintains coin-operated machines, such as beverage and cigarette machines, for the convenience of employees and customers. Operators who sign up for this service usually earn a portion of the money the machines collect.

Of course, operators must be concerned with the commission split to which the vending machine company agrees. They are also interested in the **user discounts** provided; that is, the hospitality operator would like to use these machines personally at no cost or at a reduced cost. These financial considerations, along with the services provided, are normally the deciding factors when operators shop for **vending-machine service**.

Another major consideration is whether or not operators want to buy their own machines and do all the work themselves. Operators can make a good profit with these machines, but the initial cost and the ongoing maintenance costs can be exorbitant. If the sales revenue is large, however, operators might do very well with their own machines. However, they may not want to add more tasks to their already long list: the work can be tedious, especially the maintenance aspects, which require operators to have a highly trained repair person, someone large vending-machine companies have.

A large hospitality operation can contract with an intermediary who will oversee the vending-machine program in effect for all of the company's individual locations across the United States. For instance, some intermediaries will take on the responsibility of ensuring that all locations have the latest, state-of-the-art equipment; receive the appropriate service; and earn the maximum commission split. Usually these intermediaries develop national contracts with the hospitality operation. This is quite convenient because it means that the hospitality operation will receive one report and one commission check each period. This practice also eliminates the need for unit managers to deal with several local vending-machine companies on a day-to-day basis.

ADVERTISING

Most hospitality operations use some sort of advertising—newspaper, magazine, radio, television, Web, social media, or some combination thereof. Effective use of the right mix of the tactics described here is very important for the success of the organization. Printed or online brochures, flyers, and menus all serve as advertising media. In addition, operations may need in-house promotion kits, also known as press kits or media kits, which provide information about the company.

When operators evaluate advertising purchases, an important element they need to keep in mind is the audience they intend to reach with their message. They must select the advertising medium, or media, that will reach this audience. They should not, for example, buy a newspaper ad strictly on the basis of its low price. When purchasing advertising, operators will find that it is usually best to opt for quality over quantity.

In most instances, the amount operators must pay is directly related to the size of the intended audience. They will need to ensure that the advertising medium consistently delivers the guaranteed audience size by periodically checking independent rating services' reports detailing these statistics. Reputable on-air, print, or online advertising media will issue **make-goods**, which are blocks of free advertising time or space granted to buyers when the actual intended audience size was smaller than the guaranteed one, or when there were errors in ad presentations or placement.

When operators choose advertising, one of their major concerns is the cost per potential customer reached by or influenced by the ad. The cost is difficult to compute, but the media buyer, or the medium itself, usually can come up with a reasonably accurate figure.

Another important consideration is the ability for operators to trade their products or services, such as meals and sleeping rooms for advertising. This type of exchange bartering, usually referred to as **trade-outs**, can save hospitality operators a great deal of money by reducing their out-of-pocket expenses. This is common for radio, newspaper, magazine, other print media, and outdoor billboard advertising, but not as much for television advertising.

Another question for operators to ponder is the use of soft-drink-company signs and printing. Coke©, for instance, often shares the cost of menu printing and sign preparation as long as its logo is prominently displayed. Operators must decide, then, as with all **promotional discounts**, whether they want to be closely identified with a particular supplier.

---

make-goods Free advertising time or space granted to buyers when the actual intended audience size is smaller than the guaranteed one.

trade-out Refers to bartering your goods and services instead of paying cash. This term is commonly used to refer to trades between hospitality operations and advertising firms.

promotional discount Price discount awarded to the buyer if he or she allows the vendor to promote the product in the hospitality operation. Or if the hospitality operation agrees to personally help promote the sale of the product to its customers.

Still another consideration for operators involves opportunities such as sponsoring local athletic teams, participating in fund-raising functions with local charities, and advertising in local high school and college newspapers. Many companies feel that these methods contribute to good—and profitable—public relations. To measure how these sponsorship opportunities impact a business, there needs to be an accurate review of the sales and communication effect. The most recognizable way that sponsorship can contribute to public relations is through name recognition and exposure.[4]

Operators can go through an intermediary such as an advertising agency or other **media-buying service** rather than deal with the various advertising media in person. When they select an agency, they normally discuss what they want and how much they can afford. The agency develops an overall advertising strategy and selects the various media to use. Operators pay the cost of the advertisements, and the agency often takes a percentage, or commission, of these expenditures as its fee. Usually, the agency is paid on a sliding-percentage scale. However, it could receive a flat rate. Alternately, it might be paid on **merits**; that is, its income could be directly related to the sales success the advertised product or service generates.

> **media-buying service** A type of advertising agency that helps clients develop their overall advertising strategies and selects the various media to use. Works for commissions.
>
> **merits** Refers to the way advertising is paid for. The price a buyer pays is directly related to the amount of sales revenue generated by the advertising.

■ Newspaper Ads

Some commercial restaurants purchase newspaper ads. They normally purchase an ad on a **run-of-the-press** basis, which means that the ad will be put any place in the paper at the discretion of the advertising editor, though operators can specify in a very general way what they do and do not want.

> **run-of-the-press** Refers to a newspaper ad being placed in the paper at the discretion of the advertising editor.

Nowadays, the buyer might also have the option of whether to have the ad in the print version of the newspaper, the digital version, or both.

Operators can usually save money by contracting for an ad space over a period of time, such as an ad that is printed once a week for 25 weeks. Over the long run, the cost of each of these ads should be less than the cost of individual ads purchased once in a while. As with all purchases, quantity discounts are available.

The cost and benefits of newspaper advertising are hard to calculate accurately unless operators can count the number of coupons that customers tear out of their ad in response to, for instance, a special-price promotion. Newspaper ads do serve as good reminders to customers. They keep the operation's name in the public eye.

■ Local Radio Ads

Local radio ads are charged on a different basis than newspaper ads. The most expensive radio ads run during what is known as drive time—usually 6 till 9 A.M. and 3 till 6 P.M. These are the times when people are driving to and from work and are listening to the radio—thus, these are the times with the largest listening audiences. Paying for the drive time slot on a local radio station may be worth the investment, especially if the salesperson offers an accompanying **run-of-the-station** schedule, whereby the ad may run at any time during a 24-hour period on a space-available basis. Depending on the station, the length of the ad, and the time of day desired, the price varies considerably.

> **run-of-the-station** Refers to a radio ad being sold on a space-available basis as opposed to a specific time of day.

Local radio stations can usually tell operators who their listeners are with reasonable accuracy. Newspapers and magazines cannot be as accurate because these pieces may be read by more than just the original buyer before eventually being discarded.

Radio tends to build business slowly over the long run, and it might take time for a radio campaign to generate results. However, radio is an efficient medium because specific audiences are fairly easy to target.

■ Television Ads

Network television is usually too expensive for hospitality operations except at the regional or national-chain level. Most operations, though, can afford it if they agree to run commercial messages during nonprime time, or on local independent cable stations. If they opt for television advertising, they usually need the help of a professional advertising agency or another media-buying service. It is not a good idea for operators to begin television advertising unless they can sustain it. The costs are prohibitive for a one-shot ad. For the simple production of a few commercials, they might pay thousands of dollars.

■ Magazine Ads

Hospitality operators must use magazine advertising selectively. Some magazines of the gourmet, airline, and tourist variety may reach the operators' intended market, especially if the operations tend to attract people from a wide geographical area. Other magazines are published to meet the tourism needs of a single city, and many hospitality operators find advertising in these periodicals profitable. Some trade magazines and travel indexes can be useful, especially to lodging operations that want to advertise to and solicit business from business travelers, travel agents, and companies seeking convention and meeting facilities.

■ Directories

Although not as popular anymore, some potential guests may still use hard copy directories, and therefore, the hospitality operator may still consider using this form of advertising. The main decision hospitality operators must make is whether to buy an expensive illustrated ad or to accept the one- or two-line notations most operations choose.

Many options are available, such as the AAA and Forbes travel directories, hotel/motel directories, dining directories, and local coupon directories. Approximately 6,000 directories are published in the United States each year. When selecting a directory, operators should consider the cost, the number of years it has been published, the target audience, the way it is distributed to readers, and whether they will be listed in both print and online versions.

■ Printed Brochures and Menus

Brochures and flyers are quite useful in some circumstances and for some operations. Their publication rates are usually fairly standard; they vary according to, for example, the number of colors, the quality of the paper or other materials, and the printing style.

With the availability of high-quality color printers, many hospitality operators now choose to print their own menus and brochures. This can be especially cost effective and convenient for restaurants that change their menus and specials on a regular basis. However, the savvy operator will need to consider carefully whether the staff has the expertise to design and produce professional looking documents. Although it will add to the expense, operators may also wish to hire a graphic artist to design a logo or pictorial layout, and an editor to develop the wording.

Many operations purchase such items as swizzle sticks, menu covers, sugar packets, and napkins emblazoned with their logo. These items, too, keep their name before the public. In fact, some bars may need to rely on this form of advertising and internal promotion.

FIGURE 24.4 A hospitality billboard.
©Bob Pardue-South Central/Alamy Stock Photo

■ Outdoor Ads

Billboards are especially useful when hospitality operators have continuing messages to display, such as current entertainment offerings. Billboards are also a good choice when operators want to build awareness (see Figure 24.4).

Hospitality operations along the side of or near a highway often use billboards and signs to guide travelers. However, the law strictly regulates the use of these media along highways. Some locales, such as Hawaii,[5] severely restrict the amount and type of outdoor advertising a company can display.

Numerous options and cost plans are available. For instance, hospitality operators can spend a minimal amount by arranging for a joint promotion with some related firm, such as a soft-drink company. Alternately, they might splurge on an expensive sign linked to a computer that can change messages quickly and easily. The price range between these two extremes is considerable.

■ Direct-Mail Advertising

Many hospitality operations use periodic mailings to current and/or prospective customers promoting some sort of special price, event, or other form of offering. If operators have a reasonably updated mailing list or can purchase a useful one, all they have to do is to arrange for the design of an appropriate flyer, stamp it, and mail it. These mailings can be expensive. Nowadays, most operations use an e-mail system of contacting past, current, and potential customers.

The best part about direct mail is that operators usually can develop a promotional piece whose effectiveness can be tested very easily. If, for instance, a mass e-mail includes a response option for the customer, such as a coupon, they can determine very quickly the success rate of the direct-mail campaign. If the campaign is deemed unsuccessful, it is very easy for operators to alter the e-mail message and schedule another mailing.

A common direct marketing technique used primarily by take-out and delivery operations, such as pizza and Chinese restaurants, are the use of **door hangers**. Advertisements or menus can be placed on the doors of local area homes and businesses. A derivation of this marketing technique is the **windshield advertisement**, whereby marketing materials are placed on cars in local parking lots. Be aware, however, of consumer backlash when using these techniques. Many people do not like materials placed on their property. Also, it may be considered trespassing to place marketing materials on vehicles parked on private property.

In the United States, 91 percent of adults use e-mail. Therefore, the use of digital advertising, promotions, surveys, and comment cards has increased in recent years as a less-expensive mean of reaching consumers over the previously popular snail mail option.[6]

■ Web Ads

Web advertising has become a common practice among hospitality operators. They can advertise in this manner two ways: (1) by developing their own website (or outsourcing the development) and marketing it online in review sites, portals, and/or search engines and (2) by placing ads on other related websites (this includes **banner ads**, pop-ups, and sponsorships) that their intended target market might frequent, such as a local online directory (see Figure 24.5).

door hangers
Promotional tools used to convey a business's message to potential customers. They are designed in such a way that they can be hung on a door knob. Often used as an alternative to direct-mail pieces. They are usually double-sided, have attention-grabbing styles, and have angled hole slits that can adjust to most doorknobs.

windshield advertisement
A flyer typically placed under a car's windshield wiper.

banner ad   Graphical advertisement that appears on a website that provides a hyperlink to the advertised site.

FIGURE 24.5 Examples of banner ads.
Courtesy of Vance Bell

The benefit of Web advertising is that it allows for a direct line of communication with the consumer. Browser history and cookies are able to tailor advertisements that suit the viewer's needs or recent search criteria. In addition, Web advertisements are able to educate consumers through the use of hyperlinking (transferring) to a hospitality operations website.[7] The costs associated with using this medium are comparable to traditional forms of advertising.

■ Social Media

Many hospitality companies purchase very little advertising as they rely on promoting their business through their websites and other social media sites. Examples of these sites include Twitter, Facebook, Instagram, Yelp, and TripAdvisor. These sites constitute free advertising because a hospitality organization can link directly to consumers through their personal pages (Twitter, Facebook, and Instagram). Once a customer follows the page, they can be exposed to advertising in the form of updates, posts, and pictures. Websites such as Yelp and TripAdvisor allow customers to post reviews. TripAdvisor receives more than 315 million unique views each month.[8] Many hospitality organizations employ social media analysts or coordinators to monitor the company's reviews, respond to negative ones, and ensure that the company maintains an overall positive image on social media

■ Reservation Services

With the growth of online sales, hospitality operators must carefully consider which online booking websites to use. More than 148 million travel bookings are made on the internet each year which is 57 percent of all travel reservations. Although the majority of hotel reservations (65.4 percent) are still made on hotel brand websites, such as Marriott or Hyatt, more than 30 percent of travelers book over merchant websites, such as Expedia. Hotels.com, Priceline, and Travelty. Priceline alone sells more than 22 million hotel rooms per month.[9]

For foodservice, there are many options for online reservations. The largest of these is OpenTable.com, which allows consumers to make reservations at approximately 38,000 restaurants across the country. OpenTable has seated more than 370 million diners worldwide through its platform, representing more than $14 billion in revenue for OpenTable restaurant customers. It was acquired by Priceline in 2015 but still operates as an independent brand.[10] Some restaurant review sites, like Zagat, link readers directly with OpenTable. Other online reservations services include Restaurant Reservations and Freebookings, a division of Livebookings.

CONSULTING, FINANCIAL, AND INSURANCE SERVICES

■ Consulting

Consultants abound in the hospitality industry. Some of the most typical consultants include (1) designers, (2) feasibility researchers, (3) attorneys, (4) accountants and bookkeepers, (5) operations planners and counselors, (6) energy advisers, (7) employee trainers, (8) architects,

(9) building contractors, (10) property appraisers, (11) engineers, (12) real estate advisers, (13) business brokers, (14) fire and safety inspectors, (15) data processors, (16) printers, (17) equipment rental firms, and (18) information technology (IT) specialists.

Some trade publications publish lists of consultants in some of their issues. These lists typically include national consultants, those who work in more than one part of the United States. The websites of the International Society of Hospitality Consultants (IHSC) and the Foodservice Consultants Society International (FCSI) are also good places to find information about the types of consulting services available and their member companies. As a rule, however, local firms provide most consulting work. In that case, local chapters of the American Hotel and Lodging Association (AHLA) and National Restaurant Association (NRA) can recommend allied member companies that perform consulting services.

Generally, operators tend to purchase a consultant's service whenever the task to be performed is relatively complicated, highly technical, and not part of the owner–manager's daily routine. For instance, accounting and bookkeeping, design, legal, and computer consulting services are the types of tasks operators may not be able to do very well for themselves.

A company staff member can perform some other types of consulting in-house. Many operators can easily complete such tasks as menu design and certain feasibility studies. Large organizations often hire in-house consultants as permanent staff members to handle these functions. Usually, these specialists are required to travel from one unit operation to another, solving problems, doing research, and performing several other related activities.

A user somewhere in the organization or the owner–manager normally determines the need for a **consulting service**. Purchasing this service can be tricky. In some cases, the user or owner–manager can map out exactly what is wanted, thereby occupying a relatively good position for evaluating various consultants. For the most part, however, the operator will be dealing with professionals, some of whose work may not be completely understood by a layperson.

Operators can use a certain type of bid buying when purchasing this kind of service. Essentially, this would require them to describe the problem they have and the results they would like. After that, they might ask two or more consultants to prepare a **consulting proposal** for them. The proposal would typically include such considerations as the objectives of the job, what will be done to achieve them, what the final results will be, which approach the consultant will take, the time constraints, and the fee for the consulting service. The operators' job, then, would be to evaluate the proposals and select one.

A beneficial aspect of these proposals is that they rarely cost operators anything. In addition, during proposal preparation, the consultant may help operators define more clearly just what it is they need. Some consultants assume the buyers' role by engaging in what is sometimes referred to as **negative selling**. They tell operators how severe the problem is and how busy their schedule is, but that they have to see what they can do because the operators definitely need help quickly. Operators may find themselves begging the consultants to save them; that is, operators try to sell the consultants on taking the job—and their money.

consulting service Company that specializes in helping others by giving advice and/or accomplishing specific tasks that clients do not wish to do on their own.

consulting proposal A document submitted by a company that typically includes the project's objectives, tactics, time constraints, and total price. Similar to a competitive bid for food products submitted by a vendor.

negative selling Occurs when a vendor places the buyer in a position where the buyer encourages the vendor to take the buyer's order (and money). Usually done by convincing the buyer that he or she must use that particular vendor and that there is no substitute vendor capable of handling the order. More likely to occur when purchasing consulting services than when purchasing any other type of product or service.

If operators use the proposal approach, they should try to negotiate a firm contract. Operators should examine a consultant's references and be watchful of negative selling. If they can, they should ask the consultant to perform a "trial job," an inexpensive job that the operators need done, which can be an excellent test of the consultant's future work habits and overall competence.

Operators should try to negotiate on price but should be careful not to rush the work. They might want to make a bonus offer for early completion or some other incentive for good, quick work. They should also make sure that how much money they can potentially save does not completely determine the fee because, as per the recommendation, operators might have to invest too much to save this money.

The objective is, in short, to complete the job satisfactorily. As a result, cost considerations might sometimes be a secondary concern.

Operators must sometimes use trust as their sole criterion in selecting consultants because the consultants often direct some of their money to other people. For instance, when discussing a consulting job possibility with a professional consulting firm, operators will probably talk to one of the partners, usually a seasoned veteran in his or her field. Although this partner will retain limited supervision of the job, one or more junior members of the consulting firm might do the work or it might be subcontracted to another party. This is sometimes done in feasibility studies and real estate appraisals.

The key to developing an excellent working relationship with a consultant is to be very clear about what is needed. Operators must be willing to spend as much time as necessary so that the consultant can obtain the information needed to do the job properly. Also, although operators certainly must maintain their privacy, they cannot expect positive results if they treat the consultant as an outsider.

Before purchasing a consulting service, operators might try to get it free. For instance, if the problem relates to energy, the public utilities companies might do a free energy audit and recommend ways of conserving precious fuel. The operators' trade association might have a staff member who can help them design a menu. Suppliers and salespeople are often ready to offer valuable advice. In addition, the federal government's **Small Business Administration (SBA)** sponsors consulting and similar programs for qualified small businesses.

Small Business Administration (SBA)
Federal government entity set up to maintain and strengthen the nation's economy by aiding, counseling, assisting, and protecting the interests of small businesses. Also helps families and businesses recover from national disasters.

financial service
Company that provides assistance with attaining, investing, storing, moving, or borrowing money or monetary equivalents.

■ Financial

Hospitality operators usually have flexibility when they shop for loan capital, checking services, or other types of **financial services**. Banks, for example, do not all charge the same rates and provide equal services. Even though financial institutions are regulated by law, it is incorrect to assume that one institution is as good as another. These institutions do have some discretion within the law, and the intangible "supplier services" they provide more than likely vary considerably.

Hospitality operators need bankers who will provide them with checking accounts, petty-cash accounts, payroll accounts, loans, cash management techniques, and computer services and, perhaps, monitor benefit packages for their employees. In most cases, the accountant, bookkeeper, or owner–manager negotiates for a banker's services, either with banks or, for some other services, with other types of financial institutions. In too many instances, operators hesitate to negotiate. In these situations, they often become a house account, particularly in those areas of the United States where few financial institutions exist.

Financial institutions are like any other supplier: they want a hospitality operation's business, and they want it to become a house account. They strive to make it very inconvenient for a company to purchase one service from them and other services from their competitors. Some banks, for instance, might offer a better rate of interest on a loan if operators keep a savings or payroll account with them or permit them to make a bit of income by processing the firms' payroll checks. Also, some banks' credit and debit card services may be more timely and convenient.

Typical hospitality operations usually have little time available to evaluate several financial institutions when purchasing these services. Often, an operator will tend to "grow up" with a local banker, the banker who was there to encourage and nurse the operator along during the company's early days. As long as this banker can consistently provide a wide range of services, the grateful operator will tend to remain a house account. In some situations, such an arrangement is mutually beneficial.

A large hospitality operation using one-stop shopping for financial services would be very unusual, however. These big firms usually have more time and skill for determining the combination of services and service providers most favorable to them. Moreover, the amount of cash turnover a large company deals with gives it a strong bargaining position. Like corporate purchasing directors, who have the time, ability, and responsibility to seek out better deals, corporate accountants, and treasurers have the same capabilities.

■ Insurance

Unfortunately, no single, all-inclusive insurance policy that hospitality operators can buy exists. They must purchase more than one. The typical policies, often dictated by state and local laws and codes, by lenders, and by landlords, include (1) fire and extended property damage; (2) storekeeper's liability; (3) business interruption insurance; (4) crime coverage for burglary and robbery; (5) personal injury insurance, with protection for libel, slander, defamation, or false arrest; (6) glass insurance; (7) product liability; (8) vehicle insurance; (9) fidelity bonds for those employees who handle money; (10) third-party liability insurance for bars; (11) workers' compensation; and (12) comprehensive insurance to protect against an employee's dishonesty toward customers.

Operators can purchase several additional insurance policies at their discretion. These include (1) health or life insurance for company personnel; (2) other types of policies to be used as employee benefits, such as disability insurance; and (3) extra insurance on expensive antiques, works of art, and furnishings.

Generally, when evaluating insurance coverage, operators should consider three major factors: (1) the extent of the coverage, or the amount of deductible they must pay; (2) reimbursable losses, or the types of exclusions for which they cannot collect damages; and (3) the conditions they must satisfy before they can collect.

Another major consideration involved with selecting an insurer is the number of policies operators can obtain from one source. The more they can receive under one roof, so to speak, the smaller the number of insurers they need to deal with. Thus, it is common for operators to go to one independent **insurance broker** and secure all their insurance needs through one person. Brokers work for the buyer. They deal with insurance agents and insurance companies when putting together an insurance package that will meet their clients' needs.

If operators prefer, they can buy insurance directly. This is cheaper because operators save the agent/middleman's fee; however, they do not get the advice and counsel of this agent/middleman. Companies that sell directly are sometimes referred to as **direct writers**. Vehicle and life insurance can easily be purchased directly.

Operators can also purchase insurance from an **exclusive insurance agent**. However, this type of agent represents only one insurance company. Consequently, if operators need some unique insurance coverage, they may have to deal with several exclusive agents.

If available, operators should consider joining a **risk-purchasing group**. This is a type of co-op purchasing arrangement that, essentially, enables individuals to become part of a larger group and, thereby, reduce insurance costs for all of the group members. Hospitality chain organizations can easily qualify for these plans. Independent operators might consider joining a group that buys insurance for its members, such as groups that many state and local restaurant and hotel associations maintain. Group plans are always less expensive than individual plans.

Operators can evaluate an insurance company's performance reasonably easily because most states keep records of their dealings with the various companies. Also, operators can check an insurance company's rating in one of several rating agency publications, such as *Best's Insurance Reports*. This publication notes each insurance company's history, financial performance, and other related data. Sound companies are rated A or A1. Operators should also determine the skill of the persons handling the claims. Some discreet conversations with other customers of the insurer(s) with whom an operator is thinking of dealing can give the operator a sense of the promptness and fairness of claims adjustments.

Insurance is often highly technical, and it is appropriate for operators to consult legal counsel before making a decision. Some busy managers leave much of the dealing with insurance companies to their attorneys, but this is an expensive move because attorneys charge by the hour and happily interview anyone operators send them. As with so many other complex decisions, it may be best for operators to determine what coverage they want and then negotiate the price with a limited number of reliable bidders, and in this case have their judgment backed up by their attorney. Furthermore, it is usually to the operators' advantage to shop and compare insurance policies every year or so. Our experience shows that a wide spread in prices exists for essentially equal coverage.

---

insurance broker
Salesperson authorized to represent several different insurance companies and sell their products. Usually selects appropriate insurance policies from different companies to provide all necessary coverage a client needs.

direct writer Insurance company that bypasses intermediaries, such as insurance brokers, and sells insurance directly to customers.

exclusive insurance agent
Insurance salesperson who sells only one company's insurance policies.

risk-purchasing group
A co-op that specializes in the purchase of insurance for its members.

SERVICES AND TECHNOLOGY THAT LET MANAGERS FOCUS ON THE GUEST
Sara Janovsky, Product Operations Specialist OpenTable, San Francisco, CA

Sara Janovsky, Product Operations Specialist for OpenTable, is a problem solver, working with different restaurant operators and owners to make their lives easier and to achieve their companies' financial and guest service goals. Sara spent more than 10 years in the restaurant industry, in many front of the house and management positions and for many types of establishments, especially fine dining restaurants. Six years ago, she began working for companies that provide services and technology solutions for restaurants. Sara says her restaurant work experience was important in giving her the knowledge and skills for these jobs. But earning her bachelor's degree in hotel administration helped her broaden her horizons, meet people, and develop her networking skills. The organizational skills and work ethic she learned as a student, including research, organization, and time management, have proven just as valuable to her success as her work experience.

Sara first worked at OpenTable as a Restaurant Conversion Specialist, and then was promoted to Senior Restaurant Optimization Specialist. OpenTable has been transforming restaurant reservations since 1998. With more than 38,000 partner restaurants, OpenTable finds restaurant reservations for more than 20 million people per month. The company is headquartered in San Francisco, and the OpenTable service is available throughout the United States, as well as in Canada, Germany, Japan, Mexico, and the UK. In North America, 50 percent of its restaurant reservations are made through its mobile app, available since 2008 (http://www.opentable.com/about/).

Sara's job was to assist existing customers with transitioning from using the first version of the reservation software to a more sophisticated system. With the initial system, restaurant managers specified how many reservations were available for different time slots based on their gut feeling and experience. The later version uses a more scientific approach using actual physical table inventory for optimizing the space. Sara explains that this is never a perfect science because the restaurant industry is a people business; however, using these tools allows the restaurant to save time, serve more guests, and have more confidence that the tables will be available when guests arrive. Her job was to understand the goals of the operation so she could determine the best table inventory design for it. Some of the key variables that she reviewed and evaluated with the clients to determine their business mix and best approach to taking reservations were

- Estimating turnover times based on party size.
- Determining maximum business levels (number of guests at any given time) based on what the kitchen could handle and the staff schedule.
- Evaluating the impact of large party business based on the party size and time of the reservation. If possible, large parties were scheduled so that the operation could still have two turns in the space used for them.
- Limiting party size availability of tables to help maximize seat utilization. For example, the restaurants may make certain four-top tables available only for parties of three or four people, but if they were not sold by a certain time of day, they would release them for reservations for parties of two.
- Reviewing the historical data from their electronic reservation book (ERB) to see what the turnover times were and how many people the restaurant could accommodate at a given time.

SERVICES AND TECHNOLOGY THAT LET MANAGERS FOCUS ON THE GUEST (continued)

Sara worked with many types of decision makers. In the case of independent restaurants—the majority of OpenTable's restaurants—she worked with owners and operators, typically a general manager, middle manager, lead host person, or maitre d'. When working with hotels and chains, she would often have corporate contacts such as training coordinators or sales and marketing managers, though every individual store would have a specific contact person. Training coordinators prefer all restaurants and reservation departments or call centers use the same reservations system. This makes training easier and ensures standards and consistency across the brand.

For the sales and marketing managers, a big selling point for OpenTable is that it is not just a reservation system; it is a marketing tool due to its global diner network, its name recognition, and the quality of its website. OpenTable can significantly contribute to marketing efforts, or for some operators, even replace the need for traditional marketing channels. In addition, having restaurant reviews on the OpenTable website separates it from many other reservation systems. OpenTable clients can trust its reviews because they can only be written about completed reservations, unlike many competitors such as Yelp and its SeatMe system, on which users can leave reviews without ever stepping foot in the restaurant.

For each diner who makes a reservation directly from the OpenTable website, OpenTable earns $1. Alternately, for reservations that originate from the restaurant's own website that are then connected to OpenTable, the company earns $0.25. This cost of a reservation and providing this service to the guest did not exist before the advent of Web reservation systems. Some operators may view it as an incremental cost, but now it has transitioned to a seemingly fixed cost. Many guests expect to be able to make a reservation over the Internet or through the mobile app, so it becomes an essential cost. Sara says it can also be looked at as an amenity cost, as providing online instant and secure bookings makes diners' lives easier, which is what hospitality is all about. Once part of the OpenTable network, operators tend to stay with it because it drives guests to the restaurant so well and the company provides such effective software and support.

One of Sara's favorite aspects of working for OpenTable was that it was such a creative and innovative company. The success of the table inventory program, mobile app, mobile payments, and rewards program are a result of those characteristics. She was inspired by what is possible with technology and the important information operators can leverage to improve their businesses and more important, the guest experience. One example is the possibility of having access to a diner's preferences even if they have never dined at your restaurant before. Another could be receiving alerts through mobile location and mapping tools when diners are going to be late and an estimate of how long it will be until they will arrive at the restaurant. That is real hard information to help operators make the decision—do I seat a walk-in party instead or not? These are great tools to help solve problems that operators did not even think they could solve.

She also liked that her schedule was very flexible; she could work at home and have meetings at any hour, especially with clients in different time zones. Most of the time, working over the phone rather than face-to-face was faster and more efficient. Regardless of the method of contact, ultimately, what operators appreciated most were correct answers and empathy.

After a brief time working for another company that provides management solutions for hiring, training, inventory, and other aspects of restaurant operations, Sara returned to work at OpenTable as a Product Trainer and Media Content Specialist. She collaborated with product and product marketing management teams to do product testing, manage internal training, and provide content support. She has recently been promoted again to become a product operations specialist.

Key Words and Concepts

Banner ad

Better Business Bureau (BBB)

Bid buying

Bond

Business license

Common area maintenance (CAM) fee

Construction management firm

Consulting proposal

Consulting service

Direct writer

Door hangers

Exclusive insurance agent

Extended warranty coverage

Financial service

Groundskeeping service

Guarantee

Inspection procedures

Insurance broker

Integrated pest management (IPM)

Laundry and linen supply service

Lien-sale contract

Maintenance contract

Maintenance service

Make-goods

Media-buying service

Merits

Moonlighter

Negative selling

Outsourcing

Pest control operator (PCO)

Professional employer organization (PEO)

Promotional discount

Risk-purchasing group

Run-of-the-press

Run-of-the-station

Service agreement

Small Business Administration (SBA)

Trade-out

Unconditional lien release

User discount

Vending-machine service

Warranty

Waste removal service

Windshield advertisement

Questions and Problems

1. List some disadvantages of hiring an unlicensed service provider. Are there any additional disadvantages of hiring a moonlighter?

2. Why is completion time a very important selection factor when operators evaluate potential repair and maintenance service providers?

3. Assume that an operator's real estate lease contract requires it to pay a monthly CAM fee. What is the purpose of this fee?

4. List some advantages and disadvantages of purchasing a cleaning service.

5. What is the major disadvantage, for operators, of a lien-sale type of contract?

6. What is the major disadvantage of operators' purchasing their insurance from a direct writer?

Questions and Problems (continued)

7. Briefly describe the concept of "negative selling."

8. What are some of the costs and benefits of operators managing their own laundry machinery and purchasing their own linens?

9. What is the primary purpose of purchasing a fidelity bond?

10. List some advantages and disadvantages of purchasing a maintenance contract.

11. What is the difference between a service agreement and a maintenance contract?

12. Assume you are the owner–operator of a quick-service hamburger operation with annual sales revenue of $850,000. What services would you consider purchasing? Why?

13. Briefly describe how a buyer could use an escrow account as part of a bill-paying schedule set up to pay a remodeling contractor.

14. How are the acronyms PCO and IPM related? Why do most hospitality operations hire professional PCOs?

15. What is the difference between run-of-the-press and run-of-the-station?

16. Should operators trade their products for advertising services, or should they pay cash? Why?

17. When would operators expect an advertising medium to issue "make-goods" to its customers?

18. What are some Web-based advertising services available to hospitality operators? Why would using these be preferable to traditional types of advertising?

19. A specification for pest control service could include this information:

    a.

    b.

    c.

    d.

    e.

20. A specification for vending-machine service could include this information:

    a.

    b.

    c.

    d.

    e.

Questions and Problems (continued)

21. A specification for financial services could include this information:

    a.

    b.

    c.

    d.

    e.

22. A recycling operator contacts you and offers the following deal: if you save your aluminum and cardboard and bring it to her plant, she will give you $0.45 per pound for the metal and $0.08 per pound for the cardboard. How much money would you want to earn each month before you would be interested in this deal?

23. Assume you manage a full-service restaurant. You are paying $48,000 a year for linen service, which is mediocre. Setting up an in-house laundry would cost $20,000. Operating the in-house laundry would cost $22,000 per year. What do you suggest? Also, what does the $22,000 include?

Experiential Exercises

1. Imagine that your bed and breakfast is in need of developing a new advertising model to attract new customers. What areas of advertisement are most pertinent to your business (Web, direct mail, social media)? How would you incorporate these new tools to gain the greatest impact in your market? Write a one-page summary addressing your business's advertising needs and methods you would implement to achieve them.

2. You own a small restaurant in a major city. Your sales and profits are lower than expected, and your food costs are higher than expected. What areas do you think the consultant should address to help the restaurant reverse those trends? Write a one-page proposal, from the point-of-view of the consultant, with suggestions for what type of consulting services it would provide.

References

1. Elaine Simon, "Pros and Cons of Outsourcing," *Hotel News Now*, April 26, 2010, www.hotelnewsnow.com/Article/3209/Pros-and-cons-of-hospitality-outsourcing. See also Steve Wilson, "Hospitality Outsourcing: Frequently Asked Questions," HospitalityNet.org, www.hospitalitynet.org/news/4052558.html.

References (continued)

2. M. M. Pack, "Indies Find Going Green Worth the Extra Energy," *Nation's Restaurant News*, 42, no. 32 (August 18, 2008):40–42, http://nrn.com/product-watch/indies-find-going-green-worth-extra-energy. See also eXtension.org, "Used and Waste Oil and Grease for Biodiesel," Retrieved from http://articles.extension.org/pages/28000/used-and-waste-oil-and-grease-for-biodiesel

3. Educational Foundation (National Restaurant Association), *ServSafe Coursebook 6th Edition* (Chicago, IL. National Restaurant Association Educational Foundation, 2012).

4. Eunju Suh, Curtis Love, and Billy Bai, "An Examination of the Impact of Sponsorship on Attendees' Recognition of Sponsors," *Journal of Convention & Event Tourism*, 6, no. 4 (2004), DOI: 10.1300/J452v06m04_03.

5. "State of Hawaii Billboard Statutes," New Rule Project, Institute for Local Self-Reliance, www.newrules.org/environment/rules/billboard-bans-and-controls/billboard-ban-hawaii. See also John Curran, "Exemption to 40-year-old Billboard Ban in Vt. Worries Some," *FoxNews.com*, May 7, 2008, www.foxnews.com/wires/2008May07/0,4670,VermontBillboards,00.html.

6. Amy Newman and Judi Brownell, "Applying Communication Technology: Introducing Email and Instant Messaging in the Hospitality Curriculum," *Journal of Hospitality, Leisure, Sport & Tourism Education*, 7, no. 2 (2008), DOI: 10.3794/johlste.72.191.

7. Mills Juline, Jung Kook & Alecia Douglas, "Exploring Perceptions of US State Tourism Organizations' Web Advertising Effectiveness," *Asia Pacific Journal of Tourism Research*, Vol. 12, No. 3, (September 2007), DOI: 10.1080/10941660701416820.

8. "Competition Is Shaking Up the Online Travel Market," *Forbes*, January 5, 2015, www.forbes.com/sites/greatspeculations/2015/01/05/competition-is-shaking-up-the-online-travel-market/#45f650d15846.

9. Statistic Brain, "Internet Travel and Hotel Booking Statistics," www.statisticbrain.com/internet-travel-hotel-booking-statistics/.

10. OpenTable, "OpenTable Fast Facts; as of Q2 2016," http://files.shareholder.com/downloads/ABEA-4SW9EX/0x0x394755/ed27a649-cf4e-401f-af22-b724c184608a/OpenTable_Fast_Facts.pdf

FURNITURE, FIXTURES, AND EQUIPMENT

The Purpose of This Chapter

After reading this chapter, you should be able to:

- Identify management considerations surrounding the selection and procurement of furniture, fixtures, and equipment.

- Outline the general procedures used when purchasing furniture, fixtures, and equipment.

- Describe the primary selection factors for furniture, fixtures, and equipment.

- Evaluate furniture, fixtures, and equipment based on operating characteristics.

- Consider cost and service factors when purchasing furniture, fixtures, and equipment.

- Review financing options when purchasing furniture, fixtures, and equipment.

MANAGEMENT CONSIDERATIONS

capital item Expensive FFE, the cost of which must typically be depreciated over time. Opposite of an expense item.

depreciable asset Another term for capital item.

Furniture, fixtures, and equipment (FFE) are sometimes referred to as **capital items**. Most capital items are **depreciable assets**. Unlike the cost of the nonfood expense items discussed in Chapter 23, under some circumstances, the cost of FFE items cannot be used as tax deductions in the year in which they were purchased. Instead, hospitality operators must depreciate the value of these items over a period of years; operators can take only a part of the purchase price as a tax deduction in one year (see Figure 25.1).

A capital item is a long-life item. Managers anticipate that it will last in service for more than a year, and perhaps as long as 20 years, if properly repaired and maintained. Although its value may be depreciated over, say, a two-year period, it can, conceivably, remain useful and productive for a much longer period of time under normal operating conditions.

The selection and procurement procedure for these items generally involves the typical principles discussed in this text. Of course, FFE items have an added dimension: they stay around a long time. Consequently, operators are very conscious of even the smallest potential for error. If they receive a poor batch of tomatoes, they can correct this problem relatively easily, but if they select and procure an inappropriate guest room bed, they may have to live with it longer than they care to.

On the surface, determining the types of FFE they need appears to be a relatively easy task for managers. Basically, the kinds of products hospitality operators sell—menu items, quality of sleeping rooms, guest transportation to the airport, and so forth—usually dictate the types and qualities of FFE they must have to run their businesses sufficiently. Unfortunately, this is only the first step in determining FFE requirements.

A major concern is the effect that any future plans might have on the operators' need for FFE. For instance, they might want to alter their menu. Alternately, they might wish to add more banquet rooms. Should operators select FFE today in anticipation of tomorrow's needs, or should they take care of today only and worry about tomorrow when it comes?

	Computation				End of Year	
Year	Units of Activity	×	Depreciable Cost/Unit	= Annual Depreciation Expense	Accumulated Depreciation	Book Value
2017	15,000		$0.12	$1,800	$ 1,800	$11,200*
2018	30,000		0.12	3,600	5,400	7,600
2019	20,000		0.12	2,400	7,800	5,200
2020	25,000		0.12	3,000	10,800	2,200
2021	10,000		0.12	1,200	12,000	1,000

BARB'S FLORISTS

*($13,000 − $1,800).

FIGURE 25.1 Example of a depreciation schedule for FFE.

Most operators have growth aspirations, and they all should be concerned about tomorrow because these days, FFE can become obsolete quickly. If operators do not have some foresight, their hospitality company could, conceivably, become dated almost overnight. They must balance today's budget demands with tomorrow's requirements if they expect to withstand the ebb and flow of the competitive pressure in the hospitality industry.

Another major FFE concern facing operators is the issue of capitalizing an operating expense. This means reducing a current expense, such as the energy expense, by investing today in machinery that is expensive yet will reduce energy consumption. The added investment in higher-quality equipment will lead to operational savings later on, but at what point is this trade-off economically advisable?

In the hospitality industry, most operators seem willing to invest a dollar today if they can recoup that dollar in two to three years. That is, if the operational savings are such that the original investment is paid back in two or three years, generally many hospitality owner–managers will consider **capitalizing an expense.**

> **capitalizing an expense** Term used to refer to the purchase of an expensive capital item, such as a new heating system, to reduce future operating expenses, such as the cost of energy used to heat a building.

The prediction of savings is, however, difficult. The credibility of operators' estimates must be acceptable before they trade dollars today for perceived savings tomorrow. They can never be 100 percent certain of their predictions. Also, they can never tell when operational costs will level off, drop, or suddenly rise dramatically. For example, in some properties, the initial investment in computerization is much more than the amount of labor savings that can be experienced over a two- to three-year period. Labor may be the least-expensive alternative for today, but what about tomorrow?

Several other related problems arise whenever operators contemplate the capitalization of expenses. These problems almost always involve future considerations and the operators' inability to predict them adequately. Not being able to foresee the future completely puts operators in something of a ticklish position.

Deciding on the person or persons who should select and procure the FFE items is another major managerial concern. When hospitality operations plan FFE choices, four categories of people are typically involved: (1) users, (2) owner–managers, (3) buyers, and (4) consultants.

The user sometimes is involved in the process because performance on the job may be directly related to the equipment used. In addition, because the user's job performance evaluation is critical to that worker's success in the company, it generally is a good idea to invite user input. The user sometimes is also involved as the instigator of an FFE purchase, for instance, suggesting to a supervisor that an old meat slicer should be replaced with a more modern piece of equipment.

The owner–manager makes the final decision and takes the ultimate responsibility regarding any FFE purchase so it is logical for that person to make this decision. The owner–manager will probably set the quality standards, note the preferred supplier, and oversee the receiving and installation of the items and, in general, will be more actively involved in the purchase of FFE than in the purchase of other products. Because these items are expensive and remain a part of a hospitality operation for quite some time, the owner–manager is motivated to be very careful.

If a hospitality firm employs a full-time buyer, that person typically would be involved as a technical resource person, answering such questions as: Is the desired quality available? What type of payment plans are available? How long will it take to receive the merchandise? What options or alternatives are available?

Depending on the magnitude of the FFE purchase, owner–managers may seek the assistance of one or more consultants. For instance, they may ask an accountant to prepare various installment payment options for their review. Alternately, if they are considering employee lay-offs and replacement with a machine, they might hire an accountant to prepare an estimate of future savings.

If operators are contemplating a major remodeling job, they might consider using a designer or architect to assist them in their efforts. These types of individuals normally are employed when a company is building a new facility. Multiunit hospitality companies typically have full-time designers on staff.

Consultants often are worth the added cost operators must pay to procure their services. They can detail the FFE needed, as well as determine the most effective and efficient layout and design for the specific type of operation. Furthermore, they will see to it that the FFE are installed according to existing fire, health and safety, and building codes. Because these consultants normally deal in a highly technical area, operators probably cannot get too far without their help. They do not come cheap, but the efficiency they may be able to build into the operators' design can take care of their fee and leave a bit of savings besides.

Operators can often obtain some consultants or consulting advice through FFE dealers. That is, operators can do business with a **design/build dealer** who is prepared to provide, free of charge, all the advice and assistance operators need, as long as they purchase all of their FFE from that dealer. This is a one-stop arrangement, and the operators become house accounts. There are disadvantages to this arrangement; however, these disadvantages can often be offset by better **supplier services**, as well as by a decrease in the amount of **downtime** operators might incur. This is the length of time during which operators cannot profitably conduct business because they are still waiting for some FFE to be delivered and installed.

design/build dealer An equipment dealer who has the capability of providing design and construction/remodeling services.

supplier services Services, such as free delivery, generous credit terms, and so forth, provided by vendors to buyers who purchase their products.

downtime The amount of time a piece of equipment or a facility is out of service.

foodservice design consultant Person who provides advice about FFE purchases. May also plan the final layout and design of restaurant facilities.

Another choice is selecting a **foodservice design consultant** who works for the general architect or operator and who is not a part of the FFE sale. These design consultants provide an unbiased evaluation of FFE that are available and that fit into the overall design and purpose of the operation. Foodservice design consultants typically charge an overall project fee or base their fees on a time and expense structure. The membership list of the Foodservice Consultants Society International (FCSI) is a good place to start when searching for a reputable consultant.

Determining from whom to buy is another major managerial concern. For most operators, the decision is simple: they usually satisfy their needs by selecting a reputable FFE dealer or dealers. This is especially true when they are considering a reasonably large purchase, and supplier services represent a major requirement.

Other FFE supply sources exist, though. For example, operators may be able to procure FFE through **contract supply houses**, a sort of co-op arrangement available in the lodging trade; from food and beverage suppliers who deal in FFE as a sideline; from mail-order or online catalogs; from primary sources; through other types of local co-ops; through chain head-quarters that may offer their affiliates the opportunity to purchase FFE; through consultants, such as designers and contractors, who may sell FFE; through leasing companies that can provide some items; from firms that deal in used merchandise, repossessed merchandise, and the like that may be available in the local area; through warehouse clubs; and from auctioneers, who sometimes are instrumental in liquidating FFE.

Usually, operators must balance convenience, the suppliers' reputation, and so forth with the purchase price, **installation costs**, and other related costs when making their decisions.

contract supply house
A type of buying club. It is operated by a third party that negotiates with suppliers and passes on some of the savings obtained through bulk purchasing to member buyers.

installation costs
Typical charges paid when making a major equipment purchase. Usually paid in addition to the AP price of the equipment, although a buyer's company may be able to provide these services personally for less.

With so many choices and options available, operators may find it difficult to locate those suppliers who are knowledgeable and prepared to offer the necessary level of service. The optimal supplier is critical for FFE, and to drop that person in favor of someone else can cause tremendous problems, especially time-delay problems. In our experience, the amount of supplier service and its quality are major considerations for operators in most instances.

Another major managerial concern with FFE is the question of reconditioning versus replacing these items, when such a choice is possible. In some cases, it might be economically attractive for operators to recondition, remodel, and/or rebuild some items instead of purchasing new ones. The cost of making do with an existing item may be much less than the purchase price for a new replacement.

Although the reconditioning cost may be quite attractive initially, other problems may result. For instance, reconditioned machinery does not appear to have as long an anticipated life as a new replacement, so the long-term cost of reconditioning may not be beneficial at all. Another problem might be the downtime experienced during the rebuilding stage for, say, a walk-in refrigerator. Typically, it takes longer to recondition, rebuild, and/or remodel than it does to provide a new installation. In addition, new safety and energy regulations may factor into the decision. For example, under the Clean Air Act, no new refrigeration or air conditioning units can use traditional R-22 gas, commonly known as Freon, and it will no longer be available for existing equipment by 2020. Therefore, supplies of it are decreasing and prices are increasing, so it most likely would not be cost effective to recondition an old model using Freon.[1]

In the short run, rebuilding can be the best answer, but in the long run, it may not satisfy operators' needs. They should, however, at least consider the potential of reconditioning because they do not want to spend any more money than necessary to accomplish their goals.

A final concern to management that we have experienced is the impulsive purchase of certain types of FFE items, such as furnishings. An owner–manager may return from a vacation trip with an antique clock in tow that will "be perfect for the lobby." Alternately, on visiting another restaurant there may be an attraction to the wall coverings in that establishment, prompting a bit of remodeling. Not all impulse purchases are bad, but it's unlikely that something purchased on the spur of the moment will turn out to have a positive effect on the operation.

GENERAL PROCEDURES IN FFE PURCHASING

■ Sources of Information

Preparing some type of specification for FFE is not particularly difficult for operators. Often, operators do not prepare formal specifications for replacement FFE because most of them will "look around," for instance, at trade shows, in competitors' operations, in catalogs, and in trade papers, before forming an opinion. These operators usually have a very good idea of the type of FFE they require before they actually sit down to negotiate with one or more FFE suppliers.

Usually, operators have past experience to guide them as they formulate the appropriate purchasing strategy for replacement FFE. Generally, if operators have had a good experience with the current items, they are likely to replace them with the same brand, or an equivalent. This dependence on yesterday makes it difficult for new manufacturers to gain a foothold unless they offer something unique.

> **demonstration model**
> FFE used by the purveyor or manufacturer for display purposes. Usually can be purchased at a discount.

Operators normally examine replacement FFE very closely before making their purchase decisions. For instance, many of them like to attend trade shows that cater to their industry because, usually, several FFE dealers will be in attendance with **demonstration models** available for inspection. Attending a trade show seems preferable to visiting a dealer's showroom or viewing an online video presentation. It offers the opportunity to compare and contrast several alternatives.

Visitors to trade shows typically preplan their activities to maximize their time. Because time is limited, operators are able to evaluate only a few FFE selection factors; otherwise, they will get bogged down at one dealer's booth display. Trade show visitors want to view many alternatives. To do this, they should generally evaluate only a few major factors, such as the item's functionality, quality of construction, warranties, total cost (the as-purchased [AP] price plus delivery and installation charges), and the supplier's depth of knowledge and amount of service that can be provided.

■ Extra Information to Include in the Specification

When a major FFE purchase is contemplated, specifications are normally necessary. Chances are, operators will attempt to finance part of this purchase through a lender, who usually requires them to obtain competitive bids for the FFE that will be used as collateral for the loan.

The FFE specification will include many of the selection factors we note later in this chapter. For all intents and purposes, these specifications are similar in scope to those operators prepare for food and beverage items. These requirements do tend, though, to be purchase specifications rather than product specifications. This is because the required supplier services, which are not a part of the product specification, are very important when operators plan a major FFE purchase. In addition to the major types of supplier services operators will require, the FFE purchase specification will ordinarily include further information:

> **instructions to bidders**
> Required process vendors must follow when submitting a competitive bid. Typically also includes a description of how the winning bid will be determined and the qualifications vendors need to be allowed to bid.

1. **Instructions to bidders.** The where, when, and how to submit a competitive bid are covered in the **instructions to bidders**. Included in the specification is all of the pertinent information of which bidders should

be cognizant, information that will, in turn, indicate how operators will award the project and what criteria, such as lowest cost, fastest completion time, and so forth, operators will use to make the award decision.

2. **General conditions.** Operators must note several contingencies in this section of the specification. For instance, they could detail: (a) code requirements; (b) access rights, such as whether the community will permit the transportation of heavy equipment on the roadways, or if the equipment must be delivered in pieces; (c) royalties that must be paid; (d) other local ordinances; (e) provisions for modifications; (f) the treatment of cost overruns; (g) the treatment of delays; and (h) liability coverage the supplier needs.

3. **Specific conditions.** In addition to the list of FFE needed and their desired characteristics, operators also must note delivery dates and procedures, installation dates and procedures, and other related details.

4. **Detailed drawings.** This probably is the most important distinction of FFE specifications. For a major purchase, operators typically include architectural drawings of all of the custom equipment, as well as any pertinent layout and design plans. **Detailed drawings** aid bidders. They also help to prevent ambiguity. Drawings are commonly created in **computer-aided design (CAD)** software. CAD maximizes the flexibility in designing equipment layout in an establishment. CAD enables the owner–manager to virtually move FFE within the floor plan and see the desired results immediately. In addition, hotel/casinos utilize this software to assist in the design and layout of the casino floor.

Once operators have prepared specifications, they should make a list of potential suppliers and, from that list, develop an approved-supplier list. After selecting the best supplier, operators may need to modify the specifications, monitor FFE orders and delivery, monitor any subcontracting that may be necessary, and obtain the training and other start-up help needed.

■ Direct Purchase Options

Should hospitality operators go straight to the manufacturer and purchase their FFE items, or should they make a **direct purchase** through the local dealer? The choice is not always clear. Most of the time, it is a matter of personal taste. If operators buy direct, the AP price, obviously, will be lower. Because they usually must put up the cash and provide their own transportation and installation, however, the costs can quickly increase. If they bypass the local dealer, chances are good that they will need to provide their own maintenance and other supplier services.

In our experience, too many operators have been duped into the "bypass the local dealer" routine. When their equipment breaks down, who will help them? This is not a problem if they have their own maintenance crew. However, if they do not, a middleman might be worth the added markup.

detailed drawings Documents intended to communicate precise information to assist bidders and eliminate ambiguity. Typically used when purchasing FFE and/or construction services.

computer-aided design (CAD) The use of a wide range of technological tools that help design professionals. Typically used by architects, kitchen designers, and so forth to enhance the design and construction process and make it more efficient.

direct purchase Refers to a purchased product (usually a perishable food) that, once received, will bypass the main storage facility, go straight to production, and be charged to cost on the day it's received. A perishable food item, such as fresh pastry, is an example of a direct purchase. Alternately, buying directly from a primary source and bypassing the middleman.

It is also becoming more common that equipment manufacturers will not sell directly to the end user because they do not want to provide credit or local support that the dealer or distributor can supply. In essence, they would rather focus on manufacturing and utilize the channel of distribution for selling their products. This is not to say that equipment manufacturers do not want to provide customer support. In fact, many times labels on equipment request that operators contact the manufacturer directly when serious problems occur.

PRIMARY SELECTION FACTORS

Several selection factors exist for FFE items. This is expected because the purchase of FFE is a major decision, one that operators cannot perform hastily. Fortunately, they do not need to purchase these items very often, but when they do, they must plan procedures very carefully. The major selection factors are discussed in the following sections.

> **intended use**   Refers to the performance requirement of a product or service, which is noted on the specification. Considered to be the most important piece of information on a specification.

■ Intended Use

As with all purchased items, operators must identify the **intended use** of an item so that they can detail the appropriate, relevant specifications. This is a bit more difficult to do in the FFE area, primarily because so many items must be used to satisfy several production and service requirements. Difficult or not, however, operators cannot proceed very far until they isolate the intended use of the FFE needed.

■ Exact Name

At times, this selection factor can cause a bit of confusion. For instance, operators cannot simply note the term "oven" on their specification. Rather, they must be careful to detail the specific type of oven they need. For instance, a great deal of difference exists between a standard convection oven and a convection-steam oven. Another dimension of the exact name is the model numbers that manufacturers use to distinguish similar types of equipment items. When operators compare different brands of the same type of item, it is important for them to determine the comparable model numbers.

> **equipment program**   Process whereby a purveyor allows you the free use of equipment if you purchase other products. For instance, if you purchase all your coffees and teas from a vendor, he or she may offer you the free use of the brewing and serving equipment. In some cases there may be a nominal charge for the equipment; it's not always free.

■ Equipment Programs

In the discussion of nonalcoholic beverages in Chapter 22, we introduced the concept of an **equipment program**. Recall that under this program, operators can use a company's machinery as long as they are using the food, beverage, or cleaning product that this machinery dispenses. For example, operators might be able to receive "free" use of a laundry system if they agree to purchase all laundry chemicals from a specific firm. Of course, the machinery is not "free" because the chemicals are usually priced to take into account the value of the equipment.

In some instances, operators cannot buy, for example, the juice, soap, or soda that they want without taking the machine. Because this might represent a tying agreement, some companies will sell the product without the machine, but they usually keep the surcharge on the product. As such, operators might just as well take the "free" machine because they will be paying for it anyway.

Some operators resent an equipment program arrangement because they believe that the supplier will get rich by extracting a surcharge every time they purchase the products used in the machinery. In other words, they might pay the initial cost of the machinery over and over again.

However, in some situations, the supplier may not extract a surcharge. The equipment itself might represent only a form of discount to operators. The supplier may be willing to toss in the equipment if an operator buys a large supply of products over a long period of time. Alternately, the supplier might merely be motivated to ensure that the products are dispensed properly and not be interested in earning a markup. Furthermore, most suppliers maintain the equipment, freeing operators from a costly headache.

In our experience, equipment programs have generally been advantageous to hospitality operators. We periodically compare the cost of coffee with and without machinery, and the coffee with machinery usually turns out to be only a few pennies more per pound than the cost without the machinery. So, purchasing, installing, and maintaining coffee-brewing equipment is not necessary.

■ Custom FFE

Generally, operators are motivated to purchase standardized FFE. That is, usually they do not want to purchase anything that violates height, width, veneer, and other standards.

Customized FFE items are very expensive. Fine dining or celebrity chef restaurants may desire customized FFE for its functionality, to produce specialty menu items in high volume and to create the "wow" factor for their open kitchen designs.[2] However, for the average operator, it may not be worth the extra cost and inconvenience to procure such items. Aside from the normally high AP price, other major costs of purchasing customized FFE exist: (1) the company producing the desired item(s) may go out of business, which can be troublesome if it is the only firm capable of maintaining and servicing that item; (2) if it is a very odd piece of custom work, it is unlikely that operators can borrow against its value; (3) the item may have several problems, which can increase both operating costs and aggravation in the long run; (4) probably no future trade-in value exists; (5) the manufacturer may be forced to pass on cost overruns to operators; and (6) the item(s) may not be ready on time because of a production and/or installation delay.

> **customized FFE** FFE items specially made to fit a buyer's unique needs. Typically manufactured on a made-to-order basis.

Operators might be able to save some of the expense of customized FFE if they can locate a supplier that has merchandise that is part standard and part customized. For example, some kitchen equipment manufacturers produce standard stainless steel tables that allow operators to customize them in a limited way.

Several potential advantages of customized FFE exist. These include (1) operating savings may be available; (2) the items may be easier to operate, maintain, and clean; (3) the items may be more attractive; (4) operators can customize their image; (5) usually, operators can get exactly what they want; and (6) in the long run, the lifetime cost of these items can be more attractive than that associated with their standard counterparts. In fact, a custom installation may be economical in a hospitality operation because it will fit exactly the space and need for which it was designed. The idea of operators buying standardized items is not a good one if it means getting something that is less than exactly what they want.

Appearance

Image is a precious commodity in the hospitality industry. Therefore, hospitality operators must do whatever is feasible to protect and enhance it. One way they can do this is to select FFE items that have a high-quality appearance.

Manufacturers of similar FFE items often compete strictly on superficial appearance differences. For instance, counter fixtures may vary somewhat: for example, veneers, widths, and heights may differ a bit from one manufacturer to another. These differences are not substantial, but they could be very important. If customers will see the FFE items, such as in restaurants with open kitchens and sushi bars, operators may want to spend a few extra dollars to ensure that what customers see pleases them.

Brand Name

brand name Indication of product quality. A typical selection factor for purchased items.

In our experience, most hospitality operators use this selection factor almost exclusively to purchase replacement FFE. Some operators are not necessarily concerned with **brand names** when they buy an item for the first time. However, once they have had some experience with an item, either good or bad, the memory of it remains very strong. Consequently, brand name recognition will probably always be a major selection factor.

Something can be said for the effect that some brand names might have on the operators' image. For instance, some customers may recognize high-quality brand names for refrigeration. So, if it is important for operators to display one of these brand name fixtures on their premises, their purchasing decision becomes an easy task.

Another dimension to the brand name selection factor is the "halo effect" that operators can develop as they gain experience with a certain brand of merchandise. The halo effect suggests that if operators have a positive experience with a particular brand, not only will they be predisposed to purchase the same brand name merchandise when it is time to replace some worn-out FFE, but they will also tend to feel more positive about that particular manufacturer's entire product line. Consequently, the brand name selection factor grows more important as their experience with the items increases.

If operators invite input from employees when they are developing an FFE purchasing strategy, they almost always can expect them to think in terms of brand names. Most are familiar with certain brands that some other place of employment used. Alternately, employees who attended, for example, a culinary school learned their craft on particular brands of kitchen equipment and are apt to favor these.

Demonstration Models

Many manufacturers and dealers use FFE models—items in their showrooms, items at industry trade shows, or items a traveling salesperson uses—for demonstration purposes. In some cases, operators might be able to purchase these items and save a considerable amount of money. If they buy this type of FFE, normally they must: (1) put up the total amount of the AP price in cash, (2) take the item as is, and (3) provide their own transportation and/or installation. Typically, these items are inexpensive primarily because they are used products, that is, they are somewhat depreciated already in value.

Generally, a very good savings opportunity is associated with this type of purchase. If operators can live with the absence of supplier services, have the cash in their pocket, and can handle all necessary installation chores, they should be able to save quite a bit of money.

Operators must, however, consider the downside. For example, they may not be able to obtain state-of-the-art items. Most FFE available may not fit their needs exactly; they may have to compromise too much to take advantage of the savings. In addition, they may not be able to obtain adequate maintenance contracts, or if they can, these may be shorter than they would like.

■ New versus Used FFE

Occasionally, operators may come across merchandise that, although technically classified as used, could actually have suffered little or no use. We have already considered the possibility of buying demonstration models. Similar opportunities might involve kitchen equipment that trade show exhibitors offer at **show-special prices**; this equipment may be just as good as new. Also, FFE manufacturers and dealers sometimes have **freight-damaged** items that they are willing to sell for a fraction of the original AP prices. Some of these damaged products may need a lot of work before operators can put them into service. However, many of these products may have only cosmetic damage; a couple of bumps and bruises may be inconsequential when operators are purchasing, for example, worktables.

> **show-special price**
> Another term for trade show discount.
>
> **freight-damaged discount**
> Offered if you are willing to accept an item that was damaged in shipping. The damage usually does not inhibit the product's usefulness as the damage is typically cosmetic.

Of course, many used items available for purchase have been in use for some time. In most cases, operators can purchase these items for a small fraction of their original selling prices; our experience shows that they can save as much as 70 percent of new AP prices. Again, as with most bargains of this type, operators are normally required to put up the cash and take the items as is. Often, there are secondhand dealers in the area who specialize in this type of merchandise. These persons, though, are not usually prepared to service what they sell.

Operators can sometimes purchase used merchandise from a new products dealer who makes a market in trade-in items. Quite often, a local new products dealer will have available like-new merchandise that recently was exchanged for more modern models. Operators on good terms with the dealer might receive a courtesy call from the dealer letting them know about something recently available that might be useful to them.

At times, an auctioneer is hired to liquidate some FFE. More than likely, a tax collector, or lender, forecloses on a hospitality operation and hires an auctioneer to liquidate the property to satisfy past debts. In our experience, if operators know what they are doing, they can get an extremely attractive bargain at these auctions.

Some operators seek out auctioneers and other individuals and businesses involved in **liquidation** procedures, such as attorneys, trustees, escrow companies, and title companies. These operators want to be on any mailing lists that are used to advertise liquidation sales. The obvious advantage of being on

> **liquidation** Selling off business assets to satisfy creditors. May be done via auction.

impulse purchase An unplanned or otherwise spontaneous purchase.

such a mailing list is learning about potentially attractive opportunities. The drawback, though, is the possibility of making an **impulse purchase** that will not suit the operators' needs.

The major potential advantage of used merchandise, of course, is the huge reduction in the purchase price. Also, if operators are lucky, they can obtain an item that still has a long, useful life ahead. Unfortunately, operators may encounter several disadvantages associated with procuring used FFE. They might acquire (1) obsolete merchandise, (2) an energy guzzler, (3) an item that inefficiently uses floor space, (4) merchandise that is expensive to maintain, or (5) an item that does not meet current fire, health and safety, and building codes. Operators must also consider (6) the time needed to seek out these bargains, (7) the time needed to examine the items before purchasing them, (8) the fact that the item lacks a guarantee, (9) the possibility that replacement parts are no longer available, (10) the possible damage to their image, and (11) the inability to predict exactly the amount of money needed to recondition the item, if necessary.

Buying used FFE is a gamble; operators must take a risk to reap the savings. They can minimize their risk, though, if they limit their purchases to nonmechanical pieces, as well as to small wares, such as pots and pans. Risk-averse operators should shy away from mechanical items, especially those with complex, computerized control systems.

OPERATING CHARACTERISTICS

■ Versatility

Whenever possible, hospitality operators should try to purchase versatile equipment, that is, equipment that can do more than one job. For example, tilt kettles are popular in many kitchens because they can be used to satisfy so many different production requirements. This type of kettle can be used as a griddle, a steam kettle, and a braising pan. Combination oven-steamer units are also very popular because they can perform a variety of cooking methods (see Figure 25.2).

Today, versatility is increasingly important because the cost of space in hospitality operations is very expensive. Places of business are located in prime retail areas. As a result, the cost of the real estate is high, which means that operators are motivated to reduce the size of their production facilities and increase the size of their income-producing facilities, such as the dining room and lounge. Operators cannot do this, however, unless they are willing to pay a little more for versatility.

■ Compactness

compactness An important FFE selection factor. Refers to the least amount of space an item occupies.

Expensive real estate makes it necessary for hospitality operators to purchase several FFE items that are **compact**. For instance, kitchen and laundry equipment that requires minimal space can be very valuable in the long run. Similarly, foldaway types of furniture are valuable. These items certainly will cost more initially, but operators cannot ignore their convenience and space-saving capabilities.

In a related issue, operators must be concerned with the overall weight of the FFE items they are considering buying. Their businesses may be housed, for instance, in a building structure that cannot support very heavy pieces of production equipment. Alternately, their facility may not have a sufficiently large opening to permit delivery of the equipment to its exact location.

FIGURE 25.2 A combi-oven.
©Wavebreakmedia/Shutterstock

■ Compatibility

Hospitality operators should attempt to ensure that new purchases will intermingle easily with their current stock of FFE. New FFE items should be compatible with the existing stock in many ways, such as aesthetically and functionally. Otherwise, operators might experience some production problems and/or some damage to their overall image in the eyes of their customers. In some cases, such as with a **systems sale**, operators have no choice; they must purchase compatible merchandise that will meet their specific needs.

■ Portability

This could be a very important selection factor for kitchen equipment. For instance, hospitality operations that have a good deal of banquet trade will enjoy the convenience of **portability**. Being able to quickly disconnect and rearrange the equipment to suit the specific needs of a party is a major advantage.

Mobile FFE also create another advantage: the ability to move the items so that the maintenance staff can do deep cleaning easily and effectively. Also, service technicians will be able to perform their tasks more quickly if the items are not stationary.

Mobility also means that if a piece of machinery breaks down, operators may not need to have it repaired in place. Service technicians can remove the item easily, replace it with a loaner item, and proceed to take the broken item to the shop where it can receive the proper attention. Other employees, then, do not need to sidestep someone while trying to perform their duties.

systems sale Usually occurs when buying equipment that requires parts made by only one manufacturer, usually the manufacturer that made the equipment in the first place. For example, buying a dish machine that cannot use other companies' dish racks. Over the long run, a systems sale may cost you more money.

portability Refers to the ability of an item to be easily and inexpensively moved to, and operated in, various locations. Important selection factor for FFE.

Portable equipment also tends to retain its value over the long run. Because it is easy to move, it can be removed from service and sold easily.

Of course, portable items are not inexpensive. They cost more because of their convenience and their ability to accommodate several needs. In some hospitality operations, their initial cost will generate significant savings, as well as a higher trade-in value, over the years.

■ Degree of Automation

degree of automation
The extent to which control systems (such as numerical control, programmable logic control, and other industrial control systems), are used together with other applications of information technology (such as computer-aided technologies), to control machinery and processes, reducing the need for human intervention.

Hospitality operators can earn some savings when they purchase equipment that provides some labor-saving opportunity through the **degree of automation**. For instance, they may be able to save a bit of labor cost by using automated broilers. The related labor costs, such as payroll taxes and other employee benefits, represent additional savings. Furthermore, if operators can reduce the number of required work hours, they may be able to reduce the number of employees needed, which implies that they can economize on space needed.

As we have noted before, in our experience labor saving is very difficult to attain. Unless operators run a very large facility, it is quite difficult to trim even a little bit of their payroll budget without risking alienating their guests through poor service. Consequently, it is difficult to justify automated equipment's higher AP price strictly on the basis of the potential amount of labor savings.

Instead, operators should judge automated equipment on its ability to provide standardized products and to assist their control efforts. For example, fully automated espresso machines enable operators to serve consistent coffee products quickly and easily. Furthermore, machines with enhanced diagnostic capabilities, advanced computer controls, and several digital readouts can be operated by less-skilled employees who will not require extensive training. This streamlines both quality-control and cost-control efforts.

Some automated equipment also enables operators to control the cost of sales and the cash they collect from guests. For instance, fully automated bar dispensing systems can pour an accurate, preplanned portion of liquor, record the liquor usage, and ring up the sale on the point-of-sale (POS) system.

■ Ease of Cleaning

All FFE items must be cleaned. The amount of time needed to clean these items varies with the quality of items purchased. For example, hospitality operators will pay a bit more for an item that is very easy to clean. They gain an advantage, though, when their employees are more motivated to clean it than another similar item. Furthermore, clean FFE, especially clean equipment, should last longer under normal operating conditions. The operators' lifetime cost for an easy-to-clean item, therefore, can shrink appreciably.

Further, equipment that is not properly designed could harbor bacteria, pests, and dirt in creases and corners and transfer unwanted flavors and aromas to other products. Operators should select only equipment that has an approval label (such as NSF International) that indicates that the product has been designed with cleaning and sanitation in mind.

To save labor, operators might consider purchasing self-cleaning devices. For instance, self-cleaning ovens, dispensing equipment, ventilation ducts, and exhaust fans are very convenient items to own. Operators are assured of clean equipment when they purchase these types of items, but they must be willing to pay a higher AP price, as well as being willing to incur additional energy costs over the equipment's lifetime; this is because self-cleaning items normally require a good deal of expensive energy in their operation. The convenience and labor savings, though, can easily exceed these costs.

■ Ease of Maintenance

Most equipment requires some sort of repair and maintenance. The amount required directly affects the total operating costs hospitality operators will incur over the useful life of the items. The ease of providing a service also affects the total operating cost, primarily because the labor cost involved can increase dramatically if the operators' equipment items require considerable effort to maintain.

Operators make a major mistake when they overlook the maintenance requirements of any type of FFE. Ignoring this potential problem is very tempting if they are blinded temporarily by an attractive AP price. This usually turns out to be false economy. Labor costs will continue to rise. Operators should strive to build a hedge against this inflationary expense by ensuring, as much as possible, that they minimize future labor requirements whenever they can.

■ Availability of Replacement Parts

Hospitality operators must ensure that an inventory of spare parts will be available for the FFE they want to purchase. If they have any doubt about this, they may want to either reconsider the purchase or immediately buy a spare-parts inventory to protect themselves. Maintaining their own inventory exposes them to normal storage costs, costs they would rather leave to their supplier. However, an additional cost of this type can pale in comparison to dealing with a broken machine that might need to be scrapped because of the lack of one or two parts.

In addition to the availability of parts, operators should also consider the time lag that might exist between the ordering and the delivery of a part. The lead time can be very short or, as in the case of foreign-made FFE, quite lengthy. A short lead time implies that the supplier maintains an inventory of parts locally, thereby increasing the cost of doing business. The supplier will eventually pass this cost on to operators, but that might be far less burdensome than having a broken item hampering an operation's production needs.

Operators should assume that they may not be able to obtain replacement parts if they purchase a used piece of equipment. Although this is not always the case, they should always be prepared for this possibility when buying used items. For instance, only electronic cash registers are manufactured today. Old, gear-driven models may be attractive additions to the operators' lounge, but they will pay the price for this luxury when the old registers need service and parts.

In addition, operators also may find obtaining parts and service difficult when they purchase technologically unique equipment that is just being introduced to the marketplace. These items may have bugs that have yet to be remedied. Even worse, the manufacturer of a new item may drop the line because of a lack of interest from other hospitality operators, which could leave the operators who purchased the item begging for parts and service. Furthermore, service staff may be unfamiliar with a new item.

A similar situation can develop when operators purchase customized FFE. The probability is high that they will not be able to procure parts and service without expending a great deal of effort.

■ Employee Attitude and Skill Level

Before purchasing any equipment that is complicated to use in production or service, hospitality operators must ensure that the staff is able to comprehend the operating procedures. As discussed in Chapter 23 regarding cleaning supplies, the availability of instructional materials in multiple languages may be a concern when buying FFE. At the very least, employees must possess the aptitude to learn the operating procedures within a reasonable period of time.

Operators must also be certain that everyone in their company will accept the new equipment, which represents change to the employees. Resistance to change has caused many good ideas to fall by the wayside. For instance, employees may resent an automatic bar installation. This does not mean that operators should not invest in one of these machines, but it does mean that they should be prepared to smooth the way for its implementation within the operation.

■ Energy Source

Hospitality operators can run machinery using various energy sources. For example, they may be able to utilize natural gas, electricity, steam, oil, or solar power to operate some of their equipment. In some instances, they have no choice; for example, they may be stuck with an all-electric kitchen, with no possibility of converting to an alternate energy source. If, however, operators have a choice, they should consider equipment that can be powered by a less-expensive source of energy. Many gas and electric utility companies have demonstration kitchens where buyers can examine different types of equipment and receive advice on the best models to fit their needs. Alternately, operators might be interested in using only energy that is least damaging to the environment.

Generally, to acquire equipment that can utilize less energy, an inexpensive energy source, and/or an energy source that is most favorable to the environment, operators must be willing to pay a significantly greater AP price for it. As with the potential savings of any type of operating cost in the future, usually operators must be willing to invest today to reap the benefit tomorrow. For instance, a natural gas–powered machine may cost more initially than a standard electric one. Furthermore, installing it may cost more. Operators hope, though, that they will save enough money down the road to make such an investment economically attractive (see Figure 25.3).

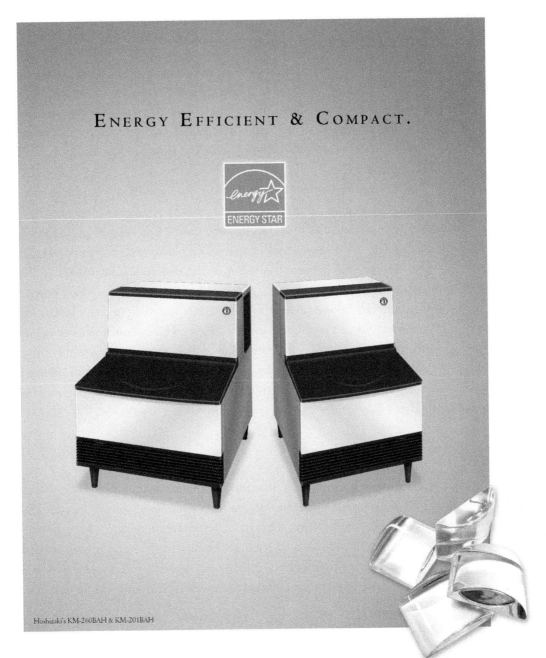

FIGURE 25.3 Operators sometimes purchase equipment because of its energy-saving potential.
Courtesy of Hoshizaki America, Inc.

■ Excess Capacity

In some cases, hospitality operators may need to decide whether they should consider the potential growth of their business when they are about to make an FFE purchase. When buying equipment, especially kitchen equipment, operators might think about the possibility that two or three years from now, they will need equipment that can handle twice the number of customers they currently serve. The question, then, is, "Should operators buy kitchen equipment that handles the current customer load only, or should they purchase **excess capacity** equipment now?"

If the larger equipment is available today at an attractive AP price, operators might consider purchasing it. If not, they probably should avoid these items for several reasons: (1) they often can buy equipment that has **add-on capability**, (2) they will waste money maintaining a larger-than-necessary piece of equipment, (3) they will have capital tied up in the larger equipment that might be best used in some other income-generating activity, and (4) they have no guarantee that their business eventually will increase according to their expectations.

Adding on to the physical space when customer count increases is more difficult. Also, the costs of construction tend to increase considerably in just a short period of time. Consequently, it may be advisable for operators to erect a physical structure that can service their future needs, but they should probably purchase the FFE as the need arises.

> **excess capacity**
> Refers to a situation where a company or a piece of equipment is producing at a lower scale of output than it has been designed for.
>
> **add-on capability**
> Feature that allows retrofitting in the future. Especially important when purchasing equipment that may need to be modified as the business grows.

■ Add-On Capabilities

If hospitality operators anticipate an increase in business in the near future, they might want to consider purchasing FFE items that can be modified and adapted easily to service the additional business. Operators should expect to pay a bit more today for this feature.

Operators might discuss their needs with their supplier and agree to purchase the added capacity later on if the supplier will take this into consideration when setting the AP price of the items that the operators currently wish to purchase.

■ Code Compliance

Local governments normally enforce several laws governing fire, health and safety, and building procedures to which all businesspersons must adhere. The FFE that hospitality operators purchase must meet the existing legal codes, including health district codes, safety codes, electrical codes, and noise pollution codes. If operators buy new equipment, they would expect it to satisfy the current legal **code compliance**. Used equipment may not, so they need to be a bit cautious to ensure that they do not purchase FFE only to find out later on that the government will not permit the FFE to be used in their establishment.

Several organizations endorse certain types of FFE. Buyers normally look for their seals of approval when purchasing these items. The most common endorsements are made by **National Sanitation Foundation (NSF) International**—sanitation certification, **Underwriters Laboratories (UL)**—

> **code compliance**
> Following the laws and regulations of a governing body. Term typically used to refer to compliance with building, equipment, and health codes.
>
> **National Sanitation Foundation (NSF) International** Provides sanitation certification for FFE items that meet its standards.
>
> **Underwriters Laboratories (UL)** Provides electrical safety certification for electrical-powered equipment that meet its standards.

electrical safety certification, **American Gas Association (AGA)**—gas safety certification, **National Fire Protection Association (NFPA)**—fire safety certification, **Environmental Protection Agency (EPA)**—energy star rating, and **American Society of Mechanical Engineers (ASME)**—steam safety certification.

In some parts of the United States, operators may need to purchase items that carry these or other appropriate seals of approval. In Clark County, Nevada, for example, all food-contact equipment used in food services must carry the NSF International seal.

COST AND SERVICE FACTORS

■ Lifetime Cost

The FFE purchase decision is a long-term investment. Sometimes, operators must plan one or more years in advance of their actual purchase. Also, the items operators are buying are expected to have a reasonably long operating life. Consequently, it is impractical for operators to consider only the initial AP price of the FFE because there are so many other expenses incurred with them over their normal life span.

When calculating the **lifetime cost** of FFE, besides the AP price, it is imperative that operators consider the following:

1. The **trade-in value** of the operators' old FFE

2. Delivery costs

3. Installation and testing costs

4. Relevant operating costs

5. Potential operating savings

6. The trade-in value of the new FFE when operators decide to replace it or liquidate it

The related costs can add up very quickly. Inexperienced buyers may not realize this. For instance, delivery, installation, and testing costs can easily be 10 percent, or more, of a walk-in refrigerator's AP price. When soliciting competitive bids, wise buyers always ask suppliers to quote the "installed, ready-to-operate" purchase price.

If the initial AP price exceeds the buyers' budget, they generally tend to forgo the purchase or to settle for lesser-quality, hence less-expensive, FFE. This may or may not be an appropriate strategy. On one hand, a new piece of equipment might improve worker productivity significantly, but if buyers are struggling under a heavy debt load, it may be unwise for them to risk bankruptcy.

American Gas Association (AGA)   Provides gas safety certification for gas-powered equipment that meets its standards.

National Fire Protection Association (NFPA)   Provides fire safety certification for FFE items that meet its standards.

Environmental Protection Agency (EPA)   A U.S. agency responsible for protecting human health and the environment by writing and enforcing regulations based on laws passed by Congress. Among its many responsibilities, this agency promotes the Energy Star Program, a voluntary program that fosters energy efficiency.

American Society of Mechanical Engineers (ASME)   Provides steam safety certification for steam-powered equipment that meet its standards.

lifetime cost   A term typically used when analyzing an equipment purchase. Along with the AP price of the item, the buyer might also examine the trade-in value of the old equipment; the cost of the energy needed to operate the new equipment; extra charges for delivery, setup, and training; how much it can sell the new equipment for when it is time to replace it; and so forth.

trade-in value   The amount of cash a supplier will give a buyer for an older model piece of equipment, which is then usually used as a down payment for the purchase of a new model.

operating costs
Day-to-day expenses involved in running a business. Alternately, the costs of using a piece of equipment.

equipment dealer
Company that purchases equipment from a primary source and resells it to hospitality buyers.

lowball bid A competitive bid that is artificially low. Vendors may lowball a buyer hoping to get their foot in the door; later on they will try to hike the AP price substantially.

Sometimes, operators can save money by setting up a personal "equipment rental" firm and purchasing all the FFE through this firm. For instance, an operator can call this firm XYZ Rentals, send a purchase order (PO) directly to a manufacturer, and usually, obtain the lowest AP prices possible. Manufacturers ordinarily quote their lowest prices to customers who will lease or resell the merchandise because those customers do not need the extra supplier services that typical hospitality buyers require.

In some cases, operators might be swayed by a low AP price only to get stung later with high **operating costs**. For instance, an **equipment dealer** might quote a low AP price, knowing full well that operators will need to purchase expensive parts, supplies, and so forth because no other alternatives exist.

Operators should be skeptical of any unusually low AP price quotations. If a quotation sounds too good to be true, they might be getting hit with a **lowball bid**.

Lowball bids can take many forms. For example, some salespersons might justify their equipment by pointing out its labor-saving potential. Labor saving in the hospitality industry is very difficult to achieve, and quite often it is illusory. For example, operators might save two work hours per shift if they purchase a floor-washing machine, but if they must fire a full-time employee to save these two hours, chances are they will find this impractical because they will have a hard time replacing the remaining six work hours of other necessary duties that employee performed per shift. Similarly, even if operators do fire a full-time person, before they know it, they have hired a part-time employee, and eventually, that person becomes a full-time employee. Plus, hospitality operators usually need a certain number of employees just to open the doors. They cannot very easily replace workers with machines. The result: operators realize smaller labor savings than originally anticipated. Usually, only the largest operations might save a bit of labor over the long run.

Other lowball possibilities operators need to consider include the following:

1. Equipment loans or sample test periods that allow operators to try equipment in actual use may spoil the persons using the equipment. Sometimes, once operators order an item and accept a loan or test period, the salesperson sees this as an excuse to stop by often to convince the users that they should have some expensive attachments. As a result, what seems economical to start with may become quite expensive in the long run.

2. The new equipment may not be compatible with what operators currently have; therefore, they may need to purchase expensive adapters to make it work.

3. If operators get a stripped-down model, the users may persuade their employer to obtain expensive options.

4. The supplier might be offering a low price because of discontinuing that particular line of equipment; where will operators get replacement parts?

warranty Another term for guarantee.

5. The supplier may put in several exceptions on any **warranty** or guarantee; for example, operators may have to pay the first $500 of any service calls during the first year.

6. Operators may find out too late that they are required to purchase a large inventory of spare parts right now. (This could be an illegal tying agreement, however.)

Generally, the issue with any capital expenditure is not what it costs initially but what it is worth over its lifetime. Judging FFE on the AP price alone is usually a mistake. Operators must force themselves to consider the FFE's lifetime cost. However, if operators plan to be out of business one or two years from now, then an overreliance on AP price might be appropriate.

■ Potential Operating Savings

Quite often, operators purchase a piece of equipment primarily to effect a savings in operating expenses. That is, they make their decision to capitalize an operating expense by investing in something today that will cause some of their expenses to decrease in the future.

Management can control several operating expenses that are good candidates for possible future reductions. For example, the cost of merchandise, labor, energy, taxes, water, waste removal, and so forth might all decrease if managers proceed to invest in something today. Operators can use several mathematical models to test the feasibility of buying equipment based on its potential **operating savings**. A typical formula that operators use to make a capital investment decision is the **payback period** formula. The payback period refers to the amount of time it takes operators to recoup the original investment. For instance, if they must invest $5,500 in an energy-saving oven today, how long—how many years, perhaps—will it take for them to save $5,500 of energy costs? If it takes them more than three years to recoup the initial investment, operators typically will not purchase the oven.

Probably, operators will find it most helpful to use the **net present value** procedure, which takes into account the time value of money: a dollar saved next year is worth considerably less than a dollar saved today. The net present value procedure requires operators to first compute the present value of the future savings. To do this, operators estimate the future savings and then discount them to take into account the fact that the longer they must wait to receive these savings, the less the savings are worth today. Furthermore, the longer operators must wait, the greater the risk of losing the savings becomes; this implies that the future savings are worth even less today.

Second, the net present value procedure requires operators to subtract the amount of the initial investment they must make today from the present value of predicted savings. If the answer is greater than zero—if today's value of the predicted savings is greater than the amount of money they must invest today—the current investment is economically attractive.

Several other types of formulas have been developed for specialized applications. For instance, some formulas tell operators in what year a piece of equipment should be replaced, and others indicate when operators need to perform maintenance. These formulas are useful, but they do require numbers; the answers are only as good as the numbers operators provide.

operating savings Refers to the reduction in costs experienced by adopting a new way of doing things, for example, purchasing a more expensive, but efficient, piece of equipment.

payback period Refers to the amount of time it takes to recoup an initial investment. For instance, if a buyer purchases a new refrigerator for $5,000 and it reduces energy costs $1,000 per year, it will take 5 years to get back the initial investment in the refrigerator.

net present value Concept that takes into account the time value of money. It is the difference between the present (current) value of any projected savings because of the investment in, for example, a piece of energy-saving equipment and the present (current) value of the price of the equipment. Ideally, the present value of the savings should exceed the present value of the price of the equipment.

Consequently, the use of the formulas is anticlimactic. The real challenge is for operators to come up with the proper number estimates. In many cases, predicting future operating savings is very difficult. Operators should, for example, consider the potential to save time and to increase the overall productivity of their hospitality firm. If they own a buffet, they might consider purchasing a more modern POS system because this might get customers through the line faster. However, some salespersons might comment, "If we get the customers through faster, we can serve more customers." Hence, a new POS system causes an increase in customers. But wait. How does this all connect? Do patrons eat in a particular place because of this speed? Are potential guests walking away from the restaurant because they see long lines? This is hard to say.

Operators must also be careful of other productivity arguments. For example, it is not advantageous for them to own a 400-slices-per-hour toaster if they sell considerably less toast than that.

Potential product savings may also be illusory. For example, someone selling automatic bars may tell operators that free pouring of liquor wastes 2 to 3 ounces per bottle. We agree with this figure. However, we do not agree when a salesperson tells operators that if they save those ounces, they can sell them at $5 each and, as a result, make $10 to $15 more per bottle, all because they have the automatic bar. Simply not wasting the ounces is no guarantee that customers will come in and buy them. Operators have only a certain number of customers. If they are wasteful, it costs them more product to serve them. Consequently, operators save the cost of the liquor with the automatic bar. Energy efficiency is another noteworthy concern. One of the potential advantages of new equipment over old is a more efficient energy usage pattern. Unfortunately, many bogus "energy-misers" are on the market. Operators must be aware of the potential for exaggerated claims. Looking for equipment with the Energy Star® label and using resources such as those provided by the Foodservice Technology Center and Consortium for Energy Efficiency can help operators avoid this problem.[3]

Sometimes, operators purchase energy-saving equipment that they really do not need. For example, it may be futile for them to purchase an expensive cook-and-hold oven that guarantees both less energy use and less meat shrinkage. By cooking roast beef in a regular oven at 250°F instead of 375°F, operators can accomplish almost the same savings. In addition, existing equipment can sometimes be modified to produce similar savings, and this modification might be a much cheaper alternative.

However, cook-and-hold ovens do have their place. They are excellent at low-temperature cooking and they are mobile, allowing for extra oven capacity that usually does not require expensive ventilation systems. These types of ovens also allow for overnight cooking with very little trouble, thereby saving money by using off-peak energy rates.

If operators are purchasing a capital item primarily to effect a reduction in future operating expenses, they must do their homework very, very carefully. Speculation about future costs is a hazardous undertaking; the pitfalls are many. However, the potential to save a considerable amount of money in the long run makes some operators eager to take their chances.

■ Warranty

It is unusual for suppliers to sell any FFE item without a manufacturer's warranty. The typical warranty covers parts and repair for 12 to 24 months from date of shipment (see Figure 25.4). It is strongly suggested that the operator contact the manufacturer or dealer after purchasing

WHIRLPOOL® DISHWASHER WARRANTY

ONE-YEAR FULL WARRANTY

For one year from the date of purchase, when this dishwasher is operated and maintained according to instructions attached to or furnished with the product, Whirlpool Corporation will pay for FSP® replacement parts and repair labor to correct defects in materials or workmanship. Service must be provided by a Whirlpool designated service company.

TWENTY-YEAR FULL WARRANTY ON DURAPERM™ TUB AND INNER DOOR

For twenty years from the date of purchase, when this dishwasher is operated and maintained according to instructions attached to or furnished with the product, Whirlpool Corporation will pay for FSP® replacement parts and repair labor for the DURAPERM™ tub and/or inner door should either fail to contain water, if defective in materials or workmanship. Service must be provided by a Whirlpool designated service company.

Whirlpool Corporation will not pay for:

1. Service calls to correct the installation of your dishwasher, to instruct you how to use your dishwasher, or to replace house fuses or correct house wiring or plumbing.
2. Repairs when your dishwasher is used in other than normal, single-family household use.
3. Damage resulting from accident, alteration, misuse, abuse, fire, flood, acts of God, improper installation, installation not in accordance with local electrical and plumbing codes, or use of products not approved by Whirlpool Corporation.
4. Replacement parts or repair labor costs for units operated outside the United States and Canada.
5. Pickup and delivery. This product is designed to be repaired in the home.
6. Repairs to parts or systems resulting from unauthorized modifications made to the appliance.
7. In Canada, travel or transportation expenses for customers who reside in remote areas.

WHIRLPOOL CORPORATION AND WHIRLPOOL CANADA INC. SHALL NOT BE LIABLE FORINCIDENTALORCONSEQUENTIALDAMAGES.

Some states and provinces do not allow the exclusion or limitation of incidental or consequential damages, so this exclusion or limitation may not apply to you. This warranty gives you specific legal rights and you may also have other rights which vary from state to state or province to province.

Outside the 50 United States or Canada, this warranty does not apply. Contact your authorized Whirlpool dealer to determine if another warranty applies.

If you need service, first see "Troubleshooting." Additional help can be found by checking "Assistance or Service," or by calling our Customer Interaction Center at **1-800-253-1301**, from anywhere in the U.S.A. or write: Whirlpool Corporation, Customer Interaction Center, 553 Benson, Benton Harbor, MI 49022-2692. In Canada, call Whirlpool Canada Inc. at .**1-800-807-6777**   11/00

Keep this book and your sales slip together for future reference. You must provide proof of purchase or installation date for in-warranty service.

Write down the following information about your dishwasher to better help you obtain assistance or service if you ever need it. You will need to know your complete model number and serial number. You can find this information on the model and serial number label/plate, located on your appliance as shown in "Parts and Features."

Dealer name_____

Address_____

Phone number_____

Model number_____

Serial number_____

Purchase date_____

FIGURE 25.4 Example of an equipment warranty.
Courtesy Whirlpool Corporation

FFE to make sure that the warranty only starts when the product is placed into service. Failure to do this could result in the warranty starting after a product has been on a dealer floor or in inventory for 6 months, and the warranty might only be for the remaining time. It is also a good idea to keep records on equipment, including purchase date, serial numbers, and maintenance/use history, in a safe place should problems arise.

The main issue with a warranty is not the warranty itself, because just about every item has one, but the convenience, or lack thereof, with which hospitality operators can receive satisfaction if they must have an item serviced. For instance, they may need to ship an item to the factory for repairs. Alternately, they may need to wait too long for the work to be performed, which can cause customer dissatisfaction when their operation has considerable downtime.

Warranties are only as good as the manufacturer's or dealer's intention and ability to honor them. In our experience, the best warranty is the supplier's reputation for ensuring customer satisfaction.

If operators purchase FFE items directly, the warranty provision might be very limited. Furthermore, suppliers may not even offer a warranty for items shipped directly. So when operators buy direct, they may have to surrender this benefit.

■ Supplier Services

service after the sale Periodic or as-required maintenance or repair of equipment by its manufacturer or supplier during and after a warranty period.

The main supplier service hospitality operators are concerned with is the proverbial **service after the sale**. FFE items will, undoubtedly, need repair and maintenance service, as well as replacement parts, during the warranty period. Also, operators must have the appropriate information on economic value, such as installation and operating instructions, where applicable.

Service appears to be one of the most, if not the most, important selection factors. Operators must have a trustworthy supplier if they do not have the capacity to handle this type of service themselves. Not only will inadequately installed or serviced FFE increase their operating costs, but it will also affect the quality of service they can provide their guests. The specter of customer dissatisfaction is fearful, and operators, generally, are not eager to suffer its consequences.

After the warranty period and the break-in period expire, operators may wish to engage other service providers to maintain their FFE. The ability to assist operators might ensure an FFE supplier's place on their approved-supplier lists. Many suppliers sell FFE, but not too many of them sell FFE and service. Operators cannot afford to discover that they have chosen the wrong type of supplier after submitting their purchase orders.

When operators purchase FFE directly, they must be willing to forgo any type of service after the sale. Although some manufacturers of highly specialized equipment give operators a toll-free 800 number to call for technical support, operators should always assume that they will be on their own when they buy direct. Operators may consider this to be acceptable for some items, such as certain types of furniture. For mechanical devices, however, if operators have any doubt about their ability to help themselves, it may be a good idea for them to seek the services of a reputable equipment dealer.

FINANCING THE FFE PURCHASE

When hospitality operators purchase capital items, almost invariably the subject of financing the transaction arises. In most cases, operators must devote as much thought to the financing of the purchase as they do to the various selection factors discussed in this chapter.

Purchasing FFE is not an everyday occurrence. Operators do not expect to pay for many of these items by writing a check on their current bank account. Rather, they often must determine the various alternative financing arrangements available and decide which one, or ones, they can use to their best advantage.

Of course, operators may indeed be able to finance some FFE purchases with money that currently sits in the property's bank account. So, one financing alternative is financing an FFE purchase through the normal cash flow of the hospitality operation. Quite often, though, operators might use a bit of cash and supplement it with some sort of installment credit. For example, operators might be able to make a down payment to a dealer and sign a personal promissory note for the balance. Operators expect to pay the current market interest rate to the dealer who is acting as their lender in this transaction, as well as their FFE dealer.

Working a credit arrangement with the dealer may be advantageous for operators for several reasons. For instance, knowing the operators very well might lead to dispensing with the normal credit checks and other costly loan application fees, thereby saving the operators a bit of money. Furthermore, operators might be able to combine some sort of discount with their purchase, such as a cash discount, if they pay the final installment before the due date.

In our experience, FFE dealers are a bit more inclined to grant favorable credit terms than food and beverage suppliers. Although not all of these FFE dealers may be willing to grant large amounts of credit, operators might consider dealing only with those suppliers willing to finance their purchases regardless of the dollar amount.

If operators arrange an installment payment plan with a dealer, the normal expectation is to make a down payment equal to one-third of the purchase price, make monthly payments (that include interest and principal), and sign a **security agreement**, which grants the dealer the right to foreclose and take back the FFE item if the operators fail to make their installment payments. Usually, the loan term will not exceed 36 months.

Some dealers and manufacturers are willing to accept credit cards for payment. However, this is an expensive option for both buyers and suppliers. Credit card interest rates are usually much higher than the rates the suppliers would charge if they extended credit themselves. Furthermore, suppliers accepting credit card payments must pay a **merchant fee**; suppliers may add this extra cost to the AP prices operators must pay for their FFE items.

Operators can use FFE as collateral for a loan from a commercial lender. This is also an expensive alternative. For instance, lenders normally require a relatively large down payment because they are unwilling to finance more than 40 to 50 percent of the value of these items. They also assess a variety of credit expenses, such as loan origination fees, and require operators to sign a security agreement. Also, if operators are dealing with a commercial bank, it might

security agreement
Contract used to secure a loan. If the borrower fails to pay, it allows the lender to foreclose and take the asset(s) used to collateralize the loan.

merchant fee Fee suppliers pay for accepting credit card payments instead of cash or check. The fee is usually some percentage of the amount charged by the buyer.

require them to maintain a non-interest-bearing checking account with a reasonably large balance; this increases the effective interest charges on the loan because operators now have the use of less money than they originally borrowed.

leasing company   Firm that purchases FFE and leases them to other companies. The typical rental plan is a rent-to-own arrangement. May be a more expensive form of financing a FFE purchase than borrowing the money and buying the items outright.

rent-to-own plan See leasing company.

Finally, operators could opt for some sort of a lease arrangement for FFE items. They may be able to secure leases from FFE dealers or **leasing companies** that specialize in this form of financing. Although not all FFE are available for lease, operators can lease a great number of items. For instance, leasing computers, ice machines, and refrigeration machinery is somewhat common in the foodservice industry, whereas leasing television sets and laundry equipment is common in the lodging industry.

Leasing is a very expensive form of financing. For example, with some leases, operators pay and pay, but they never own the leased item. With others, such as **rent-to-own plans**, operators have an opportunity, and sometimes are required, to buy the item at the end of the lease period for a specific stated amount. Lessors normally require lessees to purchase full insurance coverage for the leased items, which might be more than they would be willing to do if they owned these items. Also, unless maintenance comes with the leased item, operators may be required to spend more money for maintenance than they would consider spending if they owned the item. Furthermore, lease payments are usually based on the FFE item's list price; as a result, buyers do not have the opportunity to negotiate the underlying purchase price.

Leasing does have advantages, though. Operators do not need to put up a large amount of money as a down payment; this helps preserve their working capital. Also, operators can experiment with new technology without making a long-term purchase commitment. And, generally, it is relatively easy for operators to set up a lease arrangement: less paperwork and fewer other related problems are involved with a lease than with a loan from a commercial lender. Unfortunately, these advantages aside, leasing is almost always more expensive in the long run than buying.

GAZING INTO THE FUTURE OF FOODSERVICE EQUIPMENT

George E. Baggott, CEO, Baggott Consulting Ltd.; Former Chairman of the Board of Cres Cor, an international manufacturer of mobile foodservice equipment and developer

The growth of the middle class and longer life spans will continue to increase the size of the meals-away-from-home market. People will eat out more frequently. The foodservice industry is changing worldwide, and the equipment for foodservice operations is changing as are the dynamics in the industry. People in purchasing face issues such as high energy costs, rising real estate prices, concerns about waste disposal, pricing, performance, longevity, global political instability, and government legislations and regulations along with less reliance on fossil fuels.

Our choices are increasing, which means we have more decisions to make when choosing equipment. No longer are there three manufacturers of the oven you need, now there are fifteen. The equipment can be from Thailand, China, or India with innovations to satisfy customers' international tastes. You have more dealers and distributors from which to choose with different product offerings, pricing, and service options. The job of a purchasing agent is getting more complex every day.

GAZING INTO THE FUTURE OF FOODSERVICE EQUIPMENT (continued)

But what is really in our future? Will the equipment we buy today serve us tomorrow? What will change? We cannot predict the future, but by looking at the trends of today, we can perhaps catch a glimpse of what is to come.

Calculating Value. The equipment of the future will come with an estimated service life. Knowing the service life of a piece of equipment allows one to calculate its whole life cost, also known as life cycle cost. For example, a product that costs $100 and is predicted to last for 10 years costs $10 per year. A similar product that costs only $80, and at first seems to be a better buy because of the lower cost, but is guaranteed to last only five years at a cost of $16 per year. Based on life cycle cost alone, the more expensive product is a better value. Other variables to consider when comparing two or more similar machines include maintenance costs, energy use, required floor space, cost of replacement parts, and ease of use. It is always best to keep in mind that the lowest price is not always the best price.

Globalization of Customer Taste and Selection. Our foodservice customers are very mobile and travel all over the world physically, but also by watching travel shows on TV and online. As a result, our customers have become much worldlier, and their taste buds cry out for the spices and foods of the lands they have visited. Equipment manufacturers are going to have to adapt and redesign their products to accommodate specialized foods from around the world. They must start to pay attention to the cultures of foreign lands and understand what equipment will be required to supply the cooking, holding, and serving of these foods.

Kitchens. Space will continue to be reviewed and reduced as the bottom line calls for higher-density seating and more revenue-producing square footage. Therefore, equipment will need to perform in reduced spaces and be able to do multiple tasks. For example, a steaming unit will also act as a skillet, and a combi-oven will have several new features such as holding, steaming, and convection air and may even be able to clean itself at the end of the day.

Floor space is very expensive; use of vertical design of equipment is important. A product installed in your kitchen could be designed for more vertical design versus long horizontal (floor space usage) design.

Ventless air makeup is important. Ventless ovens are available and you can also have less heat in the kitchen by using induction cooking equipment.

Another long-term trend is that kitchens are coming into the dining room so that customers can view chefs preparing food and giving demonstrations. The equipment of tomorrow will have to be attractive as well as functional in design.

Equipment will also become more reliable as manufacturers pay attention to detail, realizing that the competition is growing and quality and performance are critical to foodservice operations. The equipment of the future will be designed by chefs and representatives of food companies to fulfill the food preparation, warming, and presentation needs of small, highly productive kitchens. Finally, much of the equipment will be self-diagnosing. When problems occur, the piece of equipment will e-mail a work order to the service provider without human involvement.

People in the United States and around the globe are concerned about obesity and other dietary issues. The foods of the future will be created with a focus on calorie count, fat and trans-fat content, and other areas relating to health and nutrition. Equipment will play a part in this with an emphasis on maintaining the vitamins and nutrients in the food.

Training. Because equipment will be multifunctional, training of chefs and employees will be crucial. The equipment of the future will be designed for ease of use, with features such as single-button operation, temperature accuracy, trouble-shooting messages, and specific information on malfunctions or other issues.

Technology. The Internet will be a key source for a purchasing director to find information about a product's design, features, and operation. An incredible amount of information is available on equipment websites, dealers' websites, and industry chat rooms. Order placement and tracking is done on the Internet. Training is offered online. Remote monitoring of a new product for troubleshooting or regular maintenance may soon be available. Communication among all parties will take place via e-mail, webcasts, and/or Skype.

An updated CAD (computer-aided design) system with exciting new features will continue to be used in kitchen design. The design can be drafted by the chef, sales professionals, or trained foodservice facility consultants. One new feature is a virtual tour option. Imagine being able to "walk through and view" the proposed kitchen layout before the lease is even signed. Or, to very clearly see how the menu fits with the equipment in relation to the flow/location of preparation areas throughout the space. CAD can also provide a look inside a piece of equipment, showing how it is assembled and operates. Directions for installation and service of equipment will be made easy due to this technological advancement. Future designer and user tools are CAD and BIM (Building Information Management).

Safety and Sanitation. All equipment will have to pass rigorous safety and sanitation tests before being distributed locally, nationally, and internationally. A purchasing agent must be familiar with local codes, the National Sanitation Foundation, Underwriters Laboratories, and others who provide manufacturers with guidelines relating to sanitation, energy, and general performance. Stockpots will have cool-down and dispensing features. Holding ovens and refrigerators will be extremely sensitive to prevent food-borne illnesses. Controls will be very exact, and tracking and paper trails on holding, transporting, and cooking will be available in a digital format for filing and review. All handheld tools, such as knives, will have a new design to protect the user. Every inch of the kitchen will have to be safe, clean, and functional with no wasted space.

Communication with Your Supplier. Trade shows and networking will continue to be important. Your contacts, not only from college but also from the daily interchange you have with fellow workers and people in the industry, will be critical. The opportunity to shake someone's hand will become more valued as many meetings and product presentations will increasingly take place online.

Energy. Where will the power come from for the future equipment of the world—solar, gas, electric, wind, biodiesel, or hydro? The equipment of tomorrow will be more powerful, cost less to operate, and be more efficient. The Energy Star® rating will tell you if the equipment falls within the energy-saving guidelines of the Department of Energy and the Environmental Protection Agency. Foodservice and equipment manufacturers may find themselves establishing funds to promote research into sustainable energy sources for kitchens. Can't you just see a solar kitchen with zero energy costs? Before too long, we may have to move away from fossil fuels.

Labor. What will the labor force of the future look like? Workers will be better trained, more motivated, and more productive due to job enrichment and incentives. They may also be motivated by the opportunity to help provide great culinary experiences for the customer. Costs for employees are a reality. Minimum wage and benefit cost increases are putting more focus on productivity and multifunction type job functions. Equipment that is safe, useful, and easy to operate can enhance employees' talents.

Waste. With anything, there is an input and an output. Where will the waste of the future go? Will it be recycled? Will it end up in landfills? Will it be incinerated in a special oven and thereby fulfill the energy needs of the kitchen? The food containers will most likely be biodegradable and reusable. Cleaning of equipment will be more automatic and powerful, and dishwashers and washing machines will require less water and detergent.

Purchasing of Food, Supplies, and Equipment. The eye of the customer will be directed toward the actual price and value-added services. The selling of products will be relationship driven in part, but will also be a function of a price/quality/service ratio. This is where life cycle costing will be involved. The products of the future will be purchased at a variety of places, a local small or large food distributor; a "box store" or wholesale club; a small ethnic-oriented specialty distributor; or a national foodservice distributor offering services and support (in person and online). Remember the lowest price is not always the best price. In many cases, products will come already bar coded or come with radio frequency identification (RFID) tags for easy receiving and inventory processing. Reorder points will be determined by computers that will e-mail orders directly to the suppliers. The equipment will be researched, quoted, and purchased via e-mail from supplier websites, catalogs, or even through online auction services such as eBay.

Your Future. Don't forget that there are job opportunities in the supply side of the industry: sales person, marketing representative, dealership manager, product designer, engineer for an equipment company, consultant. You may have to start in a low part of an organization but hours might be better, and you would have a different variety of job responsibilities and exposure to all kinds of challenges that in other sides of the hospitality industry. Websites for industry information are always available to refer to for research, data, and communications. Here are some of the more useful ones:

- North American Association of Food Equipment Manufacturers (www.nafem.org)
- Foodservice Equipment Distributors Association (www.feda.com)
- Manufacturers' Agents Association for the Foodservice Industry (www.mafsi.org)
- Commercial Food Equipment Service Association (www.cfesa.com)
- Foodservice Consultants Society International (www.fsci.org)
- Food Marketing Institute (www.fmi.org)
- National Restaurant Association (www.restaurant.org)
- American Hotel & Lodging Association (www.ahla.com)

GAZING INTO THE FUTURE OF FOODSERVICE EQUIPMENT (continued)

The future of foodservice equipment looks very exciting. Customers are seeking new and exciting dining experiences, and it will be the job of the purchasing director to ensure that the equipment is onsite to support both the front- and back-of-house operations.

■ New Products for the Future

- HotCube³™ Hybrid Hot Cabinet Hybrid mobile cabinet that does not require extension cords or generators or canned fuel when used outdoors (hot food safety in catering) www.CresCor.com.

- Holding units in various sizes—no more one-size-fits-all: www.crescor.com, www.carter-hoffman.com.

- Serve more people at one time with modular tray lines and island service. Also, new holding and pre-prep equipment will let you get 3,000 school kids fed and in and out of the lunchroom in 30 minutes: www.vollrath.com, www.eaglegrp.com.

- Conveyor hot air ovens that keep constant airflow and humidity, and provide an even distribution of air: www.middleby.com, www.hennypenny.com, www.turbochef.com, www.manitowoc.com.

- Carriers—holding units—As restaurants use more stylish dishes, the carrier/holders have had to change. New, multisize carriers and holders must adapt to different sizes and shapes of dishes to be used in kitchens and service areas: www.cambro.com, www.crescor.com, www.metro.com.

- Ease-of-use and equipment monitoring are two essentials. Today's one-button operations make for easy operation of equipment. The option for remote switches and energy monitoring give kitchen managers and chefs control from a central office or other location: www.avtecind.com, www.dukemfg.com, www.cooperatkins.com, www.haltoncompany.com.

- Modular equipment is a must for small kitchens and table side preparations: www.wilburcurtis.com, www.bunn.com, www.fetco.com.

- Filtration products for water and grease are available that result in cleaner water for drains (no more clogging), and biodiesel as a byproduct. One example is The Goslyn, an aboveground mobile compact-grease interceptor that will remove 99.5 percent of all fats, oils, and grease (FOG) from the waste water stream before it can go down the drain and clog up the drainage system. The unit has no moving parts and, as such, is a very effective, efficient, and easy product to use and maintain. The grease can be retrieved and sold to collection pickup companies for added income from what was formerly waste: www.goslyn.com.

- New filtering systems for drain type fryers. Purefry Filter Machine's state-of-the-art filtration system will extend the life of the oil, which will help reduce operating costs and ensure that customers receive great-tasting food on a consistent basis. The machines include innovative safety features to aid in the protection of employees: www.purefryusa.com.

- Monitoring the entire kitchen's energy use from a central location will help chefs and kitchen managers manage energy consumption: www.bernerinternational.com, www.controlproducts.com, www.fastinc.com, www.dwyer-inst.com, www.cooper-atkins.com, www.cdn-timeandtemp.com.

GAZING INTO THE FUTURE OF FOODSERVICE EQUIPMENT (continued)

- Chefs will need an oven that will bake special ethnic foods and bakery products in traditional ways (but with modern equipment): www.woodstone-corp.com, www.montaguecompany.com, www.vulcanhart.com.

- Coffee, beverage products (regular coffee and Asian tea units); the single-service coffee regeneration units heat up fast and have digital components and longer hold times. Plus, there is a wider range of flavors available: www.bunn.com, www.wilburcurtis.com, www.fetco.com.

- PowerPak is a portable rechargeable lithium ion battery pack used in the foodservice industry to power electric heaters for chafing dishes, coffee urns, soup marmites, and mobile equipment in banqueting or catering when unplugged from the main power sources or in transit from the transport and/or kitchen to use: www.sbarta@hsgnow.com.

- Ventless oven—Ovations "Match Box" product: www.manitowoc.com.

- Ice machine—Program the ice machine when you want ice (i.e., no ice on weekends): www.manitowoc.com.

- Round rotating broiler—display and quantity to produce (5-ft.-round footprint); if flat grill 6 ft., the revolving grill is 2 times the surface. Display/show piece: www.RMW.com.

Note: This is only a small sample of what is new in equipment. Refer to magazines such as *Food Service Equipment Reports* (www.fermag.com) or *Food Service Equipment and Supplies* (www.fesmag.com) and the associations mentioned earlier. Another valuable resource is magazines that study the trends in the industry, including *Restaurants and Institutions, Restaurant Hospitality, Foodservice Director,* and many more.

Key Words and Concepts

Add-on capabilities	Demonstration model
American Gas Association (AGA)	Depreciable asset
American Society of Mechanical Engineers (ASME)	Design/build dealer
	Detailed drawings
Brand name	Direct purchase
Capital item	Downtime
Capitalizing an expense	Environmental Protection Agency (EPA)
Code compliance	Equipment dealer
Compactness	Equipment program
Computer-aided design (CAD)	Excess capacity
Contract supply house	Foodservice design consultant
Customized FFE	Freight-damaged
Degree of automation	Impulse purchase

Key Words and Concepts (continued)

Installation costs	Operating costs
Instructions to bidders	Operating savings
Intended use	Payback period
Leasing companies	Portability
Lifetime cost	Rent-to-own plan
Liquidation	Security agreement
Lowball bid	Service after the sale
Merchant fee	Show-special price
National Fire Protection Association (NFPA)	Supplier services
National Sanitation Foundation (NSF)	Systems sale
International	Trade-in value
Net present value	Underwriters Laboratories (UL)
NSF International	Warranty

Questions and Problems

1. What are some advantages and disadvantages of leasing FFE?

2. Briefly describe the concept of "capitalizing" an expense.

3. Why would a hospitality operation hire a consultant to assist in the development of FFE purchase specifications?

4. When should an equipment purchase specification include detailed drawings?

5. What are some possible disadvantages of purchasing reconditioned equipment?

6. The lifetime cost of an FFE item could include this information:

    a.

    b.

    c.

    d.

    e.

7. Briefly describe the concept of "net present value."

8. Briefly describe the concept of "payback period."

9. Why would a commercial lender require a borrower to sign a security agreement?

Questions and Problems (continued)

10. What are some advantages and disadvantages of purchasing a personal computer direct from the manufacturer?

11. What are some advantages and disadvantages of purchasing customized kitchen equipment?

12. Why would an equipment dealer be willing to sell a demonstration model for much less than the normal purchase price?

13. When would "compactness of FFE" be an important selection factor?

14. When would "availability of replacement parts" be an important selection factor?

15. What are some advantages of purchasing portable kitchen equipment?

16. What are some advantages and disadvantages of purchasing used FFE?

17. A specification for a walk-in refrigerator could include this information:

    a.

    b.

    c.

    d.

    e.

18. A specification for a dining room table could include this information:

    a.

    b.

    c.

    d.

    e.

19. A specification for a microwave oven could include this information:

    a.

    b.

    c.

    d.

    e.

20. What are some disadvantages of using a credit card to finance an equipment purchase?

21. What type of considerations regarding energy sources and efficiency should an operator be aware of when purchasing FFE?

22. When would operators select FFE strictly on the basis of brand name?

Experiential Exercises

1. Attend a hospitality trade show, such as the National Restaurant Association Show, the International Hotel, Motel, and Restaurant Show, Catersource, or a local/regional trade show. Select one type of FFE to focus on. Speak with the company representatives, and collect information and brochures. Write a two-page paper comparing the products that the companies offer.

2. Obtain a food and beverage menu from a restaurant or catering facility. Make a list of all the back of the house and front of the house FFE that would be necessary to operate the business. Ask one of the operation's managers to review your list. Was there anything you left out? Was there equipment that you thought was needed and is not used? Write a two-page paper about your findings.

References

1. United States Environmental Protection Agency, "Ozone Layer Protection—Regulatory Programs," http://www.epa.gov/ozone/title6/phaseout/22phaseout.html.

2. Amelia Levin, "Working on Celebrity Chef Restaurants Poses Unique Challenges," *Foodservice Equipment Magazine*, June 25, 2014, http://www.fesmag.com/home -highlights/11846-working-on-celebrity-chef-restaurants-poses-unique-challenges.

3. Efficient Commercial Foodservice Equipment, http://www.sustainablefoodservice.com/cat/ equipment.htm.

Glossary

accept gifts Usually refers to buyers accepting something of value from suppliers for their personal use.

accepting a delivery Occurs when a receiving agent is satisfied that the delivered merchandise meets the company's standards. Once the shipment is accepted, the receiving agent normally signs a copy of the invoice accompanying the delivery.

actual cost of food sold Equal to: (beginning inventory + purchases – ending inventory) +/ – any adjustments, such as employee meals, complimentary items given to guests, and so forth.

additives Chemicals added or used to upgrade product quality and/or help a product resist spoilage.

add-on capability Feature that allows retrofitting in the future. Especially important when purchasing equipment that may need to be modified as the business grows.

age at time of slaughter Characteristic that affects the flavor, tenderness, and other culinary characteristics of poultry.

agency law Law that allows employees, when acting in their official capacity, to sign contracts for their companies.

aggregate buying group A group that forms for the purposes of co-op buying.

aggregate purchasing company Another term for buying club.

Agricultural Adjustment Act Legislation developed as part of the New Deal's farm relief bill. It stated that whenever the administration desired currency expansion, the president must first authorize the open market committee of the Federal Reserve to purchase up to $4 billion of federal obligations. Its primary purpose was to create an "honest dollar" that would be fair to debtors and creditors in the farming industry. Also referred to as the Thomas Amendment, named after its sponsor, Oklahoma Senator Elmer Thomas.

Agricultural Marketing Act Law that regulates the marketing of agricultural and meat products.

Agricultural Marketing Agreement Act Law that allows primary sources and intermediaries in the produce trade to work together without violating antitrust regulations.

Agricultural Marketing Service (AMS) Agency of the USDA that establishes federal grading standards for several food products, under authority of the Agricultural Marketing Act.

Agricultural Marketing Service (AMS), Live Stock & Feed Division Agency that oversees and regulates the marketing of agricultural and meat products.

alarm system Security device that alerts when something is wrong. Examples are burglary, fire, and refrigerator/freezer alarms.

Alcohol Beverage Commission (ABC) A liquor control authority that regulates the sale and purchase of beverage alcohol.

alcohol content The amount of alcohol in a beverage, expressed as a percentage or as a proof.

allocation Process whereby a distributor and/or primary source determines how much of a product you are allowed to purchase. Usually done with high-quality wines so that all restaurants have a chance to buy at least some of it.

allocation Process whereby a distributor and/or primary source determines how much of a product you are allowed to purchase. Usually done with high-quality wines so that all restaurants have a chance to buy at least some of it.

almond milk A beverage made from ground almonds. It is a cholesterol- and lactose-free substitute for whole milk.

American Angus Association An organization that serves the beef cattle industry. Its primary objective is to help the industry increase the production of consistently high-quality beef that will satisfy consumers throughout the world.

American Culinary Federation (ACF) Professional organization of chefs and cooks.

American Gas Association (AGA) Provides gas safety certification for gas-powered equipment that meets its standards.

American Purchasing Society Professional association of buyers and purchasing managers, which was the first organization to establish certification for buyers and purchasing professionals.

American Society of Mechanical Engineers (ASME) Provides steam safety certification for steam-powered equipment that meet its standards.

application service provider (ASP) A company that distributes software online from a central location to customers in other locations.

approved substitute A product that a buyer can purchase in lieu of the typical one that is usually purchased.

approved supplier A vendor that the buyer is allowed to buy from.

approved-payee list A list of all persons and companies that are allowed to receive any sort of payment from you. An excellent security precaution.

Approved-supplier list A list of all vendors who buyers are allowed to purchase from. An excellent security precaution.

aquaculture The controlled farming of plants and animals, such as fish, shellfish, and algae, in a water environment.

architect Person who designs buildings and develops plans for their construction.

aseptic pack A form of controlled atmosphere packaging (CAP). Sterile foods placed in an airtight, sterilized package. The package contains a hygienic environment that prolongs shelf life and makes the foods shelf-stable.

aseptic packaging A form of controlled atmosphere packaging (CAP). Sterile foods placed in an airtight, sterilized package. The package contains a hygienic environment that prolongs shelf life and makes the foods shelf-stable.

"as-is, where-is" condition Buying a product, such as a used piece of equipment, in its current condition. There usually are no guarantees. In addition, the buyer is usually responsible for the cost of packing up the product and having it delivered.

as-purchased (AP) price Price charged by the vendor.

as-served cost Another term for edible-portion (EP) cost.

as-used cost Another term for edible-portion (EP) cost.

auditing the inventory sales Process whereby a supervisor or manager compares inventory that has been used in production to the sales records. Ideally, the amount missing would be recorded as sold to customers.

automatic dispenser A piece of equipment that allots a portion-controlled amount of beverage.

B2B e-commerce Online interaction between businesses. Typically involves the sale and purchase of merchandise or services.

B2C e-commerce Online interaction between businesses and consumers. Typically involves the sale and purchase of merchandise and services.

backdoor selling This happens when a sales rep bypasses the regular buyer and goes to some other employee, such as the lead line cook, to make a sales pitch. The cook then exerts pressure on the buyer to make the purchase.

background check Researching personal or company history, checking for things such as reliability, unethical behavior, criminal convictions, and so forth.

backhaul Occurs when a driver delivers a shipment to a hospitality operation and then refills the empty truck with items (such as recyclable materials) that need to be delivered to another location. The purpose is to gain maximum efficiency by seeing to it that the truck is always full when it is on the road.

back order When your shipment is incomplete because the vendor did not have the item in stock, the invoice will state that the item is back ordered. You will receive the item later.

bank charges Fees charged by financial institutions for various types of services provided.

banner ad Graphical advertisement that appears on a website that provides a hyperlink to the advertised site.

bar code A computerized label attached to most food packages. The information on the bars can be read by the computer and used to track inventory amounts and values.

bar code element The lines and spaces on a bar code label.

bar code reader Device used to read labels that contain bar code elements.

barter group A group of businesses that wish to barter for products and services and use trade dollars instead of cash money to get what they need. The group is organized and administered by a third party, and a fee is usually assessed each participant whenever they make a deal. The opposite of direct bartering, whereby two or more persons get together on their own to make a deal.

barter The practice of trading your products or services for something you need. Intended to reduce your out-of-pocket expense.

basic commodity A product for which there is demand, but which is sold by many suppliers without qualitative differentiation. It is a product that is the same no matter who produces it.

beginning inventory Amount of products available for sale at the beginning of an accounting period.

best-if-consumed-by date Another term for pull date.

best-if-used-by date Another term for pull date.

Better Business Bureau (BBB) Organization that helps protect consumers from shoddy and fraudulent business practices. It also helps consumers resolve complaints they have about businesses they've dealt with.

bid buying When buyers shop around seeking current AP prices from vendors. The vendors are asked to quote, or bid, the prices they will charge. Intended to give the buyer competitive pricing information that will allow him or her to get the best possible value.

bill of lading Document that conveys title to the goods purchased.

bill-paying procedure Method used to discharge debts in such a way that payments are made on time. Payments should not be late, as that could create penalties, yet they should not be too early unless there are incentives for early payments.

bill-paying service An outside company entitled to use a company's money to pay for products or services purchased by the buyer. Bills are typically paid automatically by accessing the buyer's company's bank account(s). The service is typically used to reduce administrative expenses and to increase efficiency.

bin card A perpetual inventory record. It includes all items delivered to the restaurant's storeroom, all items issued out of the storeroom, all items returned to the storeroom, and the current balance of all items held in the storeroom.

blanket order discount Another term for volume discount.

blanket order Purchase order that contains several different products.

blind receiving When the invoice accompanying a delivery contains only the names of the items delivered. Quantity and price information is missing. The receiving clerk is required to count everything and record it. An expensive way of controlling the receiving clerk's work.

blowout sale Refers to the sale of old, defective, or discontinued merchandise that is usually sold at a huge discount.

bond An insurance policy covering cash-handling employees. Alternately, refers to a performance bond, which is insurance taken out by a construction contractor that guarantees work will be done by a certain date or else the client will collect damages.

bonded supplier A supplier that has adequate insurance coverage demanded by the local government that issues business licenses.

bonding An insurance policy covering cash-handling employees. Alternately, refers to a performance bond, which is insurance taken out by a construction contractor that guarantees work will be done by a certain date or else the client will collect damages.

bottle service Service, typically in an upscale nightclub, where guests pay a high price for a bottle of alcohol and receive VIP service and seating.

bottom-line, firm-price purchasing Method used when the buyer focuses on the total dollar amount of a purchase instead of on each item's AP price. If shopping around, the buyer will not pick and choose among several vendors. He or she will buy from the one that quotes the lowest total dollar amount of the entire purchase and will not purchase anything from the other competing vendors. The opposite of line-item purchasing.

bovine somatotropin (bST) Chemical injected into lactating cows to increase their milk production.

brand name Indication of product quality. A typical selection factor for purchased items, especially when purchasing beverage alcohol.

breaker plant Facility that removes eggs from their shells and processes them further.

break point The point at which a vendor will accept a lower price. For instance, if you buy from 1 to 50 cases, the AP price may be $5 per case, but if you purchase more than 50 cases, the AP price may be $4.75 per case. In this example, the break point is 50.

brewer Primary source of fermented beverages made primarily from grains.

brew pub Retail establishment that brews draft beer on-site and sells it to retail customers. The typical brew pub also serves food and other beverage alcohols.

Brix level A higher Brix denotes a higher sugar content, and vice versa.

broadline distributor Intermediary that provides food, nonfood supplies, and equipment.

broken case Refers to the purchase of less than one case because the vendor is willing to break open a case and sell you only part of it. Few vendors will do this for you.

broker Person who represents one or more primary sources. A broker does not buy or resell products, but promotes products to potential buyers. A broker usually represents manufacturers and processors that do not employ their own sales force.

budgeting Developing a realistic statement of management's goals and objectives, expressed in financial terms. This statement is usually referred to as a budget.

bulk pack Package containing a large amount of product. Unit cost for products packed this way is typically much less than individually wrapped products, or products purchased in small packages.

Bureau of Alcohol, Tobacco, Firearms, and Explosives (ATF) Federal agency responsible for overseeing the sale and purchase of these products and ensuring that all pertinent laws and regulations are followed.

business license Authorization issued by local, state, and/or federal governments needed to conduct business.

butterfat content The amount of fat in a dairy product.

buyer fact sheets Another term for buyer profiles.

buyer pricing Occurs whenever a buyer does not have a clear-cut specification; the vendor then helps the buyer determine what he or she needs. Will also occur whenever you engage in panic buying. This method will significantly increase your cost of goods sold.

buyer profiles Vendor files that contain information about current and potential customers. Typically used by sales reps to help them prepare the best possible sales presentations.

buying club A type of co-op purchasing. Instead of co-op members organizing and administering their own co-op, they join a buying club that, for a fee, streamlines the process and makes it more efficient.

buying plan Overall selection and procurement strategy. Includes reasons why it was selected and relevant policies and procedures needed to carry it out successfully.

buying service Another term for buying club.

buyout policy Vendors' willingness to purchase from a customer, a competitor's products, so that the customer can immediately begin purchasing similar products from them.

buyout sale or closeout sale Another term for blowout sale.

call brand Term used in the bar business to refer to a drink that customers order by brand name. Opposite of well brand.

call sheet buying Used when shopping around on a day-to-day basis. The buyer contacts several purveyors seeking their AP price quotes. He or she then purchases from the one offering the lowest AP price.

candling Looking inside a shell egg by passing it over a light to determine its quality. Part of the egg-grading process.

can-cutting test Examining the characteristics of two or more similar products to determine which one represents the best value. Alternately, an examination of all relevant characteristics of a product the buyer is thinking about purchasing.

capital cost The rate of return (e.g., interest income) that capital could be expected to earn in an alternative investment of equivalent risk. Alternately, cost incurred when purchasing land, buildings, construction/remodeling, and equipment to be used in the production of goods and/or services to be sold to consumers.

capital item Expensive FFE, the cost of which must typically be depreciated over time. Opposite of an expense item.

capitalizing an expense Term used to refer to the purchase of an expensive capital item, such as a new heating system, to reduce future operating expenses, such as the cost of energy used to heat a building.

carcass The whole body of a dead animal.

carrying cost Expenses, such as insurance, security, and spoilage, associated with holding inventory in storage.

case price Equal to the AP price for one case divided by the number of units per case. For instance, if you pay $12 for a six-can case of canned tomatoes, the case price is $2 per can. If a vendor is willing to sell you less than one case, but charges you only $2 per can, he or she is charging the case price and not a premium price for a broken (busted) case.

case price per unit Equal to the AP price for one case divided by the number of units per case. For instance, if you pay $12 for a six-can case of canned tomatoes, the case price is $2 per can. If a vendor is willing to sell you less than one case, but charges you only $2 per can, he or she is charging the case price and not a premium price for a broken (busted) case.

cash-on-delivery (COD) Paying for a shipment when it is delivered. Payment may be in cash, check, credit card, debit card, or other acceptable means.

cash discount An award for prompt payment, for paying in advance of the delivery, or using a cash-on-delivery (COD) bill-paying procedure.

cash management Procedures used to ensure that a company's cash will be tightly controlled and handled effectively and efficiently.

cash rebate Occurs when a vendor charges the full AP price for an item, but later on, after you provide proof-of-purchase documentation, he or she will send you a check for a small amount of money, or will credit this amount to your next bill.

cash-and-carry Another term for will-call buying.

cash-on-delivery (COD) Paying for a shipment when it is delivered. Payment may be in cash, check, credit card, debit card, or other acceptable means.

catalog house A very small equipment dealer that carries no inventory, or very little inventory, in stock. Buyers select items from one or more catalogs, and the dealer handles the ordering, delivery, setup, installation, and so forth.

catch weight The approximate weight in a case of product. Used when it is not possible to specify an exact weight. For instance, if you purchase a case of whole, fresh fish, you usually cannot specify the exact total weight of all pieces of fish, but you can ask for an approximate total weight of the case.

cello packed Products completely surrounded by clear plastic film. Typical packing procedure for things such as ready-to-serve salad greens. Also commonly used as an inner wrap. For instance, if you purchase a 5-pound box of frozen fish fillets, usually there will be six cello-wrapped packages, each containing approximately two to four pieces of fish.

cell pack Products layered in a cardboard or plastic sheet that has depressions in it so that the items sit in them and do not touch one another. Typically used to pack high-quality fresh fruit.

Center for Science in the Public Interest Organization that advocates for nutrition and health, food safety, alcohol policy, and sound science.

Center on Alcohol Marketing and Youth A research organization located at the Johns Hopkins Center for Public Health, which is funded by the Centers for Disease Control and Prevention.

central distribution center A large warehouse owned by a multiunit hospitality company that orders merchandise directly from primary sources, takes delivery, stocks the merchandise, and then delivers it to company-affiliated units in the area.

Certified Angus Beef ® Program Group that monitors and regulates the sale of Angus meat that has met its mandated quality standards.

certified buying Another term for USDA Acceptance Service.

Certified Foodservice Professional (CFSP) Indication that the person who holds this designation has achieved a certain level of foodservice operations knowledge and experience.

chain of operating activities The sequence of day-to-day operating activities that hospitality businesses perform. Generally, they involve the following activities, in order: buying, receiving, storing, issuing, preparation, service, customer consumption, and customer payment.

change order Used if a buyer wishes to alter a purchase order that was recently placed with a vendor. May be a written document, or it could be accomplished with a phone call or e-mail.

check padding Overcharging a customer to make up for undercharging another customer. Alternately, overcharging a customer to pocket the extra cash.

chemical additives Substances added to food and beverages to preserve flavor, maintain shelf life, and/or improve taste and appearance.

chemical standards The amount and/or type of additives a buyer is willing to accept in purchased products.

chemical tenderization Adding an enzyme to meat to change the protein structure.

cherry picking See line-item purchasing.

Child Nutrition (CN) label Indicates that the product conforms to the children's nutritional requirements of the USDA. Typically found on product containers sold to school foodservice operations.

chill packed Preservation method whereby the temperature is held at approximately 28 to 29°F, just above the product's freezing point. Usually done for fresh meat and poultry. Intended to increase the product's shelf life.

Clayton Act Enhances and amplifies the antitrust duties performed by the FTC. It also outlaws tying agreements and exclusive dealing.

closed-circuit television (CCTV) System that allows supervision of a specific area through the use of monitors.

code compliance Following the laws and regulations of a governing body. Term typically used to refer to compliance with building, equipment, and health codes.

cold chain Keeping product refrigerated from the producer to the supplier to the buyer and ultimately to the guest.

color A substance, such as a dye, pigment, or paint that imparts a hue.

commercial hospitality operations Profit-oriented company.

comminuting Process of reducing a substance into smaller, random-shaped pieces. Typical method used to produce things such as processed chicken patties.

commissary Similar to a central distribution center. The major difference is that at a commissary, raw foods are processed into finished products, which is not the case in a central distribution center. Could be considered a restaurant company's personal convenience food processing plant.

commodity A basic, raw food ingredient. It is considered by buyers to be the same regardless of which vendor sells it. For instance, all-purpose flour is often considered a commodity product, for which any processor's product is acceptable.

commodity exchange An organized market for the purchase and sale of enforceable contracts to deliver a commodity, such as wheat, or a financial instrument, such as eurodollars, at some future date.

common area maintenance (CAM) fee Fee charged to tenants. Used by the landlord to pay for facility upkeep, especially of things like the parking lot and landscaping.

common carrier An independent delivery service hired by the vendor to deliver goods to the restaurant operation. UPS is an example of a common carrier.

communal buying, co-op purchasing, or shared buying Other terms for co-op buying.

compactness An important FFE selection factor. Refers to the least amount of space an item occupies.

compensation Financial remuneration, such as wages, salaries, bonuses, and fringe benefits, paid to people for their work.

competitive pressure Force produced and exerted by companies on one another, to lower prices and/or to provide better products and services.

computer-aided design (CAD) The use of a wide range of technological tools that help design professionals. Typically used by architects, kitchen designers, and so forth to enhance the design and construction process and make it more efficient.

concentrated agricultural feeding operations (CAFOs) Facilities in which livestock undergo intensive feeding or finishing before being slaughtered.

consignment sale Allows the buyer to pay a vendor for a purchase after the buyer's company has sold the merchandise to its customers.

construction contractor Term used in the building trade. One who takes the plans and designs produced by architects and designers and turns them into finished products.

construction management firm Organization that specializes in managing and controlling the various companies (such as architects, designers, and construction contractors) needed to build a new facility and/or remodel an existing one.

consulting proposal A document submitted by a company that typically includes the project's objectives, tactics, time constraints, and total price. Similar to a competitive bid for food products submitted by a vendor.

consulting service Company that specializes in helping others by giving advice and/or accomplishing specific tasks that clients do not wish to do on their own.

contract house Another term for buying club.

contract supply house A type of buying club. It is operated by a third party that negotiates with suppliers and passes on some of the savings obtained through bulk purchasing to member buyers.

contract Voluntary and legal agreement, by competent parties, to do or not do something. In almost every case it must be a written agreement to be legally enforceable.

controlled atmosphere packaging (CAP) Process that involves placing a food or beverage item in a package, removing existing gases by creating a vacuum, and introducing a specially formulated mixture of gases intended to enhance the product's shelf life.

controlled atmosphere storage Similar to controlled atmosphere packaging (CAP). However, it can also refer to a controlled atmosphere that exists in other types of storage environments, such as controlled atmosphere warehouses.

controlled brand Products produced by a company that typically offers only one level of quality (usually a high quality). The company controls all aspects of production and distribution.

control state A state that sells beverage alcohol. It is the only purveyor of beverage alcohol in that state.

control Systems and procedures used by managers to ensure that the actual costs of doing business are consistent with the expected (or budgeted or theoretical) costs.

convenience food A food that has been processed to change its form and/or taste. It usually requires very little handling in the restaurant kitchen. It may be ready-to-use or ready-to-serve.

conventional profit markup The most typical percentage (or dollar amount) added to the cost a company pays for an item it sells, to compute the company's sales price.

conversion Converting supplies into finished products.

conversion weight Another term for yield.

corporate social responsibility The practice of a company self-regulating the effect of their practices on the environment, people, and the global economy.

corporate vice president of purchasing Person responsible for all purchasing activities for the corporation. Major responsibilities include such things as: setting purchasing guidelines; negotiating long-term, national contracts for price and product availability; and researching new vendors and products. In some cases, this person is also responsible for overseeing the central commissary and/or central distribution warehouses.

correct order size The order size that minimizes the ordering costs, inventory storage costs, and stockout costs.

correct order time The order time that minimizes the ordering costs, inventory storage costs, and stockout costs.

Cosmetics-Devices Act Law granting the FDA injunctive powers and the authority to set food standards.

cost of paying too early The loss of interest income that could have been collected if the cash were invested between the time the bill was paid early and the time it had to be paid.

cost of paying too late Includes things such as damage to a company's credit rating, late fee charges, and being required to pay COD for future purchases.

cost-plus buying The AP price the buyer pays is equal to the vendor's cost of the product plus an agreed-upon profit markup.

cost-plus purchasing procedure Under this purchasing procedure, a product's AP price is equal to the supplier's cost of the product plus an agreed-upon profit markup.

count The number of pieces in a container. Alternately, the number of smaller containers in a larger container.

coupon refund Another term for cash rebate.

co-op A business organization owned and operated by a group of individuals for their mutual benefit. Another term for co-op purchasing, shared buying, and communal buying.

co-op buying The banding together of several small operators to consolidate and enhance their buying power.

credit card payment Paying bills with a credit card instead of cash or check.

credit control Refers to government agencies dictating the credit terms that can be extended to buyers. This type of control is fairly common in the dairy and beverage alcohol distribution channels.

credit memo When a shipment, or partial shipment is unsatisfactory, the supplier will send one of these to the hospitality operation, signifying the amount of credit that will be applied to its account.

credit period The amount of time a borrower has before a bill must be paid.

credit rating Another term for credit score.

credit risk The probability that a borrower will not pay.

credit slip When a shipment, or partial shipment, is unsatisfactory, the driver will give a credit slip to the receiving clerk, signifying the amount of credit that will be applied to the restaurant's account. It eliminates the need for the restaurant to prepare a credit memo.

credit terms The type and amount of financing a vendor will provide, along with the prescribed type of bill-paying procedure that must be followed. Also included are things such as a description of late fees, penalties, and so forth.

critical-item inventory analysis Reconciling the critical item inventory daily usage with the daily sales recorded in the POS system. Discrepancies between what was used and what was sold must be resolved.

crustacean Shellfish with a soft shell (e.g., shrimp).

Cryovac aging Another term for wet aging.

Cryovac® The company that pioneered shrink-wrap technology.

customer relationship management (CRM) Another term for customer. Sometimes also referred to as customer relationship marketing. Forming personal alliances that will lead to the sale and purchase of products and services.

customized FFE FFE items specially made to fit a buyer's unique needs. Typically manufactured on a made-to-order basis.

cycle of control The day-to-day operating activities in a hospitality organization. Typically the cycle begins when products are delivered to and received by the hospitality organization and ends when they are used. Controls are established to ensure that what was received is used appropriately, with little or no loss along the way.

daily bid buying Another term for call sheet buying.

daily-quotation buying Another term for call sheet buying.

decay allowance The expected amount of a purchased product that will be unusable, yet will be acceptable to the buyer when it is shipped to the hospitality operation. The typical situation involves the purchase of fresh produce where the buyer will expect, and accept, a few broken and/or spoiled pieces in the lot.

degree of automation The extent to which control systems (such as numerical control, programmable logic control, and other industrial control systems), are used together with other applications of information technology (such as computer-aided technologies), to control machinery and processes, reducing the need for human intervention.

degree of ripeness A measure of a food or beverage product's maturity and readiness to be used in production, or to eat or drink.

delivery schedule Purveyor's planned shipping times and dates.

delivery ticket Written receipt summarizing what was ordered and delivered. It is typically written up by route salespersons when they are finished restocking the hospitality operation. Similar to an invoice.

demonstration model FFE used by the purveyor or manufacturer for display purposes. Usually can be purchased at a discount.

deposit Money, or other asset, used to ensure that future products or services will be provided. Alternately, money used to ensure that returnable items, such as reusable packing crates, will be returned to the vendor.

depreciable asset Another term for capital item.

depreciation Loss of value over time.

derived demand Refers to the notion that a buyer's demand for certain products and/or services is contingent on the needs and desires of the customers the buyer's company serves.

design/build dealer An equipment dealer who has the capability of providing design and construction/remodeling services.

designers In the hospitality industry, designers are persons typically hired to originate and develop a process for creating suitable work spaces and/or themes for the interiors of hospitality operations.

detailed drawings Documents intended to communicate precise information to assist bidders and eliminate ambiguity. Typically used when purchasing FFE and/or construction services.

digital video recorder (DVR) Electronic device that plays and copies video streams from a video source.

direct bartering When two persons trade between themselves rather than through a barter group.

direct buying Bypassing intermediaries and purchasing directly from the primary source.

direct control system System that does not rely on number crunching and paperwork. It relies on the supervisor's presence and personal supervision and direction.

directing Supervising and managing persons who work for you.

direct purchase Refers to a purchased product (usually a perishable food) that, once received, will bypass the main storage facility, go straight to production, and be charged to cost on the day it's received. A perishable food item, such as fresh pastry, is an example of a direct purchase. Alternately, buying directly from a primary source and bypassing the middleman.

direct writer Insurance company that bypasses intermediaries, such as insurance brokers, and sells insurance directly to customers.

discount operation Another term for storefront dealer.

disposable versus reusable Disposable refers to single-use products, such as paper napkins, plastic dishes, and paper cups. Reusable refers to similar products; however, they are not single-use. They can be washed and reused many times before being replaced.

distiller Primary source that produces alcoholic beverages, such as whisky, that have undergone a distillation process.

distribution channel The people, organizations, and procedures involved in producing and delivering products and services from primary sources to ultimate consumers.

distributor or merchant wholesaler A term for a vendor that purchases directly and resells to customers.

distributor sales representative (DSR) Person employed by a vendor to sell products and provide support functions to restaurant operators.

document cash paid-outs Maintaining a record of all cash removed from petty cash or from a cash register.

door hangers Promotional tools used to convey a business's message to potential customers. They are designed in such a way that they can be hung on a door knob. Often used as an alternative to direct mail pieces. They are usually double-sided, have attention-grabbing styles, and have angled hole slits that can adjust to most doorknobs.

dot system Color-coded, stick-on dots (usually a different color for each day) usually attached to inventories when they are received. They have enough blank space to pencil in dates, times, AP prices, and other pertinent information.

downtime The amount of time a piece of equipment or a facility is out of service.

drained weight Refers to the weight of the product (such as canned sliced peaches) less its juice or other packing medium. It is computed by draining the product in a specific sieve for a certain amount of time. Sometimes referred to as the edible weight.

driving while intoxicated (DWI) The criminal offense of operating and/or driving a motor vehicle while under the influence of alcohol and/or drugs to the degree that mental and motor skills are impaired. In some states the offense is called driving under the influence (DUI), operating while impaired (OWI), or operating a vehicle under the influence (OVI).

drop shipment Typical shipping procedure used when engaging in direct buying. The shipment is delivered to the back door of the restaurant, usually by a common carrier.

dry aging An expensive method used to tenderize meat and to enhance its flavor.

e-procurement Ordering products and services from various purveyors online. Alternately, ordering these things from a particular vendor who provides proprietary software to the buyer, who is then allowed to enter the vendor's electronic system.

early-morning deliveries A form of odd-hours delivery.

economical packaging Packing methods and packaging materials used that will reduce overall product costs.

economic force The effects of supply and demand, and other forms of competitive pressure, on businesses.

economic order quantity (EOQ) formula The EOQ in dollars is equal to: the square root of [(2 times the ordering cost in dollars times the amount of the item used in one year in dollars) divided by the annual storage cost expressed as a percentage of average inventory value]. The EOQ in units is equal to: the square root of [(2 times the ordering cost in dollars times the amount of the item used in one year in units) divided by the annual storage cost per unit in dollars].

economic value Represents the increase in AP (as purchased) price that occurs as a product journeys through the distribution channel. For example, 10 pounds of preportioned steak is more valuable, and more expensive, than 10 pounds of meat that has to be processed further in a restaurant's kitchen.

edible byproduct Trimmings of food items, such as meat and seafood, that can be processed into another type of menu item. For instance, meat trimmings left over from cutting steaks may be processed into sausages or hamburgers.

edible yield percentage Another term for yield percentage.

edible-portion (EP) cost Equal to the AP price per portion divided by its edible yield percentage.

Egg Products Inspection Act (EPIA) Applies to shell eggs that are removed from the shell and processed. Sets standards for sanitation and wholesomeness. Also mandates the pasteurization of egg products and requires egg production to be inspected by the USDA.

employee skill Workers' abilities to perform certain tasks.

ending inventory Amount of product on hand at the end of an accounting period.

endorsement Testimonial by an independent agency or person, expressing approval and satisfaction with a company's product or service.

end-user services Support functions provided to buyers by vendors. Includes everything except the sales effort, which is provided by a sales rep, such as a food broker.

environmentally safe packaging Packaging materials that do not harm the natural surroundings during their production, use, and disposal.

Environmental Protection Agency (EPA) A U.S. agency responsible for protecting human health and the environment by writing and enforcing regulations based on laws passed by Congress. Among its many responsibilities, this agency promotes the Energy Star Program, a voluntary program that fosters energy efficiency.

equal to or better Tells the vendor that the buyer will accept a substitute item if it is the same, or better, quality.

equal to the facing layer A receiving standard that requires all layers of a product packed in a case to look the same as the layer on top. You want all the layers to look just like the top (facing) one. You don't want the junk hidden underneath the facing layer.

equipment dealer Company that purchases equipment from a primary source and resells it to hospitality buyers.

equipment program Process whereby a purveyor allows you the free use of equipment if you purchase other products. For instance, if you purchase all your coffees and teas from a vendor, he or she may offer you the free use of the brewing and serving equipment. In some cases, there may be a nominal charge for the equipment; it's not always free.

equipment testing Evaluating equipment to determine if the item performs as expected.

escrow account Buyer funds held by an independent third party who releases them to the vendor once the transaction is completed satisfactorily. Commonly done when purchasing construction services.

ethical force The effects on businesses of fair and honest business practices and other relevant forms of competitive pressure.

ethics code A code of conduct designed to influence the behavior of employees. It typically sets out the procedures to be used in specific ethical situations, such as conflicts of interest or the acceptance of gifts.

ethylene gas Used to induce and hasten the ripening of fresh produce.

evaluating the part-time buyer Process of establishing performance objectives and appraising how well employees achieve them. In the case of part-time buyers, it is critical to establish guidelines that represent fairly the impact buying performance will have on the overall performance evaluation.

exact name Indication of a product or service's specific type, quality, and style.

excess capacity Refers to a situation where a company or a piece of equipment is producing at a lower scale of output than it has been designed for.

exchange bartering Another term for barter.

exclusive dealing Occurs when a salesperson allows a buyer to purchase the brands he or she carries, only if the buyer agrees to purchase no competing brands from other vendors. An illegal practice.

exclusive distributor A vendor who has the exclusive right to sell a particular product or product line. For instance, if you want Sara Lee brand pastries, there may be only one vendor in your area that sells it; this eliminates your ability to shop around for these items.

exclusive insurance agent Insurance salesperson who sells only one company's insurance policies.

exclusive selling See: Exclusive Distributor.

exclusive territory The geographical area in which an exclusive seller is allowed to operate as the sole vendor of certain brands of merchandise.

executive steward Oversees cleaning crews. Typically also has purchasing responsibilities for things such as soaps, chemicals, and other cleaning supplies. May also control the china, glass, flatware inventories, and single-use (paper, plastic, etc.) products.

expediting To move shipments through the distribution channel at an accelerated rate. Alternately, the process used in a kitchen (or bar) to coordinate the orders from food servers (or cocktail servers) to cooks (or bartenders) to ensure efficiency and timeliness.

expense item Relatively inexpensive nonfood item, such as glassware, the cost of which can be written off in the year in which it is incurred. Opposite of a capital item.

expiration date The date after which a product should not be sold because of an expected decline in quality or effectiveness. Another term for pull date.

extended warranty coverage Maintenance contract purchased to cover the cost of parts and service over a defined period of time.

e-commerce marketplace An online application allowing buyers to locate vendors, research products and services, solicit competitive bids, and place orders electronically.

e-commerce Refers to transactions done online.

e-procurement application Software that allows customers to select and purchase products online.

Fair Packaging and Labeling Act (FPLA) Requires consumer products' package labels to provide an accurate description of the amount of contents in the package. It is also designed to allow consumers to make value comparisons among competing brands. Sometimes referred to as the Hart Act.

Fair Trade Products produced by farmers who are compensated fairly for their work. They have the fair trade logo displayed on their packaging.

farmers' market Area where local farmers, growers, and other merchants come together to sell their own products directly to consumers.

farm-to-table The food on the table (served to the guest) comes directly from a specific farm.

favoring suppliers Giving special treatment or unfair advantages to a supplier and/or its representatives.

feathering Amount of fat streaks in an animal's ribs and inside flank muscles.

Federal Food, Drug, and Cosmetic Act (FFDCA) Provides the majority of food and drug regulation in the United States.

Federal Meat Inspection Act Establishes the ability of the federal government to inspect and label meats before and after slaughter.

Federal Trade Commission (FTC) Oversees and regulates advertising, deceptive promotions, monopolies, and unprofessional conduct in the marketplace.

FFE Acronym for furniture, fixtures, and equipment.

fictitious invoices Fraudulent bill sent to a company with the hope that the company will not check it closely and just pay it along with all the other bills it receives. May be part of a kickback scheme.

field inspector A person hired by a company to inspect products before they are shipped to the company. Typically done when purchasing large amounts of fresh produce directly from the farmer.

field run Refers to fresh produce items that have not been graded. They may be low-quality items intended to be used by food processors to make things such as juice, jam, jelly, and so forth.

fill rate Equal to the amount of items delivered divided by the amount of items ordered. For instance, if you ordered 10 items and the vendor delivered 9, the fill rate is 90 percent (9 divided by 10). A fill rate less than 100 percent indicates that the vendor is out of some items and has to back order you.

financial service Company that provides assistance with attaining, investing, storing, moving, or borrowing money or monetary equivalents.

fin fish A typical fish used in food service operations. In its whole form, this fish is ectothermic, has a streamlined body for rapid swimming, extracts oxygen from water using gills or uses an accessory breathing organ to breathe atmospheric oxygen, has two sets of paired fins, usually one or two (rarely three) dorsal fins, an anal fin, and a tail fin, has jaws, has skin that is usually covered with scales, and lays eggs.

finish Refers primarily to the fat cover on a carcass.

first-generation convenience food Value-added product that was one of the first convenience foods on the market. It has been available for many years. May be less expensive than its fresh counterpart. An example is frozen orange juice.

Fish and Game Office Local agency that certifies that fish and game products from other areas have not been purchased from unapproved sources and are acceptable to use and resell to customers.

fixed bid buying Shopping around and soliciting competitive bids for long-term contracts.

fixed-price contract Contract that does not allow price fluctuations.

flat Refers to one layer of a product. Term typically used in the fresh produce trade.

fleet management software Software that suppliers use to schedule vehicles and other equipment usage, required repair and maintenance work, and preventive maintenance activities.

Food and Drug Administration (FDA) Administers the Federal Food, Drug, and Cosmetic Act (FFDCA).

Food and Drug Administration (FDA) Office of Seafood Safety Agency that, among other things, will provide buyers with a list of approved interstate fish suppliers operating in their areas.

Food Quality Protection Act (FQPA) Provides a single safety standard for pesticide residuals in foods. It also changed the way the Environmental Protection Agency (EPA) regulates pesticides use in the United States.

Food Safety and Inspection Service (FSIS) Division of the U.S. Department of Agriculture (USDA). It oversees meat, poultry, and egg products inspection.

Foodservice Consultants Society International (FCSI) Professional association consisting primarily of kitchen designers and other related professions.

foodservice design consultant Person who provides advice about FFE purchases. May also plan the final layout and design of restaurant facilities.

forecasting An attempt to predict the future. Current and historical information is used to estimate what might happen over the near or long term. Referred to as sales forecasting when attempting to predict future sales.

formal issues system Process whereby all products a business uses are kept in a warehouse or storeroom overseen by a clerk or manager. Products can be obtained only by authorized persons who are required to present a properly completed stock requisition.

formal specification Another term for purchase specification.

fortified milk Milk to which vitamins, such as vitamin A and vitamin D, have been added.

forward buying When a buyer purchases a large amount of product (for example, a three-month supply) and takes delivery of the entire shipment.

franchise law Refers to the ability of a franchisor to require franchisees to adhere to certain standards of quality set by the franchisor.

franchises A business form where the owner (franchisor) allows others (franchisees) to use his or her operating procedures, name, and so forth, for a fee.

free on board (FOB) When buyers purchase merchandise, but have to arrange for their own delivery. The vendor will place the merchandise on the buyer's vehicle or a common carrier at no additional charge (i.e., "free on board"), but the buyer is then responsible for the merchandise and the cost of transportation from that point on.

free sample Part of the marketing strategy used by vendors to sell products. Buyers are allowed to test a product in their own facility without having to pay for it.

freezer burn The loss of moisture from a food product while it is held in frozen storage. Typically causes dry (i.e., "burned") spots on the product as well as an unpleasant odor.

free-range chicken Poultry that is not confined to a cage during its life cycle. Furthermore, it is not fed unnatural foods, nor is it injected with hormones or other chemicals.

freight-damaged discount Offered if you are willing to accept an item that was damaged in shipping. The damage usually does not inhibit the product's usefulness as the damage is typically cosmetic.

freight-damaged item A product that has been damaged somewhat during the shipping process.

freshness date Another term for pull date. The date beyond which a product (usually food) should not be used, or should not be sold.

fresh shell egg Product that is less than 30 days old.

full-line distributor A vendor that provides food products and nonfood supplies.

full-service dealer FFE vendor that typically carries a full line of inventory and is able to provide all end-user services.

futures contract Agreement to purchase or sell a commodity for delivery in the future.

gas-flushed pack A type of controlled atmosphere packaging (CAP).

generic brand The package label typically does not refer directly to the company that processed the item. Rather, the label generally highlights only the name of the item while downplaying other information. Its quality is very unpredictable. Typically, it is low-quality merchandise that is sold to economy-minded buyers.

genetically altered or modified food Food modified by bioengineering techniques. Typically done to enhance flavor, appearance, and/or uniformity of size and to increase shelf life.

glaze A thin coating of ice applied to frozen products, such as boneless, skinless chicken breasts. Done to provide protection from freezer burn.

Global Food Safety Initiative (GFSI) Launched in 2000, the GFSI seeks to ensure confidence in the delivery of safe food to consumers through continuous improvement of food safety management systems. GFSI provides a platform for collaboration between some of the world's leading food safety experts from all levels of food companies, international organizations, educators, and government.

going-out-of-business sale Held to dispose of all remaining inventory and in some cases, all the existing furniture, fixtures, and equipment (FFE). Everything is typically sold at heavily discounted prices.

goods received without invoice slip Created by the receiving agent to record a shipment when no invoice or delivery document accompanies the shipment. Without a record of shipments received, a hospitality operation wouldn't be able to calculate actual costs.

grading factors Characteristics of food or beverage products examined by grading inspectors. Used to judge and rank products.

grain-fed beef Beef from cattle that have been fed a grain-based diet, typically featuring corn.

grass-fed beef Beef from cattle that have a low percentage of body fat. Tends to be less flavorful than corn-fed beef.

green meat Product that has not had a chance to age. In some cases its use will result in an unacceptable finished product that cannot be served to guests.

gross weight Weight of product plus the tare weight.

groundskeeping service Vendor contracted to maintain all outside landscaped areas.

group purchasing organization (GPO) Another term for buying club.

grower Primary source providing fresh, raw foods.

guarantee May be expressed or implied. Assurance that a product or service will be provided. Alternately, assurance that a product or service will meet certain specifications. Alternately, assurance that a product or service will be acceptable for a specified period of time or amount of use. Alternately, assurance that parts and/or repairs needed during a specified time period will be paid for by the vendor.

Hazard Analysis Critical Control Point (HACCP) system Process used by food processors and others in the foodservice industry to ensure food safety. It identifies the areas at which foods are most susceptible to contamination and recommends procedures that can be used to prevent it from occurring.

health district Local regulator that is responsible for preventing food-borne illness and other related safety problems.

health district storage requirements Regulations established by a community's health department outlining the sanitation and food safety standards that must be maintained by foodservice operations.

heavy equipment dealer Specializes in handling large equipment installations. Carries inventory. Usually involved in the layout and design of new hospitality properties or major renovations.

heavy pack Packing product with very little added juice or water.

hedging Attempting to reduce or avoid the risk of fluctuating AP prices by taking a position in the commodity futures market.

heirloom plants Plants that are open-pollinated—meaning that unlike hybrids, seeds you collect from one year will produce plants with most of the characteristics of the parent plant. Most date from 1951, the year that the first hybrid seeds were developed, or earlier, and some varieties may be 100–150 years old.

holding court Refers to a buyer analyzing several competing products while the competing vendors are in attendance.

homogenization Process of breaking up fat globules in liquid milk in such a way that they remain suspended in the milk and do not separate out and float to the top of the milk container.

house account Term used by a vendor to identify a very loyal customer. A customer who continually buys from a vendor and is not interested in buying from competing vendors.

house brand Another term for well brand. Alternately, another term for proprietary brand.

house wine Refers to the "well brand" of wine used when customers ordering wine do not specify a particular brand name.

HRI Buyer's Guide An e-mail subscription service that notes current commodities prices being paid to wholesalers and purveyors by foodservice operations for eggs, poultry, meat, and seafood.

Hydroponic Method of growing plants in nutrient-rich water instead of chemically treated soil.

ice pack Foods packed in crushed ice. Intended to increase shelf life. A typical packing procedure used for things such as fresh chicken and fish.

ice spot A dry spot on a food product that has been previously frozen. An indication that an item that is thought to be fresh has actually been frozen, thawed, and passed off as fresh.

illegal rebate Another term for kickback.

imitation meat products Products that approximate the aesthetic qualities (primarily texture, flavor, and appearance) and/or chemical characteristics of specific types of meat. Also referred to as meat analogues, meat substitutes, mock meats, and faux meats.

importer–wholesaler Intermediary in the beverage alcohol distribution channel. Responsible for importing products into the United States, as well as into each state and local municipality. Also responsible for distribution to retail establishments, such as bars, restaurants, and liquor stores.

IMPS/NAMI number Another term for Institutional Meat Purchase Specification (IMPS) number.

impulse purchase An unplanned or otherwise spontaneous purchase.

incomplete shipments Deliveries that do not have all of the items ordered by the buyer. The missing items may be back ordered, or the supplier may have forgotten to include them with the shipments.

indirect control system Process of using overlapping computerized and/or noncomputerized receipts and other records to maintain tight control over all inventory items.

Individually quick frozen (IQF) Process whereby products are quick frozen and individually layered in the case. Typical packing procedure for things such as portion-cut boneless, skinless chicken breasts.

industry and government publications Materials printed and distributed by government agencies covering a variety of subjects useful to businesses and consumers. For example, some of these publications detail quality measures that can be used by buyers to help them prepare their specifications.

ineligible bidder Company that would like to bid for a buyer's business, but would not be allowed to bid because it does not meet certain qualifications set by the buyer. For instance, the company may not be large enough, it may not have sufficient financial strength, and so forth.

informal specification Less-precise product specification. Usually includes only information the vendor uses to describe the product.

ingredient room Area set aside in the main storeroom where an employee measures out all the ingredients needed for all the recipes to be prepared during the shift, and then issues them to the appropriate kitchen locations.

inspection procedures An organized examination or formal evaluation exercise. It involves the measurements, tests, and gauges applied to certain characteristics in regard to an object or activity. The results are usually compared to specified requirements and standards for determining whether the item or activity is in line with these targets.

installation costs Typical charges paid when making a major equipment purchase. Usually paid in addition to the AP price of the equipment, although a buyer's company may be able to provide these services personally for less.

Institute for Supply Management (ISM) Organization that offers relevant information, education, and training to supply management professionals.

instructions to bidders Required process vendors must follow when submitting a competitive bid. Typically also includes a description of how the winning bid will be determined and the qualifications vendors need to be allowed to bid.

insurance broker Salesperson authorized to represent several different insurance companies and sell their products. Usually selects appropriate insurance policies from different companies to provide all necessary coverage a client needs.

intangible force Factors that impact the distribution channels in ways that cannot be easily determined, nor can they be easily categorized.

integrated pest management (IPM) Program to systematically prevent pests from entering and surviving in a facility. It features the use of PCOs.

integrity testing Controversial method used to determine if a person is honest.

intended use Refers to the performance requirement of a product or service, which is noted on the specification. Considered to be the most important piece of information on a specification.

intermediary Another term for vendor.

Internal Revenue Service (IRS) Federal agency responsible for enforcing the U.S. tax code and for collecting taxes.

International Foodservice Manufacturers Association (IFMA) Organization whose primary membership is employed in the foodservice equipment trade. Provides relevant information and professional development opportunities to its members. Also helps ensure that their interests are represented in the marketplace.

Interstate Certified Shellfish Shippers List Agency within the Food and Drug Administration (FDA) that approves the areas where shellfish are grown and harvested. When a buyer purchases these shellfish, the container will include a tag (that must be kept on hand for at least 90 days) that shows the number of the bed of water where the products were grown and harvested.

Interstate Shellfish Sanitation Conference Voluntary program, involving federal and state agencies, that supervises the beds of water used to grow and harvest shellfish.

introductory offer A price discount offered by suppliers to buyers who purchase an item that is newly available in the marketplace. The discount may be in the form of a cash rebate or it might include a free item for every one the buyer purchases at the regular AP price.

inventory control and security Procedures used by hospitality operators to ensure that the quality and cost of all items in storage areas are maintained according to company standards. Usually involves environmental controls such as proper temperature, humidity, and ventilation as well as the use of security methods such as web cams, physical barriers, and strict accounting procedures.

inventory padding Reporting a false inventory amount by indicating that there is more inventory on hand. A fraud that is usually committed to make the actual cost of food or beverage sold appear to be less than it is.

inventory shrinkage and skimming Other terms for pilferage.

inventory shrinkage The inappropriate loss or removal of supplies.

inventory substitution Occurs when someone takes a product and leaves behind a different one. Typically done by persons who steal a high-quality item and substitute a low-quality one in its place.

inventory turnover Equal to: (actual cost of products used, or sold, divided by the average inventory value kept at the hospitality operation).

inventory usage rates When referring to food and beverages, it is the rate at which the products are produced and served to customers. When referring to nonfood and nonbeverage supplies, it is the rate at which the products have been exhausted and are no longer available.

inventory "book" value The value of inventory that is supposed to be in storage, as recorded on inventory records, such as a bin card. The value is based primarily on perpetual inventory calculations.

invoice A bill from a vendor for goods or services, often presented as the goods are delivered or after the services are performed.

invoice receiving Common type of receiving procedure. Involves comparing the invoice with the order record, and then proceeding to check quality, quantity, and AP prices of the items delivered.

invoice scams Using fraudulent invoices to steal from a company.

invoices on account Involves reconciling all invoices and credit slips received during the billing period with the end-of-period statement sent by the vendor. If everything is correct, the company pays the total amount listed on the end-of-period statement, or makes the minimum payment and lets the balance ride until the next period.

invoice stamp Information placed on the receiving agent's copy of the invoice that indicates all appropriate checks were made and that the shipment was accepted.

in-process inventory Products located at employee workstations; most or all will be used during the shift.

irradiation Controversial product preservation procedure that can reduce or eliminate harmful bacteria. It is used to extend a product's shelf life.

issuing procedure There are two types: formal and informal. The formal procedure requires a product user, such as a chef, to requisition products from a central warehouse or storage facility. The chef signs for the items and is responsible for them. An informal procedure allows the product user to request from the manager what is needed, with the manager getting the products and handling the paperwork later on. Another informal process allows any product user to enter the warehouse or storage facility and take what's needed for production and/or service.

itemized bill Invoice that indicates each item's AP price and extended price, as well as all other costs, such as delivery charges, associated with the purchase.

job description A list of duties the job entails that the employee must perform. May also include additional information, such as the job's direct supervisor, the objective(s) of the job, and guidelines that must be followed when performing the job functions.

job specification List of qualities, such as education, technical skill, and work experience, a person should possess to qualify for a particular job.

jug wine Refers to a product typically served as the house wine. Usually packed in large containers, such as bag-in-the-box containers.

Julian date The interval of time in days and fractions of a day since January 1, 4713 BC Greenwich noon. The system was introduced by astronomers to provide a single system of dates that could be used when working with different calendars and to unify different historical chronologies.

just-in-time (JIT) inventory management System that attempts to ensure that the moment the inventory level of a particular product reaches zero, a shipment of that item arrives at your back door. The main objective is to reduce carrying charges to their lowest possible level.

kickback An illegal gift given by a vendor or sales rep to someone if he or she will agree to help defraud the hospitality operation.

Kosher chicken Chicken that fulfills the requirements of Jewish dietary law.

labor availability The amount of labor that exists in the hospitality operation's location. Sometimes referred to as the labor pool.

lactose Sugar that is found most notably in milk. It makes up around 2 to 8 percent of milk (by weight).

lactose-free milk Milk that has the lactase enzyme added to break down the lactose in it.

landed cost The cost used by the vendor in a cost-plus buying arrangement.

large egg Common fresh shell egg size purchased and used by the hospitality industry. It weighs approximately 2 ounces. The typical standard recipe requiring fresh shell eggs assumes the cook will use this size.

late deliveries Shipments received after the time they were expected.

laundry and linen supply service Outside service that provides cleaning, pressing, and fabric repair. Delivers fabrics to the hospitality operation. May lease its fabrics to the hospitality operation or may maintain those owned by the hospitality operation.

layered Products packed between sheets of paper, plastic, or cardboard. Intended to protect products so that they do not break or otherwise lose quality.

layout pack Products are packed in layers that can be lifted from the case and placed in other containers for storage or production. For example, layout sliced bacon may be layered on baking sheets that can be placed on sheet pans and cooked off in the oven.

lead time Period of time between when you place an order with a vendor and when you receive it.

leasing company Firm that purchases FFE and leases them to other companies. The typical rental plan is a rent-to-own arrangement. May be a more expensive form of financing a FFE purchase than borrowing the money and buying the items outright.

legal force Legislative influence on the distribution channels establishing certain rules of conduct. Enforced by local, state, and/or federal governments.

length of service Amount of time equipment, tools, and utensils can be used before they need to be replaced. Alternately, the amount of time a person has worked for an employer.

Levinson approach Method of determining the appropriate order sizes. Takes into account forecasted sales, portion sizes, and yield percentages when calculating the amount of products to order.

Levinson approach to ordering Method of determining the appropriate order sizes. Takes into account forecasted sales, portion sizes, and yield percentages when calculating the amount of products to order.

license state A state that grants licenses to importer–wholesalers, distributors, and retailers, who then handle the distribution and sale of beverage alcohol.

lien-sale contract Allows the service provider, usually some type of construction, decorating, or designer service, to attach a lien to the entire property if he or she is not paid for the work performed.

Lifetime cost A term typically used when analyzing an equipment purchase. Along with the AP price of the item, the buyer might also examine the trade-in value of the old equipment; the cost of the energy needed to operate the new equipment; extra charges for delivery, setup, and training; how much it can sell the new equipment for when it is time to replace it; and so forth.

limiting rule Federal regulation that stipulates if a product to be graded scores very low on one grading factor, it cannot receive a high grade regardless of its total score for all grading factors.

line-item purchasing A practice of buying from vendors only the individual items on a competitive bid sheet that are priced lower than those submitted by competing vendors. For instance, if a purveyor bids on 10 items, but is the lowest bidder on only 1 of them, the buyer will buy only the 1 item. Sometimes referred to as cherry picking. The opposite of bottom-line, firm-price purchasing.

liquidation Selling off business assets to satisfy creditors. May be done via auction.

liquor distributor Another term for vendor. Purchases beverage alcohol from primary sources or liquor retailers.

liquor license Granted by a government agency. Gives the licensee the authority to purchase and sell beverage alcohols.

live-in-shell Refers to shellfish that are still alive when delivered.

localvore Person who is dedicated to eating food grown and produced locally or grown and produced personally; localvores typically are not motivated strictly by a profit motive.

logistics and mapping software Software used by vendors to outline the routing sequences its delivery drivers must follow when delivering shipments. Intended to increase delivery efficiency.

logistics management The part of the supply chain management that plans, implements, and controls the efficient, effective flow and storage of goods, services, and related information between point of origin and the point of consumption in order to meet customer requirements.

long-term contract Agreement that typically lasts at least one year.

loss leader Product sold at a much lower profit margin to attract customers who will purchase it as well as other more profitable items.

lot number An indication that packaged goods originated from a particular group, or lot. Important if, for example, you are purchasing canned goods; products coming from the same batch will have similar culinary quality whereas those from different lots may be slightly different.

lowball bid A competitive bid that is artificially low. Vendors may lowball a buyer hoping to get their foot in the door; later on they will try to hike the AP price substantially.

lug Container that has two layers of product. Term typically used in the fresh produce trade.

mailed deliveries Shipment that is delivered by the U.S. Postal Service, FedEx, DHL, UPS, or other similar delivery services.

maintenance contract Type of extended warranty coverage. For a fee, usually paid monthly, the contractor provides routine maintenance as well as emergency service. Typically purchased when the initial warranty period is set to expire.

maintenance service Outside contractor who provides repair and maintenance service. May involve the purchase of a maintenance contract, or the service may be purchased only when needed.

make-goods Free advertising time or space granted to buyers when the actual intended audience size is smaller than the guaranteed one.

make-or-buy analysis A cost/benefit analysis whereby the buyer tries to determine if, for example, it is more economical to purchase raw foods and make a finished product in-house, or whether it may be less expensive to purchase a convenience, value-added food. The buyer usually considers the cost of food, labor, overhead, labor skill available, and so forth when making the decision.

management information system (MIS) Method of organizing, analyzing, and reporting information to manage a business effectively. It typically involves the use of computerized record keeping.

managing storage facilities Procedures used to ensure stored merchandise is managed effectively and that losses due to spoilage, theft, and pilferage are minimized.

manufacturer's agent Similar to a manufacturer's representative, but not the same. Main difference is that the agent typically works for only one primary source, whereas the manufacturer's representative typically works for several.

manufacturer's representative Similar to a broker, but not the same; main difference is that the rep will typically provide end-user services, whereas the broker will not. Also similar to a manufacturer's agent, but not the same; main difference is that the agent typically works for only one primary source, whereas the manufacturer's representative typically works for several.

manufacturing grade A very low grade given to food products that are not intended to be sold as fresh items, but are meant to be used by processors to produce a finished item. For example, low-grade beef usually is purchased by a processor who makes things such as canned chili or canned beef stew.

marinade pack A packing medium intended to impart flavor, and sometimes tenderness, to foods. For instance, if you feature spicy wings on your menu, you may decide to purchase fresh wings marinated in a special sauce. When they arrive at your restaurant they are ready-to-cook; you do not need to marinate them yourself.

Marine Mammal Protection Act Law stating that tuna harvested in a way that endangers dolphins cannot be sold in the United States.

market research Organized effort to gather information about customers. Typically used by businesses to discover what people want, need, or believe.

materials budget Involves setting a dollar limit of how much a buyer is able to purchase over a particular time period. A method used to control and evaluate a buyer's performance.

maturity class Used to categorize an animal's age at time of slaughter. Important grading and selection factor for beef.

measures of quality Various rating systems that can be used to determine the appropriate product quality needed to fulfill an intended use. For instance, federal government grades and brand names can be used to denote the quality desired on a specification.

Meat Inspection Act Along with other legislation, grants the U.S. Department of Agriculture (USDA) inspection powers throughout the food distribution channels.

meat tag Used to control the usage of expensive items, such as meat, fish, and poultry. It contains two duplicate parts. One part is attached to the item when it is received and placed into storage, the other one goes to the controller's office. When an item is taken from storage and issued to production, the part on the item is removed and sent to the controller, who matches it with the other part. The item is then removed from the inventory file. At that point, the storage supervisor (storeroom manager) is no longer responsible for the item, the chef is.

mechanical tenderization A physical tenderization technique. Usually takes the form of grinding, chopping, cubing, flaking, or needling. May change the shape of the product being tenderized.

media-buying service A type of advertising agency that helps clients develop their overall advertising strategies and selects the various media to use. Works for commissions.

menu price calculation The food cost of a menu item divided by its food cost percentage. Alternately, the beverage cost of a menu item divided by its beverage cost percentage.

merchant fee Fee suppliers pay for accepting credit card payments instead of cash or check. The fee is usually some percentage of the amount charged by the buyer.

merits Refers to the way advertising is paid for. The price a buyer pays is directly related to the amount of sales revenue generated by the advertising.

middleman An antiquated term for vendor.

middleman or intermediary Other terms for vendor.

minimum order requirement The least amount of an item a buyer needs to purchase before a vendor will agree to sell it. Alternately, the least amount a buyer needs to purchase before he or she can qualify for free delivery.

minimum weight per case Important selection factor when purchasing products that may vary in weight from one vendor to another, or because of other factors, such as seasonal variations. Helps ensure that the buyer receives a predictable amount of product.

minimum-order requirement The least amount of an item a buyer needs to purchase before a vendor will agree to sell it. Alternately, the least amount a buyer needs to purchase before he or she can qualify for free delivery.

mixed-case A case that contains more than one type of item. Usually found in the beverage alcohol trade, where the vendor will allow the buyer to purchase a case of 12 bottles, but each bottle may be a different product. Vendors may allow this for products you purchase that you don't sell very quickly, such as specialty bourbons. Vendors who sell mixed cases are usually willing to charge the appropriate case price for each item.

modified-atmosphere packaging (MAP) Another term for controlled atmosphere packaging (CAP).

mollusk Shellfish with a hard shell (e.g., oysters).

monopolistic competition Refers to a competitive environment where each competitor is affected by supply-and-demand conditions because their businesses are very similar. However, each competitor is able to differentiate its products and/or services enough to establish a competitive advantage. Typical economic conditions faced by vendors and hospitality businesses.

moonlighter An individual who arranges a second job that is outside the course and scope of his or her first job. Sometimes a person may "moonlight" only with the written approval of his or her primary employer.

Mothers Against Drunk Driving (MADD) A nonprofit organization that seeks to stop drunk driving, support those affected by drunk driving, prevent underage drinking, and encourage legislation that establishes stricter alcohol policies.

move list A list of products that need to be sold ASAP. For instance, they may be on the verge of spoilage, or they might be discontinued items. If vendors have items on a move list they may call you to see if you're interested in any of them. Usually the AP prices of these items are deeply discounted.

muzz-go list Another term for move list.

National Cattlemen's Beef Association (NCBA) Trade organization representing the beef industry. Its primary purpose is to promote the sale and purchase of beef. It also is an information resource for members of the beef channel of distribution.

national distribution Clause in a national contract stipulating that all restaurants in the chain will be able to rely on getting the same types of products delivered to their back doors.

National Fire Protection Association (NFPA) Provides fire safety certification for FFE items that meet its standards.

National Livestock and Meat Board Group made up of representatives from all areas of the meat industry. Its primary objective is the promotion of all red meats (beef, lamb, and pork) through research, education, and information sharing.

National Oceanic and Atmospheric Administration (NOAA) Agency of the U.S. Department of Commerce (USDC) that, for a fee, will provide continuous inspection of a fish processor's plant.

National Restaurant Association (NRA) Trade organization that represents, educates, and promotes the U.S. foodservice industry and the people working in it.

National Restaurant Association Educational Foundation (NRAEF) Agency of the National Restaurant Association (NRA) that provides educational resources, materials, and programs that address recruitment, development, and retention of the industry's workforce. It is dedicated to fulfilling the NRA's educational mission.

National Sanitation Foundation (NSF) International Provides sanitation certification for FFE items that meet its standards.

natural poultry Poultry that must have no preservatives, have no artificial ingredients, and be minimally processed.

needling A tenderization procedure. Submitting a large cut of meat (or fish) to a machine with several tiny needles. The needles penetrate the item, tenderizing it without altering its shape. The needle marks are usually invisible once the product has been cooked.

negative selling Occurs when a vendor places the buyer in a position where the buyer encourages the vendor to take the buyer's order (and money). Usually done by convincing the buyer that he or she must use that particular vendor and that there is no substitute vendor capable of handling the order. More likely to occur when purchasing consulting services than when purchasing any other type of product or service.

negotiations To come to terms or to reach an agreement through discussion and a willingness to compromise.

net present value Concept that takes into account the time value of money. It is the difference between the present (current) value of any projected savings because of the investment in, for example, a piece of energy-saving equipment and the present (current) value of the price of the equipment. Ideally, the present value of the savings should exceed the present value of the price of the equipment.

net weight Gross weight less the tare weight.

new pack time Time of the year when products intended for sale the following year (or other period of time) are packed. For instance, canned fruits and vegetables are usually processed and packed right after harvest. Vendors then work off of this inventory until the next new pack time rolls around.

night drop When the delivery driver has a key to the facility, enters it when closed for business, leaves the shipment, locks up, and goes. The shipment is put away the next morning. Intended to reduce costs due to the efficiency of deliveries at off-hours (e.g., late-night or early-morning) and not having to pay a receiving agent.

nitrogen flush A gas-flushed pack. Using nitrogen to remove air, thereby removing all oxygen from the package. Done to enhance shelf life.

noncommercial hospitality operations Another term for on-site or military hospitality operation.

North American Association of Food Equipment Manufacturers (NAFEM) Trade organization representing companies in Canada, the United States, and Mexico that manufacture commercial foodservice equipment and supplies.

North American Meat Institute (NAMI) Trade organization representing meat processing companies and associates who share a continuing commitment to provide their customers with safe, reliable, and consistent meat, poultry, seafood, game, and other related products.

North American Meat Processors Association (NAMP) Trade organization representing meat-processing companies and associates who share a continuing commitment to provide their customers with safe, reliable, and consistent meat, poultry, seafood, game, and other related products.

number of pieces per bird Selection factor that may be important when purchasing poultry. Refers directly to the number of parts to be cut from a bird carcass, and indirectly to the style of cut that will be used.

Nutrition Labeling and Education Act Legislation that mandates nutritional and other related information to be listed on product package labels.

odd-hour delivery Shipment delivered at times of the day or week when a receiving agent is not usually scheduled to work. Buyers who agree to these types of deliveries may receive a discount.

odd-hours receiving Receiving activities that are performed when examining an odd-hours delivery.

one-stop shopping Buying everything you need from one vendor. Alternately, buying everything you need from the fewest possible purveyors.

online auction site Electronic auction, allowing prospective buyers to bid on products without being physically present. Usually all details are handled online.

online ordering system Ordering products from vendors over the Internet or directly from a purveyor using his or her proprietary software.

on-the-job training (OJT) Typical method used to teach job skills to new and continuing employees. Involves learning the skills while performing the duties in real time, usually under the direction and supervision of a trainer.

open storeroom An unlocked storage facility that can be accessed by employees as needed. Usually contains the less-expensive foods, beverages, and nonfood supplies.

open-market buying or market quote buying Other terms for call sheet buying.

operating costs Day-to-day expenses involved in running a business. Alternately, the costs of using a piece of equipment.

operating savings Refers to the reduction in costs experienced by adopting a new way of doing things, for example, purchasing a more expensive, but efficient, piece of equipment.

operating supplies Another term for expense items or nonfood expense items.

operational performance Refers to a manager's (such as a buyer's) ability to run his or her department effectively and efficiently, while maintaining company standards. Important factor considered when preparing a manager's annual job evaluation.

opportunity buy A purchase intended to save a great deal of money. The products are price discounted. A quantity discount is an example of an opportunity buy.

opportunity cost By choosing to do something, you give up the option of doing something else. For instance, if you pay a bill too early you lose the option of investing the money and earning some interest income. The loss of income in this case is considered to be the opportunity cost.

optimal inventory level The amount of inventory that will adequately serve a hospitality operation's needs without having to incur the costs associated with excess inventory.

optimal inventory management Procedures used to maintain efficiently the quality and security of merchandise.

ordering cost The amount of money spent to make an order, receive it, and store it. Includes things such as labor needed to perform the work and administrative costs such as faxing, photocopying, and cell phone charges.

ordering procedure Standardized process used by the buyer to ensure that the correct amounts of needed products are ordered at the appropriate time.

order modifier Point-of-sale (POS) software prompt that forces the server to answer questions about a guest's order. For instance, if the server enters one steak into the system, the computer will ask, "What temperature?" The server will then answer the question to complete the order before sending it to the kitchen.

organic and natural standards Organic products must meet specific standards established by the USDA, whereas the term natural is generally used for items that may not meet all standards or have not been voluntarily inspected by the USDA.

organic dairy products Products produced from milk obtained from cows that were: fed organic feed raised on land certified as meeting national organic growing standards; raised in conditions that limit stress and promote health; cared for as individuals by dairy professionals who value animal health; and not given routine treatments of antibiotics or growth hormones.

organic food Natural food grown, produced, packaged, and delivered without the use of synthetic chemicals and fertilizers. Primary sources and distributors must adhere to the organic guidelines and standards published by the USDA.

organic poultry Poultry that meets standards set forth by the USDA, which requires that the poultry must be raised under organic management no later than the second day of life.

organizing Process of arranging a company's workforce to achieve its overall business objectives.

outsourcing Identifying work that is not central to your hospitality company's primary mission and hiring an outside service to do it for you instead of doing it yourself. Things such as pest control and gardening services are usually outsourced.

overrun The amount of air whipped into a frozen product.

P. L.O.T. Acronym for potatoes, lettuce, onions, and tomatoes. These four vegetables are an average of 40 percent of all fresh produce purchases.

packaging procedure Way in which items are packed in a larger container capable of protecting the items while they are in-transit and storage.

packaging Process of enclosing or protecting products for distribution, storage, sale, and use. Alternately, the process of design, evaluation, and production of packages.

Packed Under Federal Inspection (PUFI) Seal placed on the product labels of fish items that have been produced and packed under continuous government inspection by the U.S. Department of Commerce (USDC).

packed under continuous government inspection Selection factor some buyers may specify when purchasing food products (such as fresh produce and fish) that are not legally required to be produced under continuous government inspection.

packers' brand names Very specific indication of product quality. More precise than a brand name. A packer's personal grading system. Usually intended to take the place of federal government grades.

packers' grades Another term for packers' brand names.

packing medium The type of liquid used to pack foods. Especially relevant when purchasing canned goods.

packing slip Typically accompanies a shipment delivered by a common carrier.

paid-outs A method that is fairly popular with small hospitality operators. That is, assuming that everything is acceptable when the delivery is received, the receiver reaches into the cash register and pulls out the appropriate amount of cash to pay the delivery driver. Instead of pulling out cash, the receiver could pull out a preprepared check and give it to the delivery driver. Either way, the emphasis is on paying COD.

panic buying Occurs when a buyer is in a pinch and will pay any price to get the product immediately.

par stock approach Method used to determine the appropriate amount to order. Involves setting par stocks for all items and subtracting the amount of each item on hand to calculate the order sizes.

par stock The maximum amount of a product you want to have on hand. When reordering the product you want to buy just enough to bring you up to par.

partial limiting rule Grants the federal grader discretion to invoke a limiting rule or to ignore it.

pasteurization Heating foods to the point where it kills most bacteria and harmful enzymes. (Raw milk is milk that has not been pasteurized.)

Pasteurized Milk Ordinance (PMO) Another term for U.S. Public Health Service's Milk Ordinance and Code.

patent A set of exclusive rights granted by a government to an inventor for a limited time period in exchange for a public disclosure of the invention.

payback period Refers to the amount of time it takes to recoup an initial investment. For instance, if a buyer purchases a new refrigerator for $5,000 and it reduces energy costs $1,000 per year, it will take 5 years to get back the initial investment in the refrigerator.

payment terms Another name for credit terms.

payroll service company Company that provides payroll processing and related activities for businesses that do not want to do this type of work themselves, preferring to outsource it to a firm that specializes in completing the tedious tasks associated with the payroll administrative function. This type of service is very popular with small hospitality operations.

perceived value equation Perceived value of a product is equal to: (perceived quality + the perceived supplier services) divided by its perceived edible (i.e., usable or servable) cost.

Perishable Agricultural Commodities Act (PACA) Legislation prohibiting unfair and fraudulent practices in the sale of fresh and frozen produce.

perpetual inventory Keeping a running balance of an inventory item so that you always know what you have on hand. When a shipment is received you add to the balance, and every time you use some of it you deduct that amount. Similar to keeping an up-to-date cash balance in your personal checkbook.

personalized packaging Unique packaging produced according to the buyer's specific requirements. Normally includes the buyer's company logo and/or other proprietary marks.

personal purchase Another term for steward sale.

pest control operator (PCO) Company licensed to handle and apply pesticides that are not available to the general public.

physical barrier Device, such as a lock, used to control access to a facility or storage area.

physical inventory An actual counting and valuing of all products kept in your hospitality operation.

pick-up memo Gives the delivery driver permission to pick up something from you. Typically used when you want to return a product to the vendor and you arrange to have it picked up when the driver makes the next regularly scheduled delivery of things you purchased. May also be used when a driver is delivering a substitute piece of equipment (such as a coffee urn) and needs to pick up the one you have so that it can be taken back to the shop and repaired.

pilferage Refers to minor theft. For instance, employees snatching a drink while on-the-clock, or guests swiping a wine glass.

planning Process of developing business goals and objectives, along with actions and systems needed to achieve them.

plant visit Refers to a buyer making a personal visit to a vendor's facilities to evaluate its product line and its production and distribution systems.

point-of-sale (POS) system Computerized device used to record sales revenue and maintain a considerable amount of management information, such as number of guests served, server productivity statistics, amount of cash collected, number of each menu item sold, and so forth.

point of origin Refers to the part of the world where a product originates. Important selection factor for some food items, as the point of origin can have a significant impact on their culinary quality.

political force Refers to factors that impact the distribution channels in ways that are directly related to the amount of influence channel members have on one another.

polychlorinated biphenyls (PCBs) Any of a family of toxic chemicals containing chlorine and benzene. PCBs have been found to cause some skin cancers and can become concentrated in animal flesh.

popularity index A percentage calculated by dividing the number sold of that particular menu item by the total number of all menu items sold.

portability Refers to the ability of an item to be easily and inexpensively moved to, and operated in, various locations. Important selection factor for FFE.

portal Web access point. Presents a starting point and access to multiple sources of similar online information.

portion divider (PD) Equal to an item's (portion factor (PF) multiplied by its edible yield percentage).

portion factor (PF) Equal to (16 ounces divided by the number of ounces needed for one serving). Alternately, equal to (1,000 milliliters divided by the number of milliliters needed for one serving). Alternately, equal to (1,000 grams divided by the number of grams needed for one serving).

portion-cut meat Equal to one serving. Typically refers to precut steaks and chops that are all the same weight.

Posilac A supplement of the naturally occurring cow hormone BST, that when administered to cows allows them to produce more milk.

postmix Refers to a nonalcoholic beverage concentrate, such as frozen juice concentrate or soda pop syrup, that must be reconstituted just before serving it to customers.

post-off Term used for a discount offered by a beverage alcohols vendor.

potentially hazardous food Food, especially protein-based food (such as meat, fish, and poultry), that can cause food-borne illness if not handled properly.

pouch packaging Another term for aseptic packaging.

poultry A term applied to all domesticated birds used for food.

Poultry Products Inspection Act Legislation mandating federal government inspection of poultry products sold interstate.

pouring cost The cost of beverage alcohol sold.

precosting Calculating the costs of all ingredients used in a standard recipe to determine the cost for one serving.

precut fresh produce Refers to fresh produce that has been chopped or otherwise cut, and packaged in cello wrap or other similar type of packaging material.

predatory pricing Company pricing its products unreasonably low in an attempt to drive all other competitors out of business. An illegal practice.

premium well brand A well brand that is higher quality than the typical well brand poured by most bars.

premix Refers to a ready-to-serve nonalcoholic beverage, such as a 12-ounce can of Coke.

preservation and/or processing method Preservation methods are used to extend the shelf life of a food or beverage product. Processing methods are used to enhance the product's taste and other culinary characteristics.

preservation A procedure, such as refrigeration, freezing, canning, drying, or chemical additives, used to maintain a product's shelf life and quality and, in some cases, impart additional flavorings.

preservatives See additives.

prewashed Produce that has been washed or rinsed with water during processing.

pre-employment testing Another term for pre-employment screening.

pre-employment screening Initial evaluation of job applicants to determine which one(s) should advance to the next step of the recruiting and hiring process. Alternately, determining which job applicants should be granted a job interview.

price club Another term for buying club.

price control Refers to government agencies dictating the minimum price that must be charged for a product. This type of control is fairly common in the dairy and beverage alcohol distribution channels.

price extension The as-purchased [AP] price per unit of that product times the number of units purchased.

price limits Guideline that sets the maximum AP prices a buyer is allowed to pay for products or services unless given permission to do so by a supervisor.

price maintenance Another term for price control.

primary source A supplier at the beginning of a product's channel of distribution. For instance, a farmer is a primary source for fresh produce items. This supplier typically sells items to an intermediary that resells them to hospitality operations.

prime-vendor account A consistent and significantly large account a buyer has with a vendor that, because of its size and the loyalty of the buyer, may be eligible for discounts and/or other special privileges.

problems of the buyer Challenges buyers must overcome to perform their jobs effectively and efficiently.

processed eggs Eggs that have been removed from their shells for processing at facilities called "breaker plants."

processed fish Fish that are marketed in many forms, except the whole form.

processing Producing a finished product from raw materials. Typically involves the production of convenience foods by a food processor.

processor or fabricator Company that takes raw foods and assembles them into a new product.

procurement An orderly, systematic exchange between a seller and a buyer. The process of obtaining goods and services, including all activities associated with determining the types of products needed, making purchases, receiving and storing shipments, and administering purchase contracts.

procurement performance Refers to the buyer's ability to accomplish the purchasing objectives set by management. Important factor considered when preparing a buyer's annual job evaluation.

Produce Marketing Association (PMA) Trade association representing members who market fresh fruits, vegetables, and related products worldwide. Its members are involved in the production, distribution, retail, and foodservice sectors of the industry.

product analysis Evaluating various products to determine which one represents the best value. Alternately, another term for critical-item inventory analysis.

product compatibility The extent to which a product is able to interact well with other products. A typical example would be purchasing a new piece of equipment because it would fit nicely with the current equipment.

product cost percentage Equal to: [(cost of a product divided by its selling price) multiplied by 100]. A typical example would be the food cost percentage.

product effectiveness The extent to which a product lives up to its vendor's claims. A typical example would be the ability of an all-purpose cleaner to clean satisfactorily any type of surface.

product form Refers to the degree of processing, or lack thereof, a product has when you purchase it. For instance, a buyer can purchase whole chickens or selected chicken parts. The parts typically would cost more than the whole birds.

product identification Another term for product specification.

product preservation Refers to production, storage, and/or delivery procedures a vendor uses to ensure consistent and reliable product quality. Alternately, process used to increase an item's shelf life.

product safety Refers to the level of risk incurred when using some products, such as cleaning solutions.

product size Refers to the buyer's specified weight, or volume, of a particular item he or she wants to purchase. Examples would be a 10-ounce steak or a 4-ounce hamburger.

product specification Same as a purchase specification but does not contain any information about supplier services the buyer wants.

product status Indicates whether a product is available from the vendor or if it is on backorder.

product yield The same as edible yield.

professional employer organization (PEO) Firm that, for a fee, manages the human resources function for client companies. In addition, these types of firms typically join with client companies to become a co-employer. In effect, the client's employees become the employees of the PEO. This allows small clients, such as the typical hospitality operation, to enjoy relief from HR administrative tasks, improved employee benefits, increased employee productivity, and enhanced liability management services.

profit markup The difference between the vendor's cost of a product and its sales price. Alternately, the difference between the EP cost of a menu item and its menu price.

promotional discount Price discount awarded to the buyer if he or she allows the vendor to promote the product in the hospitality operation, or if the hospitality operation agrees to personally help promote the sale of the product to its customers.

proof Measure of the amount of alcohol in a beverage. Equal to twice the percentage of alcohol in a beverage. For example, if a beverage is 50 percent alcohol, its proof is 100.

pull date Date beyond which a product (usually food) should not be used, or should not be sold.

pull strategy Refers to vendors trying to influence their buyers' customers to demand the vendors' products in their favorite restaurants or hotels. The buyers, then, will have to purchase these products to satisfy their guests.

pulp temperature Internal temperature of precut, convenience fresh produce products, such as chopped salad greens.

purchase order (PO) A request that the vendor deliver what you want, ideally at the time you want it, at an agreed-upon AP price and credit terms. May include other conditions, such as minimum order amount, cost of delivery (if any), and so forth.

purchase order draft A purchase order that includes an attached check to cover the price of the goods and/or services. A form of prepaid order.

purchase requisition Lists the products or services needed by someone in the hospitality operation. It is given to the buyer, who then goes into the marketplace to find the best deals. This requisition is typically used for things that the buyer doesn't purchase on a regular basis.

purchase specification A concise description of the quality, size, weight, count, and other quality factors desired for a particular item. Usually also includes some description of the desired supplier services a buyer wants.

purchasing activities Tasks buyers must perform in order to obtain the right products and services, at the right price and time, from the right vendors.

purchasing Paying for a product or service.

Pure Food Act Along with other legislation, grants the U.S. Department of Agriculture (USDA) inspection powers throughout the food distribution channels.

push strategy Refers to vendors who will do whatever is necessary, and legal, to entice buyers to purchase their products, usually by providing discounts and/or very generous supplier services.

quality assurance Another term for quality control.

quality control Systems and procedures used by managers to ensure that the actual quality of finished items is consistent with the expected quality.

quality standard The type of quality you consistently use and that the hospitality operation is known for. Buyers typically communicate this standard to vendors by specifying brand names and government grades.

quantity discount A price reduction for buying a large amount of one specific type of merchandise.

quantity limits provision Part of the Robinson-Patman Act. Stipulates that the amount of product that needs to be purchased to qualify for a quantity discount must be reasonable, and not so high that only one or two favored buyers have the chance to reach it.

quick response (QR) code A type of 2-D bar code used to provide easy access to information through a smart device. The device's owner points it at a QR code and opens a barcode reader app, which works in conjunction with the device's camera. The reader interprets the code, which typically contains a call to action such as an invitation to download a mobile application, a link to view a video, or an SMS message inviting the viewer to respond to a poll.

ratite A family of flightless birds with small wings and flat breastbones. Ostrich and emu are the two most common types sold in the United States. The meat tastes like beef and has less calories and fat than beef, chicken, or turkey.

ready-to-serve product Convenience food that can be served right out of the container, with no additional preparation other than perhaps thawing and/or reheating.

real estate investment trust (REIT) A legal business entity that buys, sells, and manages commercial and residential properties.

rebate Another term for cash rebate.

receiving objectives Ensuring that the delivered items meet the qualities, AP prices, support functions, and quantities ordered by the buyer, and that they are delivered at the correct time.

receiving Process of examining shipments to determine if they should be accepted or refused.

receiving sheet A running account of deliveries maintained by the receiving agent.

reciprocal buying "You buy from me, I'll buy from you."

reciprocity In the world of purchasing, it means, "You buy from me, and I'll buy from you."

recombinant bovine growth hormone (rBGH or rBST) Chemical injected into lactating cows to increase their milk production.

recycling Refers to taking a used product and/or its parts and reusing them after they have undergone a reconditioning process. Alternately, taking a used product and/or its parts and creating something new and different that can be used for another purpose.

reduced oxygen packaging (ROP) Another term for controlled atmosphere packaging (CAP).

reference check Confirming the veracity of information and personal accomplishments provided by vendors and job candidates.

referral group A type of co-op where independent operators join together to send business to one another. For instance, Best Western is a referral group that has a central reservations system available to each member. In addition, these groups typically provide some purchasing advantages, as well as other types of support, to its members.

relationship marketing Procedure that does not view marketing as selling products one at a time, that is, it does not view marketing as a series of individual transactions. Instead, it refers to the need for vendors and customers to form personal alliances that will lead to the sale and purchase of products and services that mutually benefit one another.

renaming fish A method used in the fish industry to change a seafood product's name if that name is considered a detriment to its sales potential.

rent-to-own plan See leasing company.

reorder point (ROP) The lowest amount of stock on hand that you feel comfortable with, the point that you will not go below before ordering more stock.

request for bid Another term for request for quote (RFQ).

request for credit memo A note sent by the buyer or the receiving clerk to the supplier requesting that the hospitality operation's account be credited because all or part of a shipment was unacceptable.

request for quote (RFQ) Used by buyers who shop around for the best possible deals. It is a list of items needed and their specifications, given to potential vendors who are then asked to quote, or bid, the AP prices they would charge for them.

responsible bidder Opposite of ineligible bidder. Company that is considered large enough, has sufficient financial strength, has a good reputation and history of satisfactory performance, and so forth, and because of this, is placed on a buyer's approved-supplier list.

restocking fee payment a supplier requires if an order is returned.

retail cut A small meat item produced from a wholesale cut. Alternately, another term for portion cut.

returned merchandise Items that do not meet the buyer's and receiving clerk's expectation, and therefore are returned to the supplier.

returns and allowances Amount of money representing price reductions given to customers because of goods returned and defective merchandise not suited to the customers' needs.

returns Items returned by the buyer to the supplier because they are unusable. Typically, something is returned because it is the wrong item, or the item is damaged in some way.

returns policy Vendor's procedure a buyer needs to follow to return products and receive credit for them.

RFID tags Radio frequency identification tags placed on boxes, crates, pallets, and the like. They are used by distributors and retailers to monitor automatically inventory and storage areas. A wireless technology is used—the same technology that allows electronic wireless toll payment in many states or the ExxonMobil SpeedPass wireless payment system—to transmit data wirelessly to a sensor. It could be argued that RFID tags are a major improvement over the bar code technology used by most distributors and retailers today.

rice milk A grain milk processed from rice. It is normally made from brown rice and unsweetened.

ripeness A term used to indicate that a food or beverage product is fully developed, mature, and ready to be used in production, or ready to eat or drink.

ripening process Can be natural or artificial ripening. Important selection factor when purchasing some fresh produce products.

ripening room Closed storage area used to ripen some fresh produce products, such as bananas. The storage area is sealed, and ethylene gas is introduced to induce and hasten the ripening process.

risk-purchasing group A co-op that specializes in the purchase of insurance for its members.

roadside sensor network Vehicles that contain a variety of onboard sensors that collect real-time data on current traffic conditions that can then be used to reroute automatically the vehicles' scheduled routes. Some networks also include safety warning features.

Robinson-Patman Act Legislation that enhanced federal antitrust powers that help protect small businesses.

route salesperson The driver who delivers standing orders to the restaurant.

run-of-the-press Refers to a newspaper ad being placed in the paper at the discretion of the advertising editor.

run-of-the-station Refers to a radio ad being sold on a space-available basis as opposed to a specific time of day.

résumé-checking service Company that specializes in checking employment job applicants' references and verifying information provided by them. Employers, not job applicants, typically pay the fees for this service.

sacred hours Time of the day when you would not want to accept deliveries. Usually these hours are from 11:30 a.m. to 1:30 p.m.

safety stock Extra stock kept on hand to avoid running out and disappointing guests.

safe-handling procedures Instructions typically printed on a product's package label detailing the way in which the product should be handled and prepared to prevent foodborne illness.

sales tax Taxes a company must pay to state and local governments for things purchased, such as cleaning chemicals, that will not be resold to customers.

salvage buy Buying a deep-discounted item. Usually the AP price is very low because the item is damaged.

salvage opportunity Purchase of a product that is damaged, hence sold for pennies on the dollar. Buyers must be willing to gamble that the product is usable because the item is generally sold as-is, with no guarantee.

sample Testing a small portion of a product or a shipment to determine its overall quality and acceptability. Alternately, see free sample.

sanitary Food Transportation Act of 2005 Federal regulation related to the transportation of human and animal food.

sealed-bid procedure Vendors' AP price quotations are secret until they are all opened by the buyer at the same time. Typically done with fixed-bid buying.

security agreement Contract used to secure a loan. If the borrower fails to pay, it allows the lender to foreclose and take the asset(s) used to collateralize the loan.

security problems Challenges that make it difficult to safeguard people and property. The major ones relevant to the selection and procurement function include kickbacks, invoice scams, supplier and receiver error, inventory theft, inventory padding, inventory substitutions, telephone and e-mail scams, inability to segregate operating activities, and suspicious behavior.

segregate operating activities Separating activities and assigning them to different persons and/or departments. For instance, it is common to separate the buyer from the person authorized to pay the bills. A security measure enacted to minimize the ability of employees to engage in fraudulent activities at the expense of their employers and/or customers.

selection and procurement policies These are usually broad, flexible rules a supervisor expects a buyer to follow when selecting and procuring products and services.

selection Choosing from among various alternatives.

seller co-op Refers to sellers, usually primary sources, who are legally allowed to join together to market their products. Typically found in the fresh produce trade.

server Central computer to which other computers, such as individual PCs, are networked. It communicates with all the other computers on the network.

service after the sale Periodic or as-required maintenance or repair of equipment by its manufacturer or supplier during and after a warranty period.

service agreement Covers the cost of furniture, fixtures, and equipment (FFE) defects and malfunctions during the initial warranty period provided by the FFE vendor.

shatter pack Another term for individually quick frozen (IQF).

shelf life The amount of time a product can remain in storage before it loses quality and cannot be used.

shelf-stable product A food item that is processed and packaged in such a way that it can maintain its quality for long periods of time at room temperature.

shellfish Exoskeleton-bearing aquatic invertebrates used as food. They are filter-feeding mollusks such as clams, mussels, and oysters.

Sherman Antitrust Act The first piece of antitrust legislation enacted in the United States. Prohibits any action that tends to eliminate or severely reduce competition.

shingle pack Layering product in such a way that the pieces overlap and do not completely cover one another. May be done for things like sliced bacon.

shoppers Persons whose jobs involve checking performance and service at retail and other businesses. These persons usually work for independent companies that provide mystery shopper services or secret shopper services.

shopping procedures Methods buyers use to find the correct products and services at the right prices from the right suppliers. Usually involves taking bids from several potential suppliers before deciding who to purchase from.

short orders See incomplete shipments.

show-special price Another term for trade show discount.

shrink allowance The amount of weight loss the buyer will accept in a shipment. The weight loss is due to unavoidable moisture loss during transit.

shrink-wrap Product is packed in plastic, and a vacuum is pulled through it so that air is removed and the wrapping collapses to fit snugly around the product. A type of controlled atmosphere packaging (CAP).

shucked shellfish Shellfish that have had their protective shells removed.

side A lengthwise half of a carcass.

signature item A menu item that is very popular; the restaurant is known for it.

single-ingredient, generic-brand food A product that does not carry a "name" brand label, but because it has only one ingredient, is likely to be of uniform quality and may also be equivalent to the quality of a name-brand product.

slab-packed Refers to items tossed into a container in no particular order or style. An inexpensive packing procedure, though it can cause breakage and other quality deterioration for some products.

slacked out A food item that is thought to be fresh but has actually been frozen, thawed, and passed off as fresh.

Small Business Administration (SBA) Federal government entity set up to maintain and strengthen the nation's economy by aiding, counseling, assisting, and protecting the interests of small businesses. Also helps families and businesses recover from national disasters.

snap pack Another term for individually quick frozen (IQF). When you remove a layer of frozen items from a case and drop it onto a counter, the IQF portions should snap apart easily. If they do not come apart easily and cleanly, it usually means that they have been thawed a bit and refrozen.

socially responsible supplier Vendor who uses environmentally safe products and/or procedures. Alternately, vendor who promotes social causes, supports charities, and so forth.

sole-source procurement, prime-vendor procurement, or single-source procurement Other terms for one-stop shopping.

solid pack Packing product in a container with no added juice or water.

source Supplier at the beginning of the channel of distribution. For instance, a grower (farmer) would be at the beginning of the fresh produce channel of distribution. Also referred to as a primary source.

sourcing Procurement practices aimed at finding, evaluating, and engaging suppliers of goods and services. The process used by a hospitality company to help establish a supplier. Typically done by large hospitality companies to help establish minority-owned primary sources and/or intermediaries. Alternately, the process a buyer undertakes to locate a vendor for a product or service that is very hard to find.

soy milk The liquid obtained by suspending soy bean flour in water.

specification A description of a product's required characteristics.

specific gravity A comparison of a product's density to that of water.

spoilage bacteria Microorganisms that do not necessarily cause food-borne illness but do cause product decay.

spoilage Deterioration of food by microbial and/or chemical action.

staffing Process of recruiting, hiring, and training personnel to perform specific tasks in an organization.

standard cost The expected cost. Sometimes referred to as the "potential" cost, the "planned" cost, the "budgeted" cost, or the "theoretical" cost. Typically used to help set menu prices, sleeping room prices, and so forth. Also used to compare to the actual cost incurred to determine if management is achieving its budgetary goals.

standard of fill A U.S. government regulation that indicates to the processor how full a container must be to avoid deception. It prevents the selling of excessive amounts of air or water in place of food.

standard of identity A U.S. government regulation that establishes what a food product must be to carry a certain name. For example, what a food product must be to be labeled "strawberry preserves."

standard of quality A U.S. government regulation that states the minimum quality a product must meet to earn the federal government's lowest possible quality grade. Products below the minimum standard of quality must indicate on the package label what the problem is. For instance, if canned green beans are excessively broken, the label could read, "Below Standard of Quality, Excessively Broken."

standing-order Under this procedure, a driver (usually referred to as a route salesperson) shows up, takes inventory of what you have, then takes off the truck enough product to bring you up to some predetermined par stock, enough to last until he or she visits you the next time. The driver writes up a delivery ticket after it's determined what you need and the products are placed in your storage facility.

statement of quality Information regarding standards buyers would like to have, such as product size and preservation method, when dealing with vendors who sell and distribute fresh food items that are hard to define and can vary significantly in quality from one delivery to the next. Examples of these types of products are fresh fish and organic produce.

steam-table pack Convenience food items packed in a container that can be popped into an oven or combi-steamer to reheat the food inside. When hot, the top of the container is removed and the container is then placed directly into a steam table or chaffing dish and kept warm for service. The typical container is usually made out of aluminum.

steward Manager who has food-buying responsibilities. May also be responsible for the food storage areas.

steward sale A sale of your inventory to employees. You charge them the price you paid. In effect, you allow them to take advantage of your purchasing power for their personal benefit.

stockless purchase When a buyer purchases a large amount of product, for example, a three-month supply, and arranges for the vendor to store it and deliver a little at a time.

stockless purchasing plan When a buyer purchases a large amount of product, for example, a three-month supply, and arranges for the vendor to store it and deliver a little at a time.

stockless purchasing When a buyer purchases a large amount of product, for example, a three-month supply, and arranges for the vendor to store it and deliver a little at a time.

stockout cost The cost incurred when you do not have a product guests want. Although the cost cannot always be calculated, in the long run there will usually be a negative impact on your bottom line. For example, the guest leaves without buying anything. Or the guest stays and orders something else, but never comes back.

stockout Running out of a product; not having it available for guests who want it.

stock requisition A formal request made by an employee for items needed to carry out necessary tasks. It is given to the person managing the storage facilities. A typical control document used by large hotels.

stock rotation A system of using older products first. When a shipment arrives the older stock is moved to the front of the shelf and the newer stock is placed behind it.

storage cost Another term for carrying cost.

storage space The amount of room, for example, the number of cubic feet, devoted to storeroom and warehouse facilities.

storefront dealer FFE company that carries a minimum amount of inventory. Usually specializes in handling small, portable types of FFE.

stretching the accounts payable Paying bills after the credit period has expired. This might be done by a buyer's company if it is temporarily short of cash. However, suppliers may charge interest if bills are paid after the credit term expires.

substitution possibilities Opportunities for using substitute ingredients in recipes that will not compromise the culinary quality of the food and beverage items made with those recipes. Alternately, opportunities for using substitute nonfood and nonbeverage products, such as cleaners, equipment, and utensils, to accomplish the same purposes.

supervisory style The way in which a person watches over and guides the work or tasks of another who may lack full knowledge of the tasks that must be carried out.

supplier diplomacy The art and practice of conducting negotiations between buyers and suppliers. Alternately, the employment of tact to gain a strategic advantage or to find mutually acceptable solutions to a common problem.

supplier selection criteria Characteristics a buyer considers when determining if potential vendors should be added to the approved-supplier list.

supplier services Services, such as free delivery, generous credit terms, and so forth, provided by vendors to buyers who purchase their products.

supplier–buyer relations Establishment of firm and fair business dealings and interactions between buyers and suppliers and their representatives.

supplier's costs Business expenses suppliers incur in order to operate their businesses effectively.

supplier's forms Paperwork documents or an electronic application the supplier provides to buyers, usually at no charge. They are typically intended for use by buyers who purchase products from the company providing them for free.

supply and demand Refers to a competitive environment that exists for producers of commodity items. If supply exceeds demand, purchase prices will decrease. If demand exceeds supply, purchase prices will increase.

supply chain management Process encompassing the planning and management of all activities involved in sourcing and procurement, conversion, and all logistics management activities.

support functions Another term for supplier services.

supporting local suppliers Done to maintain good relationships with businesspersons who live and work in the local community.

surimi Fish-based paste used to produce imitation lobster, crab, and other shellfish items.

surprise audit A security strategy intended to deter theft and pilferage by hiring an outside firm to make unannounced inspections.

sustainability The ability to not harm the environment or deplete natural resources. For seafood, the condition where the fish population does not decline over time due to fishing practices.

synthetic hormone Man-made chemical used as a substitute for the natural hormone produced by animals' glands. Given to animals to increase weight, milk production, speed up weight gain, and so forth.

systems sale Usually occurs when buying equipment that requires parts made by only one manufacturer, usually the manufacturer that made the equipment in the first place. For example, buying a dish machine that cannot use other companies' dish racks. Over the long run, a systems sale may cost you more money.

tare weight Weight of all material, such as cardboard, wrapping paper, and ice, used to pack and ship the product that is not part of the product itself. Subtracted from gross weight to compute net weight.

theft Premeditated burglary.

The Meat Buyers Guide (MBG) Another term for Institutional Meat Purchase Specification (IMPS) number.

theoretical inventory usage Expected amount of inventory usage based on recorded sales. For instance, if 100 steaks are recorded as sold, there should be only 100 steaks missing from inventory.

theoretical-inventory value What the inventory value is supposed to be, based on what you sold. For instance, if you had 100 steaks in inventory and the POS system says you sold 50, then there should be 50 steaks left. An actual count, though, may reveal that you have more or less than 50.

tied-house laws Legislation that prohibits liquor distributors from becoming liquor primary sources or liquor retailers.

time- and temperature-sensitive food labels Labels that typically change color when the product is too old and/or when the product has been too long in the danger zone (i.e., in an unsafe storage temperature).

title to goods Represents ownership of property which is free of claims against it, and therefore can be sold, transferred, or put up as security.

toner-phoner Term used to identify a scam artist who contacts people and misleads them into purchasing junk merchandise for a high price. A typical scam is to call and offer to sell printer toner for a bargain-basement price, hence the term toner-phoner.

trade association standard Minimum performance standards for items the association members produce.

trade relations The practice of spreading your purchase dollars among several vendors. Intended to create positive publicity for your hospitality operation.

trade show visit Attendance at exhibitions organized so that companies in a specific industry can showcase and demonstrate their latest products and services, study activities of rivals, and examine recent trends and opportunities.

trade-in allowance Amount of money a vendor credits your account when you buy a new piece of FFE (especially equipment) when turning in an older model.

Trade-in value The amount of cash a supplier will give a buyer for an older model piece of equipment, which is then usually used as a down payment for the purchase of a new model.

trade-out Refers to bartering your goods and services instead of paying cash. This term is commonly used to refer to trades between hospitality operations and advertising firms.

training Procedure designed to facilitate the learning and development of new skills, and the improvement of existing skills.

transfer slip Document used to control and account for products moved from one unit to another one within the same company. For instance, if you run a Red Lobster and you send food product over to another Red Lobster on the other side of town because it's running low, the transfer slip will credit your food cost while debiting the other unit's food cost.

transportation The movement of people and goods from one location to another.

trim Another term for waste.

truth-in-menu Guidelines menu planners use to avoid unintentionally misleading the customer by ensuring accurate descriptions and prices of all menu offerings. Alternately, refers to legislation prohibiting misrepresentations on the menu.

tying agreement Illegal contract that forces a buyer to purchase from a vendor certain items he or she may not want to gain the privilege of purchasing other items the buyer does want.

U.S. Department of Agriculture (USDA) Among other responsibilities, it has inspection powers throughout the food distribution channel. Typically concentrates its inspection efforts on red meat, poultry, and egg production.

U.S. Department of Commerce (USDC) Agency that, among other things, will, for a fee, provide to seafood processors continuous government inspection and federal grading of their fish products.

U.S. Grade A versus Grade A The former grade designation indicates that a federal government inspector has graded.

U.S. quality grades Rating system used by the federal government to indicate the quality of food products. Not all foods have established federal government quality grading standards.

U.S. yield grades Rating system used by the federal government to indicate the yield of meat products. Not all meats have established federal government yield grading standards.

ultra-high temperature (UHT) Ultra-high temperatures sterilize food by heating it above 135 °C (275 °F)—the temperature required to kill spores in milk—for 1 to 2 seconds.

ultra-pasteurized (UP) Pasteurization process using ultra-high temperatures (UHT). Used to produce a shelf-stable product that is packed in aseptic packages.

unconditional lien release Document verifying that a vendor has been paid in full. Typically used in the construction trades to protect a buyer who has signed a lien-sale contract. Once the vendor signs it, he or she is prevented from placing a lien on the property.

undercover agent or spotter A person hired to go undercover in a business to detect fraudulent actions perpetrated by employees. Sometimes referred to as a shopper, even though the two perform different services.

Underwriters Laboratories (UL) Provides electrical safety certification for electrical-powered equipment that meet its standards.

Uniform Commercial Code (UCC) Legislation outlining rules and regulations pertaining to various business transactions, such as leases, contracts, bills of lading, and so forth. Ensures consistency throughout the United States.

Universal Product Codes (UPC) Another term for bar code.

usage pattern When referring to food and beverages, it is the rate at which the products are produced and served to customers. When referring to nonfood and nonbeverage supplies, it is the rate at which the products have been exhausted and are no longer available.

USDA Acceptance Service Agency that, for a fee, will help buyers prepare meat specifications and oversee the purchase and delivery of meat.

USDA Agricultural Marketing Service (AMS) Agency that establishes federal grading standards for several food products, under authority of the Agricultural Marketing Act.

USDA Product Examination Service Agency that provides inspection of purchased meat by a federal inspector while the products are in transit.

USDA's Acceptance Service Agency that, for a fee, will help buyers prepare meat specifications and oversee the purchase and delivery of meat.

used merchandise FFE that are not new; they have been used by others but may still have some useful life left. These items are typically sold as-is, with no guarantee.

user discount Typical arrangement with vending companies that place machines, such as video games, in your hospitality operation. As part of your compensation, you are allowed to use the machines at no cost, or at a reduced cost.

user–buyer Refers to a person who is not a full-time buyer, but has some buying responsibilities. For instance, a chef who also orders the food products he or she uses in production would be considered a user–buyer.

use tax Tax charged by the state where the buyer's hospitality operation is located (i.e., home state), on products purchased from out of state. Similar to the sales tax charged by the home state. Charged by the home state to prevent companies from going elsewhere to avoid paying sales tax to their home states.

value analysis Involves examining a product to identify unnecessary costs that can be eliminated without sacrificing overall quality or performance.

value-added food Another term for convenience food.

value-added product Another term for convenience food. Alternately, it could also refer to a nonfood item that has many upgraded features, such as a kitchen ventilation system that is self-cleaning as opposed to one that has to be cleaned by hand.

variance Difference between what is expected and what actually happened. Typically used to refer to the difference between the standard cost and the actual cost.

variety meat Refers to organ meat, such as liver, kidney, and so forth.

vending-machine service Outside contractor that provides and maintains coin-operated machines, such as beverage and cigarette machines, for the convenience of employees and customers. Operators who sign up for this service usually earn a portion of the money the machines collect.

vintage Refers to the year of production. Important selection factor for some wines.

volume discount Similar to a quantity discount. The buyer agrees to purchase a huge volume of goods; however, unlike with a quantity discount, he or she buys more than one type of merchandise.

warehouse club Another term for wholesale club.

warranty and guarantee May be expressed or implied. Assurance that a product or service will be provided. Alternately, assurance that a product or service will meet certain specifications. Alternately, assurance that a product or service will be acceptable for a specified period of time or amount of use. Alternately, assurance that parts and/or repairs needed during a specified time period will be paid for by the vendor.

warranty Another term for guarantee.

waste removal service Outside contractor that carts away trash and other unwanted items. May also provide clients with trash containers, such as dumpsters.

waste Unusable part of a product that occurs when it is processed. Most waste is unavoidable, but sometimes avoidable waste occurs due to mistakes and carelessness.

water damage Products that have been injured by moisture and, therefore, are not usable.

web order entry system Refers to a method of ordering products online.

weight range Indication of the approximate size of a product the buyer wishes to purchase. Used when it is impossible or impractical to specify an exact weight.

well brand Term used in the bar business to refer to a drink that customers order by type of liquor and not by brand name. Opposite of call brand.

wet aging Shrink-wrapping meat, which allows the release of meat enzymes that soften the connective tissues.

what-if analysis Method of analyzing the potential outcome of a particular procedure without actually executing it. Normally involves the use of mathematical models.

wholesale club A type of buying club. It is a cash-and-carry operation patronized primarily by small hospitality operations that do not order enough from vendors to qualify for free delivery. Buyers usually have to pay a membership fee.

wholesale club or cash-and-carry A type of buying club. It is a cash-and-carry operation patronized primarily by small hospitality operations that do not order enough from vendors to qualify for free delivery. Buyers usually have to pay a membership fee.

wholesale cut Refers to a large cut of meat used to produce several retail cuts. It is smaller than a forequarter or hindquarter but larger than a retail cut.

Wholesome Meat Act Enhances the USDA's authority to regulate safety in the meat industry. Requires state inspection of meat production to be at least equal to the federal inspection program.

Wholesome Poultry Products Act Enhances the USDA's authority to regulate safety in the poultry industry. Requires state inspection of poultry production to be at least equal to the federal inspection program.

wild-caught Refers to any seafood caught from its natural environment or fishery, rather than from a controlled farm.

will-call Merchandise not delivered to the restaurant; the buyer picks it up at the vendor's location. The buyer may also have to pay for it when picking it up, unless the company has established credit with the vendor.

windshield advertisement A flyer typically placed under a car's windshield wiper.

winemaker Beverage alcohol company that produces fermented alcoholic products made primarily from grapes.

wine speculating The act of investing in wine for a profit-making purpose. The speculator does not consume the product; rather, he or she treats it as a valuable collectible that may increase significantly in value.

wine-dispensing unit Mechanical equipment that stores open wine and maintains its quality after opening. It can be programmed to dispense predetermined portion sizes.

working storeroom Refers to a storage area that is kept open during the shift to allow employees to enter as needed to retrieve products.

yield The net weight or volume of a food item after it has been processed and made ready for sale to the guest.

Index